MARTHA GELLHORN: A LIFE

Caroline Moorehead is the biographer of Bertrand Russell, Freya Stark and Iris Origo. She is well known for her work in the sphere of human rights, and has written a history of the International Committee of the Red Cross. She lives in London.

Caroline Moorehead

MARTHA GELLHORN:
A Life

V

VINTAGE

Published by Vintage 2004

12

Copyright © Caroline Moorehead, 2003

Caroline Moorehead has asserted her right under the
Copyright, Designs and Patents Act 1988 to be identified
as the author of this work

First published in Great Britain in 2003 by
Chatto & Windus

Vintage
Random House, 20 Vauxhall Bridge Road,
London SW1V 2SA
www.randomhouse.co.uk

Addresses for companies within
The Random House Group Limited can be found at:
www.randomhouse.co.uk/offices.htm

The Random House Group Limited Reg. No. 954009

A CIP catalogue record for this book
is available from the British Library

ISBN 978 0 09 9284017

Penguin Random House is committed to a sustainable future for
our business, our readers and our planet. This book is made from
Forest Stewardship Council® certified paper.

Typeset by Palimpsest Book Production Limited,
Polmont, Stirlingshire

Printed and bound in Great Britain by Clays Ltd, St Ives plc

Contents

List of Illustrations

Tom Matthews with Martha (*by kind permission of Sandy Matthews*)

Martha in Africa with the Pamps (*Martha Gellhorn Archive*)

Martha on the beach in Kenya (*Martha Gellhorn Archive*)

Martha and Sandy in London (*by kind permission of Sandy Gellhorn*)

Sybille Bedford (*courtesy of Jerry Bauer*)

Betsy Drake (*by kind permission of Betsy Drake*)

Edna in the 1960s (*by kind permission of Alfred Gellhorn*)

Diana Cooper (*by kind permission of Sandy Matthews*)

The two Sandys: Sandy Gellhorn and Sandy Matthews (*by kind permission of Sandy Matthews*)

Martha's cottage in Wales (*Martha Gellhorn Archive*)

Martha with her younger borther, Alfred (*by kind permission of Alfred Gellhorn*)

Martha with one of her beloved cats (*Martha Gellhorn Archive*)

Birthday party for Martha at the Groucho Club *(Martha Gellhorn Archive)*

Martha in her eighties (by kind permission of *Susan Greenhill*)

Doodle from letter written by H. G. Wells to Martha, p.112 (*courtesy of the Estate of H.G. Wells*)

TO DAISY AND MILLIE,
DAUGHTERS OF MY OWN
MARTHA

Preface

In the last years of her life, Martha Gellhorn wanted to see her friends just one way. She liked to meet them in the late afternoon or early evening, in her own flat, over drinks that could go on for many hours but that very seldom turned into dinner. Restless, energetic, always on the move, she resisted when in London leaving her own sitting room. And, since, in the over twenty-five years in which she lived in London, she never changed the bamboo furniture or the plain blue sofas, nor bought new pictures, nor allowed any clutter in the room, nor varied where she sat or what she drank, these meetings with Martha have remained absolutely distinct in the minds of her visitors. It is as if the friendship itself were contained in the passage of a Greek play, one event, in one place, at one time. It gives a peculiar frame to memory.

In 1970, when Martha was in her early sixties, she decided to stop wandering and to make London her home. She liked the easiness of the city and its parks, and it was where a few of the closest of the friends she had made while moving from country to country now lived. She found a flat in Chelsea, the top floor and attic of a tall, gabled, red-brick Victorian house in Cadogan Square. It was here that the visits took place. First, the heavy door in from the street, with its iron grille and bevelled glass, so heavy that if you were carrying flowers, you needed to push hard with your shoulder to get past. In the hall, immediately to the right, above the bold black and white checked tiles, hung a large, rather ornate mirror in which to

check appearance, for appearance, you knew, was not altogether unimportant. At the end of the hall there was a narrow
lift, that shuddered as it rose and threatened often to stall.
The fifth floor had a deep red pile carpet; three steps led down
to her front door. It was here that you would find Martha,
leaning against the door frame, in black trousers and sweater
and expensive shoes, fashionable and clean, with rather red
lipstick, her fair-grey hair, short and slightly curly, brushed
back. Her voice immediately suggested the anticipation of
pleasurable laughter; her smile was both expectant and
quizzical. She was always elegant.

The sitting room opened to the right of a large and airy
hall, empty except for a bamboo coat stand, and it gave an
immediate impression of lightness and the colour blue. Wide
1930s windows, with functional cast-iron frames, looked
across a view of the rooftops of Chelsea and Kensington as
far as the Catholic church in the Brompton Road, because
views – the low round bumps of the Welsh hills, the plains
and volcanoes of Africa, the wooded valleys of Spain – were
always necessary. Two sofas, at right angles to each other, both
covered in the same cobalt-blue linen which never seemed to
fade, with bamboo and glass tables for lamps and ashtrays in
between and on either side. Above one, an oil painting, done
by a friend in America, of a trout swimming in shallow water
over round, smooth, speckled stones; above the other a picture
of flowers by the same painter, Bernard Perlin; and on either
side bookshelves, though most of the books were upstairs in
the study or in the bedroom by her bed. The drink was kept
on a dresser made of pine: glasses on the shelf, bottles and
the ice on a tray below. It was essential to have ice. By the
window stood a bamboo screen and a tall, green plant, that,
like the sofas, never seemed to age. Tidy, clean, neutral: what
one interviewer described, to Martha's irritated surprise, as
'austere'. This outer tidiness, she would explain, was to coun-
teract the extreme disorder of her mind.

What Martha liked to do was to talk, a tumbler of Famous
Grouse whisky by her side, a cigarette in a holder, eyes slightly
narrowed against the smoke, accent unmistakably still of the

American Midwest, voice almost a drawl, full of irony and curiosity and indignation. Occasionally, there were some nuts to eat, though her feelings about weight and figure were rigid. No one, she would say, ever, at any age, should give up their physical vanity: keeping fit was both basic discipline and a 'public service'. In Martha's case, this meant good muscles, a weight of exactly 125 pounds; and great style. She was particularly pleased with her feet, which were long and so thin that she had to have her shoes made for her. In summer her toenails were red. She said that old age, once she had got over a period of loneliness and inability to write, was 'spiffing' and talked of writing a book on its pleasures. She used words like 'pooped' and 'whopping' and expressions like 'oh my'. 'If you live long enough,' she would say, 'you get to be a monument. I am now a monument.' It was a thought that she did not altogether dislike, particularly as the 1980s were a good time for her kind of writing, for the sort of hardy and solitary travel she thrived on, and the personal reporting she had made her own. 'I have only to go to a different country, sky, language, scenery, to feel it is worth living,' she wrote to a friend, explaining her need to move, to get away. '*Flâner*,' she would say, 'is as necessary as solitude: that is how the compost keeps growing in the mind.'

At around the age of seventy, in the late 1970s, after the bad spell in which writing had become so tough and the fiction seemed to have dried up, Martha began to meet what she affectionately called 'my chaps'. They were women as well as men, writers for the most part, or in some way connected to the world of writing, but television people too: not teenagers, who bored her, but people in their late twenties and thirties with work and adventures behind them, early loves dissolved, current relationships floundering, people who did things. 'That's my trouble, I can't love without admiration,' she once wrote. 'Who said: "*Je pense, donc je suis*"? Descartes? I think it wrong. I act, therefore I am. We must be the product and sum total of our actions.'

Martha liked people who shaped their own lives, who, like her, travelled to look and ask and carry back what they had seen; and after ill health severely reduced her ability to see and get about, she relied on the chaps to bring her the news she had once gathered herself, to report from the war fronts, both real and emotional. 'I believe passionately,' she would say, scornful and impatient, 'that we are responsible, here and now, for ourselves and our acts; there is no escape from that.' The capriciousness of luck she tended to disregard, particularly at her tougher moments, allowing only – and, improbably, an odd concession in someone so rational – an intervention by the stars. Scorpios, she wrote, referring to herself, were either 'geniuses or miserable or both, well known to be very spiky characters . . . for whom life is not lined with smiling faces'. Lucky people, she maintained, had lucky natures; either way, good behaviour was immutable, as was strength of character and purpose. Only the weak 'sat on their arses'; the people she liked got out there and fought. Selection as a friend was more or less instant; not everyone made the team, and not everyone had the appetite for it. Even to someone who had known her since childhood, as I had, the touches of imperiousness could feel a little like bullying.

Martha enjoyed it when people were 'in the beam', her description of being consumed by passion, yet would sometimes say that she didn't really know about that sort of tyranny and that she could not accept that any woman could be destroyed by a man. 'In the beam' was one war zone she had never visited. She liked to hear that the world was full of shits, and was a little envious of the good sex she said that she had never really had, and the *tendresse* that she had only read about. 'I've never known complete love,' she told an old friend. 'Except of course for Miss Edna, who is the true north of my life.' Miss Edna was her mother, and long after her death in 1970, at the age of ninety, Martha continued to compare herself to her, always to her own disadvantage. True north meant old-fashioned values, toughness and courage, a time of better hearts and minds and manners, and being 'gallant'.

This failure to have been overwhelmed by the anguish of real love did not stop her giving advice, that sounded worldly but was somehow too decisive, too black or too white, though even she would admit she felt on surer ground when talking about writing. Martha knew more painfully than most about a writer's life: she called the bad times 'chewing cement'. This was a war zone she had visited all too often, weeks, months at a time when the words came and later turned out duds, or did not come at all, and the hours passed and nothing happened. She felt very strongly about the craft of writing. 'You must not only know how to write,' she told a writer who was stuck. 'But you have to be privately, personally, sound at the core. Not sane, but sound. If not, it always shows. Slight smell of cheese in the air, and the work gets a limp, rotting, glazed look.' Reporting from this front line meant bearing witness; like love, it had a true north. Sloppiness, dishonesty were worse than poor behaviour: they were evil. Quoting Nadezhda Mandelstam, who said that if there is nothing else to do one must scream, Martha wrote: 'I long to scream. But where? But how? I am screaming all the time inside me and it will end by giving me severe stomach pains as it already gives me insomnia.' Cowardice repelled her. Railing against the unfairness of life was encouraged, as long as it was done with humour and grit; moaning and whining were taboo, and what she called the 'archaeology of psychoanalysis' was deeply suspect, along with all prodding and peering into childhood. Freud, she said, had done 'hell's own damage, giving everyone the right to *blame* someone else. That's a filthy way to live.' Her feminism was a simpler affair: she had never allowed the fact that she was a woman to interfere with anything she did; and she was not greatly impressed by the idea that other women could not do the same. 'Buck up' was a phrase we all heard when we strayed too near to self-pity.

She was often furious; furious with apocrophiars, a word she coined for those who rewrote history, particularly to their own advantage; furious with critics who read fact into her fiction; with trimmers and prevaricators; with those who had no guts for the fight and those who destroyed others, casually; and furious with the crassness and arrogance of governments.

Like lying, sitting on the fence was contemptible. Martha's horizons were peopled by villains, politicians in particular, men and women such as Nixon and Kissinger and Mrs Thatcher, who led the innocent into chaos and the dark night, stupidity and arrogance. She was haunted by a world out of control. 'My God, what sort of world is this?' she would ask a visitor in disbelief after some act of terrorism or political chicanery. A friend once wrote to ask her if she was ever afraid. 'No,' she replied. 'I feel angry, every minute, about everything.' Anger fed her, and she felt it her duty and her calling to keep a constant watch on injustice. As it became increasingly hard for her to do so, her sight almost gone, her hearing poor, her back painful, so she spoke of the 'relay race of history', and how she relied on her chaps to stop the human species, like scorpions, from stinging itself to death.

Her blind spot was the Palestinian cause, in which she saw nothing honourable or good. A few chaps braved the fury and challenged the magisterial dismissal; most preferred to leave the subject to one side. This clarity of right and wrong, seldom tempered by doubt, remained as absolute as it had been when she set out, in 1937, to catch a train to Barcelona and register her outrage against Franco and his fascist army. To the very few reporters permitted to interview her, and on the rare occasion she grudgingly agreed to join a discussion panel, she would speak, in tones of genuine incomprehension, of what she called 'all this objectivity shit'. How could anyone not have a view or take a side?

Before she was, as she put it, half-laughing, a little hurt, 'rediscovered by the young' in the late 1970s, Martha would say she no longer had anyone to laugh with. Laughter was like truth, not a luxury but necessary for existence. 'What happened to laughter? Do you know?' she asked an old friend as she turned seventy. 'I remember it as the central and loveliest fact of life . . . Are other people doing it still or has it gone out of fashion? I'd give anything I have to meet someone who made me laugh.' She could be cruel to old friends, quick to deliver the chilling *coup de grâce* to those who developed the fatal flaw of becoming boring, but she missed the 'helpless laughter among chums who were glad to be alive because they knew about death'. With the chaps, and particularly with the men, she laughed, and there was something pleasurably seductive in the laughter, something distinctly flirtatious, that gave the friendship its colour. One described it as 'like a great affair without the sex'. The uniqueness of the relationship of each of us with her is something that we all remember. 'I always suspected there were other doors to worlds I didn't inhabit, rooms she would go to with others where I was not invited,' says a woman who knew her well for over twenty years. 'But that was fine. What she gave me was enough. I left feeling that each visit had been a complete occasion.'

Compartments were seldom breached; even husbands and wives paid their visits alone. Separate, but also a gang, the gang she had never had, preferring to live with single friendships, accountable to no one, once writing: 'My chosen and projected status is that of an outsider. I have never seen any place or group I wanted to join: not their taboos, rules, games, ambitions . . . I am an onlooker.' It was what had lent her war reporting its edge: the independent, lucid eye, telling it how it happened, not worried about who it might offend.

For most visitors, the evening was just a drink, or many drinks, sat over long after it got dark. But there were times when she felt that the chaps needed feeding, and then terrible concoctions would appear. Martha loathed what she called the 'kitchen of life', or, in her blacker moments, the 'kitchen of death'. It made her frantic with irritation and impatience. And though the kitchen of life took in buying light bulbs and ringing the plumber, it also covered her rare attempts at cooking. She was an imaginatively bad cook. One appalling day she discovered a dish that consisted of frozen sweet corn, tuna and condensed milk. Many of the chaps, cooks themselves, took to turning up with food they would prepare, or brought picnics of smoked salmon. With the arrival of a microwave came what she alarmingly called 'microwave feasts' though she was delighted to read in a magazine that custard or gravy, left too long to heat, would explode and cover the kitchen with slime.

And at the end of the evening it was hard not to leave a little drunk, with that uneasy feeling that you had talked too much, revealed secrets you had sworn to yourself not to mention. But Martha, who had a remarkable ability never to repeat herself, and an apparently genuine curiosity about the intricacies of the lives of those she was fond of, was not, as she put it, 'leaky'. Confidences did not get repeated, and nor did she play her chaps off one against the other. Walking down the street afterwards, past the other tall irregular red-brick Victorian houses, past the gardens in which her admirer H.G. Wells and Arnold Bennett had once played tennis, you felt a little better about yourself. The disastrous turn in the ailing love affair had been in some way cushioned by her laughter and understanding; the work that was advancing so very slowly was, after all, not something to be ashamed of. You could take a certain modest pleasure in not having made a fool of yourself. The world had been sorted out and American foreign policy, always a snake pit of immorality, had been suitably denounced. A few things might perhaps need a little correction, but that could all be done in a humorous postcard. And if you happened also to come away a little bruised, suffering from some sharp rebuke – for Martha's addiction to truth telling could be merciless – then there was always the next drink at which to do better. 'She wasn't always right,' says one woman friend, 'but I miss her every day.'

Under her attentive cross-examination, each had brought to the encounter the best of themselves. The reporters had described skirmishes in inhospitable places; the travellers told of horrors and misadventures; the writers lamented over blocks and rejections; and everyone, at some point, had dipped into their personal lives. A few exaggerations, perhaps; a situation milked for its comedy. For her part, Martha would have listened, rewarded those who touched chords with her complete concentration, her eyes flickering encouragingly and very shiny, lighting one cigarette after another; she, too, would have talked, though not so personally, about journeys of her own, about new places she had discovered where she could snorkel or swim in empty and unpolluted sea, about the hell of writing, about fresh villainies heard late at night on the radio when she could not sleep, about her friendships with Capa and Leonard Bernstein and Eleanor Roosevelt, or the day she arrived in Finland as the Russians were invading. New words made her laugh with sudden delight and she was enchanted when someone told her about anhedonia, the lack of pleasure or the capacity to experience it. It was, she said, precisely how she felt, and it was also a way of touching lightly on the fact. Just as her metaphors, visually sharp and designed to make you laugh, were a safe way of belittling unhappiness. 'I do most definitely feel that my life is like walking a Pekinese,' she wrote to a woman she had known for many years. 'And it does not brighten me.' And, just occasionally, she would talk about Ernest Hemingway, to whom she had been married for less than five years, and whose shadow infuriated her to the point where she allowed no mention of his name, ever, in connection with her own. Hemingway, in her book, was the worst apocryphiar of them all.

Did her visitors ever really learn about Martha? They learnt enough to admire and become extremely attached; for some, she became their true north, the best confidante they had ever had; she gave them fun of a kind they never had with anyone else. She made *them* laugh. Her idea of friendship included perceptive generosity, cheques in the post, no discussion or thanks permitted. And it was exhilarating to be talked to with such sympathy, toughly delivered, to be told not to waste one's life, to listen while she announced that stupidity was original sin, that happiness was being fully alive, using all of oneself and getting better in the using, that contentment was a meaningless aspiration, that while fear paralysed, indignation was 'like being equipped with steady interior jet propulsion'. It made the chaps laugh when Martha insisted that they stop being led by their penises and use their heads instead. No one attended court, as the regulars affectionately called it, out of a sense of duty.

What very few of them were ever allowed to see, however, was the degree of loneliness, self-doubt and sense of failure that run like a sad refrain through a lifetime of letters, and that grew more marked in the last years of her life. It was then that she began to speak of the 'dark grey sludge pit' of the mind, 'in which no light glimmers'. Letters, like views, were necessary; they were, she said, her way of staying alive. As old friends died, and others were cast off, as her failing eyesight blighted the two enduring escape mechanisms of her life, reading and travelling, so she wrote: 'Yes, life is tough and toughness carries us through and on average I'm as tough as the next one: but the further thought is – why trouble?' She minded increasingly when the chaps failed to keep in touch. The cruelty of the world oppressed her and she began to tire of the idiocy of rulers. 'I know that I am old because passionate anger has turned into weary disgust: nothing impresses me.' She spoke of being 'permanently dislocated – *un voyageur sur la terre*.' Her body, she would say, was becoming too old for her mind. Unlike tenderness in a love affair, her looks had always been a factor; they were a source of pleasure and an acknowledged asset. Now she wrote: 'I feel very old, ugly, tired.' Being a survivor, she said, was hard work.

But she did not complain. The courage that she valued above all other qualities did not fail her. At most, she recounted, usually with marked self-mockery, the minor accidents, the falls, the aches, the spreading blur to which the world was rapidly becoming reduced. 'I am sick of my body which seems to be copying Job,' she wrote to a friend she had first met in Spain, during the civil war. The letter was typed in capitals, picked out with the help of big characters another friend had stuck on her keyboard; but to read it back to herself, she had to carry the letter into the bright light, and use a magnifying glass.

True or not, she would say she remembered nothing, unlike John Updike or Saul Bellow, writers she admired, who could recall everything they had seen or heard or smelled, adding that this was a huge advantage in coping with old age. 'Tell him,' she instructed a friend who repeated to her what a fan had said admiringly of her achievements, 'that I never look back, which is true; or anyway I only look back with heartache

on lost scenery, ruined by the travel explosion. Tell him that
I don't remember doing anything that calls for great pride.
Tell him that one reason I cultivate my bad memory is that I
remember well only what has caused me pain, hence I prefer
to live in the present. Just this very day will do me fine.'

CHAPTER ONE

A Talking Childhood

'I was never deeply interested in being a child,' wrote Martha to her agent, Gillon Aitken, not long before her eighty-third birthday, adding that, were she ever to write her autobiography, and she had no intention of doing so, this would be her opening sentence. Indeed, she never did write it, but she did leave several fragments, written both then and thirty years earlier, around the time of her fiftieth birthday, chapters later filed away and forgotten. In all versions, her attitude to her childhood is the same. Her early years were happy, and, like happy families, happy children have no history. Only violence to children, cruelty caused by history rolling over them like a tank, which with the years came to preoccupy her more and more, seemed to her worth recording in anyone's early past. In any case, she would say, her memory, untrained by either school or two years at Bryn Mawr, was more like a black hole or a compost heap than a useful implement for research, and she had no gift for introspection. Not just no gift: no taste for it either. Autobiography, the long journey through the past, for her spelt if not excessive self-love then at the very least self-absorption. It was conceit.

What never vanished into the black hole, however, was an enduring memory of talk. The Gellhorns were what she later called a 'talking' family. They told each other things, at meals in the evening at which the four children were expected to recount the adventures of their days, amusingly enough to make their parents smile. Laughter was rewarded. George Gellhorn, a busy doctor who was for a while St Louis's only specialist gynaecologist and obstetrician, would offer a penny to any one of them who could make him laugh. Alfred, the youngest by five years, remembers that Martha was the one who pocketed the most coins. When the children argued and asked questions, which they did constantly, dictionaries and reference books were fetched; most evenings, the dinner table was piled high with books. Edna Gellhorn, their mother, an early suffragette and social reformer, no less busy than her husband, encouraged their many visitors and her husband's medical colleagues to stay and eat with the family. Once they had reached the age of twelve, the children were allowed to take part; up until that day they sat on the stairs and watched the visitors come and go. But there were rules, administered by Dr Gellhorn as Speaker according to Roberts' parliamentary rules: no gossip or hearsay but everything reported from personal observation or experience; and no referring to people by their race or colour. The Gellhorn house was one of the very few white homes in St Louis where black people came regularly for meals, and Martha was encouraged to bicycle to visit a black woman friend of the family who owned a cosmetics factory, where she was allowed to try on the lipsticks forbidden at home. The food served at dinner had to be eaten and no questions were permitted about what it was. Aubergines, greyish and mushy, were Martha's particular nightmare. Telling tales on anyone was inconceivable, as was any form of self-pity, but bragging was contemptible. Martha complained later that this was why she never knew about the eminence of her brothers in adult life.

St Louis at the turn of the twentieth century was a city of some standing. Founded by a French fur trader in 1764 and named after the thirteenth-century French king, it had long since shed its rough pioneering past for a solid commercial prosperity. Beer, flour, boots, stoves, bricks, chemicals, and above all tobacco, had brought in enough money to landscape some of the finest parks in the country. It was here, on the lakes frozen in the extreme winter winds, that Dr Gellhorn took his only daughter to ice skate. Once crowded along the banks of the Mississippi and the Missouri, where the emigrants arrived by steamboat before buying tools and supplies for the long trek across upper Louisiana, the city centre had now moved west, to a pleasant district of faintly Italianate houses in timber and brick, set back from the street and surrounded by small gardens. Only the largest mule market in the country was a reminder of its pioneer days. Among the city's half million inhabitants were 100,000 Germans, which was one reason why the ambitious young German doctor George Gellhorn had settled on St Louis when searching for a toehold in the New World. The other was an introduction to Dr Washington Fischel, a local physician, who would, he hoped, help him set up a practice.

Family history has little to say about the extent to which George Gellhorn was consciously escaping the anti-Semitism of late nineteenth-century Germany. Son of a cigar maker called Adolph, he was born in the small town of Ohlau, near Breslau, in what was then East Prussia and is today Poland. An aunt, Dora Bloom, had brought him up. George had completed his medical studies at Gürzburg, then travelled for postgraduate work to Vienna and Berlin, where he had developed a love for music and a taste for wine, before signing on as a ship's surgeon to explore the world. Hating and fearing German militarism, he had nonetheless become president of his university Jewish fraternity duelling club, at a time when friendly duels meant a web of honourable scars around the face and head. At the time he decided to end his roaming life and settle in St Louis, in 1900, he was thirty-one, and not altogether prepossessing in appearance. Though tall, over six feet, with impeccable manners and a good ear for languages, he was somewhat Prussian for American tastes, with his high collars, round-rimmed glasses and heavily scarred bald pate. He had a booming laugh, a good singing voice and he played bridge. The wife of Dr Washington Fischel, Martha, found him uncouth, despite an attractive smile. She did what she could to discourage him, when her husband's new protégé fell in love with their only daughter's thick crown of reddish-fair hair, glimpsed in the sunlight as Edna walked down the stairs to greet him. Martha Fischel was convinced that Edna could have her pick of St Louis's most eligible bachelors, but Edna assured her mother that she knew, with absolute certainty, that George Gellhorn would never bore her. Boring people, her own daughter Martha would soon be saying, was a sin.

The Fischels were socially minded. Martha Fischel, whose family had been bankrupted after the civil war, was a determined, handsome woman, with arched nostrils, a strong jaw and heavy black eyebrows. Her own granddaughter Martha would later say that it was from her that she had inherited a 'tendency to beat my cane on the floor and call everyone to order'. The Fischels were founders of the Ethical Society, and the Gellhorn children, brought up in an otherwise atheist household, attended Ethical Sunday school. They were all, Martha would say, 'great swells'.

Both Edna, who had not long graduated from Bryn Mawr, and George had strong views about the world they wished to see around them. It owed much to the vision of America left by Jefferson and Lincoln and to its Constitution, which the young German doctor had studied and admired from afar. It included liberal politics, progressive education and, in the segregated and masculine Midwest, equality of every kind. When clubs or associations failed to meet these requirements, the young couple refused all offers to join, frequently going on to set up alternative establishments that did. It was to be a singularly happy marriage, something to which Martha would often refer when making the point that truly happy marriages are rare. It was another way in which the happy childhood had no history. Both she and Alfred remembered the way their mother would listen for George's return, running to stand by the front door so that she could be there to kiss him as he turned his key in the lock.

Their first child, born in 1902, was a boy, and they called him George. After him, over the next six years, came Walter and then Martha, in November 1908. Edna, who liked to read thrillers, was reading *The Circular Saw* by Mary Roberts Rinehart when labour began; Martha, who all her life insisted that she was poorly educated, complained that had her mother been reading Gibbon's *The History of the Decline and Fall of the Roman Empire* she would not have been so incurably 'unknowledgeable'. Alfred was born in 1913.

By 1910, when Martha was two, the Gellhorns owned a three-storey house in the central west district of St Louis, 4366 McPherson Avenue, halfway down a wide, tree-lined street with gardens both in front and behind. It had four bedrooms, a landing with a stained glass window, pale oak-panelled walls, Persian carpets with octagonal patterns on which the children played marbles, and heavy mahogany furniture. As in Martha's own houses later, nothing new was ever bought or added. The children had friends up and down the road. Martha from an early age protested bitterly that Tina, their German maid, was exacting and mean-spirited and taught her too early about injustice and the fatal habit of appeasement. She also accused her older brothers of bullying her. 'Walter and George tried to kill me,' read one of her earliest letters. 'If you don't do something about it, I'm going to leave home.' Martha left notes like this stuck to the newel post, most of them cries of rage and injustice about her brothers. She would hear her parents laughing as they read them.

The family lived well. St Louis was an agreeable city for the comfortably-off. Two well-endowed universities attracted scholars from the east, and one of the city's six newspapers was printed in German. There were tennis parties and Sunday excursions to a shared cabin in the woods by the Merrimac river, to which each family contributed a different picnic dish, eaten under the eaves of a huge porch. In the winter, the man who delivered St Louis's ice door-to-door opened an ice-skating rink. Martha's only spanking was delivered when she hid herself in the ice-man's horse-drawn cart and was not found until long after dark; she protested that it had only been her intention to see the world. In the summer there were baseball games between the St Louis Browns and the Cardinals.

George Gellhorn insisted on his children taking exercise, thereby instilling in Martha a lifelong concern, at times even an obsession, with fitness. His belief in the goodness of fresh air meant that the children slept outside, even in the middle of winter, on an open porch screened by canvas curtains like sails, where they had pillow fights and ragged late into the night. And, as each child reached the age of thirteen, they attended the 'Fortnightlies', dancing parties held by their teacher Mr Mahler at his house on Wednesday nights, stopping for ice cream and sundaes on their way home. Martha, tall for her age and a little awkward, was not greatly in demand as a partner, though she had pretty fair hair and blue eyes. Mary Taussig, the daughter of one of Edna's close friends, remembers her as rather clever and a bit superior, but always very elegant. Martha herself would later say that she learnt the nature of social rejection at these Fortnightlies, when she and her best friend Emily Post, one too tall, too talkative and too prone to laugh at her own jokes, the other too dumpy, with too much red hair and too many freckles, and eyelashes like those of a white mouse, hid behind the coats to avoid being singled out as wallflowers.

As a doctor, George Gellhorn owned one of St Louis's few private cars; for the most part people travelled by tram or bicycle. Dr Gellhorn's somewhat unconventional ways – he insisted on eating hot dogs and potato salad in their box at the opera, as he had done in the European theatres of his youth – were remarked on, but not held against him, though during the First World War, together with other resident Germans, he suffered mild ostracism. In St Louis, Berlin Street became Pershing Street. Martha claimed to remember nothing of the First World War, which ended when she was ten, beyond the day she came home from school to find her father sobbing: his favourite brother, also a doctor, had been interned in an English camp where he committed suicide.

Edna, like Dr Gellhorn, was half-Jewish. This fact, in a world in which anti-Semitism was an accepted feature of American life, appears to have played so little a part that none of their children seems to have been more than passingly aware of their Jewish origins. Several years after the Second World War, by which time the holocaust had forever altered the way that Martha would look at history, she tried to explain to the Russian Jewish doctor with whom she had fallen in love her first encounter with anti-Semitism; indeed, possibly her only childhood encounter, for she never mentioned or spoke of another. It concerned her first Fortnightly. Martha had a friend, a girl called Johnny Stix. When the day of the dance approached, she asked Johnny what she was planning to wear. Johnny said that she was not going, that she had not been asked because she was Jewish. On protesting to her mother about the unfairness of it, Martha was simply told that if she wished not to go either, no one would make her. In the event, Johnny was embarrassed and cross, and Martha went with her brothers, suffering agonies 'and very unpopular, due to not knowing how to talk to boys as a girl, but only as if I were another boy'. And so the question of Jewishness went away, since 'my parents had no use for society (as it used to be called)'. Not until she was in Munich fifteen years later, in 1936, did the question arise again for Martha in such a way as to trouble her, though an adolescence of partly suppressed awareness of bigotry and racial slights may explain the later sudden intensity of her feelings.

More openly memorable, and with more immediate impact, was Dr Gellhorn's attitude towards his daughter's dress. The doctor believed that modern fashion was lethal to the female form and waged what felt to Martha like a personal vendetta against everything that to her seemed desirable. She was obliged to wear special shoes, called ground grippers, shaped like feet and laced above the ankles, so that the toes were not constricted. When the age of the flapper came in, and Martha's friends wore bands of canvas clamped around their chests to flatten them, she was forbidden to wear one, with the result, she would say, that she enjoyed a brief popularity with the boys as she was the only girl with breasts, and that it never occurred to her to wear a brassiere at all until she was over forty.

The messages from these early days are contradictory. When Martha was about eight her father told her that the bones of the skull separate all human beings from each other, thereby explaining the painful solitariness of the human condition. This, together with a disposition for 'inconsolation' handed down by her Fischel grandmother and her German father in 'unhappiness genes', accounted for her 'glum' temperament, and for the fact that from early childhood on she would record each passing birthday with the thought: 'another year gone and nothing to show for it'. And yet, in countless later letters, she would write that the marvel of her childhood was that she had felt so 'entirely alive', so 'permanently excited about living that I took it for joy'. These, perhaps, were the legacy of Edna and her grandfather, 'who were all sun' and moved in an 'aura of lovingness'.

And, above it all, the single clearest memory of her happiness was Martha's love for her mother. At night she would sometimes wake in tears, fearing the day her mother would die. From the list of Edna's committees and campaigns – for wrapped bread, free clinics, smoke abatement, tuberculosis-screened milk, improved divorce laws, stricter child-labour laws – it is obvious that she must have been exceptionally busy. She managed, however, to give her only daughter the feeling that she was always there. In a short article written over sixty years later, Martha described how every fine Saturday in the spring and autumn of her twelfth year, she and her mother would take a tram for an all-day picnic by a lake known as Crève Cœur. Carrying with them a volume of Robert Browning's poetry, four sandwiches, two hard-boiled eggs, fruit, biscuits and a thermos of lemonade, they took it in turns to read the poems aloud to each other, sitting by a small waterfall, under a weeping willow. After lunch, Martha climbed on the rocks and talked, while her mother listened, watched and admired. It was 'always childhood's weather: flawless blue sky, just-right sun'. There were violets and lilies of the valley, which Edna stopped her from picking, saying that they were to be seen not owned. Nothing else 'in the city or my life was as magical as Saturday at Crève Cœur'. Martha never went back. 'As a traveller,' she wrote, 'I have learned that it is wise not to return to what was once perfection.'

* * *

Like her magnificent thick hair, piled on top of her head, so long that at one point she could sit on it, and her cornflower-blue eyes, Edna's sweet nature was legendary. By 1916, the year Martha turned eight, she was leading St Louis's campaign for female suffrage. The red scare that would follow the end of the First World War, with its strikes and talk of 'sinister and subversive agitators', and fear of all things radical and un-American, was still in the future, and women were turning cautiously to politics. Martha would remember defiantly eating her sandwiches at school on her own, feeling both pride in her mother and confusion when other little girls, warned by their own mothers not to consort with the daughter of such a dangerous radical, took their own lunches to another corner of the playground.

In March 1916 the Democratic National Convention was held in St Louis. Seven states had already granted full suffrage to women and more were on the verge of committing themselves. Edna decided that a peaceful but memorable demonstration of women's intentions would help their deliberations. She organised what the newspapers described as the Golden Lane, seven thousand St Louis women with yellow sashes holding bright yellow parasols lining the route along Locust Street the delegates had to take from their hotel to the meeting hall. On the steps at the top stood a renowned local beauty, Mrs David O'Neil, dressed as the Statue of Liberty. Below her were seven ladies in white, representing the states endorsing the female vote; below them, in grey, those who stood for the ditherers. Another row down, this time in deepest black, mourning the intransigent states, one of which was Missouri, stood a further sombre group stretching out manacled hands imploringly at the passing delegates. And somewhere out in front, dwarfed by the full dresses and the parasols, were two small girls dressed in white: these were the women voters of the future. One of them was Mary Taussig; the other was Martha.

Edna by now was becoming well known to Washington's campaigners. When in 1919 votes for women became a reality, Carrie Chapman Catt, president of the Suffrage Association, spoke of 'raising up a league of women voters as a memorial to suffrage pioneers', and invited Edna to become its first president. Pleading family ties, Edna refused, but there was no local position on suffrage boards, or indeed on every other kind of civic undertaking, that she did not in the years to come occupy. She seems to have been a woman without guile or vanity; she was energetic and immensely practical, born, as Martha might have said, with the lucky nature that invites a lucky life. As Martha's second husband Tom Matthews would observe many years later, when you were with her you somehow felt not just better about yourself but about the whole human race.

When Martha was about twelve, she came home one day from the Mary Institute, the girls' private day school attended by the daughters of St Louis's professional families, with a new biology textbook. Leafing through it, Dr Gellhorn was irritated to see in the pictures of the human body that everything below the navel was a blank. It was the spur that he and Edna needed to push for a new school, coeducational and progressive, to match the reforms sweeping through the city's institutions, and in keeping with the progressive school movement in vogue in America. John Burroughs School, named after a well-known naturalist, with a curriculum that included a course on the life of the city, designed to foster a sense of pride in St Louis and prevent young people departing for the east coast as soon as they could get away, opened in the autumn of 1923. There was much talk of the 'beautiful religion of service', and both boys and girls gardened and played baseball in the eighteen-acre grounds, the school following Dewey in maintaining that there was no difference between male and female physique. Martha and Alfred were among its first pupils, paying the then considerable fees of $1,000 a year. Martha was one of a dozen in the top form. The two children caught the tram, the 'special', from near their house for the fifty-minute ride to the suburbs, and Alfred remembers that Martha forced him to walk on the other side of the road and not stand too near her because of the embarrassment of having a little brother. Soon, John Burroughs School had a debating society, a school council and a magazine; on all of these Martha took a leading part, becoming speaker of the Assembly and president of the Dramatic Association, saying later that she always wanted to be leader of anything she became involved in, as she preferred bossing others to being bossed. Following Dr Gellhorn's house rules, she drafted the new school's constitution and she contributed to the first issue of the school magazine a review of a collection of Galsworthy's stories, a short story of her own about life in Russia under the tsars, and a poem with a mournful refrain:

> 'Peace! do not mourn the dead,
> They're in a happier land,' I said
> And be a man! (yes, be a man)
>
> But when to me great sorrow came
> It seemed the case was not the same
> Forsooth, why should I be a man? Why? Why?

In an essay she wrote breezily and with weary sophistication during her sixteenth year, she described the world as a 'hypocritical hole, blackened by lies and deceit'. But poetry, at this stage, was where she had decided her future lay, and she was fortunate in that John Burroughs School had attracted two exceptional English teachers (one of them the future novelist Stanley Pennell), both of whom encouraged her writing. Edna having demonstrated to her the rewards of boldness, Martha sent some of her poems to Carl Sandburg, asking for his opinion. He must, she wrote later, have been not only a wise man but a nice one. The poems came back with a short handwritten note. 'If you must be a writer,' Sandburg had scrawled, resorting to a safe Delphic utterance, 'you will be.' When she wasn't writing, Martha read, mainly books belonging to her father, such as Knut Hamsun's three-volume *Growth of the Soil*, which Dr Gellhorn kept in the lavatory, or a collection of horror stories, found in her brother Walter's room.

As the children grew up, family life began to be marked by

quarrels between George Gellhorn and his eldest son. The young George was restless and unpredictable, irked by his father's ambitions for him. At sixteen, perhaps to general relief, he left home for Annapolis, from where he joined the Navy, and seldom came home again. Walter, more pliant and bookish than his older brother, got on better with his father, but neither felt much affection for the other. Walter went off to college at Amherst, then on to what was to become an outstanding career in the law. Alfred was his father's natural heir. On Sundays, Dr Gellhorn took the young boy with him on his rounds of black patients, pausing at one of the city's museums on the way home to show him a single object of beauty or interest. Alfred loved his parents' company. Having been persuaded by Walter to follow his father into medicine, he chose to pursue his medical studies in St Louis, in order to live at home. It is with great love that he remembers his father, working late every night at his desk, sitting at his typewriter and wearing an eye shade.

When Alfred was twelve, and Martha seventeen, George Gellhorn decided that the moment had come to show his two younger children his native Germany. Having crossed the Atlantic by ship, they rented a red Mercedes-Benz and drove to Breslau and Würzburg. She and Alfred, Martha wrote later, behaved like 'barbarians'. Alfred only wanted to swim or to eat. Martha, by now interested in young men, 'mooned around, looking at everything but not inquiring as to what I might be seeing'. At the Alte Pinakotek in Munich, she announced that Rubens made her feel sick; at the Bayreuth Festival she said that she loathed opera. The Germans she found 'shockingly ugly'. 'My father,' she wrote, 'struggled bitterly, despairingly and heroically against us.' Having longed for 'wakeful, interested and original minds' he was forced to conclude that his children were 'lumpish'.

For her part, Martha would complain that her father was a perfectionist, setting for himself and others the sternest standards. She knew its drawbacks all too well, for what he termed 'divine dissatisfaction' was something that she shared. Writing later to a friend, she confessed that she had a great deal of her father's blood in her, and 'he was a man who used to inform people that their doorbells were broken, and run his finger thoughtfully if silently over dirty surfaces and also look at people with friendly interest, as though they were under microscopes, and tell them they looked as if they drank/ate, or whatever, too much'. For her mother, who loved, admired and encouraged all her children, whatever they did, Martha felt lifelong love; but it was really her father, she would say, who taught her about justice, independent thought and compassion. He gave her the gift of curiosity and a taste for excellence.

* * *

With suffrage had come domestic freedoms of a kind American women had not experienced before the war. Even if there was no sudden rush of young women into offices and public life, the drudgery of housekeeping had been agreeably diminished by the arrival of tinned food, commercial laundries and Hoovers. Magazines and popular books in the early 1920s portrayed men and women dancing cheek to cheek or sitting together in speakeasies, drinking the fashionable new cocktails. There was a vogue for wearing rouge and powdering your face in public, and the fashion for straight, long-waisted dresses included skirt lengths that rose steadily season by season towards the knee. Manufacturers concentrated on finding new fabrics, easy on the working girl, rather than on lavishly decorated hats. Men and women now not only drank more often together, but drank more, especially among the young prosperous classes. The gay twenties, the 'time of wonderful nonsense', brought in jazz and a craze for mahjong. At the theatre, especially in New York, were staged plays about adultery and homosexuality, in which sex was openly and cynically discussed. 'Face-lifting' had been invented, and sunbathing was said by Coco Chanel to improve the looks; cropped, bobbed and shingled hair was more popular than the long plaits favoured by St Louis's pioneering suffragettes. Young women were also now beginning to leave their parents' homes and set up house on their own. All this fed Martha's growing restlessness, as did the family's frequent journeys. Like many of the sons and daughters of St Louis's more progressive families, Martha was sent to Europe during several long summer breaks. On one of these early visits she took against London, where it rained and she considered the food disgusting and the hotels depressing, but when she caught a train to Cornwall and rented a bicycle to ride between the country villages her spirits lifted. She had started to notice the weather.

Martha spent her seventeenth summer in France, with a chaperone called Miss Johnson and a biddable friend whom she rapidly decided she hated. By her own admission, Martha must have been extremely trying, refusing to join them in any of their excursions, and sneaking out of the hotel on her own to wander and stare. She had been saying for months how she longed to see Paris, but now found it too 'quick and sharp' and complained that it failed to provide her with the signal she expected that she had suddenly become a woman.

The signal was not long in coming. Martha was by now not exactly beautiful but striking to look at, with very long legs, very fair hair and a bold manner. In Grenoble, where they went next, a boy called Freddy, who was training to climb the Dents du Midi, kissed her; Miss Johnson, who widened her nostrils whenever she became angry, told her that she was behaving like a 'fallen woman'. Walter's brotherly strictures about not letting herself be kissed in 'summer rushes' were forgotten. She was delighted to be chosen as the 'summer love' by three Oxford boys who, like herself, wanted to spend hours discussing the world. What happened to the obedient friend is not recorded. Already, what Martha wanted to do was talk, and in Europe the young talked 'at any time, anywhere . . . life was light and quick, improvised, exploring and all roads led somewhere good'. Among Martha's papers is a telling letter from Edna, written during the Grenoble summer and evidently in reply to an indignant letter from her daughter describing something she had witnessed: 'You show yourself a hot little insurgent when you revolt at conditions of poverty . . . hot indignation is all right – as long as there is something to lead

it in a definite direction . . . Learn all you can about the system
that produces unjust poverty and find out how to go about
working for a change.'

Martha returned reluctantly to St Louis from her French
summer feeling 'itchy' and 'resentful' to find her parents cross
that she had taken up smoking and wearing earrings, but
convinced that she had finally glimpsed in 'the land of Europe'
something that had particular meaning for her. Personal rebellion, she wrote later, had always seemed to her so natural and
easy that it barely counted: it was little different from choosing
one's own clothes. Graduating from John Burroughs in June
1926, she contributed a last ponderous but rousing poem to
the school magazine.

> And you have hopes, Adventurers all, with yet
>   undaunted hearts,
> That life must be
> As strong, and proud and beautiful,
> As the magnificent sun.

* * *

Martha might perhaps have left St Louis rather sooner had it
not been for her attachment to her mother, and what was
already a marked need to live up to her parents' expectations.
It may also have been that the various conflicting forces in
her character, her longing to roam and her uncertainty about
herself, were making her path rather harder than she let on.
In a letter written to Edna in the spring of 1929 she refers to
having had a 'nervous breakdown' at the age of seventeen and
to 'my extreme selfishness, which made me indifferent to you
and to everyone except myself.' There is no other mention of
any mental problem, but even a brief encounter with depression could explain why she hesitated.

At all events, having failed her first college exams, she sat
them again and won a place at her mother's old college, Bryn
Mawr. In the autumn of 1926, shortly before her eighteenth
birthday, she caught the train east. In her luggage was a letter

from her mother, loving letters to accompany people on their travels being a charming family tradition. It contained a message that stuck in Martha's mind. 'You only possess,' Edna had written, in her looped and slanting hand, having found the saying in a book of Chinese proverbs, and possibly referring to her own close feelings for her wilful daughter, 'what you set free.' Edna seems to have been just as strongly attached as Martha. 'My dear and only girl child,' she wrote. 'How I long for your complete happiness – the tragedy of motherhood is that it can't protect what it most cherishes, and give the joys that it most longs to provide . . . Don't stop loving me . . . I am as dependent on you for my happiness as any of those who weep and moan about their loneliness.' Alfred, who was an affectionate observer of his family's entwined relationships, would later say that of all her children Martha was the one to whom their mother was most devoted. Devoted, and, perhaps more significant, it was a devotion without conditions, possibly the one true commitment that any human being can give another. 'I realise,' Martha wrote after Edna was dead, 'she approved me always – she alone, in my whole life. Yet she did not approve all my acts; only she gave me the benefit of the doubt, saying that she could not believe my motives would ever be ugly. She said I made endless mistakes and the main loser and sufferer was me; but she did not blame me for my nature, the basis of my mistakes . . .'

Bryn Mawr was not a success, and Martha did nothing to make it so, though she was beginning to perceive that hard work could be wonderfully distracting. There was little of the good talk she believed existed in Europe. In *What Mad Pursuit*, a first novel written in her early twenties and later suppressed as embarrassing juvenilia, she has her nineteen-year-old college student heroine, Charis Day, describe her intention 'to make a triumph of living'. We 'just were, don't you see, free to do what we liked', she has the initially cocky Charis explain, 'but it was always going to be a success'.

At the end of a course on English literature in which she wrote disparagingly about Wordsworth but was nonetheless praised for her 'effective style', she switched over to French and discovered a maxim of Malraux's, which she read and reread, copied out, stuck on her wall above her desk, and forever afterwards quoted, on all occasions and to all new friends: '*Travail – opium unique.*' The welcome stupor of hard work: it was a message she never forgot, however happy or preoccupied. Nothing in her later life would ever equal its unique gift of conferring forgetfulness.

And Bryn Mawr – before she failed a set of exams, then passed them with high credits at the second attempt, reached her senior year and grew 'bored' – did provide her with a much loved and admired older friend. This was a woman poet and lecturer called Hortense Flexner, little read today, who was published in *The New Yorker* and *Vanity Fair* and married to a small, genial cartoonist named Wyncie King. Always in search of models, Martha found in the Kings her second example of a truly happy marriage. 'Teecher', as Martha was soon writing to her, signing herself 'Gellhorn', was an old friend of Edna's, and evidently of the same independent and uncomplaining mould. Over the next forty years, long after she had abandoned either reading or writing poetry, Martha wrote her several hundred letters, as intimate as any she wrote in her life.

* * *

Some time towards the end of her junior year at Bryn Mawr, Martha became ill and was moved into the infirmary, 'for no known reason' as she explained to her mother in a letter 'except that I suddenly felt too rotten to continue the academic life'. She found the work not so much hard as 'unlimited in quantity' and despite an excellent memory for facts protested that 'one never gets through'. Bryn Mawr had come to oppress her; then, as later, she was convinced that the kind of intellect it fostered was useless on its own: you needed 'spirit' to turn it from heavy stone into bread. Not surprisingly, given her already pronounced aversion to the unpredictable regions of the mind, Proust, whom she had started reading, irritated her; Ibsen, on the other hand, impressed her with his 'triumph of youth dreams and hopes, over the old and worn out', as she wrote in an exam paper. In any case, she had turned her mind to quite another life, one in which she hoped to win her father's approval with her resources and talents, because along with her impatience at what she labelled intransigence she felt an uncomfortable need to make him proud of her. 'Blondes,' Dr Gellhorn had once said to her, 'only work under compulsion.' The sternest of her critics, he was constantly urging her to stop thinking so much about herself, and to leave adolescence behind. 'But how can you do that, my dear, as long as your person is covered with gigantic letters spelling EGO, as long as you *feel* that . . . the earth exists solely to furnish your pleasure.' His taunts hurt enough to leave their mark, and evidently served to strengthen her by now considerable need to impress him.

She had been writing off to newspapers around the country asking for a job and in June 1929 she announced that she would be leaving Bryn Mawr after her junior year, saying that a college degree would only qualify her for precisely the sort of job she would never want. 'I'll get something, somehow,' she told her mother. 'And I'll use it as a stepping stone to get a job abroad . . . Oh Gosh! how I ache to get over there. It's a real malady.' The *Emporia Gazette*, in Kansas, turned her down, saying that what they needed were writers who could spell local names and knew the difference between 'Herefords and Durhams and Jerseys', but the prestigious *New Republic* in New York offered her a summer job reading galley proofs, an occupation she found so excruciatingly boring that she let in 'more typos than ever in the history of the paper'. However the *New Republic* did publish her first article: a mocking and very youthful parody of Rudy Vallee, America's heart-throb crooner, brashly written and full of confidence; and then a second article about a train journey out of Grand Central Station in New York. In this, she drew a pitying contrast between the 'stale and dead' American commuters, who, like animals on cattle trains, lacked all lustre and curiosity, and the 'alive and talkative' passengers on European trains, who enjoyed 'the elements of the impossible . . . the uncertainty and the fascination of travelling'.

In November, shortly after her twenty-first birthday, she went as a cub reporter to the *Albany Times Union*, to cover women's clubs, the police beat and, on what she casually referred to as better days, the city morgue, where she stared at the corpses on the slabs, with their 'grey, marcelled bobs' and 'narrow shoulders' and speculated about their former lives. Stories about people and their lives were beginning to intrigue her. The first time, before she became blasé about the morgue assignments, 'I found myself growing cold, and shaking. I wanted to scream that it was all too ghoulish to be true.' The only girl reporter on the paper, she fought off the advances of the city editor, who was always drunk, and, like her heroine Charis, felt awkward and out of place in the rowdy, heavy-drinking newsroom. But she got her stories and everyone talked about her long legs and fair good looks, and an Irish police reporter called Joe O'Heaney nicknamed her the 'blonde peril'. Martha kept notes on her time in Albany, full of snatches of dialogue and quick sketches of people; she was now acquiring a sure ear for the telling phrase and the comic aside, and a great deal of what she saw made her indignant.

One day she followed up the story of a woman who had lost custody of her only child to her husband, because she smoked, worked as a waitress and liked to play bridge. Assuming that she would be instructed to do battle on behalf of the 'underdog', she reported to the city editor that the bigoted old judge had 'mistaken himself for Solomon'. When he told her simply to 'drop it' she complained bitterly. Keen rivalry between competing newspaper chains produced papers more concerned with exposing sensational crime stories, divorces and natural disasters than reporting serious news or social issues. After her days in court or the morgue she went with the other reporters to a 'one-armed joint' where they drank coffee and grumbled about their lives.

When Martha had been in Albany six months, a family friend persuaded her that her time was being wasted 'hobnobbing with odd persons who wore loud checked suits'. He told her that her parents were making themselves ill with worry about her. With extreme reluctance, she agreed to go back to St Louis. She was so cross that night that she got drunk on five highballs 'and all I could think about was that I had recanted on all my principles and I felt pretty sorry for myself and pretty put upon.' (In *What Mad Pursuit*, Charis Day's departure from her paper was rather more glamorous than Martha's from the *Albany Times Union*: having taken the side of a striking union employee in a clash with the police, Charis is fired by a corrupt newspaper proprietor and when later offered her job back, stalks self-righteously from the office. The underdog and injustice: two promising themes were developing.)

At first, it was fun to be home. Martha remarked on the comfort of her own bathroom and clean sheets, and the way food arrived regularly on the table, and she remembered all over again how much she loved and admired her parents. But before the end of her first week home she decided that the houses along McPherson Avenue were unbearably ugly, and that the Catholic cathedral nearby had hideous decorations. She secretly rented a room in a boarding house for $3 a week, and installed her typewriter, at which she sat writing short stories about love and a long poem in blank verse about windows and the need to escape. At lunch time, she hurried surreptitiously home. '"Life is terrible," murmured one of the freshmen,' Martha later wrote in *What Mad Pursuit*. '"Idiot!" Charis snapped. "There's absolutely nothing wrong with life. It's the way that people live that's ghastly."'

It was February. Her friends had jobs or were still at college. The more fortunate had gone east or abroad. When one day Martha started to tell her father of her outrage at a scene she had witnessed in the street, in which someone had been mistreated, she was shocked when he told her that he didn't want to hear about it. She assumed he was being selfish; only years later did she understand that he had been exhausted by her vehemence. But she kept on writing. The months in Albany had provided her with the useful lesson that for a writer there is no short cut. 'Write all the time,' she told her stepson many years later. 'Rework what you write. Hack it to pieces, cut and change . . . Writing is a self-conducted apprenticeship.' Writing, at this stage, seems to have held no terrors for her, beyond that of being boring.

It was absolutely inevitable that she would soon move on: there was nothing in St Louis that she wanted, and much that she wanted elsewhere. The end came suddenly; already Martha was becoming impatient with all forms of prevarication. Many years later she described the actual moment when she knew she was going. Walking along the street one day with her mother, she suddenly found words pouring out of her, exploding, hurtling crazily all around her. She told Edna how she hated St Louis and how she could no longer bear to live a life that had everything to do with them and nothing to do with her; she said that she felt as if she were dying when all she wanted to do was be alive. She said that she hated the city and the way that it was lost in flat land and the way that the air moved about it so slowly. She said she loathed the 'un-minds' she brushed against and their 'fearful half-thinking', their tiny rules and regulations, their laziness and bloodless-ness. Her mother said nothing and went on walking. Appalled at herself, Martha heard her own voice becoming shrill. Everything, she announced, was 'part of that death – even you'. When she stopped, her mother calmly asked what she planned to do. She replied that she was leaving for France, immediately. She longed to ask for her mother's forgiveness, but knew that if she did she would never get away. 'I had meant it all,' she wrote many years later, 'and I knew that sentimentality was horrible because it led to sacrifice which was a great sin. A sin practised by little cowardly people.' Europe was where people laughed.

After her outburst, events moved quickly. Martha did not discuss her plans with her father, believing that he would never understand. He made her feel, she wrote, 'fire-crackery and soft'. In any case, he went into a 'hard, destroying rage' at the pain she was causing her mother. At twenty-one Martha was already refusing to pretend that things were other than what they were, however ugly or uncomfortable. As with her reluctance to conceal her impatience with those who bored her, her directness left an impression on her contemporaries that she was somehow older and clearer about what she felt. Even as a young girl, she made them feel that she was bound for a different world: it was just a question of where and when she would leave.

Not long after Christmas 1929, Edna lent her the money for her train ticket to New York. Both her parents went with her to the station, where Martha tried, and failed, not to cry. When she turned to kiss her father, he leaned away. She tried to concentrate on her hat, which she considered too homely for her new life and had decided to throw out of the window as the train crossed the Mississippi.

New York was crowded, prosperous and full of new skyscrapers. Her spirits rose. Her brother Walter gave her the sofa in his apartment, and she bought a new hat, in which she visited the offices of the north German Lloyd shipping line and offered them an article on their service in exchange for a berth in what was then known as College Steerage. On the ship a few days later she simply sat and thought. 'I just waited . . . I knew I was getting back to something I had missed, something that had roots in me and was part of me . . . I was waiting for a kind of light I remembered, a grey light . . . And more than that, I knew that now I was free. This was my show, my show.'

If her formidable mother had convinced her of anything, it was the importance of never allowing yourself to be defeated, a lesson she would try again and again to impart later to the young. 'Don't fear death, my Sandy,' she wrote fifty-three years later to her stepson. 'That's a sure way to cripple life. Don't fear anything if you can possibly help it; or anyhow think about your fear and get it into shape, where you can handle it. Fear is a hideous burden and useless. Fearing something does not stop it; it only makes the time of living ugly and menaced. Self fears are really diminishing, to one's dignity as a human being, to one's chances of living hard and fully.'

Nowhere, in any of the fragments of memoirs, or in the many early letters, is there a shadow of self-doubt. Thomas Wolfe's words, which she would use in her first book – 'the hunger that haunts and hurts Americans and makes them exiles at home and strangers wherever they go' – could have been written with Martha in mind: she was a visitor in life, she would say, by constitution, and home life bored her. 'I had a theory,' she explained many years later, 'that you can do anything you like if you are willing to pay the full price for it.'

CHAPTER TWO

In Search of a Hero

In the spring of 1930, when Martha arrived in Paris with two suitcases, a typewriter and $75, France was much envied by the rest of the world. The leading economic power in Europe, second only to Britain for the size and wealth of its colonies, its army was strong, its franc solid and French industry was said to be growing faster than any other. There was very little unemployment, so many Frenchmen having died in the trenches of the First World War, and there were many more women than men. A long tradition of a centralised and protectionist civil service, even though widely recognised to be corrupt and inefficient, had effectively blinded the French to the fact that their train system was chaotic and their telephones antiquated. No one appeared to care that French newspapers were more interested in scandal than in serious reporting.

The constitution of the Third Republic, which came to power in 1875, had strengthened the French parliament at the expense of the ruling government, with the result that, between the wars, ministries lasted on average a little over six months. In March 1930, the large radical party, conservative on almost every issue, had as Prime Minister their hero of the First World War, André Tardieu. Tardieu's bulging forehead was said to owe its exceptional size to the number of brilliant ideas it housed, but the rest of the radicals were popularly known as radishes, 'red outside, white inside, and sitting in the middle of the butter dish'. At the Quai d'Orsay, Aristide Briand preached peace and rapprochement with Germany. There was as yet little sign of a depression.

Following the publication of Ernest Hemingway's *The Sun Also Rises* in 1926, young Americans in search of inspiration had begun crossing the Atlantic to settle in small hotels on Paris's left bank in search of inspiration for their novels. Martha was neither the first nor the last Bryn Mawr girl to arrive with a typewriter and a dream of escape. Saint-Germain, not so very long before the quarter inhabited by the French literary world, was now home to the largest American colony in Europe, and though Scott Fitzgerald, John Dos Passos, Ezra Pound and Nancy Cunard had all come and gone, Sylvia Beach still sold her books at Shakespeare and Company, and Archibald MacLeish or Gertrude Stein could occasionally be seen drinking at Les Deux Magots. New cinemas were opening on the Champs-Elysées, showing films by Luis Buñuel and Jean Cocteau. Radclyffe Hall's *Well of Loneliness* had been turned into a play and duly praised, while in *Sido*, Colette, a 'traveller who tells of an unknown land', had introduced her many readers to the surprising pleasures of nature. Picasso, torn between wife and mistress, was painting two-faced women, one side sensuous and beautiful, the other harsh and frightening.

On Friday and Saturday nights, the young Americans went dancing at the *bals musette* around the Luxembourg, or dropped in on the new nightclubs to listen to jazz or practise the charleston or the shimmy. Theatres kept their foyer floors highly polished, and provided orchestras, so that audiences could fox trot in the intervals. Musical reviews were more lavish than they had ever been, the dancing girls wearing great sheaths of feathers and plumes: at the Casino, Josephine Baker, an 'unforgettable female ebony statue', had already made her first appearance naked but for a single pink flamingo feather, in a show that included a live cheetah, a flight of trained pigeons, some roller skaters and an aerial ballet of stout Italian dancers. According to the Duc de Brissac, a guest at a Parisian dinner party had just twelve seconds' grace before having to produce witty answers to questions about monetary policy, Apollinaire or astronomy. So essential were the fashions dictated by Chanel and Molyneux, that *The New Yorker* ran a regular column on what smart Parisians were wearing: lipstick, even by day, brightly coloured silk stockings, nail varnish, and perms that rippled the hair like a beach at low tide. Life was glamorous, full of experiments and agreeably cheap. It was all a very long way from St Louis.

Martha had been to Paris twice before, but both times it had seemed to her a lifeless city, 'mountainously blocked out' by her travelling companions. Alone, it was full of possibilities, 'a door opening into the lovely glad-bag world'. As she walked around, she spun stories about herself and the people she observed, for it was people rather than places that already caught her attention. Leaving her suitcases and her typewriter at the station, she looked for a cheap hotel near the flower stalls of the Place de la Madeleine, eventually being forced to settle on a room so garishly furnished and so squalid she marvelled at the complete lack of French taste. It had a mirror on the ceiling and no central heating.

Dressed in brogues, an old college coat and tweed skirt, with a bunch of violets she bought instead of breakfast so as to look rich and successful, she went directly to the offices of the *New York Times* and told the bureau chief that she could start work immediately as a foreign correspondent. After six months on the *Albany Times Union* and two articles in the *New Republic* she believed herself highly experienced. After he had finished laughing, he turned her down; and on hearing her description of her hotel, he explained to her that it was a *maison de passe*, a brothel, and suggested that she would do better somewhere on the left bank. Finding a job as a very junior assistant in a beauty shop, occasionally interpreting for lost Americans, took her a week of wandering the streets, knocking on every office or shop with a sign of a vacancy. Her second hotel, in the rue de l'Université, had flowers in a vase in the hall and a grand piano at which a series of tearful young men played Chopin, and it was not until an American college friend visiting Paris explained to her about homosexuality that she realised why she was the only woman guest and why there seemed so much emotional tension. But the room cost $6 a week, and included one bath, and she felt safe among all the young men, so there she stayed, going out to eat at a nearby white Russian restaurant.

The beauty salon job lasted two weeks, and was followed by a spell writing copy about a slimming bubble bath for an American advertising agency on the Champs-Elysées called Dorlands, before she moved to the United Press, where she took down the stories of the 'provincial rag-pickers' phoning in their copy. She was clear about her own plans. 'I wanted to go everywhere and see everything and I meant to write my way.' UP let her do a few stories, and at lunchtime she went out along the Boulevard des Italiens to a restaurant where meals were paid for by tickets, bought by the week, and where a napkin cost an extra fifty centimes. She had no money for movies, the theatre or clothes.

Something of the ease and brashness of these first weeks comes across in an account of a trip she made to Tunisia with a young American lawyer called Campbell Beckett, who turned up one day in Paris and took her off to stay with the French military governor and his countess wife in an Arab house in the old part of Tunis. It was only later, when she was herself irritated by the self-centred ways of the young, that she realised what an undesirable guest she must have been. Her clothes had been embarrassingly unsuited to formal diplomatic life – a deep blue taffeta dress with a cascade of ruffles and a fish-tail sweeping out behind for the evening, a purple flowered housewife's cotton dress and sneakers for the day – while her manners had been loud and casual. One evening in the governor's house she fainted in her bath, and had to be carried, naked, by two Senegalese men servants, to her bedroom. 'Years later,' she wrote, 'I understood that the Countess had presumed Cam and me to be lovers, and had been horrified by the brazen unworldliness of the arrangement, and had catalogued me as a girl who would come to a bad and deservedly bad end.'

Returning to Paris, Martha was soon fired from UP, after a visiting South American tycoon, in some way linked to the news agency, made a pass at her in a taxi and she complained to her boss. 'When I was young,' she wrote many years later on a scrap of paper, 'alone and tempting, at the start of my travel career, I thought men a blight. Men and boys, the lot. They interfered with my liberty of action; they made me feel foolish.' Later, she turned the sacking into a short story in which the heroine, Jane, informed by her editor that her writing is not professional enough, watches 'her pride, her complete assurance, wilt'. She spends her last fifty francs on lilac. 'No money. Jobs hard to get. What the hell.' Martha herself had by now saved a little money. It was early June. She decided to find somewhere cheap to live on the coast where she could start her novel, having already decided that while journalism might make her money, the writing she considered real was fiction.

In the early 1930s, the French Mediterranean, explored by the Fitzgeralds and the Murphys, was a coastline of fishing villages, sandy coves and umbrella pines, smelling strongly of wild herbs. It was largely deserted, particularly in summer, fear of the heat, octopuses and sewage keeping foreigners away, though Colette, who had bought a house in St Tropez in 1926, spoke of it as a place for siestas and making love. Martha found a pension by the sea, brought out her note book and sat waiting for inspiration. Nothing happened. She did not wait for long, having already understood that, for her, the way to escape despair was to walk rapidly away from it, so she packed a knapsack and took to the empty roads, paying her way by making up fashion articles and posting them to American magazines. One, on the latest Parisian style in men's pyjamas, invented while staying in a hut in the hills, earned her a much needed $25. She had taken a volume of Nietzsche with her, and, as she climbed the pass leading from France into Andorra, she thought profound thoughts about the bridge between man and superman. She was twenty-one.

On her way back, terrible blisters from ill-fitting boots and the rigours of a twelve hour climb over the pass, part of it in snow, served only to make the small, deserted coves awaiting her along the French coast more entrancing. Mistaking a red rash across her chest for syphilis – though a doctor's daughter, she had a vague idea that syphilis came from drinking out of dirty glasses – she found a clinic in Marseilles and waited in a long queue of Arab and French sailors until a laughing doctor told her that she had prickly heat. It was all useful material for the great American novel, and soon her heroine Charis Day observed a red rash of her own across her chest; only in her case it was indeed syphilis.

* * *

Martha was happy, she had discovered, on her own; happy, but already aware of the particular dangers of prolonged solitude. Real life, she assumed, something that continued obstinately to elude her, must ultimately mean being with other people. After five weeks wandering along the Mediterranean coast, she returned to Paris.

During the spring she had made friends with an older woman called Gi, who had been lent a house on the edge of Paris, and Martha now went to stay with her, hating the gentility of her suburban surroundings but loving and admiring her hostess whose hopeful and self-mocking attitude towards the future should, she noted later, have served as a model to her. Instead, she simply enjoyed the pleasure of being with her, and learnt nothing, sitting all day over her note book, struggling with Charis Day's process of self-discovery. She had decided that her role was to be 'the spokesman for a generation' of young Americans. Martha had fallen in love with a journalist called Pierre de Lanux, a forty-three-year-old Parisian who, scrupulous about the difference in their ages, 'held me off, wisely and firmly'. She maintained that she was lonely, and felt herself unwanted.

Then, one day, in de Lanux's office, her life did change. Among Martha's papers, filed away after her death, is a rough diary of the most important dates in her life between 1930 and 1939. The page for 1930 consists largely of the names of towns and villages in France, Switzerland and Italy. Halfway down the page is a single line: 'July 14 (circa): met Bertrand.'

Bertrand was Bertrand de Jouvenel, whose republican father Henri was a politician and, as editor of Le Matin, one of

France's most influential journalists. His mother, Claire Boas, had a salon on the Boulevard St Germain where she entertained Henri Bergson and Gabriele d'Annunzio and where politicians came to discuss Franco-German rapprochement. Milan Stefanik, Eduard Beneš and Jan Masaryk, architects of Czech independence, were her friends. Bertrand himself, Jewish on one side and Catholic on the other, was already a successful journalist, writing about politics and the economy, and author of a first book, *L'Economie Dirigée*, in which he had outlined what he saw as the hopes of his generation. Five years older than Martha, he was outspokenly in favour of a united and peaceful Europe, and strongly against Mussolini; and he had opposed France's occupation of the Ruhr in 1923. Bertrand spoke excellent English, having read foreign academic journals for his father and compiled dossiers of extracts from them when Henri de Jouvenel was a member of the Senate foreign affairs committee, and he had then gone on to work for Beneš in Prague.

Bertrand was married to a woman called Marcelle Prat who was twelve years older than himself, something that no one found surprising. What everyone knew about Bertrand was that at the age of sixteen and a half, a shy, bookish boy studying for his baccalaureat, he had been seduced by Colette, his father's second wife. The seduction had taken place the day that Claire had sent her son to ask Colette to intervene with his father on her behalf, as she wanted to keep the name de Jouvenel, which Henri was opposing on the grounds of her increasingly embarrassing political manoeuvrings. Later, Bertrand would write that Colette had first struck him as 'small, stocky, quick', and that he had immediately noticed her imperious forehead and slanted eyes, and the thick lines of kohl she wore around her eyes. The impression she gave him, he said, was of power, not age.

It was Colette, then reaching the height of her fame and popularity, who had given Bertrand his literary education, during long summers spent in the country and on holiday at the oasis of Bou-Saada in the Algerian desert. Colette called Bertrand her 'little leopard' and her 'great whippet of a boy' and became obsessed with his weight, trying to feed him up on lobster and cream. When Martha first met him, she was in fact somewhat put off by his reputation as one of Paris's most desirable lovers, but he was a good-looking man, slender, with the body of a runner, high cheekbones and eyes that looked either grey or green, depending on the light. At the time of their affair, Colette had been forty-six, and even as it was going on, life imitating art, *Chéri*, her story of the seduction of an exquisitely beautiful boy by an older woman, Léa, was being serialised in *La Vie Parisienne*. Like Chéri, Bertrand never saw Colette naked. But then Colette herself, unlike the youthful and svelte Léa, was decidedly fat. In his own auto-biography, *Un Voyageur dans le siècle*, published in 1979, Bertrand makes little of his seduction by Colette, though he admits that he surrendered to her instantly and totally. What he felt about the portrait of the spoilt and tyrannical Chéri, whose beauty was matched only by his narcissism, is not recorded. Much as Colette overfed Bertrand in real life, the emotionally generous Léa pressed on to Chéri the rich food he craved. 'A mon fils CHERI Bertrand de Jouvenel,' Colette wrote in the flyleaf of the copy of *Chéri* she gave him.

By the summer of 1930, Bertrand's affair with Colette, which had lasted five years, lay in the past, having been brought to an end by Bertrand's mother, when the suggestion of a scandal threatened to tarnish all their political lives; but Colette had retained a motherly concern for her boy lover, telling friends that she was proud of the way she had opened up the world to him. 'I rub him down,' she told her friend Marguerite Moreno, 'stuff him, scrub him with sand, and burn him in the sun.' The affair had effectively finished her marriage to Henri – it was rumoured that Henri found them in bed together – but Bertrand continued to see his stepmother from time to time. Marcelle, to whom he had now been married for six years, was also a writer and it was said in Paris – and repeated later by Martha in a long, confessional letter to a friend – that Marcelle, in contrast to the considerably older Colette, had always seemed to Bertrand young and virginal, and that in any case he had inherited from Colette the 'habit of being *taken* and looked after'. When it came to his living habits, Bertrand was simply, as she rather coldly put it, a '*poule de luxe*'.

He was also, however, a clever and remarkable man, and his encounter with Martha in the summer of 1930 played a significant part in his long and controversial life. For the rest of July, Martha haunted Pierre de Lanux's office, hoping to conquer him; Bertrand haunted it too, 'staring at me' as Martha wrote later, 'reaching for me, almost maddening me with his love'. When he kissed her, 'behaving like a starved man with food', she struggled 'like a caught fish'. Already, Bertrand had perceived in her something that he felt he lacked and longed for: 'For we live on different planes, you and I,' he wrote to her, using the formal *vous*. 'You live impulsively, I calculatingly. You deliciously overturn everything that you lay hands on, while I force myself, small-mindedly, to rearrange things that look to me untidy.'

Something about his intensity terrified her and on 1 August she escaped to go walking in the Vosges with an American college friend called Ibby. She did not tell Bertrand where she was going. They were joined by another Bryn Mawr friend, and the three girls rented bicycles and pedalled around the chateaux of the Loire, until Martha began to find her old friends 'tight-lipped and narrow and full of the most cement-like prejudices', and took off once again on her own, saying that they doubtless found her 'fallen apart' and a 'tower of corruption'. Wherever she turned Martha now seemed to feel at increasing odds with her surroundings.

It was in this restless, self-doubting mood that she reached the lake of Annecy, near Geneva, with her knapsack. Funds were once again very low, but she kept going on windfalls, which arrived from her parents in the guise of dividends or bonds, and which she only later realised were simply their way of sending her money without wounding her pride. Once again, she found a small pension by the water and settled down to write. But Bertrand had learnt that she had been bound for Annecy and appeared one day in the prow of a motorboat 'like Lochinvar', having stopped in the villages all around the lake asking whether anyone had seen a tall, fair-haired American girl with a knapsack. Martha blamed her upbringing for what happened next, though less for the event itself than for her reaction to it.

Her parents were too intelligent and too sophisticated to be strict moralists, but they had brought their children up with a 'great love of nobility'. Her father, in particular, had somehow conveyed to her – she never explained exactly how – that men suffered when they wanted a woman and were refused. When, day after day, Bertrand begged her to sleep with him, 'in a state of anguish, something terrible, something I did not know about', she felt she was being selfish. Selfishness, like lying, was unacceptable. 'I haven't the right to refuse,' Charis Day says to herself when a poor North African student she meets asks her to sleep with him. 'He's brave and his life is unbearably hard. It doesn't matter about me, I don't count. If he needs me, I must help him.' And so, one night by the lake of Annecy, Martha slept with Bertrand.

Added to her sense of shame – for her father had imparted mixed messages, guilt if refusal, shame if acceptance – was a fear that since she herself had neither wanted nor enjoyed the experience there was something wrong with her, 'something not quite like a woman'. She followed her usual instinct: she fled. Before dawn, while Bertrand slept, she packed her knapsack and crawled out of the window 'embarrassed in a way so profound' she later wrote, 'that I doubt if I can ever describe it'.

Bertrand followed her. He wept, he pleaded, he told her he loved her. And, little by little, because Martha was young and adventurous, and Bertrand a nice man, they started to have fun. He had never owned a knapsack and was charmed by hers. They went to Sils Maria in the Swiss Alps, Nietzsche country, and walked round and round the black lake, discussing Zarathustra; they travelled down to Lugano in Italy and were arrested by the border police while trying to climb over the fence with a bar of soap in order to wash in the lake; they waded into Lake Como where Bertrand, revealing too late that he could not swim, was only saved from drowning by his brand new knapsack, which acted as an unexpected float. But while Bertrand wanted her as a woman 'almost too much, but I don't know, I have no way of knowing, what is the right and correct amount', Martha thought of herself as a man, on whom everyone depended, and believed that without her constant 'effort, organisation, planning, will', life would 'whirl into chaos'. Everything in her upbringing had suggested that life must be governed by conscious and unselfish intent, informed by intelligence and reason; the random and anarchical nature of love presented loss of control of a kind that nothing had prepared her for. Was it more than the simple fact that she, unlike Bertrand, had not fallen in love? Whatever the reason, Bertrand's huge need for her, as well as her own sense and language of abnegation and duty, created an unhappy undertow for their long relationship to come.

* * *

In 1930 it was still perfectly possible to believe in a League of Nations. The Depression that had already devastated America and was threatening to destabilise the entire West had not yet bitten deep in Europe, while the principle of collective security was still more or less intact. Japan's attack on Manchuria lay more than a year in the future. Neither Hitler nor Stalin had yet travelled very far towards their dreams of totalitarianism. Supporters of the League could still maintain that peace in the world could be achieved by peaceful means alone.

Both Henri de Jouvenel and Bertrand had often written, with considerable enthusiasm, about the League's affairs, and in the early 1920s Bertrand had served for a while as vice president of its student federation. Martha, whose liberal family had understood all too well the dangers of the Treaty of Versailles, was soon as passionate about an organisation that, for the moment at least, promised permanent peace. From Paris, to which she and Bertrand had returned at the end of the summer, she arranged with the *St Louis Post-Dispatch*, then a newspaper with a considerable reputation in America, to visit Geneva and write a series of articles on the League's most prominent women delegates.

Martha liked Geneva. She had enjoyed her earlier summer vacations in the city and kept in touch with friends from that time. Returning now in some triumph, not long before her twenty-second birthday, as an accredited journalist with access to whatever caught her imagination, she wandered down the corridors of the Hôtel des Bergues, where the more important delegates were staying, making notes about their appearance and behaviour. She recorded that the Chinese bore expressions of 'piteous cynicism', while the Japanese appeared lordly.

Like many other aspiring young women journalists, Martha was adamant that she was not interested in the 'woman's angle', and she deplored the way that enterprising women were discussed rather as if they were performing dogs. She called her commission for the *Post-Dispatch* 'harmless whoring'. It was perhaps a little disingenuous, in that she had kept herself financially afloat at least in part on occasional fashion articles, but Geneva gave her the chance to define in print precisely what she felt about modern feminism. In the second of two long articles, she drew an admiring portrait of Mlle Henni Forchhammer, the Danish woman who had been the first female delegate to the League back in 1920. Mlle Forchhammer, Martha coolly observed, was not a glamorous woman. She was small, shy and white-haired and she wore her old-fashioned watch pinned endearingly to the front of her dress with a safety pin. The hem of her skirt was coming down. But Mlle Forchhammer was a worker, a knowledgeable, intelligent delegate who went about her job without fuss. 'It would not occur to Mlle Forchhammer,' wrote the twenty-one-year-old Martha in an article running to two full columns, 'to make an issue of herself as a woman: she is a human being, living in the twentieth century, with certain obligations and certain abilities.' This small, unprepossessing Danish woman was in fact the symbol of modern feminism, neither trading on nor ignoring her femininity. The days of the suffragette and the blue stocking were, wrote Martha with youthful assurance, over.

The two articles written, Martha did not waste any more time on the women. What interested her far more was the power she saw exercised by the delegates every day in the Assembly, and the collection of reporters whose job it was to translate their words into stories that would appeal to readers. The two, she reasoned, were inextricably connected. It was all a question of reaching the people who had interesting things to say, and doing your homework beforehand. For all her apparent casualness, Martha was extremely conscious of her looks, and not against using them when they might be useful. A very young and blonde American girl, with no apparent timidity, was not a common sight in the League of Nations. Schooled by Bertrand to recognise the faces of the political leaders attending the meetings, Martha was entranced when, sitting in the press gallery, she heard Aristide Briand declare: '*Tant que je suis où je suis, il n'y aura plus jamais de guerre.*' She had no hesitation in going up to him afterwards and telling him how much she had admired his speech. Briand invited her to dinner. The evening went well and she enjoyed his fatherly manner and his indiscreet gossip about fellow delegates, but she had expected sonorous pronouncements about the state of the world, and a certain weariness from bearing the weight of world peace on his shoulders. It gave her a first glimpse of the ordinariness of leaders, and of the way that power seemed to have so little to do with inspiration, and she never forgot it. Afterwards she walked around the city, eating hot cheese tarts and hoping that Briand had a good heart. Then she went to look for the other foreign correspondents, who sat together drinking between sessions in the Café Lutetia, and was extremely pleased to note that this illustrious group seemed perfectly willing to accept her as one of their own. She was getting a first taste of that particular excitement that all journalists experience, when they suddenly feel they have understood a complicated story, perceived its underlying truths and become party to its innermost secrets. 'I believed,' she wrote, 'that if everyone knew the truth, justice would be done.'

* * *

After Geneva, Bertrand took Martha to Italy. He had left Marcelle and now, whenever parted from Martha, wrote her loving letters. 'My beloved, I am so happy – We have such a marvellous life – Your work – my work – our car – our Sundays – our nights – our friends – We're independent – we're free – we're proud – we're young – we're in love – we stand out from all others . . . Oh my love.' He called her 'rabbit'. She called him Smuf. They travelled down the coast to Rapallo, then back up again to Tuscany. Under Mussolini's disastrous economic policies industrial production was falling rapidly and there were said to be huge parts of Italy where children were barely kept alive on tomatoes, bread and olive oil. But what Martha would chiefly remember about the journey was the day in Florence when they had been planning their future and a telegram came from Marcelle announcing that she was pregnant, and begging Bertrand to return home. What Bertrand would remember was that Martha seemed little interested in her surroundings, and preferred to sit in cafes.

Compared with her new friends, well versed in the complexities of modern European politics and culture, Martha felt herself to be extremely ill educated. Knowing the pleasure that it would give her father, and encouraged by Bertrand who, after a brief spell with Marcelle, was again back with her, Martha enrolled at the Haute Ecole des Sciences Politiques on their return to Paris. Remembering her enjoyment of Nietzsche during her walks in the South of France, she chose to study the German philosophers. It took her little more than a couple of weeks for her to realise her mistake. It was not that she had trouble with either the French or the German language: it was the content of the classes that baffled her. She sat impatiently through a number of lectures, listening to sentences that had no meaning for her; before the end of term she left, saying she would attend political meetings, of which Paris was full, instead. Debate and analysis: neither appealed to her in the way that people did, and how they lived.

Yet her uneasiness about her new life had increased over the months. Her early friends, scruffy, eager, tentative like herself, had scattered and been replaced by Parisians, well-informed, highly politicised people who were at the same time chic and confident. She felt that her clothes were wrong. More and more, she had the uncomfortable feeling that things were expected of her that she had no idea how to deliver. Good 'livers', she told Bertrand, and the words have a ring of sadness to them, were 'even more scarce than good writers'. Writing to her at about this time, Bertrand spoke of his desire for her, his 'wild will to possess'. 'I have learned,' he wrote, 'to coat it with light laughter and playfulness. But it's brutal, it's carnal, it's damn real.' To Martha it felt all too real. 'I was stuck,' she would write, 'with a lot of maddening emotional problems which I did not want. I began to feel like a plaything of destiny which made me at once gloomy, angry and confused.' Sometime towards the end of the year, she realised that she, too, was pregnant.

There was no question of marriage, Marcelle having made it clear that she would not give Bertrand a divorce; in any case she wanted him back. Though an abortion would have been easy to fix in Paris – France in the 1930s had the highest number of abortions in Europe – Martha felt 'in every way trapped'. After Christmas, she booked herself a cheap passage on a ship going to America. She had been in France for ten months. 'I knew myself to be old and failed,' she wrote with the sense of drama and tragedy that she sometimes went in for during these early years. 'My life had come to nothing, I did not have whatever it took to live.' Instinctively shrewd about herself, which often made her appear older and wiser on paper than in her behaviour, she concluded that it was all due to a constant need for heroes. 'Despite my best efforts to turn everyone I met into a hero, people sensibly enough did not feel like playing the part thrust on them . . . Since others would not perform as I demanded or expected, I had to do it myself and act heroically.' Like her father, Bertrand had failed to live up to her ideal.

CHAPTER THREE

A Little Hungry for a Long Time

Martha's diary for December 1930 consists of one short entry. 'Xmas(?)' it says. 'St Louis (ill and pregnant).' Dr Gellhorn was evidently angry and unforgiving about his daughter's involvement with the married Bertrand; at some point, according to the pages of memoir written at the end of the 1950s, he called her 'selfish scum'.

In January she went to Chicago for an abortion. Beyond one reference to the actual event, Martha wrote nothing about it, neither then nor later. In keeping with her self-imposed stoicism and with her refusal to allow herself to complain, she seems to have treated the loss of Bertrand's child in her customary brisk, matter-of-fact way. It had to be done; the thing was to do it efficiently, quickly and with the minimum of fuss. To do otherwise would have been unacceptably self-indulgent. One can only speculate about what this may have cost her in terms of real pain, grief stored up and not allowed to surface.

Martha was not in a happy position. In America, as in France, society was at a moment of rapid and confusing change. The Coolidge prosperity under which she had grown up had seen young women for the first time earn decent salaries, move around freely and unchaperoned and live in apartments on their own. She had read *The Great Gatsby* and *Babbitt*, and the new literary magazines, such as *American Mercury*, that were published in the 1920s, and laughed with H.L. Mencken at sentimentality and academic pomposity. 'I rebelled naturally,' she said many years later. 'I understood experimenting: my whole life has been an experiment.' With Einstein, Freud and Bertrand Russell had come the heady new thought that not only was there no such thing as unquestionable right or wrong, but that certainty of any kind was an illusion. And even if the Wall Street crash of October 1929 had returned a measure of formality and conservatism to American life, the Gellhorns personally had been little hit by the financial upheavals. There was a family story that Dr Gellhorn had once acquired some stock on a friend's advice, but having forgotten its name, spent hours at the breakfast table with his children trying to guess which one it was.

As part of their liberal tradition, the Gellhorns had brought up their only daughter with clear views about tolerance, censorship and racial and sexual equality, and certain immutable standards of personal behaviour. On to these, while with Bertrand in Paris, she had grafted a new and less rigid morality, one that involved few obligations, beyond that of listening to one's own instincts and desires. Bertrand saw their love affair as excitingly bound up with the freedoms of postwar Europe; Dr Gellhorn saw it as painfully self-centred and ultimately destructive. Martha herself lay uneasily somewhere in the middle, still needing her parents' approval, and, what was more, genuinely convinced that she was applying their standards to her own life, yet believing that what she and Bertrand had together should not be sacrificed to respectability. Neither she nor her father was prepared to make concessions. 'My mother,' Martha wrote later, 'loved us both and was miserable for us both.' But even Edna, who was 'much smarter than anyone I know', did not seem to sympathise with her conflict of loyalties. 'I think I am probably sexually repressed and all queer because I have scrambled sex and aesthetics and morals and fear into a stinking mess and I'm suffocating somewhere at the centre,' she wrote to a friend, evidently struggling to sort out the contradiction she felt between her very obvious attractiveness to men and her own lack of responsive feelings.

Once again, she was rescued by work. For the next four months, living on somewhat strained terms at home, she filled her days with her novel, and with short stories and articles, of which she would produce dozens of fragments, all neatly typed, in the next few years. Some were written in the first person; some were set in America, others in Paris; many revolved around the lives of cub reporters, young women writers, their parents and brothers and sisters, and the tensions between them, or around friendships between older and younger women. There are ones about abortions and about college life. The tone is often a little lofty. The heroines, dark haired and silent, have 'infinitely languid' eyes. 'I wrote as I breathed and saw,' Martha later noted in a diary, 'very fast, not worrying, it was as easy as a worm's digestion. I swallowed the world around me and it came out in words.' There was not a great deal of room for feelings.

None of these stories appears to have been published, and it is possible that none was even submitted for publication. But it was not in Martha's nature to brood. Sometime in April 1931, deciding that she needed a break from St Louis, she persuaded the *Post-Dispatch* to pay her $25 for every story they took for their Sunday magazine, and the Missouri Pacific Railway to give her a free Pullman pass in exchange for publicising their routes to the west. Alone, a roving correspondent in a 'brand new outfit' of a blue cotton shirt and full skirt, with sneakers on her feet and a small suitcase she decided more suitable to her new role than a knapsack, she 'bounced across the continent to the Pacific coast and back . . . and America looked vast, beautiful and empty'. She paused in Texas, Nevada, New Mexico and California, interviewed a girl bullfighter called Juanita, and sought out three of her heroes: Tom Mooney, the imprisoned union leader, the heavy weight boxer Jack Dempsey, and the poet Robinson Jeffers, whose message about man's egocentricity and indifference to the beauties of nature had struck her keenly. All three made 'flashy prose' soon speeding its way back to the *Post-Dispatch*. The first story to appear was about a town in east Texas, where a sudden discovery of oil had brought 'human bedlam . . . a forest of oil wells, towers eighty feet high . . . machinery scraping, chugging, pounding' and where the three Texas

Rangers in charge of law and order kept their drunken prisoners chained by the leg to a peg in a circle of dust. 'The gaunt new millionaires,' wrote Martha, 'sat in rocking chairs on their crumbling porches, bemused', their fingers thickly covered in diamond rings. At night, she slept in a derailed Pullman car, eating cold baked beans out of the tin, watching the oil men gamble 'while greenbacks fluttered down like falling leaves'. They addressed her as 'little lady' and apologised for their bad language.

In Reno, 'land of the lotus eaters', she wrote about 'women with indiscriminate hips, clothes by Sears Roebuck, speakeasies serving dago red called sparkling burgundy', and complained that never before had she been so bitterly bored. She was fending off the 'eternal male: the pursuer (Ugh)'. In Ciudad Juarez in Mexico, she talked to a heavily pregnant French prostitute, dowdy and to her twenty-two-year-old eyes very old, who was reading Alexandre Dumas and André Gide as inspiring prenatal influences on her unborn child. When she at last reached California, she wrote to Stanley Pennell, her English teacher from John Burroughs School, who sometime that spring had fallen in love with her. 'Palm trees along the boulevards, and God bountiful with greenery. But as usual humanity is a stench in the nostrils of the knowing . . . I have developed a Doubting Thomas complex (he was the pooh-pooh guy wasn't he?). But can still get pretty bright-eyed over the way the hills move up from the earth, and the wind blows.' She described life as 'damn funny and almost fun'. Pennell had sent her Evelyn Waugh to read on her journey, and she wrote that for him life was 'all swill . . . but laughing swill . . . and if one forgets to laugh swill becomes noxious, unendurable, whereas it really isn't important enough to be that'. To Pennell, her tone was breezy, mocking. She ridiculed the nasal voices, people who were 'cow-like' or openly too enthusiastic. 'Avoid Dubuky. Avoid almost all cities, towns, hamlets. Wherever mortals squat together, forming clubs, and breeding with Presbyterian refinement, life smells.' Never again would she sound quite so young or sure of herself; but she was learning important lessons in writing and reporting, training herself to observe and remember, and if her actual words could be off-putting, it was becoming clear that the thoughts behind them were pertinent and perceptive.

Not everyone succumbed to her easy manner and blonde hair. In Nevada, various people she had hoped to interview turned her away. 'I find myself walking with my chin high,' she told Pennell, 'my mind seething with hate and ennui.' She was frequently lonely, saying that she felt like a miserable small child. But her clear eye for her own impulses and reactions, as well as for the effect she had on others, seldom failed her. Later in the trip, when she paused in Bryn Mawr, she wrote a shrewd and confessional letter to Pennell. 'This thing called "breeding" fascinates me. I have no breeding. I am just plainly a freak of environment, and an ability to giggle. But the "bred" take me in as do the "unbred". And I feel always like a spy, because I am watching them, thinking about them, never accepting them, and someday I shall have things to say about them, criticisms and laughter . . . My dear, I shall need you always, and give you nothing in return . . . And this urge to run away from what I love is a sort of sadism I no longer pretend to understand.' Though she had largely abandoned the verse she had poured out at college, she sent him a poem called 'Spleen':

> I have said that I laughed
> at the damp, overheated emotions
> common to the mean average.
> It is so.
> But can I not find some high, dignified hysteria.
> Some easy harmony of lust and love,
> breath and body,
> brain and beauty, with never a suppressed hiccough,
> a gaseous stomach,
> a fan-shaped sneeze,
> to corrode the scheme?

Martha was never in love with Pennell – his name does not appear on a short list she later wrote of the men she loved in the 1930s – and she told him that she was trying to forget Bertrand, to whom she had taken to referring as her 'angel of destruction'. But Pennell's own diary makes plain his own feelings. 'I believe I love her still' he wrote over a year later, in July 1932, 'but nothing could come of it'. He sent her *Zuleika Dobson* and reflected that she had at least inspired him to write the best sonnets he would ever write. As for Martha, her long solitary train journey across America was fast restoring a sense of her own worth, as well as developing a lively journalistic eye, alert to subtleties of meaning and the telling visual detail. And she had become increasingly watchful of any tendency, in herself or anyone else, to rewrite history, or avoid facing the truth, however unpleasant.

Back in St Louis she was seized by a sudden misgiving that she had not been absolutely frank with Pennell, and wrote in unambiguous terms of her lack of loving feelings for him, quoting Hemingway's words in *A Farewell to Arms*: 'You're brave. Nothing ever happens to the brave', words that together with Malraux's epigram became an early mantra in her life. Already, she was talking of travel, of her 'need of the far lands', as the 'only thing besides writing which is worth the sweat'. What she could not blot out with work, the sense of panic 'over what I can no longer confine or understand', Martha now kept at bay with constant movement. She had seen in herself an unsettling pendulum that swung between a craving for the company of amusing people and a real need for solitude. It took her, that summer of 1931, to house parties in Bryn Mawr, to theatres and nightclubs in New York, and, towards the end of June, back on to the Missouri Pacific Railway for one last story for the *Post-Dispatch*, this time to Mexico. She spoke no Spanish, received none of the necessary vaccinations, had no tourist card and was a young girl travelling on her own, each on their own enough to make the trip hazardous. At the frontier she was asked for a letter from her family giving her permission to travel. She brazened it all out, telling the police that she was engaged to the American ambassador's son and that he was waiting for her in Mexico City. They let her through.

Mexico was everything that she most liked. She was capti-vated, writing delighted letters to Pennell about the perfect sun, the armfuls of roses and canna lilies she had bought for forty cents in the market, and the people with 'faces which say something'. 'I spun like a top,' she wrote later. 'I did not know where to begin.' Even food poisoning did not spoil her immediate sense of pleasure.

She had heard that Eisenstein was making a film about Mexico's history and took first a train and then a mule to find him at work in the desert. There was nothing in her long piece for the *Post-Dispatch* about the Russian film maker that suggested either her youth or her ignorance of film making. It was authoritative and thoughtful, with none of the almost childlike zest that still filled many of her letters. The same sober, professional tone ran through what she wrote about Diego Rivera, who was painting a mural in the National Palace in Mexico City when she tracked him down one day. She climbed a scaffolding and perched next to him, marvelling at the contrast between his delicate hands and the 'gargantuan proportions of the man', and envying an occupation she later decided was the 'least stuck in the kitchen of life', which for her was even then ultimate praise. They talked about the glories of American machinery, and the need to wean Americans from their dependence on European art. She wrote in her notebook that he was wearing a dark blue polka-dotted shirt and that his laugh was an 'absurdly pleased chortle'. Later, she had dinner with Frau Wills, wife of the German minister, and noted that she was wearing 'one of those special, flat, infinitely life-less fox furs one sometimes sees in European provincial cities slung about her shoulders like a knapsack'. Already, the bones of what was becoming her particular style were being laid: the subject picked out by the memorable and seemingly insignif-icant detail, jotted down on scraps of paper or in little note-books, which would later turn into a talent for describing the ordinariness in tragedy, the horror of war framed by the smallest of scenes.

Martha's contract with the *St Louis Post-Dispatch* was now at an end and she returned home to spend the summer with her parents by the sea, fooling lazily with her brothers Alfred and George, getting sunburnt and swimming naked. Now that she appeared to have given up Bertrand, her relations with her father had greatly improved. She stopped smoking, ate green vegetables, put on three pounds, talked loftily of feeling 'Olympian – imperturbable and remote', and was merely irritated when the *New Republic* turned down a proposed article on the grounds that it was not 'valuable commercially'. 'Great Christ,' she asked, 'what is?'

The holiday was almost over when she heard from Bertrand that he was arriving in New York at the end of September. Learning of the proposed visit, the lovesick Pennell was reproachful. Martha's reaction was one of impatience and irritation. She told him that he was 'gruesome' in implying that she had been less than honest with him. Given the general uproar that had descended on the Gellhorn household with the news of Bertrand's visit, she declared, the very least Pennell could do was have the guts to be properly angry.

* * *

It was in his mother's salon in Paris, among the radical deputies and the advocates for a united Europe, that Bertrand had taken his first political steps. A biography of Zola that he had written was published in the spring of 1931, and he was now writing for a number of magazines and newspapers of the left, warning against the continuing dangers of the legacy of the Versailles treaty, and anxious that no one was taking Hitler seriously enough. The depression was only beginning to bite in France, but the once rich Americans were leaving the cafés in the St-Germain, selling their flats and their houses, and drifting home. In the rue de la Paix jewellers and art dealers were losing fortunes on cancelled orders. Janet Flanner, *The New Yorker* writer, reported that women had been seen paying for their own cocktails in the Ritz bar. Bertrand, who had been missing Martha acutely, had decided that the moment had come for him to observe and write about the American Depression at first hand, driving through the Southern corn belt.

He arrived in New York on the *Ile de France* at the end of September to find Martha waiting for him on the quay in a blue linen dress. Both their families had objected strongly to their plan to drive south together so, as Martha put it in her memoirs, they went out and bought a platinum-coloured vintage Dodge for $25 and set off. Bertrand felt about America the way she felt about Europe: it was a place to laugh. He led the way, proposing routes to take, listening, writing notes; she followed 'doubting and criticising and worrying' and later said she remembered very little about the trip beyond a feeling of space and that 'nobody had taken root or possession of the land'. The South seemed to her 'full of determinedly ignorant dreamers'. Never having minded poverty when on her own, she now found something repellent and corrupting about it. 'Poor *à deux*,' she noted, 'is a disaster.' For once, she seems to have taken little heed of the devastation they passed through.

Driving through Mississippi late one night, trying to reach a town called Columbia where they hoped to find a reasonable hotel, they broke down in the middle of the countryside. For several hours, no one passed by. The mosquitoes were ferocious, and they sat gloomily by the roadside, smoking to fend off their bites.

A truck eventually appeared, and its driver stopped to offer them a lift, explaining that he was on his way to a lynching, that of a nineteen-year-old black boy called Hyacinth, accused of raping a white plantation owner in her fifties. They climbed on board and the truck soon stopped under some trees. They could see a crowd gathered around a tree not far away, with a car parked directly underneath its branches. Martha and Bertrand stayed in the truck. 'We did not speak to each other,' Martha wrote later. 'I have a memory of trying not to be sick and trying not to believe any of this. We had heard children's voices too.' Eventually the driver returned, and they went on.

In New Orleans they rented rooms in the old part of town, in what had once been a grand colonial house with high ceilings and wrought-iron balconies. For a while, they both took jobs in a cafeteria, where 'every new American expression' filled Bertrand with 'ecstasy'. By the end of the year they were in Hollywood, where the orange trees were already covered in fruit and houses came in the shape of French chateaux, English cottages and Italian villas; they moved into a Spanish-looking bungalow, in order for Bertrand to write his articles for *La République*, and to start work on a book. Every day, wearing nothing but a bathing dress, Martha sat at her 'deadly novel'. This was how she liked to write, in the full sun, getting brown, wearing as little as possible.

When they ran out of money they went to the film studios, where there was a current craze for costume dramas, requiring a vast number of actors, and joined the pool of extras, getting occasional parts at $15 a day. During the 1930s, Hollywood's golden age, the studios produced over five thousand feature films. Bertrand was much in demand as an elegant bachelor, kissing hands and leaning against pillars, or as a Cossack, in a tall fur hat. Having long since abandoned their vintage Dodge, they bought a grey touring Cadillac. One weekend, they were invited by new friends to go panning for gold, and had to agree to having their eyes covered so that they would not know where they had been. After a long hot morning in the sun, a religious hermit they came across told Martha that her destiny was to raise her voice someday for the dumb. In her memoirs, written almost thirty years later, Martha remembered declaring firmly that she loathed animals, but that if by dumb he meant voiceless and poor people, then of course that was exactly what she planned to do.

They were always short of money. But when the day came that Martha was auditioned for a part in a nightclub scene, in which she was supposed to swing her long legs and say 'Look at me, I'm full of sex' – and they turned her down, on the grounds of her firm, clear, Bryn Mawr tones – she decided that she had had enough of Hollywood. Leaving Bertrand behind, she took the car and drove up the coast to Carmel, where she rented a two-room cottage by the sea and at once 'floated off into that state of exalted daydreaming' which invariably came to her with solitude. Writing to tell Bertrand that when he joined her he would have to keep up appearances by taking a room in a nearby hotel, she added that he would also have to look after himself, because she *'seriously hated'* disorder and in any case needed to be alone to write. *'Viens vite!,'* she wrote. 'I may not be able to live with you but I surely can't live without you.'

Their love affair had moved into an uneasy phase. While Bertrand seems to have felt nothing but pain at being without her, Martha alternated between longing for his presence and guilt that she did not miss him more. 'You've given me everything and I've given you in exchange faint, grudging thanks, so little warmth. My dear, forgive me,' she wrote from her cottage, adding that she would not mind if he decided to have an affair. 'Please be a conqueror for a bit; forget me. I'm a shit face; and make yourself realise again what you knew before I came.'

One day, while still in Hollywood, Bertrand read in a paper that a young woman living on her own in Carmel had been kidnapped, and spent many frantic hours believing it might be her. He spoke of the 'dread, anxiety, regret' he felt whenever he was not with her and at times feared what his great attachment to her might do to their future. For her part, she was at last working hard on her novel, though she worried ceaselessly that it was bad, and never in her life had she tried so hard or for so long to make something good. She referred to her work as the 'foulest *crotte*', and to herself as an amateur of fourteen, for whom the 'bloody words would not walk straight'. She was frightened about the future, sensing that there was no longer anything to which she could return 'spiritually', that she was no longer a *'jeune fille'* and could not live without a man because her body, if nothing else, called for its 'accustomed food'. She had found Colette's *La Vagabonde* in the basement of the Carmel library, and wrote to tell Bertrand that she considered his stepmother to be her *'chèr maître'*: 'Even in matters of style I can find many gropings in me which look like her finished product. Moreover, we have both got one obsession: the individual. She has no "*thèse*" and neither have I; the life of any man or woman being in itself the highest unreason and therefore mystery, wonder, beauty.' Only, she added, Colette 'should have left you alone'.

In April 1932, having been in America six months, Bertrand decided that he needed to return to France for his work. Martha was finding her rift from her family increasingly hard – Dr Gellhorn had told her that in his view there were 'two kinds of women, and you're the other kind' – and Bertrand agreed to ask Marcelle again, more pressingly, for a divorce.

Bertrand's meeting with Marcelle did not go well. Unlike Martha, she had decided against an abortion, and a son, a big blond baby she said bitterly looked very like Martha, had been born and named Roland. She was adamant that there would be no divorce. Bertrand, shocked by Marcelle's haggard and sickly appearance, withdrew. He sent Martha a telegram begging her to join him despite his failure to push Marcelle harder, and was again miserable when she accused him of not trying hard enough. 'You are built for fights,' he wrote back. 'And you have had but too few occasions for fighting . . . You are throwing away an almost unique chance: the chance of a grand fight on both fronts, of a challenge to prejudices as to private behaviour as well as to established interests on the political and social plane . . . I want you. Find out for yourself whether you want me.

'I think you do.'

In the middle of June, Bertrand wrote directly to Edna, telling her that in the circles in which he moved in Paris marriage was more or less out of date, but that nonetheless his greatest wish was for Martha to be happy. He could see how wretched this pulling backwards and forwards was making her. He also recognised that while she felt 'no wild passion of any description for him', she did need the intellectual life they shared, 'considering that she lives mainly by her brain'. What he proposed was that Martha should return from America to Europe, where she was happier, but go to live in Berlin, while he, from Paris, helped her write and place articles in French papers about the political situation in Germany. If necessary, if Martha met someone suitable whom she could love, he would step out of her life.

Edna's reply is lost. But early in June Martha borrowed $1,000 at 6 per cent interest from a friend and booked a passage on the *President Roosevelt*. Evidently the possibility that Bertrand might still be able to get a divorce in Russia, and marry Martha there, had been raised, and Martha's lawyer friend Campbell Beckett had offered to go to St Louis to discuss it with the Gellhorns. 'Ah my beloved, my beloved,' Martha wrote to Bertrand. 'Sweetheart, I've missed you so . . . I'm coming, I'm coming, I'm coming.'

*   *   *

Martha and Bertrand planned to meet when her boat docked at Le Havre in July, and to go walking in Germany. The elections for the Reichstag were due to take place at the end of the month, and Bertrand wanted to see Berchtesgaden. When Martha walked through customs Bertrand was 'more scared than I have ever been', as he later told Edna. He had left Martha in California brown and healthy; three months later she got off the boat thin, frail and her voice weak. His first thought was that she might have tuberculosis. Sometime during the crossing from New York, she had in fact caught an ear infection; but the strain of being tugged between Bertrand and her parents was beginning to tell. She suddenly seemed to him uncharacteristically fragile. They drove across France and into Germany. Berchtesgaden reminded Bertrand of Disneyland, a place of gingerbread houses, where men wore lederhosen, and boy scouts celebrated '*la culture du corps*'. On 10 July, they listened as Hitler made a speech; Bertrand felt sure he was hearing the death knell of the European partnership that he so believed in.

Martha's ear grew steadily worse. It was before the day of antibiotics and the pain became unbearable. They found a doctor who lanced the abscess and prescribed morphine. When the time came for Bertrand to return to Paris, he set off reluctantly, leaving Martha in Germany as he had promised her parents. A few days later, she felt so ill that she took herself into a clinic. It is at this point that one of her early fragments of memoir comes to an abrupt end. 'My faith in doctors . . .' begins a sentence, and then stops. She would later say that it was remarkable that she did not lose her hearing in that ear, and that the doctor in the Munich clinic had been a Nazi and tortured her most savagely. 'I am terribly tired,' she wrote to Bernard. 'I would like to die.' By 21 July the pain was so terrible that she could not stop crying. One day she fainted. Her head felt as if it were full of swords, her hand shook so violently she could barely write and she had stopped sleeping. 'It is this endlessness,' she wrote, 'which I cannot bear. Two more months of this would unhinge my reason.'

She decided to go south, to the warmth. She went first to Etretats, with a new French doctor and his wife, provoking a burst of jealousy from Bertrand, who pointed out that Etretats was the place where he had once stood for parliament and where Marcelle's uncle lived, and that there would be gossip. 'There are things you can't and which I won't let you do,' he wrote. 'And weekending with men is one of them. If you will insist upon it, we must separate.' Mollified by a loving letter, he was soon angry again. On 14 September, he wrote her an eight-page letter, full of reproach, despite her entreaties that he should not upset her while her ear was bad. 'I can't live a monk's life. I shall be driven to leading a dissolute life, to taking a succession of mistresses. This displeases me . . . I think it all so messy. But unavoidable. I could hate you for never perceiving the consequences . . . you haven't got a clarity of vision because you don't want to have it.' It was all very well to want to share the good things in life with him, but what about the ugliness?

At this moment ugliness, for Martha, consisted of little beyond the pain in her ear, and she dealt with that stoically. The infection had spread again, and her new doctor gave her more injections, wrapped her head in bandages and instructed her to rest. She told Bertrand not to come to see her, saying that she felt like an animal sneaking away to get well, and that she had to be alone. Bertrand was sending her what money he could, and she accounted for it scrupulously in her letters:

3.30F every day on cigarettes, 1F on a newspaper, 5F on tea, 12F on five thrillers. 5F for a weekly bath. She was wondering whether she could afford some vigorous Swedish massages for her stomach muscles. Even with her aching ear, she remained acutely conscious of her appearance.

At last, the swelling in her ear subsided. Feeling better, she travelled on south to Zaranz near the Spanish border to meet a friend called Ruth. The two young women walked, and on fine evenings they lay in the fields and looked at the stars; one day they went into St Sebastien to see a bullfight. Martha felt that she had come home: 'I have refound my childhood,' she wrote to Bertrand, 'but with peace.'

As the weeks passed, and they remained apart, so Martha began to think that she would have to make a choice between Bertrand and a life of solitude. 'I know there are two people in me,' she wrote, in one of her periodic moments of confession and self-knowledge. 'But the least strong, the least demanding, is the one that attaches itself to another human being. And the part of me which all my life I have shaped and sculpted and trained is the part that can bear no attachment, which has a ruling need of *éloignement*, which is, really, untamed, undomesticated, unhuman . . . Since I was a child people have wanted to possess me. No one has . . .' They had seldom been so distant, one from the other. Struggling to meet deadlines for his newspaper articles in Paris, Bertrand complained that his life had turned into a relentless race against time. 'And because our life is so badly managed, I turn upon you, with resentment and bitterness, because you bring into it neither order nor tranquillity, because you do not make the best of it, either materially or morally, because your discontent is ever present, like a restless dog wandering through the room . . . It's not courage that you lack . . . It's rather the art of living.'

Towards the end of October, he went south to visit her. He found her ear still rather swollen, and her chest sunken. She was also thin and sleeping very badly; the long, hot southern summer she so loved was turning cold. On returning to Paris, he wrote again to Edna, blaming at least some of Martha's ill health on her acute unhappiness at having to live alone, divided from both him and her parents by their intransigence. He argued that he should bring her back to Paris, where he could look after her, and where he could help her to find the sort of serious work that she thrived on. 'Let her steep her vagrant soul in stable, uneasily-influenced, obstinate and enduring France,' he wrote, saying that St Louis did not provide her with enough to feed her intellectual curiosity.

Like her earlier answer, Edna's reply is lost. But a letter she wrote to Martha at around this time must have made painful reading. In her whole life, Edna wrote, she had known three 'great devotions' – for her own father, for her husband and for Martha. (Martha, interestingly, wrote that she wanted the good opinion of three people: her mother, Bertrand and herself; of these her own self-approval was the most important.) These three great loves, said Edna, had made her life happy, simple and secure. But with Martha's affair with Bertrand had come a whole new set of different values, ones that she had great difficulty absorbing. 'By my standards you have taken what *legally* belongs to another woman . . . You say love is not a matter of law and that B. belongs to you not to Marcelle. I can generalise and rationalise and speak glibly on *your* side, but I feel and *live* by mine – mine is for the world, yours for the individual – I think, I suppose, in terms of . . . the greatest good for the greatest number – you live and feel for the greatest immediate good for M.G. and B de J.' The rift between them, she added, was made; it was too late to change it. What was more, she said that she and Dr Gellhorn never talked about her any longer. For a loving mother, Edna, perhaps in keeping with her strong views about honesty, could be surprisingly brutal, but Alfred remembers the misery she felt about Martha's estrangement and how once she said to her husband: 'If you make me choose between you and Martha, I'm going to choose Martha.'

Her ear aching, sleepless and always short of money, torn between the jealous Bertrand and the unbending Edna, Martha's spirits remained low. Other young women in her position, not yet twenty-four, in pain, alone in a foreign country, might well have given in and gone home. Instead, as soon as her ear improved, Martha returned to Paris and took a job as general helper on the fashion pages of *Vogue*, where she could, as she put it, 'limber up' her journalistic muscles. She called herself a *'femme de ménage littéraire'*. She wrote to her mother to tell her that she had put on weight, and that with her pink cheeks and long blonde hair she looked like a fine example of young German womanhood. She was sending articles back to American magazines, and dashing around like a 'crazed squirrel', having resolved never again to allow bad health to overcome her. Nor did she ever again intend to stop work, because only in work 'can one have a real sense of life, of the wonder and surprise and joy of being alive'.

A new tone, brisker, less vulnerable, entered her letters. There was less time for ruminating about her feelings. When not in the office, she was out meeting new people, no longer casual and easy-going young Americans drifting their way across Europe after college, but Parisians, more elegant in appearance and many of them, like Bertrand, both socially well connected and highly political. Gaston Bergery, a close friend of Bertrand's, was engaged in founding the Front Commun, bringing together radicals, socialists and communists in a coalition against fascism, attempting to do what Léon Blum did two years later with the Front Populaire. He, too, had an American companion, Bettina, to whom he was not married, and the two women had become close friends. With their rich American clients impoverished by the Depression, French fashion houses had adopted a number of pretty young women of good background as their unofficial models, lending them evening dresses in return for publicising their collections. Martha, tall, strikingly thin despite her words to her mother, was much in demand by Chanel and Schiaparelli, newly arrived from Italy and captivating Paris with her shocking pinks. Even Colette seems to have been willing to receive her stepson's mistress, talking to her about the difficulties of writing fiction, and urging her to waste no time worrying about whether a book was good or not until it was finished. *'Je crains que vous êtes trop intelligente,'* she told her.

Martha, who admired Colette hugely as a writer, took strongly against her as a person. She said that she had a 'mean, bitter little mouth' and found it hard to forgive when Colette, having looked her up and down, told her that she absolutely must pencil in her faint blonde eyebrows in heavy black, drawing the lines so that they almost met in the middle. Martha obeyed. It was three days before a kind friend told her that she looked grotesque. Martha was sure that Colette had done it on purpose, and that she was not merely malicious but jealous.

Martha was not only working on *Vogue*, writing articles and leading a social life of considerable glamour, for smart Parisians had responded to the spreading economic depression by throwing ever more lavish fancy dress parties, at which guests came as fish, or mermaids, or wisps of smoke, or went away with lion cubs as prizes. She was also still trying to finish her novel, and she had decided that she wanted to try her hand at a thriller. Whenever she could, she escaped to Bertrand's house at Le Lavandou, near St Maxime in Provence, where she would walk for hours along the coast, climbing on the rocks, lying naked in the sun, working all night and going to sleep at dawn, noting the delicious fresh smell of the earth after rain and the profound quiet. When there, she tried to lose weight, saying that without him food lost all pleasure and eating became the 'job of a stoker, shovelling coal into a boiler'. She would choose times when Bertrand's articles took him to Germany, or when he was in Rome, working with his father, who had been named French ambassador. Then their letters would resume, more loving and more settled than before, talking of how they wished they could marry and how perfectly close they felt. 'I love you,' Martha wrote. 'I think I offer you a fairly superior brand of love, it's the best I have ever managed to produce.' Even so, Bertrand found it hard to curb his jealousy. One day, discovering that she had been out on her own late at night interviewing unemployed people, he wrote frantically to say that he had been so anxious that he had missed an appointment to interview Hitler. As conscientious about his work as Martha, he constantly berated her for ruining his concentration.

In June 1933, the World Economic Conference opened in London. Huge war debts were owed by virtually all of Europe to the USA, and the Conference was intended to bring an end to constant economic warfare, and an agreement on plans to fight the Depression. At Bertrand's urging, Martha caught a boat across the Channel, to write about the delegates, to see something of England and to call on newspaper editors in order to try to place future articles. It was the start of a life-long love affair, for England was to become the country to which she always returned, where she loved the peace of the countryside while deploring the climate. Already, at twenty-four, she minded intensely about weather, hating and fearing the wet and the cold, her spirits constantly turned by the presence or lack of sunshine. 'On the whole,' she wrote on one of her more tolerant days, 'I think the weather in Britain is a national catastrophe borne bravely by the inhabitants.' In a small notebook of the kind that now went with her on all her travels, she wrote about the 'goodness' of the people, the efficiency of the buses, the tranquillity of the green land. Travelling, under a constant downpour of chilly summer rain, round Dartmoor and the cathedral towns, she made notes about how much people earned and what they ate. When the Conference opened in London, she made notes on what the American delegates looked like and where their wives were staying. It was the detail that caught her eye, as it would always, the expressions on people's faces, the way they talked, the adjectives they used; there is little in the notebook about economic policy. Walking up and down the corridors, looking for people to interview, she complained that she felt like a 'dejected wastebasket'. She was greatly taken with Ernst Hanfstaengl, Hitler's foreign press chief, though she remarked that he was Nazi down to his tailoring, with a milk chocolate-coloured suit and matching shirt and tie. She had no difficulty getting invitations to the nightly round of diplomatic parties, and was later reported by columnists to have worn the first backless evening dress ever seen in London society, lent to her by Schiaparelli. At the social gatherings she wandered among the guests making mental notes about the women's jewellery and the medals worn by many of the men. It all reminded her, she said, of a film of court life in Transylvania. The precision of her memory for such things, colleagues were already noting, was astounding.

Sometime in the late spring or very early summer of 1933 Martha appears to have found herself pregnant once again, 'and I don't really mind,' she wrote to Bertrand, 'as long as there is an ocean between me and my parents'. This time there was no suggestion that she should go back to America to have the abortion, and she wrote quite cheerfully to Bertrand that she felt so well she could see that she would have children 'rather comfortably'. But evidently not this one, for she told him that she found it comic to be paying for an abortion with her salary from *Vogue*, and that she intended to spend the week it would take living on her own in a hotel in Paris. Once again, she seems to have wasted no time on regret or speculation.

In July, she and Bertrand went with Gaston Bergery and Bettina to Spain, and then on alone to Italy for another long, hot summer by the Mediterranean, Martha sitting writing in the full sun in her bathing suit. They now tacitly behaved as if they were married, and, with Marcelle away in Mexico, she had taken to calling herself Madame de Jouvenel, even occasionally signing her pieces this way. A sour note seems to have been sounded when she discovered, from her old friend Johnny Stix's mother, who passed through Paris, that in St Louis the Gellhorns were denying that she was really married. It prompted an immediate and angry letter. 'If you wish to go on thinking my life is ruined and that I'm a martyr to B.'s brutal selfishness that's your prerogative,' she wrote to her mother. 'But I have no sympathy with such an attitude. It's false and troublesome, as insulting to me as to B . . . I consider myself married, and resent your point of view towards my husband. I shan't discuss myself and B. anymore with you; it's no use. Also we won't worry you by coming to St Louis . . . Ever since I realised clearly that it was denial and falsehood and fear and creeping around and being anxious about Mrs Jones' opinion which was destroying me, and stopped feeling or caring about those things, I have been secure and happy . . .' To Bertrand, to whom she showed the letter, she added that since her first loyalty was now to him, she would regard her parents as 'old, confused people', and that they could no longer hurt her. No more than Edna was Martha prepared to compromise.

Martha, when trapped, could be belligerent. She was not yet twenty-five, and clearly torn between the conventions of her strong family and a genuine desire to explore and enjoy a world her instincts told her she was perfectly suited to. Not surprisingly, her behaviour comes across as contradictory. Though nothing quite explains why she signed her articles with Bertrand's surname, this does explain why, to this day, there persists the confusion as to whether she was or was not married to Bertrand. Like others faced by similar pulls, she adopted a strategy she would use all her life, though never with great success: unless absolutely forced to do otherwise, she took the path of least resistance. When with Bertrand, it was easier to pretend they were married: she loved him, she wished they were married. But to have his baby would have been impossible. Martha does not emerge from these evasions particularly well – it was, after all, hardly fair to criticise her morally perfectly clear parents as 'confused' – but the evasions are understandable. It was only Martha's genuine pursuit of and admiration for honesty that made them appear slippery.

That September, Martha and Bertrand were on Capri and Martha stayed on until the middle of October on her own, writing. She had temporarily abandoned the novel for short stories, saying that she had no interest in plots and preferred to draw pictures of people, 'just a scene, a mood, something felt and forgotten within half an hour but real and important while it lasts'. She was pleased with one called 'Honeymoon in Italy', and said that she was now writing best about lovers and about tenderness, an emotion Bertrand had accused her of not understanding, and that in years to come would cause her some perplexity. When the weather broke, and the autumn storms hit the island, she missed Bertrand's warm and comforting physical presence, saying that she knew he 'coddled' her brain into fatness and sloth, but that just the same her spirit was starved without him. Something of her earlier insecurity about writing, her constant fear that she was simply not good enough, had been replaced by a calmer idea about what she was trying to do. 'The great temptation is to do what I call "fine writing",' she wrote to Bertrand, 'the beautiful mellow phrases and the carefully chosen strange words. That I must avoid like the plague; only the simple words; only the straight clear sentences. I am terribly frightened of "style".' What she wanted to be was a 'faultless carpenter', a goal she clung to all her life.

The coming winter had been planned in her mind. The days were to be spent quietly in their flat, with no time wasted on casual outings with other people, keeping healthy and fit and taking care of her face and her body, 'because I know how much they matter to me, in my attitude towards myself . . . I must keep them as lovely as possible as long as possible'. *Mens sana in corpore sano*, her father's much repeated adage; and a paring away at style, until the writing, too, was clean and healthy. 'I see perfection as a complete aliveness,' she would write. 'Being alert and eager, wanting all things to mean growth and intensity . . . I want to keep my body and my mind muscular; surely one can do both at the same time? I want to love you actively, not passively, not holding on to you fearfully as a protection against loneliness and boredom.' Martha was still not quite twenty-five and had published very little; but she was already absolutely certain that, for her writing to amount to something, it would have to come from some deep feeling of necessity, a need to write so powerful that not to do so would be too painful to bear.

* * *

During the early 1930s, before Hitler became Chancellor, and for a short time afterwards, French liberals continued to urge close relations with Germany. Many of the politically minded young, *la jeunesse française*, with some six hundred often small and very different organisations throughout the country, supported Briand and his calls for negotiations, believed in the League of Nations' assertion that only disarmament could ensure lasting peace, and told each other that there would be no European war provided the French and their German neighbours remained on good terms. Reared on the nationalistic teachings of de Gobineau, Proudhon and Georges Sorel, they tried hard to convince themselves that National Socialism was the necessary answer to Marxism, talked about rejecting the established order and how they deplored the drift into chaos they witnessed around them. Martha had kept her word and continued her education in the smoky meeting rooms of the poorer Parisian districts, where she listened to many speeches about how badly Germany had been treated at Versailles, and how it was still all a question of showing the younger German generation a little respect.

The day came early in 1934 when an invitation arrived to the young in France to send a delegation to Germany, to cement these ties of friendship. Spanning the entire political spectrum, from the Catholic right to the neo-socialist left, twenty-eight French men and women in their twenties were asked to visit Berlin and talk to their contemporaries. Jean Luchaire, an ambitious journalist who at this stage genuinely believed in Franco-German rapprochement, but was later bought by German funds and executed by the partisans after the war, was to have led the party, but at the last minute was obliged to back out. Bertrand, whose articles about the League and European friendship had won praise among the young, took his place. Martha went with him to Berlin, as did Drieu la Rochelle, another bright journalist and novelist, destined, like Luchaire, to end up among the fascists. Drieu was an interesting, clever and profoundly self-destructive man, veteran of the First World War, who had spent much of his youth reading tales of Napoleonic grandeur and military heroism and was the successful author of novels extolling a union between intellectual life and political action. Aged thirty, and thus somewhat older than the others, he was more sophisticated and formidable than his companions. The party set out for Germany towards the middle of January.

The group on the train were in boisterous spirits, eating the food they had brought with them wrapped in old newspapers, until they reached the frontier with Germany, where the border guards inspected, and then confiscated, many of the books and newspapers the young delegates had brought with them. After that, according to Martha's notes, they filled the time by shouting '*Vive la Liberté*', and singing 'La Marseillaise'.

They had expected to be greeted by young Germans like themselves, of relatively modest means and not very well organised, having evidently failed to grasp the fact that by the winter of 1933 Germany's youth movement was enormous – over four million boys and girls – fanatically active and boundlessly energetic. The Hitler Youth alone, to which several of their hosts belonged, had well over 100,000 members and was rapidly moving to absorb and then outlaw competing groups. Like the storm troopers, the young Nazis were already spending much of their free time motoring around the countryside in hired trucks, singing, waving banners and addressing crowds. Waiting at the station in Berlin were a collection of neat, clean, well-fed young men and women, most of them in immaculate uniforms, who could speak enough French to reassure their guests – falsely, as was soon made clear – that they had no formal links to Hitler, and took them off to a comfortable hotel in a fleet of taxis. The young French had very little experience of such luxury.

Among their German hosts was Baldur von Schirach, who was jovial and expansive and kept offering them champagne; von Schirach, whose American grandfather had been an honorary pallbearer at Lincoln's funeral, had an older brother who had committed suicide because he could not tolerate Germany's humiliation in the First World War. Von Schirach was twenty-six, a year older than Martha. He was somewhat stout, and wore a uniform: Rebecca West once said of him that he looked like a 'neat and mousy governess'. 'We thought him a vast joke,' Martha wrote later. 'He ran an organisation for babies, as far as we could see, the Hitler Jugend, who got out of diapers and into brown shirts.' Organiser of a National Socialist student *Bund* at Munich University, von Schirach had however been appointed head of the Hitler Youth in 1931 by Hitler himself, with the rank of *Gruppenführer*, a salary and expenses, rewards for the help he had given the Führer during the elections.

There was also Otto Abetz, a blond and amiable teacher of drawing from Karlsruhe and his French wife, Suzanne, who was homely and earnest. The Abetzes told their new friends that they were Catholic socialists. Abetz had a smiling expression, and wore his fair hair combed severely back; he was a Francophile who liked to quote Romain Rolland's words: 'Germany and France are the two wings of the west – whoever breaks one of them, impedes the flight of the other.' Both Martha and Bertrand took to Abetz. They liked his wit and intelligence, and the way that he deflected the pomposity of his German friends and assured them that once they had been softened by a little contact with their more sophisticated French visitors, they would become more sympathetic. In honour of the delegation, a play was staged, a tale in which a Nazi youth rescued a pure fair-haired maiden. Although the French had watched this with embarrassment, a man got up and gave a warm speech of welcome and the whole audience, perfect in word and tune, sang 'La Marseillaise'. Then Drieu addressed a large gathering of Hitler Youth and other Nazi student groups on the subject of racism. His words were not openly anti-Semitic, but they came uncomfortably close.

On the train home to Paris, the French group split in two. There were those who, like Martha, had found the entire visit repugnant, and now could not wait to abandon all thoughts of rapprochement; '*au fond*,' as one young man put it, '*c'est une race d'enmerdeurs*.' And there were those who, like Drieu, continued to think that there were possibilities of closer links between the two countries. Bertrand lay somewhere in the middle, reluctant to abandon his long-held dreams, but worried

by what he had seen. He had, as Martha would later tell a
friend in the secret services, 'such a feeling for underdogs that
he managed to be in every movement while it was a failure
and to leave it the minute it looked as if it were succeeding'.
He was, she insisted, entirely and scrupulously honest, seeking
neither fame nor money for himself. Nothing in the trip had
changed his friendship for Drieu, nor his growing liking for
Abetz, who became a regular visitor to Paris, where Martha
and Bertrand continued to enjoy his sardonic and worldly
conversation. That summer, Abetz joined the Hitler Youth,
then met and became close to the future foreign minister
Joachim von Ribbentrop, but he continued to preach and
promote closer ties between the two countries. He came often
to Paris but never in uniform. It was Abetz, Martha wrote
later, who lulled the young French 'into suicidal sympathy for
the German form of government'.

By early 1934, French politics had reached a new low. Briand
was dead, the League of Nations had finally been discredited
by the Japanese in Manchuria and by its twenty-seven different
rejected schemes for disarmament, while the Depression which
had reached France later than elsewhere was now beginning
to cause real hardship. The slums around Paris were said to
be the worst in Europe. Unemployment was climbing towards
two million. Industrial production had declined by 80 per cent.
While governments formed and promptly fell – there were six
in two years, many of its members simply switching portfolios
– strikes were called by textile workers and miners, the
communists led a hunger march from Lille to Paris and
extremist movements, several openly fascist in their views,
became increasingly active. Anti-Semitism was becoming more
outspoken too, both on the extreme right and on the extreme
left. Many early advocates of European rapprochement were
beginning to drift into other ranks. Then, in February, France
was gripped by a scandal whose roots seemed to lie in both
politics and the criminal underworld.

Serge Alexandre Stavisky was a crook, a financier who
floated fraudulent companies, liquidating the debts of one by
the profits of its successor. He was a Ukrainian by birth but

now a naturalised French citizen, long associated with drugs, fraud and corruption. The newspapers described him as having the 'eyes of a gazelle'. His influence among the judiciary was such that he had managed to have a case against him postponed nineteen times. Some time around the new year a story appeared that Stavisky had sold bonds worth two hundred million francs based on the assets of Bayonne's city pawnshop, greatly helped by the mayor of Bayonne, Joseph Garat, and the radical party government minister for the colonies, Albert Dalimier. The public demanded an inquiry. Then Stavisky disappeared. On 8 January, the police admitted that he was dead, having apparently shot himself as they forced a door in a villa in Chamonix where he was hiding. The *Populaire* announced that Stavisky had been 'suicided', in order, so it was assumed, to protect high-level political accomplices. As he had been Jewish, there was talk of Dreyfus and anti-Semitism. Demonstrators gathered near the Palais Bourbon, amid rumours of bomb plots and insurrection, calling for cleaner politics. The government fell.

On the afternoon of 6 February, just as the newly elected Prime Minister Edouard Daladier rose in the Chamber to address the deputies, complete chaos erupted. There were catcalls, jeers, yells; fights broke out. However, far worse was taking place just across the river, where demonstrators from the many extremist groups had joined up with communists, ex-servicemen and some of the unemployed in the Place de la Concorde and had started throwing stones and bricks at the police, who had barricaded the bridge and were now cowering behind their vans. Those on the left were loudly singing 'the Internationale'. Martha, who, with Bettina, was in the middle of it, would later say that she personally enjoyed the day hugely, leaping into the fountains when the Garde Mobile brought in fire hoses and horses and charged the rioters. Friends nicknamed the two young American women '*les déesses de la révolution*'. Later, it all got more violent, the iron railings along the Jardin des Tuileries were pulled up and used as javelins, marbles and fireworks were rolled under the horses' feet, the Ministry for the Navy was set on fire, and the Garde

Mobile began to shoot. By the end of the day, 328 people were seriously injured and fifteen were dead. It was indeed, as Martha wrote, the 'bright opening burst of disorder'.

That same evening Bertrand, Martha and a group of journalists met in a friend's flat and decided to do what many of the articulate French protesters did in the 1920s and 1930s: start a new magazine. They called it *La Lutte des Jeunes* and proposed to use its pages to campaign for more scholarships and for paid holidays for students and to explore, cautiously, continued programmes of friendship with Germany, as well as question the reasons for the continuing failure of the liberal nations in their fight against the Depression. As Martha remembered it later, they had convinced themselves that the Hitler Youth should be given the benefit of the doubt, particularly since they seemed primarily interested in sport and physical fitness. Bertrand was appointed editor of the new magazine, and Drieu wrote a series of articles calling for left and right to unite in a 'fascist' organisation that was not of the right politically, but only in the sense that it was a 'necessary stage in the destruction of capitalism'. Fascism as he saw it was against everything that was currently destroying society, and should bring together everything that he believed in – youth, friendship, physical health and leadership. Still pushing for a united Europe, Drieu talked of a strong Germany at its head.

How far Martha agreed with Drieu is hard to say, for she left no comments about him. But she did believe in a federated Europe, and remained for the time being a pacifist. Helped by Bertrand, she researched and contributed three short pieces to the magazine. Neither of them appears to have paid much attention to the warnings all too visible in Germany, where Dachau was taking in its first political detainees and the works of Jewish and liberal writers had already gone up in smoke. Martha addressed the contradictions in her own life, writing about fashion for *Vogue* by day and listening to left-wing speeches by her journalist friends by night, by writing a mocking article called *'Politique à la mode'*. French politics, she wrote, had at last been made really fashionable – by smart

Parisians wearing checked taffeta, polka-dot hats and piqué collars and cuffs and if you knew the right people you could get a seat in the Chamber of Deputies for an all-night debate, conveniently dropping in on the way home from the theatre. 'Over tea-tables, bridge-tables, dinner-tables; in restaurants, in salons; at clubs, at the coiffeur, at the races; wide hats bend towards each other. Women discussing politics.' At Colonel de la Roque's Croix de Feu mass meeting, she wrote, the size of the women's hats had made it impossible for anyone to see what was going on, while the colonel himself had trouble making himself heard above the 'faint ripplings of taffeta, swish of silk, and the tiny gentle noises a woman makes when she turns her head'. As for the fracas around the Place de la Concorde, French women had more than proved themselves worthy of the vote – which they still didn't have – by racing before the bullets and the police horses, wearing the latest tight skirts and the dizziest hats, demonstrating amazing agility by climbing in and out of the fountains, despite their extremely high heels.

* * *

From her earliest days in Paris, Martha's letters often carried the same yearning for the countryside, for a house outside the city, where one did not feel 'despairing, strangled', and where one could have 'wind on one's face'. She wanted to walk, to smell the grass, to get away from the kind of people who seemed always to wander in 'narrowing circles, intent on escaping themselves and all that's valuable in life'. She found these acquaintances 'ugly – and mostly so bloody stupid', just as she would say that she felt at odds with the scheming and always rational French, so unlike Americans, who belonged to a race of 'people who go mad, or drift into gutters or suicide, from broken hearts'. Paris, a city she later turned against, was never more to her, she would say, than simply the place where her real life began. On the other hand, she loved Bertrand's house in the Midi, the Villa Noria, to which all through 1933 and early 1934 she got away whenever possible and where some of her happiest and most loving letters to him were written. 'I tell myself a story until I'm sick of it,' she wrote one day. 'And it always consists in money and children and a house in the country and lots of time alone with you. But in my story you're thrilled to be alone in the country instead of scratching to get away, back to your pursuits and pals; politicians and economics and world without end amen. Poof. I should have married a musician or a painter or a guy with a SOUL; it's just my luck to get a bloody reformer.' The contradictions in Martha's character, pulling her towards domesticity, then violently away from it, towards people then as passionately away from them, were now becoming more marked. Her strength and her natural impatience made the prolonged company of others hard, even as her gregariousness and love of talk made her seek them out. At no point would she ever find relationships easy, though she felt great affection for friends and real interest in their lives and predicaments.

Bertrand too was capable of outbursts of irritation against the pressures of his city life, against the deadlines and the worries about money, but it mattered to him that he was seen to be the kind of professional journalist who delivered his copy on time and never let an editor down. He had never worked harder than he did in the spring of 1934, nor been so active politically, turning out for the many demonstrations that brought the capital to a halt after the Stavisky riots. He was arrested several times and once quite badly beaten up by the police. Editing La Lutte des Jeunes on borrowed funds – he suffered from the fact that, like Luchaire, he was forced to accept gifts of money, except that in his case it was mainly from his father – writing his weekly columns and interviews, constantly in demand for his views on the current political situation, on which he was now considered an expert, he would write to Martha very late at night, or at dawn, having walked home through deserted streets after seeing the paper through the presses. 'My needs are simple,' he wrote to her one night, sitting down at his typewriter in preparation for an all-night session, 'I need you, and provided I have you or news from you, I can discharge the simple duties of living.' What he could not do, however, was join her as she wished him to, in the Midi. 'War? Yes, and before five years. Run away to enjoy the last years of bliss? Is that what aristocracies were made for? Oh darling, I'll take my stand. My chosen one, won't you stand by my side?'

Martha was beginning to wonder whether she could; indeed, whether she really wanted to. She sometimes felt that she had become nothing but a 'bed-warmer', and though she blamed herself – she never wavered from her conviction that people must take full responsibility for everything that happens to them – she saw her life as a betrayal of 'my youth, my love and my dreams'. Blaming Marcelle for destroying Bertrand's peace of mind, and her family for destroying hers, she wondered whether it would ever be possible to regain the 'purity and fire of those first days'. That Bertrand was indeed a rebel she had no doubt; her fear was that she was a puritan, 'in my blood, my upbringing' and that she could never change.

And the sex between them had never been good. Over the years Martha had consulted several doctors about her lack of desire and the fact that she found making love painful. Long afterwards, she would say to a friend about Bertrand: 'Physically, for me, it was nothing, ever.' Each felt guilty about the other. Martha was conscious of having failed him, 'being unable to give you complete joy in sexual love', as she wrote to him. But while Martha had been faithful to Bertrand, he had not only slept with Marcelle the time that she had summoned him back to her side from Florence on the grounds that she was pregnant – a lie, as it turned out, but she became pregnant that night – but he had also had an affair with a woman called Suzanne, who had also become pregnant.

From the Villa Noria, on 29 April 1934, at much the same time as Bertrand was writing to her from Paris about standing by his side, Martha wrote a very long and different kind of letter to her American lawyer friend Cam. It is a strange document, both perceptive and oddly chilly. It is also extremely bleak. She had suddenly, she told Cam, been overcome by a need to write to him a letter about the French, or more exactly about the de Jouvenels; but it was really all about Bertrand.

'I don't know what to do about B. because I have turned coward. Not coward about him; I writhed too much over his pity ever to want to go in for pity myself. I'm sure on that point; pity is the one great crime because it destroys two people sloppily . . . I should hurt him somewhere deeply; but that hurt is part of life and not to be feared.

'The cowardice is about myself . . . You see, I have chalked it up too well, and see where and how I am caught – and how tightly. Through ignorance, carelessness, pride and generosity: and the passionate desire to burn all boats, to prove that I had no intention of retreating . . .

'The root of the trouble is the body. Our minds and spirits are comfortable together: and between us we have two bodies, one eager and demanding, the other polite and often kind – but you can't bully emotion or rather you can't bully passion . . . I have no desire for affairs. My body very curiously has no need of that food – not at least now. I am happy with myself, you see. I have enough in me to fill my life. But all my life boils and simmers, stews and burns, because something is asked which I cannot truthfully give.'

Martha was now working on a second novel – set among the French and German pacifists – and making yet further revisions to the first. Four American publishers had turned down what had now been definitively given the title *What Mad Pursuit* (earlier titles had been worse: *Tarnish*, *Knight Without Armour* and *Tender Croppes*, after Chaucer), saying that the sex was too explicit, the medical problems too detailed, the love scenes too revealing and that it was altogether too 'bold'. On the advice of the writer Michael Arlen, who lived not far from the Villa Noria, she had reluctantly agreed to tone it down and was busy 'slashing out sex right and left', removing the abortion, and throwing 'syphilis into the wastepaper basket'. The novel, she complained, was going to be so clean that 'they'll use it as a text in Sunday schools'. What she wanted was for it to sell, in order to pay for a larger flat and perhaps a small car, and to stop being a financial burden to

Bertrand. On the other hand, these last months of work had proved that she was not lacking in 'will'. 'Anyone who can go over a book as I've gone over this *another time* is by way of being a bloody worker,' she wrote to Bertrand. 'That's comforting. Nothing else is.'

In June, Edna arrived on a visit to the Villa Noria. She and Martha had not seen each other for two years. They stayed on in the Midi, watching the hot summer settle in, and though Bertrand was unable to join them, sending apologies to Martha that he could not send her more money to make her mother's visit more luxurious, he did meet Edna briefly in Paris and the encounter went well.

Bertrand's thin, restless good looks were extremely attractive to women. From the time of his seduction by Colette, he had always managed to convey the impression of a man dominated and led by far stronger women, though there were friends in Paris who maintained that this was a skilfully contrived illusion, and that in the end Bertrand always did precisely what he wanted. With Martha, it was all rather different. Through nearly five years of his letters to her runs a vein of unsatisfied longing, of anguish and apprehension, and of a very adult realisation that she never quite felt the same way about him. Of the two, Bertrand was undoubtedly the better educated, with a quick understanding of intricate problems and a philosopher's love for discourse. This, Martha knew; compared to him, she would say, she was 'intellectual jelly'. He understood her very well, once telling her that he loved her precisely because she combined an 'ever-flowing deep rage against injustice, imbecility and weakness', with an odd lack of real compassion. Few people ever saw this in Martha more clearly, nor phrased it so neatly. There were things about him that she loved too: his affectionate nature, his solicitude, the way he made her laugh; but she was not in love with him. And when his enormous need for reassurance made his demands urgent and almost desperate, then she felt inadequate. Instinctively, weakness already repelled her, and she resented being cast into the role of the 'strong one'. 'He is so weak,' she told a friend, perhaps with unintentional cruelty, 'that it is like having cancer, it is an incurable and killing sickness.'

One evening, at the very end of June 1934, Bertrand went out to Fontainebleau to walk at dusk in the forest and to think. He then went home and wrote Martha a long letter, to wait for her at Le Havre, where she was planning to see Edna off on her ship to New York. It was very generous.

The moment had come, he told her, for her to leave him. She should board the ship with her mother and go back to America. Marcelle was never going to give him a divorce. The causes for which he fought so hard were not Martha's causes; he had not managed to become the hero she so badly wanted. 'My beloved, you do not love me,' he wrote, adding that he knew only too well that she had been unhappy for a long time.

'You told me once that I was standing in your sun, keeping its light from you. I remove myself from it, dear love. The world is so limited with me, so wide open, so limitless if you're alone. Take this chance, my little one. Escape.'

Martha did not leave with her mother on the boat. And though she wrote in her diary that in July she 'decided to leave Bertrand', she added, on the same line: 'Returned.' But the end had come. She spent August travelling around England, pondering possible stories and wondering whether she could interest British newspapers in portraits of Colette or the film director René Clair, or an article about 'France's Mussolinis', the 'little crowds of pseudo-Mosleys', as Bertrand described them. She also started an affair with an earl, whom she never named, but whom she liked, she told a friend, in spite of all his money. In October she packed and left for America.

At first, 'taking the temperature' of her heart from her letters, Bertrand believed that he had been wrong, that she loved him still and would return; but as the weeks and then the months passed, he began to understand that he had finally lost her. By December he knew that she was not coming back. In *Ways and Means*, the outline of a memoir of her first twenty-five years that she never wrote, Martha bracketed Chapters 14 and

15 together: 'More France. Waiting for things to happen, which couldn't happen in such an old country. Closing down of the atmosphere.' Chapter 16 has a single word: 'Escape.'

Bertrand had never really been able to understand what it was that could have made her happy, he wrote later; had he understood, their history might have taken another turn. They remained friends until his death in 1989. Martha was always loyal to him, during the war and for some years afterwards, when his sympathy for underdogs and his refusal to turn his back on his ideals or on his friends led to accusations of fascism. Long after other liberals had abandoned their hopes for rapprochement between France and Germany, Bertrand was still clinging to the notion of civilisation represented by Europe as a whole. A son, Hugues, born later of a second marriage – for Marcelle did finally agree to a divorce – believes that, apart from his mother, Martha remained, together with Colette, the great love and influence of his father's life; and that even in old age, Bertrand never doubted it.

But, in the summer of 1934, as she told Cam, Martha wanted to live. She felt that she had been a 'little hungry' for a very long time. 'Great God!' she wrote, 'what an eagerness and energy I have to live; how much living I can stand and must have . . .'

CHAPTER FOUR

The Trees Don't Grow Tall Enough

In later years Martha would often say that she had decided to go home in the autumn of 1934 because she realised that the poverty she witnessed in Europe was happening in her own country, and she wanted to be there to write about it. How much of a part this played in her next move is hard to say. But within a week of docking in New York on the *Normandie*, an old ship that bucked and rolled its way slowly across the Atlantic, she was in Washington, being introduced by Marquis Childs, a journalist friend, to Harold Hopkins, a key figure in Roosevelt's New Deal. And by the end of the month of October she was on the road with a new job. She had also found a heroine, in the shape of a tall, ungainly woman of fifty, with wispy hair, no chin, protruding teeth, terrible hats and startling reserves of energy. Her name was Eleanor Roosevelt.

By October 1934, Franklin Roosevelt had been in the White House for nineteen months, hailed by many as the last desperate hope for a country in a state of economic and social collapse. Seventeen million men were out of work. Steel plants were at a virtual standstill. Seventy per cent of the country's coal miners were idle. In some parts of Massachusetts women garment makers were working for five cents an hour. Thirty-eight states had closed their banks. And while over a quarter of the population was without any work at all, many children were not being educated, but spent their days in the streets, picking through rubbish dumps, and fighting over scraps of food. Skin diseases, syphilis and tuberculosis were all spreading, and the Ku Klux Klan found willing audiences for their lynchings among people reduced by poverty to apathy and a profound sense of hopelessness. Americans were angry, wretched and frightened.

To make it all worse, the great plains of the Midwest had been hit by a severe and prolonged drought. It had started in 1931 and by 1934 was affecting a dozen states. That summer, the temperature stood at over 100 degrees for thirty-six consecutive days. Oklahoma, Texas, New Mexico, Colorado and Kansas had become a 'dust bowl', over which, for thousands of miles, rolled waves of earth and sand that filled people's ears and eyes and noses with dust and suffocated animals. It was almost dark in the middle of the day. In the winter, the snow that fell over Maine was red. The countryside had become a desolate, barren stretch of dead trees and drifting brushwood. Farmers went bankrupt, and were dispossessed of their farms. As those who could no longer afford their mortgages and rents lost their homes, so there spread around the major cities, along the river banks and railroad sidings, camps widely known as Hoovervilles, built out of cardboard, corrugated iron, old tyres and sacks. A whole new generation of migrants was on the move, over two million hobos or Okies going west towards the Pacific and the warmth, looking for work.

President Hoover, elected to the White House in 1928, had told the voters that a planned economy was witches' brew, emanating from the 'cauldrons of all three European collective forms', communism, socialism and fascism. Roosevelt captured their imagination by telling them that the only thing they had to fear was 'fear itself – nameless, unreasoning, unfinished terror which paralyses needed efforts to convert retreat into advance', a sentence that Martha would often quote in the years to come. He understood that his immediate task was to halt any further slide into poverty, and to set up as rapidly as possible the administration of relief on a scale never previously attempted. One of his first steps had been to appoint a brains trust of practical and imaginative advisers. Among these was a shrewd social worker called Harold Hopkins, a dishevelled and argumentative young man whose eyes bulged and who chainsmoked and drank too much coffee and who, like the President, saw that the moment for voluntary help was long since past, and that the only way to pull the country up out of the morass was for federal government to intervene. Both men were of the view that relief, handed out simply as charity, would ultimately undermine character and encourage dependency, and that what was needed was to find ways of creating work.

Within weeks of coming to power in 1933, Roosevelt was shaping and pushing through government bills and measures to reform the trust laws, water conservation, banking, taxation, insurance, trade, industry and agriculture. Later, under a Civil Works Administration, men would be put to building roads, clearing slums, digging canals, constructing bridges, sewers, hospitals, power plants and prisons.

Meanwhile, under Hopkins, and based on his earlier experiences with emergency relief while Roosevelt was still governor of New York, a Federal Emergency Relief Administration – FERA – had been set up in May 1933, under which social workers of 'sympathy and training' would administer a vast programme of public relief. FERA was given $500 million to help states meet their relief needs, divided between matching funds and absolute donations to those states too poor to contribute. By the autumn of 1934, the salaries of congressmen had been cut, as had been the defence budget, and, in order to drive down the dollar and make exports more attractive, the US had been taken off the gold standard. Five thousand local emergency relief bureaus around the country were trying to determine the needs of families and tailor relief to meet them. FERA paid rents and provided money for medicine and doctors' bills and above all it gave out food. And, wherever possible, it provided work.

But there was more to it than that. It was the whole American spirit which seemed to those in power to be threatened by the Depression, the very self-reliance and energy of people who had come from everywhere to build the most prosperous and forward-looking industrial nation on earth. And federal intervention, in the hands of enlightened social workers recruited from the best of the charity organisations and among urban reformers, would, if effectively conceived and run, not only restructure a society in danger of falling to pieces, but restore a sense of self-worth to the people. For this, however, Hopkins, who was going through what Martha later called his 'social conscience period', thought he needed a better picture of the human tragedy of unemployment, what it was actually costing in terms of broken families, alcoholism and disease, what it actually felt like for a man to lose his job, his savings and his house and to watch his family sink into misery. At what point did he simply give up and become 'downhearted and brooding and dangerous'? Only then did Hopkins believe he would really be able to take the pulse of the nation and devise a sound relief programme for the 'third of the nation' that was 'ill-nourished, ill-clad, ill-housed'.

To know just what impoverished, unemployed America was feeling, to construct what was essentially a vast demographic portrait of the Great Depression, Hopkins turned to the statistics on rural poverty that flooded into his office in Washington from Oregon and Colorado, Utah and North Dakota, Illinois and Massachusetts. His rural research supervisors analysed data; his statisticians collated figures; and his caseworkers put together family profiles. He was deluged by facts. But Hopkins wanted something more, something more intangible and descriptive, something that was about impressions and thoughts as well as about health and physical conditions. And so, in the summer of 1933, he hired an erratic, tough, forty-one-year-old newspaper reporter called Lorena Hickok, who smoked a pipe and had a rasping cough, and had once been described by a colleague as a 'big girl in a casual raincoat with a wide tailored hat, translucent blue eyes, and a mouth vivid with lipstick'. She was built, said Martha, like a tank, and weighed almost two hundred pounds, and she played poker and drank bourbon with the boys. The daughter of a butter maker from Wisconsin, Lorena Hickok was a close friend of Eleanor Roosevelt, having covered her side of the election campaign and declared herself much impressed by her good sense, humour and determination. Hopkins gave her the title of chief investigator and sent her off to tell him what she saw and heard, while never for a moment forgetting 'that but for the grace of God, you, I, and any of our friends might be in their shoes'.

Over the next twelve months Lorena Hickok visited every part of the country except the northwest, mostly by bus but then, once she had learnt to drive, in a battered old Chevrolet, banging and rattling her way across the immense distances of America, stopping to talk to farmers and teachers, officials and housewives, factory workers and policemen, children, blacks, Hispanics, the sick, the elderly. The letters she sent back to Hopkins were breezy, irreverent and engaging. Late at night, using capital letters for emphasis, she wrote about the 'gaunt, ragged legion of the industrially damned. Bewildered, apathetic, many of them terrifyingly patient.'

Hickok's reports soon convinced Hopkins that he was right in his hunch that this was the way to learn things about the Depression that no amount of facts would ever teach him. He started to recruit other newspaper reporters, novelists and writers, people accustomed to listening to what people said and writing it all down simply and clearly. While Hickok had all America as her beat, the newcomers were assigned either a region or a major city and its immediate surroundings.

There was Louisa Wilson, daughter of a missionary to China, a star Washington profile writer, whose girlish clothes and manner concealed ambition and determination; Wilson was assigned to the automobile centres of Detroit and Michigan, and to Ohio. There was Ernestine Ball, who had published a much-acclaimed series of articles about Aimee Semple McPherson, the religious revivalist. She was given upstate New York. Wayne Parrish, a Pulitzer Prize travelling scholar with a passion for aeronautical engineering, got New York itself. David Maynard, one of the two economists on the team, who had worked for the League of Nations, was allocated the Midwestern industrial towns of Cleveland, Cincinatti and Indianapolis. And Martha, at twenty-five one of the youngest of the investigators, and their sixteenth member, was dispatched to the textile areas of the Carolinas and New England. Their instructions were all the same: go to wherever unemployment and poverty are to be found; talk to everyone you see; write down what they tell you and what your impressions are; and send it in. Their pay was $35 a week. Those who had cars took them. The others, like Martha, cadged lifts from local FERA social workers, or caught buses, trains and streetcars. Sometimes they went on foot. What they came back with was a haunting picture of despair.

* * *

It was in the textile mill towns of North Carolina that Martha finally found the writing voice that she had been looking for. It was clear and very simple, a careful selection of scenes and quotes, set down plainly and without hyperbole. Nothing particular; there were many other writers who did the same just as well. What made it her own was the tone, the barely contained fury and indignation at the injustice of fate and man against the poor, the weak, the dispossessed. Nothing so enraged her as bullying, superiority, the misuse of power; nothing touched her so sharply as people who had become victims, through the stupidity or casual brutality of others, or children who were frightened, in pain or who did not have enough to eat. In Gastonia, among those who had lost everything, she at last had her subject. For the next sixty years, in wars, in slums, in refugee camps, she used this voice again and again, to great effect, handling it with such a sure ear for nuance that only very rarely did she stray over that fine line into the mawkish or shrill. Unmistakably, it became her hallmark.

Before leaving Washington, Martha was given vouchers for her trains to the South and $5 a day for food, hotels and local travel. Broke as ever, she had no money with which to buy sensible clothes and stout shoes suited to tramping round derelict towns in the late autumn. So she went with what she had, which happened to be the discarded dresses and tailor-made suits from Parisian couturiers, worn once by models during the collections, then sold cheaply to fortunate customers of the same size. She reached her first destination, Gaston County in North Carolina, 'flat and grim as can be expected', in a Schiaparelli suit, with a high Chinese collar fastened by large brown leather clips, and on her head a brown crochet hat out of which rose a brightly coloured plume of cock pheasant feathers. Her face was thickly made up, with plenty of mascara, eye shadow and lipstick, as worn in fashionable Paris. It says much for her complete disregard for the effect she made on others that no one seems to have held her flamboyant appearance against her, and that it took her some time to realise that her turnout was odd.

Martha had a knack for total absorption in work. Soon, she was engrossed by what she was doing, interviewing up to five families a day among the thousands of mill hands and sharecroppers scrounging for jobs that no longer existed, along with factory owners, doctors, union representatives, teachers and relief workers. Meticulously, she noted rates of pay, levels of relief and the story of each family. In her elegant Parisian shoes, she trudged around slums of tumbledown shacks, where latrines drained into the well from which all drinking water came; she looked at 'houses shot with holes, windows broken, no sewerage, rats'; she listened to children so listless with malnutrition that they could barely stay awake, trying to recite the Gettysburg Address for her by heart; she heard doctors talk about rickets, hookworm, anaemia and pellagra, the skin disease of vitamin deficiency and the starving, and the way that it had become endemic after months on a diet of pinto beans and corn bread, and about tuberculosis, which was spreading fast through the villages. In one factory, she found three young women lying on the lavatory floor, their eyes closed; they told her they had come in to rest for a few minutes because the eight-hour shifts on heavy machines with no breaks was making them faint. And as she travelled around, so her indignation rose and so her reports began to include more observations and conclusions of her own, more recommendations for action, in tones of outrage that grew ever more precise and icy. A doctor, she wrote, had told her that his patients were 'degenerating' before his eyes. 'The present generation of unemployed,' she went on, 'will be useless human material in no time. Their housing is frightful (talk about European slums); they are ignorant and often below-par intelligence . . .' Returning from a mill town where those fortunate enough still to have jobs were forced to pay half as much again for their food at the company store, she added: 'It is probable – and to be hoped – that one day the owners of this place will get shot and lynched.' The people who really touched her were those who, too proud to go on relief, unable to understand why their entire lives had collapsed around them, were desperately keeping going on occasional part-time work, while their children slowly starved to death. This was an America Martha did not know. The flappers and cocktails and mahjong parties popularised by Scott Fitzgerald and the fashion magazines had touched only the thinnest surface of society. Country roads were seldom paved and were often unpassable in snow or heavy rain. It was another world.

Everywhere she went, Martha found cases of syphilis. In one town a doctor told her that it had reached the level of an epidemic, and that unless the government decided to treat it as an emergency, as with smallpox, there was no way to halt it. She saw twelve-year-old girls with open syphilitic sores, a baby paralysed by it, syphilitic families sleeping four to a bed. She discovered that while the blacks referred to it as 'rheumatism', the whites called it 'bad blood'. And as she went from one sick family to the next, with 'morons' in every generation, and a new baby every year, so she began to write back to Hopkins about the need for birth control, urging him to explore ways of breaking this nightmarish cycle of sickness and overcrowding. 'Birth control is needed here almost more than in any other area I have seen,' she wrote from North Carolina. 'There is one village where half the population is pathologic, and reproducing half wits with alarming vigor.' Like syphilis, mental retardation began to obsess her. 'Another bright thought: feeblemindedness is on the increase . . . out of every three families I visited one had moronic children or one moronic parent. I don't mean merely stupid, I mean . . . fit only for sanitariums.'

Like Hopkins, Martha carried in her mind a vision of a strong and purposeful America, seeing behind the daily scenes of malnutrition and apathy the collapse of the great American dream. The 'foreign born' or first generation Americans, she noted, still proud of their few possessions, were standing up better to the Depression than the 'natives', whose 'homes are quickly going to hell' under filth, decay and demoralisation. She reported being told by social workers that the unemployed on relief were becoming entirely dependent not only on the dole itself, but on the people who handed it out. And yet, she added, 'with all this, they are a grand people. If there is any meaning in the phrase "American stock" it has some meaning here. They are sound and good humoured; kind and loyal. I don't believe they are lazy; I believe they are mostly ill and ignorant . . . It is a terribly frightening picture . . . It's terrible to think that the basis of our race is slowly rotting, almost before we have had time to become a race.' In the 1930s, it was still possible to write of such things.

If this was much what Hopkins suspected and feared, Martha's next reports touched on far more sensitive matters. On 5 November, she reached Boston and for the next ten days she travelled around Massachusetts, worrying that, by moving so quickly all she was sending was a 'bird's eye view' and a bird flying high and fast at that. On the 25th, she sat down to her report. The picture, she began, was 'so grim that whatever words I use will seem hysterical and exaggerated'. All the families she had seen were in the same condition of 'fear – fear driving them into a state of semi-collapse; cracking nerves; and an overpowering terror of the future . . . I haven't been in one house that hasn't offered me the spectacle of a human being driven beyond his or her powers of endurance and sanity . . . It is hard to believe that these conditions exist in a civilised country.' There was more. It was not only the poverty that was at fault: it was the administration of relief itself. And that, in Massachusetts, was 'so definitely and blatantly bad that it was an object of disgust'. Here Martha abandoned all efforts at restraint. 'It is impossible,' she wrote, 'travelling through this state and seeing our relief set up not

94

to feel that here incompetence has become a menace . . . It is a bum business from every point of view . . . The Public Welfare very probably gets the laurel for low type human animal in this job . . . Politics is bad enough in any shape; but it shouldn't get around to manhandling the destitute.' The greed and stupidity of those in power: already, for Martha, a picture of the world was being formed. It looked to her very bleak.

At the beginning of December, Martha reached Providence, Rhode Island, and found a hotel. Her spirits had never been so low, and though she got dressed in the morning she spent the 'dark' day lying on her bed, 'numb and doubting'. In a long letter to Bertrand, written on the portable typewriter she carried everywhere with her, she talked about the modern world as a disordered and final battle for the survival of the fittest, in which there was little to tell between the vulgar, narrow and priggish ruling class, and the 50 per cent of the unemployed, who were below normal intelligence, sick, treacherous to each other, resentful and reproducing more 'in these empty days than ever before'. 'I thank God,' she wrote, 'I have no children and I want none. This mess is unworthy of new life. As for me: I am ill – principally from nerves, and because my brain is rushing in unhealthy circles . . . And very sick at heart; and very alone. Another myth: America is beautiful. Oh Christ what a thought. It's ugly, horribly ugly; raw and unkempt; nasty, littered, awkward. The trees don't grow tall enough and the land is torn and dishevelled. It moves endlessly ahead, without shape or grace; and over it are spread the haphazard homes of a shifting, unrooted, grey people . . . People are ugly too; ugly and vulgar; and poor, Smuffy. Poor the way I mean it; there are too few faces with warmth and intelligence, some harmony between experience and spirit.

'Gawd, you can see I'm low . . . I have no one here to talk to – think of it, 120,000,000 people; and the rabbit hasn't found a pal. Well, well, no doubt there's something wrong with the rabbit.'

* * *

Alone, despondent and angry, Martha decided that she had
seen enough. She returned to Washington and, according to
her own account, stormed into Hopkins's office and harangued
him about the way relief was being administered, before giving
her notice, adding that she had plans to write and expose what
she had witnessed. By all accounts Hopkins was a calm and
sensible man. He told her that he had sent her reports to Mrs
Roosevelt; why didn't she discuss it all with her? Edna Gellhorn
and Eleanor Roosevelt were friends from college days, and
Martha had grown up to admire her selfless campaigning.
Invited to dinner at the White House, she grudgingly accepted.
When she got there, she was outraged at the apparent luxury,
and particularly at the gold and white china.

Mrs Roosevelt was a little deaf. A terrible moment came
when she rose from her place at the long dining-room table
and shouted down to her husband at the other end, her voice
high and patrician like the President's. 'Franklin, talk to that
girl. She says all the unemployed have pellagra and syphilis.'
There was silence; then an explosion of laughter. The President,
trying not to smile, listened politely while Martha, more angry
than embarrassed, talked about her travels through the mill
towns. He asked her to come back and tell him more. And
when, not long afterwards, Mrs Roosevelt persuaded her that
she could do far more for the unemployed by sticking to her
job, it marked the beginning of a close friendship, one of the
most devoted attachments of her life. 'She gave off light,'
Martha would write many years later. 'I cannot explain it
better.'

What Mad Pursuit had at last appeared, the publishers,
Frederick A. Stokes having accepted Martha's reluctant last
round of cuts. Even so, her world-weary story of three college
girls in search of something to believe in, and their brushes
with syphilis, adultery and drink, caused a not altogether flattering stir among reviewers, though the St Louis Post-Dispatch
listed her name among those of outstanding local women,
together with Betty Grable. The Buffalo Evening News called
her heroines 'hectic', and most newspapers drew attention to

her respectable St Louis origins, her elegance, and the fact that she had married the Marquis de Jouvenel. Edna was quoted as saying that her daughter was a 'knight without armour' and never afraid of the truth and, somewhat more disconcertingly, that she was already 'writing much better'. The most perceptive review appeared in the *New York Times*. 'Crude as it is, there is something fresh and appealing about this book. It would be more likable if Miss Gellhorn were not so enamoured of her own heroine, and if she did not dabble so ineffectually with questions of social justice . . . If she does not go to Hollywood, as she easily might, she may do good work.' Martha had no intention of going back to Hollywood, but she minded the reviews and the poor sales, though she dismissed the reviewers sharply as 'immature and unreasonable'. 'When I think of what went into making the book, and see how little it counts, I am dismayed before the future,' she wrote to Bertrand.

What Mad Pursuit, 'palpable juvenilia' as a reviewer noted, was consigned to a closed past: Martha never listed it among the things she wrote, and made sure that once it went out of print it stayed there. It was 'petit-point', little stitches laboured over, only to be ripped out, and she had wasted three years on it. But, read today, it is not a bad book, with its insights and passages of lively dialogue, and it laid down a marker for many of the themes that would occupy her life: the weather and the moods it shaped, the need to survive the unsurvivable, the parameters of loneliness, exile, the obligations of friendship, and injustice in all its forms. It also defined the way she would henceforth write fiction, drawing heavily on her own life and experiences – on several occasions too heavily for the comfort of her friends. Though Martha always denied that her heroines had anything to do with her, it is possible to follow the events, places and people of her life through her tales of troubled relationships and disillusioned women.

Deft at shutting doors, Martha now moved firmly on, to the next of her trips for FERA, writing to Bertrand her old refrain: 'I want so much more out of life. I want to give and take more.' Though before she set out again she seems to have had what two papers called 'nervous exhaustion' and took to her bed, 'feeble as spaghetti', for a month with a very low blood count in a friend's house in Bryn Mawr. Slowly her mood picked up. As she felt stronger, she wrote to Lorena Hickok that she could not wait to get back to 'our happy family'. Hickok, she told a friend, reminded her of the captain of a girls' hockey team.

On her earlier travels around the country, Lorena Hickok had detected 'extensive communist activity'. Hopkins's investigators were therefore asked to keep their eyes out for signs of 'organised revolt'. Travelling through the South in the autumn, Martha had come across repeated expressions of admiration and respect for the President, and a genuine belief that he was on the side of the unemployed. Six months later, visiting some of the same areas, she encountered little but despair. Even union meetings had become 'sad and dispirited'. 'I can only report,' she wrote, 'that there are no organised protest groups: there is only decay. Each family in its own miserable home going to pieces . . . It seems incredible to think that they will go on like this, patiently waiting for nothing . . . Grim is a gentle word: it's heart-breaking and terrifying.' It was now the children who most disturbed her. 'I cannot write too feelingly of the physical condition of small children.' What schooling there was, she told Hopkins, was a 'joke'. The young no longer had any resources, either 'within or without'; they were waiting for nothing and they believed neither in man nor in God. She was also coming across increasing numbers of girls who, having grown up 'against a shut door' were becoming prostitutes, sometimes just for a glass of beer.

Martha herself remained angry. One day, in a little town on a lake in Idaho called Coeur d'Alene, she talked to a group of men, farmers and ranchers in their former lives, who were being exploited by a crooked contractor. They told her that while they shovelled dirt, he threw their shovels into the lake, then told the authorities that they had been broken, and collected commission on each new consignment. While waiting for their new shovels to arrive, the men were again out of work. That evening, Martha bought them beer in the bar, and told them that the only way to make themselves heard would be by doing something dramatic, like breaking the windows of the FERA offices. The next morning, she moved on to Seattle. The men did exactly what she had suggested, and broke the windows of their local FERA office, and immediately the FBI, alerted to a possible communist uprising, terrified that the jobless would stop being docile and turn violent, descended on Coeur d'Alene, where they were told that it had all been done at the suggestion of the relief lady. Before long, the contractor was arrested for fraud, the men went back to work, and Martha was recalled to Washington and sacked. She had become, she wrote to her parents in triumph, a 'dangerous Communist'. As she saw it, it was an 'honourable discharge'.

Fearing that others might not see it that way, the Roosevelts sent over a note, which arrived as Martha was clearing out her desk at FERA's headquarters, inviting her to stay with them. Since what she now planned to do was write a book about the 'defeated army of the unemployed', she accepted.

* * *

It was a good moment to stay at the White House. Roosevelt's early decisiveness, his rapid measures to mobilise industry and distribute relief, had all restored a sense of hope. Some of this had to do with his nature and style. His 'fireside chats', authoritative yet intimate radio talks during which he spoke reassuringly about the health of the nation, his own public battles against polio, and his pleasant, open manner had convinced people, as Martha had seen on her travels, that he at least was on their side. Though Roosevelt had his detractors – the *Chicago Tribune* once famously described Hitler, Stalin, Mussolini and Roosevelt as the Four Horsemen of the Apocalypse – in the winter of 1934 there was nothing to suggest that he would not win a second term comfortably.

H.G. Wells, a frequent visitor to the White House in the 1930s, observed that it had gone from being a 'queer, ramshackle place like a nest of waiting rooms with hat stands everywhere' to a comfortable private house. Comfortable perhaps, but not elegant, and certainly not lavish. Though Eleanor Roosevelt was an attentive hostess, always on the watch for a guest who felt uneasy or intimidated, she was unpretentious and frugal by instinct, and in any case anxious to demonstrate her solidarity with the country by running a spartan household. To help her, she had recruited a former political ally in the League of Women Voters, Henrietta Nesbitt, a graceless and tetchy woman who waged war on all foreign visitors and on any semblance of good food. Meals were distinctly odd. The porridge tasted like gruel, the soup like water, and no more than one glass of white wine and one of red, always American, was ever served. Joseph Alsop, the Washington columnist, once complained that he found pieces of marshmallow in his salad. Tea, with passable chocolate cake, was said to be the best meal.

Mrs Roosevelt's own version of the fireside chat was a column called 'My Day' syndicated in 135 newspapers, and a regular question and answer piece for *Women's Home Companion*, in which she invited readers to write in freely. Three hundred and one thousand did so in the first six months. The 'My Day' columns, which, when read together provide an evocative picture of American life in the 1930s, consisted of homely, pacey pieces about manners, happiness (never a goal, only a by-product), responsibility and learning how to be useful – and food. Nourishing but inexpensive menus were recommended, having been tried out in the White House. In 1933, not long before Martha's first visit, Mrs Roosevelt and Mrs Nesbitt experimented with a seven and a half cent lunch, which consisted of 'hot stuffed eggs' in tomato sauce, whole-wheat toast, mashed potatoes and prune pudding. It was, said Mrs Roosevelt, a wholesome meal, and very nourishing.

The mixture of rather formal dress in the White House – black tie for dinner – and extremely informal manner, the sparse, even shabby leather- and cretonne-covered furniture with a great deal of clutter, appealed to Martha, whose own taste was becoming increasingly plain. She was given one of the faded chintz bedrooms, and a bathroom with an old-fashioned tub on clawed feet, and told that she could come to meals or not, as she preferred. When she did, particularly on Sundays, when Roosevelt's formidable mother came to lunch, she would find the President skulking in the cloakroom among the coats with favoured guests, mixing lethally strong martinis amid a great deal of laughter, for his mother disapproved of drink and, as Martha recorded critically, seldom bothered to be pleasant to Eleanor either. In the cloakroom, the chosen few giggled and chattered, Martha wrote later, 'as if we were all bad children having a feast in the dorm at night'. For a while she became, she told friends, the President's 'mascot or pet or poodle'.

To Martha, Eleanor Roosevelt seems to have behaved like a very nice headmistress. She was solicitous, helpful, motherly and keen to learn from her new young friend, treating her as 'bringing the news from Ghent to Aix'. 'I have moments of real terror,' she had confessed earlier in the year, 'when I think we may be losing this generation.' Mrs Roosevelt needed people in order to understand about causes. She made certain that Martha was comfortable and that she met the right people. 'She must learn patience and not have a critical attitude towards what others do,' she wrote about Martha to a mutual friend, much as if she were filling in an end of term report. 'For she must remember that to them it is just as important as her dreams are to her.'

At night, after the guests had left – there were always guests, some of whom stayed for months – Martha sometimes sat in Mrs Roosevelt's exceptionally austere room at the end of the corridor, still in evening dress, helping her to answer her vast post. Anything relating to Missouri went off to Edna to be dealt with in St Louis, as Mrs Roosevelt used her friends around the country as informal helpers. A lot of it came from women, as Mrs Roosevelt used her column, as well as her radio broadcasts, to plug women's rights, so that during the Roosevelt years, New Deal Washington gave the impression of having an informal political sisterhood. But much of it came from people in trouble, and copies of some of these letters wound up many years later in Martha's own files. There was one from a Mrs Moore in Chicago, asking for a little milk and fruit for her five children, all of them ill with measles and pneumonia; another from a Douglas Doss of Minnesota, who had lost an arm in a hunting accident and could no longer help his younger brothers and sisters, who needed clothes in which to go to school; Doss wondered whether Mrs Roosevelt could provide him with a horse. 'This is a direct appeal to you,' wrote seventy-nine-year-old A.H. Charles from Texas, whose relief money had been stopped, 'not knowing no other to appeal to.' Until it became impossible, Mrs Roosevelt answered the letters herself; she was, Martha later said, so pathologically modest that she felt she only had the right to anyone's affection if she was being useful.

After the letters came a brisk walk around the grounds with the dogs before bed, Mrs Roosevelt striding out ahead with her long swinging gait. (Martha did not care much for dogs, and these dogs, which nipped, snarled and bolted, were frightful, but Mrs Roosevelt refused to part with them until they had lunged at several children and bitten at least one diplomat and one senator.) The Roosevelts did not share a room, the President having started an affair with his wife's social secretary, Lucy Mercer, over twenty years earlier. ('I have the memory of an elephant,' Mrs Roosevelt told a friend. 'I can forgive but I can never forget.') When not actually in bed, Mrs Roosevelt was always on the move, usually at a run, with her secretary Tommy – 'gray,' noted Martha, 'like old gray cardboard' – running behind her, taking down in shorthand her next column. Occasionally she knitted while she dictated, but either way the whole process never took more than an hour. Throughout the White House years, it would be said, Mrs Roosevelt ran a parallel administration concerned with the domestic betterment of American families, placing memos about things she thought needed doing by her husband's bed each night. Martha, who admired hard work, marvelled at Mrs Roosevelt's utter self-discipline, her readiness, always, to do the sensible thing, even if it was unconventional. She was touched by the columns and the little talks, none or them especially well written or well delivered, for despite lessons in public speaking, her voice remained uninspiring, but direct and without guile. They reminded her, Martha wrote later, that 'America was a simpler, humbler country then'. She liked Mrs Roosevelt's huge modesty and lack of all affectation. 'I loved her,' she wrote after her death. 'I doubt that she believed she was ever loved for herself, and, more than that, I doubt if anyone knew who that self was.'

Except, perhaps, Lorena Hickok, with whom Eleanor Roosevelt exchanged 3,500 letters during the thirty years of a friendship that is now accepted to have been very loving and dependent. It was Hickok who had persuaded Mrs Roosevelt to get help in writing from a professional journalist and turn her letters into the 'My Day' column. Whenever Hickok was in Washington, on breaks from her FERA reporting, she stayed in the White House, sleeping on a day bed outside Mrs Roosevelt's room. Occasionally, she persuaded the First Lady to travel with her, to see for herself what the Depression was doing to America. In town, the burly Hickok dressed well, her long hair pulled back, with coral red lipstick and bright silk scarves, and she had good legs, in spite of her weight; but on her travels she wore tweeds and trousers. Mrs Roosevelt's letters to her, unlike those to Martha, are far from head-mistressy; on the contrary, many are sarcastic and snide, evidence of a less kindly but more amusing woman who, when crossed, could be icy. She was clearly not the saint Martha seemed to take her for, and she was certainly not always charming. Hickok, for her part, was shrewd, with a direct and quick humour. The relationship between the two women, though sometimes bumpy, was trusting; and they sought, and for the most part, succeeded, in avoiding gossip.

*　　*　　*

It was not so much that the writing went badly for Martha as the fact that there were too many distractions. It was hard to sit upstairs trying to conjure up the shantytowns of South Carolina, while along the corridor people were discussing world politics. After observing life in the White House for a few weeks, Martha packed her bags and moved into a holiday house belonging to a friend called W.F. Field, an expert on China, in New Hartford, Connecticut. Here she spent most of the next four months writing her book about the Depression. This time, she knew precisely what she had to do. She wanted to tell the world what it felt like to have lost the job you had always assumed was yours for life, and with it your house, your possessions, your security and your dreams; and what you thought about when you saw your wife ill, your children hungry and uneducated. The material was fresh, dramatic and intensely present in her mind. It was a question of distilling it. She had been haunted by what she had seen; now, she had to haunt others. She decided to cast it as fiction, on the grounds, she told an interviewer later, that the way you make facts come alive is by showing their effects on people, through stories, though her characters were so closely modelled on real people that they were for all purposes real. For most of the time she was alone, writing late into the night, sleeping late in the morning. None of her letters to friends at the time suggests that she was lonely, but on 8 November, the day of her twenty-seventh birthday, she wrote down in a notebook: 'I tell you loneliness is the thing to master. Courage and fear, love, death are only parts of it and can easily be ruled afterwards. If I make myself master of my own loneliness there will be peace or safety: and perhaps these are the same.'

Even in her mid-twenties, Martha's control of language and ear for tension were remarkable. The four long stories, their titles taken from the characters, are among the best things she ever wrote. Very little happens in them. Six or seven characters in all, drawn in sharp, brief lines, shine on the page. There is a union representative called Joe, who is laid off work in a soup factory after leading a strike, and Jim, hurt and baffled as he watches his family fall apart, until the day he steals a red dress so that the girl he loves can marry him in finery; and Ruby, the little girl who becomes a prostitute so that she can buy a pair of roller skates but who, even after she is sent to reform school, still does not quite understand what she has done wrong. No character in any of Martha's fiction was ever to be more poignantly drawn, perhaps, than Mrs Maddison, who, at the opening of the book, is preparing to visit the relief office in search of something for her granddaughter to wear. 'Mrs Maddison stood before the mirror and tried tipping her hat first over the right eye and then over the left. The mirror was cracked and Mrs Maddison's reflected face looked a bit mixed up. But the hat was clear. It was of white straw, the pot shape that is cheapest and commonest; it had cost thirty cents and Mrs Maddison herself trimmed it, with a noisily pink starchy gardenia, in the centre front, like a miner's lamp.' There was pity in the writing, but no sentimentality; never had the small, still voice been better used.

How far was Martha plunged into this intensity of writing by a need to prove to her father, who had made it clear that he did not approve of *What Mad Pursuit*, that she was a serious writer? Their relations, since she had left Bertrand, had improved, but she had not spent much time in St Louis. A very long typed letter he wrote to her at about this time exists; it was tough, even harsh, and though loving must have made unhappy reading. It was about her character. Bertrand is quickly disposed of: 'your affair with that little French runt that gave you so much "valuable experience" and us so much real pain'. It is how she will handle her life after his death, given that there will be no money for her to inherit, that worries him. 'It will be pretty dark for you if you remain in the groove you have been ploughing these past six or seven years. Strangely, that has been the only thing you haven't got tired of, this self-deception . . . I am ready to bet that many of the people who are now fascinated by you would be rather surprised, I mean disillusioned, if they knew that you are almost 27 years old. The impression of a precocious and altogether bewitching child would vanish . . . it's you and only you that can pull you out of this slough of self-pity and self-abasement and make you a person of lasting worth . . . "I want to write, I want to write" that is your eternal wail. Then why the devil don't you? If you really *want* to write, write by all means, but do it *NOW* . . . instead of capitalising your yellow hair and your lively, spicy conversation, you should have the pride of wanting to *show* the world that you can hold your place with anybody else, not only while you are young and attractive to men, but at any time.'

In New Hartford, Martha wrote as she never had before. In a little more than four months the book was finished. Dr Gellhorn, when she sent it to him, remarked that he was unable to read the story about Ruby because it was too painful; but that he had hastened through the first part 'without stopping and with breathless interest'.

For once, the timing was fortunate. Some time in December 1935, not long after he had finished reading her manuscript, Dr Gellhorn began to feel pains in his stomach. In January, they decided to operate and Martha travelled back to St Louis to see him. The operation appeared to go well and she returned east, leaving him convalescing in bed. On the 25th, while asleep, his heart failed and he died.

Dr Gellhorn had been much loved in St Louis, particularly by his black patients, and his skills as a physician were renowned. Of all his children, Alfred, then twenty-two, was the one most affected by his death, saying sadly – but quite wrongly – that with his father's 'enthusiasm and love to push me along, I think I might have amounted to something'. Alfred became a distinguished doctor and medical researcher. Martha herself left almost no record of her own feelings about her father, though, many years later, not long before her own death, she remarked that of all her regrets one of the most painful was a feeling that she had failed him.

After the funeral, Martha stayed on for a while in St Louis, keeping her mother company, but she had no intention of remaining and Edna did nothing to keep her. Edna's working life had blossomed, and her name had been engraved on a bronze tablet honouring the city's women who had helped secure female suffrage, but her love and need for her daughter had not diminished. 'She loves you so thoroughly that it makes me ache,' Alfred wrote to Martha. 'She has more pride in your accomplishments than in any of the rest of us, and she is completely confident in your ultimate success.' But Martha needed a job, and wrote disconsolately to Teecher – her now usual form of address for her poet friend and tutor Hortense Flexner – that she was 'terrified of this slime I use for brain; of the jobless future; of the fact that I am twenty-seven and have produced two stinking books only. And that the shining adventure that was *Life* at twenty is now an endurance contest . . . But goddam it, I want to write great heavy swooping things, to throw terror and glory into the mind.' The language was still brash; but the ambition remained keen.

Her ear, which had given her so much trouble in France two years before, was again painful, and she went briefly into hospital for an operation. Towards the end of April, she boarded the train for New York, where a grudging publisher told her that he would take her book of stories about the Depression, but only out of a love of literature, and warning that it would never sell. 'I have been job-hunting,' she wrote to a friend of her father's, Dr Edward Schumann, 'which is an experience everyone should have, because it makes you tender towards all humanity (except employers) . . . I loathe it. I feel constantly like a gold fish who has been bought on approval.' She was waiting to hear whether *Time* magazine was going to offer her a staff position, having asked her to write a trial story for them.

In September, *The Trouble I've Seen*, the title taken from the Negro spiritual, was published in America. Contrary to the publisher's forebodings, it was reviewed in virtually every major city in the country, respectfully and with admiration, and sold extremely well. The *Saturday Review of Literature*, which put a photograph of Martha on its cover, praised her 'profound and sympathetic understanding'. Its reviewer, Mabel Ulrich, observed that the book seemed to be 'woven not out of words but out of the very tissues of human beings'. To interviewers who came to write articles about the elegant St Louis-born Marquise de Jouvenel – in spite of Martha's attempts to make it clear that she and Bertrand had never actually married, newspapers insisted on using the title – she said that she had wanted to 'jar the hell out of the populace, shatter them out of their smug complacency'. Mrs Roosevelt mentioned the book in three separate 'My Day' columns, saying that America badly needed Martha's understanding and interpretation 'to help us understand each other'. 'I cannot tell you,' she wrote, 'how Martha Gellhorn, young, pretty, college graduate, good home, more or less Junior League background, with a touch of exquisite Paris clothes and "esprit" thrown in, can write as she does.' In Paris, where it appeared as *La Détresse Americaine*, it was referred to as 'one of the great books of the day', and one reviewer linked Martha's name with those of Dostoevsky, Dickens and Victor Hugo. It was a book, wrote Lewis Gannett in the *Herald Tribune*, that 'lives and dances in the memory'.

* * *

The Trouble I've Seen had in fact first appeared in London, where Graham Greene in the *Spectator* devoted considerably more space to its 'amazingly unfeminine' style and its lack of 'female vices of unbalanced pity or factitious violence' than to reviewing its content. Putnam had been the publishers, through the intervention of H.G. Wells, who contributed a preface, drawing attention to the author's 'lucidity and penetration'. Wells had undertaken to make all the arrangements for her and had first interested Hamish Hamilton in the project, taking the book away from them after they appeared doubtful about possible sales – Hamilton talked about an initial five hundred copies – and proposed an advance of only £30. Putnams came up with £50.

H.G. Wells was an interesting figure in Martha's life, neither hero nor lover, as often wrongly supposed, but with some touch of both, with fondness and admiration on Martha's part, and, for a while, fanciful infatuation on his. There was something fatherly in Wells's efforts to school Martha in his own vigorous work habits – Martha was never shy of work, only erratic in her methods – to which Martha responded with affectionate mock obedience. She told a friend he was the most intelligent man she had ever met. His nickname for her was Stooge, as in a dogsbody, someone to fetch and carry and boss around; she wrote to him as 'Wells darling'.

They had met in Washington at the White House in 1935, on one of Wells's periodic visits to America, where he had numerous friends, particularly in California, and a large following. He had decided that he liked and approved of the Roosevelts, 'unlimited people, entirely modern in the openness of their minds and the logic of their actions'. Martha was then still working for FERA, perching in a rather pleasant, large flat, with four light rooms. Wells was sixty-nine, a short, round man with a straggling moustache, a squeaky voice and feet that barely touched the floor when he sat down; Rebecca West, his former mistress and the mother of his son Anthony, had said of him that he smelt of walnuts and that he frisked like a nice animal. Martha was then twenty-six and a whole head taller. Wells, already widely known for writing books – *The Time Machine, The War of the Worlds* – which translated the new discoveries in science into a language ordinary people could understand, and which also looked into the future, had parted from Odette Keun but was embroiled with Moura Budberg, Gorky's former mistress. ('My story of my relations with women,' Wells once wrote with surprising honesty, 'is mainly a story of greed, foolishness and great expectation.')

Not long before they met, Wells had written that, though not usually an unhappy man, he was never absolutely safe from occasional attacks of acute misery: 'and there is no one to whom I can go with the assurance of that envelopment and refuge and comfort for which the distressful heart craves'. Martha, he thought, might become that one. She made him laugh, and he liked to ask her questions about 'American youth'. For her part, she admired the way he maintained that women could accomplish anything they wanted to, and she had enjoyed *Ann Veronica*, his daring novel about the rela-tionship between the sexes in which he had poked fun at the more strident feminists, caricaturing their self-importance and muddled thinking. Martha, too, found their seriousness faintly comic.

After he left Washington, he wrote to her from New York: 'I'm sorry to leave you behind. There was something queer and acute that happened between us. I leave something of myself in Washington with you. What is liking? What is love? I dunno.' And again: 'I am strongly moved to ask you to pack up and come to England and to bed with me . . .' From his flat in London, at 47 Chiltern Court, he wrote regularly, letters full of seduction and doggerel and the little comic sketches, 'picshuas', that he drew in the letters of the women he was taken with. He told her that he felt closer to her intellectually than to Rebecca West, and that she was '*important*. You count. You are responsible for yourself. You are one of US', all welcome words to a young writer. (Martha once asked Rebecca West why she had not had an abortion. West told her that since she had been young and healthy it seemed the 'reasonable and right thing' to have the baby. Martha put it down to West's 'constant instinct towards self-destruction', a remark that says much about what she must have felt when faced with the prospect of having Bertrand's child though not married to him.)

After receiving an unhappy letter from Martha from St Louis, Wells wrote: 'A sunny beach, Stooge getting sunburnt, me getting sunburnt, Stooge very much in love with me and me all in love with Stooge, nothing particular ahead except a far off dinner, some moonlight and bed – Stooge's bed. A long, lazy, week long talk about everything.' To her letters of outrage about the misery she observed in the South, he warned against 'accumulated indignation' but brought the letter back, as he often did, to himself: 'At bottom,' he wrote, 'I'm glummer than you my dear. You are young and valiant and you still think that somewhere in the whole darkness there is light and righteousness . . .' The amorous letters kept coming. One day there was a single line: 'Stooge I love you.' Martha's letters back were, like his own, affectionate and flirtatious; they exchanged news about friends, particularly the Roosevelts, about their travels, about books written and read, and about themselves.

In the autumn of 1935 Wells returned to America. Martha was by now in Connecticut, writing hard. It was snowing. Wells came to stay. Exceptionally disciplined about his own work, he now followed Martha around the house, talking without cease, demanding her attention, preventing her from getting on with her book. She wrote later that she remembered thinking bitterly that he started at breakfast with the Ice Age and ended after dinner with Henry James. At last, noticing her irritation, he told her that she would be sorry, after he was dead, that she had not paid more attention to him and learnt more. When she could stand the talk no longer, she sent a telegram to his old friend Charlie Chaplin, whom she had never met, telling him that Wells would undoubtedly welcome an invitation to California. One arrived and Wells departed, having first to be dug out of a snowdrift by Field, her host, who generously came up from New York to collect him. 'Martha in ski-ing trousers with her shock of ruddy golden hair in disorder,' Wells wrote later, 'her brown eyes alight and her face rosy with frost is unforgettable.' From Chaplin's house in Hollywood, he wrote again: 'I'm restless and bothered. Why don't you make love with me and smoothe me down and make me altogether happy? . . . I wish I was attractive to women. Why have I of all men to wander about the world without a responsive Stooge to talk to and sleep with and love? . . . You weren't given that nice body of yours just to fritter it away.'

The amorous letters continued to arrive. 'I am now deeply in love with you, deeply and permanently . . . It's as good as fresh violets.' At some point Wells seems to have given Martha $500, to act as his 'eyes' in America, and when *The Troubles I've Seen* was finished, and she was looking for a job, he suggested, in rather touching terms, that while becoming an 'Important' writer, which she certainly would, she might like to be his 'fag'. 'Suppose there is a dozen years of vitality left in me. Would it be a sacrifice or an apprenticeship for you to become . . . something between a Shulamite and a mental secretary, an accessory conscience. But you're restless . . . You aren't ancillary enough . . .

'Stooge what are we going to do about it? . . . I've glimpsed something between us too good to lose. The sort of thing that is always getting lost in life.'

Wells was constantly trying to work out what exactly he

wanted the women around him to be – mistress, *passade* (his name for fleeting infatuations) or wife; but Martha, for her part, was not proposing to be any of them. Only many years later did she realise that Wells must have been lonely and weary; at the time, with the hurry of her age, and her particular eagerness for life, it never occurred to her that 'anyone could be old, famous, rich and working hard, and still be in trouble'.

She turned up in London in June 1936, and, presumably reassured by being told that 'Moura and I have an ineradicable affection but for profound but inexplicable reasons this isn't going to come between you and me', went to stay in his immaculate new house in Hanover Terrace, painted white and sparsely furnished, from where the lions could be heard roaring in the zoo nearby. She talked to him about Bertrand, whom he had already met, and about the 'attractive young gents' who came to take her out every night; he told her that she had to stand alone and that the world was a 'cage of apes'. He insisted only that she got up in the morning, never something she did willingly, to have breakfast with him, and, one day, after being nagged about getting down to work, she sat down and wrote an article about the lynching she and Bertrand had narrowly avoided witnessing during their travels through the American South, which, like the stories in *Troubles*, had an intensity all the more powerful for being so simple. Only, she wrote it as if she had actually seen it. 'From beneath,' she wrote, 'a group of men, shoving and pushing, got Hyacinth's limp, thin body up to them. He half lay, half squatted on the car roof . . . Now he was making a terrible sound, like a dog whimpering . . . Then he snapped from the back of the car, hung suspended, twirled a little on the rope . . . I went away and was sick.'

There are two versions of what happened next. In one, recounted to John Hatt in January 1990, Martha left London for Germany the next day and Wells, knowing that her article was based closely on fact, sent it to the *Spectator*. The *Spectator* published it and it was then reprinted in *Reader's Digest*. After this it was picked up by *The Living Age* in the US, where it became a leaflet for the anti-lynching campaign which was fighting hard to combat the Ku Klux Klan, which had carried out thirty-three lynchings in 1933 alone. When Martha returned from Germany and found out what had happened, she was too ashamed to confess that she had not in fact personally watched the lynching, but she did refuse an invitation to appear as a witness before a Senate Committee on the anti-lynching bill.

In the other version, as told to Eleanor Roosevelt in a letter written on 23 November 1936, Martha sent the article to her agent in London, who sold it to the *Spectator* for £50. It was then published in Germany before appearing in the *Reader's Digest* and *The Living Age*. Explaining, with some embarrassment, her 'muddle-headedness' to Mrs Roosevelt, Martha wrote: 'Around now, I feel that I have attended twenty lynchings and I wish I'd never seen fit to while away a morning doing a piece of accurate guessing.' In this account, she said that she had fused two separate incidents – meeting a drunken truck driver on his way home from a lynching, and, later, talking to a man whose son had been lynched – into a single story. Mrs Roosevelt advised her to say nothing and let it all blow over.

It was not until many years later that Martha admitted publicly that she had never actually witnessed Hyacinth's death, but she added that her real regret was not that she had allowed people to think she had, but that she had done nothing at the time to protest. 'I do not forget nor slur over my cowardice,' she wrote in her fragment of memoir. 'That crowd could not have been stopped; but I could have stood up and spoken my hatred of them and their abomination of cruelty.'

Whatever the literal truth of what took place, what is interesting is what it says about the way that Martha blended fact and fiction all her life. Whether she did in fact see incidents with such vivid clarity, in her mind's eye, that the line between what was imagined and what really happened genuinely blurred is impossible to say, but it would, in the future, lead her into difficulties. The story of the lynching and the fact that she, who held so strongly to the truth, had lied, returned to haunt her; and after her death it was used by her detractors, out of all proportion to the event, as evidence of hypocrisy.

As for Wells, he undoubtedly played a role in Martha's early writing, though there is nothing to suggest – as Martha's critics have – that she ever used her friendship with him to advance her work, or was indeed ever greatly interested in his fame. Friends were what they were to her: it was one of the things that made her approval so rewarding. What Wells did do, however, was talk to her constantly about work, agreeing that it was the 'best thing in life', and told her that she should be sharpening herself on her experiences, making her 'moods do their exercises' in short stories and articles. She was disconcerted when he wrote to tell her that her technique was greatly increased 'in cunning'. After Martha had been staying with Wells, Edna noted in her daughter a new sense of discipline and wrote to thank him: 'You have accomplished more than I have ever achieved – up at eight, and writing!'

Romantically, Wells did not quite give up hope for several years. At one point he seems to have proposed marriage, but Martha 'gently and politely pointed out that it would look pretty funny', after which they settled down to a mildly flirtatious correspondence and friendship, on Wells's side somewhat wistful, which lasted until his death in 1946. Martha, who had by now met Moura, and greatly taken to her, suspected that Wells was simply using her to 'enrage Moura or make her jealous or punish her'. The two women laughed merrily after Wells told Moura, referring to Martha, 'I am not having her now.'

Neither then, nor, Martha always insisted, ever; and her affairs were matters over which she was scrupulously honest. Wells, to the young Martha, had seemed 'older than God'. 'Why the hell would I sleep with a little old man when I could have any number of tall beautiful young men?' she wrote irritably in a letter to Victoria Glendinning many years later.

At some point in the 1930s, Wells wrote what he called a 'Postscript' to his autobiography, to which he gave the subtitle 'On Loves and the Lover-Shadow', an expression he said meant a 'continually growing and continually more subtle complex of expectation and hope'. Among the many women he had been involved with, he listed Martha as one of the less important 'women I have kissed, solicited, embraced and lived with, have never entered intimately and deeply into my emotional life'. In a manuscript of some four hundred pages, she appears half a dozen times, as a promising, vivid young writer, with an 'adventurous honesty'. 'And I have never had more amusing love-letters.' About his stay in Connecticut, he wrote: 'We two had a very happy time together for a week, making love, talking, reading over her second book.' Later, 'we parted – indeterminate . . . She is extremely incidental.' All words which say much about the part played by fantasy in Wells's relations with women, and about the many different meanings conveyed by the language of affection. For though Martha never actually had an affair with Wells – though of course it is her word against his that she did not – she was certainly more than 'incidental' in his life.

In 1983, nearly fifty years later, Gip Wells published his father's Postscript. Writing to tell Martha what he intended to include, he received a furious reply. 'I'd have swum the Pacific rather than get involved with him beyond friendship, and not too much of that . . . He was my father's age and not, you will agree, physically dazzling. I had a constant supply of attractive young gents and have never been lured by men who were smaller than me . . . He was fun unless he was bullying intellectually, and I was very fond of him but the rest is rubbish.' He was also a bit of a bore. She regretted having been shown his words, because they made her 'dislike Wells and I had fond memories and sad memories of him'. She would sue if he suggested they had had an affair. When the book appeared, with no mention of her name (but a few meaningful asterisks) she read it through and wrote to tell Gip that Wells came across as so caddish and selfish that she doubted 'his right to be the great ideologue of Utopia'. As for his affairs with younger women, Wells was older and it was up to him 'to keep his overanxious and over-excited penis in control'.

Yet the myth of their affair continues to be repeated by

successive biographers, anxious to add another lover to Wells's already ample collection.

* * *

Martha was having a restless year. *Time* had not offered her the staff job she hoped for, and the proposal of a piece on Europe to *The New Yorker* had been turned down on the grounds that the timing was wrong, though Katherine White wrote warmly to say that she had liked Martha's book and hoped she would try them again with other ideas. Martha replied that she would indeed, for there was no magazine she more admired, if she could ever again find anything to be cheerful about. After her stay with Wells in London – among the 'attractive young gents' whose names are mentioned in her diary were Bill Astor and a man called Anthony Winn – she went back to Paris in July, where Léon Blum was now at the head of a Popular Front coalition of socialists and communists and where the city was constantly shut down by strikes. She was thinking about going back to the novel about peace she had started while with Bertrand, and wanted to walk around the battlefields of the First World War.

Since his brief visit to America the previous year, Bertrand had written regularly; but their affair was finally over. Coeur d'Alene had been, as he put it, their 'swan song', and they had moved, by uneasy stages, into an affectionate friendship. Bertrand was, as ever, generous, though he clearly sensed that, of the two of them, she had taken the more successful turn. 'You are a very great person,' he wrote to her, 'far greater than the woman Sand or than Colette . . . Darling, let no one ever tell you you haven't the genius. It's there, and no force on earth can prevent you from howling what you have to say.' As for matters of the flesh, if not the heart, he urged her to take lovers 'till one day you find some tenderness and beauty where you bargained for none'. Martha now took to consulting him over her affairs, and he patiently wrote pressing her not to turn her men into Siegfrieds, nor bully them into saying only what she wanted to hear. 'For Christ's sake don't give the impression you're prowling around, trying to pounce upon men . . . And don't experiment too much. Lest you grow hard and cynical just because you've knocked at the wrong doors and found them bolted.' Later, Martha would write that her five years with Bertrand had taught her many useful lessons, not least how important it was never to give in to anything; and that it was by observing 'le grand monde' in Paris that she had learnt to despise society.

Bertrand, meanwhile, by a single interview in which he was manipulated by forces far subtler and more calculating than he would ever be, had taken a turn that would colour the rest of his life. In 1935, having won acclaim for his coverage of the economy both in France and in the English-speaking world, he had been taken on by *Paris-Midi* to conduct interviews with European political leaders. On 6 February 1936 he had received an invitation to interview Hitler in Berlin. Hitler talked warmly and at length about his friendly feelings for France, and his hopes for closer ties between the two countries, ties which, he insisted, would remain unaltered even if France chose to go ahead and sign a pact of friendship with the Soviet Union. 'I plan to alter my foreign policy which is based on an understanding with France,' Hitler told him, explaining that the French should not fear the hostile attitude towards them that had appeared in *Mein Kampf*. After the interview was written up, it went to von Ribbentrop for checking and when it came back Bertrand found that part of it had been altered: the new version suggested that in the case of a Franco-Soviet pact, Hitler's views on friendly relations with France would change. In the event, Bertrand's article did not appear until after the pact was signed, which had apparently been von Ribbentrop's intention all along, making it possible for the Germans to say that the French had been kept in ignorance of Hitler's views on the matter. The interview made Bertrand famous; but not pleasantly so. He was widely accused of having acted as Hitler's spokesman, a view all the easier to sustain because of his continuing loyalty to Otto Abetz and openly fascist French intellectuals such as Drieu la Rochelle and Jean Luchaire.

After German troops marched into the demilitarised Rhineland in March, Bertrand did repudiate National Socialism, writing in the *Daily Mirror* that the occupation was an offence against the sanctity of treaties and the dignity of France, and urging England to intervene as mediator, but it all came a little late. In France at least he was now regarded as a fascist and newspapers, other than those owned by Nazi sympathisers, closed their pages to him. As Martha later wrote, Bertrand was 'the long-term lamb amongst wolves', 'a man lacking in all judgment'; but 'his heart was clean'. There was, in Bertrand's character, such an endless longing for things to work out for the best that he often appeared curiously innocent.

As for Martha, somewhere around this time, she seems to have embarked on a love affair with Allen Grover, a journalist writing about business for *Time*. Grover was eight years her senior, and, like Martha, had fled St Louis as a young man, and if they had not actually met in the country club they both hated as children, then their families had certainly known each other. He was tall, thin and had almost black hair, which he wore in Hollywood style, shiny with grease and plastered smoothly to the side; he was energetic, gregarious and his eyes were rather pouchy. He was also married, to a painter, and had a small daughter called Lorraine. He and Martha laughed when they were together, and each helped the other over matters of work. Feeling herself to be the more involved of the two for a while, Martha soon pulled away from him, writing to reassure him that he had ceased to be her breakfast and was now only the cream in her coffee. 'The only terms on which to take you are the instalment plan ones,' she wrote, as their affair became progressively less intense, and then developed into friendship. From Paris, which she had now decided that she hated, Martha moved on to Stuttgart to work in the Weltkriegsbibliothek, and then on to Munich. She was becoming increasingly conscious of the brutality and unpleasantness of Nazi rule. One day, reading in the library, she saw its new director arrive on horseback, galloping across the grass in a crisp new Brown Shirt uniform, a young good-looking man who made a lot of noise when he entered the building. He made her uneasy, and when in the newspapers she read an account of the 'Red swine dogs', the Republicans, in Spain, she was so angry she felt she could stay in Germany no longer.

She was lonely, but she was also looking for 'gaiety', and she found it in casual affairs among men who gave her 'company, laughter, movement, the sense that life was an open road and you could run very fast on it'. Writing nearly twenty years later about those uneasy prewar months, Martha's verdict was tough: 'No one reached out for me, really, not for what I was or wanted to become, but grabbed for my body . . . It was also never any good. The only part I ever liked was arms around me and an illusion of tenderness. But I could not make much illusions, and arms didn't last; and the rest happened to someone else (it was always painful) and except for two men I never saw anyone again afterwards because the debts were paid and everything was ruined anyhow and I only wanted to go away.' As for the two men she did see again, one was a 'monster and a brute . . . and I was like a canary with a boa-constrictor', while the other was an Englishman called Paul Willert who made her laugh and 'I could almost talk to him'. But Willert too had a wife and kept hesitating about asking her for a divorce, and when that, too, ended, on 'an unclear dying note', she went back to America to write her book on peace, still troubled about the future but in no way chastened. 'I want life to be like the movies,' she wrote to Bertrand, 'brilliant and swift and successful.' Eleanor Roosevelt, hearing of her emotional entanglements, noted crisply that Martha should not be allowed to 'get sorry for herself and become just another useless, pretty, broken butterfly. She has too much charm and real ability for that.' She need not have worried: self-pity was never in Martha's nature. Nor much compassion for the wives of the men she took up with. They play so little part in her musings and observations on the affairs of those years that it is often hard to keep in one's mind how many of her lovers were in fact married. That both Willert and Grover had wives, who did not want to lose them, is never mentioned.

Something of her emotional toughness in these years comes across in an unguarded letter she wrote to Allen Grover about Willert's failure to leave his wife. 'I want to see what kind of guts and independence he has. (HATE people unless they are free of me, I want nothing to do with anyone except my superiors. I have a real physical loathing of people who are morally weak. A man is no use to me, unless he can live without me . . . Bertrand was enough for life of the little boy, who needs his nurse.)' Such vulgarity and toughness on her part, Martha volunteered, was bound to condemn her to a lonely future with a monkey and a dachshund for company. Tough, certainly, and self-mocking; but not repentant. Already conscious that she needed periods of time alone, she went off to the Tyrol for a week to walk and look at the mountains and brood about what she saw as a 'lull to end the war to end wars, and the war to end Europe'. Her novel about German and French pacifists was not going well, but she felt her mind to have become sharper and clearer and, she told Allen, 'I have lost my usual pity, lost it hard.' Then she went back to Paris, and lunched with the women who had been her daily companions with Bertrand, and found them handsome and amusing as they discussed mascara and communism with equal fervour. After lunch they went off to visit a fortune-teller, and that evening she dined with Drieu la Rochelle, who was 'in love with war and sexy as a satyr'. They went on to the Louvre, to look at sculptures of women's breasts. 'I don't belong in an air so strange,' Martha told Grover, 'so languid and so intense.' She reported that she felt utterly alone, and that her women friends assumed that she had become a lesbian.

* * *

Martha had not been the only one of Hopkins's reporters who had sifted through the daily scenes of poverty in search of the erosion of the American way of life. All the writers, in their own fashion, talked about the humiliation, so acutely expressed in Mrs Maddison's gestures, suffered by people reduced to accepting relief. In their reports, they all took the view that the only way back to dignity was through work, a conclusion that played its part in helping Hopkins frame his campaigns for work projects, old-age pensions and child benefits. And the reports were certainly read and taken in by Roosevelt, and, perhaps to a greater extent, by Eleanor. The New Deal was not without its dark sides, its brushes with social engineering, and Martha was among those later criticised for concentrating too much on birth control, syphilis and feeble-mindedness, and too little on the racial minorities. But the picture that emerged from the 107 final reports constituted a remarkable history of the Great Depression. Taken together with the work of photographers like the Pulitzer Prize-winning Walker Evans, and writers like Dos Passos and Steinbeck, they showed the death of an earlier, simpler America, which would now vanish before the march of industrial and technological advance.

Though Roosevelt was not popular with the entire electorate – a man was said to have taught the tiger in the zoo in New York's Central Park to roar whenever his name was mentioned – the country as a whole endorsed his humanitarian handling of poverty and unemployment by returning an unprecedented majority for the Democrats. The Depression itself was at last easing, though it would bite again in 1937, and Hopkins and the New Dealers were slowly starting to focus on longer-term measures to introduce the benefits of modern technology to farmers, and to try to put in place safeguards against anything of the kind ever happening to the country again. By the middle of the 1930s the administration, intent on fending off the red menace at home, was observing Europe's political upheavals and Japan's seizure of Manchuria, and feeling increasingly isolationist. Within two years, the House Committee on Un-American Activities would be seeing a communist in every trade unionist.

Martha went home to St Louis in December, Edna having told her that she had enough money to keep them both for a while, so that Martha could write without financial worry. Their relations were again loving, the unhappy breach over Bertrand long past. Alfred was living at home, his medical studies almost finished. Edna and her two younger children decided to spend Christmas in Florida, since this was their first Christmas without Dr Gellhorn. They didn't much care for Miami, and so they caught a bus to Key West, where the swimming was good and it was all rather more casual. One evening they went for a drink in a bar called Sloppy Joe's. Sitting at one end was Ernest Hemingway, a 'large, dirty man in untidy somewhat soiled white shorts and shirt', as Martha remembered later, reading his mail.

CHAPTER FIVE

To War with the Boys

It is hard to remember – now that Hemingway's name evokes a masculine swagger, an increasingly drunken slide into belligerence, depression and suicide – that for a whole generation, the 'lost generation' whose malaise he so perfectly captured, he was regarded by many as the finest writer of his age. Something in his direct, spare narrative, the ease with which his words seemed to flow, struck a chord with readers bewildered and repelled by the horrors of the First World War, hoping to find a saner and more honest message in his self-aware heroes, battling to the limits of their endurance but impotent against circumstances over which they had no control.

Martha was not the only young writer to pin a photograph of him on her college wall, quote from his books and to observe that her style had been 'affected' by his, nor the only one who bought and read all his books as they came out, seduced by their clarity and the economy of his prose, every line of which seemed to reject the cant and rhetoric of the generation which had allowed the war to happen. (Though she would add that he was no good at describing people who really knew how to talk.) Even as some critics wondered why Hemingway chose to write about bullfights and safaris, when Americans were enduring the privations of the Depression, there was nothing he wrote that was not widely read. When *The Snows of Kilimanjaro* appeared in *Esquire* not long before Martha went to Key West, Dos Passos wrote to tell him that it had made more people cry than anything since the Armistice.

The first thing that people remarked on when they met Hemingway was his bulk and strength. He was big, six feet tall and about two hundred pounds in weight, with hard muscles that bulged and a stomach that had spread a little with time, and he already had the weathered looks of a man who has spent much time outdoors. His hair was dark, in some lights almost black, as was his beard, which had not yet turned the familiar pepper and salt colour that it would later become, and his eyes were brown and very watchful. He was endlessly energetic, though somewhat clumsy, and talked about the way that the modern writer and man of action should be fused into one. Though clearly happy in the company of men, whose courage he enjoyed, sometimes cruelly, measuring it against his own, and with whom he could explore his fascination for violence and competitiveness, he also admired courage and stoicism in women. He liked his women to do things, and he liked them to be independent, healthy, happy, loyal, selfless, tanned and not overly made up. It helped if they were clever, at least clever enough to follow his jokes and allusions; to be intellectual was to go too far. His temper was sharp and unpleasant. 'He's a big powerful peasant,' James Joyce once said of Hemingway, 'as strong as a buffalo.'

At the end of 1936, Hemingway was thirty-seven, married to his second wife Pauline Pfeiffer, a journalist who had written for *Vogue* and *Vanity Fair*, for whom he had left his first wife, Hadley, in 1927. He had three sons: John, born in Paris in October 1923, known as Bumby; Patrick – Mexican Mouse – who was now eight; and Gregory, or Gigi, who was five. It was Bumby who had originally called him Papa, the name by which he was now known by his circle. Neither Hadley, tall, auburn-haired and eight years his senior, nor the small and slender Pauline, now forty-one, was exactly beautiful, but both had something in common with Martha. Hadley, who came from St Louis, had also been to Bryn Mawr but dropped out early, and Pauline was a journalist. Both women had a literary bent, and both had been caught up in the Hemingway cult.

That autumn, Walter Winchell had mentioned in his column that Hemingway, as a supporter of the republican cause, was planning to go to Spain to the civil war, which had prompted the North American Newspaper Alliance (NANA) – a syndicate which supplied material to sixty papers, the *New York Times* among them – to invite him to cover the conflict for them. For Hemingway, who had long maintained that novelists who pontificated about politics never produced great art, this represented a new kind of commitment. Agreeing to a fee of $1,000 for each longer piece of around 1,200 words, and $500 for short cabled reports, he was now raising money to buy ambulances. 'I hate to go away,' he wrote to Pauline's parents, 'but you can't preserve your happiness by trying to take care of it or putting it away in mothballs and for a long time me and my conscience both have known I had to go to Spain.' Together with Lillian Hellman, John Dos Passos and Archibald MacLeish, he was involved in setting up a company called Contemporary History, whose real purpose was to find the money to make a documentary about the war, with the Dutch film director Joris Ivens.

In Key West, the island of lush tropical flowers and shrubs to which he had been introduced by Dos Passos, and where the fishing was superb, Hemingway spent a lot of time drinking in Sloppy Joe's. The first meeting with the Gellhorns went well, though Hemingway at first assumed that Alfred and Martha were on their honeymoon – Martha looking younger than her age and Alfred older – and had come off a yacht. Before they parted, he offered to show them round the place, with its old white frame houses and palm and banyan trees. They had already taken to its soft, faded charm. The air smelt of the Gulf Stream, and made them think of Nantucket and the early whalers. Privately, Hemingway said later, he had already resolved to get her away from the 'young punk' and believed that, given three days, he could do it.

The Gellhorns were introduced to Pauline and shown the Hemingway house on Whitehead Street, and when Edna and Alfred set off back to St Louis a week later, Martha decided to stay on for another fortnight, to work at her novel about the French and German pacifists in the winter sun. The story itself, she was certain, was good, but she had doubts about her 'technical ability' to make it work. Matthew Josephson, a drinking friend of Hemingway's, observed that to him Martha looked as if she had a 'touch of the bluestocking'.

With the excellent reviews for *The Trouble I've Seen*, hailed as the literary discovery of the year, Martha was a match for Hemingway, particularly as her wanderings in Europe had made her very conscious of the Spanish war. They talked about his books, about the Cuban revolution and about hurricanes, and he gave her his new manuscript to read. Its dialogue made her 'weak with envy and wonder', but she wanted to avoid parodying his style, however superior it was to all the others 'I have been trying on lately'. Hemingway told her that he never used anything in his writing that he didn't think was accurate and that she should stop worrying about her book so much and have the courage to abandon it if it was no good. Martha found him, as she wrote to Eleanor Roosevelt, an 'odd bird, very lovable and full of fire and a marvellous story teller', but she really had her eye on a young Swede, a 'bum' who was 'gay, swum beautifully, danced beautifully'. She saw Hemingway only as a 'glorious idol', adding, rather improbably, that she felt shy in his company and found him hard to talk to. Before the fortnight was up, Martha later admitted, 'I did my usual gesture: I paid my debt for ten days of companionship, amusement, laughter' and went to bed with the Swedish bum. Then she could bear the young man no longer and wanted to get away. Hemingway does not seem to have been on her mind.

Towards the middle of January, a family friend offered her a lift for the first leg of her journey back to St Louis. Hemingway, inventing urgent business in New York, caught up with her in Miami, where they ate steak and travelled on together as far as Jacksonville. When they parted, he kissed her on the forehead and said: 'Goodbye daughter.' Martha's thank-you letter to Pauline for her hospitality in Key West is effusive but it can hardly have been reassuring. Referring to Hemingway as Ernestino, and his books as 'pretty hot stuff' and the 'tops', she went on: 'What I am trying to tell you in my halting way is that you are a fine girl and it was good of you not to mind my becoming a fixture, like a kudu head, in your home.' Hemingway's style had not altogether been successfully resisted. Nor would Pauline have greatly enjoyed reading Martha's letter to Mrs Roosevelt. 'If there is a war then all the things most of us do won't matter any more. I have a feeling that one has to work all day and all night and live too, and swim and get the sun in one's hair and laugh and love as many people as one can find around and do all this terribly fast, because the time is getting shorter and shorter every day.' She and Hemingway had agreed, she told Mrs Roosevelt, that as a war in Europe came ever nearer, there 'seemed terribly little time to do anything'.

In New York Hemingway, busy with preparations for Spain, saw Maxwell Perkins, his editor at Scribners, and asked him to read one of Martha's short stories, 'Exile', about an awkward German refugee who comes to America because he dislikes the Nazis' attitude to Heine, but finds the sense of displacement too painful. When Charles Scribner wrote to tell her that he would like to take the story for *Scribner's Magazine*, but that it would have to be cut, Martha was both pleased and 'peevish'. 'I do not write so well that every word is essential,' she wrote to him, 'but I hate having to change things when they have already been done as carefully as I can do it.' A sense of clarity about her own work, and an absolute need to control every word, was beginning to mark her exchanges with editors. This time, she gave in. 'Books matter,' she observed, 'but magazines are for people on trains.'

All through January Martha sat in her room on the third floor of the Gellhorn house on McPherson Avenue and lived the hermit life of a 'yogi', protesting crossly about the ghastliness of St Louis and planning to finish her book as quickly as possible in order to go to Paris and get 'all the facts tidy once more'. She set herself a quota of ten pages a day, regardless of how she felt. One day, from New York, Hemingway phoned her every five minutes all through the day because 'he was a little lonely and very excited' about his forthcoming journey. Then he went back to Key West to an increasingly apprehensive Pauline, who proposed that she accompany him to Spain. He was evidently not keen. Martha and Hemingway were now exchanging letters and she wrote to say that she felt left behind, growing moss, while the world 'hums at a great distance . . . I hope we get on the same ark when the real deluge begins. It would be just my luck to survive with the members of the St Louis Wednesday Club.' Martha too now decided to go to Spain, telling friends that she had known where her sympathies lay from the moment she had heard the Nazis chanting slogans in Munich about the Spanish loyalists, calling them the 'Red swine dogs of Spain'. Spain was, she told friends, the 'Balkans of 1912' and she fully assumed that she would die there. But as the time for Hemingway's departure approached, she grew increasingly nervous. 'Please don't disappear. Are we or are we not members of the same union? Hemingstein, I am very very fond of you.'

Fretting over her novel, which refused to 'jell', she received an affectionate letter from Mrs Roosevelt, urging her not to keep rehashing her material all the time. 'You do get yourself into a state of jitters . . . Mr Hemingway is right. I think you lose the flow of thought by too much rewriting.' As it happened, Martha had had more than enough of the book, of St Louis and of being alone. After Allen Grover, to whom she had sent a draft, told her that it read more like a political tract than a novel, she abandoned the pacifists and went off to join a picket line with the striking women workers of the National Underwear Company. And at the end of February, feeling as if she were at last emerging from a long period in prison or Siberia, and in a 'great hurry to be . . . in any sort of trouble I can find anywhere', she set off for New York, Hemingway having begged her to get there before he left. 'I did', she wrote later. 'And I entered into Ernest's world which then seemed odd and glamorous and later came to seem the most deadly waste of time and the enemy of all private feelings.'

New York with Hemingway was not what she had expected. In Key West there had been time for long flirtatious meetings, time to talk seductively about writing and political commitments. In New York they were always in a crowd, everyone drinking, rushing in and out, answering the telephone, going to the Stork Club and Twenty-One. 'Oh it was very dashing – and vulgar.' She was frantic herself. She needed papers for Spain, and with some difficulty eventually persuaded her friend Kyle Crichton at *Collier's* magazine to give her not exactly a job but a letter identifying her as their special correspondent. *Collier's*, an early critic of prohibition, was a loyal supporter of Roosevelt and the New Deal, and its editor-in-chief Bill Chenery, a distinguished stiff-necked Virginian, and its editor, Charles Colebaugh, a short and stocky Scot, were both men who set great store by good writing. The success of the magazine, currently more than holding its own against the older, stodgier *Saturday Evening Post*, showed how keen the public was becoming for more liberal and wide-ranging magazines. Martha also needed money for her boat ticket to Europe. *Vogue* obligingly commissioned her to write an article on the 'Beauty Problems of the Middle-Aged Woman' – Martha was just twenty-seven – which involved acting as a guinea pig for a new experimental skin treatment, the skin peeled away chemically, leaving fresh layers underneath. (It ruined her skin, she told Diana Cooper many years later, but it got her to Spain.) Someday, she told a friend, 'I shall be a great writer and stick to misery which is my province and limit my reforming to the spirit and the hell with the flesh.'

There was nothing now to keep her. Before boarding her ship, she wrote to Mrs Barnes, a family friend in St Louis: 'Me, I am going to Spain with the boys. I don't know who the boys are, but I am going with them.'

* * *

When the Popular Front coalition, promising widespread reform, had assumed power in February 1936, Spain was a vast, backward country where people still believed in witchcraft, and where wealthy landowners, a corrupt and lazy bureaucracy and an immensely powerful Church ruled with the help of the civil guard, men who wore tricorn hats and tall, polished boots. There were few tarmac roads. Priests, who were often feared and hated, regarded universal literacy as dangerous and had been known to stop children from learning to read lest they be corrupted by modern progressive ideas. Spain was also a country exceptionally given to political passion, from the anti-Semitism of the extreme nationalists to the puritanism of the anarchists, who held that all measures were legitimate in the struggle to free Spain from fascism. There were dozens of political parties, whose initials varied from place to place, and whose positions shifted from month to month.

Less than half the country had actually voted for the new republic. The new Prime Minister, Manuel Azaña, was hampered by regional calls for autonomy by the Catalans and the Basques, by violent anti-clericalism, which had already led to several atrocities committed against priests, nuns and churches, and by a communist-led uprising of miners in the Asturias. By the summer of 1936 strikes, clashes and random violence had erupted into full-scale fighting, bringing the youngest European general since Napoleon, Francisco Franco, to the head of a nationalist force which was now fighting its way across Spain, committing atrocities as it went. Though the loyalist forces of the republic committed atrocities of their own, Léon Jouhaux, the French trade unionist, coined the memorable phrase of a struggle 'of the light against the night', and many people were soon repeating it. Spain became the place in which one talked in opposites: fascists against democrats, religion against atheism, the rich against the poor, bosses against workers. For loyalists and nationalists alike, the civil war was a crusade, and even as André Malraux, Martha's hero and author of the Prix Goncourt-winning *La Condition humaine*, was prophesying that fascism would spread 'its great black wings over Europe', not just Spaniards but people all over the world began to project their own hopes and fears on to a conflict that grew more divisive and more murderous day by day.

By the end of July 1936, the nationalists had taken Burgos, Segovia, Avila, Saragossa, Teruel, Pamplona, all of Navarre and much of Estremadura, their experienced troops facing untrained, disorganised men equipped with primitive weapons and led by ordinary soldiers in the ranks, most military officers having joined the rebels. On 14 August, the nationalists took Badajoz, on the frontier with Portugal, herded all the men they suspected of fighting against them into the bullring and opened fire with machine guns. Eighteen hundred bodies were counted; the blood, according to Jay Allen of the *Chicago Tribune*, flowed as deep as a man's palm. By the end of September they had taken Toledo and were pushing on towards Madrid.

Once it had become clear that, for all their military victories, they faced courageous and determined opponents, the nationalists had appealed to Hitler and Mussolini for weapons and equipment. Supplies poured in. The Germans sent their famous Condor Legion and airlifted Franco's Army of Africa to mainland Spain in Junkers – the first major airlift of troops in military history – while Mussolini, building on his recent triumphs in Abyssinia, sent soldiers, ostensibly 'volunteers', as well as aeroplanes, pilots and tanks. For their part, the European democracies stood by and did almost nothing. When the democratically elected legal republican government begged them for supplies, they drew up a non-intervention pact. One hundred and twenty-seven countries agreed to remain 'neutral', a pact neither fascist Italy nor Nazi Germany made any pretence of honouring. Stalin, having at first joined the pact, later announced that he would sell weapons to the republic, in return for substantial amounts of Spanish gold. (It was only well over half a century later, when the Russian State Military Archives were finally opened, that the extent to which Stalin short-changed and double-crossed the republic, effectively swindling it out of several hundred million dollars in arms' deals through the secret cooking of accounts, became clear. As did the manner in which the Soviets sent in secret police and military intelligence, setting up a network of secret prisons, in which they tortured and murdered those they considered hostile to communism.)

And as the fighting spread, so foreign volunteers – whether refugees from Hitler or Mussolini, or idealists, or democrats, or left-wing sympathisers or simply those who, like Martha and Hemingway, saw in Spain a prologue to another world war – arrived in Spain to stand beside the republicans. By early November, when a concerted attack on Madrid by rebel troops began, and the government fled to Valencia, the Moscow-based Comintern helped organise these foreigners – many of whom had never held a gun before – into the International Brigades.

By the end of March 1937, when Martha prepared to leave Paris for the Spanish border, republican morale was perhaps at its highest in the entire war. Four Italian divisions supporting Franco had taken part in a third attempt to encircle Madrid, and been overwhelmingly routed at the battle of Guadalajara, north-east of the city, in part due to the tenacity of a battalion of Italian anti-fascists, the Garibaldi, who had outmanoeuvred and outfought Mussolini's fabled Black Flame division. For a moment, it looked as if republican fortunes could still turn. Madrid, for the time being at least, was safe.

The Poles and the French, the Germans and the Swedes, the Americans and the Greeks – fifty nationalities in all, some 40,000 men, the youngest seventeen, the eldest sixty, and a few women, among them Simone Weil – came to fight in the International Brigades on the republican side because the Spanish war brought to the surface all the complex political philosophies and humanitarian dreams of a generation sick of slaughter and conscious of the need for a fairer world. In their wake, throughout 1936 and 1937, came writers, poets, journalists and a few artists, drawn, like the volunteer soldiers, by a belief in civil rights and democratic government and universal literacy. They came because, like Martha, they had witnessed for themselves what the Nazis were capable of and were appalled, because they sensed that this was probably the last chance to halt the slide towards a full European war, and because Spain represented something in human values that seemed lacking in their own world. 'Our spirit,' wrote Louis MacNeice in *Autumn Journal*, 'Would find its frontier on the Spanish front / Its body in a rag-tag army.' To go to Spain was to be in at the birth of a new and better social order. The burning of books by the Nazis in 1933, and the exodus of writers from Germany and Italy, only confirmed to them that art could not flourish in a reactionary atmosphere, a feeling expressed by many of the writers canvassed in 1937 by Nancy Cunard for a symposium on the Spanish civil war in *The Left Review*. As Hemingway would soon tell the Congress of Writers in New York: 'There is only one form of government that cannot produce good writing, and that system is fascism.'

Very few of those questioned by *The Left Review*, and very few of those who actually went to Spain, supported the rebels, though George Santayana, Ezra Pound and Paul Claudel were all writers who hoped that if the republicans were defeated this would mean the destruction of the menace of communism; and many Catholic intellectuals, though repelled by Franco's desire to rid Spain of 'heretics', agonised over the killing of priests and the burning and desecration of churches. Most of the 1930s intellectuals, particularly after Spain's great poet, García Lorca, was executed by the nationalists, shared Léon Jouhaux's image of a struggle between light and dark, and agreed with Cecil Day-Lewis that Spain was about freedom made 'In the image of simple men who have no taste for carnage / But sooner kill and are killed than see the image betrayed'. Fascism was unreason, the denial of light.

For many, it was exhilarating to have found a cause, a direction in a decade of chaos and uncertainty, and they never forgot it. 'I know, as surely as I know anything in this world,' Herbert Matthews, the American reporter, would write after the war was over, 'that nothing so wonderful will ever happen to me again as those two and a half years I spent in Spain . . . It gave meaning to life.' Bertrand de Jouvenel, in an elegiac letter to Martha shortly after his own visit to the war, drawn like Drieu to notions of unity through thought and action, wrote: 'I've been happy. The hunger, the thirst, the fatigue, the fear, the horror, all of it was one grand tragedy and I felt alive and I loved all the actors, those who killed and those who were killed . . . the time for civil wars has come. For wars where at least you know whom you are killing. Rabbit, you will think I have gone off my head . . . But ah if you'd marched with the Legion, shooting, burning, looting and raping. Darling you would have thought it fine . . . that intensity of feeling one develops in the war I experienced sometimes with you, *quand je t'aimais à fond de train*.' And if much of the vast literature to emerge from the Spanish civil war was indeed sensational in language, sentimental and too polemical, novels like Malraux's *L'Espoir*, or the personal narratives of Koestler, Bernanos and Orwell, written later with full knowledge of the treachery, betrayals and atrocities, did reflect the real complexity of the issues.

But all that came later. For the moment it was enough to be there, to witness, to write. 'We knew, we just *knew* that Spain was the place to stop Fascism,' Martha told Phillip Knightley many years later. 'It was one of those moments in history when there was no doubt.' One interesting question for Martha, Hemingway, Matthews and others, was how far 'all that objectivity shit' – a phrase she surely coined in that war – would actually make it impossible for writers who had been trained to see and record the truth to ignore the atrocities carried out not only by the Nationalists, but the Republicans and their supporters as well.

* * *

Paris, by the spring of 1937, had become the jumping-off point for the Spanish war, and it was here, in the cafes on the left bank where the émigrés from Nazi Germany and Mussolini gathered, that Martha went to look for other writers or reporters with whom she could travel to Madrid. She waited for a few days, held up by the delays of the French in issuing her with papers to cross the frontier – since the drafting of the Non-Intervention Pact it had become harder to get into Spain – then bought a map, decided on a route, caught the first train going south, then changed to a second one bound for the border at Puigcerda, and set out on her own.

Wearing grey flannel trousers and a windcheater, and carrying a knapsack and a duffel bag full of tinned food, she crossed the border on foot at Andorra. She had $50, and spoke no Spanish. It was very cold. The train to Barcelona had no heating. At six in the morning, she saw from the windows the first trees covered in white and pink blossom. 'At seven', she wrote in her diary, 'the snow was falling like petals. By eight the trees were of glass and the fields were white and the snow blew flat over the land.' The train was full of young recruits on their way to join the Republican forces. On 24 March Martha was in Barcelona, which was crowded 'like an oil boom town' with soldiers and militia in every kind of uniform, rifles slung over their shoulders. The walls of the buildings along the Ramblas were covered with political posters, and the hotels, intensely cold because Barcelona had run out of coal, were full of young Americans and Englishmen on their way to the war, 'looking like hell, and very happy and intense and busy and friendly'. The Ministry of Foreign Propaganda found her a room and she slept right through a bombardment; next morning she went to look at a factory, where women were sewing for the troops, and a prison. There was sugar to be found in the hotels, she noted, but no butter.

After two days she was eager to press on. It was all rather too cosy. She found a truck carrying munitions leaving for Valencia, and there she encountered Sidney Franklin, a sandy-haired young American bullfighter who had become a protégé of Hemingway's while he was in Spain before the war writing *The Sun Also Rises*, and who now offered her a lift in his car. Piling up the roof and the back seat of a car with six Spanish hams, 10 kilos of coffee, 4 kilos of butter, 100 kilos of tinned marmalade and a 100-kilo basket of oranges, grapefruit and lemons, they set off for Madrid. 'When you are in Spain,' Martha wrote, 'you always have a feeling of coming home, but home is a place you hoped would exist and you were never sure.' As they drew near, they could hear artillery sounding like blasting in the clear mountain air; they climbed out of the car and stood in the sunshine, listening.

The boys, when Martha and Franklin had negotiated their way past roadblocks and sentry posts, were at dinner in a former hotel storage basement on the Gran Vía, where the journalists, the '*extranjeros de la prensa*' ate on long wooden planks, together with carefully vetted police agents, army officers and prostitutes, whom Hemingway referred to as 'whores de combat'. The long room was noisy with people talking about the day's shelling and blue with cigarette smoke. If Martha was not annoyed at being greeted by Hemingway, who was surrounded by admiring young men, with the words 'I knew you'd get here, daughter, because I fixed it so you could', it was because she took this to be 'one of the foibles of genius', this 'large' way of ignoring the truth and shaping it to a 'self-congratulatory end', and she accepted it with 'interior shining tolerance'. He had told Joris Ivens that his beautiful new girl-friend had legs which began at her shoulders.

She was soon installed in the Hotel Florida on the Plaza de Callao, the gathering place for visiting foreigners, where Hemingway kept two rooms, 108 and 109, on the corner of the third floor at the back, under jutting balconies, which he maintained were out of the line of vision of the fascist artillery positions on the hills outside the city. (The rooms at the front, looking out over the tiled roofs and buff-coloured towers and cupolas of seventeenth-century Castile, were considered more hazardous, and cost less.) Here, at various times of the day, he could be heard pecking at his typewriter. Franklin, an ebullient man, described not altogether fondly as 'buoyantly mindless', who acted as Hemingway's major-domo, slept in one of them with the provisions, while a Swedish girl, who spoke seven languages and wore men's clothes, came and went.

On the first night, Hemingway locked Martha into her room. There was a bombing raid and she hammered on the door to be let out. When Hemingway finally came, he explained that he had locked her in for her own good, because the hotel was full of pimps and drunks and she might be taken for a whore. Martha was furious, writing later: 'I should have known at that moment what doom was.'

Two weeks later they went to bed together, apparently for the first time. She was not in love with him, and did not find him physically attractive, but she admired him – much, she wrote, as she would have admired a surgeon in an operating theatre – and she was grateful to him for teaching her about war. And, as 'just about the only blonde in the country', it was much better to belong to someone.

Regular hotel guests, who held on to their rooms permanently, making expeditions to the various front lines but keeping Madrid as their base, included John Dos Passos who, to Hemingway's considerable irritation, had just made the cover of *Time* magazine, Joris Ivens, working on his documentary film, and Sefton Delmer, in whose room people collected late at night to drink whisky and beer, listen to Beethoven's Fifth Symphony and to taste the fine wines ransacked from King Alfonso's cellars. Delmer, who worked for the *Daily Express*, was a big man with a florid complexion: Hemingway referred to him as a 'ruddy English bishop'. Martha was occasionally irritated by Delmer, complaining about his laugh and the way he held his head on one side.

Herbert Matthews, a long-limbed, studious American working for the *New York Times*, who would become one of the most admired reporters of the war, was about to move into a penthouse flat on the edge of the Retiro park, with a terrace from where, at night, you could watch the flashes of artillery on the horizon and listen to the trace of the shells as they spun into the city. Hemingway later used Matthews partly as his model for Robert Jordan in *A Farewell to Arms*, the American explosives expert who blows the bridge behind nationalist lines. (The other part was Major Robert Merriman, of the 15th International Brigade, a professor of economics from California.) Matthews, who had a long, thin nose and thinning hair, and wore espadrilles and peasant trousers, suffered from terrible migraines and in the evenings Martha would massage his neck to ease the pain.

There were writers too among the foreigners who joined the republican forces as soldiers or ambulance drivers, men like W.H. Auden, J.B. Priestley and Sean O'Casey, and many of these dropped in on the Florida when on leave, either to have baths – it was said to be the only place in Madrid with hot water – or to eat some of Hemingway's supplies, the rich smell of ham and eggs frying on Franklin's small stove drawing them up to the third floor. By early 1937 food in Madrid was very scarce – the meals in the Gran Vía restaurant were widely agreed to be revolting, with salami and rice for lunch, and salami and beans for dinner, and the occasional sausage stuffed with sawdust or mule steak. Within days of arriving Martha was remarking how hungry she felt. In the shops only oranges and shoelaces were on sale; bread, meat and cigarettes were rationed and there was no coffee, soap or milk to be had anywhere but on the black market. The cafes had been taken over by waiters' collectives. Spring had started, and the broad avenues and squares were full of trees coming into leaf.

Among the visiting men from the International Brigades particularly liked by Hemingway and soon well known to Martha were Gustav Regler, the rugged and somewhat battered young German novelist with a deeply-lined forehead and the jaw of a prizefighter, who had been in Moscow during the first purge trials the previous year, and who was a political commissar; and General Lukàcs, the *nom de guerre* of a stocky forty-one-year-old Hungarian short-story writer called Mata Zalka Kemeny with pale blue eyes and a bristly yellow moustache, who was Hemingway's favourite. Professor J.B.S. Haldane, the British scientist, appeared one day, wearing a very tight pair of breeches and a tin helmet with a broken strap left over from the First World War, and was obviously, Martha noted without false pride, taken by her. Another day, H.L. Brailsford, the political writer, came by looking 'like a little grey chipmunk'. There were soon complaints that it was all getting more and more like Bloomsbury, with the correspondents clucking over the rubble, studying each other 'like crows'. Most of the reporters worked for morning papers, and filed their stories at around nine in the evening, writing them after listening to the daily five o'clock briefing by the Junta de Defensa de Madrid, and so they rose and breakfasted late. 'Of all the places to be in the world,' wrote Herbert Matthews, 'Madrid is the most satisfactory.'

The city was in the fifth month of constant bombardment. Having failed to take it in March – it would stay in loyalist hands until the end – Franco had decided to clean up the northern provinces first. But Madrid, situated on a plateau with the Guadarrama Mountains to the north, was still surrounded on three sides by the rebels, who shelled at conveniently regular hours – after breakfast, just before and just after lunch – while people went on queuing for the little food to be had, or talking in the streets, or going to the cinema, where *The Gay Divorcee*, with Fred Astaire, enjoyed a long run. Martha, observing her first city at war, was full of admiration for the calm and resignation of Madrid's inhabitants.

The front line had halted two miles from the main shopping district in the university quarter, and the journalists sometimes caught a tram part of the way, walking the last few hundred yards along a honeycomb of trenches that filled with mud and water during the rains, and baked hard in the summer months. Many of the foreigners used Baedekers to find their way around. In some places, the trenches were so close that the men on both sides taunted each other by megaphone after dark; the fascists had the better gramophone and played a song called 'Kitten On The Keys' again and again. The anarchists held the golf course. Some of the International Brigades were stationed in the university quarter itself, and this was now filled with émigrés, political refugees who had made their way to Madrid from Vienna or Berlin or Milan, Jews, members of the German Communist Party, many of them survivors of Dachau, the concentration camp opened by Hitler in 1933. Others were camped near the park. '*Madrid sera la tumba del fascismo*' read the posters on the walls. 'Had a fine heavy late breakfast with H,' Martha wrote soon after she arrived, 'and then set out for the park. Forgot the war and the vague strange restlessness which is mixed up boredom and a kind of personal footlingness, not knowing who I am, or what I love, or why I live.' There was an acid smell of explosive permanently in the air, and Hemingway tried to think up words to capture the sound of gunfire, the 'rong, cararong, rong, rong' of the machine guns, and the 'tacrong, carong, carong' of rifles.

Censorship was strict – no reference to Russian armaments – and the censor's office was run by a nervous and cadaverous man called Arturo Barea, who later wrote memorably about the war, and a plump Austrian woman called Isa Kulscar, who sang Schubert songs and dealt fairly with the correspondents. Barea observed that Hemingway, for all his bonhomie with fellow journalists, seemed 'remote and somewhat sad', with the anxious look of a worried boy. The two censors themselves frequently learnt about the day's events from the dispatches brought in for checking by the journalists in the evening. The only two lines to Paris and London, from where the messages would travel on to their destinations, were stationed in the Telefonica, a white, thirteen-storey steel and concrete building not far from the Gran Vía, said to be the tallest building in Europe. Though frequently hit, the Telefonica continued to stand, surrounded by the skeletons of once fine buildings, and crumbling houses, in which several floors had been sliced off but where the occupants hung on, watering the plants that still grew on the balconies and feeding their canaries. In the grander apartments whose rich owners had fled many months before, lived refugees from the worst hit suburbs, several families to a room.

* * *

As America's best-known writer of war fiction, correspondent for a syndicate of important newspapers and producer of a forthcoming documentary about the war, Hemingway was regarded – and regarded himself – as the foremost foreign journalist in Spain. While others had trouble finding transport to take them to the front, Hemingway had a car, and sometimes even two, at his disposal, and plenty of petrol, and the military in the field were flattered and delighted by his visits. Franklin found him extra food and did his typing. Petra, the Spanish maid at the Florida, cooked the game he shot in the hills when there was a lull in the fighting: his bag one day consisted of a partridge, four rabbits and an owl he mistook for a woodcock. All this provoked a certain amount of envy. Noël Monks of the *Daily Express* complained that Hemingway was 'uncouth and of a bullying temperament', and Josephine Herbst, who had staggered into the Hotel Florida under a heavy suitcase and a large typewriter a few days after Martha, objected that he was not exactly a 'benign influence in a wartime hotel'. There was, she wrote later, 'a kind of splurging magnificence about Hemingway . . . a crackling generosity whose underside was a kind of miserliness'. After two pots of jam disappeared from his cupboard one day he made a major scene. Some of this asperity spilled over on to Martha, whom Herbst described with unconcealed bitchiness as sailing 'in and out in beautiful Saks Fifth Avenue pants, with a green scarf wound round her head'. Franklin, who was very fond of Pauline Hemingway, was not much taken with Martha either, but Gustav Regler found her 'witty and humane'.

It was not long before it was perfectly clear to everyone at the Florida that Martha and Hemingway were having an affair. One night, not long after her arrival, the fascist shells scored a direct hit on the hotel. It sent dozens of prostitutes scuttling out from various correspondents' rooms on the landing that overlooked the well of the hotel, where Antoine de Saint-Exupéry, magnificent in a vibrant blue satin dressing gown, solemnly handed each of them a grapefruit from his private store; and it brought Martha and Hemingway out together from his room. Martha noted in her diary that the scurrying prostitutes had made her think of beetles, emerging in the dark, 'crying in high voices like birds'. Dos Passos was wearing a tartan dressing gown, and Martha described herself as 'in pyjamas, uncombed, with a coat on'; they made coffee and ate Saint-Exupéry's grapefruit and some chocolate and went back to bed. 'Somehow the vilest of all is the exhausted tension inside one, the coldness, the waiting, the fear,' she noted. 'Better to sleep.'

By now, Martha was calling Hemingway Scrooby, from 'screwball', a private joke she shared with Matthews, and Delmer observed that she treated him with robust good humour rather than the servility shown him by many of the others. He called her 'daughter', or 'Mooky'. When not out filming scenes for their documentary with Ivens, who liked to get shots of bursting shells from dangerously near, he would take Martha to the various battle fronts, usually with Matthews and Delmer, their car packed with cotton pillows on the petrol tank to make the back more comfortable and flying two flags, the Union Jack and the Stars and Stripes. Hemingway wore a canvas hunter's cap, old buckskin boots and thin gold-rimmed spectacles. 'Ernest is quite childish in many respects,' Milton Wolff, the man who would become the Abraham Lincoln Brigade's last commander, wrote to a friend. 'He wants very much to be a martyr. Matthews is in love with Martha . . . and is peeved by her seeming coldness, and she lays it on pretty thick.' Wolff would soon become a good friend of Martha's and remain so until her death.

One fine spring day they drove through villages which had been destroyed by shelling, stared at by children covered in sores and clearly hungry, and then parked and watched from the hills of Guadalajara as rebel soldiers, like hurrying ants, climbed a bluff across the valley. On another, they went to visit four separate front lines, riding on horses for part of the way, sleeping in the soldiers' encampments. Hemingway would stop to show the young volunteers how to hold their rifles and how to fire them, lying down alongside them in the mud. Gustav Regler, the German commissar, thought that he was having a good time. 'Hemingway had the calming effect of a buffalo straying shaggily over the tundra,' he wrote later, 'knowing its water holes and its pastures. For him we had the scent of death, like the bull-fighters, and because of this he was invigorated in our company.' Knowing that Hemingway, after witnessing the First World War defeat of the Italians at Caporetto, had been convinced that all Italian soldiers ran away, Regler made a point of introducing him to some of Mussolini's refugees, brave men who had held the fascists off during the March battle for Madrid. Wherever they went, Hemingway would stop to explain to Martha the tactics of war and how to take cover; he told people that she was the bravest woman he had ever met, but that she had not yet undergone a true baptism of fire. Later, Franklin remarked sourly – and inaccurately – that no foreign woman reporter went to the Spanish front after Martha, because her visits had proved so distracting.

For the first few weeks Martha made no attempt to write

for publication. She visited a hospital set up in the former Palace Hotel, now stripped of its brocade hangings and gilt furniture, where boyish-looking soldiers lay on primitive army cots under cut-glass chandeliers in wards that had once been salons and banqueting halls. The nurses were untrained peroxide blondes with long, brightly-coloured nails, Madrid's regular nurses having all been nuns and now serving on Franco's side. The smell, she wrote later, was of cabbage and ether; there was no morphine and the marble steps had blood on them. 'People in pain,' she wrote in her diary, 'give me a strange feeling of nausea, it is the noise they make I suppose . . . Note the thinness that goes with a steady pain. The real undeniable eating away of the human body.'

She went shopping with Virginia Cowles, like herself an American, who dressed in black and wore heavy gold jewellery and shoes with extremely high heels. Cowles had come to cover the Spanish war for the Hearst newspapers and was already famous for an interview she had done with Mussolini a week after Italy's invasion of Abyssinia. Since this had been followed up by a talk with Marshal Balbo, the new Italian governor in Libya, Cowles had acquired a reputation for journalistic prescience. Like Martha, she was tall, attractive, energetic and drawn to war. Her intention in Spain, she said, was to report both sides of the war, which, almost uniquely, she did. 'With Ginny, went and priced silver foxes and got desperately greedy wanting them . . . At three a shell ricocheted from the Telefonica and killed five women in front of the Gran Vía . . . Home, after a bitter seance with the shoe man. How those shoes have turned out, like gunboats for a clubfooted pregnant woman . . . Got a little tight with Hem and Dos and grew pontifical about modern Spanish art, and dinner was foul with all the spinach having run out because the Duchess of Atholl's party got served first.' The Duchess, known to the English press as the 'Red Duchess' for her socialist sympathies, had come to Madrid with a delegation of British women politicians. The night of their visit, shells killed a number of people at the door of the restaurant.

Martha went to the hairdresser with Lolita, a 'real born

whore, with a basic respect for *ces messieurs*', and found that all the women were having perms, because the lotion used for perms was on the point of running out.

And she listened and watched and asked questions, going back to the Florida at the end of each day to write up her notes, fearful always that 'I would forget the exact sound, smell, words, gestures which were special to this moment and this place'. Unlike Virginia Cowles, who preferred discussion and analysis and the rounded article, reflecting all sides of an argument, Martha wished only to record, to bear witness, and so perhaps to influence people with the strength of her descriptions. Already, she was noting that particular element in war reporting, the mixture between brief moments of intense drama and the long patches when nothing happened. She saw developing in herself a capacity for boredom, stronger than she had known before, and a clearer instinct for what brought it on. Most press officers and all but a very few generals were 'boring and liars and fakes'.

On 2 April, she noted: 'At lunch there was no more room at the table, due to influx of shits now that all is quiet. Herbst and two Seldes and a nice handsome dumb named Errol Flynn who looks like white fire on the screen, but is only very very average off.' And on the 3rd: 'I find everything except the actively involved people very bad, and I have reached the state where human society is again trying for me. I am not a very good person.' Four days later, she continued: 'Odd how really inwardly, almost all the time, unless I am seeing new things, looking at beautiful country or above all writing, I am bored. I have never yet really found the people who do not tire me in the end, and I know inside myself that I can always go away and if I never see them again it will not matter . . . I get homesick for places, for the way mountains look and for the color of the sky over Paris, and for the air in New York, but I do not think I would get on a train and go anywhere to see anyone, except Edna.' 'I do nothing here,' she wrote again, 'eat, sleep, grow fat, spend money, loaf and am like any woman at Cannes in season.'

But for much of the time Martha, like Hemingway, was

cheerful. There were drinks with friends on leave from the International Brigades, surprise visits to Madrid by amusing writers and journalists, and wonderful weather, always important to her and a permanent feature of her notes. The random events that filled their evenings are memorably evoked in her diaries. On 14 April, having bought Pope's translation of Abelard's letters to Eloise in a shop near the hotel, and taken a bunch of camelias to a wounded young man in hospital – letting him imagine she was a little in love with him – she changed her clothes at the Florida and went back to the hospital, to dine with the doctors, nurses, chauffeurs and orderlies, then went on to a party at military headquarters, where an officer asked her whether she would become a spy for them. There was singing, 'so beautiful, the men's voices and the feeling in it', and a Russian called Petrov, who sent his translator to tell her that he was not 'indifferent' to her, did a little Russian dance 'like a small bull. Very belle of the ball, having missed all this at Princeton and Yale, finally in Fuencarral, I got it. Funny as hell.' The password, when they were stopped by a sentry on the way home, was '*El Fascismo se alimenta con sangre*'.

But then the day came when Hemingway and Matthews suggested that she write an article for *Collier's*, since that was what had brought her to Spain in the first place. Martha protested that she knew nothing about war or military matters, only about ordinary people doing ordinary things. Why would that interest anyone? It was just daily life. 'Not everyone's daily life', Hemingway is said to have replied. So she wrote a piece about what she saw about her in the streets of Madrid, about the courage of the civilians who went on living their ordinary lives in the midst of such fear, and about how bleakly and abruptly these lives were being destroyed. Her article, which has all the spare simplicity of her best reporting, contains a marvellous passage. Shells have been falling on a square, roaring as they hit the granite cobblestones.

'Then for a moment it stops. An old woman, with a shawl over her shoulders, holding a terrified thin little boy by the hand, runs out into the square. You know what she is thinking: she is thinking she must get the child home, you are always safer in your own place, with the things you know. Somehow you do not believe you can get killed when you are sitting in your own parlor, you never think that. She is in the middle of the square when the next one comes.

'A small piece of twisted steel, hot and very sharp, sprays off from the shell; it takes the little boy in the throat. The old woman stands there, holding the hand of the dead child, looking at him stupidly, not saying anything, and men run out toward her to carry the child. At their left, at the side of the square, is a huge brilliant sign which says: GET OUT OF MADRID.'

She sent the article to *Collier's*, who took it and published it under the title 'Only the shells whine'. Then she sent them a second, and they took that as well, and put her name on their masthead. *The New Yorker* agreed to take two other pieces, one on the zoo that she and Hemingway had visited the day they walked in the park, the other a description of going with a doctor to take blood for transfusions to the front. In everything she wrote, she explored what she felt about this war in carefully observed details, and about war in general; and in these early days of their relationship, when Hemingway's presence made her feel safer, she seemed to take pleasure in playing with his style and adapting it to her own purposes. 'You knew that pain was as solid as rock, for instance,' she wrote in 'Madrid to Morata', which appeared in *The New Yorker* that summer, 'that it had weight and shape. You knew, too, that someday the newspapers would announce peace instead of war, but that the pain would have been there, like mountains, and that it could not be denied or disappear quickly, and that it would form all these men and through them Spain and whatever happens next.' Driving home that night from delivering the blood, they had caught up with a line of tanks, their shape 'ominous' in the dark. 'We cleared them carefully, and later, when I looked back, it was as if six boats, with only their harbor lights showing, were tied together, riding a gentle sea.'

Martha was no longer a 'war tourist'. She had joined the

boys, and at the age of twenty-eight, covering her first war, she was writing a good deal better than many of them, and in many ways better than Hemingway, the professional war reporter, whose stories from Spain were often contrived and self-centred. 'I like writing,' she observed in her diary. 'In the end it is the only thing which does not bore or dismay me, or fill me with doubt. It is the only thing I know absolutely and irrevocably to be good in itself, no matter what the result.'

* * *

Guernica, lying far behind the front lines in northern Spain, was a small town of great symbolic importance to the Basques, for it contained a sacred oak tree that was said to stand for the undying nature of Basque democracy. The Basques, over the years, had insisted on their right to autonomy and at the start of the war the loyalist government had granted them the status of an independent republic. General Mola, at the head of the nationalist forces, had called for complete Basque submission. The Basques had stood firm.

On the afternoon of Monday 26 April 1937, squadrons of German Junkers and Heinkels, flown by German pilots, bombed Guernica. It was market day. Those who survived the bombs by escaping into the surrounding fields were strafed from the air by machine guns; later came the incendiary bombs. No one has ever established how many people died or were seriously injured, but the figure for the dead is said to lie somewhere between one and two thousand, roughly a fifth of the town's inhabitants.

As it happened, a small group of journalists were in the area and, drawn by the flames, drove to see what had befallen Guernica. The next day, newspapers in Europe and North America carried the story. Though Mola and the nationalists denied responsibility, blaming the republicans for bombing their own people for propaganda purposes, Guernica, later painted by Picasso, became overnight a symbol of the brutality of fascism, the moment when indiscriminate bombing of civilians became an acceptable and terrifying tactic of war.

Italian planes had bombed civilians in Abyssinia, but not with such devastating precision. And not all nationalists were keen to refute what they had done. Later that year, Virginia Cowles was told by a nationalist officer: 'We bombed it and bombed it and bombed it, and bueno, why not?'

If doubt was cast about the perpetrators of Guernica's destruction, it was because newspaper editors in the Western democracies were often more concerned with appeasing German sensibilities than facing the truth of what was happening in Spain. Guernica thus became easy prey for sensationalist propaganda. Propaganda – invented battles, stories of reprisals, atrocity reports of every description – was used vigorously on both sides. In Paris, the talented Agitprop director Willie Munzenberg fabricated accounts of fascist torture and executions and fed Arthur Koestler and Claud Cockburn fictitious events to use alongside real ones. The fascists, meanwhile, published their own newspapers in Burgos, Salamanca and San Sebastian, and pushed out a steady flow of invective and lies night after night from radio stations in Germany, Portugal and Italy. Confronted by all this, newspapers either gave news from both sides – though it was relatively rare for a paper to have two correspondents, one with the republicans and another with the nationalists – or simply used their own special reporter in the field, the best of whom tended to be with the republicans and were based in Madrid. And these reporters, who for the most part felt exactly like Martha and believed that a victory for the legitimate republican government might just halt fascism and prevent a second world war, faced the daily dilemma of what and how much to write. They were not helped by their editors who were sometimes reluctant to believe or print articles too hostile to the nationalists, and Herbert Matthews in particular was vilified by the strong Catholic lobby in America, who called him a 'rabid Red partisan' and tried to get the *New York Times* to recall him. (Martha, outraged like his many admirers, wrote a ferocious letter to the paper, saying that Matthews was 'by far the most careful and competent man in the country, and when you want to know really what happened and why,

Matthews is the man to ask.') Nor were they helped by sensationalist reporters, desperate for horror stories, who were more than happy to repeat rumours as facts.

Martha almost became an unwitting pawn for Frederick Voigt, the correspondent for the *Manchester Guardian*. Voigt maintained that Madrid was littered with the bodies of people executed by the republicans. When pressed, he admitted that he had not actually seen any himself. The other reporters were scornful. However, he asked Martha when she left Madrid to take an article for him to Paris to post from there, saying that it would be quicker than relying on the Spanish mail. Hemingway advised her to show it first to Barea. Voigt had not, of course, passed it by the censors. When opened, the article was found to contain a fulsome account of the bodies of men and women killed as collaborators by the republicans littering the streets. Hemingway was so angry, both about the dishonesty and the risks to Martha, that he had to be restrained from punching Voigt. In point of fact, Voigt was alert to the undoubted republican and Russian atrocities which many of his colleagues chose to ignore. Yet the *Manchester Guardian*, like other English language newspapers, was remarkably unforthcoming on the subject of atrocities committed by either side, though it did report at length the bombing of Guernica and the new weapon of aerial warfare. One of the only references to republican reprisals during the late spring and early summer of 1937 was a brief statement that more people were being executed in this war than were dying either in the fighting or in the bombing, and that at least 10,000 had been shot in Madrid alone. Similar figures were quoted, just as baldly, about the rebels. Even Voigt, like his colleagues, concentrated on battles, advances and retreats, refugees and the effects of the Non-Intervention Pact, with occasional swipes at the unwarlike Italian fascists. The world was in any case becoming familiar with atrocities: the Italians in Abyssinia, Stalin's purges and show trials, the Nazis crushing all dissent in Germany. Appeals were issued from time to time by the Western democracies to 'humanise' the Spanish war, but this was largely with regard to the bombing of civilians from the air.

And so, day by day, the correspondents walked a thin and nervous line between truth, evasions, bias and propaganda, telling each other that though it was not all right if things were made up and presented as true, it was acceptable to describe what you wanted, provided it was true and provided your readers were aware of your position. As Matthews put it, good reporters should write with their hearts as well as their minds.

'All that objectivity shit' – Martha's much used shorthand phrase to describe her impatience with the idea that it was possible for an honourable journalist to remain neutral – was not quite as lucidly simple as she chose to maintain. Given that she and Hemingway longed for the republic to behave heroically and within the law, and longed for the democracies to break the Non-Intervention Pact and supply them with arms, how far consciously or unconsciously did they distort reality? For what neither she, nor Hemingway, nor Matthews, chose to do was to report the persecutions, torture and summary executions that were also being carried out by the republicans. This contradiction – choosing not to write what you knew to be true in order to promote a greater good – was something that Martha would avoid confronting all her life. That they knew what was going on is evident from Hemingway's play *The Fifth Column*, written later that year during lulls in the bombing and set in the Hotel Florida, in which a nationalist spy is caught and tortured, and from Robert Jordan, the hero of *For Whom the Bell Tolls*, who learns in excruciating detail about the atrocities committed by both sides. André Marty, the French communist and commander of the International Brigades at their headquarters on Albacete, who as a young man in 1919 had played a part in the mutiny of the French fleet in the Black Sea, and who later admitted to executing five hundred 'spies' in Spain, is mentioned by name and described in the closest detail. Hemingway hated Marty. He was, he wrote in his novel, an old, heavy, large man with watery eyes, in an oversized beret, his grey face with a look of decay 'as though it were modelled from the waste material you find under the claws of a very old lion'. André Marty,

Hemingway has a Spanish soldier say, was 'as crazy as a bedbug' and had killed more people than the bubonic plague (an opinion borne out by the documents later found in the Russian Military Archives, which show Marty to have been a rigid Stalinist, suspicious of everyone and quick to shoot those he suspected of treachery). And Martha herself, making no mention of any of this in the pieces she was now at work on, wrote blithely in her diary about a sinister figure called Pepe Quintanilla as the 'Executioner', though she did tell Eleanor Roosevelt that some of the communists were 'sinister folk and very very canny'.

It was not until the autumn of 1938 – by which time he had left the Spanish war for good – that Hemingway admitted that it had been a 'carnival of treachery on both sides', and not until the late 1990s that the full extent of the Soviet manipulation of the Spanish war was properly documented, showing how the officers in the Brigades were also officers of the Red Army, intent on turning the international troops into a Soviet army within Spain. How far Martha and Hemingway realised this in the late 1930s is not clear.

At the time, however, Hemingway's blinkered approach could turn unpleasant. John Dos Passos had an old friend called Jose Robles Pazos, who had translated his books into Spanish. Robles, a colonel with the republicans, had been arrested by counter-espionage in December 1936, and Hemingway agreed to try to find out what had become of him. He told Dos Passos that he had been assured that Robles would receive a fair trial. In fact, Robles had already been executed and Hemingway neither chose to question why nor to break the news gently to Dos Passos, doing so, on the contrary, very publicly and in such a way as to suggest that Robles had got what he deserved. Later, he dismissed Dos Passos, who was angry and upset, as having a 'typical American liberal attitude'. Dos Passos, understandably, never forgave him. The two writers went on attacking each other, for years to come, through their books.

When, earlier in the war, General Mola had coined the phrase 'la quinta columna', or fifth column, he had been boasting about a secret, unseen group of men within Madrid who were said to be waiting for the arrival of his four fascist columns in order to rise up and assist them. After Mola's notable failure to capture the city, there was much speculation among the correspondents about who these spies might be and whether they really existed. Much of this spy hunting centred around Gaylord's Hotel, where the Russians who acted as advisers and technical experts to the loyalists were based. Gaylord's was not as cosy or as ramshackle as the Hotel Florida, but the food was better and there was vodka. For breakfast, favoured visitors were served eggs, ham and chopped liver, luxuries unobtainable anywhere else in the city. It was at Gaylord's, where Hemingway and Martha were invited to a party, that she met Mikhail Koltzov, officially correspondent for *Pravda* and *Izvestia*, but in fact, as she wrote later, 'Stalin's man, Stalin's eyes and ears on the spot'. In 1994, when her sight was failing, she wrote what she referred to as the last article she would ever actually see to write. It was called 'Memory', and it was about the party at Gaylord's with Koltzov.

Koltzov, she wrote, was a 'small, thin man, with thick, well-cut, grey hair', wearing a good dark suit, and with the 'quiet manners of complete confidence'. He wore horn-rimmed glasses and his hair was crinkly. Koltzov, later called Karkov in *For Whom the Bell Tolls*, was brilliant and witty, and quick to mock dogma and rhetoric. While tucking into caviar on bits of 'real' bread normally unheard of in Madrid in 1937, she began talking to Juan Modesto, the republican general. She found him 'intensely attractive'. She went on: 'Hemingway suddenly appeared beside us wearing an ugly, shark smile, the first time I had seen it.' He challenged Modesto to Russian roulette, and Modesto accepted, but before the two men reached the door Koltzov intervened and Hemingway and Martha were bustled into their coats and out into the street, Martha now furious at being ousted from the warm room and the delicious food, and enraged at being treated as a possession to be bartered. They were not invited again. What news was to be gleaned at Gaylord's now had to be learnt from Regler. She did meet Koltzov's mistress again, however, an 'ominous' German with long, almond-shaped eyes she described as cold and blue at the time, but later remembered as green. Both she and Hemingway liked Koltzov, whom Hemingway later wrote about as a man who believed in the 'humanising possibility of benevolent intervention'.

There had always been cracks in the republican alliance, and by the late spring of 1937 clashes between communists and anarchists reached a peak in Barcelona, the communists conducting a heresy witch-hunt, later described by Orwell in *Homage to Catalonia*. (Published only with some difficulty – Victor Gollancz, the left-wing publisher, having turned it down – it had sold only six hundred copies by Orwell's death in 1950.) After intense fighting in the streets, POUM, the Marxist Workers' Party, was outlawed and its leader, Andrés Nin, was caught, tortured and killed, along with his more important associates. Then came attacks on anarchists and Catalan separatists, the way they were treated providing a frightening vision of Stalinist terror tactics. None of this featured in Martha's diaries, letters or articles. Nor did the presence of Stalin's police, sent to Spain to take control of the Spanish economy and government, and to get rid of Spaniards and any other foreigners who opposed their plans. Exactly how much Martha and Hemingway actually knew about the torture and assassinations is impossible to say. Certainly they did not want to know.

By now, in any case, Martha and Hemingway had left for Paris, en route to New York, where both had plans to raise support for the republic. *The Spanish Earth* sequences had all been shot and the film needed to be edited and dubbed. And Pauline, who had used Hemingway's absence to build an enticing saltwater pool at their house in Key West, was expecting his return, evidently anxiously aware that Martha had been with him in Madrid. From Paris, on 10 May, Martha sent an excited note to John Gunther. 'There are practically no words to describe Madrid, it was heaven, far and away the best thing I have ever seen or lived through . . . I want to do a book on Spain fast and I want to go back.' With her new role as war correspondent, the boredom had evaporated; her pacifist novel was to be used as 'fire wood to keep me warm in winter'. To Allen Grover, who now acted as a critical editor of her writing, she cabled: 'Returned today. Spain superb. Plans vague.' Grover sent it on to Edna, adding laconically: 'Just what she means by Spain being superb, I would not want to guess . . . She was probably there during the heavy shelling of Madrid last week.'

Paris, when they reached it at the beginning of May, was in a frenzy of preparation for the opening of the International Exposition along the banks of the Seine. On one side of the Pont d'Iéna stood the German pavilion with its seven-metre high statues of naked Teutons and an immense bronze eagle perched 150 feet up in the air. Dr Hjalmar Schacht, the German Minister of Foreign Affairs, who arrived to open the pavilion, said that it would prove to the world that the Germans loved work. On the other side the Soviets had placed two giant workers made of stainless steel, holding a hammer and sickle. The British pavilion, by contrast, was embarrassingly puny, with a cardboard cutout of Neville Chamberlain fishing, and a buttery serving roast joints flown in daily from London. The Spanish had sent Picasso's black, grey and white painting of Guernica, seven and a half metres long, three and a half wide. The food shops were full of cream and butter and steak, and the cars looked sleek and expensive. Schiaparelli had toppled Coco Chanel to become queen of Paris fashion and Parisian ladies were wearing Fauvist orange, yellow and shocking pink. On their heads perched vegetables, and they carried handbags shaped like telephones. One celebrated evening dress was made out of white satin, with a large pink lobster. It was all a long way from Madrid.

CHAPTER SIX

Only Kind People Should Be Kind

'The Loyalists will win in Spain simply because they have an apparently unlimited supply of guts,' Martha told reporters who met the ship bringing her back to New York in May 1937. Her account of the war was determinedly upbeat, with warm and admiring stories of the courage of Madrid's women in the midst of shelling and of the fairness of republican justice. 'In one prison,' she said, 'I saw the Fascist prisoners taking sun baths, playing games and listening to a phonograph.' Both she and Hemingway still appeared to believe that the republicans could win the war. While he now left for Key West and Bimini to see Pauline and the boys and to fish, Martha wrote to Eleanor Roosevelt to try to persuade her to intervene on behalf of five hundred Basque children, many of them orphaned by the heavy fascist bombing of Bilbao, and have them brought to homes in America. Ever sensible, Mrs Roosevelt, whose outspoken sympathy for the republicans was attracting increasing opprobrium in the isolationist mood of the country, suggested that the children would do much better in their own country, with funds raised in the States. Martha, she added, should not so readily allow her emotions to warp her judgement. 'Emotional women are bad news,' Martha replied contritely, agreeing that she had not thought the question through. 'It is hard nowadays not to get emotionally terribly involved in this whole business.' Later, she admitted that right up to the Spanish civil war she still had the impression, however 'erroneous, that we could do something, the sense of urgency, you had to make people see. We had no self-consciousness. We were young nobodies but that didn't stop us from seeing all the top people and yelling at them.' Fearless about speaking her mind, seldom intimidated by anyone, she remained convinced that if you minded about something enough, you could convince others of its rightness.

Hemingway came back to New York from Florida in time to attend the Second Congress of American Writers, held in Carnegie Hall early in June. There was an immense gathering of people, 3,500 crammed into the auditorium and a thousand more turned away. Since the first congress to discuss ways in which writers could confront the apparent march towards war, held in the spring of 1935, Abyssinia, China and Spain had all seen fighting. Telegrams from Thomas Mann, C. Day Lewis, Upton Sinclair and Albert Einstein, read out to the audience by Archibald MacLeish, reflected growing fears about fascist violence, and the feeling that it had now become impossible to discuss art in the absence of politics. When Hemingway spoke about writers in Spain, it was the first time that many in the audience had heard him express a political opinion. MacLeish himself called for help for those who 'truly fight our battles *now* – *now*, not in some future war – *now*, *now* in Spain'. The Hearst newspapers next day called the Congress a Moscow plot. The poet and playwright Dawn Powell, excellent chronicler of American life, described the scene to a friend with a more comic eye. 'About 10.30,' she wrote, 'all the foreign correspondents marched on, each one with his private blonde, led by Ernest and Miss Gellhorn, who had been through hell in Spain and came shivering on in a silver fox cape chin-up. Walter Duranty had to leave his outside (blonde not cape) and John Gunther could only get his to the corner of the platform and of course Archie's own blonde was lost somewhere, but those who had none could take pot luck on Muriel Draper or go eat peach-pit . . . Ernest gave a good speech . . . and his sum total was that . . . writers ought to all go to war and get killed and if they didn't they were a big sissy. Then he went over to the Stork Club, followed by a pack of foxes.'

Martha had spoken in public before, but never to so many or to such distinguished people. Less apparently nervous than Hemingway, she was called on the second afternoon. 'A writer,' she told the several thousand people sitting before her, 'must be a man of action now . . . A man who . . . has given a year of his life to steel strikes, or to the unemployed, or to the problems of racial prejudice, has not lost or wasted time. He is a man who has known where he belonged. If you should survive such action, what you have to say about it afterwards is the truth, is necessary and real, and it will last.'

Martha was never an intellectual in the way of Simone Weil, but like Weil she was increasingly conscious of the need to experience for herself what she wanted to write about, and increasingly convinced that only experience mattered. The strengths, her lack of self-aggrandisement or the need to put herself constantly into the picture, that would make her a better reporter than Hemingway – though never nearly as good a novelist – were now becoming more pronounced. After going on to address a convention of librarians, again on the subject of Spain, she wrote to Mrs Roosevelt. The tone of the letter is resigned, even sad, but it carries a new understanding about herself. 'All the time (hating public speaking and being frightened),' she wrote, 'I kept wondering what use it was at all, I don't think one really touches people, they have to feel it themselves before they can understand the same way . . . And if it is useless to work so hard at the different things which trouble me, then it is a poorish life. Because there isn't much time left for fun, for friends, for leisure, for enjoying what is lovely and can't be deformed . . . I suppose I will go on doing humbly and rather badly the kind of thing I do, whether it is purposeful or not, because I don't know what else to do, and because I can never forget about the other people, the people in Madrid or the unemployed or the seven dead strikers in Chicago or the woman who sells pencils in the subway. I wish I could forget, but I don't know the technique for that.'

The Spanish Earth was being edited in New York, in the Columbia Broadcasting laboratories, Hemingway having written the commentary and recorded it after Frederic March and Lillian Hellman announced that they found Orson Welles's voice too polished and theatrical for the stark words. During editing, so Pindencio de Pereda, one of the sound editors, later said, it was Martha rather than Hemingway who did 'most of the courting' and that Martha seemed the more attached of the two. One night, Martha helped Ivens produce the whistle of incoming shells for the soundtrack, using a football bladder, an air hose and fingernails snapped against a screen.

Because of her lobbying, Eleanor Roosevelt had invited them to the White House to show the finished version, and on 8 July, Martha went with Hemingway and Ivens to Washington, insisting on stopping on the way to eat three fat sandwiches, saying that the dinner was bound to be revolting. She was right. Hemingway later described it as 'rainwater soup followed by rubber squab, a nice wilted salad and a cake some admirer had sent in'.

The screening, attended by both Roosevelts and Harold Hopkins, went well, and the President impressed Ivens and Hemingway by advising them to provide more in the way of context and background, thereby making the film more strongly anti-fascist. (One newspaper ran a headline next day: 'Communist Director Invades White House'.) Hemingway was taken with Mrs Roosevelt's great charm, but found her husband 'very Harvard charming and sexless and womanly like a great Woman Secretary of Labor . . .'. He sent a telegram to Pauline: 'White House still same colour but enthusiastic we charmed Papa.' Martha, as their 'scribe', wrote to thank Mrs Roosevelt, referring to her two companions as her 'trench buddies', and saying that she had felt like a mother with her two infant prodigies. Ever since her frequent stays at the White House during the Depression, she seemed to feel no hesitation about approaching the Roosevelts for every cause and on every occasion, saying later that it never hurt to give the President first-hand news, and that he 'understood and responded to adventure, excitement, bravery', while Mrs Roosevelt knew all about suffering and what the 'derring-do really cost in human pain and misery, and fear, and hunger, and wretchedness and all the rest of it'.

Martha did not go with her buddies to Hollywood, however, where Hemingway and Ivens went on 10 July to show the film at Frederic March's house, and where the politically committed turned out in number to watch the scenes of struggle in Spain. Hemingway, who according to Fitzgerald spoke with 'nervous tensity', asked the audience of writers and film people to help fund ambulances for the republic, saying that he guaranteed that $1,000 put one vehicle on the front line. Dashiell Hammett was the first to offer his $1,000. Dorothy Parker, a founder of the Algonquin Hotel Round Table in New York and already famous for her acerbic and witty short stories, and who had already given $500 towards the making of the film, came up with another $1,000. The evening ended with twenty new ambulances pledged for Spain. Martha, who had stayed behind to raise funds on the east coast, complained that the New Yorkers were apathetic and that she was treated like a 'cuckoo idealist'.

She had brought piles of notes back with her from Spain, planning to start her book, but despaired at her own writing which grew, she told Hemingway, 'lousier and lousier'. Everyone, she reported to her old family friend Hortense Flexner, was telling her that she wrote just like Hemingway, and this was enough to turn her from writing for life, for though he wrote like the 'heavenly host', she preferred to write 'like mud, and have it be a poor thing but my own'.

She was longing to go back to Spain. She and Hemingway 'tried steadily though in vain to be discreet', and she met him in secret and communicated mainly by letter and telephone. When they arranged to set off back to Europe, they travelled separately, Hemingway on the *Champlain* on 17 August, and Martha the following day on the new, luxurious *Normandie*, recently relaunched with exotic curtains of cerise wisteria and petit point Aubusson chairs. Dorothy Parker was on board with her husband, Alan Campbell, and, loathing physical exercise herself, remarked on Martha's energetic workouts in the ship's gym, where 'all of Ernest's ladies began their basic training for the life partnership'. Dorothy Parker, who didn't much care for Hemingway, had taken a liking to Martha, to her 'looks and her spirit and her courage and her decency', and invited her for a drink in first class. Lillian Hellman, whose play *The Children's Hour* had recently ended an eighty-six-week run on Broadway, was also on the *Normandie* on her way to Spain, and observed sourly that Martha's trousers were 'well-tailored' and her boots 'good', and that she looked as if she were off to cover the war for *Vogue*. Martha found Hellman 'sullen'.

Martha met Hemingway and Matthews in Paris, which was crowded with visitors to the International Exposition and where there were parties with the Murphys and Janet Flanner, and Ring Lardner's son, soon to be killed on the Spanish front. 'He is a nice kid,' Hemingway said about him, 'but he is awfully gloomy to make a soldier.' Obliged one evening to have a drink at the Meurice with Dorothy Parker as an 'anti-gossip ploy', Hemingway fled to join Martha and Matthews, loping 'towards us, closely resembling a horse that has escaped from a burning stable'. Martha escaped for a few days on her own to swim at Le Lavandou, where she had been so often with Bertrand in the early 1930s. By 6 September she and the trench buddies were on their way south, to cross the border back into Spain.

* * *

The news in Spain was dark. Franco had taken the northern provinces, Bilbao and the Basque country: two-thirds of Spain now lay in nationalist hands. Italian planes and submarines, attacking shipping in the Mediterranean, had further cut off desperately needed supplies. The Vatican had recognised Burgos as the seat of the official nationalist government. Republican losses were mounting all the time, and among them were men who had become friends to Martha and Hemingway. One of these was Werner Heilbrun, the gentle and charming German doctor who was the chief medical officer of the 12th Brigade, once described by Hemingway as a 'weary beggar-monk'. 'I thought I knew everything about the war,' Martha told Hemingway, 'but what I didn't know was that your friends got killed.'

Madrid was bleak, dirty and, as the autumn advanced, increasingly cold. The city, wrote Dos Passos 'has a grim look as if stamped on iron'. The death carts were now out every night, collecting the bodies in the streets, and one evening Martha found a dead horse and a dead mule in front of Chicote's, the bar where they liked to go and drink, and the 'smear where they had cleared up a dead man'.

Fighting had stalled along the front in Aragon, and immediately after reaching Madrid, Martha, Hemingway and Matthews set out to visit Belchite, scene of an earlier republican victory and still triumphantly in loyalist hands. The sky was pale and clear, and they drove slowly down dirt roads, through valleys with poplars and willows, planted with rows of cabbages dark green against the reddish earth. In the late morning, they stopped the car and ate food straight out of tins, washed down with local wine. That night, they slept on mattresses in an open truck, parked in the courtyard of a farmhouse, and cooked food over an open fire. It was bitterly cold and an 'orange-coloured September dust' blew steadily. Writing later about Belchite, where they were the first correspondents to arrive, Martha recorded that the houses had slumped in on each other in the shelling, and that soldiers were digging out the dead. 'You could pass a high pile of rubbish and smell suddenly the sharp rotting smell of the dead. Further on would be a half-decayed carcass of a mule, with flies thick on it. And then a sewing machine, by itself, blown out into the street . . . It was sunny and quiet and the whole place was infinitely dead.' Later, they looked out at Brunete, now in fascist hands, over a land 'still tawny with summer' and Martha could see, through her binoculars, nationalist soldiers wandering around the deserted buildings, while the other way, in a hollow in the hills, republican soldiers washing in a stream. 'Even here, I thought, it is beautiful,' she wrote.

Hemingway and Matthews had many friends in the Abraham Lincoln Brigade, and while they discussed military tactics with the officers Martha walked through the olive groves observing the faces she knew so well from 'Mississippi and Ohio and New York and California and hearing the voices that you'd heard at a baseball game, in the subway, on any campus'. She was not always welcome in the trenches, one officer pointing out that the men had been in the front line for many weeks and that a visit from a woman might provoke a mutiny. In her article for *Collier's* on the International Brigades, Martha speculated about these 'men who came all this distance, neither for glory, nor money and perhaps to die', and the way that they 'knew why they came, and what they thought about living and dying, both. But it is nothing you can ask about or talk about. It belongs to them.' Again and again, she returned to this idea of certainty, the reassuring sense of knowing why you were doing something, and that what you were doing was right. Sending the article to St Louis for her mother to read, Martha added a brief note: 'Matie dearest: Bad weather, bad tummy, cold feet and weltschmerz, otherwise all fine.' In her diary, she wrote: 'So now the long winter starts. Winter is something to endure, and summer is something you can almost always waste.'

On his return to Madrid in the autumn of 1937, Hemingway praised Martha for her stoicism and indifference to discomfort. He appeared proud of her, and she continued to treat him with her own kind of wry and affectionate detachment. But now, from time to time, there was something about her that seemed to infuriate him, and then he would rage and threaten and bully. One night, over dinner, he was suddenly overcome with irritation at her plans to return to America to lecture on the Spanish situation, calling her money-grubbing at the republicans' expense. 'Dinner,' wrote Martha later, 'was a meal like scratching your fingernail over the blackboard . . . For an hour perhaps he put on, without opposition, a really excellent show but the kind of show usually reserved for enemies.' They walked back from the Gran Vía to the Florida in silence, 'with plenty of street between us'. But it was not over. 'Someday I must learn to describe E. as hyena because I know it is a marvellous thing . . . It was very hyena indeed, with everything called out and spat on, and the first round ended with a side swipe at the electric light which crashed beautifully all over the room.' Later they made love, but that was never very good. As Martha told a friend, all through the months in Spain she went to bed with Hemingway 'as little as I could manage: my whole memory of sex with Ernest is the invention of excuses and failing that, the hope it would soon be over'. At the time, what she felt was loneliness and fear, 'a terror that things thought or spoken in anger must have had their beginnings somewhere, when the mind was calm: and then the terror that if the beginnings can come, what is the end . . . So no doubt he and I will wear each other out, as millions have done so well before us, chipping a little each day, with just a little dig or a minor scratch . . . Oh God, either make it work or make it end now. What the trees can do handsomely – greening and flowering, fading and then the falling of leaves – human beings cannot do with dignity, let alone without pain.'

After the war was over, Martha wrote a short story about a young woman reporter being invited to the front by an Italian *commandante*, who shows her around the trenches. As they scramble along the ground, spent bullets buzz around their heads, 'like June bugs in the dark, fast purposeful June bugs'. The *commandante*, a large, cheerful, rather attractive man makes heavy passes at the American girl. In 'A Sense of Direction', the title she gave to her short story, the *commandante* is called Giorgio. Giorgio was in fact Randolfo Pacciardi, a handsome Italian officer in the International Brigades, first commander of the Garibaldi Battalion and in civilian life the leader of the Italian republican party. One day Pacciardi invited Martha out to his sector and, during the drive back to Madrid, kept trying to get her to put her hand on the front of his trousers, while she shrank back against the seat in horror and in silence, not wanting to embarrass the driver by protesting. Pacciardi laughed merrily at her scruples. Hemingway was jealous of Pacciardi's attentions.

But it was not always sad or quarrelsome. Often, Hemingway and Martha walked together around Madrid, buying silver and jewellery 'like speculators', picking their way over the new shell holes, or wrote their articles before going off to drink sherry or gin at Chicote's, or talked to the many visitors who continued to pour into the city in the autumn of 1937. On Sunday mornings the flea market sold canaries in paper bags. The young American volunteers continued to use the Hotel Florida as their base, men like Alvah Bessie, the scriptwriter and novelist, who called Hemingway the 'Great Adolescent' and Martha his 'long-legged moll', or Milton Wolff, at twenty-two the rising star of the Lincoln machine-gun company. And then there were the British and American celebrities, the war tourists, some of whom they already knew and some who they longed to avoid. Dorothy Parker came wearing a cyclamen-coloured hat shaped like a sugar loaf. And after dinner, when they were alone, there would be 'Mister Scrooby, as friendly as a puppy and as warm as fur'.

Lillian Hellman was one of the war tourists they did not much care for. Hemingway, who knew her from Hollywood, was respectful and asked her to dinner, but Martha had taken a dislike to her during the crossing on the *Normandie*, 'with her thin upper lip, and the lids flat over her eyes and the insulting darkened teeth and the expression of polite spite'. She sensed that her 'forked tongue' would cause trouble between Hemingway and herself. 'I am angry at Miss Hellman,' Martha wrote in her Madrid notes, 'who has no reason to hate all women simply because one man left her. It has happened to other women and will happen again and it would be a very dreadful world if this abandonment affected all women as it affects Miss Hellman.' While Hemingway 'paid homage', Martha fumed at the way their guest contributed nothing to the dinner and spread an atmosphere of grumpi-ness. Many years later, Lillian Hellman's visit to Spain would become the subject of an acid literary row. Better by far the evening that Koltzov, the enigmatic *Pravda* correspondent, came to dinner in Hemingway's room. He told them a story about being given poison to administer to any wounded Russian in case the nationalists took Madrid, to conceal the fact that there were Russians with the loyalists, and another one about a Spanish general who refused to carry maps, saying that he kept the map of his country in his heart.

That autumn, all Spain was hungry. The queues for beans grew longer. Though the republican forces urged the people of Madrid to leave, very few did so. Sad families could be seen making their way along the pitted streets, in mud that reminded Martha of chewing gum, pulling barrows or donkeys behind them piled high with what remained of their possessions, their homes in the outlying suburbs of Rosales and Arguelles having been flattened by fascist artillery. Some brought sheep and cattle with them and put them to graze in the parks, between the trenches. Even the fascists on the hills were hungry. A platoon of Franco's Moorish soldiers, who had fought their way into the University and taken the medical research laboratories, came down with typhoid after eating the monkeys and guinea pigs kept for experiments. It snowed in the mountains and, as a sharp wind blew through the now treeless avenues, women could be seen chopping the beams of the shelled houses for firewood. In the restaurant on the Gran Vía, the menu was down to bread and chickpeas cooked in olive oil with onions; occasionally there were a few lentils or beans. At the Capitol they continued to show the Marx Brothers; the Paramount was doing well with Chaplin's *Tiempos Modernos*. The constant shelling from the fascist batteries on Mt Garabitas went on, and Martha and Hemingway would listen to the whine of the spent bullets and the crash of the shells as they burst against the stone and metal of the buildings. Along the avenues, the bright yellow trams were still running.

The 8th November was Martha's twenty-ninth birthday. Matthews presented her with a large basket of flowers, and produced a meal of caviar, *pâté en croûte, marrons glacés*, ham and Christmas pudding. Hemingway found champagne and Château d'Yquem. The day was kept from being 'horrible' only by Matthews' efforts, because Martha had heard from America that there was now much malicious gossip about herself and Hemingway. She noted grimly that she could think with pleasure only of death and that she had sworn 'never again to get into such a thing and again I am in it up to the neck'. She was worried principally about Edna; but about

Pauline and the boys too. She feared her next visit to New York, when she would have to 'squelch it all'. Hemingway was worried too, 'but only I know how bad it is going to be'.

Once again she was 'busy with clothes and lazy like a disease', fretting about her own idleness, her visits to the dressmaker and furrier, and about a taffeta skirt 'in which to dance later in some other city, with people who will understand nothing of all this and care less'. 'Stupid day,' she wrote on the 9th. 'Grey, cold, nothing. Stupid day, stupid woman. I am wasting everything and now I am twenty-nine.' She decided to eat no lunch, 'because of my bottom and also because my stomach is tired of digesting rich food from cans'. Often, she could not sleep at night, thinking of all the young men now dead and how terrible things would be when she went home to America; and then she would take what she called 'dope' at 4.30 and sleep through until lunch next day. 'The days are long,' she wrote on 12 November, 'and waiting is hard and yes the days are long. No, they're unbelievably short but nothing gets done and I am rotten with laziness and not worth spitting on.'

She was being hard on herself. She was now not only writing for *Collier's* and *The New Yorker* but broadcasting to America about life in Madrid, an unnerving undertaking both because she found the performance daunting and because it involved a dash across the road to the Telefonica, at the moment of peak evening shelling. But she never seemed to mind much about the danger, dismissing a direct hit on her room at the Florida when she was out one day as unimportant. It was the boredom and the future that she feared.

It was better when they found something to celebrate, and the four of them, she and Hemingway, Delmer and Matthews, would eat themselves 'warm' on the tins left in the cupboard – down to soup, sardines, spinach and corn – and talk about movie stars. When the shelling started, they would open the windows so that the glass wouldn't break, wind up Hemingway's portable gramophone and play a Chopin mazurka. For the rest of her life, wherever she was, Martha associated Chopin with Madrid during the civil war. It was better too when she forced herself out of the hotel and into the city, visiting the hospitals, or walking around with the team of architects and builders whose job it was to inspect what was left of the houses after each day's shelling, and pronounce on their safety. Then she would stare at the mounds of brick and kindling wood, the old rags and scraps of paper, the pieces of plaster and slivers of glass which had once been homes. 'You had a feeling of disaster,' she wrote, 'swinging like a compass needle, aimlessly, over the city.'

During the empty days in Madrid in October and November, when there was little happening at the front and not much going on in the city, Hemingway started to write a play. He called it *The Fifth Column*, after Mola's hidden weapon, and it was about a grubby American secret agent called Philip Rawlings, with big shoulders and a taste for bully beef and raw onion sandwiches, living in room 109 at the Florida in Madrid and working for the republicans during the civil war. Rawlings' room was a replica of Hemingway's, and his cupboards were full of tins of milk and corned beef and soap. His chambermaid, like Hemingway's, was called Petra. In the evenings, he played Chopin's mazurka in C minor on his portable victrola. Rawlings takes part in an underground operation and winds up helping the republicans and their foreign advisers torture a fascist spy to death. There is a character called Antonio, a thin-lipped, aristocratic-looking man in dove grey, wearing horn-rimmed spectacles, clearly modelled on Pepe Quintanilla, the man they knew as the 'executioner'. More interesting than what this says about the loyalists and what Hemingway knew of their conduct in this dirty war, however, is the light it sheds on Pauline and Martha. Hemingway had sent messages to his women this way before, and the message to Pauline, now, was unmistakable. 'Where I go now I go alone,' Rawlings declares, 'or with others who go there for the same reason I go.'

There was little comfort to be had in *The Fifth Column* for Martha either, though she seems to have chosen to read into his portrait of the heroine, the tall, handsome, blonde Dorothy Bridges, with the 'longest, smoothest, straightest legs', nothing more than an affectionate parody of herself. But Dorothy is, in Rawlings' view 'lazy and spoiled, and rather stupid and enormously on the make', a 'bored Vassar bitch' who can't cook, but who can write quite well – for a magazine called *Cosmopolitan* – when she is not too idle. Dorothy has had 'men, affairs, abortions, ambitions' and is now desperate to marry Rawlings. At the end of the play, having decided not to make an 'absolutely colossal mistake', he abandons her; she is, after all, only a 'very handsome commodity . . . a commodity you shouldn't pay too high a price for'. 'You're useless really,' Rawlings tells her. 'You're uneducated, you're useless, you're a fool and you're lazy.' Harsh words that perhaps should not have been taken so lightly. Though it is in Dorothy's mouth that Hemingway puts the most memorable words in the play. 'Oh don't be kind,' she says to him. 'You're frightful when you're kind. Only kind people should be kind.'

Martha and Hemingway were in Barcelona, on their way home to the States, when the loyalists launched their long expected attack on Franco's forces at Teruel, a pretty, small town on a plateau which in winter looked like the surface of the moon. It was mid-December and snowing heavily. Hemingway went with Matthews and Delmer to watch the assault from a nearby hill, then followed the soldiers into the town as they stormed the buildings with hand grenades and dynamite. Martha was not there, writing later to Hemingway that it would hurt her forever that she was not at Teruel with him, but she was waiting in Barcelona for them to have a Christmas dinner together before he put her on the train for Paris.

She was back in New York for Christmas itself, where she visited the parents of some of the young Americans of the Abraham Lincoln Brigade, delivering presents and reassuring them that their sons were safe. 'I, pure from the war, muff everything, get underpaid by radio, *The New Yorker* asks me for money back, *Collier's* wants some rewriting,' she wrote to Hemingway. 'Ho for the Causa.' She had been right to dread the repercussions of her now public affair with Hemingway, for Pauline had decided to follow him to Spain, and by the time he reached Paris himself, she was waiting for him at the Hôtel Elysée. Their reunion was stormy. Hemingway was feeling ill, and had something wrong with his liver; he was also anxious about his articles for the NANA, and *To Have and Have Not* had just been published in the States, to poor reviews. Pauline threatened to jump off the hotel balcony. She told Hemingway that Martha was egoistic, selfish, stupid, childish, phoney, and 'almost without talent'. The Hemingways travelled home together on the *Grisholm* and Hemingway admitted to Max Perkins that he was indeed in a 'gigantic jam'.

In January, Martha set off on a tour of lectures on Spain and the lessons of the war, and in her talks, praising the young Americans who had flocked to fight with the republicans, she returned to her old theme about the sense of dignity and morality 'which only comes to people who know why they are there'. On 7 January, she was at the University of Minnesota, speaking to three thousand people; three weeks later, she reached St Louis, where the *Post-Dispatch* described her as an 'honest partisan', and quoted her as calling Franco a 'butcher'. Everywhere she went she was interviewed, and the articles that appeared in local papers were admiring. She brought to the platform, observed the reporter in Louisville, 'the voice, the culture, the art of pose, the poise, gesture, diction which succeed upon the stage at its best', adding that this 'slip of a girl' had been the best performer of the evening. The *New York Times* listed her among the very few popular women lecturers of 1938, and everywhere she went Martha warned of worse things to come, if the nationalists were allowed to defeat the democratically elected republican government of Spain. 'Martha Gellhorn Predicts US Will Soon Be In War' announced one headline. But the mood of America was not on her side, and even Eleanor Roosevelt, who had become an ever more passionate advocate for the republicans, was now under attack by the Catholic hierarchy, while Roosevelt refused to countenance any softening of the embargo.

In February, exhausted by delivering twenty-two lectures in under a month, angry about America's isolationist foreign policy, sick of seeing herself as 'Moses with the tablets of stone', and having lost twelve pounds, Martha pleaded ill health, cancelled her last few lectures and fled to Florida with her mother, to lie in the sun. But not for long. To Mrs Roosevelt, who had written to urge her to 'stop thinking for a little while', she replied that she had no mechanism to do so, and, what was more, she felt she had no right to stop thinking. 'The only way I can pay back for what fate and society have handed me is to try, in minor totally useless ways, to make an angry sound against injustice.' On 4 March she met Hemingway in Miami. When news reached them that Franco had retaken Teruel and was driving a wedge through to the Mediterranean, splitting the loyalists forces in two, they hurried back to Spain. Pauline did not go with them.

On board the *Queen Mary*, her handwriting uneven in her evident haste to write, Martha covered twelve pages in a letter to Mrs Roosevelt. It was a furious cry about Spain and what she was now sure was a coming European war. 'The young men will die,' she wrote. 'The best ones will die first, and the old powerful men will survive to mishandle the peace . . . And all the people I love will finish up dead, before they can have done their work . . . I wish I could see you. But you wouldn't like me much. I have gone angry to the bone.'

The front line was the place to be now; there she did not have to think.

* * *

Long after the war in Spain was over, Martha wrote a short story called 'Till Death Do Us Part'. It was about a war photographer called Bara, an elusive Hungarian who wore flamboyant clothes and whose past was sealed off to everyone, together with all talk about his wife Suzy, killed in a nationalist raid in Spain. Bara was an attractive man, with glossy black hair, and he spent money, lots of money, with no regard for anything. He had a very good friend, a 'hit and run' photographer like himself, a Pole called Lep, and an American girlfriend, Helen, a pleasant, reasonable woman, who was desperate to marry him. But, crucially, Bara had another friend, a woman he called Marushka, a war reporter he had met in Spain. Marushka and Bara were never lovers, but they had a friendship of great intimacy. They quarrelled over everything and they shouted at each other, but they minded a great deal whenever the other was in trouble. 'Marushka,' Bara tells the frantic and jealous Helen, 'is my brother. Or my sister. My sister *and* brother.' Of all the short stories she wrote Martha liked this one the best. 'I love it for what and who it is about,' she told a friend, 'knowing that it is truer than truth.'

Martha met Robert Capa in Spain, probably in Barcelona, soon after returning to the war in September 1938. Capa, a Hungarian by birth, the son of a dressmaker in Budapest, was by then Spain's most famous war photographer, his 'moment of death' picture of the loyalist soldier caught as he is shot and begins to fall, having been picked up from *Vue* by *Life* and reprinted all round the world. Like Martha, what drew Capa was the effect of tragedy on ordinary people; like her, he was not all that keen on objectivity, saying that as a reporter 'you must have a position or you cannot stand what goes on'.

During a bombing raid, Martha and Capa sat together in a darkened room in a hotel, Capa wearing a double-breasted coat with brass buttons, Martha telling him that it was vulgar, and Capa replying that he had always wanted a coat just like it, and that if he was going to die he wanted to die wearing it. Capa was twenty-four, almost five years younger than Martha, and spoke poor English. Hemingway liked him, and Capa said he felt like his adopted son. Soon he had become one of the 'trench buddies'. But for Martha it was more than that; it was a friendship of a very particular sort. Writing to Rosamond Lehmann in the early 1950s, she explained that she had had five friends in her life, all men, 'when it is as if you were nearly the same', and of these Capa had been 'the best, the nearest in every way'. He was, she often told people, 'my brother, my real brother'. Neither for Capa, nor for these other men, had she felt the slightest sexual attraction, but 'they and the dead have always mattered to me more than any lovers ... Lovers somehow never seemed serious; there was something

I couldn't quite believe – and even in the most anguishing intoxicating depths of a love affair, I would always rather be with my friends, who were my own people and where I belonged . . . I only loved the world of men – not the world of men-and-women.' Wars belonged to the world of men, and it was in wars that Martha found her closest friends.

Like Bara in the story, Capa had a wife, Gerda, killed by a reversing tank in Spain. In the sixteen years before Capa stepped on a mine south of Hanoi and was killed, he and Martha had a lot of fun. They talked about many things, Capa in his broken English, but they never talked about Gerda. They laughed all the time. Capa had a great photographer friend, David Seymour, whom he called Chim; and after the war, back in America, Ingrid Bergman fell very much in love with him, and wanted to marry him, telling Martha that she had never before met 'a free human being' like him. But Capa slipped away from her.

Barcelona, already a city reduced by war to extreme poverty and hunger became, in March 1938, the scene of the most sustained aerial bombing of the Spanish war, providing an image of what was soon to follow throughout Europe. At 10.15 on the night of the 16th, under a full moon, Heinkel bombers began to pound the city. In the next forty-eight hours, they carried out eighteen raids, and many of the bombs fell on the city's most densely inhabited quarters, where tall buildings, housing dozens of families, lined narrow streets. People were trapped under falling beams and bricks and mortar. At daybreak, reporters described scenes of carnage, and blood literally flowing down the gutters. Matthews later wrote in a dispatch that he had witnessed 'things which Dante could not have imagined'. Soon, Barcelona's hospitals were full of badly injured and dying survivors, and when Martha went to visit one ward she found 'all the children silent in the white tiled room, white with huge black eyes'. Barcelona had almost no food left and everyone was hungry. It had long since run out of soap, and later Martha would remember the terrible smell, and the way that in the Hotel Majestic where they stayed, the linen, filthy and stained, would be ironed and put back on the beds.

The loyalist troops were forced to retreat, and Martha and Hemingway followed the line of smashed and abandoned trucks, taking shelter behind low stone walls to watch the fascist bombers, 'high and bright like dragon flies' glinting in the sun far above. When they came in to drop their loads, they made an echo that circled around the mountains. One day they drove through the olive groves to the Mediterranean, where the water was as flat as glass, leaving a thin lacy white line of foam along the sand, and where the umbrella pines stood in clumps along the shoreline. The pink almond blossom was out. They came on Modesto's headquarters, and talked about the campaign with the general, who was wearing espadrilles and seemed dirty and tired, eating mutton chops and salad with sardines, and drinking wine from an empty tin. Later, they drove back to Madrid, and visited the hospital where Freddy Keller, a short, tough, American boy with mouse-blond hair who they were both fond of, and who had rescued eighteen of his men by twice swimming across the Ebro under fire, was recovering from a bullet wound in his thigh.

On 15 April, Franco's troops reached the Mediterranean, splitting Barcelona from Valencia and Madrid. The rebel victories across Catalonia were emptying villages one after the other and there were refugees everywhere, struggling along the roads, crouching in the ditches, taking shelter in bombed-out houses. 'There were those who came with only a bundle,' wrote Martha that day, Good Friday 1938, 'pink or yellow or blue or dirty grey, and all strange shapes, clutched under their arms or balanced on their heads, some walking fast and others wearily . . . leaving behind them everything to walk down mountain footpaths away from the enemy, in the dark. Their faces were the same, children's faces and the faces of the old men in twisted black stocking caps. Sad and tired and frightened but as if they had been frightened for a long time . . .'

On 18 April, the Italians captured Tortosa and Martha and Hemingway, standing peeling hard-boiled eggs and eating oranges in an olive grove, watched as twenty-three bombers, small, delicate and white against the sky, dropped their loads. Along the route there were pockets of loyalist soldiers, some of the newer recruits still children, and men from the International Brigades, reading maps, smoking quietly, planning to make a last stand to give others the time to retreat. Borrowing her language from Hemingway, Martha wrote: 'And maybe history is a stinking mess and a big injustice anyhow, and the victory is always wrong. But one thing is sure: good men are as absolute as mountains and as fine, and as long as there are any good men then it is worth while to live and be with them. And one cannot feel utterly hopeless about the future knowing that such people exist, whether they win or not. Though every day war seems more loathsome and the destruction of good people . . . more tragic and useless.' There was no time, now, to be bored.

Martha wanted to stay on in Barcelona to write about the refugees and the evacuation of the wounded, and sent a cable to *Collier's* that it was all very like the 'last days of Pompeii'; but world attention had moved away from the dying Spanish republic. 'Not interested Barcelona story stop,' *Collier's* replied. 'Stale by the time we publish.' They wanted her to go to France, and then on to England and Czechoslovakia, to see what the rest of Europe felt about a war. They offered excellent rates – $1,000 for each piece they accepted – and in any case she could hardly turn it down. But she had come to love and care about Spain, and was still thinking of writing about it in the way she had written about the Depression, and she still believed that what happened in Spain was 'the affair of us all, who do not want a world whose bible is *Mein Kampf*'. Leaving for Paris, she wrote to Mrs Roosevelt: 'The war in Spain was one kind of war, the next world war will be the stupidest, lyingest, cruellest sell-out in our time.'

* * *

Martha had now been immersed in the politics of Europe for almost a decade, much, she wrote later, as a tadpole is involved in a pond. She had travelled round Germany and Austria, visited England, driven through Italy, covered much of Spain and most of France. She spoke excellent French, adequate Spanish and some German. Her contacts were good, particularly in France, where some of the young journalists and politicians she had known with Bertrand now held positions of authority, and she had friends among the foreign correspondents who covered European affairs, in whose club she firmly belonged, and whose easy life she loved. She also had an extraordinary amount of influence, because *Collier's*, with a readership of around ten million, was regarded as one of the most serious of the popular American magazines. And she was still young, striking looking and bold; the uncertainty that marked her first *Collier's* article from Spain had gone, leaving in its place decisiveness and a powerful sense of indignation.

In May, leaving Hemingway to make his own way to Paris, Martha crossed back into France at the border near Perpignan and hired a car, planning to gauge the mood of France for *Collier's* by her well-tested method of wandering and talking to whoever she came across. 'Aix: happy' she wrote in her diary. Soon, she was telling her editor that she had enough material to write a book, and that she could 'give Baedeker pointers'. By the 26th she had reached Paris, where Hemingway was already waiting for her, and where she lunched with the Aga Khan and went to the races and a cocktail party 'for the bright or social end' of the article, before interviewing Jacques Doriot, the former communist and now founder of the Fascist Parti Populaire Français, and Maurice Thorez, the general secretary of the communist party. Apologising for sending off a 'monumental' article, far longer than had been commissioned, Martha warned *Collier's* that the French were 'in a mess from the war material point of view', with only about a hundred decent planes, the others being badly built and far slower in the air than those being manufactured with such efficiency in Germany. Her fears for France were reflected in her closing words. France, she wrote, had 'won wars before and knows there is nothing in it – nothing but heartbreak and calamity . . . There is neither victory nor defeat; there is only catastrophe.'

Hemingway, unable to postpone his return to Pauline any longer, now sailed for New York, and Martha wrote to her mother that she was being 'what the French call "reasonable". There isn't anything left to be, I have tried everything else. I believe he loves me, and he believes he loves me, but I do not believe much in the way one's personal destiny works out.' By early June she was in Prague, staying at the Hotel Ambassade, with all the other foreign correspondents come to witness Czechoslovakia's struggles to survive. She wanted to get the visit out of the way, she told *Collier's*, before the threat of war: 'to be cut off there in those mountains with people who speak a preposterous language is more than I'll risk . . .'. Her lightheartedness quickly evaporated; soon, the fate of the Czechs, like that of the Spaniards, came to haunt her.

Surrounded on three sides by German territory, Czechoslovakia was home to some three million so-called Sudeten Germans, whose lands in northern Bohemia had been transferred from Austrian to Czech rule after the First World War. Hitler's plan was to reunite this rich industrial region and its German-speaking people with the Reich, using Konrad Heinlein, the Sudeten leader, to provoke violent confrontations with the Czechs, and to keep putting pressure on the President, Dr Eduard Beneš, to make concessions. Beneš, seeking help everywhere, and particularly from France which was bound to Czechoslovakia by treaty, was using the weeks of procrastination to mobilise and to build up defences on the border with Austria. It was, Martha quickly realised, just the kind of story she most enjoyed, with a heroic David and a villainous Goliath, and a very clear issue of right and wrong. She travelled around the border area, noting the barricades and the guards on every road, remarking that the map of Czechoslovakia looked like a kite with its head, the Sudetenland, resting in Germany. She found the soldiers in high spirits, ready to defend their country, whatever the cost. 'The country is a fortress,' she wrote to Mrs Roosevelt, 'and the atmosphere is of someone waiting in an operating room for the surgeon, who will come to work with a blunt knife and no anaesthetic.' In her article for

Collier's, she wrote of the 'authentic, desperate, makeshift feeling of war', but said there was no panic, just a 'marvellous feeling of will'. Taking her title from the refrain of a song she heard everywhere she went, 'Come Ahead Hitler!', she warned that if the war started – though her 'ifs' now sounded more and more like 'whens' – this 'green and gentle plain will be Flanders'. The Czechs, she added, could do nothing except wait: 'And hope. And watch the former house painter who now holds the lightning in his hands.'

Martha still had her article on England to write. 'What do they think of Fascism or Aggression or the possibility of war?' Charles Colebaugh had written, asking her to find out whether the British were now alarmed about the prospects of war. Her own feelings of contempt for Chamberlain and appeasement had been growing and her newfound friendships among dissidents in Czechoslovakia had done nothing to soften them. She set out from Prague in a belligerent mood, accompanied by Virginia Cowles, who had been writing a series of articles on Czechoslovakia for the *Sunday Times*.

It was June and in England the roses were out. The two women, tall, stylishly dressed, with their American accents and their brisk efficiency, drove to the Midlands and worked their way north towards Newcastle. Everywhere they stopped, in villages, town centres, pubs, tea rooms and dockyard restaurants, at farms and in libraries, they chose people at random and asked them what they felt about the possibility of war. France had maddened Martha by its lack of foresight; England struck her as criminally complacent and English politicians as cynical and opportunistic. Though the country was clearly in desperate need of more ships, aircraft and arms, everyone they spoke to told them that war was inconceivable, that Chamberlain was a fine man, and that Churchill's pleas for more vigorous rearmament were excessive. Soon, Martha's questions became confrontations; then the confrontations turned into lectures. In her autobiography, written many years later, Virginia Cowles recalled their trip chiefly as Martha haranguing total strangers on the evils of Hitler and the irresponsibility of appeasement. In Yorkshire, where they had been invited to tea, Lord Feversham, then Under-Secretary for Agriculture, laughed at Martha's indignation and told the two women that they were warmongering, stirring up the country. Martha replied that she had every intention of stirring it up a great deal more, starting with his own peasants. 'In England,' said Lord Feversham smugly, 'we call them farmers.' On this bickering note, the tea party moved to the fields, where obliging elderly tenant farmers assured Martha that all talk of war was absurd.

When she sat down to write her article for *Collier's* Martha was scathing. Britain, she wrote, was suffering from the fact that it had not been invaded for a thousand years and 'there is no terror to climb back into in the memory of her people'. British phlegm, a grotesque misplaced sense of calm, was effectively crushing all instinct for realistic self-preservation. 'It rose from England like mist: it was as real as London fog: everything's going to be all right – somehow. And at last I thought, well, they certainly believe it, so maybe it's true: the Lord will provide for England.' To her mother, Martha wrote dismissively: 'I think that England is a kid glove fascism worse because of its hypocrisy and the fact that all the people are fooled all the time . . . As Laski said, "The first economy an Englishman makes is on thought."' Chamberlain she considered to be the most 'hateful figure in modern times'.

Collier's, who had found her monumental French article 'jumpy' and undigested, but praised her Czech piece as 'swell', wanted her to keep going. Feeling she needed a break first, she was having a brief holiday with Hemingway, on the stretch of coast between Le Lavandou and St Tropez that she loved so much, when news came of the Munich Pact. Beneš, 'under unbelievable pressure', had accepted the French and British proposals and ceded the Sudetenland to Germany. She hurried back to Prague to find German forces occupying the border regions and Czechs fleeing the Sudetenland; between 1 October and 10 October, the German army took over 11,000 square miles of territory. Everywhere there was a feeling of war.

George Kennan, who had just taken up a post with the American Foreign Service in Prague, recalled later that he had been in his office one morning when 'an attractive young lady wearing a collegiate American fur coat and tossing, in her indignation, a most magnificent head of golden hair' burst in and berated him and his colleagues 'for our sleepy inactivity'. Why, demanded Martha, 'don't you *do* something about it?' Long after they became friends in the 1950s, Kennan remembered that at that time he had simply thought Martha was exaggerating and belonged to 'the category of ignorant, impractical do-gooders' and that he had been much relieved when she left.

Collier's had asked Martha to see if she could talk to Beneš, and perhaps get him to write an article; having met him with de Jouvenel, she now went in search of him. On a wooden bench in a corridor of the Hradcany Palace, she found Koltzov, the *Pravda* correspondent whom she had known and come to like in Madrid, who told her that he was bringing Beneš a message from Stalin that, if the Czechs would fight, the Soviet army would back them against Hitler. Koltzov had been waiting for four days: he looked shrunken, his former ebullience gone. They sat in the corridor talking in French, as Martha described her last impressions of the refugees in Catalonia and the way that Barcelona was starving to death. Koltzov stared at the floor and said nothing. When it became clear that Beneš was not going to see them, Koltzov took Martha to dinner in a workers' restaurant and over bowls of soup and 'thick, greasy food' spelt out to her what he thought would happen next. Writing about that evening almost half a century later, Martha remembered how accurately he had foretold the future, and how despairing he had sounded. Afterwards, on a dark street corner, they shook hands and said goodbye. She never saw Koltzov again. In the spring of 1939, Martha sent Maria Olsen, Koltzov's girlfriend, enough money to buy a railway ticket for Moscow, where he had been arrested for treason. She later heard that he had been shot.

In the days that followed Martha made one more attempt to reach Beneš, hiring a car and driving out to his country house. But she was stopped at the gates by plainclothes police, and Beneš eventually sent out word that he was seeing no one.

From friends in the government, Martha now got hold of some documents and notes written in the days leading up to Munich and had them translated into English. 'It is a story like a third rate police grilling,' she wrote to Charles Colebaugh. 'Nothing so shocking that I know about in history . . . England planned to sell out Czechoslovakia all along, and . . . the mobilisation of France, the mobilisation of the English fleet, the mobilisation of the Czech army (which was ordered by England) were all part of a vast comedy to terrify the people of the world and make the Munich pact seem a last minute rescue of peace, whereas it was a long planned betrayal.' But she knew, she said, that this was not what *Collier's* wanted from her. 'Perhaps I am wrong,' she continued, in a long, weary letter written after her return to Paris on 22 October, 'but I have always tried to be as non-political and pictorial as possible for you . . . The story of Czechoslovakia is, really and finally, the story of the dishonesty of the Chamberlain government and the cowardice of Daladier: but I am writing you a picture of a destroyed state . . . It is the grimmest and most complicated story I ever saw: and worst of all, the war is now certain, and when it comes it will be a far worse war . . . Chamberlain has given Europe to the dictators, and there seems very little hope that democracy will survive on the continent.' Most of her friends in the government, supporters of Beneš, were leaving the country, knowing that concentration camps were the 'next step'; Beneš would surely follow, if he were able to get away alive. To H.G. Wells, she wrote: 'Why don't you shoot Chamberlain? What a man, with a face like a nutcracker and a soul like a weasel. How long are the English going to put up with these bastards who run the country?'

And then she sat down and wrote about the refugees, the frightened Jews who had already fled once from Austria and Germany, and now had nowhere else to flee to, the Czech patriots beaten up by the Sudeten Nazis, the clerks and school teachers who never had a chance to fight, the children whose parents had already disappeared into the camps. The story was, she said, 'as moving as anything I ever saw', but Beneš had failed his people, and the Czechs should have been allowed to fight. She called it 'Obituary of a Democracy', and *Collier's* used her title. About Beneš, she wrote that he 'knew surely what his people know now: that this is no peace, there is no safety and no justice and no permanence in it'. Beneš, praying at the grave of Tomáš Masaryk, founder of Czech democracy, before leaving for exile in England, had 'perhaps prayed in mourning for the democracy of all Europe'. The disease that had killed it was something 'called cowardice'.

* * *

For the few remaining months of 1938, Martha was constantly on the move, writing follow-up pieces on France and England for *Collier's*, swearing that she would never again set foot on 'their cursed island'. 'Gellhorn is renouncing England,' she told H.G. Wells. 'As for a free press, mother of God, you don't need Goebbels.' Her mood was black, and she was obsessed with the number of refugees now trying to escape fascism. In letter after letter to her mother and Mrs Roosevelt, written in short, urgent sentences, she talked on and on about treachery and corruption and betrayal. 'I am so angry and so disgusted that I feel dazed.' She had lost not just all sense of optimism but all the belief she had ever felt in pacifism. War, she was convinced, must be better than fascism, at least for those who still believed in 'any of the decent words'.

In October she was in Paris, where the flags put up to welcome King George VI and Queen Elizabeth for their state visit in July had been taken down, and where the walls were now covered with posters calling on people to prepare for national defence '*pour sauvegarder la patrie*'. France, battered by social strife and political upheaval, was drifting towards war lacking most basic equipment and weapons. Martha had written a formal report on the Czech refugees – the ten thousand or so earlier refugees from Austria and Germany, and the newer ones, the Jews, the Catholics, the Social Democrats and the anti-Nazis – and had delivered a copy to Sir Neill Malcolm, the League High Commissioner for Refugees, who had visited Prague and not met, she claimed, a single refugee. Writing to her mother, she described the way she had pounded on his table and shouted at him and pleaded. Though she had managed to arrange a meeting between him and General Sirovy, the Czech Prime Minister, and persuaded General Faucher, the former head of the French Military Mission, to attend, nothing had been done for the refugees for fear of offending Hitler. 'I'll maybe lose my mind with the fury and helplessness,' she wrote. On *Kristallnacht*, 9 November, the night that the Nazis burned synagogues, looted Jewish businesses and murdered their owners throughout the Reich, she was in Paris, writing her stories for *Collier's*.

As if nothing were happening over the border in Germany, Paris was very lively. The hotels were full of American and English tourists, and at a costume ball given by Comte Etienne de Beaumont guests were asked to come dressed as characters from Racine. With Hemingway, Martha paid one more visit to Spain, where the loyalists had suffered huge casualties during the nationalist push towards Valencia, and where Negrín had disbanded the International Brigades, hoping that Franco might do the same with the German and Italian soldiers on his side. It was becoming clear that Stalin had failed in his goal to take over and run the Spanish government, economy and army and that Spain had not been turned into a Soviet People's Republic, even if the International Brigades had wound up close to being a Soviet army within Spain, many of its leaders and advisers officers in the Red Army. Many now were fated to become victims of Stalin's purges, recalled to Moscow, imprisoned and shot.

There was an emotional farewell parade through the streets of Barcelona, 200,000 men of the International Brigades marching before a stand on which stood Negrín and his war cabinet, with women in tears throwing flowers, while planes above dipped their wings in salute. The men looked, wrote Martha, 'very dirty and weary and young, and many of them had no country to go back to'. Watching them, she reflected that the guilt of the democracies was like a sense of sin. Forty thousand foreign volunteers had served in Spain, and a third had given their lives for '*la causa*'; one of the last was Jim

Dr George Gellhorn, Martha's father

Martha's mother, Edna

Martha in St Louis, aged two

George, Walter and Martha

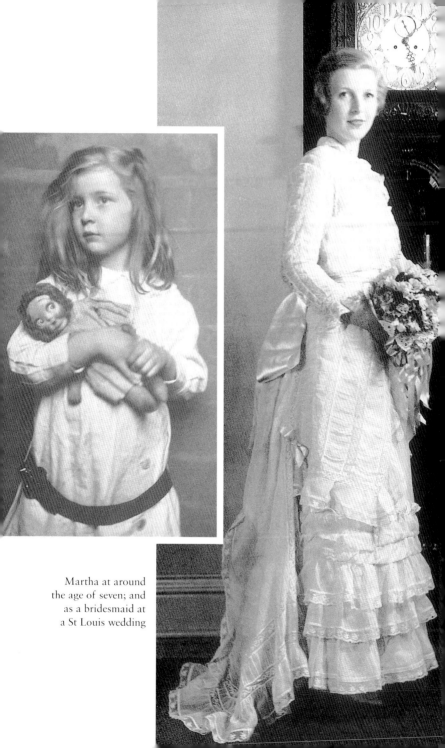

Martha at around
the age of seven; and
as a bridesmaid at
a St Louis wedding

Martha in Paris in the 1930s

Bertrand de Jouvenel, who fell in love with Martha in July 1930

H.G. Wells, whose friendship with Martha began in 1935

Allen Grover in New York in the late 193[

Martha during the Spanish Civil War, 1936

Robert Capa, 'my brother, my real brothe[

The early years with Ernest Hemingway:
Martha in Cuba (*above*) and at Sun Valley (*below*)

Robert Capa's photographs of the Hemingways at Sun Valley, taken for *Life* magazine at the time of their wedding, in November 1941

Top right: Martha with Hemingway and his three sons, John, Patrick and Gregory

The Hemingways on honeymoon in China.
Above: with Madame Chiang Kai-shek; *below*: visiting the war zone

Lardner, the young American with whom Hemingway and Martha had travelled down to Spain. Among the parading men they saw Pacciardi, the Italian officer who had pursued Martha in Madrid, and he told them that he would have to return to France, stateless and penniless, since fascist Italy was closed to him. Pacciardi had stood firm against the takeover of the Brigades by the Soviets, and insisted on regarding the Garibaldi fighters as a symbol of Italian anti-fascism. He looked, Martha wrote later, tragic, but he said little and did not complain.

It was an important moment in Martha's feelings for Hemingway. That evening, in their hotel room, she heard him, leaning against the wall, weeping. It was the only time she ever saw him cry. 'They can't do it!' he was saying, 'They can't do it!' Hemingway was crying for Pacciardi, for what Spain had done to him, and what would now become of him. At that moment, said Martha later, she really loved him.

Madrid was still in loyalist hands, but Martha chose to stay in Barcelona, to write about refugees, the 'very old women, talking to themselves with soft lips over their gums, crazy and pitiful', and about the children, most of them very frightened, and all of them hungry. She painstakingly collected statistics, as she would gather them all her life, filling her notebooks with lists and figures: 870,000 Catalonian children of school age and under; 200,000 of them undernourished, 100,000 in a 'state of pre-famine'. From very high in the pale blue winter sky, the Italians bombed, day after day. 'I cannot yet understand why there must be so much suffering,' she wrote to Mrs Roosevelt, 'I shall never be a good writer, the human animal escapes me.'

By the middle of December she had seen enough; she was 'tired in the head' and wanted to go home, to find somewhere quiet to sit and write, probably fiction, though she was afraid that her voice might have become too 'intense'. 'There will be millions like me who will never know what to believe again,' she wrote in a letter, 'or what to do for their beliefs or whom to serve . . .' Like Herbert Matthews, she had been profoundly changed by Spain, and all her life she would be grateful that she had 'been young and there, at that time; I think we got something out of history that is more than anyone has a decent right to hope for. We got that fusion, so often attributed to the human body (but so rarely achieved except in literature) of body and soul; of living one's life and believing with one's whole heart in the life around one.' And though she felt keenly that she had been powerless to help any one of them: 'I could remember for them.'

CHAPTER SEVEN

Flint and Steel

The Spanish civil war was not over yet, and it would be several months before the defeated loyalists, 300,000 soldiers, civilians, women, old people and children, hungry and exhausted, crossed the border into camps in France, where they were put behind barbed wire, as Janet Flanner wrote, 'on a treeless beach, on the edge of a muddy, soiled sea'; but it was perfectly clear that Franco and the Falangists were on their way to victory. Then Madrid fell; and the killings by Franco's execution squads began.

The events of the autumn had convinced Martha that there would be war in Europe before long; she wanted no part in it. Disapproving of Roosevelt's foreign policy, she nonetheless felt, for perhaps the only time in her life, some pride in being American. Like Hemingway, she thought the moment had come to retrench, take stock, find a way of using the material gathered in the last few years to record her own perception of the immorality of European political leaders and the fragility of those they so casually destroyed. She was already more pessimistic than he was about the power of journalists, and had finally abandoned her youthful conviction that, by writing persuasively enough, an honest reporter could shape public opinion. It was once again in fiction that she was now determined to translate and use her experiences. It had worked with her tales of the Depression; it could work again for refugees and those made casualties of Western political ambitions and conflict. A lifelong pattern of alternating pulls between fiction and reporting was now established, though for Martha the pull towards fiction would always be the stronger and the ambition to write a good novel the greater goal.

She spent a family Christmas with her mother and her brothers and their wives in St Louis, and Martha and Edna then drove south for a short holiday, before Martha went back to New York to help returning members of the Abraham Lincoln Brigade find jobs with employers sceptical after their service with the Reds. 'I can't do anything evidently for large causes and issues,' she wrote to Mrs Roosevelt, 'can help no one, so at least I can be temporarily useful to my own.' She visited the White House, where Mrs Roosevelt told her that she longed for the day when Martha might 'write something that will not make one really feel ashamed to read it'. Privately, Martha kept remembering the dead in Spain, their dying made useless because 'democracy itself didn't want to be fought for'.

And there was her life with Hemingway to sort out, put to one side in the recent confusing months. Many years later, in a letter to Hortense Flexner, Martha said that Hemingway had proposed marriage to her in Madrid, three weeks after her arrival in Spain in the spring of 1937. Now, nearly two years later, he was still married to Pauline, living some kind of family life with his children when at Key West, but it was apparent to visitors that he was restless and irritable. Leicester, Hemingway's brother, noted that he was drinking between fifteen and seventeen Scotch and sodas in the course of a day. Pauline, a conciliatory woman and much attached to their friends, who were becoming highly critical of Hemingway's behaviour, carried on much as if nothing were happening. Archibald MacLeish, who, together with the Murphys and John and Katy Dos Passos, would soon feel increasingly estranged from him, remarked that he 'sucked the air out of a room as he entered it'.

After an uneasy Christmas, Hemingway went to New York, where he met Martha and worked on *The Fifth Column*, finally in production with the Theatre Guild, complaining to everyone that the director and actors were ruining it and that he should have written it as a novel, and that reviewers ganged up on him. Grenville Vernon, reviewing it for *Commonweal*, called it trite, and declared that it proved that Hemingway could not write love scenes. Dorothy Bridges, Hemingway's compliant heroine, seems to have taken on other attributes in his mind, for in his introduction to the published version he wrote that 'her name might also have been Nostalgia'. (Initially dedicated to Martha, the dedication was withdrawn in deference to the fact that he was still married to Pauline.) Declining to attend the tryouts in the provinces, Hemingway returned briefly to Key West, before crossing to Havana, where he planned to write in the peaceful atmosphere of the Ambos Mundos, a hotel he had stayed in off and on for the ten years he had been coming to Cuba. Pauline, Mexican Mouse and Gigi stayed behind, together with a pair of pet raccoons and six peacocks. Hemingway was at work on a series of short stories, with five done and the outline of two more in his head, one on the Spanish war, the other about an elderly fisherman who struggles for four days with a marlin, only to lose it to a pack of sharks when it proves too heavy to haul on to his skiff. He booked one room in the Sevilla-Biltmore, where he slept, and a second on the fourth floor of the Ambos Mundos, where he wrote. Hemingway loved Cuba. He was happy in its cool hills, with its semi-tropical gardens and the deep-sea fishing in the Gulf, only half an hour away by boat.

In her brief record of dates, Martha noted that she joined Hemingway on 18 February 1939, though Hemingway's biographers have tended to claim that she reached Havana only in April. As she and Hemingway were still attempting to keep their affair private it may have seemed more tactful to suggest that there was a longer break. Either way, she arrived to find him settled in his two rooms in spreading mess and dishevelment, relishing the lack of telephone and the irresponsibility of hotel life, surrounded by fishing tackle and old newspapers, stockpiling a large ham and quantities of cured sausages, much as he had done in the Hotel Florida. Prepared to tolerate any discomfort in war, Martha was too fastidious to bear dirt and disorder for long, and she was in any case no longer the unsure figure of the early days of their affair. Spain and Czechoslovakia had altered her. In her dealings with the world, there was a new note, older, more defined and more purposeful.

Before starting work herself, she began to look for somewhere for them to live and soon saw an advertisement in the local paper for a fifteen-acre property in the village of San Francisco de Paula. It was called the Finca Vigía – the Watchtower – and stood on a slight hill, with views down to the sea. At night, from the front steps, you could see the lights of Havana. The house itself was a one-storey Spanish colonial limestone building, with a fifty-foot sitting room and a large library off it, and had been built in the 1880s by a Catalan architect called Miguel Pascual y Baguer to help his grieving wife get over the death of their two young sons. Nearby stood a small white frame guesthouse.

The Finca Vigía had not been lived in for some years. It was dirty, its paint peeling, the swimming pool silted up, the surface of the tennis court cracked. There was a smell of drains. The garden, grown into jungle in Cuba's tropical climate, was littered with rusty tins and empty gin bottles. But it had a majestic ceiba tree growing from the wide front steps, with orchids sprouting from its trunk, which was the colour and texture of an elephant's hide. The terrace had a trellis bowed down with bougainvillea, and flowering vines hid the front wall. There were hummingbirds making their nests in the deep foliage. Martha was charmed. The ceiba alone, she said, made it worth it. She showed the Finca to Hemingway, whose first reaction was to say that the rent of $100 a month was far too high, and to go off fishing, but she took it anyway, and used the money she had saved from *Collier's* to have the place cleared and cleaned, and to order mahogany furniture.

The '*flamboyantes*', as she called them, the flowering jacaranda and bougainvillea, flourished in the hot brilliant sunshine she thrived on, and one day she counted eighteen different kinds of mango growing on the slope up to the terrace. She had the house painted a dusty shade of pink; and, for a while, she loved it. A wary sort of love perhaps: in a letter to Hortense Flexner, she sounded as if she felt she were only perching in the Finca, without possessions, telling her that 'When I leave, they can be seized by the first comer.' But she was happy, feeling 'serene and relaxed' for the first time in years. They moved in, Hemingway keeping his address at the Ambos Mundos for the sake of discretion, though this effectively marked the end of his twelve-year marriage to Pauline.

Both Hemingway and Martha were now writing hard. Hemingway, when asked, always gave 1 March 1939 as the day he started work on *For Whom the Bell Tolls*, having temporarily abandoned his fisherman for an American dynamiter in the Spanish civil war. From the first, the story went extremely well. Within three weeks he was reporting to his editor Max Perkins that he had finished 15,000 words, that he was proud of the way it was going but that he didn't want to talk about it because it might bring bad luck. Martha, having regretfully given up her plans for a Spanish novel as too raw and hard to shape, had transferred her setting to Prague and was building a story about refugees around a central character of an American woman journalist sent to cover the collapse of Czechoslovakia.

The two writers led a disciplined existence. Hemingway rose early and started working soon after first light, keeping going until two or two-thirty; he chose to use their bedroom as his study, a pleasant room with yellow tiles and windows that faced south. Martha marvelled at the way he protected himself, going into a shell of silence 'exactly as if he were dead or visiting on the moon', as she wrote to Hortense Flexner. 'He handles himself like a man who is about to do the world's championship boxing match. He has been I may say about as much use as a stuffed squirrel, but he is turning out a beautiful story. And nothing on earth besides matters to him . . . I learn a lot as I go on.'

She herself was having trouble with her book, again nagged by the feeling of being outside the stream of life, and had told the servants that she would 'spit small particles of hot steel' at them if they spoke to her in the mornings. She worried constantly that her writing was flat, and her own vocabulary bored her. 'The empty pages ahead frighten me as much as the typed pages behind,' she told a friend. Only her 'dog determination and pride' and the conviction that her subject mattered, that the now 'terrible and usual' spectacle of refugees on the march across Europe had to be described, kept her going, and she forced herself to put down 1,250 words every day. 'I have been thinking about writing until I am dizzy and a little ill. And have decided that what I have is patience, care, honor, detail, endurance and subject matter. And what I do not have is magic. But magic is all that counts . . . without magic who will weep and who will protest? Oh hell.' Hemingway, she said, had magic. When she read bits of his new novel, she could see it, 'clear as water and carrying like the music of a flute'.

In the afternoons they played tennis on the newly surfaced court, or went into Havana and drank in the Floridita or walked down the Prado, a wide boulevard of oaks and benches where people sat and talked, with boys selling papers and lottery tickets, and where each evening the negritos, small black birds, arrived in swarms from the surrounding canefields to settle in the laurel trees. And sometimes they went out on the *Pilar*, Hemingway's forty-foot green and black cabin cruiser, to fish for marlin in the deep, or took a day off and had a boating picnic with the Basque pelota players who lived in exile in Havana, who brought chicken and rice to cook on an open fire on the beach, and got 'blotto drunk' on wine from gallon straw-covered flasks and sang Basque songs. When Martha swam she wore motorcycle goggles so that she could watch the shoals of tiny, iridescent fish. She and Hemingway were extremely conscious of their weight, reporting to friends and to each other every pound gained or lost.

The final collapse of Czechoslovakia in March found Martha and Hemingway at their desks, as did Franco's proclamation of victory in Spain on 1 April. Gustav Regler, watching on the French border as weary and defeated loyalist soldiers and civilians came down from the mountains and were finally allowed over the frontier into exile, spoke of a scene 'like a mediaeval picture of the Crucifixion', with mimosa blooming on the hillsides and the camps waiting to receive them, mile upon mile of barbed wire and sand. The fascists had won, taking with them the hopes not only of the Spaniards who had voted for the republic but of the foreigners who had been prepared to die for it. 'A humorist in this world is whistling by the loneliest graveyard and whistling the saddest song,' Dorothy Parker told a reporter in Los Angeles. 'There is nothing funny in the world any more.' Martha, feeling that the moment had still not come when she could put down on paper what the war had meant to her, wrote to Hortense and Wyncie King: 'Nothing in my life has so affected my thinking as the losing of that war. It is, very banally, like the death of all loved things and it is as if a country that you had worshipped was suddenly blackened with fire and later swallowed in an earthquake . . . Spain has really broken my heart.' Like Herbert Matthews, she would talk all her life about Spain as the place and the time when she had learnt about war and come to value liberty, and she went on exchanging letters with men who had served with the International Brigades – Freddy Keller, Milton Wolff – until her death. But for now Europe, and its cowardly retreat before fascism, was to be held at bay in her mind; democracy was destroying itself and she did not want to watch it happen. The Finca Vigía was where she wanted to be, a 'beautiful desert island with mod cons'.

*   *   *

Sun Valley, in central Idaho, was the kind of countryside sportsmen dream of. Taking its name from a small village near the mining town of Ketchum, it was a vast and beautiful plain, with the Sawtooth Mountains all around; there were partridge, duck, snipe and pheasant in great number and fish in the winding creeks; the riding was excellent and the slopes provided good skiing. In 1936, Averill Harriman, president of the Union Pacific Railroad, had started developing the area into an all-year-round resort, and, encouraged by agents hired to publicise the venture, was now inviting his more famous friends to sample its delights. There were shops, restaurants, a heated swimming pool, hotels and a number of Swiss-style chalets; and in nearby Ketchum a roulette wheel. But there were still very few people. Hemingway, with his fame and his love of fishing and hunting, was the ideal guest.

By the middle of August 1939, Hemingway had written 76,000 words of his Spanish novel, while the first draft of Martha's book was done, though she worried about how to prevent it becoming too bleak 'because it must be kept varied, light and dark, and it is only a dark story'. She had found a title, A Stricken Field, from a medieval chronicle of battle that Hemingway had been reading. Sending one copy of her manuscript to her mother and another to Hortense Flexner for safekeeping, repeating to both of them, as she always did at this stage in a book, that it still needed many months of rewriting, Martha agreed to accompany Hemingway to Sun Valley. After a miserable holiday in Wyoming with Pauline and the boys, Hemingway had announced that he wanted a divorce; he and Martha talked about marrying in the spring. Both of them needed a break.

They arrived late at night along the dusty, unmade roads in his black open Buick, packed high with guns, fishing rods and books, and were given Suite 206, one of the more luxurious rooms, with open fireplaces and views over the mountains. For the next six weeks they settled into an agreeable routine, writing until midday, then taking a bottle of wine and some sandwiches before going riding, shooting or playing tennis. Martha became a 'devotee of the horse' and Hemingway taught her how to shoot. She made friends with Tillie Arnold, wife of the resort's official photographer, who was soon describing her as a 'barrel of fun and sharp as a tack'.

In October, when early snow speckled the higher mountains, Collier's asked Martha to go to Finland to write about the threat of Russian invasion. With Leningrad twenty miles from the Finnish border, Stalin had decided to expand west and was now demanding territorial rights. Martha, not yet the experienced foreign reporter she was keen to appear, was not even quite certain where Finland was. Tillie Arnold would later tell reporters that she had urged Martha to turn down the assignment in order to stay with Hemingway, but that Martha had told her she wanted it more than anything in the world. Though towards the end of her life Martha admitted to a friend she had accepted principally because it gave her a chance to get away from Hemingway, this was with the hindsight of a failed relationship. More likely, as she told her mother at the time, this 'dull assignment in the frozen north' was a way of finding herself again as a reporter and of making some money. After she left, Hemingway rechristened their suite 'Hemingstein's Mixed Vicing and Dicing Establishment' and turned it over to games of craps and poker. He told friends that he was 'stinko deadly lonely' without her.

On 10 November, having to cancel a dinner party at the White House at the last minute, Martha boarded the *Westenland*, a Dutch ship carrying wheat to Belgium. There were just forty-five passengers on board, rather than the full complement of 544, and Allen Grover, her friend from *Time*, saw her off, having provided her with letters of introduction to various *Time* employees in the European offices. She also carried with her a letter from Roosevelt, written on green paper and addressed to American foreign service officials asking them to assist her. Writing to thank Grover, Martha reported that her bunk had clearly been constructed for pygmies, and her mattress stuffed with nails, but that, far worse than the Arctic temperature of her cabin, the revolting food and the lack of all exercise, was the boredom. The 'happy family' of forty-five had yielded only one friend, a nephew of the art historian Bernard Berenson. If the ship were interned, as the last one doing the same run had been, she would certainly prefer to die. Her war aim was simple, she wrote: 'Come home quick.'

When, after ten tedious days, the *Westenland* reached British coastal waters, it paused in order not to cross the heavily mined Channel by night, since another Dutch ship, with six hundred passengers on board, had struck mines the previous day and blown up. From the deck, Martha watched the mines bobbing about, and caught sight of some of the bodies still floating in the water. In another letter to Grover she remarked that she was far too stupefied with boredom and insomnia to feel afraid, and that in any case she didn't have the kind of imagination to experience fear before anything happened. She had spent part of the trip thinking about the war, and had realised that in order to stay sane she would have to suspend all feeling and turn herself into 'a walking tape-recorder with eyes'.

From Belgium she flew to Stockholm and then on to Helsinki, reaching her hotel, already sealed in blackout paper, in the absolute dark of a far northern winter afternoon. Apart from the unrelenting cold – which Martha loathed with more than usual vehemence – she quickly found much to admire in Finland. The Finns struck her as steady and stoical, and as she watched mothers packing their children off on buses to places of safety in the forests, without fuss, it made her marvel again at the resilience of ordinary people at times of war.

At three o'clock on her first afternoon, despite a curtain of fog, the Russians attacked. Planes came in low over Helsinki and bombed four blocks of flats. There were shouts that the clouds of smoke rising from the burning buildings were poison gas and Martha found herself running through the streets with an Italian aviator who had fought in Abyssinia and with the fascists in Spain. Her first sight of a dead body, a 'shapeless and headless' man, his leather shoes neatly mended, reminded her of the 'small man with rope soled shoes' whose corpse she had seen in the street in Madrid.

'It is going to be terrible,' she wrote to Hemingway, 'the people are marvellous, with a kind of pale frozen fortitude. They do not cry out and they do not run; they watch with loathing but without fear this nasty hidden business which they did nothing to bring on themselves.' Missing him, telling him how she loved him, she said that she felt very alone, and that none of the journalists in Finland was particularly sympathetic. It was raining, and the white fog had settled over the city. One day she had the satisfaction of being taken close to the front line at Karelia – her letter from Roosevelt giving her unique access – where she watched the soldiers, camouflaged in white and on skis, preparing for a surprise pincer attack on the Russian lines. She was greatly enjoying her sense of being different – 'snotty and superior' as she reported to Hemingway – and when Geoffrey Cox of the *Daily Express* was detailed to wake her one night because the journalists were being evacuated in anticipation of a Russian bombardment, she told him to leave her alone. Cox, recalling the scene almost sixty years later, remembered how very glamorous she looked asleep in a pale yellow silk nightdress, and how very firm she had been that she preferred to stay where she was. Before he had even left the room, she had turned over and was asleep again. To Hemingway, she wrote scornfully: 'My God, if they begin being scared pissless of probable dangers now, what are they going to do later when it really breaks loose on them?' Hemingway had trained her well. He now wrote proudly to Max Perkins that Martha might not be the best military reporter, but 'boy she got out to that front when not a single correspondent had been there'.

Soon, Martha was filing her own kind of stories back to *Collier's*, descriptions of staunch civilians, small boys who showed nothing but anger, women who volunteered for all the auxiliary jobs. 'If people wept in Finland,' she wrote about seeing villages and the forest in flames, 'they would be weeping for the waste and cruelty of this: but would not be weeping from fear.' When the skies cleared and the sirens sounded, she was hurried off together with the others to take refuge in the forests, where her fur-lined gloves, leather jacket and heavy fur coat did little to keep out the cold. She longed to be back in the warmth of Cuba, in touch again with Hemingway's Spanish novel, with which she felt herself to be deeply involved. 'This book is what we have to base our lives on,' she wrote. 'The book is what lasts after us and makes all this war intelligible . . . And as I love you I love your work and as you are me your work is mine.' She asked him to take care of her mother for her, 'because she is ours too, like the book, something we have to take care of together', and she begged him 'let's never never leave each other again'. Whenever they were apart, Martha seemed to remember only the good times. To Edna, she wrote that she was feeling fat and ugly and old-looking and that she had reached saturation point with her reporting of the Finnish war.

But there was no simple way to leave Helsinki, now that

the war had begun, and she grew restless and bored. The optimism of the Spanish days had left her, and she felt only resigned and weary. When she ran into Frank Haynes, an American military attaché, in a restaurant one day and he asked her whether she would like a flight out, she jumped up, called out 'Christ, yes' and flew to her hotel to pack. From Sweden she sent Hemingway a telegram: 'Happy New Year and all of it together beloved.' She broke her journey in Paris, having heard that Gustav Regler had been interned as an enemy alien in a French prison, and tried in vain to use her good contacts to get him released. Then she pressed on. She paused again in Washington to describe to Roosevelt the fortitude of the Finns and to urge him to send help. 'It is my sort of repayment to these people for their goodness to me,' she explained, 'and their elegance and courage in undertaking this war rather than be kicked around.' The Czechs, she continued to say, ought to have stood and fought.

On 19 January she reached Cuba. That same day, she drafted a humorous and somewhat poignant letter. 'I, the undersigned, Mrs Martha Wasp Fathouse Pig D. Bongie Hemingstein,' she wrote, 'hereby guarantee and promise never to brutalise my present and future husband in any way whatsoever, neither with weapons nor pointed instruments, nor words, nor uncalculated sudden phrases nor looks . . . I promise equally to cherish him, and not only to cherish him so that I know it . . . and that also I recognise that a very fine and sensitive writer cannot be left alone for two months and sixteen days.' She signed it 'Martha Gellhorn Hemingway'. Eight large mauve orchids had sprouted on the trunk of the ceiba tree, and she had become, she wrote to Charles Colebaugh, 'wondrously fat'. 'It is perhaps wrong to be so happy in this present world, but my God how I love this place and how happy I am.'

*　*　*

Soon after Martha got back to the Finca, Hemingway told her that he intended to let his hair grow until his Spanish novel was finished. No doubt in part a genuine desire to focus his mind on the need to press on to the end, this was also an excellent way to tease Martha, who continued to object to his general grubbiness and air of mess. Twenty-three chapters were already written, well over half the book's final length, and a title had been chosen, after some thirty had been tried and rejected. Leafing through the Bible, Shakespeare and the *Oxford Book of English Prose*, Hemingway had come upon Donne's Meditation 'No man is an island'. He had been taken by the line 'never send to know for whom the bells tolls; it tolls for thee' and had written to Max Perkins proposing the middle phrase, asking for reassurance that people would not think of 'tolls as long distance charges and of Bell as the Bell telephone system?' Perkins cabled back that the 512 pages he had read so far were 'magnificent strange and new' and that the title was beautiful. 'I am so damn happy with Marty,' Hemingway told him, 'that it seems that it made everything work better. Sort of as though there were a lot of you that never was really used before and that is all working now. I'm a damned lucky bastard to be alive.'

The weather in Cuba was exceptionally cold and Hemingway had taken to writing his book in bed. In the afternoons, they resumed their games of tennis, and once a week, usually on Sunday, they spent a long evening drinking hard with the Basque pelota players at the Floridita, Hemingway justifying these binges by saying that he needed to let off steam after the sustained daily labour of writing. Martha reported to Hortense Flexner one morning that she was still recovering from a 'wonderful drunk' the previous night, in which they had sung their way happily through the streets of Havana with a stranger from Miami and a French whore, and that it had lasted until five-thirty that morning. Martha herself was capable of heavy drinking, but never in a sustained or serious way; she felt too ill the next morning and there was in any case something in the loss of control that repelled her, both in others and in herself. Allen Grover, with whom her affair had turned naturally into an affectionate friendship, came to stay and impressed the Basques with his tennis and Hemingway with his 'splendidly constructed' physique.

In March, Hemingway's three sons arrived in Cuba for a visit. It was their first meeting with Martha since her visit to Key West with Edna and Alfred in December 1936. Martha wrote with delight to Hortense that she was revelling in having become an instant mother of three, all of whom were 'as funny as their papa'. Bumby, at sixteen the eldest and taller than Hemingway, had a 'body like something the Greeks wished for'; Patrick, who was eleven, was a keen reader and compared all his books in size to *The Green Hills of Africa*; and Gigi, now eight, was a passionate dice player. All three were good shots and eager fishermen and in the evening Hemingway and his sons did target practice on the negritos as they flew past on their way to spend the night in the laurel trees in Havana. One evening, on their urging, she shot a hawk and a black-bird 'in a very dégagée and confident manner'. The boys appeared fond of Martha, referring to her as 'The Marty', and they later remembered the way she treated them as equals, and though firm about discipline and manners, was also fair. 'I don't care about going to war now,' Hemingway wrote to Perkins. 'Would like to live a while and have fun after this book and write some stories. Also like the kids very much and we have good fun together. Also would like to have a daughter.'

That same month, *A Stricken Field*, Martha's novel about Czechoslovakia, was published. In 'My Day' Mrs Roosevelt called it a 'masterpiece'. Ostensibly, the book was about Europe's betrayal of the Czechs, but as Martha herself repeated in many letters to friends, it was also the book that she had wanted to write about the Spanish civil war. It told about how she had felt about the betrayal of the republicans, the death of Spanish friends, the destruction of the ideals born and nurtured during the months in Madrid – all transposed to Czechoslovakia. She remained obsessed by the idea that her generation had been deformed by what had happened in Spain, because it was in Spain that their hopes for a better world had been shattered; what she could not quite explain to anyone was why she had chosen not to give the book a Spanish setting.

Early reviews were tepid, critics remarking that the novel

was more like reporting than fiction, and that the story of a journalist trying to intervene on behalf of Czech refugees in a 'world hurrying between large disasters' was really only a portrait of Martha and her work for *Collier's*. In the *Saturday Review*, Marianne Hauser wished that the heroine had been 'less noble and more real'. They might have complained more vigorously had they fully taken in how faithfully Mary Douglas's appeal to Lord Balham to win a reprieve for the refugees mirrored Martha's own dealings with Sir Neill Malcolm. Later reviews were warmer, Lewis Gannet in the *Herald Tribune* saying that for all its unevenness, it was 'one of the powerful books of the year', and that in her picture of an American girl who wasn't afraid to try, 'there is a startling splash of sunlight'. Another reviewer called Martha 'Walt Whitman in a woman's dress'.

Whatever pleasure Martha might have taken in the praise – and, like many writers, she found praise very hard to hear – was destroyed by a malicious personal piece which appeared in the book pages of *Time*. Devoting a full half-page to an account of her life with Hemingway, and bringing in her friendship with the Roosevelts and Harry Hopkins, it was the first public exposure of Hemingway's separation from Pauline, who immediately threatened to keep the boys away from Cuba. Martha was outraged and dispatched a furious cable to Grover, now a senior editor on the magazine. This was just the beginning. Her next and many subsequent letters blamed him for his magazine's deviousness and accused him of leading their reporters to the story. To Mrs Roosevelt, apologising that her name should have been dragged in, she added defiantly, 'I intend to outlast *Time* and far outlast it.' Grover, who was not the culprit, infuriated Martha still further by making light of the scandal, which provoked her to fire off several more long and angry letters on the subject of loyalty and friendship. She minded, she told him, not so much for herself as for Hemingway, who was currently 'writing smoothly, with ease and magic and like an angel', turning out the 'finest novel any of us will read in this decade', saying that to upset him at such a time was a 'stinking crime'. 'I think it's barbarous,'

Martha wrote, 'and the mark of microscopic minds, to confuse the man and his works . . . I do not understand the mentality of people who want to ruin other people, unless the people they want to ruin are themselves destroyers.' She accused Grover of believing in *Time* in the same unquestioning way communists believed in the Party, and said that it was bad luck that her friend – implying a *real* friend – Tom Matthews had been away from the magazine at the time. She also demanded that it never happen again. Publicity had always made her uneasy; coming as it had, in the guise of a book review, was unpardonable. In the course of her life, Martha would shed several friends for lesser perceived crimes, but with Grover, after a number of tough letters, she pulled back from a final breach. 'Myself, I am just an individualist,' she concluded, at last running out of steam, 'and have always thought my friends, no matter who they were or how they lived . . . deserved my first loyalty. I am not a newspaperman, evidently.' She was mollified by steadily improving reviews, and a cable from Scribners telling her that *A Stricken Field* had been taken by one of America's leading book clubs.

'She was afraid,' Martha has Mary Douglas think to herself early in the novel, 'she would be reporting disaster and defeat her whole life.' Hemingway was now urging her to take on less bleak subjects and Martha wrote to Colebaugh at *Collier's* suggesting that one way to avoid being branded as a 'disaster-girl', a writer who not only was blind to everything else, but even seemed to invent catastrophes, would be for her to write about America and subjects 'which are cheerful . . . written gaily and happily'. She proposed to join local rabbit hunts and swimming parties and lodge dances, and perhaps write about Ketchum and the arrival of the very rich in Sun Valley. It was one of the last times she would feel able to write of her country that 'we are the last large so-called civilised country on earth with a lot to save and a lot to lose'. Colebaugh was not impressed. His reply, though humorous, was firm. 'You say you're having a swell time . . . but we are people of action living in a great world and the life of the vegetable soon palls . . .' On the contrary, replied Martha, the life of the vegetable was exactly what everyone was looking for; she signed her letter 'the lucky vegetable'.

Just the same, she was restless. Hemingway remarked that Martha was like a racehorse with just two speeds, either running away or asleep. She began to spend her mornings doing what she called 'five-finger exercises', which meant practising the kind of writing she believed she was worst at – dialogue, humour and sex – by setting down brief pictures of something she remembered or observed. To Grover, with whom she was again on affectionate terms, she said that she had taught herself to write about landscape and country this way, so why not sex? Soon, the exercises began to turn into stories, even if some of them remained little more than descriptions – of a drunken evening with the pelota players in Havana, of a walk in Madrid during the civil war – with an emotional charge to lend some bite. But two are revealing, both for their content and their edgy tone. 'Portrait of a Lady' is a bitter tale about an attractive American reporter who seduces a heroic Finnish aviator, only to find herself discarded with disdain. The second of the longer stories is 'Good Will to Men', in which the heroine – another American woman reporter – travels home to the States from an assignment in Finland, stopping in Paris where she hopes to persuade influential friends to intervene on behalf of a sick, interned, former soldier with the International Brigades, unmistakably a portrait of Gustav Regler, now confined in a French camp and ill. What stands out about both stories, apart from the fact that they are so largely autobiographical, is the nastiness of the characters and the unpleasant taste they leave in the mouth. Six years of observing and writing about the suffering of powerless people had left Martha with profound misgivings about the selfishness of those with power.

Some time during the spring of 1940, Hemingway bought a radio so that he and Martha would 'get our disasters shrieked fresh and on the minute' without waiting for the newspapers to arrive by the mail boats. Martha, in particular, wanted to follow the war in Europe and tried to persuade an increasingly reluctant Hemingway to involve himself in world affairs; but Hemingway found the daily bulletins intrusive and finally banned the radio from the house altogether saying that he wanted no news until his book was finished, and the war would still be there waiting for him. She found his detachment irritating and though she greatly admired the bits of the book he had allowed her to look at, she complained that he was like an animal with his work, keeping it hidden away in a drawer. Evidently there had been difficulties between them, for Hemingway wrote her a long letter of apology for having been 'thoughtless, egotistic, mean-spirited and unhelpful' over the past eighteen months, putting it down to pressures of the book, and telling her that he would absolutely understand if she decided that she didn't want to go ahead with their marriage. It was a generous letter. 'Much love from your Bongie,' he wrote at the end, 'who loves you and who understands whatever you want to do even if you don't want to marry him. Although I'll swear Bongie that if you do I will bore you less and amuse you more . . . I only brag when I am on my ass.'

In June, Martha took off for New York, saw her friends and her publishers, and lunched with Allen Grover. She was there at the fall of France and talked gloomily about 'those goddam maniac bastards' destroying the beauty of Paris. When she returned to Cuba, after a few nights in the White House, she took with her Edna, who liked Hemingway and got on well with him. They went out on the *Pilar*, and one day saw a rare whale shark, as big as the boat, which swam alongside as 'if something from the Smithsonian woke up and began plodding around the ocean'. Martha reported happily to Hortense Flexner that as the days passed her mother looked better and younger and happier than at any time since her father had died; she said that she now felt in an odd way as if she were the older of the two, and tougher in the sense that she was less startled by evil, and 'not being a very good person myself I can take a lot of non-good'. There was one outburst, when Hemingway failed to turn up for dinner and Martha stormed into the bar in Havana where he was drinking and bawled him out for keeping Edna waiting, but Cuba had rarely seemed to her such an agreeable and tranquil place, nor her need to live a simple and private life more acute.

In September, Hemingway went alone to New York to prepare for the publication of *For Whom the Bell Tolls*. Scribners had cleared their shop windows on Fifth Avenue and given the entire space over to a display of his work, and the first printing of 75,000 was already sold out by the time he arrived. Maria's blonde hair, 'like a wheatfield in the wind', was perceived to be very like Martha's own, but in all other ways Hemingway's modest and compliant heroine could not be mistaken for the assertive and independent Martha. There were offers from Hollywood for the film rights, and at some point there was even talk of Martha – to whom, together with Herbert Matthews, the book was dedicated – taking the part of Maria. The *New York Times Book Review*, in a front-page article, called it the 'best, deepest, and truest book' that Hemingway had written. Only a small number of communist reviewers attacked the book, accusing Hemingway of exploiting the loyalist cause. His old friend Alvah Bessie was one of three veterans of the Abraham Lincoln Brigade who signed an open letter denouncing him for 'mutilating' the cause of democracy by slandering André Marty, maligning La Pasionaria and exaggerating the influence of the Soviet Union on the republicans. None of this had a negative effect on sales. As Hemingway wrote to his first wife, Hadley, 'book selling like frozen Daiquiris in hell'. From Martha, still in Cuba, came loving letters, saying she felt that the two of them were now like 'peas in a pod', and that it felt lonely and very chilly without him.

In the autumn of 1940, taking the boys with them, Martha and Hemingway returned to Sun Valley. The mountains looked to Martha like lion skin and had a cool blonde light hanging over them. Hemingway, liberated from his book, organised daily expeditions along the creeks and up into the mountains. Locals referred to him fondly as the 'General'. Bumby fished 'as if the whole fate of mankind depended on it', Gigi was a boy clearly 'geared to get on', but twelve-year-old Patrick was the boy whose character most intrigued Martha. To Max Perkins, she wrote that he would certainly go somewhere, and that wherever that was it would be 'a place to envy . . . a fine ungrabby certain kind of place'. She thought they were 'rare' boys, borrowing a word that Hemingway had used all the time in his novel, and said that Hemingway had a huge talent for being a father, bringing them up with 'genius and not obeying any of the rules'. For their part, the boys seemed increasingly attached to her, finding that her naturalness with children made her an easy companion. Many years later, Bumby told a reporter that she was the first 'attractive lady I ever heard use the "f" word'.

They were joined at Sun Valley by Dorothy Parker and her husband, with whom they played tennis, and by Gary Cooper, who had starred in the 1932 film version of *A Farewell to Arms*. There was talk that he might now take the part of Robert Jordan in the proposed film version of *For Whom the Bell Tolls*. There had also been rumours that Dorothy Parker might write the script, but Hemingway had never liked her writing; Ingrid Bergman was now being suggested for Maria, and Martha wrote to Hortense Flexner that if 'Greta were a braver actress I think she might do Pilar, without eyelashes, but with all the strength there is in her, unused and never to be used'. Martha went on loving the untouched country all around, and the local people, whom she considered to be 'individuals without being Dali', but she found the 'famous folk . . . a pain in the ass', and was appalled by their constant talk of box office returns. 'I begin to feel my family is directly descended from Martin Luther,' she wrote to Max Perkins, 'as I get angrier and angrier about such idiocies.' She was maliciously delighted when Cooper's wife, Rocky, told her how much she sympathised with the central character in Henry James's *The Portrait of a Lady*. 'Having a living bitch meet a fictional bitch and feel the sisterhood at once, is my idea of doing a good job.' Martha decided to divide up the 'movie element' around her into the 'good' and the 'intolerable' and one night lectured them all, after a prolonged bout of heavy drinking, which often made her extremely bossy, on the evils of Hollywood for serious writers. Money was about to start pouring in for the film rights of *For Whom the Bell Tolls*, and she and Hemingway agreed that there was very little they actually wanted to spend it on, other than a new ice box for Cuba, some binoculars and a sleeping bag. If she was jealous of Hemingway's huge success, she showed no sign of it.

For all her protestations about a peaceful life, however, Martha had no talent for being a happy vegetable. With France now partly in German hands, with the Italians entering the war, and with the British enduring nightly bombing raids, she longed to be in Europe. 'Oh Hell and Highwater,' she wrote to John Gunther. 'How I wish I were a journalist again . . . that life of rushing and asking questions, trying to tell the liars from the ones who maybe know the facts . . . Sun Valley is a kind of Shangri-La, without the Tibetan odors. (But where I want to be, boy, is where it is all blowing up.)' To Grover, she wrote that she so hated 'not to be part of history (I don't want to be elected or anything or mentioned in the papers, I just want to be where history is happening, to see it, to know about it for myself, to do whatever small goofy usually futile thing I can do in order to make some minor events easier for unknown people.)'

News of Hemingway's uncontested divorce from Pauline on grounds of desertion came through on 4 November, and Robert Capa arrived soon after to take photographs of them for *Life*. They show Martha, her hair windswept, wearing a slightly rueful smile, in various different sporting settings, often in shorts, her long legs stretched out, and they caught a look somewhere between happiness and self-mockery. Martha told Hortense Flexner that being engaged gave her a feeling of permanent youth, and her new diamond and sapphire ring was 'snappy as hell'. 'Scroob says, you might almost say that people who haven't at least started a baby before they're married are slackers,' she wrote. '(Don't get any ideas. I want to go to the wars.)' Perhaps reflecting on the unpleasantness of Hemingway's divorce from Pauline, she seemed rather unsure about the marriage itself, writing to Grover, 'I would rather sin respectably, any day of the week . . . Allen, it's awful, isn't it, the way you can make someone pay you in stocks and bonds and furniture and Christ knows what all, for not loving you. I thought if people stopped loving you, you went into a corner like a sick animal and held yourself very tight, so as not to break . . . Myself, whatever grand things I have gotten from men, I did not consider that you could deposit any of it in a bank: since when can pain be paid for in dollars? . . . I like it better clean: I think sin is very clean . . . There is all the deadly obligation of one human being to another, but there is no insurance. You are probably less free, socially, but anyhow you feel awful simple and straight in your heart.' Her misgivings upset Hemingway, who wrote her a brief note one day about her ratting on their plans, and giving him a 'good sound busted heart'. The moment passed. Edna, also clearly very anxious about the marriage, tried hard to persuade them to wait until they were quite certain; but by now the train was moving.

On 21 November, in the dining room of the Union Pacific Railroad at Cheyenne in Wyoming, Martha and Hemingway were married. Martha was thirty-two, Hemingway forty. There was an affectionate telegram from the Roosevelts, and several newspapers carried the story, listing Martha's achievements as a writer and adding that she had been married once before, to Bertrand de Jouvenel. One reporter called it a 'pairing of flint and steel'. 'Ernest and I belong tightly to each other,' Martha told Mrs Roosevelt. 'We are a good pair and we are both crazy about being married.' Scott Fitzgerald, on hearing of the event, remarked that it was very odd to think of Hemingway married to a 'really attractive woman. I think the pattern will be some-what different than with his Pygmalion-like creations.' After the short ceremony, they ate roast moose for dinner.

* * *

Many years later, when Martha was approaching seventy, she wrote a book about the horror journeys of her life, *Travels with Myself and Another*. It is the funniest of her books, full of comic stories of punishing discomfort, embarrassing situations, paralysing boredom, excruciating delays and bitter and heartfelt clashes between travellers condemned to share ghastly experiences in some foreign and distant land. Perhaps the most comic expedition of all is an account of a trip to China with Hemingway, very soon after they got married, which he insisted on referring to as their honeymoon. The three months she spent in the Far East, Martha later said, taught her a new lesson about war, and about what utter hell it was for all the people who were not fighting. What is most memorable about 'Mr Ma's Tigers', her chapter on their journey, is its affectionate, appreciative and self-mocking tone. Given that biographers have tended to paint Martha's relationship to Hemingway as quarrelsome and exploitative, it is an agreeable and wholly convincing account of shared laughter.

At *Collier's* Colebaugh had asked Martha to go to China, Hong Kong, Singapore, the Dutch East Indies and Burma to report on the 'Chinese army in action' and assess the state of the British defences against future Japanese attacks, now that Japan had joined the Axis powers. She was to start on the Burma Road, the 715-mile track that connected Kunming in China to Lashio in Burma, along which travelled the only supplies into China. She had never been to the Far East, but had filled her mind with imaginary pictures of the Orient ever since childhood; and she was anxious to keep paying her way as a journalist. 'I am going to the Burma Road,' she wrote to Averill Harriman, 'isn't it a miracle?' Hemingway, who was just beginning to enjoy the success of his book, was not so certain, but agreed to do part of the trip with her and write some articles for *PM* magazine, the American publication having become more interested in the area since the passing of the Lend-Lease Act in 1941, which authorised Roosevelt to provide equipment to any nation 'whose defense the President deems vital to the defense of the United States'. In 1937, Henry Luce, who had been born in China of missionary parents, had put Chiang Kai-shek and his wife, who were Christians, on the cover of *Time* as Man and Wife of the Year, and the

Generalissimo, desperate to shore up central government against insurrection while ostensibly bent on defeating the Japanese, was now making ever more exigent demands on America.

Martha went to Washington to arrange visas, stayed at the White House, collected a number of introductions to useful contacts, and had her typhoid injections. Before joining Hemingway in Havana, she spent a fortnight with her mother in St Louis, where she gave a talk on individual freedom to the pupils of her old school, John Burroughs. She was home in time to see through the purchase of the Finca Vigía, for $12,500, using some of the huge sums from sales of *For Whom the Bell Tolls*, and from the film rights, for which David O. Selznick had offered $100,000. Hemingway and Martha flew to Hollywood to talk to Gary Cooper and Ingrid Bergman about their possible roles, and were invited to a banquet to listen to Cecil B. de Mille speak; and early in February boarded the *Matsonia* in San Francisco for Honolulu. Martha, still obsessed by news of the war, was almost desperate to get back to active work, writing later that she had felt 'a driving sense of haste: hurry, hurry, hurry before it's too late . . .'.

The tribulations which would years later make such splendid copy started soon after the *Matsonia* cleared the harbour. Martha and Hemingway had been pleasurably imagining all the stylish luxury of prewar cruises: what they got was a dismal ship, high seas and the rolling motion of a dolphin which, as Martha remarked, was fine in a dolphin but terrible in a ship. They were shuttled about like ping-pong balls, and finally took to their berths and lay there drinking. Hemingway complained that if anyone had warned him about the Pacific, he certainly would not have come. When they reeled off the boat in Honolulu, eighteen garlands of flowers, one after the other, were strung around the neck of a by now snarling Hemingway, 'grinning like a wolf with bared fangs'. 'The next son of a bitch who touches me,' he told Martha, 'I am going to cool him.' The ship was met by Hemingway's aunt who took them to lunch; there was nothing to drink and Martha began to think she was going to faint with boredom. In Pearl Harbor, they were shown warships 'nudging each other', and planes parked 'wing-tip to wing-tip'. Hemingway gave a number of interviews, drinking rather too much in order to calm himself, and sounding like a character from his own books.

When they arrived at their old-fashioned hotel on the seafront in Hong Kong, with paddle fans and antique bathrooms, their spirits lifted. Martha thought of Somerset Maugham's stories of colonial life. Hemingway quickly settled down to the sort of life he most enjoyed, gathering about him a group of jovial hangers-on, with whom, over a good deal of drink, he could swap stories and laugh. He arranged to go pheasant shooting in the hills. Despite the war between China and Japan, now in its fourth year, acute overcrowding, shortage of food and a cholera epidemic, the colony was flourishing, with rugby and cricket matches most days and smart, well-attended race meetings. Martha called it a 'continuous circus'. She preferred to gather material her own way, and set off with her notebook, filling it with snatches of conversation, odd sights, facts, details, figures, and taking, as Hemingway put it, the 'pulse of the nation'.

The Chinese National Aviation Company (CNAC) had a contract to fly money and important passengers between the part of China not occupied by Japan and the outside world. To avoid Japanese attack, the planes, piloted by a collection of eccentric Americans, flew over the Japanese lines by night and very high. At 4.30 on a freezing morning in March 1941, Martha joined a flight, leaving Hemingway, who was now enjoying himself greatly, with his pheasants. Her destination was the very end of the Burma Road, the nine-foot wide single-lane highway scratched out of the mountainsides by hand by 200,000 men, women and children, and her first impression of the Chinese National DC2 that was to fly her there was that it looked like a small beetle. After takeoff, cloud the consistency of thick cream gathered. At 14,000 feet, the plane bucked and the air speed dial froze, and the pilot was forced to open his window and peer out in an attempt to establish their speed, telling Martha that if it fell below 63 m.p.h. the plane would spin out of control. They passed through a storm, the hail pummelling the fuselage like a threshing machine, then emerged into bright sunlight. On both journeys, out and back, they landed at Kunming, where the airfield was routinely bombed by the Japanese. Martha returned safe and elated to Hong Kong, and sent off a first piece to *Collier's* about the service, and the extraordinary pilots who kept it open. She found Hemingway surrounded by his new buddies, boxing, enjoying Chinese food and practising Chinese English, and delighted by a supply of firecrackers which he let off in their room.

At this stage, Martha was also having if not a good time, an extremely interesting one. Her idea of taking the pulse of the nation was to do so, as she put it, from the bottom. Leaving Hemingway sparring with his buddies, she set out to explore dance halls, markets, factories, brothels and an opium den, where she found a girl of fourteen with a pet tortoise filling the pipes. Everywhere she went, she made notes about what the people ate and earned, how they lived and what things cost. 'There is a very good story right here,' she wrote to Colebaugh. 'The city is jammed, half a million extra Chinese refugees. It is rich and rare and startling and complicated . . .' She was overcome by the sheer number of people, the squatters living in the streets, the small children working in terrible conditions and her next piece for *Collier's*, 'Time Bomb in Hong Kong', carried a note of urgency. Hemingway told her that her problem was that she saw everything through her own eyes; what was hell for her was not necessarily hell for others. Hemingway himself was more concerned about the cholera, particularly after an apparently drunken woman staggered in front of them in the street before collapsing, vomiting blood, and he now insisted on double injections against all possible diseases. 'Life is awful jolly,' Martha wrote to Alexander Woollcott, the critic and a founding member of the Algonquin Hotel Round Table, whom she had met in the White House. 'Ernest goes about really learning something about the country and I go about dazed and open mouthed. Everything smells terrific. I have never been happier, only a little weary.' Simply being on the move was enough to keep her mood buoyant.

Permission at last came for them to travel to the front line, where the Japanese offensive, after its earlier victories in the east, had come to a halt before China's rugged mountains, in spite of a vastly better equipped army. Martha bought Keating's Flea and Lice Powder, disinfectant, mosquito nets and thermos flasks. Their interpreter was a Mr Ma, a small, round man with a round nose and round glasses and a maddening smile. Together with Mr Ho, who was in charge of transport, they set out across the Seventh War Zone, which covered an area the size of Belgium. There were no roads. The footpath along which they drove was a river of treacherous mud; a fine rain fell; the wind blew. There were frequent stops for courtesy calls on military establishments and local dignatories, during which Martha, as a woman, was expected to remain silent, and Hemingway made speeches.

From Shaokwan, in an ancient truck with four teenaged soldiers to guard them from bandits, they bumped and jolted their way to the river, where they boarded a derelict Chriscraft. Since there was no cabin they sat perched on coiled ropes, while the many other passengers hawked and spat and Martha retched. The towrope, with which they were pulling a crowded sampan, snapped, and they were forced to moor for the night; at daybreak they caught sight of a black flag flying, the sign of a cholera epidemic. After the river, they moved on to ponies, so small that Hemingway pointed out that he could walk and ride at the same time. The ponies kicked and squealed and tried to bite the coolies; in her notebook Martha wrote down that they were 'obstinate, iron-mouthed and mean natured', that this was clearly the mosquito centre of the world, and that the rain was now driving across 'the face of flat carved green furred mountains' both ways at once, so that you got wet in front and behind. She asked Mr Ma what the trees were. 'Ordinary trees,' he replied.

They visited barracks, parade grounds, and a cadet school, where they found portraits of Goering, Mussolini and Chamberlain, and at one stop were greeted by a banner: 'Welcome to the Representatives of Righteousness and Peace.' 'Soldiers,' noted Martha, 'always look like sad orphanage boys'; they wore cotton uniforms and were clearly hungry. In some units, they had one blanket for every five men.

At night, they slept in their wet clothes on board beds, dozed until six, and pushed on, with occasional pauses for boiled hot water but no food. Martha asked Mr Ma why the hills were all burnt black. 'They do that to get rid of the tigers,' he told her. 'Tigers, Mr Ma?' 'Yes, many, more or less . . . tigers eat some kind of tender little roots and sweet grasses, and when it is all burned, they get hungry and go away.' One day Hemingway's horse fell over. Hemingway picked it up and started walking with it. 'Put that horse down,' said Martha. 'You're insulting the Chinese.' The rain went on. There were more parade grounds. The whisky ran out. One night, lying on a board in her wet clothes, fighting off mosquitoes and flies, Martha said to Hemingway: 'I wish to die.' 'Too late,' he replied. 'Who wanted to come to China?'

And so it continued, more rain, more speeches, more entertainments, more slogans. They decided that the one they liked best was: 'Democracy only survives Civilisation.' At one point a full-scale mock battle was staged for them, and a banquet held at which they ate sea slugs. Mr Ma told them a story about eight girls who had been raped by the Japanese. 'Since village girls are very particular about their virginity, they resisted furiously. But they were nuded and very seriously raped.' By now they were drinking the local rice wine, a 'menacing pink colour, thickish, slimy'. One evening, about to pour herself a glass from the stone jug, Martha heard something scrape along the bottom. It turned out to be a snake, the local delicacy. There was also bird wine, which contained cuckoos. Back on the Chriscraft at last for the return journey, roosting like chickens on greasy bunks she had covered in Keating's Powder, Martha shouted to Hemingway over the roar of the motor: 'The worst is over.' 'You go on hoping,' said Hemingway. 'They say hope is a natural human emotion.' The following night thirty feet of a stout steel cable wrapped itself round the Chriscraft propeller. They were held up again in Kweilin, in the Palace Hotel, where the lavatory had long since overflowed, bedbugs crept around the board beds and

Hemingway said that had he had his gun, he would have shot them. Martha wrote to her mother: 'China has cured me. I never want to travel again . . . The real life of the East is agony to watch and horror to share.'

In Chungking, China's wartime capital, where they were stranded next, Martha noticed that the skin between her fingers seemed to be rotting and oozing yellow pus and blood. A doctor told her that it was a particularly virulent fungus, not unlike athlete's foot, and he gave her a foul-smelling cream to put on, adding that she should wear gloves at all times. From then on, she walked around in large white gloves, while Hemingway kept as far away from her as he could. 'Honest to God, M. You brought this on yourself. I told you not to wash.' It was in Chungking, a city described by Hemingway as 'grey, shapeless, muddy, a collection of drab cement build-ings and poverty shacks', humid in summer, muddy the rest of the year, and at all times dirty, smelly and rat-infested, that they lunched, alone, with the Generalissimo and Madame Chiang Kai-shek. The Generalissimo had no teeth and they were later told that it was a great honour to be received by him without his dentures. They were also led, in great secrecy, to meet Zhou Enlai, founder member of the Chinese Communist Party, hiding in the city, about whom neither knew anything, but who was the one Chinese they met who they felt at home with. Hemingway later wrote a long, thoughtful appraisal of Chiang Kai-shek for Henry Morgenthau, Secretary of the Treasury, describing the hostility that existed between him and the communists, and saying how charming, brilliant and able he and Martha had found Zhou Enlai. It was only later that Martha learnt that the meeting and the article had given them a reputation as fellow travellers of the left.

In Rangoon, after a last terrible flight, in which eighteen Chinese and the Chinese co-pilot were sick, she and Hemingway parted, he to go back to Hong Kong, she to visit military installations and to fly to the west coast of Burma, which she found 'hotter than the inside of a steam boiler'. 'I am lost without you,' wrote Hemingway to Martha at the end of a long letter about arrangements. 'Can't sleep, don't want to move; just straight aching miss you all the time. And with you I have so much fun even on such a lousy trip.' Still gathering material for *Collier's*, she stopped in Singapore, where she noted the wonderful luxury after the weeks of mud, endured a number of cocktail parties, wrote a long piece about the snobberies of British colonial life and wondered how they would all cope once their uniforms got dirty. The truth, she decided, was that Singapore was virtually defenceless while believing itself to be impregnable. She marvelled at the daily tea dances in Raffles Hotel and the way that everyone insisted on pretending that all was well. She then moved on to Guam and Manila, and some weeks later met Hemingway in June in New York. She had been on the road a little over three months, and put together two long pieces for *Collier's*. 'I felt it was pure doom to be Chinese,' she wrote later. 'I longed to escape from what I escaped into: the age old misery, filth, hopelessness, and my own claustrophobia inside that enormous country.' To Grover, she said that the people she had really disliked were the English: 'If you are not nuts for the English in England, you are close to vomiting over the English in the Orient.' Physically tough, certainly, and extremely uncomfortable, but when the long trip was recalled thirty years later, it was remembered as a time of happiness.

Their return was slightly spoiled by an altercation over their articles, Bill Chenery at *Collier's* accusing Hemingway of having 'scooped' Martha in his pieces for *PM*. Hemingway reacted with customary belligerence, blasting back: '. . . the only reason I went along was to look after Martha on a son of a bitching dangerous assignment in a shit filled country'. Peace was restored only after a letter came from Chenery assuring Martha that he had never intended to be 'disconcerting, insulting, imputing, chiding, up-braiding or even disesteeming . . .' When Hemingway had calmed down, he admitted to Chenery that part of his ill temper had stemmed from an absurd claim by a writer called John de Montijo that he had stolen the story of *For Whom the Bell Tolls* from an unpublished film script of his during a reading at a party in Hollywood.

Martha was not altogether pleased with everything she had written. Years later, she admitted that she had not been 'candid' when it came to her account of the meeting with the Generalissimo and his wife. She had known perfectly well at the time that Chiang Kai-shek's regime was brutal, corrupt and inefficient, and that he was more interested in making his own rule safe against insurrection than in pursuing the war against the Japanese. Far from admiring them in an unqualified way, as she had suggested, her chief impression of the Generalissimo and his wife had been one of ruthless determination. If anything, she found them 'inhuman' in their conversation. 'Madame Chiang that great woman and saviour of China. Well, balls,' she wrote to Grover. 'Madame Chiang is the Clare Booth of Cathay, different colouring, different set of circumstances. Perhaps more health and energy. But far far far from Joan of Arc . . .' What had prevented her from writing what she perceived as the truth was the fact that she had been a guest of theirs, she said, and like any guest she could not have the bad manners to criticise her hosts.

And so neither she – nor Hemingway – came clean about the brutality of the Chinese nationalists, though Hemingway did relate stories about graft and bribery among senior bureaucrats. The 'objectivity shit' had taken a new direction, and the whole question of how much can and ever should be written clearly troubled her, though not so uncomfortably as to force her to face up to it in print. 'There is so much shit written in our business,' she wrote in a long and revealing letter to Grover, soon after returning from the Far East, 'that finally you feel very ashamed: you cannot write the straight truth because people resent it, and are conditioned (by the shit) not to believe it. So, finally, you write a certain amount of evasion yourself, carefully shirking the definitely dung features of journalism . . . You have to be very young, very cynical and very ignorant to enjoy writing journalism these days.' She herself was no longer any of these things.

CHAPTER EIGHT

The Last Toughness of Youth

The only literary advice Martha ever received from H.G. Wells, she told her new editor Max Perkins not long after her return from China, was never to use commas unless there was no way of avoiding them. In Cuba, where she found the proofs of her collection of stories waiting, she discovered that they contained 'enough commas to sink a ship', and settled down to weed out all but the essential ones. She was pleased with her title for the book, *The Heart of Another*, taken rather surprisingly from a letter of Pauline's, in which she had written that the 'heart of another is a dark forest', a quotation she and Hemingway variously attributed to Dostoevsky or Turgenev (but was, in fact, by Willa Cather). She was equally pleased with Scribners as her new publishers, having cheerfully left Duell, Sloane and Pearce – referred to by Hemingway as Dull, Slum and Pus – and told Perkins that the stories were her most adult book so far and that they filled her with hope. By now she had extremely clear views about the appearance of her books, and warned Perkins that she had a horror of fussiness, and was waiting to vet the colour of the cloth for the binding, the jacket design, the blurb and the advertising copy. Hemingway had agreed to take photographs of her for the back jacket, and she reported that the first ones made her look 'Isadora Duncanish . . . with masses of wild hair and an expression of combined bewilderment and sunstroke'. He took a close interest in her hair, and wanted her to cut it straight, with a severe line of fringe, in the current Hollywood style.

The fishing expeditions on the *Pilar* resumed, and though

Martha felt 'pooped' after hours of bracing herself against the groundswell and driving rain, she watched one night with excitement as Hemingway fought but failed to land a two hundred-pound, eleven-foot-long marlin. Hemingway told Perkins that he was happy with Martha, that it was good to have both a loving wife and a sporting companion and that she had told him that she wanted to 'chuck correspondent's work now and stay home. But don't tell that to anyone.' With the pigeon shooters, Martha took to referring to herself as *'la fille du régiment'*.

In a long article about Hemingway published in the *New York Post* that spring, Earl Wilson described Martha as having a 'startlingly breezy manner'. Even though she had never met him, she called him 'Pal' and 'Mr W.' and when asked for an amusing anecdote about the writing of *For Whom the Bell Tolls* had replied: 'There's nothing very amusing about writing a book, you know, Mr W.' Hemingway himself told Wilson that the character of Robert Jordan was pure fiction – 'when you make it up, you have all the advantages of God' – and outlined his by now much quoted view of what made good writing: 'I take my example from the iceberg. It ought to be seven-eighths under water and one-eighth out. If you omit something you don't know, it shows, it's hollow. If you omit something you know, it's as though it's in.' The iceberg had become a rule in Martha's own writing. Hemingway was still being hounded about plagiarism over the book, and an article had appeared saying that he had submitted the film version to Franco for his approval. Fuming against these 'fools and crooks' and comparing their lies and 'cheap spirits' to Goebbels, Martha berated Hemingway's friends for not standing up for him in public. 'What's the matter with you people . . . Are both loyalty and truthfulness so outlawed that everyone must be mum despite such outrages?' That Martha herself was now something of a public figure is clear from an invitation she received in April asking her to speak on individual freedom in democracy at the Astor Hotel in New York, with Wendell Wilkie and Norman Thomas.

* * *

Martha had come back from China, her fourth war, increasingly confused about her own feelings on the fighting in Europe. 'I wonder all the time what sort of world is going to come out of this,' she wrote to Mrs Roosevelt. 'The great crime the Nazis have invented is this one of filling the world with hate, because the hate will stay like an infection in the blood, even after the killing is over.' Returning to her thoughts about the syphilitic families she met during her travels in the Depression, she speculated about whether there might be ways – short of extermination – of diluting blood on a national scale, so that what was dangerous was bred out. But as the weeks passed, and she and Hemingway settled back to their agreeable Cuban life, broken only by visits from friends, and late-night binges with the Basque pelota players, so a torpor of detachment seemed to settle on her. 'I find in myself a total inability to retain interest . . . right now it all sorta stinks . . .' she wrote to Allen Grover. 'Do you think it is possible after all these years of caring so intensely about how people live and how the world goes, to relapse into total cosmic indifference? . . . The glory and the faith have all gone, it seems to me: there is nothing now except the waste. Ah, balls. I don't want to think about it.' Both she and Hemingway were touchy about their failure to engage in the war, and quick to dash off prickly and defiant – and in Hemingway's case rather belligerent – replies to letters from friends asking them about their plans. It did not help to receive a jocular message from Charles Colebaugh asking Martha whether Hemingway was not 'champing at the bit? Does he smell fire and paw his stall at nights?'

In September, Hemingway set off ahead of her for their annual visit to Sun Valley, leaving her in 'bachelor splendor', as she told Hortense Flexner, and 'my Christ how I enjoy it'. Once again stupefied by a hangover after a night out in Havana 'drunk as a goat' with the pelota players and a 'whore who looked like a sharecropper's wife', she said that what she longed for was a life divided between absolute solitude in which to work, and a life 'almost explosive in its excitement, fierce and hard and laughing and loud and gay as all hell let loose'. 'I do not want to be good,' she wrote. 'Good is my idea of what very measly people are . . . I wish to be hell on wheels, or dead . . . Only a fool would prefer to be actively achingly dangerously unhappy, rather than bored: and I am that class of fool.' In this, she told Hortense, she was all too like Hemingway, and so, she added briskly and rather ominously, they were afraid of each other, 'each knowing that the other is the most violent person either one knows, and knowing something about violence we are always mutually alarmed at the potentialities of the other.' Her fear was that one of them might at any time burst into 'loud furious flame'.

Martha was beginning to turn against Sun Valley, where Averill Harriman's publicity deal had come to an end, and the Hemingways had moved to more modest rooms in the Challenger Inn, where Hemingway complained that the ducks on a nearby pond disturbed him. One day he took Martha and the boys to hunt antelope in the Pashimeroi Valley in eastern Idaho, where they rode through marvellous country full of ducks and shot jack rabbits, and where they felt far away from the blackness of the war. Still, Martha felt uncomfortable with the pointless round of social events, writing irritably that she hated the place 'like holy hell' and that it was 'the west in an ornamental sanitary package'. When a reporter phoned to ask her what she felt about being dropped from the 1942 Social Register, she replied sharply that it could not have mattered to her less. To Max Perkins she wrote that the stars were fine if you happened to like them, but that when it came to finding someone to talk to, the place was like a desert. 'Max,' she added, referring to Scott Fitzgerald, who she had met with Hemingway, 'Hollywood *ruined* Scott, unless he was terribly dead before.'

The Hemingways were still at Sun Valley when *The Heart of Another* was published, once again to mixed reviews. Several critics remarked on Martha's considerable talent for evoking scenes and emotions, but there was hardly one who failed to say that her stories were heavily influenced by Hemingway, who cast a 'Svengali spell' over her writing, and the *New Republic* objected that her style sometimes broke down 'through aping into mush'. Not one of them seems to have been unduly struck by the bleakness of the stories, most of which centre around loss and disillusion. She was delighted by the book's appearance, telling Perkins that for the first time in her life she had not felt sick, or disappointed, or full of regrets when the finished copy arrived. As for the criticism, 'finally (and after each new book again) the hell with it . . . We are still writing to fill a big waiting place in our own selves and lives: and for no reviewers and really no one.' 'Martha is fine and very beautiful and happy,' Hemingway told Charles Scribner towards the end of November.

On 3 December, Martha and Hemingway took off to see the Indian country in Arizona. Crossing the Texas border on their way to San Antonio, they stopped to drink daiquiris in a scruffy little bar. As they sat idly talking about raising cattle, a ragged Indian child came in selling newspapers, calling out: '*con la guerra, la guerra*'. They called him over and learned that the Japanese had bombed Pearl Harbor. Next day, America was at war. The last two years, E.B. White now wrote, had been time spent in a doctor's waiting room; everyone knew that it had to end, and were relieved when it did. 'It seemed a dreadful way for a great nation to get into a war,' wrote Martha, many years later. They set off back to spend Christmas in Cuba, with Hemingway's sons, Martha's friend Virginia Cowles and Howard Hawks and his wife. Bumby, now nineteen, was of an age to go to war.

For Whom the Bell Tolls had not won the Pulitzer Prize, as Hemingway had hoped, but it had already sold over half a million copies. Not yet ready to start work on another novel, anxious about future writing, and still extremely reluctant to engage in the war of which America was now a part, he started to collect stories and articles for a war anthology of the kind that he felt would have inspired him during the first war. He and Martha had both been intrigued by Madrid's Fifth Column and they now talked over the idea of setting up some kind of counter-intelligence group in Havana, where many of the large Spanish colony were openly anti-American and pro-Axis, 'violent Falangists'. With German submarines said to be sinking Allied tankers and cargo ships, and fishermen in the Gulf Stream reporting that they were surfacing to demand fresh water and fish, Hemingway proposed to recruit informers among his friends in the Havana bars. Rather more wildly, he also concocted a plan to equip the *Pilar* with bazookas, grenades and machine guns and to cruise off the shores of Cuba, pretending to be gathering scientific material for an American natural history museum, while in fact hunting Nazi submarines, with the idea of dropping grenades down their conning towers. Despite Martha's scepticism, Hemingway set about enlisting an eight-man crew of Catalans, Cubans, Spaniards and Americans, who shared, in some discomfort, the *Pilar*'s seven bunks, and persuaded the FBI, through their agent in Havana, Robert Leddy, and the new American ambassador to Havana, Spruille Braden, to contribute $500 a month to cover the expenses of the weapons and fourteen paid informers. He decided on the name 'Friendless' for the operation, after one of his favourite cats, but it was more often spoken of as the 'Crook Shop'.

Martha had always enjoyed the company of the exiled Basques, but as the Finca became the headquarters for the Crook Shop, with noisy drinking parties lasting far into most nights and the garden full of furtive looking strangers lurking behind the mango trees, she grew impatient, quick to quarrel with Hemingway, even about writing, a subject which more often united them. 'I'll show you, you conceited bitch,' Hemingway shouted at her one day. 'They'll be reading my stuff long after the worms have finished with you.'

Charles Colebaugh had been urging her to do more work for *Collier's*, but with the American military so totally opposed to women war correspondents, it had been hard to come up with a good subject which would not require their permission. When Colebaugh rather improbably suggested that she do a little submarine hunting of her own, travelling around the Caribbean and writing about preparations for war, she was delighted, and immediately began to study military and naval tactics and strategy, artillery, insignia and the geography of the islands. 'I am in a state of bliss,' she wrote to an old friend of Hemingway's, Bill Davis. 'I love the life of the wandering journalist very much.' She planned to take a number of 'clean and cool white dresses' with her, and Proust, whom she had still not managed to read. Isolation had been fine for a while, but now that it was coming to an end she felt nothing but relief. 'If you have no part in the world, no matter how diseased the world is, you are dead,' she wrote very late one night, unable to sleep. 'It is not enough to earn your living, do no actual harm to anyone, tell no lies . . . It is not enough. It is okay. It is not dirty. But it is dead.' She still believed that journalists changed nothing by their writing; but that, paraphrasing Donne, one could not, should not, stand outside history. 'I want,' she wrote, 'to be part of what happens to everyone.' Perhaps, too, she wanted a break from the quarrels, the now uncertain happiness; and flight, always, was her preferred solution.

Before she left, she wrote an acid attack on a pontificating French commentator for the *New Republic*, in which she returned to what would always now be one of her most passionate crusades: the villainy and stupidity of governments, and the sterling qualities of ordinary people. 'France,' she wrote, 'was always better than her rulers and still is . . . It is France that counts. Not the *couloirs* of Geneva and Paris, the wonderful eloquence without results, nor the Radical–Socialist conventions, nor poor Blum falling over himself and the Front Populaire . . . Our first step is to see that the people of France get France back; and after that we can pray that the best of them and the bravest and cleanest will rule it and keep it.'

Learning that Robert Capa, who as a Hungarian had been classified an enemy alien in the United States when Hungary declared war on the Allies, had been ordered to turn in all his photographic equipment to the police, Martha characteristically sent off urgent letters to all her friends in the administration, begging them to use their influence to help him. Capa, for whom this would have spelt an end to all his war photography, was desperate. Through Martha, J. Edgar Hoover arranged to have the cameras released and Capa was able to return to Europe.

And then she went on holiday to Florida with Edna, to swim off deserted beaches and stroll along the dunes watching the pelicans and dolphins. An order had gone out restricting private travel for civilians and she believed that this would be the last time she would see her mother for the duration of the war.

* * *

Even as they were attacking Pearl Harbor, the Japanese had begun their offensive across South-east Asia, encircling Hong Kong, occupying Thailand, landing in northern Malaya and bombing the Philippines. By the middle of January 1942, they had reached the Dutch East Indies and were advancing into southern Burma. Singapore surrendered on 15 February; Rangoon fell on 8 March; by 12 March the conquest of the Dutch East Indies was complete. Listening to the defeats on the radio, Martha wrote to Mrs Roosevelt: 'Are we going to rat out on the Dutch too? . . . If so, it is heartbreaking: not only morally, but practically . . . Are we going to adopt the English fetish of retreat?' And during all this time, there was talk of enemy submarines sinking ships not only along the eastern seaboard of the United States and in the Gulf of Mexico, but in the Caribbean as far south as Brazil. Martha, having identified a corner of the war that the American military would not begrudge a woman correspondent, now proposed to roam the Caribbean and report on submarine warfare. It was, she told friends, a sideshow; but it would get her away from the Nazi hunts being boozily plotted at the Finca Vigía, and it was something new. If not actual war, which she would greatly have preferred, it was at least travel, and travel was increasingly her way to escape boredom and *schadenfreude*. Only many years later did she discover that it had not been quite the sideshow she imagined: while she dawdled around the Caribbean for two hot months in the summer of 1942, enemy submarines sank seventy-one ships in sixty-one days. 'Gosh, gosh it is fun to be going again,' she wrote to Colebaugh. 'Boy, give me the life of the itinerant journalist.' She reminded him that all her articles were to be signed Gellhorn, 'always: that is what I always was, and am and will be'.

Survivors from the torpedoed merchant ships were being taken to Puerto Rico, now an immense naval base, to recover and rest before being assigned to new vessels. Martha persuaded the navy to let her join a Flying Fortress on anti-submarine patrol, but it was tame stuff after her CNAC flight over Japanese lines. In Puerto Rico, she wandered along the seafront, listening to the sailors' tales of survival, and then went to see the slums, liking the local people she talked to and noting their extreme poverty, 'like a constant smell, like a constant embarrassment and sadness'. 'War,' she wrote about the thin and ragged people in her first article of the series for *Collier's*, 'is just a little worse than peace. It is a hungrier time.' She told Hemingway that she was working entirely on his iceberg principle, and that she had heard such balls from the military people that if all the brains she had encountered were boiled up together they would amount to no more than 'two drops of grey matter'. She worried about her article being stunningly boring and badly written, and the fact that it had no story to it, beyond hunger and misery and waste. Colebaugh, however, liked it and cabled her to keep going.

Like Hemingway, Martha was now looking for action, to see for herself a prowling enemy submarine, and all her dormant instincts as a journalist had come alive. Examining a map, she saw that there was a string of islands, with exotic names like St Bartholomew and Virgin Gorda, stretching between St Thomas, which she could reach by plane, and Antigua, some 275 miles away. There being no official means of transport between them, she would have to hire her own boat. And so began a second horror journey, remembered and recounted with affection and comedy many years later. Before setting out, she wrote to Hemingway: 'I am driven to this unceasing looking, these twelve hour days of inspection, not for *Collier's*, but because of some terrible curiosity, a real desire to know what it is all like. And all the time knowing I will not know . . . Finally one is very alone.'

Hurricanes threatened, then heavy rain held her up on St Thomas, but at seven o'clock one morning, with a supply of tinned beans, sardines, crackers, a Superware Sanitary Pail and a large black umbrella, Martha set sail on the *Pilot*, a thirty-foot potato boat with one sail and a hold for the cargo. There was a crew of five barefoot black men, in ragged singlets and shorts, but no life belt, sextant, log, barometer or chart. The single sail looked like a patchwork quilt. Few people would have embarked on this expedition without profound misgivings. Martha's heart 'rose like a bird', as it inevitably did when she felt she was about to fall off the map. It was enough, she told Mrs Roosevelt in a last letter before setting sail, to make her 'spin like a top with happiness'.

And so they set out, Martha in her white cotton dress clutching Proust, the crew marvelling at the absurdity of the outing. The days passed, very slowly. She was bitten by a swarm of lethal red ants, and, having lost her umbrella overboard, she scorched in the baking sun as the *Pilot* lay becalmed for two days and two nights; then it rained, in great torrential sheets of water, and she was soaked. The boat's relentless rolling kept her permanently queasy. Meeting another small sailing boat far from land one day, the old man at its helm called out to ask where they were bound. 'Right roun de globe, boy,' called back Martha's captain, Carlton, as she recorded later. 'What you cargo?' asked a second man in the other boat. 'De lady,' replied Carlton, and all men on both boats howled with laughter. 'I was past caring,' wrote Martha later, 'slumped in the lethargy of compounded discomfort and boredom that is the trademark of the genuine horror story.'

But as they moved from island to island, an enchanted world opened up before her, of silent, deserted coves ringed by palms, where she could swim naked and lie in the sun and watch the dark blue hummingbirds flitting among the tropical plants. From time to time, they landed in peaceful little ports, where she met oddball refugees from the world's bustle and frenzy. For a while, she wrote, 'I forgot the war. It was somebody else's nightmare. I was in that state of grace which can rightly be called happiness. This occurs, as a divine surprise, in travel.' For the islanders she met and talked to, no war seemed to exist. On St Bartholomew she acquired a small cat, which then travelled on with the *Pilot*. From Basseterre on St Kitts, conscious of her need to justify her expenses for *Collier's*, she filed an 11,000-word article – 5,000 was their maximum – not about submarines, for she had seen none, but about the people she had encountered. Later, Colebaugh told her that such was the laughter in the office over her article, and the universal sense of relief among the staff that it was her and not they who were on the *Pilot*, that it was worth her expenses twice over. The true horror, however, was still to come.

On Saba, hurricanes threatened again and Martha slept in a room on shore. When, at dawn, she hastened down to the seafront, she found that the *Pilot* had slipped away in the night, leaving her marooned in a tropical paradise, with no means of escape. Soon, paradise came to seem more like prison. The hurricane arrived in the shape of a gale. It rained, in torrents. There was no café, no restaurant, nowhere to sit. She had finished her last book and taken such a loathing to Proust she could not bear to read another word; he was, she said, artificial and dead. Three days crawled by as Martha, never patient, grew frantic. When a derelict motor launch, caked in grease, called the *Queen Mary* crawled into the port, she happily spent $60 on persuading the elderly sailor at the helm to take her to Antigua. There she was able to catch a plane to Surinam, where she quickly researched and wrote an article about the Americans and bauxite, and about the Dutch preparations for their last stand against the Japanese. Her relief on being on the move again was boundless.

Waiting for her were several letters from Hemingway. They were for the most part extremely loving and very domestic, full of private words and nicknames, with news about the cats – her favourite had died – about the pelota players and the Crook Shop, and the way that he had been teaching his son Gigi how to splice knots and how to read with such concentration that he would always remember what he read. One included a plaintive cry about her long absence. Alone, he wrote, he had been unable to avoid thinking, something he had only ever resorted to before when in hospital. 'I think thinking . . . is probably fatal to me as a writer. The worst of Tolstoi I've found is the thinking. I think with my nose, my hands, mouth, ears and eyes.' Not all his letters, however, were as peaceable. Evidently goaded by one from Martha complaining about life in Cuba, he fired off a long burst of semi-comic but clearly heart-felt resentment. 'Boy can you hit. Can you hit and do you know where the heart of another lives . . . boy how my hero can hit cuando no hay enemigo and who you are giving it to loves you like a fucking dope.'

Before leaving Surinam, Martha happened to see on a map that the upper reaches of the Saramoca river appeared as an uncharted white patch of territory. Exploration seemed a natural and pleasant extension of travel. She looked around for someone to take her. Guided by a smarmy city boy, who arrived to collect her wearing dark glasses and a homburg, she was paddled in a very grubby hollowed-out tree trunk by a crew of boys wearing what she referred to as knitting needles in their hair, through dense jungle. Above her unseen birds squawked raucously. Swarms of mosquitoes descended and began to bite. At one point, rounding a bend by a village, she was stoned. It was, once again, agonisingly boring. She wished she had never come. On the fifth day, by which time she had decided that she now revered true explorers for their sheer powers of endurance, but was convinced that they were totally insane, Martha saw that her ankles were swelling. Soon they felt, and looked, enormous. She assumed that she had picked up elephantiasis. Then she developed a fever which left her shivering and unable to move for the pain in her joints. Thrashing out in her sleep, she fractured a wrist. The horror journey ended in a mist of pain. When she finally reached a doctor, it turned out that she had caught dengue fever.

Many years later, Martha returned to the same Caribbean islands. She found yachts and rubber Zodiac dinghies, plastic bottles on the seabed, casinos and boutiques in the sleepy ports, and great bald patches of land, stripped for development, where once all had been jungle and green. It was, she wrote sadly, a world lost.

* * *

Returning was always good. There was something explosive in both their characters that was making it hard for Martha and Hemingway to live calmly together, but in the late summer of 1942 they loved each other enough to enjoy periods of real happiness. Though always careful to forge no unbreakable ties to the houses of the men she lived with, Martha was immensely fond of the Finca, where the garden had been tamed and the house was as she wanted it, full of books and Hemingway's collection of modern art, which included a Braque, a Klee and a Miró. Both she and Hemingway liked cats and the resident population was growing fast – 'one cat just leads to another', as Hemingway wrote to Hadley, with whom he was on friendly terms – with names as fanciful as the nicknames they gave each other. There was Tester from a cattery in Florida, Dillinger, a black and white tom found in a nearby fishing village, a Persian cat that looked like a snow leopard called Uncle Wolfer, Thunder, Boise, Furhouse, Friendless and Friendless's brother. In their letters to each other, the Hemingways referred to the cats as 'cotsies'. Uncle Wolfer and Boise had been coaxed to take up positions on top of the pillars on the front porch, and sometimes condescended to drape themselves decorously one each side, looking like a pair of lions in a circus. Though the cats were in charge, there were also several dogs, six love-birds, three tree ducks, forty-two pigeons and a rooster and his hen. Martha, happy to be back, recovered from her dengue fever and finished her articles for *Collier's*. She was depressed to find waiting for her a letter from Bertrand de Jouvenel, telling her of a Jewish friend who had taken poison and died after learning that two other Jewish friends, to whom she had been taking food, had been arrested. The woman had been, she wrote to Allen Grover, 'round and soft and pretty and vain and utterly charming and brainless and wonderfully kind'.

In October, having convinced herself and Hemingway that she needed a break, Martha went to New York where she took a room at the Lombardy, had her hair cut and curled by Monsieur Jacques from Paris – after frequent consultations with Hemingway – shopped, and lunched and dined with friends. One night she had dinner with Harold Ross, the legendary editor of *The New Yorker* ('terrible bore') and Dorothy Parker ('so gold star'): 'I regretted every word I said.' She wrote fondly almost every day to Hemingway, telling him that she wished they could be alone for a while. Hemingway's replies were equally fond. 'Dearest beloved I love you because your feet are so long and because they get cold and because I can take good care of you when you are sick also because you are the most beautiful woman I have ever known . . .'

From New York Martha went to spend a few days at the White House. The autumn leaves were turning and in the early evening the light over Washington was a deep purple blue; it reminded her of Paris. Washington itself had been transformed by the war. The people working in the capital's new agencies had nearly doubled in number. The telephone system was overloaded and there were neither typewriters nor taxis to be had; the laundries were turning customers away. Interesting newcomers had descended on the capital, and there had never been so many or such desirable cocktail parties and receptions. People talked of Washington as being like the court of Louis XIV, but while the French king had entertained his courtiers at Versailles, the Roosevelts had withdrawn from the social circuit and left the courtiers to entertain themselves, choosing instead to give small informal dinners to selected guests, to whom they fed turkey and candied yams, Mrs Roosevelt having taken wartime economies to heart. She had wanted to go to Europe to do relief work after the fall of France, but had been prevented in case she was kidnapped by the Nazis. She was now with New York's mayor, Fiorello LaGuardia, newly in charge of civilian defence, trying to persuade the American public to contribute 'an hour a day for the USA'. Roosevelt's administration continued to attract criticism, while Eleanor herself had further irritated Washington's hostesses by proposing that domestic servants form a union to bargain for better hours and wages. After Pearl Harbor, the Liberals and the New Dealers were not as popular as they had once been.

While in Washington Martha caught a bad cold and retired to Lincoln's bed on the second floor, saying that she felt embarrassed and insolent to be in it, emerging only to gossip with Alexander Woollcott, the podgy, amusing critic, hero and star of George Kaufman and Moss Hart's *The Man Who Came to Dinner*. After Martha left, Woollcott took over her room, writing to Rebecca West that it was dear to him not because Queen Elizabeth had recently slept in it, but 'because it had more recently been occupied by Martha Gellhorn'.

The American military were still refusing to accredit women as war correspondents at the front, and Martha was once again without a commission. Back in Cuba, she spoke of being the 'good little wife' and not wanting to leave Hemingway, 'who is my job', and toyed briefly with the idea of setting up adult education classes for soldiers stationed at the nearby San Antonio base. Hemingway, engrossed in his Crook Shop, came and went on mysterious missions in the *Pilar*, and Martha used her solitude to read as she had not read for years, a book a day, choosing Koestler, Nelson Algren and Ira Wolfert as writers who were 'full of juice, with good sharp eyes'. She reread Henry James and greatly admired his 'perfect dazzling accuracy in detail' but was conscious that she dared not read too much of him when she was writing herself, or she would find herself 'happily and insanely tied into sentences like pythons'. She also continued her military education, preparing for the moment when she might be allowed to go to the war front, and redecorated the Finca, repairing the house where roots had pushed up the floors, and planting pine trees, oranges, limes, figs and breadfruit. 'One thing time has not removed from me,' she wrote to Grover, 'the last toughness of youth, and that is to live alone. I am glad of that; I would be scared to death if I found I was really needing people . . .'

One day, suddenly overwhelmed by the rising number of cats, she took several of the toms into Havana and had them spayed. Hemingway, away at sea, was furious, saying he would have preferred to have shot them. (Later, he would say of one of the cats that it hated 'wimmies', since it was a 'wommy who sent him to have his balls cut off'.) Reporting her feelings of guilt to H.G. Wells, she received back a disquisition on 'normality'. 'No tom cat,' wrote Wells, 'is happy until the urgency of sex is lifted from it. Then it becomes a serene and comfortable philosopher . . . There is no "*normal* life" for any animal. Life on this planet is a continual adjustment of animal types to changing conditions . . .' In the spirit of their earlier letters, he urged her to write down what she imagined to be the 'normal' lifecycle and food of an elephant, a water rat, a horse, a cow and a human being; and then to compare her own life with that of an Elizabethan woman her own age.

In the middle of December, Martha went to St Louis to see her mother, leaving Hemingway to spend Christmas with Gigi. She was so conscious of the closeness of her relationship to her mother, and of Edna's need for her, that when, on her return journey, her connecting flight home was cancelled in Chicago by heavy snow, she turned round and went back to St Louis by train in order to spend a few more days with her, though she was longing to get back to work. 'I guess I'm not a real writer,' she wrote to Hemingway, 'because in the end I care more about Mother's sad, hurt (but not showing it) face . . . I can't imagine a life that she's not in and when I see her so white and all I get terrified.' Her brothers were now scattered between New Jersey and Baltimore in the States, and Argentina, and she was worried about leaving Edna, now in her sixties, so much alone, though Edna was in fact busier than ever, pursuing an ever growing number of civic causes, and surrounded by friends. Torn also by missing Hemingway, she wrote to him as her 'darling, house-broken cobra (cobra because no one knew where it would strike next) . . . Take care of yourself beloved and the childies and the animalies . . . and the vegetably garden . . . and I will be home quick as a winklet.'

Sometime late in 1942, after several months in which she had felt completely unable to write anything, which, as she told Alexander Woollcott, made her 'not only sad but vicious as well as blind with panic', Martha had started work on a story, though not before her ill temper had provoked Hemingway into an outburst about the importance of a writer simply getting on with the job, much in the same terms her father had once used. The story was about a mulatto girl of exceptional beauty called Liana, living on a French Caribbean island; taken as a kind of trophy to live with a rich white planter, she falls in love with a young French teacher. The story kept growing; the way it flowed made her feel 'at once exhausted and full of love for the human race'. In the New Year, back at her desk at the Finca, she wrote to tell Perkins that she and Hemingway were both excited about its progress. 'It is the first time that I have ever written all the time with pleasure . . . I had three weeks on it and they were almost like a beautiful drunk, they were so happy . . . I always used to see E. so tired but so happy when he was writing, and I was usually just tired and doubting.' The story, she told him, was 'just about people, not about the war or anything.' To friends, she confided that she felt bad to be writing such a very small story, when everyone else was writing of dying and war '. . . no social awareness nor nothing. I am entranced by the furious miseries people make for themselves in their own heads.'

By the end of January, she had written a little over 20,000 words, perhaps half the length she wanted it to be, but was now worried that it was too short for a proper novel. Perkins comforted her by telling her that *The Great Gatsby* had only been 40,000 words long. All through the spring and early summer of 1943, she kept writing, in bursts of confidence when the words seemed to spin themselves with ease, followed by patches of intense self-doubt, when she felt she had to go back and throw out long self-indulgent passages, like 'draining a swamp and trying to make solid ground'. In those moods, her characters spoke with 'pedestrian dullness', the writing was thin, the 'knowledge, the ear and the juice' were all lacking. She had been having injections for a hormonal problem and they were making her not an 'ovaried banana but only a

bloated capon'. Even the ceiba tree she loved so much irritated her by sprouting fronds of 'repulsive silk' amongst the
new leaves. To Hemingway, again at sea on the *Pilar*, contradicting her own earlier protestations about her need to be
alone, she wrote: 'Oh my am I homesick for you . . . have a
huge stock of loneliness . . . a hollow place waiting to be filled.
Do not believe much in loneliness (same way you do not believe
in suffering) . . . really believe it is man's fate, in whatever
doses it comes.' Hemingway tried to steady her nerve, again
telling her that writers who indulged themselves in too much
wallowing in self-doubt were contemptible. Martha seldom
allowed herself to sound vulnerable, especially with
Hemingway. But now, nearing the end of her book, she had
a moment of frailty. 'I wish we could stop it all now,' she
wrote to him, 'the prestige, the possessions, the position, the
knowledge, the victory. And by a miracle, return together under
the arch at Milan, you so brash in your motorcycle sidecar
and I badly dressed, fierce, loving . . . That loud reckless
dishevelled girl was a better person . . . You have been married
so much and so long that I do not believe it can touch you
where you live and that is your strength. It would be terrible
if it did because you are so much more important than the
women you happen to be married to.' Their letters to each
other, at this point, were still fond. On 23 June, Hemingway
wrote to describe the camp he and his two younger sons had
set up on an island, where they had caught and penned two
giant turtles and were fattening up a pig, which went swimming in the sea. One day, he wrote to tell her that he had
dreamt that he had made love to a bear, 'a lovely silvery
colour', whose claws felt 'strong and smooth and clicky . . .'.
He was still very uneasy about his position over the war in
Europe. 'You have a fine time at wars and love them maybe
or happiest at them . . . But by God I hate them.'

On 27 June Martha put down the last words of her novel.
Writing to tell Perkins that it was finally done, she said that
it had come out at 90,000 words. When he asked her for a
couple of sentences for a blurb, she replied: 'It's about love
and loneliness, I think, but who can say?' It was also about

the rottenness of governments. In a refrain that was now making its way into all her writing, Martha has the young French teacher Pierre say: 'People are good and governments are bad.' To H.G. Wells, Martha wrote that she was sorry for her heroine, betrayed by both the men in her novel, 'but on the whole I am sorry for women. They are not free: there is no way they make themselves free.' Freedom, solitude, responsibility: the dicta she grew up with, shaped by the twists in her own life.

There were now struggles to find a good title, and *Share of Night, Share of Morning*, from a poem by Emily Dickinson was settled on, though Hemingway urged her to consult Ecclesiastes and Proverbs, saying that while the New Testament had been exhaustively mined, the Old Testament still contained much that might be useful. There was a moment of anxiety, when readers at Scribners worried that sales might be affected because the heroine was a mulatto, and Hemingway objected that the book was seriously short of commas, and reduced the galleys to a red battlefield with squiggles on every page; and then the novel was done. Martha dedicated it to her mother.

Hemingway had not spent much time at the Finca that spring, but when he was there he drank heavily with his *Pilar* submarine hunters, or went off to spend long evenings in the Floridita. By now he had quarrelled with most of his writer friends, and preferred to spend his time with fellow sportsmen. Their marriage was beginning to show signs of strain, with Martha no longer as ready as she had once been to overlook Hemingway's boundless egotism. She was now openly scornful of his spying activities, and accused him of becoming boastful and self-aggrandising; she hated the stories he spun and weaved over the whisky during the drunken evenings, which had long ceased to be the companionable drinking, smoking and talking together, far into the night. She was finding his grubbiness and the dirtiness of his clothes almost impossible to bear. He, in turn, told her that her cleanliness was obsessive. He complained to friends that she did not understand about money, saving 'terrifically' on pennies and spending larger sums without a thought. The laughter and jokes were not as much fun any longer. One night, after a row about his erratic drunken driving, she insisted on taking the wheel of his much loved Lincoln Continental. He slapped her and Martha drove it slowly but deliberately straight into a tree, got out and walked home, leaving him with the wreck. Making love with Hemingway had never been much pleasure for Martha, who still found sexual relations less a matter of happiness than an awkward obligation. She told a friend many years later that she had been astonished to discover, talking to Tillie Arnold during one of her visits to Sun Valley, that making love was actually something women could enjoy. From remarks made at various times by both of them, it seems probable that Martha had an abortion at about this time. The moment for them to have the daughter Hemingway had wanted had clearly passed, though whether it had ever really existed for Martha is impossible to say. Restless, feeling herself isolated from events in Europe she longed to be part of, and now frequently quarrelling with Hemingway, Martha was not in a mood for children. 'You write about them so well and so poignantly,' he told her, 'and don't give a goddam about them.'

The good times were not quite over; but they were growing fewer. Even so, Hemingway was angry when Martha told him that she had decided to go to Europe for *Collier's*, to report on the war, even without formal military accreditation. She pressed him to go with her, but he balked at the idea of leaving Cuba and the submarine hunting. With some annoyance, accusing her of picking quarrels in order to justify her longing to get away, and telling her that she had turned into a prima donna as a writer, he made plans to spend her absence on a wider sweep of the sea, lasting three months.

Just the same they parted on an amicable, even tender note. 'I will think of you so carefully all the time that you will be protected,' Martha wrote as she left for New York, where she was to meet Colebaugh and Max Perkins and see the page proofs of her novel. She begged him to be careful of the bright sun reflecting off the sea, saying that she was happy to be his daughter, but did not wish to see him become Milton. '. . .

You belong to me,' she wrote. 'Some time the war will be over . . . We have a good wide life ahead of us. And I will try to be beautiful when I am old, and if I can't do that I will try to be good. I love you very much.' Hemingway's reply was equally fond. 'Live alone makes jumpy,' he wrote back, 'we will unjumpy ourselves . . . in the six foot bed and all the long hours talking by the pool.' They had agreed on a code for Martha's letters from Europe, so that she could tell him where she was going without falling foul of the censor: a visit to Capa would stand for Africa, while Herbert Matthews would mean Italy. Sometime before she left, Hemingway wrote a letter in which he reminded her of Rilke's lines: 'Love consists in this: that two solitudes protect and touch and greet each other.' Then he went on: 'I haven't protected you good and touched you little and have been greeting you scoffingly. But truly I respect and admire you very much and of this date and hour have stopped scoffing; which is the worst of all I think.' Hemingway's own plan to leave Havana had fallen through, and he was going to be staying on alone at the Finca, as he told Charles Scribner, sleeping on the floor with the cats, who hunted for mice in his beard. He had now written nothing for over a year and was beginning to doubt that he would write anything at all until after the war.

By 3 September, having done the proofs for her novel, its title now changed to *Liana*, Martha was installed in the Berkshire, a smart hotel on New York's East Side, where she embarked on a concentrated regime of exercises, face treatments, vitamin injections and dentist and hair appointments, having decided that her gums were receding, that her hair was too dry and that she would have to get her handmade shoes rebuilt to withstand the rigours of the war correspondent's life. After many consultations by post with Hemingway, and appointments with different hairdressers, she had her hair cut very short, permed around the sides and coloured a 'tawny brownish gold'. When not out buying grey suits and fashionable hats, shaped, she complained, as for gnomes, or having the skin under her eyes peeled and her neck and chin tightened, she lunched and dined with friends. But she was soon complaining to Hemingway that the months in Cuba had left her ill at ease with New York society life; she felt bored and boring, and nothing was fun in the way she had hoped it would be. As often when low and gloomy, she felt ill and fretted about her weight and the fact that her face looked 'jowly'. New York, she reported, was full of horribly thin and unescorted women and she found the whole thing scary, which made her reflect how much she missed Hemingway, 'really sickeningly; I'm like somebody who crossed the river Styx by mistake and got in with a lot of spooks and left its real comrade elsewhere.' One evening she had drinks with Dorothy Parker – who put away eight martinis in a couple of hours – and was once again both captivated by her 'evil fascination' and repelled by her 'worthless, self-pitying and unwashed' presence. When fifteen-year-old Mousie was able to take a day out of school, he came to New York and, as ever with Hemingway's sons, Martha was fond and appreciative.

By the end of the third week in September, when her passage for Europe had still not come through, she moved to a small suite at the Gladstone Hotel, which at $175 a month was cheaper than her room at the Berkshire, and which she filled with plants to make it look more like home. As Bumby would later observe, Martha was always excellent at making nests, being someone who felt insecure if her immediate surroundings did not please her, even if she was not always so good at running them. A friend sent round her maid to do her mending and washing. As the days passed, she added new bits of furniture – lamps, trays, glasses – and pinned photographs of Hemingway, the Finca and the cats up on the walls, writing to tell him that she felt joined to him as to a Siamese twin and that she could imagine no future that did not include him. Apart, and feeling a little guilty, she quickly forgot the rows.

When not shopping or having beauty treatments, Martha was seeing her novel through the last stages before publication. She was irritated when a preview referred to her only as the 'wife of Ernest Hemingway', but the signs for the book were all promising: a Swedish publisher had asked to buy the rights, the Theatre Guild had expressed an interest, Paramount was talking about a film and the Book of the Month Club was considering it. Her much loved brother Alfred was teaching medical students for the war effort and very short of money, and she was planning to give him the $15,000 it would bring in if selected. She was miserable when she learnt that she had been passed over. She appeared to mind less, however, when the renowned Miss Helburn of the Theatre Guild interviewed her in a lordly manner and informed her that since her story of love and betrayal between a mulatto girl and two white men smacked too strongly of miscegenation, the part of Liana would probably have to be rewritten as a white girl if the Guild were to take it. 'There is no more brains or talent or courage in the theatre than in the movies,' she noted crossly. 'It's all shit. The way I feel is: all passes, books alone remain. A book is a hard beautiful unperishable thing.' After Max Perkins chose a photograph of her sitting on a rock laughing, her hair flying in the wind, she said it made her look like an aging Colette. She was just as sharp with her new agent, telling him that all decisions, however small, about her work were to be left to her, and that he was not to interfere.

The days of waiting turned into weeks, but by now she was back in the swim of New York, frenetically keeping up with parties and old friends passing through on their way to the war in Europe; and spending weekends in Washington with the Roosevelts, who introduced her to ambassadors and other useful contacts for London. Her old boss Harry Hopkins, who had been very ill, was now more or less permanently resident in the White House, as was Lorena Hickok, and Eleanor Roosevelt, as driven and active as ever, continued to cook scrambled eggs herself on Sunday nights for a passing assortment of friends. Martha's meetings with Colebaugh had gone well, and he had asked her to do one long piece on England, and then any number of shorter ones of a thousand words or less, 'the easiest thing for me to write . . . specific stories of specific people: what they wear, eat, say, how they are amused etc'. Her confidence, which had been leaking away as she waited, bounced back. 'I've got back my looks,' she told

Hemingway, 'not from treatments but just from being alive.' Reflecting on the past year, she realised that the two aspects of life she most valued – loving the right person and doing the right work – had at last come together for her. She was longing to leave, longing to get on with the next stage in her life. 'This bad city, this loud curious flashing city,' she wrote to Hemingway, 'does very deforming things to the mind. I do not like what it does to people, nor want what it gives to them . . . I have really a very great desire for cleanliness, every kind of it, and here you get corrupted and lose the something – simpleness, honor, decency, whatever – which must be the basis of people or they are not really people.' Hearing of the death in action of a French friend, and the stoicism with which his family had greeted the news, she noted: 'In the greatest disasters one does not forget one's manners, nor the trained-in manners of one's heart.'

Finally, seven weeks after reaching New York, she boarded the Pan Am clipper bound for London, a seaplane with berths. The journey took twelve days, pausing in Bermuda and Portugal where she went dancing with the Pan Am captain, co-pilot and radio engineer and looked up an old friend from Spain called Gi de Castro, only to find that he had become a supporter of Franco. The clipper stopped again to refuel in Ireland. She was, as she told Hemingway, in a state of great merriment, and her letters had an eager note of expectation, a tone that had not been present for a very long time; but there was something wistful in them too. 'Just feeling ahead already the strange places,' she wrote, 'I am happy like a fire-horse . . . But like woman, and your woman, am sad: only there isn't anything final is there, and this is just a short trip and we are both coming back from our short trips to our lovely home and our lovely cotsies. And then we'll write books and see the autumns together and walk around the cornfield waiting for pheasants and we will go to all the palaces and be very cosy in them . . .'

CHAPTER NINE

An Honourable Profession

Martha had last seen England in the late summer of 1938. Then it had seemed to her an impossibly complacent country, and she had been enraged by the mood of calm superiority. Something in the phlegmatic character of the English offended her sense of passion and commitment and she had returned with some relief to what she perceived to be the Roosevelts' honourable attempts to engage with the world's injustices. But she had always loved London as a city, and carried with her in her mind a memory of its prewar charm and orderliness, even if she felt a particular loathing for the English weather and the unheated houses her friends mysteriously tolerated. She found London pleasing and manageable.

The city she returned to almost five years later was a very different place. The months of heavy bombing in the autumn and winter of 1940 had left many of the familiar landmarks in ruins; and though much of the rubble had been cleared away, jagged edges of masonry and unexpected gaps had altered the skyline. Rationing, in force since early 1940, meant that there was not very much to eat and even restaurants, where it was still possible to find unrationed luxuries like lobster and partridge, were now restricted to a single course. Cigarettes, alcohol, oranges, eggs, envelopes, fountain pens, toothbrushes and needles were almost impossible to come by. Londoners, the men restricted to a new shirt every twenty months, the women forbidden pleats to their skirts, were beginning to look a little drab, while an acute shortage of hotel rooms had made finding a bed nearly impossible and even

Allen Grover, pulling all his *Time* magazine strings, had only been able to reserve two weeks for Martha at the Dorchester in Park Lane. What struck her most immediately however was the blackout: London, on her first November afternoon, had sunk by four o'clock into a sea of treacherous darkness, broken only by faint pools of light around the bottom of street lamps or the much-dimmed headlights of the very few cars still on the roads. Ghostly figures crept along streets from which the railings had long since gone for metal for the war, with the uncertain help of torches shrouded with tissue paper.

The life, too, was utterly different from the way she remembered it. The city was full of people in uniform, from the cerise berets and sky-blue trimmings of the parachute regiments to the scarlet linings of nurses' cloaks, and most noticeably full of American GIs, who were now gathering for the awaited push into occupied Europe. By the autumn of 1943, the Allies had cleared North Africa and the Italians had changed sides. Though France, Poland, Luxembourg, Belgium, Holland, Norway and Finland were all still under Hitler's control, the Soviet army had recaptured Kiev and was pressing on towards Germany. Martha, who had been delighted when Churchill replaced Chamberlain, was greatly impressed by a new buoyant mood she detected in the British, with none of the smugness she had so disliked before. 'I think it is true,' she wrote later, 'that nothing becomes them like a catastrophe . . . Slowness, understatement, complacency change into endurance, a refusal to panic, and pride, the begetter of self-discipline.' It made her think of the critic Edmund Wilson's phrase: 'The moral top of the world, where the light never quite goes out.'

London was full of American journalists, too, as well as dozens of Allied and British reporters, waiting for the next phase of the war, back on leave from the Italian campaign or veterans of the war in North Africa. There was every shade of correspondent from Chester Wilmot of the Australian Broadcasting Corporation who liked the broader picture, to the small gnome-like Ernie Pyle of the Scripps-Howard agency, who was interested neither in military affairs nor strategy but wrote memorable stories about individual soldiers. She met Irwin Shaw, then a dishevelled private, and they ate in the French Officers' Club off St James's. In the Dorchester and the Savoy, where the *New York Times* and the *Herald Tribune* had their offices, and which had become the unofficial meeting places for American reporters, Martha found correspondents she had known in Spain and Czechoslovakia. Some she was pleased to see again; but the years in Cuba with Hemingway had sharpened her feeling of apartness, and made her more intolerant of bores and more openly scornful of self-promotion and vanity. She made no effort to conceal her contempt for Quentin Reynolds, who had preceded her to Europe for *Collier's*, and written, Martha said, as if it was just him and not London which was being bombed. Nor did she care for Clare Booth Luce, whose demanding ways she claimed were partly responsible for giving women reporters a bad name. Her dislike of self-promotion was absolutely genuine, and neither in the tone of her articles nor in her attitude towards her own work did she set out to promote herself personally; ambitious, certainly, but for the pleasure of the story rather than her own glory.

And the nature of war reporting itself had changed enormously since Spain, which Martha continued to mourn as a time when the issues had all been clear and reporters free to roam. In Spain, she wrote, 'all men were equal and all were serving and none were getting photographed or writing heroic letters home which are then retyped and sent to every gossip column and magazine in town'. On both sides of the Atlantic much thought had gone into the question of censorship and how far reporters could be trusted or how wise it was to rely on their patriotism and good sense. Gloom, like mockery, was much frowned on. Correspondents could not enter a theatre of war unless accredited, and the only way to be accredited was to submit all copy to the censors, overworked military men more used to reports from soldiers than daily journalism, and on the whole extremely cautious. As an American, Martha had listened with misgivings to Archibald MacLeish, who had been appointed Librarian of Congress, exhort writers to abjure critical and disillusioning views of war as seen by Dos Passos and Hemingway, and she shared with E.B. White his fears that the truth was fast being lost under conjecture and rumour and conflicting statements. By the autumn of 1943, there were not many writers – apart from figures like Cyril Connolly and Edmund Wilson – who had not to some extent succumbed to a sincere and earnest tone, singularly lacking in irony and satire, with the result, as Steinbeck later complained, that the public was given very little taste of 'the crazy, hysterical mess' going on.

Seeking her own position in all this, Martha had written not long before to Max Perkins: 'If a writer has any guts he should write all the time, and the lousier the world the harder a writer should work. For if he can do nothing positive, to make the world more livable or less cruel and stupid, he can at least record truly, and that is something no one else will do, and it is a job that must be done.' It was as a witness that Martha had come to the war in Europe. And *Collier's*, a highly successful, lavishly illustrated weekly magazine, which combined middle-brow short stories with serious writing to great effect, was an excellent magazine to work for. What was more, they liked her articles about the minutiae of people's lives, admired her gift for memorable images and simple, passionate statements, and paid her generously to wander and follow her interests. She did not, and would not, analyse; but there were other writers happy to do that.

But it would not be easy. Accustomed to the freedom of Madrid and the Spanish civil war, Martha would not take kindly to the determination of the military to keep close track on the correspondents they accepted, nor to Eisenhower's attempts to win over correspondents by declaring them to be 'quasi staff officers', nor to the ban on women at the front. However strongly she felt about the rightness of the Allied cause, she was by nature impatient at any attempt to curtail her movements or direct her interests. She was now thirty-five, and had covered four wars and many battle fronts; conscious of her standing and her good looks, her manner towards authority had become a mixture of irony and slight arrogance. She thought that she would start quietly, by writing about how four years of intermittent bombing had affected the English, the kind of story about the lives of ordinary people she most enjoyed, for she had never lost her admiration for people in adversity. But after that, she wanted to go where the other correspondents, the men, went. The role of excluded spectator was not one she ever welcomed, and particularly not now that she had at last made it to London. 'It is too hard to sit on the outskirts and watch what you can neither help nor change,' she wrote many years later. 'It is far easier to close your eyes and your mind and jump into the general misery, where you have almost no choices left, but a lot of splendid company.'

She was lucky in being fresh to the war, while other correspondents, after four years on the road, were exhausted. Even Ernie Pyle was tired, worn down by a war that never seemed to end, that 'finally worms its way through you and gradually starts to devour you'. And so, on her first morning in London, after breakfast with Virginia Cowles in the Dorchester, Martha set out to buy her uniform with its patch with a C for correspondent on its left jacket pocket, and pick up her papers of accreditation to the army, which carried with them the honorary rank of captain, so that she would not be shot as a spy were she captured by the enemy.

* * *

Of all the branches of the British armed services in the winter of 1943, Bomber Command had the worst odds for survival. Twenty-four of every hundred pilots and crew could expect to survive. And as Martha observed when she went to Lincolnshire to write about their night missions over Germany, they were absurdly young, looking like good, tidy children doing their homework as they waited in their mess, with their slang and private jokes and their to her inexplicable taste for huge shaving mugs of tea, that 'sweetish, ghastly lukewarm drink that seems to mean something to them'.

Late one evening, watching the Lancasters take off, one after the other, 'enormous, deadly, black birds going off into the night', then waiting for the drone of the returning aircraft, she remembered the hours of waiting in Madrid, that odd mixture of boredom and fearful anticipation that she had come to associate with war. Waiting, she wrote, 'gets to be a thing you can touch'. The article that went off to *Collier's* had her by now characteristic twist in its tail, a phrase that drew the reader personally into her message. When the war at last came to an end, she wrote, 'let them have that lovely life they want. Let those of us, who have never been where they have been, see to it.'

Edward R. Murrow had managed to join a night bombing mission to Germany and reported that Berlin had been a 'kind of orchestrated hell, a terrible symphony of light and flame', and Martha briefly toyed with applying to be taken too; but then she decided that she was simply too scared. During her days at Bomber Command's airfield she made friends with a shy young Scot. Not long after she returned to London, she heard that he had not come back from Germany, and she was haunted by thoughts of what it must have been like for him at the end. 'It is making, slowly and suddenly, a very deep impression on me,' she wrote to Hemingway. 'I'm so glad to be here. I'd never have understood anything otherwise.'

In December, Martha moved into a small flat in Rex Street, in London's West End, but was so disgusted by the 'unwashed' and 'unwashing' maid, and so miserable in the extreme cold of the unheated building, that she fled back to the Dorchester, where they agreed to extend her stay. Even in wars, Martha remained extremely fastidious. She spent much of her time with Virginia Cowles, who had become her 'good, close pal', and through her met Duff and Diana Cooper, who would become one of her closest lifelong friends. As the famously beautiful Lady Diana Manners, daughter of the Duke of Rutland, Diana had served as a nurse during the First World War and later taken a leading role in Max Reinhardt's play, *The Miracle*. Diana 'is over 50', Martha wrote to Hemingway, 'and so beautiful you wouldn't believe . . . He's a little guy in an absurd high collar with a fine honest head . . .' The Coopers were on their way to Algiers, where he had been made British representative to the French Committee of Liberation, of which de Gaulle was now President, the idea being that after the war he would be appointed British ambassador to Paris.

Forced to take to her bed for over a week by acute gastric flu, Martha rose in time to have dinner with H.G. Wells, getting lost on the way and arriving two hours late to find him bored and not very friendly. London's wartime social life was beginning to entertain her, though she told Hemingway that she profited from the glory and power of his name and that the people she met liked her because he had chosen her. She felt herself to be regarded as an oddity, 'the very ordinary wife of a very extraordinary man'. One night she dined with Arthur Koestler, writing later to Hemingway that his 'ghastly abstraction talk' reminded her of Gustav Regler, but without Regler's sweetness: 'he evidently thinks that he alone has a corner on the Light and the Way. I absolutely loathed him and made it clear, and it was mutual.' She felt no more warmly towards Cyril Connolly, deciding that he was the ugliest man she had ever seen and 'not my dish of tea', in spite of his attentiveness. But she was delighted with most of Virginia Cowles's friends, and exhilarated by all the stories that were there to be written, even if she soon wearied of the 'important people with big intellects' who seemed to have gathered in London. 'I am in love with the human race again and thank God for that,' she wrote to Hemingway. 'It was getting sort of dry inside my head, but the dryness is gone.'

After her article on Bomber Command, others followed fast one after the other, each illustrating the impact of some aspect of the war on the lives of ordinary people, though she grumbled that she really preferred to spend more time with those she wrote about, until she felt that she understood and belonged to them. She found three Polish refugees, who told her about the Jews being pushed on to cattle trucks and about the Warsaw Ghetto, and wrote that 'it is unbearable to realise the effort and the pain of others and not be part of it. I think of the countries we have known and loved as if they were people being killed.'

She talked to fourteen-year-old Cockney boys who were working in the war industries in order to free older men for the services; she visited Archibald McIndoe's burns unit in Sussex and wrote about his determination to restore a will to live to young men whose faces had been destroyed beyond recognition; and she listened to the stories of men and women who had escaped from occupied Holland and had founded a club in London. Every few days, she sent off another long and affectionate letter to Hemingway, begging him to join her. 'I believe you will feel very deprived, as a writer, if this is all over and you have not had a share in it . . . and you remember how we want to drink Tavel and read *Le Sport* in the café in Paris, as soon as possible.' To her mother and Mrs Roosevelt she wrote about the difficulty of being a journalist and yet still be a 'good woman for a man', often mentioning the names of Dorothy Thompson and Clare Booth as 'terrifyingly' tough. Hemingway, still alone at the Finca, was spending his days shooting and drinking heavily. He told Edna he was so lonely that he felt he was dying a little every day. To Martha, he wrote less and less frequently.

Martha's suggestion that he offer a series of articles on the war to *Collier's* was all the more generous as it would mean that his coverage would take precedence over hers. But Hemingway was not about to budge, though he repeated to MacLeish and to Max Perkins how lonely he was without Martha. He observed to his son Patrick that Martha was a 'selfish and ambitious' woman. 'Haven't done a damn thing I wanted to do now for well over two years,' Hemingway wrote to Perkins, 'except shoot live pigeons occasionally, but then I guess no one else has either except Martha who does exactly what she wants to do wilfully as any spoiled child. And always for the noblest motives.'

In January 1944 , *Liana* was published in New York, Martha having decided at the last minute that *Share of Morning, Share of Night* was too fussy. The Theatre Guild had in the end turned down the idea of a play, and Paramount had failed to bid for movie rights, but the first printing of 27,000 sold briskly, and *Liana* was soon on the bestseller list. Reviews were good.

There was no talk of miscenegation and several critics remarked that the novel represented a new and mature step in Martha's fiction in that, for the first time, she had created a heroine who was not an extension of herself. The *Washington Post* commented that she had 'come artistically of age', while the *New York Herald Tribune* praised *Liana*'s 'splendid sultry grace'. In the inevitable comparisons with Hemingway's fiction, Martha held her own, one critic saying that she handled her characters with more restraint and subtlety than did her distinguished husband. Reflecting on herself as a writer, pondering over the differences between them, she wrote Hemingway a long and perceptive analysis of their different strengths. Utterly without conceit, its tone was rather wistful. Journalism, she said, though perhaps the wrong occupation for him, was the right one for her, because, 'deviously, everything I have ever written has come through journalism first, every book I mean . . . I have to see before I can imagine. I feel and act like a hardworking stenographer and I feel kind of happy about it in a grubby hardworking way . . .

'It is an honourable profession . . . even when not pleased with what I write, I am immensely pleased with what I have understood.

'. . . I have to live my way as well as yours, or there wouldn't be any me to love you with. You wouldn't really want me if I built a fine big stone wall around the Finca and sat inside it. I'm the same person who wrote articles for a steamship line paper to buy a third class passage to France in 1929. I'll never see enough as long as I live. And though my vision of the world is a Cook's tour vision, and yours is *en profondeur*, you are fair enough to concede mine as I respect yours.' Just the same, she worried that she had lost the knack of taking herself 'importantly and this is a bad loss, as people take you exactly as you take yourself'. In the years to come, friends would sometimes say of Martha that she lacked self-knowledge, or at least a willingness to perceive a true picture of her own behaviour. Yet all her life she was capable of genuine insights about herself; and now, as with Bertrand earlier, and other men later, it is possible that she preferred not to know too much, not to reflect too closely on what her long absences might mean to Hemingway and to their marriage, or what they said about her feelings for him. If she perceived a risk to their relationship, she made no reference to it.

At the end of January, having written six articles for *Collier's* and fearing that she was in danger of turning into the 'Dorchester correspondent', Martha set out for Italy, where the Allies were stalled below Cassino. She stopped on the way to visit the Duff Coopers in Algiers. 'Am really dead tired and sort of sad,' she wrote to Allen Grover before she left, though a last letter to H.G. Wells was more cheerful, saying that she had never enjoyed London more, that she had learnt many fine things and that the people she had met had restored her faith in the human race. After the freezing austerity of London, and her first experience of fog so thick she could not see her feet, the North African light and colour were almost over-whelming. There were palm trees and morning glory, and the mimosa was in flower. The city was full of generals and commanders and ADCs, and the Coopers, who had turned a formal Arab mansion into a delightful setting for parties, were busy entertaining the many French, waiting impatiently for the liberation of their country. At a dinner for de Gaulle there was caviar, sole, meringues and excellent white wine. Harold Nicolson described André Gide in his diary as 'looking old and ill but gay as a peroquet'. Writing of Martha's visit, Diana Cooper spoke of her as a 'packet of fun, yellow hair en brosse, cool slim lines and the most amusing patter imaginable'. The actress Joyce Grenfell, on tour for the troops, also admired Martha's 'divine' hair, but considered her to be 'affected, surface bright and worthless', in her war correspondent's uniform, though later, when 'we were girls together' she found her altogether more sympathetic.

When the Allies had landed at Salerno in September 1943 they had expected little resistance. Instead, they met a fero-cious German defence. By the end of the year, they were still only halfway up the Italian peninsula, constantly bogged down in the valleys, while the Germans held out on the high rocky hills above. Martha reached Naples from Algiers to find that it had been raining steadily for many weeks. She joined a French transport officer returning to the French sector of the front near Cassino, and they drove north through valleys slimy with the deepening mud that follows armies in winter, many of the bridges washed away. It was extremely cold.

The villages along the way had been reduced to little more than rubble, first by Allied shells, then, after the German retreat, by German artillery. With mines occasionally detonating around them it was, she said, like a land full of snakes. The countryside was strewn with abandoned equipment, discarded rations, the corpses of horses, mules and pigs, blood-stained bandages and burnt-out lorries. Under the olive trees, their trunks pitted with bullet holes, the fields were scored with deep ruts from the heavy vehicles moving north. Sardinian soldiers from a mountain artillery regiment had taken on the task of supplying the Allied troops who had fought their way to positions high on the mountains; they carried up their food, water and ammunition, and brought down the bodies of the dead, tied on the backs of mules. After visiting a tent hospital, and writing about a dead French ambulance driver, 'her hands crossed on a sad bunch of flowers, and her hair very neat and blond, and her face simply asleep', Martha spent the night in a cellar, seven kilometres from Cassino, sharing military rations with an American major and a French doctor, listening to music from Berlin on the radio. It was the sort of battle front Martha most enjoyed, moving with French soldiers who were less stuffy about the presence of women reporters, dodging the shells from the German batteries, looking up at the snow line, which made the mountains shine as if they were covered in moonstones. One day she stood watching as Allied planes bombed Monte Cassino, clouds of dust and smoke rising into the clear sky. And then she went off to search for Virginia Cowles, who had managed to join up with the American sector, where she, too, was dodging officious military press officers, before starting back for Cuba and home.

Martha did not want to leave, and greatly feared that she would miss the landings in France, but she needed to get back to Hemingway, who was pursuing her with cables. He missed her, and he wanted her to stay at home with him. But she was determined to 'blast him loose from Cuba' and bring him back to the war in Europe. 'My beloved Bug,' she wrote, 'you are such a sweet and lovely man . . . I'll court you until you are weary of it.' Complaining about the five months she had been away, Hemingway wrote back: 'How many times would you have divorced me if I ever left you for that?' He was still angry, telling her that he would do as she said and join her as soon as possible: 'will organise the house, close down boat, go to N.Y., eat shit, get a journalism job, which hate worse than Joyce would, and be over. Excuse bitterness.' On 31 January, he said that he felt like a good, sound, but old race-horse, being 'saddled again to race over the jumps because of unscrupulous owner . . . So long, Bong,' he wrote, ending on the bitter note that now filled many of his letters, 'maybe will see you soon maybe not.'

Collier's occasionally devoted a column to the comings and goings of their more important writers. At the beginning of March they wrote about Martha, saying that she stood out 'among gal correspondents not only for her writing but for her good looks. Blond, tall, dashing – she comes pretty close to living up to Hollywood's idea of what a big-league woman reporter should be.' A photograph showed Martha at her neatest and prettiest, the perfect portrait of a star from the days of silent movies.

Liana's overtones of feminism – a young woman treated as a child and abandoned by her lover when the masculine world of war proved more alluring – did not fit in with *Collier's* quaint view of the sexes, but it was to their credit that they acknowledged and promoted her increasingly assured and distinctive voice. Between 1938 and the spring of 1944 they published twenty-six of her articles, in which a recognisable 'I' had steadily emerged, as storyteller, guide, moralist and witness. Witness of a particular kind, however: Martha, like the other war correspondents of her day, focused on the more edifying aspects of the war. *Collier's*, like *Look* or *Life*, preferred tales of heroism and pluckiness to those of blunders, desertion, drunkenness or cowardice. As the poet Delmore Schwartz had noted in his diary in 1942, 'winning the war without criticism' would be the final victory for Henry Luce.

In the column devoted to Martha, Hemingway, asked for a comment, was generous about her writing and her fortitude and paid tribute to her ability to make her readers feel that they were witnesses with her of all that she described. 'She gets to the place,' he said, 'gets the story, writes it, and comes home. That last is the best part.' It was a nice note on which to go home.

* * *

This time, the return to Hemingway was not as good, though she said that she liked the bushy pepper and salt beard he had grown in her absence. The submarine hunts on the *Pilar* had not yielded even one sighting, and if fifth columnists were lurking in the back streets of Havana, they appeared to be causing little mischief. To the relief of the CIA, as it later transpired, Hemingway decided to call a halt to the Crook Shop and disband his men. They had accomplished nothing, but at least, Leddy, the FBI man in Cuba, was able to report to his superiors, they had caused no harm either by uncovering evidence of American links with corrupt Cuban officials. Clearly embarrassed by the futility of the enterprise and resentful of Martha's good time in Europe, Hemingway was sour and belligerent. His temper was not improved by Bumby's remark that Martha was now the writer in the family, or by his own heavy drinking. The Finca was a mess, and he refused to be mollified by the fact that *For Whom the Bell Tolls* had sold three-quarters of a million copies in the United States, more than any other American novel except for *Gone with the Wind*.

When Martha had been home a week, Hemingway wrote one of his more sententious letters to Edna, full of heavy-handed mock concern. Finding his wife much altered by her six and a half months away, he said 'for a while I thought maybe she had paranoia.' There had been such loss of memory and such inability to think about anything except herself that he had come to think of her as 'just plain spoiled and inhumanly selfish'. Martha, said Hemingway, loved war; she had never been happier in her life. Yet in all that time she was away she had never seen a dead body – a taunt he wrongly made several times. 'Nothing outside of her self interests her very much. . . . she seems mentally unbalanced; maybe just borderline. If it is just pure, straight, hard, unmoral selfishness then there is nothing to worry about . . .' What Edna felt about receiving such a letter is not recorded, though it cannot have been easy for either her or Martha that the exchange took place.

The Hemingways fought. They fought over money, over the house and work, and they fought over his drinking. He bullied her, snarled at her and mocked her; she ridiculed his submarine hunting and railed against his boastful lying. Then Hemingway suddenly announced that he had decided to go to Europe after all, and that he would be writing articles for *Collier's*, a choice Martha herself had originally proposed but, now that their relations were so bad, she saw as full of spite, since he could have had his pick of the papers. This way he effectively jeopardised her position on the magazine, which in theory at least was allowed only one accredited journalist at the front. What she also found hard to bear was the fact that since Hemingway had agreed to write about the heroism of the RAF pilots, the RAF was prepared to give him a rare plane seat to London. As Martha herself had fixed this for him with Roald Dahl, then air attaché at the British Embassy in Washington, with whom she probably had had a brief affair during one of her wartime visits to the capital, she felt further left out. 'The way it looks,' she wrote to Mrs Roosevelt, 'I am going to lose out on the thing I most care about seeing or writing of in the world, and maybe in my whole life. I was a fool to come back from Europe and I knew it.' Missing the invasion, for which she felt she had spent the autumn and winter preparing, was going to take 'an awful lot more humility and good sense than I now have at my command'.

The relationship between Martha and Hemingway was now

very unhappy. Martha, all her life reticent about the physical side of her affairs with men, said little about Hemingway. He, on the other hand, talked about her freely, finding coarse and tawdry stories with which to entertain his entourage of hangers-on, later repeated, with obvious relish by the more voyeuristic among them. As the marriage fell apart, so his cronies in the Floridita listened to his drunken maunderings and stored them up for later.

Neither Martha nor Hemingway stayed long in Cuba. Hemingway hurried to New York to catch his seaplane for Shannon and London, telling Martha that the plane was taking no women passengers. It turned out that the actress Gertrude Lawrence was on board, bearing a dozen fresh eggs for deprived friends in England, all of which broke on the journey.

With some difficulty, once again appealing to Allen Grover for help, Martha found a place on a Norwegian freighter carrying amphibious personnel carriers and dynamite, part of a convoy crossing the Atlantic. The voyage would take twenty days. She was the sole passenger. There were no lifeboats, the ship was dry, she was forbidden to smoke on deck and only the captain, an anxious and garrulous man, spoke a little English. While the freighter nosed its way gingerly through thick fog, 'blowing our whistle waspishly at everyone (the whistle says, for Christ's sake don't run into me, you baboon, I'll explode)', as she wrote to Hortense Flexner, Martha slept, rested and read *Lady Chatterley's Lover*. Lawrence, she decided, was a 'dreadful and undisciplined writer', but the novel itself not a bad study in boredom and marital distaste. Frieda Lawrence's foreword, on the other hand, was the 'most godawful tasteless mindless' rubbish and made her feel sick. She had also taken on board with her *The History of Rose Hanks*, a novel by her old teacher and admirer from St Louis, Stanley Pennell, from which Max Perkins had forced Pennell to remove long passages quite transparently about Martha, on the grounds that Hemingway would kill them both if they stayed in.

'I feel myself that man is mad and the phrase quo vadis is engraved upon my mind in neon lights,' Martha wrote to Allen

Grover, 'and very little makes sense to me any more . . . I wish peace would be at least as purposeful and moving as war.' She spent hours at a time on deck, pacing up and down between the amphibious personnel carriers, either writing short stories in her head or ruminating about Hemingway. 'I find I cannot think of him in kindness but only with dread,' she wrote in her diary on 10 May. 'Stayed in bed till afternoon,' she noted on the 12th. 'Terrible depression last night – cldn't sleep for sadness – regretting it all so terribly.' One day she wrote a long, valedictory letter to Hortense Flexner about herself and Hemingway. 'He is a rare and wonderful type; he is a mysterious type too and a wise one and all sorts of things. He is a good man, which is vitally important. He is however bad for me, sadly enough, or maybe wrong for me is the word; and I am wrong for him . . . I am wondering now if it ever really worked . . . I feel terribly strange, like a shadow, and full of dread. I dread the time ahead, the amputating time . . . I do not want the world to go dark and narrow and mean for either of us . . . It is, note, my fault: I am the one who has changed. Or maybe I was changing all along, so slowly that it was like getting a callous; but now the callous is there where there ought to be a softness and trust and love. And I am ashamed and guilty too, because I am breaking his heart . . . We quarrelled too much, I suppose . . . It is all sickening and I am sad to death, and afraid . . . I only want to be alone. I want to be myself and alone and free to breathe, live, look upon the world and find it however it is . . . I want my own name back, most violently, as if getting it back would give me some of myself . . . And do not worry and do not feel badly. We are, basically, two tough people and we were born to survive.'

As so often when coming to the end of a relationship, Martha's mind was now rich in stories; one day she sat down and wrote seven pages, which left her sweaty and tired but exhilarated. 'It's a curious thing,' she noted in her diary, 'but now it's like dope – the stories begin *after* something.' Icebergs were sighted, and she was enchanted to see them take the shape of white pigeons, their wings dipped towards the water.

It was not in her nature to grieve for long, or to be destroyed easily by regret. As the boat neared the coast of England, she rose at four and went on deck to watch the land emerge out of the darkness. 'Such a feeling of wild happiness,' she wrote.

Martha docked at Liverpool to learn that Hemingway had been in a car accident and was in hospital. After a party of Capa's in Belgrave Square, he had accepted a lift back to his hotel from a Dr Peter Gorer, who had been drunk. It was three in the morning and the streets were black. The car went straight into a steel water tank: Hemingway was thrown hard against the windscreen and knocked out. Both his knees were injured, and he had a deep gash across his scalp, which needed fifty-seven stitches.

Martha went to visit him in the London Clinic and apparently hurt his feelings by laughing at the huge bandage wrapped like an enormous turban around his head. When, a couple of days later, he returned to the Dorchester with terrible headaches, he accused her of neglecting him, but the truth was that she was repelled by all the drunken parties and not much amused by the people. She was never a drinker in the way Hemingway was and little repelled her more than groups of people out of control. Nor did she like gangs or packs. Though forbidden alcohol because of the concussion, Hemingway resumed his heavy drinking, and was once again enjoying one long continuous party, filling his room with old friends such as Capa, and the writer Irwin Shaw, as well as new cronies and acquaintances. One of these was William Walton, a young reporter sent over from New York to cover the landings for *Time*. Another was a thirty-six-year-old journalist, the wife of an Australian reporter called Noël Monks, who had come to London to write feature stories for the *Daily Express* and then moved over to *Time*. She was American, from Minnesota, a small, pretty woman, with short curly hair, and she had turned her room at the Dorchester into a meeting place for the *Time-Life* reporters. Her name was Mary Welsh.

Looking for ways to goad and needle Martha, Hemingway staged offensive scenes that reduced her to tears and embarrassed their friends. One evening, as a gesture of apology, he asked her to dine with him. On his way to collect her from her room, for they had rooms apart, he bumped into Mary Welsh. He took her to dinner instead.

*   *   *

The Allies had been preparing for the invasion of France for over two years. By the early summer of 1944, two and a half million men were ready in Britain, gathering for the weather and the tides. Poised to cross the Channel with them, jostling for position, having called in favours and made deals, were 558 accredited writers, radio journalists and photographers, reporting to censors provided by the military on board the assault crafts. Martha was not among them. As a woman, and now junior to Hemingway on the staff of *Collier's*, she had no right to a place at the front. Just the same, she got to France, and landed, and came back. Hemingway did not get there; and nor did many others.

On the grey and cold morning of 6 June, together with others who had not been granted places with the invading forces, Martha waited in London for the moment when the signal would come through to say the invasion had begun. In her diary, she noted the actual moment. '9.46 or so: In 5 seconds the command will be given to the world . . .' The briefing over, and having no particular place to go, she wandered around the city for a while, listening to the bombers overhead, 'the sound of a giant factory in the sky'. 'Abbey – soldiers – Red Cross,' she wrote. 'Weather raw and cold . . . Before 11 – no one in front of palace except crowd of soldiers & officials going in for investiture . . . Now getting scared. Worried for E.'

Then she decided to set out for the coast, to see if she couldn't find her own way to France. Late that night, on the docks, she was stopped by a military policeman. She explained that she was going to interview nurses for her magazine, indicating a white painted ship with huge red crosses on its side. He waved her through.

She boarded the ship, found a lavatory, and locked herself in. After some time, she heard the ship weigh anchor and move; she emerged to find night had fallen and that the ship had cleared the harbour. 'The weather gets rainier and colder every minute,' she wrote. 'Badly spooked . . . The sweating it out period before leaving then paid off. Was drinking a lot of whisky . . . I was very scared, drank, got unscared.' At dawn, she watched as they sailed into a 'seascape filled with ships . . . the greatest naval traffic jam in history . . . so enormous, so awesome, that it felt more like an act of nature than anything man made.'

No one questioned her presence on board. The hospital ship – the first to cross the Channel – was a civilian vessel that had once carried passengers between Harwich and Holland, manned by a crew from the Merchant Navy, with American doctors and nurses newly arrived from the States. 'Double & triple clap of gunfire,' she wrote. 'Unseen planes roar. Barrage balloons. Gun flashes. 1 close shell burst . . . Explosions jar the ship.'

The ship anchored in the American sector, at Omaha Red. On the beach, bulldozers were scooping up and detonating mines, while naval guns fired overhead at the high bluff beyond the beach. Martha watched bodies bobbing in the choppy water round the ship's bows, face-down, 'swollen greyish sacks', infantrymen who had leapt too soon into the water and drowned under the weight of their packs. And then the hospital ship went to work. Landing craft appeared alongside with casualties who were winched on board in wooden boxes looking like lidless coffins; the ship's own water ambulances brought back others. In the surgery on board, the doctors began to operate. Martha helped where she could, interpreting for French and German wounded, fetching water for the thirsty, and organising two young cabin boys in bright red monkey jackets to make corned beef sandwiches for those not too badly injured to eat. 'Dr doing duty but without sympathy,' she wrote, watching the German casualties being loaded and talking loudly to each other. 'When they giggled too much I said "Ruhig" on dr's orders and they were all instantly silent. We are helpless against our own decency really.'

When night came she went ashore with the ambulance teams, wading through water up to her waist, to collect casualties ready for embarkation at first light. Walking up a marked path that had been cleared of mines, she smelt the 'sweet smell of summer grass, a smell of cattle and peace and the sun that had warmed the earth some other time, when summer was real'. She thought of all the people who had once lain on this beach, and swum in its warm waves. Red flares lit up a scene that now looked to her like a 'deserted junk yard, with the boxy black shapes of tanks, trucks, munition dumps'. The noise of gunfire was deafening. 'Village really smashed – church like collapsed paper bag.' At dawn, the hospital ship's 426 bunks all full, the doctors having operated all night, they set back for England. In her diary, Martha noted: 'Great speed & efficiency of loading. Special tenderness towards coloured wounded . . . Burn cases. Blood soaked bandages. Everyone watching in silence. Mass of German prisoners marching to POW cage . . . terrible seedy bunch. Kids – old. German prisoners ward. Almost all complained very much of pain.'

On getting back to port, Martha watched the first German prisoners disembarking, unhealthy, undersized men of the Wehrmacht, not the blond giants she expected. Under the Geneva Convention, journalists could not question prisoners of war, in order to spare them the indignity, so she simply stood and stared. They were not, she thought, 'like us. They take advantage or they take orders; there is nothing in between.' She returned to London to write two long pieces for Collier's, the first about the hospital ship, full of admiration for the calm efficiency and dedication of the medical staff, the second about the flaccidness of the German prisoners. And then she was arrested by the military police for having crossed to France without permission, and sent as punishment to an American nurses' training camp outside London, where she was told that she could cross to Normandy only when the nurses were ready to go.

D-Day saw an outpouring of words. From the accredited journalists alone came over 700,000 written words, while the

BBC had put forty-eight reporters into the field, with Chester Wilmot in a glider and Richard Dimbleby with the RAF. Hemingway had not fared well, though a reader would not have guessed it from the story he filed for *Collier's*. On the wet night of 5 June, his head still bandaged and limping from the injury to his knees, he had boarded an attack transport called the *Dorothea M. Dix*, from which he had been transferred to a landing craft delivering troops to the beach. Though he did not make it to shore himself, the issue of *Collier's* that carried both his and Martha's first stories had Hemingway's name on the cover as their special correspondent, and a large photograph of him talking to soldiers, with his bushy grey-flecked beard, looking rather like a military Father Christmas.

Written assertively in the first person, his report spoke of helping a reluctant and jumpy young first lieutenant locate their destination, and of their assault on the heavily mined and defended Normandy beach in broad daylight. Without his guidance and calm demeanour, the article suggested, the craft would probably never have made it at all. Nor did Hemingway resist the dramatic touch. 'I saw a piece of German about three foot long,' he wrote, 'with an arm on it sail high up into the air in the fountaining of one shellburst.' Before the article appeared, he discovered that a German division had been sent 'just where *Collier's* correspondent landed.' 'We hit it right on the nose,' Hemingway cabled.

By contrast, Martha's tones were muted and extremely effective; they contained her by now usual coda, which this time had something of the resonance of a younger Hemingway: 'Day merges into night,' she wrote, 'and the invasion, which is brand new, is something we have always had, so that no other condition of life seems imaginable.' As descriptive war reporting goes, hers was very much the better.

Hemingway was not pleased when he heard that Martha had landed on Omaha Beach. He continued to feel sour about the way she had belittled his injuries, while she was feeling increasingly distanced from him by the *Time-Life* crowd who filled his room at every hour and by his obvious interest in Mary Welsh. Having managed to escape her captors by rolling under the American nurses' camp's perimeter fence, she was now looking for ways to get away from London. Most of her own friends were in France, and she had had a depressing last visit to Wells, whom she had found wearing a white panama hat with a blue ribbon round it, looking ill and sad, painting a frieze of devils round his garage walls, giving them the faces of Churchill, Stalin and Roosevelt. His memory seemed to have gone and he had forgotten that he had ever owned his house in France, Lou Pidou. He seemed very unhappy. 'They have never listened to me, never,' he said to her sadly.

On 14 June, she wrote a reassuring letter to her mother, telling her that Hemingway was alive and happy, that he had crossed to France in the first wave in the most perilous circumstances, but that she had not seen much of him as he had 'masses of his own pals'. Knowing that her letter would be censored, she went on: 'I may, after a while, go back to my old haunts where I was before I returned to Cuba. The only kick I have here is that women correspondents are treated too much like violets and unless that relaxes a great deal the other place may be better for a bit . . . Anyhow just know I am well and wildly busy, that my own affairs go comfortably, and I am happy as a goat.'

To others she did not sound quite so goat-like. 'Am really dead tired and sort of sad,' she wrote to Grover. Work, once again, the '*opium unique*' of her twenties, came to save her. She had taken *Collier's*' deference to Hemingway without complaint, and her name was now listed next to his on the masthead, as 'invasion correspondent'. Having lost any form of military accreditation, as well as travel papers or ration entitlements, by her illicit crossing to France, she would spend the remaining year of the war in Europe, sometimes in uniform, sometimes out of it, ducking and dodging from front to front, using her energy and charm to win over officers into allowing her to travel with their regiments, scrounging lifts and filing stories whenever she could cajole wireless operators into giving her a line. Her looks, her obvious courage and her utter disregard for authority came in very useful. Far fewer doors, she later admitted, would have opened for a man.

Determined to get back to Italy, where she sensed she would have more freedom, Martha now made friends with an RAF pilot returning to the Italian campaign. Inventing a piteous story about a fiancé, she hitched a lift to Naples on his plane. Before leaving London, she wrote a formal letter of protest to the military authorities about the 'curiously condescending' treatment of women war correspondents, which, she said, was as ridiculous as it was undignified, and was preventing professional woman reporters, with many years experience, from carrying out their responsibilities to their editors and to 'millions of people in America who are desperately in need of seeing, but cannot see for themselves'. To Allen Grover, she added crossly that female journalists were now seen as lepers.

The Allies had made considerable progress against the Germans in Italy in the four months she had been away. On 4 June, two days before the Normandy landings, they had taken Rome and were now pressing on north towards Perugia and Florence. Martha was charmed by the 'huge hodgepodge' of nationalities that made up the Eighth Army, New Zealanders and Indians, South Africans and soldiers from Basutoland, Canadians and Poles, who, having fought their way through the sandstorms of the African desert and the mud of the Italian winter, were now 'very neighbourly men'. She attached herself to the Carpathian Lancers, the cavalry regiment whose men had escaped from Poland over the Carpathian Mountains and had switched from horses to tanks in Egypt, later becoming the heroes of Cassino, and rode with them in their jeeps.

In the evenings, camping in fields among the haystacks, she went foraging for ducks and geese and red wine, and listened as the Poles sang the songs they had composed at every stage in their long war. It was full summer, and the weather in Umbria was wonderful. In between skirmishes with the retreating Germans, she swam with the soldiers, picking her way down to the water across beaches littered with mines and splashing in the warm pale sea. 'Lying on haystack talking nonsense,' she wrote in her notebook. 'Shells coming over – Peace itself with shells coming over . . . whistling over like great birds. Afternoon – all danger hidden (big mines looking like carpenters tool chests) blue sea and sky . . . dust unbelievable . . . Waiting, waiting, white w. dust & everything packed – like life in a circus. Happy regiment – main feature. Soldiers all so independent.'

As they travelled north, she interviewed the men about their lives and what they thought would happen to them after the war. Martha's particular trademark was now on all her pieces, her ability to weave the daily scenes of war into an infinitely large picture made up of history and memory and hope. Of all the men now gradually fighting their way home across liberated Europe, the Poles had the most to fear from what they would find waiting for them. After they had sung their songs at night, accompanied by one man's violin and another's accordion, they told her they did not believe that Russia would ever relinquish Poland, and that they feared they would be sacrificed, as Czechoslovakia had been in 1938. 'There they all stood, the officers and the men, friends and partners,' she wrote of a church service one Sunday morning in a small village, 'each one with his long journey behind him and each one with the long uncertain journey ahead.'

This was the kind of war reporting Martha most enjoyed, travelling with soldiers she admired, through wonderful countryside and under a hot sun, away from Hemingway's manipulative intrigues and uncertain temper, and always moving. She seldom indulged in fears about the future. She was busy, and alive, and, like a Hemingway character, it was good and she was happy.

By August she was in Florence, which the German and the British forces had tried to preserve reasonably intact, and where soldiers were still fighting, street by street. She was billeted with an elderly American resident in his house on the hills at Bellosguardo and from a stone bench in his garden she looked out across the city towards Fiesole, where the Germans were firing their guns. A British captain, who was commanding a battery in the garden, played Chopin on the piano, while the American's wife sang Italian songs of the seicento, and the 'outgoing shells whistled over the house like insane freight cars'. Martha's notes from Florence, scrawled in pencil, were clearly written in haste. 'Water supply. Partisans. Ponte Vecchio all damage. Germans take all transport including hearses and animals – Dead buried in handcarts. Procession – man killed going out to buy vegetables. 1400 Jugoslavs imprisoned by Italians – now disappeared . . . The people of Florence could weep for the destruction of their city. So drab & soiled in war . . . Uffizi Gallery w. hole showing ceiling paintings.'

One day, having clambered across the ruins of the Ponte Vecchio into the centre of the city, she went to bed with a twenty-six-year-old major 'tall and beautiful and funny', in the totally deserted Hotel Excelsior, and they made love to the sound of mortar and machine-gun fire in the streets outside. As the days passed, she talked to the Florentines she met in the streets, in a rudimentary Italian remembered from holidays with Bertrand, about their experience of the German occupation. She wandered around the Bóboli Gardens where the dead, left unburied because the Germans held the cemeteries, were stacked naked in open pits, and watched the young partisan boys in their shorts and sandals, wearing arm bands and red handkerchiefs, carrying machine pistols abandoned by the Germans. The Pitti Palace had been turned over to the many refugees who had taken cover from the fighting in the surrounding countryside, and in the huge staterooms mattresses lay in between the marble busts. 'Washing hanging on railings of main court,' Martha noted. 'Shuttered, silent, sheets.'

By now she had attached herself to a Canadian regiment and it was with their jeeps that she crossed to the Adriatic coast, in a great sweep of tanks and armoured vehicles grinding their way over the mountains in clouds of dust to attack the German Gothic Line, recording for *Collier's* 'a jigsaw puzzle of fighting men, bewildered terrified civilians, noise, smells, jokes, pain, fear, unfinished conversations and high explosives'. She worried 'for the young men killed now when the end of the war was at last in sight'. One day she took a book and a bottle of sweet Italian rum and sat in the hot sun on the beach looking out across the Adriatic, watching the pilot from a burning plane float down towards the ground in his parachute, out of a brilliant blue sky. 'The weather is lovely,' she wrote, 'and no one wants to think of those who must still die and those who must still be wounded in the fighting before peace comes.'

On 25 August, while the Eighth Army was beginning its offensive on the Adriatic, General LeClerc liberated Paris. Martha, anxious to learn what had happened to her Parisian friends through four years of occupation, hitched another lift on a military plane going to Lyons, where she met up with four intelligence officers leaving for Paris. On the way, the jeep went over an embankment and she was thrown out, breaking a rib and badly bruising herself. But the party pressed on. She entered Paris to find Hemingway installed in the Ritz, which he claimed to have liberated as commander of a band of 'irregulars'. Mary Welsh was in a room along the corridor.

Martha took a room at the Lincoln, and set out to walk around the fashionable streets she remembered so well, noting the 'couture and hats, fine smooth faces, gleaming hair . . . How shocked one is,' she wrote, 'absolutely beautiful clothes, material, buttons, beads. Everything non utility. Georges V – poor little poules coming in. Old lady in lace hat and wooden shoes eating crumbs of bread on sheet.' In her notebook, Martha recorded what there was to be bought in the shops and what it all cost. Paris was remarkably unchanged, a city of open spaces, statues and trees in leaf, and few of the beautiful buildings had been marked by shellfire. The booksellers were in their stalls along the banks of the Seine, and there was make-up in the shops, but since there was no leather for shoes, women clattered about the streets on platform soles made of wood, sounding like horses' hooves. The young intellectuals were all wearing ski clothes, and turbans for hats. There had been hunger, and drabness and cold, but no starvation, and no severe bombing, but there was hunger now, and cold, the blackmarket having largely disappeared with the Germans, and there was very little coal or gas about. In restaurants, you could see Parisians in their overcoats dining on carrot and turnip soup. As the weeks passed, the shortages grew worse and when salt ran low, so did charcuterie, as the Bretons, traditional providers of Paris's famed sausages and hams, were no longer able to salt their pigs. 'Way everyone now become a great FFI or partisan and way no one has served the Germans . . .' Martha wrote. 'People saying to each other in Paris "What did you do during the war?"' With her distaste for cliques, she kept away from the smart hotels, like the Prince de Galles, where soldiers she dismissed as 'very braided', the non-fighting generals and the quartermasters, went to drink, all of them 'punks and grafters'.

She also kept carefully away from Hemingway, though it was hard to ignore his hostility. He was not a man accustomed to being left by women, and his furious accounts to friends of their crumbling marriage made it plain that he was determined to emerge as the one who had had enough. 'I hate to lose anyone who can look so lovely and who we taught to shoot and write so well,' he wrote to his son Patrick, at boarding school in the States. 'But have torn up my tickets on her and would be glad never to see her again.' Though not always very pleasant to Mary – one day he told her she looked like a spider – he addressed her affectionately as 'Small Friend' and, when not drinking with his entourage, took her on drives to see the Paris he had loved in the twenties.

The Allies, who had commandeered seven hundred hotels for their own use, had designated the Hôtel Scribe as press headquarters, and it was here that petrol was stored, along with coffee, champagne and K-rations, and here that reporters brought their stories to be censored. Martha, though still a pariah in the eyes of the military, managed to slip in some cables for Collier's. Harold Acton, to whom fell the task of censoring them, later said that her stories were among the most acute that he passed. After the Allies revealed that they had discovered Gestapo torture chambers in the grounds of the Ministry of Aviation, in the Avenue Foch and at Chaton in the suburbs, Martha joined a tour laid on by the press office and later wrote about what she called the 'wounds' of Paris. Very simply, she described seeing dark, wet tunnels, much of the ground under water, where captives were held until they died; a cemetery, where men and women wandered, searching for lost relations, taken away during the war by the Germans; and a shack still brown with dried blood, where a prisoner had scratched on the wall 'Revenge me'. In the years of their occupation, the Germans were said to have shot 30,000 people and tortured many others, some to death. Now the '*épuration*' of those who had helped them was under way, the head shaving and summary trials and executions.

The formal trials of writers and journalists who were considered to have collaborated were about to begin. On 9 September, two weeks after the liberation, a manifesto of French writers, signed by fifty-nine leading intellectuals, among them Paul Valéry and François Mauriac, called for the 'just punishment of usurpers and traitors', and by October it had 156 names on its blacklist. The trials of writers proceeded quickly, if only because it was a simple matter to read what they had written.

Bit by bit, Martha learnt what had happened to those friends of hers and Bertrand's who had been so much in favour of an alliance with Germany before the war. Some, she discovered, had disappeared abroad, like Bertrand himself, who, having served as a private on the Maginot Line, had gone to Switzerland in 1942 after realising that he could not actually prove that he had remained friends with Otto Abetz solely in order to provide information to the Free French. Abetz had been appointed German ambassador to Paris in 1940. Among these former friends, now abroad or lying low, were the 'passive' collaborators, writers such as Gide or Henri de Montherlant who had seen in the French defeat something more profoundly wrong with France than military unpreparedness, and had simply tried to make the best of the occupation. Others, such as Sacha Guitry, Jean Luchaire or Robert Brasillach, editor of the pro-Nazi *Je Suis Partout*, were already in prison, and would soon be executed.

Abetz himself was under arrest, and would receive a twenty-year prison sentence from a Paris military tribunal. Responsible for the 'Otto List' of some 1,200 banned French and foreign books – including most English translations and all books written by Jews – Abetz would also be held accountable for the deportation of Jews from Drancy, the suburb of Paris from where the trains left for the concentration camps. Bertrand's offer to appear as witness at his trial was refused. Not long after his release, Abetz died in a mysterious car crash on the Cologne–Ruhr autobahn, when the steering on his car failed; it was said to have been tampered with as a revenge for the deportations.

Martha's other friend, Drieu la Rochelle, the man who on her last visit before the war had reminded her of a sexy satyr and who had taken over *La Nouvelle Revue Française*, had tried to kill himself two weeks before the liberation. He would try again while in hospital, by cutting his wrists, and was again saved. He would succeed eight months later, on his third attempt. Having returned to Paris where he was ostracised by his friends and summoned to appear before a tribunal, he swallowed three tubes of sleeping pills and turned on the gas. 'He failed with his death,' wrote a reporter for the Resistance *Franc-Tireur*, 'as he failed with life.' In the winter of 1944, after his second attempt at suicide, Drieu had kept a secret diary. 'I do not want to be an intellectual who prudently measures his words,' he had written. 'We must dirty our feet, at least, but not our hands . . . I am no ordinary patriot, no limited nationalist: I am an internationalist. I am not only a Frenchman, I am a European.'

Even Colette, whose husband Maurice Goudeket was Jewish, had a slight cloud hanging over her, because she had written for the collaborationist paper, *Le Petit Parisien*. And both Arletty, the singer, and Coco Chanel, who had taken German lovers and lived in the Ritz, were briefly arrested. Arletty had had her head shaved.

In 'A Honeyed Peace', a short story written after the war about Paris soon after liberation, Martha is less absolute and censorious than in much of her earlier fiction. The story centres around two foreign women, one English and one American, who return to Paris with the Allies and discover that their close French friend Evangeline has been ostracised by smart society as well as by local tradesmen because her husband

Renaud has been arrested for collaboration. As the two women explore their own reactions and those of their former friends, there is both compassion and cynicism about the reckoning and the settled scores.

On 4 September, the Allies took Brussels, and Martha travelled in their wake, once again eager to escape Hemingway and the drinking parties. She found the city in a frenzy of celebration and the Belgians more apparently delighted at their liberation than the Parisians, perhaps helped by the discovery of 80,000 looted bottles of the finest claret in the city's cellars. When, three days later, Antwerp was taken, the lion house at the zoo was emptied of its lions and their places in the cages taken by Germans and collaborators: one cage for German officers, a second for privates, a third for Belgian collaborators and a fourth for their wives and daughters and women who had slept with Germans. The captives sat on the straw, staring through the bars.

By the middle of September, Martha was on the move again, following behind the British ground forces waiting to link up with the airborne divisions dropping at Arnhem, driving across the flat land through villages that looked, under the grey sky, like the industrial north of England. Nijmegen, a small Dutch town obliterated by shelling, looked, she wrote for *Collier's*, as if it had been 'abandoned years ago following an earthquake or a flood', and 'not even a cat would want to slink through the shopping district'. She went to the hospital and saw silent children with head wounds, and then to the morgue. Then she visited the prison, 'the collaborators' jail . . . the stupid ugly looking woman who slept w. Germans. One slept w. 5 in 3 mo.s. Awful smell of unwashed bodies. Always the poor. Only well dressed Fascists I've ever seen were at Drancy . . . Driving home at night feeling scared mainly because of the dark. Very alone.'

Not all the reporters who had descended in their hundreds on Paris were quite as keen as Martha to move on. Hemingway, after delivering a number of gung-ho and self-regarding accounts of his adventures at the head of his irregulars, and a lyrical description of his part in liberating Paris from the Germans, had lent his typewriter to another journalist and declared that he was giving up writing. He was, his friends observed, having a good time; war, 'grace under pressure' as he famously wrote, suited him perfectly, and the *Time-Life* correspondent William Walton found him at his best at this time, both fun to be with and an 'educated warrior'. To Edna, Hemingway wrote a letter full of recriminations about Martha's 'silly inhumanity', saying that she 'loves to leave people. It is the bad scene that she plays best', and that he did not want his life smashed up any longer by heartlessness, selfishness, carelessness 'nor even just good clean ambition and hatred of team play'. To Bumby, he wrote more lightly, saying that he was now looking to trade his equity in Martha for 'a good fleece lined jacket and an extra pair of sox. Or would swap her for two non beautiful wives I might occasionally have the opportunity of going to bed with.' Marlene Dietrich had taken a room in the Ritz as her base from which to tour the troops, and Capa, Irwin Shaw, George Orwell and many others came and went, starved for the prewar meals that were available at a price, and delighted to find the restaurants they remembered open again.

At some point in the autumn Martha returned to Paris where an unexpectedly friendly Hemingway asked her to dinner in a restaurant with some of his entourage of soldiers and reporters. The evening started well, but was soon soured by Hemingway's malice; he talked, as Martha later recorded, 'like a cobra until the boys melted away with embarrassment'. When she broached the question of divorce, he became threatening. Martha returned to her hotel in tears, and was found by Capa on his way home from a poker evening. 'Phone the Ritz and ask for Mary Welsh,' he said to her, crouching on the floor counting his winnings. 'When Hemingway answers, I'll tell you what to say.' She followed his instructions and when Hemingway 'began to vituperate', Capa told her to put the phone down. 'It will be all right now,' he said and indeed the divorce went ahead. (Capa's own friendship with Hemingway did not survive the war: Capa did not care for Mary Welsh, and told Hemingway that he failed to see why he had to marry her. Hemingway threw a bottle of champagne at him.)

But Martha's mood remained low, and though Diana Cooper, now installed in the British Embassy, where Duff Cooper was ambassador, told her she would look back on the day she and Hemingway finally parted as the happiest of her life, she wept in desperation. 'Who shall I talk to and who will tell me why I am doing what I am doing,' she wrote in a long and despairing letter to Grover. 'There is no one to marry, and if God has any benevolence for me he will spare me further horrid errors of the heart, when one tries to make permanence. I wish only to be unmarried; it seems neater. I am so free that the atom cannot be freer, I am free like nothing quite bearable . . .

'On the other hand I want a child. I will carry it on my back in a sealskin papoose and feed it chocolate milk shakes and tell it fine jokes and work for it and in the end give it a hunk of money, like a bouquet of autumn leaves, and set it free. I have to have something, being still (I presume) human . . .

'I also do not believe in what I do, realising too well the fine protective layer of the human mind and heart, a thing made of ferro concrete and built to resist knowledge. I write like someone screaming, my articles are horrible, and unread and inefficient. I do not even know what I scream against, except the barbarousness of the human animal. I scream for kindness. Let there be kindness. There is bloody little and never at a high enough level.

'One cannot stop anything or help anything and only finds oneself a little mad – with always the fine shrewd disgusting self-protection that halts madness before it becomes heroic – and lonely and afraid not of the usual things, but of the unseen things, the dark series of days, the long days and the long years and all the time ahead which will be no better than this time.

'And what happened to the fine gilded hopes when one expected to be like other people with a place to come back to, someone to trust, someone to whom one could say anything without shame: what happened to the desired never existing always comforting loving trusting arms that were to be guaranteed forever against nightmares . . . Oh Allen come and hold my hand and I will hold yours. Life is as long as war.' How deeply Martha minded being childless is hard to say, given her reticence on the subject and her apparent refusal to have a child by Hemingway; but, as she told Grover now, her feeling of loneliness was made much worse by her uneasy realisation that, at thirty-eight, there was not a great deal of time left in which to get pregnant. What does come through, however, particularly in these letters to Grover, at this time perhaps her closest confidant, is both how hurt she felt by Hemingway's vindictiveness and how culpable about the breakup. Had she ever really loved Hemingway? Probably not as he had loved her. Certainly she had longed for the marriage to work, and even, for a while, convinced herself that it would; but the fact that she seemed willing to abandon it so readily now suggests that what she was left with was more grief about herself than any real sense of loss. On the surface at least, Martha was very skilled at relinquishing an unsatisfactory past; and it was rare that she allowed herself such confessions of frailty as she confided to Grover.

Martha and Hemingway had a further bruising encounter during the Battle of the Bulge, when both were unpleasant to each other and Hemingway harangued her about her ignorance of military matters. Later, Hemingway justified his boorishness to William Walton, who was present, by saying that you couldn't expect to use a bow and arrow to hunt an elephant. Later that night, Hemingway stripped to his long johns and, putting the hotel chambermaid's bucket on his head and brandishing her mop, appeared outside Martha's room. Through the door, she told him that he was drunk and to go away. They met again, very briefly, at the Dorchester in London, to discuss details of the divorce, when Martha was in bed with flu. And then they never saw each other again. Gigi, Hemingway's youngest son, later said that Martha had ultimately been driven away by his father's megalomania, and that it was only once he had finally destroyed their relationship that she abandoned him. Writing to Perkins, Hemingway observed: 'Funny how it should take one war to start a woman in your damn heart and another to finish her.'

To her mother, Martha wrote fiercely. 'I simply never want to hear his name mentioned again; the past is dead and has become ugly; I shall try to forget it all entirely, and blot it out as with amnesia.

'A man must be a very great genius to make up for being such a loathsome human being.'

CHAPTER TEN

The Pale Empty Colour of the Future

'When you were very young,' Edna once said to Martha, 'what interested you was France, and you found or were found by the most complete Frenchman available. Then you were interested in writing, so you found or were found by what you thought the finest writer. In the war, you were interested in bravery and you found or were found by who was considered perhaps the bravest of all.' The bravest of all was James Gavin.

At thirty-six the youngest divisional commander in the American army, Gavin was a lean, fit, boyish figure, over six feet tall, which was unusual for the parachute division, the 82nd Airborne, which he commanded. He was the stuff of heroes, the soldier who always jumped before his men, who was idolised for his unruffled good humour and his military precision, and Martha needed heroes, as Bertrand had sadly observed when she grew restless in his company. And Edna was right: Martha had always been drawn to the most absolute of things, and in particular to absolute professionalism. It was part of what made her such a remarkable reporter, doing more and more research where others felt that they had covered enough ground. Gavin, obsessed by all things military, enviably clear about his purpose in life, would have been attractive to her even without his considerable charm; but he had a great deal of that too.

The 82nd Airborne had been at the centre of many of the war's worst campaigns. One of the first divisions into Sicily, it had fought its way up Italy, taken part in the Normandy landings and been one of the three chosen for the attack on Arnhem. By the winter of 1944, it was based in a drab, stony village called Sissone, three miles from Reims, where it was to rest before the final push towards Berlin. A sudden call for assistance had come for the 82nd to help establish a corridor through which to extricate the four American divisions trapped by the Battle of the Bulge, the large bump carved by the Germans out of territory already held by the Allies in the thickly wooded Ardennes. It cost them heavy casualties, and they returned to Sissons four thousand men fewer. The weather by now was unendurably cold: daily snowstorms and winds so bitter that men froze to death at night in their foxholes, and the plasma for blood transfusions was found solid in the mornings. Sodden blankets became as rigid as boards.

At some point Martha, who had installed herself in an empty house in a village and joined a couple of sergeants going out on night patrol, was found wandering around the area with her notebook, without a pass or any kind of military accreditation, and not in uniform. She and Gavin met when she was taken by the military police to his tent, where she expected a dressing down and probable deportation to the States.

Martha was now, like Gavin, thirty-six, and she no longer cared, to the extent that she ever had, how she came across. Not bothering to concoct some saving lie, she told Gavin the truth about her paperless state. He laughed and remarked that, with her obvious talent for living off the land, she would make a fine guerrilla fighter. Later what she remembered was that there was something curious about the pupils of Gavin's eyes, which seemed to grow larger while she was talking to him. It gave her a physical shock, as if he had touched her. Gavin reassured her he would pretend that he had never seen her, and that she was free to pursue her own private war. She left his tent, replying to his question about where she was based by saying that she returned to Paris from time to time and stayed at the Hôtel Lincoln.

The last year of the war was the most intense and military of Martha's life. As the weeks passed, and the Allies advanced steadily through Germany, so the military press officers began to relax their restrictions towards women. Martha wandered at will, mostly on her own, sometimes joining other correspondents for a couple of days, knowing that her energy, her looks and her considerable charm would secure her access to most of the places she wanted to be. She followed close in the wake of the Americans, describing for *Collier's* readers what the soldiers called 'wonderful Kraut killing country'. She had few fears, and none at all of being on her own.

At some point early in 1945 she took off briefly for Toulouse and the Spanish border, where half a million loyalists had been living in camps – fed, as she angrily noted, on the 'soup of starvation' – since 1939. She had heard rumours that the refugees were about to launch, without help from anyone, an attack on Franco. Talking to the sad inmates of these impoverished and unhealthy settlements, she was told of all those who had been shipped off to Germany as slave labour and about the thousands who had originally decided to risk staying on in Franco's Spain and since been executed.

On her way back, alone, driving a beaten-up old coupé liberated by Allied soldiers who had lent it to her, a front tyre blew and the car went over a high bank and turned over. Martha was briefly stunned, but eventually pulled herself back on to the road and found a farmer who brought his oxen and righted the car. Remarkably, it was still working and she drove on. Later she found that she had broken several ribs.

In her article, quoting the Spanish refugees, she used 'thou' when reporting their speech, as Hemingway had done in *For Whom the Bell Tolls*. Her piece for *Collier's* ended with her customary ring of hope: 'These people remain intact in spirit. They are armed with a transcendent faith . . . they have never accepted defeat . . . and you can believe quite simply that, since they are what they are, there will be a republic across the mountains and that they will live to return to it.' A typescript of Martha's article is filed in *Collier's* archives. Across the top, someone has written 'This is not bad for tear jerker sort of stuff'.

Ever since returning to Europe before D-Day, Martha, for

all her misgivings, had wanted to fly with the air force on a mission to Germany. Her requests had been turned down, mainly on the grounds that she was a woman; and once she lost her papers she had not wanted to draw attention to herself. Now, with nothing to lose, she talked her way on board a Black Widow on a night flight over Germany, becoming the first woman correspondent to do so. 'Terrified beyond belief', she noted that the plane was very beautiful, like a 'delicate deadly dragonfly'. 'The bombed factories and houses, the pitted ground', she wrote in her notebook, once the ordeal of takeoff had been accomplished and she was wedged on a cushion behind the pilot in an agony of discomfort, clutching an ill-fitting oxygen mask over her face. 'Burning smoke and the Rhine ugly and flat here and like a sewer river . . . In this immensity of sky C-47s like plough horses . . . This land is a desert and these people who loved order and finally insanely wished to impose their order, are now given chaos as a place to live in . . .' She felt that her stomach was being flattened against her back, and that she was about to be strangled. At dinner after the mission, the pilots talked about what would happen to them after the war, and about how long babies were when they were first born because one man had just heard that he had become a father. '7 men down – no one spoke of it. Drinking and singing "I want to go home".'

There was a new note in her articles, an undercurrent of defeat and sadness. She had seen too much misery, and she was very conscious of being a single woman again and of having lost the Finca, the one house she had really loved and made her own. She wrote to Allen Grover: 'when I'm alone sorrow drowns me. This is a grief I did not know I could feel and it is very hard to bear.' In January she wrote a long letter to her editors at *Collier's*, explaining why she needed a break. To her indignation, they published it in full in the magazine, without consulting her, under a photograph of her of the Hollywood starlet kind she most disliked, smiling, her hair a neat, blonde crinkly helmet. 'There have been too many wars and they are all too long and finally one cannot endure it for the other people. There seems also to be a kind of selection backward, so that surely the bravest and the most innocent will be utterly destroyed.

'Today I saw pictures of two bodies, dug up from some boneyard in Toulouse. They were the bodies of what had once been two Frenchmen aged 32 and 29, but they had been tortured by the Gestapo until they died. I look at anything, you see, because I do not admit that one can turn away: one has no right to ignorance, one has no right to spare oneself. But I never before saw faces . . . with gouged out eyes. I thought I'd seen it all but evidently not . . .

'Oh, what a world! To think that Our Lord bothered to die for it! And is anyone going to make it fine? Is anyone able to prevent the massive insane cruelty from going on, like poison in the blood of humanity?'

Then she went back to work. She was passing through Paris in March when Gavin tracked her down at the Hôtel Lincoln. It was his third attempt. The 82nd Airborne was stationed near Rouen, recuperating from the long campaign in the Ardennes with half its men as casualties, and he now sent his plane to Paris to fetch her. Their meeting, in his dingy barracks, was awkward. Martha, who 'on principle' had never had much to do with generals, resented being summoned 'like a package and pushed into bed', which was what she decided the general did with all the women he liked. She turned him down; and so they began to talk instead, and Gavin realised that Martha understood a great deal about the 'madness and the miracle' of war, and that she could be a friend to him as well as a lover, while Martha was captivated by his unexpected modesty and his vast knowledge of military matters. 'I was crazy about him as a soldier,' she wrote later. Then they went to bed, 'on a basis of high mutual esteem'.

By April, the 82nd Airborne were positioned on the west bank of the Rhine. A pontoon bridge linking east and west had been put up across the river and called the Ernie Pyle, in tribute to the much-loved correspondent who had just been killed by a sniper in Okinawa. Gavin's men discovered warehouses full of food, crates of Portuguese sardines and cheeses the size of cartwheels, as well as piles of top hats and stacks of bicycles. Soon paratroopers were to be seen peddling along the towpaths in top hats. Though there was little left of Cologne other than rubble and the jagged remains of bombed buildings, the villages along the river were for the most part surprisingly intact, with adequate supplies of coal and food. 'The Germans are nice and fat too,' Martha wrote for *Collier's*, 'and quite clean and orderly and industrious.' Like other correspondents advancing with the Allied troops, she remarked on the way that no German ever admitted to having played any part in Hitler's war. 'No one is a Nazi,' she wrote. 'No one ever was.' In her diary, she noted: 'The eternal mystery (what does a man die for?). Girl – we are not afraid – there were no Jews here – many Communists – we are not afraid of Americans, why should we be, we were not Nazis . . . We are all shocked morally by these people.' The roads were solid with people fleeing the advancing Russians, who were regarded with terror as barbarians, and with former slave labourers, who had been liberated before there had been time to set up centres to feed and house them. Gavin noted that he now had 'prisoners like some people have mice'.

When the Russians reached the Elbe, some of the correspondents got hold of small boats and crossed to meet them, and the reporter Lee Carson described the Russian soldiers about whom so much had been heard as 'overgrown, bearish children, good-natured, abrupt and direct'. All the journalists were struck by the size and shape of the women soldiers, who seemed to them as sturdy and rugged as the men. Martha, who spoke German, Spanish and French, could find no common language with these affable new allies, but quickly learnt to recognise '*Niet*' as she tried to cajole her way to the local Soviet headquarters. Unlike the officers she was used to, who invariably succumbed to her persuasion, their Russian counterparts were amiable but adamant. Gavin was delighted with his first encounters with them. 'Their music is excellent', he wrote to Martha, 'and their vodka supply limitless.'

On every occasion they could, Martha and Gavin seized a few hours together. He wrote her long and loving letters and they exchanged news about Capa and William Walton, bumped into from time to time as the division moved and the correspondents came and went, covering the progress of the war. She sent him Evelyn Waugh's *Brideshead Revisited*, and, whenever she was able to join him, she hung pictures on the walls of his bare quarters, trying to make a home for them. They played gin rummy in bed. Martha told Gavin that he had taught her 'what I had guessed, read about, been told about; but did not believe; that bodies are something terrific', and that though she continued to feel inhibited and ignorant, there was something in the physical pleasure they took in each other that was 'wild and crazy and fierce like war'. Gavin, whom she assumed found it all less satisfying than she did, nonetheless seemed to take their affair more seriously. He wrote that their love was 'the only rock in a great deal of quicksand'. He had an estranged wife, Peggy, with whom he had not lived for ten years, and a daughter called Barbara, and was planning to get a divorce as soon as the war was over. 'You are the purpose of my life,' he wrote to Martha one day. 'You have become my life itself.' And on another: 'Darling, give. Write me a letter, goddamit, you are breaking my heart.'

Their encounters were not always smooth. One day, while on her travels, she came across the 82nd where she had not expected it to be, and happily moved in to stay with Gavin for a few days. He had been ordered to deploy his men as a sort of decoy, to draw German troops away from a vulnerable American position. There were many casualties and Martha, who had by now made friends with many of the men, railed against what she called a needless massacre. She and Gavin quarrelled furiously. Gavin, as her commanding officer, finally ordered her to go to her room and forbade her to mention the subject again, either to him or to anyone else. Later, she realised that she had been in the wrong and she apologised. But the row left her with an uncomfortable feeling that their minds worked differently and that, for all their shared physical attraction and their fascination with war, they would never really understand each other.

Martha was forced to move on, and there was in any case no time to reflect on what had happened. She was now constantly travelling, at one point returning briefly to London where she bought a small house in South Eaton Place, thinking that England was the only country she could bear to live in after the war. The winter of 1945 was Arctic-cold all over Europe and in London the Thames froze. Martha found the city ragged and austere, with long queues for still inadequate supplies of food, everything from eggs to gloves still rationed and Mayfair and Belgravia, where she found her house, much damaged by bombs. Number 21 South Eaton Place was mustard-coloured, with chunks of plaster falling off, rusty railings and streaky shutters, 'a sort of house by Charles Addams for *New Yorker* loonies' as she told a friend. She felt about her new acquisition rather as an old man might feel about a beautiful young girl, wanting to cover her in diamonds.

Some time during the spring, she spent three weeks with Virginia Cowles, like herself anxious about money and future work, and the two women decided to write a comedy about their experiences as women correspondents, set in the press camp at Sessa Aurunca they had visited together during the Italian campaign. It made them laugh to write it, and they filled it with all the grievances they felt about the military and all the competitiveness they had endured from their male colleagues, and they told each other that after the war it would make their fortunes. Knowing nothing at all about how to construct a play, they went to a London matinee, timed it, copied out stage directions, and then sat down to their typewriters, joking as they went, writing at great speed, each creating a caricature of herself, then splicing the two versions together with Sellotape.

* * *

For many months now, all through the summer and autumn of 1944, the war correspondents had been hearing about the concentration camps. Among the refugees trudging west along the roads were men and women who talked about places where

Jews and other people Hitler did not want were taken, and where they starved to death, or were so badly treated that they died of their injuries. Early in 1945, Martha had come across a young Frenchman who had managed to escape from one of the camps, and he told her about the way that 2,700 people were gassed every day, and about how the smell of burning flesh from the bodies packed into incinerators had made him retch. He described the dignity of the people as they walked to the gas chambers.

Though the Russians had liberated Madjanek, outside Lublin, in July 1944, and had gone on to take Belzec, Treblinka and Sobibor that same summer, and Auschwitz in January 1945, these camps had been frantically dismantled by the retreating Germans as they left, and their prisoners driven westwards on death marches, so the full horror of what had been done was not apparent. There had been articles in European newspapers, of course, and statements in the House of Commons, and rumours circulating since the spring of 1942, but it was not until the British entered Bergen-Belsen on 15 April 1945, where a typhus epidemic had left thousands of skeletal bodies rotting in the open, and shot films which were then transmitted around the world, that the full extent of the German atrocities became clear. It was only now that the world was really forced to know.

What the reporters accompanying the liberating troops saw was so shocking that writers whose normal style was colourful and emphatic were stupefied into careful, controlled prose. The early reports were quiet and very precise. There was no need for adjectives. 'I pray you to believe what I have said about Buchenwald,' Ed Murrow said in his broadcast for CBS. 'I have reported what I saw and heard, but only part of it. For most of it I have no words.'

On 29 April, the US Seventh Army reached Dachau. A thousand prisoners had been murdered as the Germans fled, but 33,000 remained, some of whom had been there for the past twelve years. In the woods nearby, the Allies found two rooms which had been used as torture chambers. Dachau was Hitler's model SS camp, set up in 1933 to hold people in 'protective custody', his euphemism for political prisoners. Léon Blum, the former French President, had been in Dachau, and Stalin's son, Jacob, and the Protestant priest, Martin Niemöller. Dachau was where Martha's German friends in the International Brigades in Spain had lost their nails and teeth. In her wanderings around Germany, seeing for herself the legacy and the victims of Nazi rule, Dachau had become for her its symbol, something to hate with a 'single-hearted passion'. Opening its gates had been her 'personal war aim'.

She had therefore long planned to make her way to Munich as soon as possible. She had no interest in being the first correspondent at the camp – Marguerite Higgins, a reporter for the *Herald Tribune*, would later boast that she had liberated Dachau herself – and no regard for scoops. She approached the camp slowly, reaching it early in May, a couple of days behind the American soldiers. 'Behind the wire and the electric fence,' she wrote, 'the skeletons sat in the sun and scratched themselves for lice. They have no age and no faces; they all look alike and like nothing you will ever see if you are lucky.' Dachau was the camp where the Germans had carried out their experiments to see how long people could survive without oxygen, or in very low temperatures, or with streptococcus germs injected into wounds in their legs. Martha was taken around the medical rooms while a doctor described to her in great detail how each experiment had been done. She visited the '*Nacht und Nebel*' cells where people were kept in total isolation, and she saw the crematorium where the clothing had been found neatly stacked in piles, but the naked bodies dumped like garbage to rot in the sun. Her article, which appeared in *Collier's* in June, was very calm. 'We are not entirely guiltless,' she wrote, 'we the Allies, because it took us twelve years to open the gates of Dachau. We were blind and unbelieving and slow, and that we can never be again . . . If ever again we tolerate such cruelty we have no right to peace.' She felt her own share of the guilt keenly, telling Teecher that she would never lose that sense of guilt for the fact that 'I did not know, realise, find out, care, understand what was happening'.

Martha was with one of the doctors when 'what had been a man' dragged himself into the room. He was a Pole, the only person to survive the last transport from Buchenwald, and found by the soldiers who opened the doors still just breathing under the pile of bodies. He told her how the people dying of thirst inside the locked boxcars had cried out and tried to fight their way free and how from time to time the guards fired into the cars to stop the noise. 'Everyone is dead,' he said to her, beginning to cry. 'And the face that was not a face twisted with pain or sorrow or horror,' she wrote for Collier's. And then he said again: 'No one is left. Everyone is dead. I cannot help myself.'

Something changed for Martha that day; something to do with what she felt about memory and the past, and her own sense of optimism, and perhaps even about being Jewish. It was in Dachau, she said, that she really understood for the first time the true evil of man. 'A darkness entered my spirit,' she explained later to Hortense Flexner, and 'there, in that place in the sunny early days of May 1945' she stopped being young. 'I do not really hope now,' she wrote. 'Not really; I only feel one can never give up.'

When, after a few days, she fled Dachau, unable to bear the weight of her feelings any longer, she had lost her belief, carefully protected and nurtured – against all odds through wars and the Depression – in the perfectibility of man, the instinctive certainty she had clung to all her life that truth, justice and kindness would always, in the end, prevail. She no longer felt they would; and she never did again.

A quarter of a century later, Martha jotted down on a single sheet of paper a short statement about herself and what Dachau had meant to her. For purposes of self-preservation, she explained, she had done her best over the years to dull and bury the memory of what she had seen that day. But now, twenty-five years later, she knew that she could do so no longer. 'It is as if I walked into Dachau and there fell over a cliff,' she wrote, 'and suffered a lifelong concussion, without recognising it.' To Flexner, she added: 'Looking back, I know I have never again felt that lovely, easy, lively hope in life which I knew before, not in life, not in our species, not in our future on earth.' It had crushed for ever the very mechanism by which she had lived, the sense of excitement and movement, the redemptive power of laughter, that had sustained her even in her bleakest moments.

While she was standing in the infirmary in Dachau, the same fragile figure who had described the death train to her shuffled into the room. In Polish, he whispered a few words. The doctor translated: the war in Europe had ended. On 13 February, while Churchill, Roosevelt and Stalin were meeting in Yalta, the RAF dropped three-quarters of a million incendiary bombs on Dresden, creating an artificial tornado which sucked people into its centre. On 21 April, the Russians had reached the suburbs of Berlin; on the 26th Hitler vanished in the ruins of the Chancellery. On 4 May, at six o'clock in the evening, at Lüneburg, Montgomery signed the terms of Germany's surrender: the war, which had lasted five years and eight months, was over.

Though she left Dachau in shame and revulsion, Martha was consumed by a need to know everything. She went to Belsen and watched the bulldozers burying the bodies of those found dead in heaps, and those the Allies had found alive but had been too late to save. She saw the first women home from Ravensbrück, shrunken and dressed like scarecrows, with grey-green skin and the 'sorrowing eyes' of people who had almost died. She looked and talked and asked questions and read, and on her travels around a country in which fifty large cities lay in ruins, with no electricity, gas or running water, in which 90 per cent of industry was at a standstill and no trains ran, in which there was very little food or medicines for civilians and everyone was hungry and sick, she felt no pity at all, ever, for the German people.

She spent VE day in Paris, walking alone among the vast milling crowds, the babble of voices and shuffling of feet drowning out the church bells, until she met a French acquaintance and went back with him to the Hôtel Scribe, where she lay crying in his arms, talking about Dachau, saying that nothing, now, could wipe out that cruelty. The *épuration* was coming to an end, and the French couture houses were preparing new collections, modelling their clothes in miniature, on dolls, but three million French were either dead, missing or not yet home from the war.

* * *

Early in August 1945, Gavin was given the command of the American forces in Berlin. 'Well, the town is ours,' he wrote to Martha, 'what is left of it.' The precise status of the city, capital of Germany since 1871, had been left somewhat vague at the Allied conferences of Tehran and Yalta, beyond the agreement that Germany would be governed by an Allied Control Council and that Berlin itself would lie within the Soviet zone. Though the dead had long since been cleared from the streets, and the Russian army had effectively looted everything that could be moved, the city was full of rubble and the debris left by many months of incessant shelling, through which paths had been cleared. In some parts virtually nothing was left standing. The water mains were said to be leaking in three thousand places. Gavin was conducted around his sector, introduced to his Russian counterparts, and went off to drink Armagnac with Capa, who was photographing the tattered city and its furtive and terrified inhabitants. He told Martha that he had been entrusted with the care of 887,000 'very hungry but rather docile Krauts', and that he had to find six hundred tons of food every day to feed them. He was excited by his first discussions with the Russian command about fuel and supplies. 'I love this work,' he wrote. 'At last we are doing together – I pray – humanity some permanent good.' He wrote to her nearly every day, long, pressing letters, on a typewriter, with a large, scrawling signature at the bottom. 'Darling, I love you, I love you, I love you. It is a good love now. It is sturdy, dependable and solid, something that one can count on.'

In the early autumn Martha joined him. She was given a room close to his in the staff quarters of the 82nd Airborne, on the excuse that she was writing an article on its exploits for the *Saturday Evening Post*. They resumed their games of gin rummy, discussed the war endlessly, laughed a lot, and together inveighed against the incompetence and tyranny of governments. Martha wandered around what was left of the streets, writing notes. 'Oct. 3. Sortie to dig dead out of flooded subway. I've given up deads since Dachau. The desolation – women working in the rubble. The women with dyed yellow hair & that grey thick German skin . . . Hospital – 30 hunger cases out of 960 patients. Germany should be a colony – will never be a democracy. Forecast Russo-American war . . . Danced 9 hrs.'

One day she saw Freddy Keller, her Abraham Lincoln Brigade friend from the Spanish civil war, in the Alexanderplatz, a market for loot in the Russian sector to which Gavin had forbidden Americans to go. Martha was trying to sell a hideous brown tweed suit belonging to Capa, who was being held captive in the Hôtel Lincoln in Paris until he could raise the money to pay off his poker debts. 'Running into Freddy Keller,' she noted in her diary, 'paying off w. huge bankroll.'

Gavin was eager to make plans for a shared life after his command in Berlin came to an end early in 1946, but Martha was far from certain that she could contemplate an existence on an American military base. In letters, in her diary and note-books, even in her articles for *Collier's*, she returned again and again to the theme of adjustment to a future without war. In her diary she wrote: 'It is really my own uncertainty about how I will adjust to American life that makes me wonder about others . . . How & where will I ever live normally?' When she flew briefly back to the States to spend a week with her mother on the Merrimac river, getting a lift in a C.54 transport from Scotland by agreeing to write about the wounded American soldiers returning home, she ended her piece on a surprisingly unsure, sentimental note. 'We said good-bye to one another too warmly, too long; we promised to visit one another . . . For the war, the hated and perilous and mad, had been home for a long time too; everyone had learned how to live in it, everyone had something to do, something that looked necessary, and now we were back in this beautiful safe place called home and what would become of us?' War had been the best opium of all. With Cuba gone, the London house not yet ready, St Louis relegated to a past she had no wish to return to, there was no place she herself called home. In her diary of 10 October is a short entry: 'What shall I do when this easy comradely life goes to pieces? Am really unsuited for anything else.'

In November, pursuing her unhappy desire to know all that there was to know about the Final Solution, Martha went to the opening of the Nuremberg trial, where 250 journalists had gathered. Twenty-one defendants – the twenty-second, Dr Robert Ley, who was in charge of the Reich Labour Front, hanged himself in his jail cell – had been brought together in one wing of Nuremberg prison, and allowed to appoint their own defence lawyers. Goebbels and Himmler had committed suicide earlier. Between the two daily court sessions came a two-hour break for lunch, and Martha used this time to walk around the grim, dusty ruins of the town, where ten thousand corpses were said to lie still buried under the rubble, questioning people about the trial. A doctor told her that in his view the Germans had been 'too strong' in their treatment of the Jews; a businessman assured her that ordinary Germans had known nothing about what had been going on; a twenty-year-old ex-soldier described seeing people return from the camps fat and brown. He agreed that the Jews should not have been killed, but pointed out that they were never known to have done any real work, but only to have changed money 'in a tricky way'. 'Who wept at Dachau – Auschwitz –' Martha wrote down. 'Who wept for the countless dead of slave labour?'

After the opening address by the chief American prosecutor, Justice Robert Jackson, the trial began. In the dark-brown courtroom, with its heavy green marble doorways, Martha, who was covering it for *Collier's*, sat in the press gallery making notes about the appearance and behaviour of the accused men as they sat on two long wooden benches, in the order in which they were listed in the indictment. One by one, she inspected them all: Frank, with his 'small cheap face' and sleek black hair; Keitel, who was 'nothing, a granite bust badly made of inferior stone'; Hess, 'weird, inquisitive and birdlike'; Fritsch 'with a sensitive fox's face, vain perhaps, wearing a romantic sadness like a minor poet who has killed his mistress'. She wrote: 'Frank cries & is not a true German. Faces – shocking weakness of Schirach & Papen, handsome faces.' Martha well remembered von Schirach, head of the Hitler Youth, from her visit to Germany with Bertrand in 1933. 'The Giaconda smile of Goering. Hess's giggles . . . Streicher goes on chewing gum & looking like a Jew. Sauckel listens violently. Frick has no earphones – looks like a dog with dewlaps . . . Goering has the ugliest thumbs I have ever seen – possibly also the ugliest mouth.' Harold Nicolson, another observer, remarked that the defendants looked drab and ill, like people who had travelled third class in a train for three nights.

In the court, the air-conditioning was kept on high and Martha felt permanently chilled. 'How wearing it is,' she noted. 'One realises the strain on the defendants. But it is a cold court – no pity is possible.' It was during the trial at Nuremberg that Goering confirmed that Guernica had indeed been the testing ground for the Luftwaffe: 'It was a pity; but we could not do otherwise, as we had nowhere else to try out our machines.' Justice Robert Jackson had spoken of the men in the dock as the 'living symbols of racial hatreds, of terrorism and violence, and of the arrogance and cruelty of power', and told the court that civilisation could not afford to deal ambiguously or indecisively with them. The arrogance of power was something that Martha was increasingly concerned with. Though all the defendants would plead innocent, none would attempt to refute the evidence: they tried instead to put the blame on others.

When Martha felt that she had seen and heard enough, she went back to Berlin where she had once again become, as she put it, 'la fille du regiment', though this was quite another army. Gavin was an attractive man, and Martha was not the only woman to find him so. Sometime that autumn Marlene Dietrich, who had apparently long had her eye on him, arrived in Berlin and was 'sick with rage' to find Martha installed as his mistress. According to Dietrich's daughter many years later, Gavin had sent her mother pressing messages to join him.

When not at work on her article about the 82nd Airborne, Martha had been spending her days with the other foreign correspondents, loafing about the city, an activity she had enjoyed since her first days as a young reporter in the press gallery of the League of Nations in Geneva. In particular she went around Berlin with a man who worked for CBS called Charles Collingwood, who made her laugh. Gavin, she would say later, did not make her laugh. Soon, Dietrich informed Gavin that Martha was really in love with Collingwood, and a furious Gavin, telling Martha he was going out for a short walk, went to call on Dietrich and stayed away all night. Jealousy was not an emotion Martha had experienced before. But, recognising the 'disgusting, cheap, ugly' sensation that now overcame her, she left Berlin for Paris, declaring that no relationship with a man was ever going to work for her and that henceforth she would stick to friendship. To a weaselly letter, in which Gavin tried to spread the blame for his misadventure on mutual friends, gossip and the times, Martha responded with a ferocious blast. She was also clearly hurt, and astonished to find herself so. Marlene Dietrich, she said, was a cobra. As for herself, she had been foolish enough to love, trust and admire Gavin, and the moment she realised that he had gone to bed with Dietrich, 'I stayed in that room weeping as I really did not believe I ever could or would again . . . and every night since it has come back to me the same way, like a pain that hurts too much.' She was, she declared, through with him. Her plan was now to return to England 'to build myself a sound adult life'. 'I have decided that men really want tarts and tarts is what they are going to get . . . You can sleep with everyone you like including sing-song girls and goats . . . After all, none of this matters much, does it. We are only two people, not desperately important people, and we always have a lot of work. Luckily.'

Gavin began by sending first one aide and then another to Paris and when this failed to move her, he followed himself. They went to bed. It was, wrote Martha later, 'more exciting physically' than it had ever been, but in part of her mind and heart she had already begun to draw away from him. In any case, they had very little time together in which to absorb what had become of their relationship, because Gavin was coming to the end of his posting in Berlin and Martha had arranged to write an article for *The New Yorker* about the Japanese surrender in Bali.

Early in March 1946 she set off for the Far East, later describing the surrender as an event of glorious confusion, in which the Americans behaved with spectacular lack of dignity and efficiency, and the surrendering Japanese, neat, elegant and impassive in their pristine uniforms, handed over their swords rather as if they were giving away fountain pens. When the American troops saw that the Balinese girls had bare breasts, they broke into loud cheers; all breasts throughout Bali were at once covered.

To Robert Sherrod, correspondent for *Time* and *Life*, who had helped Martha with introductions in the Far East, she reported from Singapore that she felt she now needed to be alone for a bit, that she was 'all shredded up inside' from the war and her parting from Hemingway, and that she had invented a new phrase she rather liked: 'the pale empty color of the future'. She did not take to Indonesia, referring to it as 'that stinkhole', warning that the nationalism she saw everywhere was a fever chart by which to measure the sickness of the postwar world, and complaining that the Indonesians were niggardly, mean and lacked stature. Something of the old bounce in her letters to close men friends had come back, a particular combination of intimacy, carefully circumscribed by self-deprecating humour, and distance, the repeated reassertion of independence, that occasionally made her sound flippant. She told Sherrod that she never intended to write another word about the Orient, or indeed ever to go there again. 'It is hopeless and shitty; give the country back to the ants, I say.'

That night, she dreamt that she was in a Japanese prison camp and that she killed a smiling woman guard who had plunged her teeth into her arm.

What she really wanted, she wrote to Sherrod, using the throwaway asides that characterised the letters of her younger years, in which the things she minded about were packaged up as jokes, was a little white house, with a picket fence around it and some toddlers; but she had probably already blown that, and was condemned to eke out the remaining years in the company of the 'semi-important middle-aged'.

To add to her sense of being alone, she received several long letters from Bill Walton, who had been in New York when Gavin led his 82nd Airborne Division, 'natty and drilled like the Rockettes', in a great parade up Fifth Avenue, on a brilliant January morning, to cheers from the crowds lining the streets. The day had been declared a holiday by the city for the event.

Walton described a dinner given for the officers by the mayor, and the many parties attended by Charles Collingwood, Irwin Shaw, Allen Grover and Capa that had followed, at which much drink had been consumed by all. 'Capa has a thing with Ingrid Bergman,' Walton wrote. 'I think she really broke his soft Hungarian heart.' Dietrich, whom he referred to as 'the movie queen', had not been sighted. Walton himself was now pursuing Martha, though he kept his tone extravagantly self-mocking. 'My little duck,' he wrote, 'the real trouble with me is that being with you has spoiled me completely for other women.' He told her that a limerick about one of her introductions in the Far East, to the Lieutenant Governor-General of the Dutch East Indies, was now doing the rounds of their New York friends:

> Bulletin from Belgravia
> Marty's gone to Batavia
> With a guy named van Mook
> Who can't even Fook,
> Which is most unusual behavia!

* * *

Martha, caught up emotionally with Gavin, brooding about the collapse of Germany and the concentration camps, had thought little more about her play, though it had been written, as she told Grover, in her 'life's blood'. She and Virginia had given it to a young actress called Penelope Dudley Ward to read and been delighted when they heard her laugh out loud. Since then Virginia had efficiently found both an agent and a director, fresh from directing *Charlie's Aunt* in the prisoner-of-war camp in which he had spent the war. In June 1946 *Love Goes to Press* – a title they both hated – opened at the Embassy Theatre in Hampstead. Virginia's part, that of the reporter Jane who coolly beats her male colleagues to a scoop, was played by a girl who had been touring the troops with ENSA, while a then unknown Californian actress called Irene Worth became Annabelle, or the part of Martha. All the cast except for Worth were able to save on costumes by wearing their own war uniforms. It was a nice group of actors, Martha wrote to a friend, 'with no fairies in it, which is a rest in London'.

The first night audience were appreciative of the antics of the two irreverent women who tied their male colleagues in knots of vanity and pomposity, and Annabelle's sardonic one-liners and self-deprecating asides made them laugh as much as did Martha's own with her friends. Words and expressions very familiar to those who knew Martha – 'happy as a goat', 'oh my' 'chums' – filled dialogue which if neither profound nor subtle was nonetheless funny. The critics were full of praise. Martha and Virginia, though delighted by the laughter and the cheers, fled the theatre when called to the stage to speak at the end of the performance.

Martha was now doing up her house off Eaton Square, describing what she called her 'little sewer' as 'quite lovely', elegant and white inside, though she told Robert Sherrod that the outside still looked like 'a camera study of blasted Europe'. It was her eleventh home and after months of combing London for unobtainable luxuries such as paint she was determined that it would be the last place she would ever redecorate. By some strange alchemy, she wrote to Sherrod, she felt unhurried and at peace in 'this rain sodden burg' and was hopeful that at last she was in sight of that 'shining and always diminishing goal: roots, a place of your own, peace'.

Like Virginia, she was convinced that she was unsuited for American life, telling Sherrod that neither of them could imagine getting ahead if they went back to the States, 'being unable to see where the getting got you', a somewhat disingenuous remark from one of the most successful – and hardly retiring – woman journalists of the day. To compensate for the shortages and drabness of everything, and for the grey skies, she went out a great deal, to restaurants and to parties and dancing, with friends made through Virginia, fighting off a growing feeling that her working life was going nowhere and that Gavin, who came to London to see her, was not the man for her to marry. Already, she was finding him less and less fun. Her women friends, on the other hand, she did find fun, somewhat to her own surprise, 'all so worldly and so funny, disabused, unexcited, uncomplaining and a pleasure to look at'. Martha had never felt very close to women before, so much preferring her men friends that it was no longer entirely as a joke that she talked of herself as being one of the boys, and more like a man than a woman. She was wary of the intimacy of women, their affection, the patterns of conciliation and tentativeness.

One night she went to a masked jamboree at the Albert Hall, renting a gypsy costume and taking with her some of the Carpathian Lancers she had met in Italy, wearing rented chefs' costumes. When she was invited to the fiftieth anniversary dinner of the *Daily Mail*, she wore the backless Schiaparelli evening dress she had worn at the World Economic Conference thirteen years before. She wrote to a friend that her spine 'was the most visible thing in the room. I got waved at, drunk to, and talked about by Mr Churchill (who said, "Ah, so it's Farewell to *His* Arms".) If my bosom had been bare too, I have no doubt I'd have been made a Peeress.' From across the room she watched Luce, founder and proprietor of *Time*, 'with skin like blotting paper'. The room, she went on, had a 'very strong odour of decay'. Next day, Lord Beaverbrook telephoned to invite her to 'that dreadful palace of his'.

Love Goes to Press had done sufficiently well to transfer to the West End, where it opened at the Duchess Theatre to good reviews and much applause. The two authors told each other that it was now only a matter of time before the play went to Hollywood and made their fortunes. In the autumn, an American producer did indeed appear and arranged to take it to New York. The cast, longing for the glamour of a city that had not been at war for six years, crossed the Atlantic, leaving behind only Irene Worth, who had her eye on Shakespeare and Stratford.

Shortly before Christmas, *Love Goes to Press* opened on Broadway. It was a disaster. London audiences, tired and subdued by shabbiness and rationing, longed to find things to laugh about. They needed satire. New Yorkers found the play tiresome. The *New York Sun* called it a 'struggling and straggling little comedy, one of the weakest of the West End exhibits to come along in quite a while'. It was enough, the critic wrote gloomily, to start 1947 off in a bleak theatrical mood. Rosamond Calder in *Theatre Arts* went further. If this was the way Gellhorn and Cowles had behaved at the front, she wrote, then 'it would seem wise for the high command to banish all women journalists from the next war'. The characters, she added primly, suffered from 'incredible human callousness'. Audiences kept away. Then it snowed heavily. After five performances the play folded. Martha, mortified for the actors, had already decided that it was in fact a 'big and unrewarding bore' but told Max Perkins that the suddenness with which it was all over shocked her. When, soon afterwards, Virginia proposed that they write a second play, about Parliament, since she had just married a politician called Aidan Crawley, Martha hesitated but decided that the theatre was unlikely to become the 'get-rich' scheme she had hoped for; besides, she really preferred the movies. She worked out that her share of the play had made her just £30.

For the first time in many years, Martha's work was not going well. She calculated that her entire income for 1946 had come to $244. Her longtime editor at *Collier's*, Charles Colebaugh, who had prized good writing and stood by her sometimes eccentric expenses, had died, and she was at odds with the people who had taken his place. *The New Yorker*, saying that they did not like pieces written from tours with other journalists, turned down her article on Java, which she had been obliged, for reasons of safety and permits, to do in the company of others. And *The Heart of Another*, published in England in December, had received, as Martha's novels invariably did, very mixed reviews. The *Daily Telegraph* called her stories 'little more than a glorified cocktail bar in picturesque and exciting circumstances'.

For what she hoped would not be her last piece for *Collier's*, she now went off to Paris to write about the Peace Conference, where she was immediately struck by the air of defeat and animosity that filled the Palais du Luxembourg, and by the way her old Parisian friends dismissed the proceedings with contempt. 'More like preparation for another war than making a peace,' she wrote in her notebook. 'No compromise – only distrust and fear – more cynicism than 1919 – no one cares about human rights.' In 1947 human rights were the new catchword in postwar politics, soon, under Mrs Roosevelt's direction, to become the Universal Declaration. For the rest of her life, Martha would follow their progress with interest. She sat in the press gallery, watching the speakers, just as she had at Nuremberg, observing their mannerisms and appraising their characters, reflecting that her interests were far more those of a novelist than a reporter. 'How much I look *at* people,' she wrote, 'and how without love I am. Am becoming a terrible dry character.' She thought they all looked half-asleep and sickly, though the Russian delegation seemed to her more vigorous and attentive. 'Molotov's fine and lovely hands. How from the front he has a good face & from the side, the bulging forehead which makes him look like a mean baby.'

Among the notes in her neat writing, slipped into the pages of her usual small black book, are passages about herself; they have an apprehensive tone. 'The increasing feeling of living in a dream (nothing really works, nothing is real) . . . Remember Bettina saying: "You wake up in the morning with white eyelashes *touchante*." One is *touchante* when young; *piteuse* afterwards . . . Is *anyone* happy? *All* governments are bad. But where does contact fail; where does it become impossible to govern for human happiness? Why is the business of running people the most unsatisfactory of all businesses? My dyed hair worries and sickens me. I am at last, am I not, middle aged?' (She was thirty-eight.) When she radioed her article to *Collier's* its tone was muted. The conference, she wrote, had never had any power, but it had at least sounded a great alarm bell, warning people that 'our world is dividing in two, cleft by fear and mistrust'. Only by waging peace with the same energy and courage that had gone into fighting the war could nations hope to survive. She had seldom, even at the height of the fighting, sounded so gloomy. She had even turned against Paris itself, telling Diana Cooper that she now considered it to be 'the toughest spot outside Sing-Sing'.

And her affair with Gavin was over. The general himself, Slim Jim as he was known to the American press, had no wish to end it, and kept pressing Martha to return to America with him, but she had long felt that he 'belonged to the war', as had their love affair. Peace had only sharpened her realisation that they were very different creatures and that she had nothing but distaste for the 'pitiful army-barracks world'. Bored, she became cruel. On one of Gavin's visits to London, she refused to sleep with him, the boredom 'acting on my body as on my mind'. Her final letter is not dated, but it is a good letter, and though firm is also tender. 'Dearest Love, dearest Jimmy and darling . . . I simply could not be a good army wife. It is sickening to realise that two people alone are not a world or even a life . . . I am too definite and too old and too spoiled and too intolerant to be a good wife when good wife principally means good mixer . . .

'I cannot see, now, where I belong; I think possibly I am doomed to live alone because there is no place where I can imagine living. But I am already depressed by this life I see ahead of me; the best that can be said for it is that it will not irritate me; it may easily freeze me to death. My feet are cold every night, without you, and presently I suppose I will be cold throughout. We may always be in love, some way; but we won't be able to make a partnership that will last day after day and day after day'. In her partings, even from Hemingway, Martha was honest about herself and generous. Like Edna, she was never mean spirited, and her cruelty came rather from impatience, and perhaps a certain arrogance, than from unkindness. But she was disconcertingly clear, and she very seldom prevaricated, and though she continued to see Gavin from time to time, her chapter with him was definitely over. 'I am more dependent on laughter, or even giggles, certainly giggles, than anything else,' she wrote to Diana Cooper, 'and somehow J. and I didn't seem to make things funny enough together . . . I must say I hate being out of love, and looking forward to a long life with a pair of parrots, but there it is.' She was restless; uneasy. War had always seemed to her a solution, because during war her own life became a pleasant casual joke; to find it centre stage once more was unsettling. Fiction offered her another kind of escape.

For some time now, perhaps on some level ever since the day she had walked through the gates of Dachau, Martha had wanted to find a way to write about the shock of realising what the Nazis had been capable of. What was now developing in her mind was a novel based on the experiences of two American soldiers, an amiable lieutenant-general and his driver, a young Jew from St Louis – Martha seldom strayed far in her fiction – called Jacob Levy, who, having entered Dachau with the liberating forces, finds the sole possible expression for his rage in an act of sudden violence. She would use Jacob's story as a 'memory-cleaner': unable to endure any longer being locked up in her mind with memories she knew she could not live with, she would commit them to paper and hand them over to others, so that they would become no longer hers alone.

Martha had never been to Portugal, but she knew that she needed solitude, the bright winter light of the southern Mediterranean and the blue sea; and she had no fear of being alone. Paring down her possessions, travelling light and without plans, was a remembered pleasure of her summers in Europe; and her life in London, with its surfeit of parties, had begun to sicken her. She took off for a sardine fishing village called Praia de Rocha on the coast of Portugal, which had an unspoilt beach and a cliff top where she could walk, and here, alone but more content than she had been for some years, she began to write, sitting in the sun at her typewriter, the way she liked to work. There were a few cats around but almost no people, and certainly no 'kitchen of life', no hateful chores of domesticity. As always in a new and strange place, she felt excited and full of energy, and kept well away from three other single women she had caught sight of in local hotels 'going through the appearance of being alive'. To Max Perkins, she wrote: 'My life is a beauty: I find myself without visible means of income, on the verge of bankruptcy, in a second rate hotel someplace by the sea in Europe; alone, and writing as if the whole house were burning down.' She was as conscious now as she had ever been that only when her writing was going well could she ever feel truly happy. She really needed a jailer, she told Charles Scribner, and Hemingway had had his uses, by keeping her in one place, without people to distract her, while she was trying to write *Liana*; perhaps Portugal could be her new jail. Soon, she also began to plan a number of short stories around the theme she found so troubling: the bitterness and loneliness that came with peace. Before going on with the writing, she took stock of her life, and drew up the balance in a series of lists written in a small black notebook. Though it was now two years since her parting from Hemingway, he remained painfully in a corner of her mind, a source of pinpricks of doubt about herself and the past.

'Basically,' she began, 'what is wrong is that I do not take myself seriously, neither what I am, or what I believe. It is also perhaps a want of faith, but that lack of seriousness removes a sense of direction from life.' Two weeks later, she added another entry: 'What I now know:

1) I have lost my credit at *Collier's*. To have a job there, I shall have to start over and earn it. Possibly already too late.

2) I cannot live in London (therefore my house is worthless) unless I have a regular full time job which keeps me there.

3) I am happy about 'Jacob Levy' because of the *act* of writing (as escape from all problems). I wanted to do a novel because a novel meant the chance of fame (more than money) and showing Ernest.

4) A lot of my thinking & acting has been based on showing Ernest. For fear that I reached my highest point, with & through him, and that in every way I am only sinking into obscurity little by little.

5) I need a permanent anchor because I need a human place in the world. And because, truly, I lack continuous judgment & guts & confidence. This is the purely selfish side of it.'

There was then a pause, before she added a final page; reading her words, what stands out is how hard she was on herself, and how modest. 'What I am going to do,' she wrote, underlining the words:

'1) Ignore entirely for now:
   a) *Collier's* & job problem
   b) money problem
   c) personal future
   d) mother & summer.

2) Finish this book, as soon as possible, but not driving it. Make it the *best* I can do now.

3) Think of myself as someone new; with no credit balance. (Ignore the debit balance; people's memories are short. Must remember not to torment myself about past failures and mistakes. Consider everything is to be earned, as of now.)

4) Also get over the last-chance feeling. Work steadily, modestly, sincerely – but not desperately. It is not that I have all the time in the world: it is that panic will ruin the remaining time.'

And then she got down to work.

* * *

After three months she had tired of solitude. But the writing had gone well, the novel was mapped out and she had several new stories towards a collection, perhaps among the best she ever wrote, about cynical and vindictive survivors coming to terms with lives that if not exactly happy are at least bearable. Neither likable nor admirable, the characters in these postwar stories are defined by failure and resignation. They are the bleakest of her fiction, and the cruelest.

Now she needed to see what had become of her 'little sewer' in London, which she gloomily noted had cost her $3,200 to buy and $15,000 to do up, and which she was beginning to realise had been a mistake. But first she wanted to spend a long holiday in America with her mother. By May, she was back in the States and had persuaded Edna to take leave from her many projects – Edna was sixty-nine and still very busy – and the two women set off in a seven-year-old Plymouth for the South, Martha having agreed to send back two articles to the *New Republic* on their travels. Edna was trying to persuade her to settle in America, saying that she feared expatriates were unhappy people; the very word, Martha agreed, had a 'seedy' ring to it, but she felt herself to be without roots, and, apart from her mother, without real family ties. She was very fond of Alfred, with whom she exchanged affectionate letters, but almost completely detached from George or Walter, whom she complained was unbearably stuffy, and she much disliked his wife Kitty.

Together again after so long, without constraints of time, Martha and her mother returned to the pattern of their earlier lives: they talked without cease, they read, they walked and they made each other laugh. Martha took notes. Edna collected shells for her grandchildren. They were each other's preferred travelling companion. 'For several weeks now,' Martha began her first piece for the *New Republic*, 'we have been driving through the American Way of Life.' They wandered at will, without plan, through New Jersey, Pennsylvania, Maryland, Virginia and the Carolinas, at first charmed by the faded brick and white wooden houses, with their dogwood and flowering chestnuts, and by the fields lying 'combed and sleek' around them, and later appalled by the insularity and ignorance of the Southern whites, the middle-aged women they sat next to in restaurants, smug, stout matrons in ornate hats. In North

Carolina, they visited the barracks of Gavin's 82nd Airborne, where Martha found old friends from Berlin, twenty-two-year-old veterans of the Battle of the Bulge. In Charlotte, they came across the women's branch of the Elks holding their annual convention, sporting orchids and printed silks. They hastened through Texas and its oil boom. Whenever they came across a particularly pleasing spot, they settled down for a few days, to sightsee and go to the movies. In the evenings, they unpacked their portable cocktail shaker and sat on their beds giggling, as Martha wrote to Mrs Roosevelt, 'like a pair of Peter Arno charladies'. From time to time, Martha worked on her novel, though she wondered why she instinctively chose to make both her heroes men. 'Perhaps it's because I've never lived in a proper woman's world, nor had a proper woman's life, and so – feeling myself personally to be floating uncertainly somewhere between the sexes – I opt for what seems to me the more interesting of the two,' she wrote to Mrs Roosevelt, in words that recalled her musings over Capa and her preferred early friendships with men. 'Or is that right? Women are just as interesting as men, often more so; but their lives seem to me either too hard, with an unendurable daily exhausting drab hardness, or too soft and whipped cream.' Martha, so intrigued by the infinite complexities of people's lives, remained oddly deaf to the intonations of feminism.

Her articles for the *New Republic* were not easy ones to write. Wherever she and Edna went, through tranquil countryside and well-fed villages, Martha saw the bombed-out houses, the cratered roads and the hungry children of the continent she had just left. What she sent back to the magazine was evocative, but it read uncomfortably. There was too much to say, and this was not the place to say it. America, she concluded, a little lamely, was a far better place than its image of greed, righteousness and fear suggested; and as a country it would do well to be generous, 'since it is not safe for one nation alone to be so blessed'.

Martha's divorce from Hemingway had come through shortly before Christmas 1945, and Hemingway was now married to

Mary Welsh and still living at the Finca in Cuba, where the original collection of cats, the Thunders, Furhouses, Friendlesses, Uncle Wolfers and Boises, had multiplied many times over. He had taken on a new maid called Martha, and told Charles Scribner that he took great pleasure in ordering her about. He was evidently still needled by the fact that Martha had been the one to leave him, and, when drunk, he continued to regale friends with shabby tales and limericks about their marriage, and to use caricatures of her in his fiction. In 1999 Jeffrey Meyers, an American biographer of literary celebrities, used the pages of *The Virginia Quarterly Review*, an otherwise serious publication, to repeat a comparison that Hemingway had drawn between Martha's vagina and the neck of an old hot-water bottle. It was not the worst of Hemingway's vulgar and abusive cracks about Martha, written mostly in his letters to Buck Lanham, his military friend from the Normandy landings, to whom he declared that Martha definitely belonged among the 'whores de combat'. And in one short story Hemingway had his hero Thomas read a letter from his hated third wife – a journalist covering the war in the Pacific – and say to his cat Boise: 'She's a bitch.' For her part, Martha remained surprisingly unmoved, and continued to say unprompted how she admired his writing, though she was infuriated by his continued refusal to send her the things she had left behind at the Finca, and she changed publishers when she suspected that Hemingway was using Scribners as a way of spying on her movements. He did, however, write her one pleasant message, 'Dearest Mook: No matter what hatred or justifiable contempt you feel for me I tell you it cannot be as much as I feel for myself . . .'

Martha, who had considerable self-discipline when it came to shedding the past, wished to hear nothing more about Hemingway. For the rest of her life, any interviewer bold or foolish enough to mention their marriage would be instantly squashed. Hemingway's name alone evoked a steeliness even friends found unnerving, though with many of them she was more humorous: 'I hope Ernest weighs 300lbs,' she said to Charles Scribner, after Hemingway refused to send her some papers she had asked for. 'He is a pig . . . God will punish him by making him fat.'

Whatever she said in public, Martha's verdict on their short marriage was and remained, as the years passed, pitiless; but she was always dignified. She refused to take part, ever, in what she called the 'necrophylia' that increasingly surrounded Hemingway. She was aloof about his suicide later, saying only, in neutral tones, that she understood how and why it happened. After his death in 1961, she was invariably dismissive of the many biographies that appeared, saying that their gross inaccuracies, inventions and exaggerations were his own fault, for having consorted with 'spivs' and sycophants. She added that Mary had been a fool to make a career of possessing Papa, and that the role of Countess Tolstoy was never a becoming one (and that she wished that the Count had not had her, along the way). To William Walton she once described Mary as one of the historical maggots who feed off the dead. She did consent to see Carlos Baker, Hemingway's first serious biographer, but later complained that Baker had got the Spanish civil war hideously, superficially, wrong; and that he wrote 'cheaply'. He had depended far too much, she said, on the memories of Sidney Franklin, the bullfighter cum majordomo, and Franklin, at the end of the day, was a 'very cheap kind of liar'. In one of her very rare references to her former husband, in the *Paris Review* in 1980, she wrote that Hemingway had a fair amount of hyena in him, that his boastful lies grew like Topsy as he got older, but that he 'made good jokes and was valuable cheerful company' in Spain, and 'no more boring than we all are the rest of the time'.

In private, Martha would tell friends somewhat ruefully that she did not much care for the way in which she seemed to be going down in history as a second-rate witch in the Master's life. And she could, at unexpected moments, be generous. But not often. 'He wasn't present except in the flesh,' she would later tell a friend. 'He needed me to run his house and to copulate on. (I use the adverb advisedly, not with but on) and to provide exercise in the way of a daily tennis game. There wasn't any fun or communication, none. When I thought I'd

go mad from loneliness and boredom, I slipped off to war.'
To Bernard Berenson, she clinically dissected his 'sneering
tone', mean pomposity and marked vulgarity, 'where it counts,
in the heart'; as he grew older he wrote, she said, 'with both
feet in his mouth'. A cold appraisal, without tenderness; but
in public, she was silent.

Hemingway himself was less courteous. Evidently very fond
of Edna, he continued to write to her after the separation, and
when *The Old Man and the Sea* was published in 1952 he
made her a present of the manuscript (which she, having no
understanding of its value, returned to him, with warm praise
for the book, telling him that she already owned a copy). He
had never cared to look at Martha sleeping, he told Bernard
Berenson, for ambitious career women were too restless to
'sleep pretty'. Some of the final words about their marriage
are to be found in *Across the River and Into the Trees*, which
appeared in 1950. 'She had more ambition than Napoleon and
about the talent of an average High School Valedictorian,' he
wrote about a woman clearly intended as Martha. 'You lose
[women] the same way you lose a battalion; by errors of judgment; orders that are impossible to fill, and through impossible conditions. Also through brutality.'

In the autumn of 1947, having decided that the London experiment had been a failure, Martha took a house in Georgetown
in Washington and began an affair with William Walton, the
Time-Life writer whom she had made friends with tobogganing
down the slopes of Luxembourg during the last months of the
war. Though affectionate, she remained detached and the affair
retained for her all the pleasing camaraderie that she associated with her most enjoyable friendships. Walton's wife was
ill and in and out of mental hospitals, and his daughter Frances
lived with him. Martha and he played gin rummy in bed, just
as she had once with Gavin; and he made her laugh. She later
said that their affair had been 'sweet and safe and jolly', but
that it had not included being in love; she called it a 'love
affair *d'automne*'.

Walton, unlike Capa, was one of the few people who

remained friends with both Martha and Hemingway. He was, Martha wrote later, a very sane, naturally happy, life-eater and she admired the strength and kindness with which he handled his wife's suicide attempts, saying it taught her that all of life, including the filthy bits, could in some way nourish the human spirit. Something of her detachment at this time, her wariness about commitment, must however have struck her friends. In her archives is a typed letter, written at this time; because its signature is smudged beyond recognition, its writer is unknown, but from its affectionate, intimate tone, it seems clear that he or she knew Martha well. 'Nobody can help you much,' it says. 'There's a great wide desert between you and the outside, and I doubt very much that anyone has ever crossed it. I wonder what it's like, where you are. But writers are made that way, particularly the good ones.'

Martha might have derived more comfort from these perceptive words – though she appears to have brushed them aside, as ever keeping excessive self-scrutiny at bay – had she not been in her usual state of panic and doubt over her war book. She told Allen Grover that it was sloppily written and that every time she looked at it, it grew worse. To her great sadness, Max Perkins had died suddenly of pneumonia and heart failure, leaving many bereft authors for whom his absolute attention had been a constant solace. Scribners, from whom she had not yet parted, though liking her manuscript, were worried about the intensity and unremitting horror of the passages about Dachau. With Grover's help, she spent the autumn in Washington redrafting the ending – in which Jacob Levy, incoherent with misery about what he has seen in the camp, drives at a laughing group of Germans, killing three – but she was determined not to soften by one word the sense of outrage. 'I am working like a bulldozer,' she wrote to Charles Scribner. 'Some days very pleased and some days suicidal, as is normal. I really cannot tell about what I write. Do you think all proper writers can? And are free of doubt? And full of joy and confidence? . . . I wish I knew how it was with others. All I ever really knew was Ernest: and as you know he never suffered from questions, but always felt that he was delivering the

Tablets of Stone, in the best possible style.' As always when worried about her writing, she felt ill and her bones ached. She was smoking heavily, and was too tired and too nervous to eat. Martha had wanted to call the book *Point of No Return*, after an air force technical expression describing the moment when a pilot has no choice but to continue or crash – here referring to Jacob Levy's arrival at Dachau – but was having trouble persuading Scribners, who insisted that no one would buy a novel with such a grim title. She promised to deliver the finished manuscript 'by December 15 or die'. At the end of January she was in Florida, 'awfully, awfully tired', with two chapters still to go. And then at last, at midnight one night, the book was done. 'This is a miserable book,' she wrote to Wallace Meyer, her new editor. 'I haven't any of the usual feelings, delight, pride, relief. I feel exhausted and full of doubt.' She had clearly forgotten the sense of despair and anti-climax that accompanied the delivery of all her books.

She now began to fret about the accuracy of the military details, about her uncombed hair and ugly mouth in the photograph that her publishers wanted to use on the jacket, and the possibility that it might appear at the same time as one of Hemingway's books. She had come up with another title, *The Wine of Astonishment*, from a Gideon Bible she found in a motel bedroom in Florida ('Thou hast shewed thy people hard things; thou has so made us drink the wine of astonishment') – but even she hated it and would say, until in later editions she was able to change it, that it spoiled the book for her. 'I'm through with war,' she told Meyer. 'I'm a conscientious objector. And I'm just about through with the human race. I want to lie beside a swimming pool, and dream about nice things like chocolate marshmallow sundaes.'

In March, she accompanied Edna to Bryn Mawr, where Mrs Roosevelt was giving a talk, and Martha, 'delirious with boredom' by the academic world and fiercely sober on a thimbleful of sherry, told a distinguished former dean, Helen Taft, that she herself had loathed the place and that it was perfectly plain to her that 'time had only solidified its loathsomeness'.

Martha had always railed against governments. The

stupidity and corruption of the mighty was a theme which would preoccupy her all her life, growing stronger with time. The United States, under Roosevelt, had enjoyed a long period of immunity from Martha's critical eye; but with Truman in the White House, a moment of reckoning was about to come. The worthlessness of Washington's political leaders, the evil they did, would in time become a consuming passion in her life. But the affair with America began well.

At first, Martha liked Washington. She enjoyed playing tennis in the lazy afternoons and was amused to observe the politicians and the worldly reporters who wrote about them; the city seemed to her to possess an energy absent from the flat postwar world she was continuing to have trouble adjusting to. But she was soon forced to notice that the political world had an unpleasant new edge. If in March 1943 *Life* had called the Russians 'one hell of a people', who 'look like Americans, dress like Americans, and think like Americans', by 1947 no one thought so any longer. By the time the American troops had been shipped home, the Republican right had successfully created and nourished a fear that there was treason abroad and that it was coming from the Russians, who were busy working from within to undermine and destroy the American way of life. It was the 1920s all over again, only more virulent, with Senator Joseph McCarthy and his reactionary isolationists playing on the frustrations and credulousness of the American people. The Marshall Plan, the Atlantic Pact, the New Deal, communism and Jews, all became targets for slander and attack. Washington, drifting towards paranoia about subversion and loyalty, confusing political naivety with treason, was just embarking on what would become a four-year witch-hunt of naming names and drawing up lists.

Martha, at first uneasy, became increasingly outraged. Everything in her was repelled by McCarthy and his methods. In theory, the 'tuberculosis' of the prewar world, the way men were accorded no dignity, had been eradicated. But something as terrible was now threatening, a bullying viciousness, and Martha despaired that all good people were now either dead or too tired to do the work that needed to be done. There were very few of her 'co-religionaries', people who felt the way she did, around. 'The mental climate in the US at this point reminds me only of a St Louis landmark called the River des Péres,' she wrote to a friend. 'The river wound through the park and the snappiest possible residential section and many fine plants grew alongside it and thick trees shot up from the rich mud of its banks, but the simple fact about the River des Pères was that it was an open sewer.' When the Hollywood Ten came to Washington, Martha renewed her friendship with Alvah Bessie, whom she and Hemingway had known in Spain.

One day in October she went to watch the House Committee on Un-American Activities, a collection of men she quickly labelled bigots, reactionaries and racists, question Hanns Eisler, the composer and German political émigré, about his application for membership of the German Communist Party in 1926, and the fact that he had failed to mention it upon arrival in the States in 1940. It was the sort of occasion she detested, the bullying of a 'dumpy, perspiring foreigner', as she described Eisler later, with his bald head, pudgy, bewildered face and heavily accented English. At one point a Congressman shouted at Eisler: 'You knew Charlie Chaplin! You met him many times! What did you two do?' in tones of sneering accusation. He had to repeat his words several times before Eisler understood. At last, very confused, he replied: 'Ve playt chess.'

To relieve her sense of revulsion, Martha sat down and wrote a piece, published soon afterwards by the *New Republic*. It was Martha at her best, excoriating, lucid and absolutely morally clear. The hearing, she observed, was not just sordid and filled with the baying of dingy and shabby minds, but it was evidence of a terror tactic, as yet small, but one that needed to be watched. 'For perhaps these men in the House Caucus Room are determined to spread silence: to frighten those voices which will shout no, and ask questions, defend the few, attack cruelty and proclaim the rights and dignity of man . . . If these things should come to pass, America is going to look very strange to Americans and they will not be at home here, for the air will slowly become unbreathable to all forms of life except sheep.' Having 'vomitted' her fury against these 'Congressional oafs', she returned to her tennis and her affair with Walton, but the charms of Washington, as it descended into a new Dark Age, what Dalton Trumbo would call 'the time of the toad', were fading fast. As she said to Mrs Roosevelt, she had not felt safe since the death of President Roosevelt, guardian of the conscience of the world, in 1945.

The Wine of Astonishment, competing to her dismay with other war novels like Irwin Shaw's The Young Lions and Norman Mailer's The Naked and the Dead for sales and review space, was published by Scribners in late October. She feared, she told Wallace Mayer, that they made her novel look like the 'idiot song of an idiot canary'. Early reviews were luke-warm, and Martha concluded, with wry resignation, that she had yet again failed to produce a bestselling book. But the next reviews were favourable and soon critics were remarking that she was now in the first rank of American novelists, and that The Wine of Astonishment was a clear indictment of war and brutality, which was a subject its author handled with great skill. It was taken by the Book of the Month Club, which praised Martha's 'deep disillusioned wisdom about life, love and death'. The Atlantic Monthly called it 'one of the most authentic novels of the war'. Several reviewers remarked on how well she understood the psychology of men, though none, surprisingly, drew attention to the markedly Hemingway-like tones of some of her war passages. 'But as the fierce boredom of war drove you,' reflects Lieutenant-Colonel Smithers, one of the two heroes, early in the book, 'anything was better than waiting; you had to move, you had to do something; and action was their job and you hoped that if you pushed and didn't stop you could get this over, get out of it, get free, escape from waiting in all the worst places of the world for nothing except more fighting.'

By the time the book appeared Martha had fled Washington, whose village life and political nuances she had decided she could no longer bear. She could have stayed and fought, supported her friends against wild accusations of communism, but she was tired of fighting. She was in Mexico, where she had rented a house in Cuernavaca, a mountain resort of white houses, brilliantly flowering plants and perpetual blue skies. She was delighted with the flowers, which not only grew in profusion, but could be bought extremely cheaply in the market, so that for once she felt she could always have enough. Parting from Walton, she wrote him a fond but realistic vale-dictory letter. 'Dearly beloved Cat's Paw' – Walton was the recipient of her more absurd endearments, which included Napoleon Slice, Pickle and Pissoir Attendant – 'I love you. I love you a lot more and a lot better than you know and if I were younger, nicer and more sure of myself, I would force you to love me. But it seems a pointless operation, from which no good can come, and so I think it wiser to love you from a distance. But I miss you, quite outstandingly . . . It would be a better sun and a brighter light, if you were going along.' Later, Martha wrote that this time had been 'filled with men whose names I no longer remember belonging to anyone'. In 1971, looking through her diaries of the immediate postwar years, Martha identified one as containing '3 major love affairs (I mean involving passion and the decision NOT to marry), four minor affairs and getting pregnant by an eighth (honest to God), and that year I spoke constantly to myself of knowing no one, being alone'. Whether or not this was actually the year that Martha was in Washington is not clear, but it very well might have been. The end of the war and the months that followed were a rootless, unhappy time. She was still rattled by Hemingway's intense nastiness towards her, and, after her failure with Gavin, no longer certain what she was looking for. She never gave a name to the eighth man, by whom she became pregnant, but she did not allow that abor-tion to haunt her any more than the earlier ones had done. Abortions remained events to be dealt with efficiently and without fuss.

Martha was now working on a short story about a '52 year old English widow in a desolate winter resort town in

Portugal', she told Wallace Meyer, and she was intending to deliver him an entire volume of stories, all on the same gloomy note, for publication the following autumn. She was sure, she said, that happiness was something that could be willed, provided that you did not indulge yourself in remorse and regrets. 'The days float past, and all is merriment and peace . . . I sunbathe and swim and doze and take leisurely walks, and the future is a dimness.' That is, when she could persuade herself not to think, not to indulge in 'unnecessary anguishes of the mind'. She was reading Milton and copied down a sentence: 'The mind is its own place.' Her own personal conclusion, she told Meyer, was that 'it is a hell of a place and one should get out of it'.

CHAPTER ELEVEN

Nothing with Mirrors

'The *flamboyante* trees blossomed orange red, the crepe myrtles were pink or lavender bouquets. The flowers of the casalmate lay like snow along its branches. Big purple morning glories grew down the side of barrancas . . . Our lawns had resumed their billiard table perfection and our gardens were bowers.' Writing of the arrival of the rains in Cuernavaca several years later, Martha described her Eden, a small town on the slopes of the Morelos valley, ringed by blue mountains, where the weather was always warm, the Indians ceaselessly interesting, and the pace of life exactly as she wanted it after the last four agitated years of war. Morelos was the Mexican state given to Cortés by the King of Spain as a gift in recognition of his conquest, and Cuernavaca was where Cortés built for his second wife, Doña Juana Ramirez de Avellano y Zuniga, a palace decorated to reflect his splendour. Returning there from her occasional trips to the States, driving past the great volcanoes of Popocatepetl and Ixtaccihuatl, up to the mountain rim where even in summer it could be very cold, then dropping out of the mist into the brilliant sun of the semi-tropical bowl of Morelos, through wooded hillsides yellow with mimosa and fields of sugarcane and neglected plantation houses covered in bougainvillea, Martha was always elated. Cuernavaca, the ancient Cuauhuahuac of the Indians whose name the Spanish found too hard to pronounce, was the place she spent the happiest four years of her life.

Martha began her Mexican life in the Hotel Marik, which had a sun porch and a swimming pool, for which she paid

$6.50 a day, Cuernavaca having already begun to attract visitors, drawn by the climate, the flowers and the palm trees, and by Diego Rivera's murals on the walls of Cortés's palace. From here, she moved on, somewhat irritably, to a rented house, where the mustard-coloured walls depressed her and where she stuffed the heavy, tasteless furniture away into cupboards and filled the bare rooms with flowers. She was again thinking of buying a house, or perhaps a plot of land on which to build, drawn as always by the need to live in surroundings that pleased her. She found a maid, Maria, who delighted her, and she told Hortense Flexner, that, though she had never yet had a really happy love affair, she was always very lucky with servants. She acquired a four-inch-long kitten, and was enjoying, she said, a brand new romance with peace.

She spent Christmas 1948 on her own, 'happy as a goat', sitting naked in the sun, wearing a large sun hat and reading a frivolous novel. Twice she went to a small, white, gold and red church near the market where the Indians celebrated Mary's search for shelter with two little boys looking like 'Mexican Huckleberry Finns'; ten others, raggedly dressed but with voices like flowing water, sang by the church doors. 'I had forgotten what it means to be moved to tears,' she wrote to Walton, telling him that she had stood at the back of the little church, weeping, she who had never found anything in a church except architecture. Released from the 'gilded sewer' of New York, she was adamant that she would never return to live in America. 'I'm all right again,' she wrote to Hortense Flexner, 'I know who I am . . . here, where I am really alone, I am not lonely. Whereas in the US, I feel the whole time that something is desperately the matter with me.' Laughter had not, after all, vanished from the earth.

Mexico was cheap after Washington, but Martha was running out of money. Her income for 1949 had come to $11,000, of which she had spent $8,000, and she had written only a handful of articles in the past two years for the *New Republic* and *Collier's*, having failed to secure the 'favoured nation status' deal with *Collier's* she hoped for. There never seems to have been any question of alimony from Hemingway.

But it was now that she discovered in herself an unexpected talent for what she was soon describing to friends as 'bilgers' or 'ordures of untruth and horror', popular stories about titled English ladies and Italian gigolos, or naive young American girls on their first visits to Europe. Principessas in black, speaking perfect if accented English, made many appearances, as did draughty palazzos, loyal retainers and winsome donkeys. 'I have discovered how to write bilge of the paying or golden sort, a form of literary whoring,' Martha wrote to Diana Cooper, no longer at the Embassy in Paris now but perhaps the closest of her women friends. 'I wanted a jeep, perhaps with the same intensity that inspires people who want love or fame. So I sat down and wrote a short story composed of fudge, high life, virtue and women wearing carefully described clothes. I am wallowing in gold and dishonour and expect God to strike me dead any minute.' She was right: the stories were fudge, but neither then nor later did she let the boundaries between her bilgers and her more trenchant stories blur. And bilgers made good money. *Good Housekeeping*, the first magazine to bite, paid her $1,500 – a considerable sum in 1949 – for a story called 'Alone' in which the much married Mrs Michael Macdonald has a maid called Greta who moves 'across the silvery gray carpet as if it were a field of flowers'.

Delighted with her new jeep, charmed by the unaccustomed ease and speed with which she could conjure up Italian counts, fur capes and Dio Button motorcars, she soon produced three more stories, in which both *Good Housekeeping* and the *Saturday Evening Post* were interested, though the last story made her want to be sick all over her typewriter. 'It is the purest s . . . t,' she told Wallace Meyer at Scribners. 'My mind is a pudding.' She was now looking for land to buy and had calculated that she could live on $3,600 a year, spending half of it in Mexico and the other half in Europe, with visits to her mother in America. When the bilgers flowed, she could turn out two in ten days. She told friends that she had no plans to submit to the hell of another book, and that she never intended to break her heart over 'real' writing again.

Then she was distracted with another kind of broken heart.

Sometime early on in her Mexican life, Martha met an American film producer. Nowhere in her letters or papers is there any mention of his surname. He was married and lived in Hollywood; he kept a boat, and had had an affair with Bette Davis. He was also much younger than Martha. They had a few nights together, staying in a hotel called the Majestic and hiding from local acquaintances; and then the producer went back to Hollywood and to his wife. Martha, as if in love for the first time, became frantic; she took to her bed, with fever blisters, saying that her body felt that it had broken into bits; she began to knit him a dark blue sweater, though her knitting was hopeless; and she wrote to him, long, untidily typed letters of growing desperation as the days passed and she heard nothing.

Was she just another Bette Davis in his life, neither beautiful nor famous, but as adoring? Had she made the one mistake her friends had always told her not to make, that of telling a man who didn't love her that she loved him, thereby so repelling him that she had driven him away? She told him his silence made her feel like a whore, a passing cloud, and that she regarded being a cloud as a kind of despair. 'I dug this grave with my teeth,' she told him, 'and it has broken my heart.' He had not understood 'about bed . . . I think, surely, you have had so much better . . . I cannot give my body as entirely or easily as I gave my heart, and yet my heart is the more valuable of the two because I haven't taught it any tricks.' Come back, she wrote, 'come back come back, come back because I need you so'. He did not come back. He sent her a postcard, on which he wrote 'I love you'. She wrote every day now, long letters about love and sex and whether or not he had thought that she was cold, because she was so slow to feel pleasure. Every morning, she sent her maid Maria to the post office; but there was never a letter. She felt 'mowed down', she wrote, and lay in her bed, unable to move.

Six days after he left, she wrote: 'I want you so. It is even worse in the daytime. For at night I tell myself stories and am almost convinced you are there, or soon coming; but in the daytime I know the truth.'

They may have met once again; from the dozen or so letters among Martha's papers, it is hard to say. Three months later, Martha wrote one last letter. 'You cannot help yourself; you are forced to break my heart without meaning to. A broken heart is such a shabby thing, like poverty and failure and the incurable diseases which are also deforming. I hate it and am ashamed of it; and I must somehow repair this heart and put it back into its normal condition, as a tough somewhat scarred but operating organ.

'I wish you every happiness . . . long or short, deep or shallow, however you want it and find it.

'I have a strange feeling of saying goodbye to a turned back, but I say it nevertheless, with love.'

Martha, so unyielding over the frailties of others, was implacable about her own. She seemed to have a remarkable ability to discipline her emotions, an utter contempt for self-indulgence and regrets. The producer had gone; she had loved him, and they might have been happy, but it was not to be. Not one minute more was to be wasted on memory or remorse.

Martha longed to feel the certainty of real love. It perhaps says something about what she feared was true in herself – an inability to experience unconditional love – that she fell in and out of what she took to be love so easily. Cuernavaca again came to seem to her like Eden, and the endless days of warmth and sun enchanted her. Occasionally worrying about her growing taste for solitude, and the way that she cared for fewer and fewer people all the time, she noted that the ones she was genuinely attached to, her mother, William Walton or Capa, she now cared about more keenly. When Dorothy Parker came to Cuernavaca, Martha grumbled about having to look after such a 'dreamy creature, not given to the ways and means of life', and she took immense pleasure in describing to Walton, in tones of scorn, the royal progress of Clare Booth Luce across the Morelos valley, stopping to call on Martha for a lunch party to which she had invited herself. She missed Walton, and the gin rummy in bed, and rather wistfully urged him to pay her a visit, though she remained clear that there would never be anything between them except a love affair '*d'automne*', full of pleasure and fun, but no passion; in any case, she doubted she possessed the staying power for a long love affair, particularly one that burned hard and bright.

On her own, she walked up and down the valleys of Morelos, mulling over ideas for stories, looking up at the mountains she had decided looked the colour of lions to the east and blue to the west, and she read as she had not read for years, keeping up a flow of criticism and appreciation in her frequent letters to Walton, Wallace Meyer and Diana Cooper, whose letters made her laugh, and whose wry, self-deprecating view of life seemed so like her own. She discovered Freud and found him 'perfectly killing' and wondered whether perhaps Marx, whom she also seemed to have missed, might provide her with the same degree of 'unexplored merriment'. Norman Mailer's *The Naked and the Dead* filled her with 'dazed and humble admiration'. She read Camus and thought him a finer writer than Sartre, and Salinger delighted her. She was now trying to write a short story – of her more highbrow kind – about Cuba, the fifty-two cats and Hemingway, who had at last sent on her papers, stuffed, to her fury, in old bags, leaving her to pay the charges.

A story of Hemingway's was being serialised in *Cosmopolitan*, and she read it one evening, fortified by a large whisky. It was, she said, 'revolting'. It made her, she told Walton, 'shivery sick' with its 'abject bottom-licking narcissism', and it made her weep for the eight years she had wasted in his company and for 'all that is permanently lost because I shall never, really, trust a man again', a remark that suggests that she was still very pained by the bruising parting from Hemingway. His story had, she declared, 'a loud sound of madness and a terrible smell as of decay'. Not that she really expected to need to trust a man again, because the men she now met seemed to her poor creatures, and though they looked like men, she knew better. Furthermore, she had grown so fat she could hardly waddle, while her stomach, swollen as by an enormous watermelon strapped around her middle, could hardly fit into the local peasant skirts. Fat, for Martha, meant an extra few pounds.

As for her hair, in a moment of madness, not liking what she saw in the mirror, she had had it cut short in Cuernavaca, and then permed tightly, so that she now looked as if she had a 'huge blonde Persian lamb cream puff' all over her head. 'I haven't got a grown-up lover and those days may be over,' she wrote to Diana Cooper. 'I can hardly think what I would do with one if I had one, except talk and listen and that would get very wearing. Naturally if someone who looked like Gary Cooper and had the mind of Dr Oppenheimer and the soul of Paddy Finncane crossed with St Francis, rang at my garden gate and offered himself, I doubt if I'd slam the door in his face.'

* * *

Someone far more appealing to her than a man, and for a while considerably more engrossing, now came into Martha's life. He was not exactly offered to her, and nor did he wander through the garden gate, and she had to work extremely hard to find him. But when he appeared she was ambushed by a love she had never believed herself capable of.

Increasingly, Martha had been envying such of her friends as Virginia Cowles and Diana Cooper who had children. 'I am almost certain that . . . the only private thing that gives people real joy is their own brats,' she had written to Diana soon after arriving in Mexico. 'It's what one needs: someone, or several, who can take all the love one is able to give, as a natural and untroublesome gift. As for men, they seem to me on the whole confused and feckless creatures.' Martha was now forty. Edna, recognising a profound loneliness in her only daughter, was urging her to adopt a child, or, better, two. Mulling over the ease of her own life, remembering the children playing in the rubble in Naples, the bold little boys who attached themselves to the American soldiers, Martha decided to go to Italy and see what might be possible. 'There had been too much dying and destruction,' she wrote. 'There had been enough to disgust the mind and break the heart. The only hope was to take care of life.' It was her duty, she decided, the duty of all healthy, responsible people, to care for children made orphans by the war. And if she did adopt a child, it was to be a boy, because boys, she improbably told her friends, were more independent. And there was something about small Italian boys that charmed her, something in their pluckiness and dark good looks. They were eager, and they tried hard, and they did not complain, all crucial ingredients in her lexicon of good character.

Italy in 1949 was a country still crushed by war. Money was pouring into industry and agriculture through the Marshall Plan, but the fabric of the country, its houses and roads and bridges, lay in ruins. Where German and Allied troops had passed, shelling and looting as they went, leaving rubble in their wake, there was still all the detritus of war. Many of the railway lines were destroyed; all but the main roads were full of craters. Even the fine, still, blue weather of the Italian summer, with its fields of wild flowers and the nightingales singing in the valleys, could not hide the fact that, in the south particularly, ordinary Italian families were destitute. Tuberculosis had taken hold and many of the children, to be seen scavenging in rubbish bins and begging by the roadside, were hungry. People lived in caves, in shacks, in the ruined remains of their houses.

Capri, however, was untouched; it had never been bombed and five years of war had halted the inexorable progress of tourism, so that the port and its surrounding hills had all the comfort and charm of prewar life, when visitors came for a weekend and stayed for fifteen years. With Princess Margaret due to pay a visit, and the eighty-two-year-old Norman Douglas still the doyen of the foreign writers, Capri made a possible article for one of Martha's American magazines. Martha spent ten days on the island, striding around with her distinctive, purposeful gait, interviewing the mayor, the nine policemen and the waiters in the restaurants along the seafront, pausing from time to time to swim in a sea so blue it enchanted her. Sybille Bedford, a new friend met in Rome on her way south, joined her for a few days. Meeting Martha, Sybille wrote later, was like being exposed to a 1,500-watt bulb. She gave off 'vitality, certainty, total courage'; her talk galloped, slangy, wry, dry and often funny. She was brown from the sun, and graceful. She also told Sybille that she was thirty-six, four years younger than her actual age, a small and absurd lie, but of a kind that people would later find annoying.

One evening Norman Douglas, who beckoned those he liked the looks of to his table in the one good trattoria, summoned the two women over. He called Martha 'my poppet', and they talked about Nazi collaborators. The bedrooms in their pensione were stuffy and unpleasantly hot, the only windows high under the ceiling and reached by clambering on to stools. When the two women went to bed, Martha, who wanted to talk, suggested they stand on the stools, facing the windows, opened to let in as much air as possible and with it the sweet night smells of jasmine, citrus, oleander and warm stone. And there they perched, their toes dug into the sides of their stools, craning like two giraffes towards the night air, talking, or rather, Martha talked, about the Spanish civil war, the Dorchester in the bombing, her night flight on the Thunderbird, the Italian campaign and Cassino. She talked about her love for her mother and about the hell of being married to Hemingway. Sybille, who was exhausted, listened entranced.

Next day Martha bought some clothes – 'ah such clothes, to wear for no one' – and went on with her interviewing, ending up with Edda, Mussolini's daughter, whom she predictably took vehemently against but added approvingly that there was 'nothing dull, nothing weak' about her. *Everybody's Happy on Capri* was, Martha told Walton, a 'solid mass of shit', but it was taken by the *Saturday Evening Post*. It is not her best piece, for Martha was never at her best where her passions were not engaged. Capri's beautiful people had mildly amused her, but she did not find them interesting.

A first money-making article delivered, Martha made her way slowly north. She anticipated no difficulty in either finding or adopting a child, should it turn out that this was what she really wanted. Nothing, however, had prepared her either for the sheer number of orphans, or for her own uncertainty about them. There were thousands, tens of thousands of small abandoned children, in orphanages set up in villas, convents and old schools, for the most part looked after by nuns. There were children blinded by shell blast and mines, children missing arms and legs, children with rickets and scabies, children traumatised by what they had seen. Wherever she went, the nuns would produce children coached to recite their own tragedies in flat, unemotional voices. Martha was profoundly moved. But, though more than ever convinced that it was her duty, as a well-off woman, to take and care for a child, the magic did not come. The children were not as she had seen them in her dreams, neither irresistible nor in some indefinable yet essential way what she sensed she needed. 'It goes on and on; it is a whole world of children who will never, as long as they live, stop paying for our grown-ups war,' she wrote in an article on Italy's orphans for the *Saturday Evening Post*. 'Their eyes are hard to meet. They could so easily be full of laughter, but instead they are bewildered, wary, frightened, sad.' She felt guilt; but the personal passion was not there.

Through friends in Rome Martha met Flavia della Gherardesca, an Italian woman who had very recently lost her husband in a car crash. Flavia was happy to show Martha the sights, and to take her to stay at Bulgheri, her family estate south of Livorno, and to help her look for her child. Like Sybille, she remembers being dazzled by Martha's energy, drive and outspokenness. It was soon clear that Martha, focused only on finding a child, had no interest in monuments, and preferred to sit talking about the adoption in restaurants or to make trips into the countryside.

One day the two women went in search of Capa, who was staying with friends north of Rome. Flavia found Martha very restless, and sensed that her impatience concealed a great need for reassurance. 'What amuses me about you,' she wrote to Martha soon after they met, 'is a quality of unexpectedness. *Tu n'es pas monotone*: there is a constant stream of worry which to someone who takes you too seriously, as I do, is a source of stress and anxiety, but, now and then, to relieve this, there is a light, charming touch and, often, a completely unexpected, and to me, rather comic gambol.'

Recounting to Walton scenes of her Italian life, Martha observed that the ancient nobility – who played such a prominent part in her bilgers – though affable, led 'idiot lives', insisting on speaking French to one another, and pretending to be penniless while living in palazzi that looked like dirty stage sets for gloomy Chekhov plays. In Rome, Martha had switched hotels, having grown tired of her blood-red bedroom walls at the Inghilterra, and was now in the Anglo-Americano, where she found, to her annoyance, that her new room was her most hated shade of mustard. She was eating too much pasta and had put on ten 'softly lush' new pounds. 'It is too hot,' she wrote crossly to Walton. 'Am homesick. People are fine but not as exciting as when I was younger . . . I have done no sight-seeing here, and am a lump. But this adoption thing obsesses me.'

By now Martha had realised that, should she find her child, her problems would only be beginning, though the problems she had in mind were all about acquiring the child, and curiously little about what she would do with one once she had him. One would have thought, she said to Walton, that she was trying to eat an Italian child, not adopt one. In a still fervently Catholic country, she was neither Catholic, nor even a believer; and she had discovered that there was an Italian law stating that any single woman wishing to adopt a child had to be over the age of fifty. It was not in her nature to be daunted by obstacles: she pressed on. Hearing that there were orphanages in an area near Florence where the children were mainly Protestant, she set off north, driving with Flavia over the potholes and craters of the Via Appia, to stay in Fiesole with Alan and Lucy Moorehead, friends from the Italian campaign.

Martha had found a lawyer to help her with the adoption and his assistant offered to drive her around and interpret for her, though the young woman was clearly sceptical about the whole enterprise and kept pressing her to look for a poodle instead. They visited Protestant children in villas in the hills around the city.

Lucy Moorehead later remembered the sense of sickening hopelessness when one day, having accompanied Martha to an orphanage, the two women found themselves peering through wire mesh at a pool of upturned, sad, pinched faces, as a crowd of small children, wearing little more than rags, struggled to get to the front, stretching their thin arms imploringly towards them. Even Martha had now had enough. 'This was too terrible,' she wrote. 'This was against nature. No one was meant to go from one pitiful place to another, from one cruel place to one which was only dirty or sad and inspect children as if pricing meat . . . They ought to declare war on grown-ups, who killed their childhood.'

She had visited fifty-two orphanages, and she felt too old for such misery. She had no doubts that the children were 'the bravest people possible, and beautiful and quick and cheerful in the center of hell, where they lived'; but something was missing. Besides, Martha, who as the years went by grew to hate staying with other people, was finding her friends' houses increasingly uncomfortable. The Mooreheads' sixteenth-century Villa Diana in Fiesole, she complained, was 'pure hell', horribly reminiscent of the appalling discomfort of English country houses. She wanted to go home to Mexico.

On one of the last mornings, the lawyer's assistant, still extolling the pleasures of keeping a poodle, drove Martha to a small orphanage attached to a hospital in the town of Pistoia. Unlike many of the homes she had tramped around, this one was cheerful, and though the twenty or so small children running around a dusty courtyard looked grubby and poor, they were laughing. In the middle of the yard, under the shade of the only tree, there were four babies lying together in a cot. One was a 'blond fatty', stretched out on his back playing with his toes. She put out her hand and the baby, looking up at her 'with interest and friendliness', took her fingers and held them. His hair was tawny like her own. Martha fell in love.

'I've found my child,' she wrote to Walton. 'At last. In Pistoia there is a shabby Foundling Home and therein dwells my heart's desire. His name is Alessandro. His age is either fourteen or seventeen months. He is as fat as two sausages, blonde like Botticelli's folks (gilt shining blonde) with grey eyes, a snub nose, a delicious mouth, and bowlegs. He is covered with prickly heat and normally dressed in an old flour sack. He walks, waving his arms and grunting with pleasure, like an old gent who has palsy. His smile is not to be believed; it looks as if he had invented the whole idea of smiling . . . It makes me come over weak to consider the fat character . . . I do not give a hoot about his parentage; I just want him. He may grow up to be very short and stout and of moderate brightness; but I think he is always going to be happy.' Bold words, but then Martha, like the people she liked in life, was bold.

For the next ten days, Martha returned to play with the baby every day. Her lawyer finally stopped her by saying that the word was going around Pistoia that there was an American millionairess come to adopt ten children. Like the doctor in charge of the orphanage, the lawyer had doubts about the wisdom of taking Alessandro, about whom nothing was known beyond the fact that he had been deposited with the nuns by his mother in a state of near starvation, that she had left no name or address, and that he was illegitimate. Nothing could put Martha off. And so he drove her away from Pistoia while setting in motion what turned out to be an extraordi-narily complicated process of adoption, involving the inter-vention of Eleanor Roosevelt and letters guaranteeing Martha's character from the Bishop of Missouri and the American ambassador to Rome. 'I never needed help like this before,' Martha wrote to Mrs Roosevelt. 'I never wanted anything as much.'

It was not until over three months later, on 8 November, Martha's forty-second birthday, that she was informed she could collect Sandy, as she had decided to call him. She drove to her lawyer's office in Florence, with a knitted woollen trav-elling suit for the baby, a nanny hired for a couple of weeks to teach her how to care for him, and Flavia, who had no baby either. The two women waited. A tense hour and a half later, there appeared a nun from the orphanage carrying Sandy. This was a very different child from the laughing baby who had played with his toes in June. He was pale, wheezing and unsmiling. A doctor was summoned; he diagnosed bronchitis and measles and ordered Sandy straight into a clinic. There he stayed for twelve days, still watchful and unsmiling but uncomplaining. It was clear that Sandy was, Martha wrote exuberantly to friends, 'brave as a lion'.

The flight from Rome to New York, where to Martha's fury the immigration officials would give the baby only a two-week visa, was dreadful, and Sandy, who was teething, cried for twenty-one of the twenty-eight hours, covering himself and Martha in syrup and oatmeal and working his way out of his ineptly folded nappies. Martha, handling him sometimes like 'rubber, sometimes like Venetian glass', arrived ragged and exhausted, saying that caring for an infant on a flight was considerably tougher than covering the Russian attack on Finland.

But the day came when Martha, Sandy and the ever resourceful and calm Edna flew to Mexico, a contented Sandy asleep across the laps of the two women. And there, in an article that is extremely touching but absolutely unsentimental, Martha wrote: 'He blooms more beautifully than any flower I ever saw.' To the Flexners, together with a charming photograph of the small boy, sitting beaming on the steps in immaculate dungarees and sandals, his tawny hair cut becomingly round his ears, she added: 'I sure waited a hell of a time to fall fatally in love.'

* * *

As with the children of Italy, Martha felt that the struggle of the Jews had been too grim; they were entitled to whatever the civilised world would give them, and more. To deny them this was not only unjust but evil. And so, shortly before Sandy's arrival in Cuernavaca, while she was waiting for the adoption papers to go through, Martha went to Israel. She would go there in all seven times between 1949 and 1971. She went to look, to listen, to wander and sometimes, but not always, to write. After the Six Day War she contemplated, for a while, a book about the Jews, to describe and explain their great courage and what they had left behind them in the ruins of their countries and their communities. But the book never took shape, and the most she ever wrote were a number of articles for the *Guardian* and American magazines and papers, a long unpublished piece about her feelings, and several entries in various diaries, increasingly black as the years went by. The personal guilt she had felt in Dachau never left her, and writing a novel to free herself from its memories had not brought absolution. Dachau had made her fear the human species, a darkness of spirit that she came to believe was what separated the old from the young.

More committed than almost any journalist of her generation to promoting the cause of oppressed people everywhere, more in sympathy with their sense of displacement and loss, and more profoundly sickened by torture, Martha was, however, deaf and mute when it came to the Palestinians. Able to reduce most moral problems to clear black and white, on the question of Israel she carried this certainty to an uncomfortable extreme. Palestine, and the rights of the Arabs whose lands had been taken away, their houses knocked down, their children locked up, was not a subject that could be discussed. It became a blank on a map otherwise rich in irony, humour, self-deprecation and curiosity.

In November 1947, after the United Nations announced its plans for the partition of Israel, the Mufti of Jerusalem, attempting to coordinate Palestinian opposition, declared a jihad against the Jews. By the spring of 1948 the Arab League had agreed that its members would intervene in Palestine as soon as the British withdrew. On Friday 14 May 1948, General Sir Alan Cunningham, the last British high commissioner for Palestine, left the country: at midnight the British mandate ended. The minute state of Israel, beleaguered, defiant, surrounded by over thirty million enemies, was born. It was new and it was independent; but none of the issues that had led to that independence had been resolved.

Israeli terrorists, fighters seasoned by their campaigns against the British, intensified their attacks on Palestinian targets. The Arab countries sent troops, but remained unco-ordinated and confused. The Israelis, vastly outnumbered as people, had nonetheless as many soldiers and were better trained and better led. There were truces, brokered by the United Nations and Count Folke Bernadotte, the UN mediator in Palestine, until he was assassinated by Israeli extremists. Early in 1949, an armistice of sorts was drawn up. Half the original Palestinians were deprived of their lands, and became refugees who scattered into Lebanon, Syria, Transjordan, Egypt and Kuwait. Some four thousand Israelis had died; while no reliable figure has ever been established, the Arab dead numbered at least four times as many.

For Martha, watching these events unfold, there had been nothing but a sense of relief and admiration. Israel was a country founded on the bones of six million dead Jews, murdered because there had been no place for them to go. It was as a human being, more than as a Jew, which even now played a remarkably small part in her thinking, that she felt so strongly. About to be tied to home by her links with her new son, she wanted to use her last weeks of freedom to see Israel for herself.

'Tel Aviv, river of sand,' she wrote in her notebook, as the plane came in to land on her first visit. 'Powder puff clouds then a long patch of spotless sea and sky . . . excited and happy again. A new world.' Capa was waiting for her at the Hotel Armon, which was small and shabby and close to the seafront; he had already discovered a bar with good whisky and martinis. They drank and talked about being Jews, the 'feeling of Jewishness'. Capa introduced her to Moshe Pearlman, a journalist who had been at London University and had come to Israel the moment the new state was declared to run the press department for the Foreign Office and the army. He was funny and energetic, with a Groucho Marx moustache, precisely the sort of friend Martha most enjoyed.

The three of them wandered around the streets of Tel Aviv, Martha stopping to question the people they met. 'I look for passion,' she wrote in her notebook, 'failing that, for amusement. British Ambassador: Pfui.' One evening, drinking in a rather scruffy bar after a day in the Negev desert, discussing the fact that a soldier and his girl had been killed along the same stretch of road only hours after they had driven along it, there appeared an elegant figure in white tie and tails. It was Leonard Bernstein, whose sister Capa knew in New York. Another day, Pearlman introduced them to 'a young, curt, blond captain', slender and with an eye-patch, called Moshe Dayan. To Martha and Capa, it seemed like old times in Spain. They belonged, not so much because they were Jews, but because they so profoundly shared Israel's hopes; it was a country, wrote Martha, that was not separate from her, and so instinctively familiar that she did not have to keep wondering about it. 'We were all merry and elated. Something good had come out of the endless horror of the Second World War, a new country full of young, brave, gay people and of hope. The courage was breathtaking.'

They went to Jaffa, to Haifa to see children learning Hebrew, to a kibbutz, to a Druze village, to a settlement of immigrants. One night they attended a Hanukkah party. 'Very gay,' wrote Martha in one of the two closely written notebooks that she kept of the trip, adding: 'I still don't really do well at a dance.' What struck her repeatedly was that everyone seemed happy, 'sometimes like music in a hymn, sometimes like music to dance to', which was what made Israel different from other places. Italy was about its churches, Greece its ruins: but Israel was about surviving, and about feeling glad.

One night, Capa said to her that she should leave Mexico, that time was running out and she should be in closer contact with the world. 'But I don't want to,' she wrote. 'Why does everybody tell me this: is there some doubt or unhappiness about me, of which I'm not aware?' But she was restless; and her fatal tendency to grow impatient when too long in the company of others was returning. Three days later, she continued: 'it is too ghastly to admit, I feel bored and frustrated. Something must be old and finished inside me, burned out. Because I am no longer open as once I was.' After this, the two notebooks are full of references to feeling 'dreary', 'heavy', 'pretentious' and 'self-centred'. Israel, the new world, with its energy and sense of adventure, was immensely seductive; but Martha's tastes and interests, if not her sympathies, lay with the old.

* * *

Martha wrote many letters about Israel, about the courage and the gaiety of the Jews, and about the stories of their lives, 'a gold mine the equal of which I've never before seen'. 'I am now certain,' she told Walton, 'that gloominess and cowardice go together.' She had laughed as she had not laughed in years with Capa and Pearlman and Bernstein, but she had not fallen in love, and all good journeys, she declared, ought to include falling in love; perhaps those days were over. Indeed, she said to Walton, her role these days was not so much that of sex queen as Queen Ant.

Once back in Mexico she was frantically busy, gnawed with worry about how to raise the $7,000 needed to get proper residence papers for herself and Sandy. With a small child and a nanny to look after, and Edna a frequent visitor, Martha had moved into a larger rented house on the Avenida del Parque, a cream-coloured bungalow she described as the nastiest of the eight houses she had lived in since 1930. But its walled garden and flowering vines enchanted her and she painted it white and filled it with plain furniture, obsessively consumed by a need to get every detail perfect before she felt right in it.

Martha remained overwhelmed by the love she felt for Sandy, and sent cards to friends with his photograph on which she repeated his humorous sayings, and her own efforts to make him bold, by getting him to stand up to an imperious two-and-a-half-year-old neighbour. He had all the advantages of not having inherited her genes, she said: a sanguine nature, irresistible laughter and huge enthusiasm. And he seemed to love and need her, which made her feel cheerful. She bought him clothes in the market, red and blue dungarees which ran when they got wet, so that his skin was coloured like a rainbow and he wove about on his short, stout legs like a drunken gangster. She felt insanely proud of him, of his fat little body and his new words and the way he looked and smiled. She had not expected such happiness. Only Edna's steady presence and a flow of reassuring letters from Mrs Roosevelt prevented total frenzy every time he sneezed or came out in nappy rash. Her only worry now was whether she could afford it all. 'A child is clearly twice as expensive as a yacht and a built-in mistress,' she wrote to Walton.

The bilgers were going well. After a ferociously boring local luncheon party with ten very old ladies and five old men, she resolved to stop writing about good innocent people, 'the ones whom life does in because they are victims', and write instead 'in high shrill hysterical notes about the people who are all right, and should be slaughtered. The ones who make life into a vast grey blur . . . the sprightly living dead, the utterly idle.' The vast grey blur of life had a particular terror for Martha, and it was growing stronger.

She had turned against journalism and its intrusiveness, and her mind was filled with short stories, though the one about Hemingway and his many cats refused to take shape, and she had rented a room nearby in which she wrote furiously, with all the intensity of a love affair 'only more solid'. When, a few weeks later, first *The New Yorker* and then the *Atlantic Monthly* turned down her '*good* stories' she was mortified. 'I don't want to be a bad writer, struggling in splendid isolation (and in vain) to do good work,' she wrote miserably to Walton, to whom, together with Wallace Meyer, she sent almost weekly letters. 'I'd rather know, and be a lousy writer, rolling in dough and idleness; I'd rather be something complete, not a grisly effort towards something not intended. Oh dear, do understand that sentence.'

Soon after Christmas, and with great reluctance, for she found the idea and the process of writing personal pieces a form of torture, she agreed to do an article about finding Sandy for the *Saturday Evening Post*. Linking a writer and his work was not only false, she insisted all her life, but limiting, and she was embarrassed in case friends found the story mawkish. But the *Post* were delighted, and sent her a cheque for $2,250. 'Little Boy Found' is a charming piece, very plain, utterly without sentimentality, and they published it together with a large photograph of Martha, looking down with a smile of quizzical pride at a very small, beaming Sandy, who is sitting on some steps in the sunshine.

After Edna left to go back to St Louis, where she came down with hepatitis, Martha resumed her more solitary life, built now around Sandy's meals and bedtime. While he slept, she read, books found in Cuernavaca or sent from New York by Meyer, and it was with him that she kept up a literary correspondence, praising Rebecca West, her current heroine, for saying she was in favour of pleasure, enjoying the *Goncourt Journal* because it reassured her that life was just as lousy in the nineteenth century, and brooding over Mizener's life of Scott Fitzgerald which reminded her all over again about how badly his friends had behaved towards him and how ashamed she felt of Hemingway's part in it.

She had begun to keep notes on Cuernavaca's foreign community, filing them alphabetically on index cards, and these would later make their way into a Mexican novel. More clearly than with any other book, perhaps, they show the extent of Martha's reliance on real characters for her fiction, the very sharpness of her reporter's eye lending a depth her imagination did not always provide. There was one woman, who gossiped disapprovingly about her neighbours, and Ernesto a 'lamentably indiscreet but v. kind doctor', who was accused of poisoning someone's wife. The tone of many of the entries is neutral; but Martha's eye could also be harsh. Ross and Vera 'finally married when Vera five months gone. She very ugly he drunk, pretentious, lives off her. Incredibly beastly.' The unfortunate couple's card has several entries: 'Vera: vital, common: the way she dresses, exposing those vast bosoms . . . The party for Allan's mother (in purple velvet) all fairies. And dismal.' Allan was another fairy, with the look of a fox. There is something chilling in the neatness of the index cards, and in the thought of Martha returning to fill them in with fresh observations after dinner parties.

Surrounded by foxes and fairies, Martha preferred to stay

at home with Sandy, whose first sentences in English she delightedly relayed to friends in long letters about the pleasures of motherhood. People were put on earth for only four reasons, she observed to Walton; to laugh with, and this she put first; to give a jet propulsion to the mind, because their minds were richer, faster, stranger and deeper; to love, and this, interestingly, she placed third; and to go to bed with. Interestingly, children did not rate a mention. Since Cuernavaca provided her with none of these, she kept her company for Sandy, except when visitors came through from abroad, though Dorothy Parker's brief stay in the town was enjoyed by neither of them.

One of these visitors was Leonard Bernstein, who turned up unannounced, proposing to move in; he brought with him a grand piano. Martha had admired his looks in Tel Aviv though she remarked to Walton that he was 'reported to like men (also women and goats)', and that he was about as natural as a '20 minute permanent wave' but full of talent and neuroses, 'ai, such neuroses'. As for any possible relationship between them, it was obvious that he looked on her only as a beautiful, placid middle-aged woman, honest as the trees and full of homely wisdom.

Never one to feel easy with visitors staying in her house, Martha moved him smartly into a house up the road, with a large pool, in easy walking distance. He wanted to play Scrabble, which she resisted, hating all games except for gin rummy, but one night, after he had been told by local musicians that marijuana made the music flow faster, they got hold of four joints and prepared to experiment. Since they were both terrified of what might happen, they decided to boost their courage by having a few martinis first, generously poured into water tumblers. After a while, beginning to feel ill, Martha crawled towards Bernstein's spare bedroom. As she reached the bed, she heard Bernstein fall heavily in the sitting room and lie still. All night, she was sick; when she fell asleep, her nightmares were appalling. Next morning, she crept home to Sandy, leaving Bernstein still unconscious on the sitting-room floor.

Bernstein recovered, and his stay in Cuernavaca provided Martha with a great deal of fun. Through him another friend entered her life, an athletic, handsome former journalist and playwright called Robert Presnell, on holiday from Hollywood. The three of them played tennis and sat in the sun and talked, and it reminded Martha that such friendships were now the most important thing in her life, apart from Sandy and Edna. To a letter from Bernard Berenson, whom she had first met while in Fiesole with the Mooreheads, and who had asked her 'what males she lived with', she replied that there were none in Mexico apart from old gentlemen and fairies, and of course the Indians, but that not being a 'D.H. Lawrence lady' – presumably a reference to Dorothy Brett – she regarded them with interest and admiration but no lust. She was absurdly happy, she told Berenson, because she was fortunate enough to have hermit blood, because she loved Sandy so much and because he made her laugh. When she had the time, she sat naked in her walled garden in the sun.

* * *

The wise Edna, outlining Martha's search for the absolute in men, had ended her list by remarking that the day might come when Martha actually found a man who was an absolute in nothing, whom she could really love. She was now forty-one, and though Sandy had indeed brought her an emotional dimension that continued to ambush her, she was also lonely. When, after several days alone with the little boy, she ventured out, she found herself talking too much, and too violently, unable to control the pitch of her voice. In one of her more open and honest letters to Walton, whom she pressed constantly to come and stay with her, making none of her usual attempts to hide behind self-mockery, she wrote: 'I am horribly lonely in a way, but it is being lonely for some place that never was, for people who are dead or changed or that I never knew . . . I do not want to move from here; I do not believe there is anything to move for or towards. Life is deep as a well now, not wide as the sky; one must stay put and dig until one finds water. But

I would like to laugh with someone. With whom? About what?'

In the early spring of 1950, when the long dry season was coming to its end and the blue jacaranda and magenta bougainvillea were again in flower against the grey-green leaves of the eucalyptus trees, Martha was introduced to an American doctor, on a brief holiday in Cuernavaca. David Gurewitsch was the son of Russian Jewish immigrants and a friend of Eleanor Roosevelt, whose doctor he had become after the death of the President. He was tall, spare, 'not withered but wand thin', wore a blue silk jacket and a cravat and had recurrent bouts of tuberculosis. He was married and had a daughter; once again, as with Allan Grover and Paul Willert, the fact that Gurewitsch had a wife seems to have played no part in her thinking, a reflection more of Martha's very low opinion of marriage than anything else. It was, however, quite simply as if his wife did not exist. Gurewitsch and Martha talked to each other all evening. They talked about the need for adventure and the freedom to reinvent life; he said he felt weighed down by the pressures of being a doctor in New York, and that he wanted time to think, to write, to live. That evening, after dinner, his wife Nemone sang for the guests. By the time Martha went home that night, she was in love; she believed she had at last 'found water'.

When David left Cuernavaca, fifty hours later, they had become lovers. Martha was bewildered, frightened and wobbly, and could fall asleep only after large doses of Seconal. She said that she would have married him immediately, had he been free.

It was not love as Martha knew it. She trusted him, and she was not accustomed to trust the men she loved. Whatever he said, she felt she understood it, by a sort of instinct. She did not have to keep explaining herself, as she had with Gavin, or protecting herself, as she had with Hemingway. And because nothing ever made sense to her unless she wrote it down, she began a letter to him as soon as he left, to keep the conversation going, to understand what had happened to them, an outpouring of feeling, memory, hope and confessions. Martha's letters to David Gurewitsch are the most passionate and open that she ever wrote. All the fears, of never having been really close to someone, of not having enjoyed sex, of feeling profoundly alone, flowed out, and with them expressions of need and tenderness she had never used before.

The first morning she was alone, she went to her workroom, a little heavy from the Seconal, and typed out a fourteen-page letter. She told him that all her life she had felt herself to be a displaced person, one who expected to move wherever she liked, easily, watching, loving, laughing or raging, but who always came home to loneliness; that she dismissed the fact that he was a Jew as she dismissed it in herself: belief, not categories of blood, was what counted in life; that she liked movies, bad tennis and, in some moods, detective stories. She asked, meekly, whether he would mind having to share a bathroom with her, in the new house she was planning to build for them both; and whether he knew of a book he would like her to read so that she would give him more pleasure when they made love, because she only knew how to receive pleasure and not how to give it. 'I want to be everything,' she wrote. 'I want you to love me so much that there will just be us, as man and woman, in the whole world.'

Having written the fourteen pages, she waited a few hours, took Sandy swimming, and started writing again, fretting that she had not yet heard from him. Afraid of overwhelming him with her letters, she went on writing them, and then put them in her drawers. She was overcome with a desire to be totally honest with him, and decided to write a long narrative letter about the people she had loved before him, carefully analysing her time with Bertrand, Hemingway and Gavin and telling of the '*amour d'automne*' she had had with Bill Walton. In the last three years, she told him, she had made love nine times, concessions 'to the nervous needs of the body, or the depression of the mind'. There was no mention of the film producer; and it is very clear that this was different, not like anything that had come before. 'I am very ignorant about love,' she said, 'very new to it; I do not even know what one must know, I have no way of comparing; I have no one to ask.' Alone in her workroom, she missed him, imagining him back in New

York with his patients, 'putting off thoughts and remembrance'. No matter what happened next, she said, 'one thing is there for me always: I won't die without knowing what it is to be in love with a man, and want to give yourself to him, and not be afraid of him and of the act of giving. You have already made that revelation to me and I think of it as a miracle.' Martha had never sounded so submissive nor so gentle; out of control for the first time, she was scared. Later, she would say to a friend that it was the first time in her life – at the age of forty-one – that she had enjoyed going to bed with a man.

David Gurewitsch appears to have been no less in love, but he had a job and a marriage, and if Nemone was reported to Martha to have had affairs, she was also a woman who had a horror of being alone and who was dependent on her husband. Grania, their daughter, was twelve. The days passed and the letters Martha longed for did not always come and though she made some efforts to ration her own, few hours passed without her sitting down to write. 'You are not dependent,' she wrote one day. 'I don't want to be dependent; I don't want it . . . If I were you, I'd run from me. No man wants a volcano for company. I don't want myself.' She said that she felt, for the first time in her life, like a woman, able to imagine what women felt when there was only one man for them. She told Walton that she was in love, and then she told Lenny Bernstein, who in return confided in her that his own problem lay not 'with love but only with sex . . . the wrong sex, really'. Then she went to watch Bernstein at a rehearsal in Mexico City, and for a few hours was glad to find that she could think about something else, that work and art still had the power to restore to her some sense of balance. When David's letters did come, she was able to turn back into a 'decent human being and not a fierce greedy one', and get on with the plans for the new house; but then, with the recurrent fever of being in love, the pressure of her need for him built up again and exploded on the page in expressions of love and longing and confession. She felt permanently a little ill, listless and she could not sleep without Seconal.

Two weeks later, David returned to Cuernavaca. He arrived with a new Corona typewriter for her, talking about books he planned to write himself. Martha's plague of ghosts and echoes fell silent. He stayed five days and when he left promised to return in May. No mention was made of Nemone. 'We must be as well rooted as trees and as inevitable and right,' wrote Martha. 'We must do nothing with mirrors; we must follow our hearts and our instincts.'

She wrote every day, remembering how he looked, the shape of his eyebrows and his nose. Their sex had been 'lovely, lovely', the happy pairing of a 'sex maniac and a *demi-frigide*'. She was appalled to discover hideous bumps and lumps on her own face, and apologised for having veins on her cheeks that looked like roads.

When Marlon Brando came to Cuernavaca, to study for the role of Zapata in a new film, Martha was asked to dine with him and Bernstein. She noted dismissively that his shoulders and neck seemed to have something wrong with them because they were so big but was delighted later when Bernstein told her that Brando had said he wanted her, 'because she was lovely and comforting to be with'. For her part, she said, she had felt ancient, surrounded by famous young men, a cross between Buddha and Grandma Moses. She told Gurewitsch that she would never consider being unfaithful to him, because there was no other way to feel. She belonged to him. In their letters, they discussed where they would live when they were very old, when he was boney and stooped and she fat as a pudding, waddling along behind him. But she was not always serene. It was not in Martha's nature to feel safe, and nothing gave her a greater sense of unease than her own character. From time to time she fretted not about her ability to love him, because that had become a fixed constant in her life, but about her capacity for permanence, about the deadliness of her own restlessness, the scorpion's tail that made her capable of destroying the very happiness she had so longed for. 'I wish I could trust myself as I trust you,' she wrote to him. 'I wish I could count on myself as I count on you.' The tides of her own mind alarmed her.

David returned to Cuernavaca in May, as he had promised, and again in June. He met Edna, and the two liked each other. He and Martha talked about the next step, where they would live when they married. David wanted her to sell the Mexico house and come to live with him in New York with Sandy, and Mrs Roosevelt, hearing of the plan, encouraged Martha, pointing out that it would ease the matter of Sandy's US citizenship, which continued to pose problems. Martha, however, remained utterly opposed to America. It was not only McCarthyism that continued to repel her, but a fundamental conviction that New York would destroy her. When she and David were apart, now, she was occasionally assailed by terrible fears about dependency and being trapped; but when they were together she forgot she ever had them. She had gone back to writing her bilgers, and was oozing out, she told David when he left, 'a flow of poisoned marshmallow sauce', which only proved that she was a literary whore with a huge supply of cheapness and badness about her.

A calmer note had entered their relationship, one of mutual reassurance and gentleness. 'I am happy that you are in the world,' she told him. Sometimes, now, the anxiety shifted to him. 'A poor letter, but a loving one,' she wrote one day. 'I stretch out a hand to make a little scratching on your arm, so you'll feel better. And I love you, not exactly as you want, but love anyhow.'

And so their affair went on, the pendulum swinging a little deeper into the troughs of uncertainty, as the time passed and nothing was resolved. Martha, increasingly, was emerging as the stronger and more decisive of the two, and in a long, unhappy letter, written not long after his departure for New York in July, she talked about the way she had a horror of cowardice and that she always feared she might be contaminated by it. She could only ever feel really safe, she said, with a man who was stronger than she was. One night, she dreamt about Hemingway and woke terrified. In her dream he had been staring at her, with 'a sort of obsidian hate' and he wore his 'ugliest smile'. When Edna returned to Mexico, Martha rejoiced in her company, her mother lending her a sense of balance that she sometimes felt she had lost.

It was after this visit that she began to feel impatient with David's hesitations. She found herself overcome with an unpleasantly familiar craving to 'wake up and sleep and eat and walk and look at the world alone, always alone'. Then came an attack of doubt: 'We either have to find a happy way to be with each other, or we have to amputate.' He was no use to her, miserable. Tough words, and she did not quite mean them. When several days went by and no letter came, she was again filled with terror that she might lose him and remembered with disbelief and horror the way she had told him that he bored her. But something had for the moment altered, and she felt impelled to spell out all the nuances of her changing moods. 'Mrs R.'s problem is a craving to be loved,' she wrote, on 8 July, when he had been gone two weeks. 'Mine is a craving to find someone who can make *me* love him. And I admit that I am like a cactus and all I can say is: I never saw any reason for any man to love me . . . If you want me, come and get me; seduce me, vamp me, bully me, do whatever seems necessary; but don't go on *talking* about it. I *talk* better than you, so if you keep it on that basis you are done for; I can talk myself *out* of anything . . . I'd love to be conquered by you and I know that's exactly the only way you'll get me, so hurry up and conquer or else drop it . . . You are the family psychologist, not me. I am the family's untamed horse; it is your business to know how to ride.' Elsewhere, she remarked irritably that she was not a guaranteed vacuum cleaner: if he wanted her, he would have to take the product at his own risk. They had become figures in a dream, in her mind, the two of them, dancing in quicksand.

David was evidently much thrown by this sudden assertion of independence, and some of his nerve seemed to give. Martha, for her part, soon swung back, helped by her unfailing support, work. She took to buying and reading American magazines, the 'stinkiest' she could find, in order to master the techniques of their contributors, saying that the short stories were as silky as Chevrolets. For a while, she believed herself to be pregnant, but was not sorry when it proved a false alarm, for neither

her mother nor David had shown much enthusiasm for a baby. In August, she joined him briefly in America, but was greatly relieved when the fortnight was up and hurried back with pleasure to Sandy; in September, he returned to Cuernavaca. Nemone, who was now aware of what was happening, was behaving like a 'gentleman', but she was prone to depression and clearly unwilling to accept a divorce.

Martha, by now, had swung back and was feeling optimistic again and, while David returned once more to New York, began to make plans for their wedding. Though David was not divorced, and had never in fact proposed marriage, Martha delighted in imagining the ceremony in Cuernavaca's royal palace, the reception at which he would wear a white silk suit, and their future, with him working as a doctor four days each week in Mexico City, returning to the hills at the weekends. She intended to earn enough money for the two of them and Sandy. What she would not do, however, not for David nor for anyone else, was return to live in New York. Day after day now, and sometimes twice a day, she wrote to urge him to hurry, to take the plunge, to cast off. 'Come to me,' she wrote early on 28 September. 'Let everything be clear. Let us be together . . . I am heartsick, so empty, so anxious, so unknowing . . . David, for God's sake, *seize* everything.' At two that same afternoon she wrote again: 'Life isn't forever long and we are not twenty; we are still pretty and healthy and I want to *eat* life with you, while we can.'

In New York, David worried. He worried about his work, about Grania, and about whether Martha really loved him; he worried about whether she might not lose her nerve again. 'There is an apprehension deep inside,' he wrote to Mrs Roosevelt, 'unexpressed and without reason, but it is here.' And, five days later: 'Cannot commit myself to an expression of how I feel, not even to you – I imagine this is because I do not know myself.' Letters of doubt, anguish, reassurance and protest went backwards and forwards. Meanwhile, Sandy learnt new words, Flavia della Gherardesca came to stay, a bilger sold to the *Saturday Evening Post* for $1,850, an English-language weekly in Mexico described Martha as a well-known communist, and *Collier's* turned down her proposal to go to the Middle East for them. Still David hesitated.

In between her entreaties, Martha worried about whether she was sexy enough for him, and worked at losing weight. She was delighted when a local admirer told her that she was '*une vraie femme fatale*', but rather less so when another, who had been trying to get her to go to bed with him, announced that she exuded a kind of virginity, an aura of detachment. Shortly before her birthday in November, she sent David a sad note: 'I don't know if I am randy. I'm terribly, terribly lonely.' She took to waking in the middle of the night, brushing her teeth, taking a sleeping pill, smoking a cigarette and then writing letters. 'Sometimes I feel like a very small engine,' she wrote, 'pulling many freight cars, all too heavy, trying to pull them up mountains where one can see the view.' She was upset when Flavia told her that she was a terrible person to love because she was a taker and not a giver, an impression that Martha, when at her most single-minded, was quick to give.

It might, perhaps, have come right. But David would not take the risk of abandoning his medical career in New York, and Martha was too realistic about herself to believe that her love for him would survive a move to America. Week by week, her letters grew a little sadder; she was resigned, but seldom reproachful. 'I love you, want you,' she wrote. 'There isn't terribly more to say.' She stopped urging him to explore the possibilities of practising as a doctor in Mexico. On 19 December, waking with her mind whirring inside her head like a sewing machine, she complained that 'her *vie intérieure*' had become a bargain counter of conflicting thoughts. She would have preferred a wasteland.

The long letter she wrote that morning is painful to read. 'If I had to choose between you and the certainty of being able to write, I would take writing; you better take New York . . . There isn't any happiness, I was all wrong; there is only a deep, private, silent bitter satisfaction in having *conquered* something: having conquered one's medium and oneself, of having brought something from nothing by sheer effort, will, talent, magic, whatever. I wrote the books and all the rest and one day I thought: this is mad, because there is also life. But now I see I expected too much; there isn't life: there is work.'

Edna came to Mexico for Christmas and Martha's spirits picked up. Christmas Day itself was spent with Lenny Bernstein, who had just got married to an actress called Felicia Montealegre, and he made the women laugh so much that they covered their white napkins with mascara. Afterwards they went to church and watched a procession of small boys dressed as angels singing carols. 'There is nothing good in sacrifices,' Martha wrote sadly to David. Sacrifices were for saints and neither she nor he were saints. Life could not be lived as a sandwich, a thin strip of happiness wedged between conflicting pressures.

The end, now, came quickly. One day Martha woke to find that she could bear the uncertainty no longer: it was making her ill. Looking back over his letters, she realised that even when he wrote, he was now really silent. So she did what she always did at such moments: she began to make plans. She would go to London, she told her mother, to the Middle East with Flavia, to the Caribbean, to the deserted island where *Liana* had been set, to Rome. She would immerse herself in Sandy. 'You are a free man, Davilita,' she now wrote to David, 'and I take back my freedom. I hate to lose the dream of us. It was a wonderful dream; but it is somehow lost. We have not enough faith, either of us, to make it come true.' They had dawdled and worried it away, and now its shine was lost. Martha hated muddle, and she hated all forms of attrition; she preferred sharp pain to prolonged uncertainty, and once something ceased to hold its promise, she wanted no further part in it. 'Be advised,' she wrote, 'love passes, work alone remains.' She had spent nine months believing that another life was possible, but she had been wrong: and now she would depend on no one. She would not be able to afford to do so again. She would be sad, but at least she would be sad alone. 'The heart may get sort of numb,' she wrote, 'but it does not break.'

Despite his suggestions for places and times when they could meet, she told David that she would not see him again, for

343

fear that the agonising sense of futility in loving someone only to lose them again might overwhelm her. Martha's last letters to him, written towards the middle of January, were some of the saddest she ever wrote. 'Say to yourself simply: she doesn't love me enough . . . Say that, and believe it, and forget me. Maybe I could forget you too, and think it was a love affair that did not grow, it was the best and loveliest love affair I ever knew and it must be remembered like that, with gratitude: and life is something else . . . Alas, alas.' Four days later, she wrote again. Happiness, she wrote, 'is a sort of miracle and one must be glad of it, however it comes and however long it lasts. I am. I am terribly glad of it.' She asked him to return her letters, for safe-keeping. The last letter is dated 29 January. 'I do not expect to hear from you anymore, but I send you a cloud of good wishes, to keep you company on your way.'

CHAPTER TWELVE

The Habit of Living

'You know,' Martha wrote to Hortense Flexner, 'I don't believe that one about it being better to have loved and lost. Damn sight easier just to scrabble along, without the pain of memory, without memories at all . . . I do know that the brave people stay and fight; but to be brave you need faith. I've lost it.' How much did Martha ever really mean these denials of hope and feeling? She never lacked courage, or so seldom as not to make it a question; but she was very impatient with uncertainty – and extremely easily bored. Yet she needed dreams; her disappointment when they lost their shine amounted to anguish. Only her relationship with her mother had never failed her, and work, in the sense of the activity of working rather than any success at it.

And so it was to work that she now briskly returned, not least because she needed to make money, having earned only $2,000 in the last six months. She managed to sell a short story to the Saturday Evening Post, about a visit she had paid to friends from the Carpathian Lancers who had stayed on in Grimsby in Lincolnshire after the war, and she pulled together a somewhat lacklustre article about Eton, demonstrating again how, more than many writers, she found it hard to write when her passions were not engaged. Like Capri's beautiful people, Eton's privileged schoolboys did not much interest her. She had by now collected almost enough of her good stories – the boundary between 'real' stories and 'ordures' remained precise – for a new volume around a theme that had preoccupied her since the last year of the war: the pain of return and the emptiness of all that came in its wake. 'How do you pick up the habit of living, once you had lost it?' asks her American heroine in Grimsby, bitter and awkward in her postwar reunion with the Poles to whom she had once felt so close. Martha was also working on a novel about Cuernavaca's foreign residents, intending it to stay ominously close to the originals and their quirks, still carefully filed away on her reference cards. She told Sybille Bedford that she had her first sentence: 'The Countess decided to give a kosher dinner party'; but where was she to go from here? If on some days she complained of flailing around like an apprentice juggler with slippery words that refused to fly, she also confessed to Berenson, who was taking Meyer's place as the confidant of her literary letters, that she had never really doubted that she was born to write. 'The only question is: write how, well or badly? . . . A certain amount of vitality and hope disappear when one finally decides one is not going to be Tolstoy.'

Her mood was fragile. When Wyncie King and Hortense Flexner arrived in Cuernavaca and rented a house to be near her, Martha conscientiously made all the arrangements for them and bothered about their comfort; but she soon tired of their company, irritated by the way they told her every morning exactly what they had eaten for dinner the night before, and by the little presents they insisted on bringing with them when they came to see her. Wyncie's wisecracks grated on her. 'How can one write of the dying of a friendship, when there is no cause but the passage of time?', she wrote in her notebook. 'I love them and they bore me, and I have behaved like a hyena.' She now found herself looking at Cuernavaca's aging expatriates as if they were leeches, and shrank from their 'sloppy mindless small talk'.

Only Leonard Bernstein continued to make her laugh, and he was struggling himself, drinking and taking sleeping pills, fearing that what was making him so wretched was that his marriage was not going well. He told Martha that Felicia lacked 'a sort of stimulation which I have always expected from people, and have always gotten from those I chose to see repeatedly'. Bernstein once spoke of his friendship with

Martha as 'our own peculiar sexless love affair'. Like her, he relied on it for laughter and reassurance. 'You have GOT to be there, please, please,' he wrote to her from California, on his way back to Mexico. 'I have withstood an awful lot of bad sessions and troublous times through the thought that I can see you.' Martha noted that she had become a 'laughing nanny to this troubled pair'.

Sandy was now three. He had started nursery school in Cuernavaca and Martha continued to be charmed by the unpredictability of his three-year-old's conversation, and his stalwart approach to the world about him. 'He is bliss, bliss, bliss,' she told Sybille. 'I do not deserve anything so perfect.' He was the ideal food for her heart. Sandy's own first memories are of great happiness: loved and played with by Martha, spoilt by the Mexican couple who looked after them and by Edna on her frequent visits to Cuernavaca. After her nine unguarded months with David, Martha now felt as if she were pulling the house, the gardens, the mountains and the bright blue sky of Mexico down over herself and Sandy, under which they would huddle together. Tensions had been growing in Korea, and the world seemed to her once again on the edge of war. She dreamt of digging an enormous cave for Sandy, and guarding its mouth like a tiger. Korea was a conflict she would not cover, but she was haunted by the idea of more people dying. 'It is a terrible strain to go on, acting orderly and reasonable, in a mad world,' she wrote to Sybille. 'It is a terrible strain to have to arrange for a future when there seems to be no future.' She had resolved to plod on, healthy, neat and sane, she told friends, for Sandy's sake, and as an act of defiance; and she would fill her days with reading Freud, who continued to make her giggle, and the Bible, and about Mexico. She felt that her life had entered a long stretch of open river, in which time passed without ripples.

Martha needed ripples. Boredom was a far more malevolent enemy to her than change. War reporting had, for the moment at least, lost its attraction; but travel, to new places where she could swim and write, while escaping the ensnaring kitchen of life, was becoming the one prospect that unfailingly brought the promise of pleasure. In February 1952, while Edna was on one of her regular visits to Mexico, she decided to leave Sandy with her and his nanny, Nana, and travel for a couple of weeks on her own to Haiti. She remembered the island from her Caribbean wartime journey as an enchanted place of green mountains, cobalt sea and white houses festooned with flowering vines and bougainvillea. It was, she wrote many years later in a rueful article for *Granta*, a careless choice; her days on Haiti could certainly have earned a place among the horror journeys of her life.

The twelve years that had passed since she was last in Port au Prince had not treated the town well. The houses were crumbling, the roads were dusty and full of craters, the government was notoriously corrupt. The 'vibes', she said, were 'very bad'. There were no other tourists. Though the night air was soft as fur and the stars looked like diamonds, the food in the Pension Croft tasted revoltingly of garlic and sugar. Her landlady was icy. The sheets smelled sour. Her room had no window. The man in the next cubicle hawked and spat all night, and no one spoke to her, and if she spoke to them they did not reply.

On the beach, where she went to swim, little boys stole her clothes and scattered them around the hillside, jeering, and when she slipped and sprained her ankle it swelled up and only got worse after a doctor injected it with a syringe used for horses. The days passed and she felt increasingly hysterical, but could find no way of leaving the island. At last she was able to bribe a pilot to fly her to a half-Dutch, half-French island called St Martin, where she found a deserted cove and swam naked in the aquamarine water. But what she had received, in her days trapped in the silence and hostility of Haiti, was a lesson in racism, and she did not really regret it: to be white, she had come to see, was to be on the receiving end of apartheid. When Haiti's small children stoned her and shouted '*Blanc! Blanc!*' she knew what it felt like to be 'black in a bad place'. Instead of writing her novel, as she had planned, she lay and brooded about race and colour until summoned back abruptly to Mexico after Nana, in the throes of a family row, took rat poison.

Martha had now been in Mexico for nearly four years. Though for the rest of her life she would see that time as her golden age, and mourn it as the colour of happiness, she was growing restless. Her ivory bungalow had come to feel like a mausoleum, and the countryside she had so loved to walk in had become 'unbreathable with memories'. 'I am tired, lonely, depressed and one hundred years old,' she told Sybille, and she was in need of the 'chit chat' of real friends. On a single sheet of paper, found among her notes on Mexico, are the words: 'Finally there is no one to talk to . . . so I must talk to myself.' The time had come to move on, and because Martha never dawdled the end came quickly to Cuernavaca too. 'The point of no return has been reached,' she wrote to Hortense Flexner. And she added, on a sad note: 'I reach it everywhere, sooner or later.'

But where would they go? America was not a possibility, because, as Martha told Berenson, she felt ungainly there, eight feet tall and always as if she were walking backwards. England was murky and dull and wet. The Israelis delighted but did not entertain her. The French, since the war, she found a bit repellent. This left Italy, and though she felt like a ghost, who had died young, returning to her wartime haunts, and though she despised Roman men for their maddening charm, she had friends in Rome, its weather was excellent, and the Italian contessas would continue to supply her with fresh plots for her 'ordures'. Since Cuernavaca's memories of David would not dissolve, she would run from their sadness. She wished to God, she told Mrs Roosevelt, from whom she had been slightly estranged since the end of the affair with David, that she had been born with no emotions, for she had not been given the equipment to handle them with detachment. Too much emotion, suggested Martha, was a sickness; and though Edna had provided her daughter with reason, intelligence and humour, she had not thought to give her the cure for such an affliction. Freud made her laugh, but he does not seem to have made her think.

'I wish I were a young man setting off for London,' she now wrote to Sybille, 'with my clothes tied to a stick, and my cat at my heels.' It was a refrain she would return to many times in her life, that of longing to be free, and young, and a man, embarking on a future without plans. And she added, echoing Iris Origo's famous phrase about the terrifying shortness of life, and also its unbearable length: 'Life is not long at all, never long enough, but days are very long indeed.'

* * *

Flavia della Gherardesca remembers Martha and Sandy arriving in Rome in July 1952, in the full heat of summer. They had six crates of books and toys and had stopped in the States on the way. Martha was extremely agitated about Sandy's American citizenship, and it was beginning to look as if it would take a special act of Congress to get him an American passport. She was also tired and a bit rattled by travelling with a small child. Though Sandy was out of nappies and easy and affectionate, he was accustomed to the attentions of a nanny, and Martha's unencumbered journeys had not prepared her for the rigours of moving with a three-year-old, nor for his sense of utter desolation when she parked him with a stranger and took off for a holiday with Flavia. Often, in these early years, Martha appeared curiously detached from the real implications of her new responsibilities: it was as if she neither could, nor wished to, think them through. The fact that a three-year-old, parted from his own mother as a baby, might suffer acutely from new partings and new places did not seem to occur to her. Nor had she thought to find a house for them in Rome before they left Mexico. She was grateful when, over lunch with friends, she was offered a house at Grotta Ferrata, in the cool of the Alban hills, for three weeks. Bernard Perlin, a very young painter living in Rome in the early 1950s, remembers meeting Martha and Sandy at this time, and how delighted they seemed to be with each other, Martha very loving and protective. When one day Sandy jabbed his eye with a reed Martha 'went berserk with terror', rushed to Perlin, who took the two of them on the back of his scooter to an eye doctor in Rome. Perlin was much struck by the mixture in her character between a most adult, strong, almost masculine mind and odd moments of almost childish behaviour.

Flavia's cousin Clarissa was married to a Tuscan landowner called Mario Incisa – these were the aristocratic Italians whose dusty palazzi Martha had found so chilly and uncomfortable on earlier stays. Incisa owned a farm at La Storta, twenty kilometres north of Rome, along the Via Cassia. The main house, L'Olgiata, was seldom used by the family. In late August, their stay at Grotta Ferrata over, Martha and Sandy moved into a flat in the farmhouse across the courtyard. Martha set about her usual feverish redecorating, cheered by having a home to make not for herself alone but for a child, and much taken with the thought that at L'Olgiata Sandy would be able to bicycle down a safe country drive to school with the farm children in his regulation white smock and blue bow, and that the seven-hundred-acre property would give him the sense of peace of an earlier world. It would be instructive, was how she put it to Mrs Roosevelt.

The farmhouse rooms were small, with wooden floors and open fireplaces, and some were also pleasingly panelled. Large windows looked out over trees, racehorses grazing in a paddock and a herd of the whitish-grey Maremma cattle with their long horns; beyond, the hills curved and turned yellow in the late summer light. Martha bought curtains and lamps and had an oak table carried to a room at the top of the house, where she put her typewriter and her books. With money from a story sold to the *Saturday Evening Post* she bought a Topolino, a squat pram of a car barely large enough for her and Sandy, and in this she bumped her way into Rome and back. 'Darling Napoleon Slice', she wrote to Walton, still the recipient of her more fanciful endearments, telling him that her new flat reminded her of Georgetown and listing her house improvements, 'I do not know why I care so much except that I am an egotist and a perfectionist.' It was the twelfth house she had taken over and done up.

Rome in the early 1950s was an extraordinarily beautiful city. The Marshall Plan was beginning to return Italy to its prewar level of prosperity and money was now pouring into restoring the little damage caused to the city itself by the war. Rome, *città aperta*, open city, had not been shelled and its ochre and terracotta buildings, dusty and a little shabby in the bright sunlight, looked magnificent. There was very little traffic, though the first Vespas, with comfortable back seats for passengers to perch on, were starting to be seen weaving around Rome's narrow backstreets. The markets were full of fresh vegetables, fruit, olive oil, cheeses and wine. It all looked, and smelled, and tasted, wonderful. In the shop windows were chic and frivolous dresses designed by Emilio Pucci, who had survived torture by the Gestapo after smuggling the secret diaries of Count Ciano, foreign minister and Mussolini's son-in-law, out of Italy, and who now teamed up with American managers and businessmen to enter the mass market. In America, Diana Vreeland, *Vogue*'s influential editor, ran flattering articles on Italian fashion.

Under De Gaspari and the Christian Democrats, the Italians, humiliated by the German occupation, ashamed of the support they had given the fascists, were beginning to enjoy the new industrial and economic improvements. Life for foreigners was cheap and the Americans who had settled in Paris in the 1920s now came instead to Rome, where they rented flats in the great dark palazzi in the centre and covered their roof terraces in climbing geraniums. The Italians were pleased to have them: they brought with them memories of the final Allied victories, foreign currency and new investment; in turn, the Americans appreciated the politeness and good temper they encountered and enjoyed feeling proud about what they were contributing to the new Italy. Plane travel made the journey easy, and in 1950, the first postwar Holy Year, pilgrims and tourists flocked. Among these Americans were refugees from McCarthyism, men and women like Martha who were appalled by the witch-hunts and the hearings, or were drawn to the apparent freedom of postwar Europe and had been charmed by the romantic beauty of Rome, as seen in the movies now being made by

Hollywood directors eager to make the most of low labour costs and the royalties on their earlier movies, blocked first by war and now by export restrictions.

Rome was alive with politics, for postwar Italy was also voting communist and Palmiro Togliatti was popular with the new voters. The old fascist film studios and lots out at Cinecittà, along the Via Appia towards Albano, had been cleared of the refugees billeted there by the Americans and were again at the centre of a thriving film industry, with large numbers of extras taken on for the historical biblical spectaculars that now proved so popular; and in the cool of the evening the actors, directors and expatriates hoping for parts came to sit and drink in the cafés of the Via Veneto, just below the Porta Pinciana, and to talk about the new postwar Italian vogue for movies such as *Paisan* and *The Bicycle Thieves*, films that were realistic and poignant, with no real hero, no happy ending and no stardust. The Dolce Vita lay just around the corner. Rome, it was said, was becoming Hollywood on the Tiber, and Gore Vidal came to Cinecittà to write the script for William Wyler's *Ben Hur*.

Sandy bathed and in bed, Martha and the Topolino would set out for Rome, to call on Judy Montagu, Princess Margaret's friend, in her flat on the island in the Tiber, to see Flavia della Gherardesca, or go to a party given by Jenny Crosse, Robert Graves's daughter, whose terrace above the Forum was turning into a literary salon for the new Italophiles. Randolfo Pacciardi, the Italian commander who had made passes at Martha in Spain, was now Minister for War in Rome. 'I like his wife enormously,' declared Martha, who had strong views about not getting involved with the husbands of women she was friends with. Pacciardi was charming but a philanderer: '*Il la trompe à faire claquer les vitrines.*'

Gradually, Martha rediscovered the laughter she had missed in Mexico. Her friends took her to see astrologers, much in vogue in Rome in the 1950s, and she consulted Waldner, the most popular among them, who told her the dates on which her writing would go well. (Martha, the most rational of women, had a curiously soft spot for astrologers.) The women went, in a group, into a clinic to have their faces peeled, playing cards while they waited for their treatments. Martha also dined with Bernard Berenson, at eighty-seven still making visits from I Tatti to Rome, who had, she told Teecher, developed an 'odd sort of prying passion' for her. She told him, with her usual candour, that he was 'too *fabriqué*', too 'perfectly hand-tooled' for her taste, and that his overtures were nothing but lying flirtatious salesmanship. After this rejection, Berenson told Martha that the only other person who had ever attacked him this way was Gertrude Stein. He would have minded more had he but known that Martha had decided to study him 'as a phenomenon' and was putting notes on him into her card catalogue, hoping to detect 'wisdom, a steady cool light of knowledge' and finding only politeness, an exceptionally good memory and a view of life as an interminable dinner party. He was a 'little Tanagra man, spoiled all his life by smart second-rate people', neither interesting nor inspiring, and she felt worse, not better, when she had spent time in his company.

Chim – David Seymour – Capa's photographer friend, turned up at L'Olgiata one day with Ingrid Bergman, who was neither glamorous nor witty, Martha wrote unkindly to Walton, though she was certainly nice. When Capa came through Rome, she joined him on an expedition to Ravello where he was taking photographs on a film set, and the intense enjoyment of his company reminded her that her men friends were what mattered to her most in life. Her only real worry was Sandy, who had clung to her since leaving Mexico and who had taken a strong dislike to his new Italian nanny: one afternoon he crept into her shuttered, empty room and strangled her canary in its cage.

All through the winter of 1952, Martha and Sandy lived at L'Olgiata. Sandy had started school and he now spoke Italian better than English; he had a bicycle on which he rode up and down L'Olgiata's long drives. The farmhouse was unheated, in the way of Italian country houses in the 1950s, and its stone floors made it bitterly cold. Martha, wrapped in blankets and sweaters, wrote furiously and productively, eight hours a day 'at white heat', both good short stories for the collection she was planning, and bilgers to make money, and she complained to Walton that she had been as chaste as a nun since David, 'not in tribute but from an increasing fussiness which bids fair to last for the rest of my life'. The men in what she referred to as the 'Roman Nobles Trade Union' were all identical and, what was worse, they kept repeating themselves. To Berenson she wrote: 'And why are there no men, B.B.? Can you tell me that? Why in heaven's name can't they make them alive enough and brave enough and funny enough and good enough to use up a woman's life? But they aren't. They don't exist. And they seem paler to me every year, until I could weep with despair, thinking how ghastly women will become in this world of inadequate men.'

When summer came, Martha took Sandy south, to a house on a beach near Naples, where they made garages in the sand and addressed each other as Mr Smith and Mr Jones, weaving stories about their imaginary lives. She then deposited Sandy and his nanny in a children's chalet in Cortina and drove the Topolino down the Dalmatian coast, first to a small village in the hills and then on to a hotel in what was then Ragusa and is now Dubrovnik. Her spirits rose, as they never failed to on a journey. The heat was intense, the quiet soothing, the freedom intoxicating. Her idea was to settle somewhere by the sea in order to swim and to continue with her novel.

She had not expected to meet anyone she knew, but when she learnt that Mrs Roosevelt was not far away, at Brioni, she drove over to see her and was startled to find that David Gurewitsch had accompanied her to Europe as her doctor. When he walked into the room, Martha found herself trembling; she had not seen him for a year and a half. To Mrs Roosevelt's evident displeasure, she and David disappeared to spend the night together, but when Martha woke next morning very early she fled in the Topolino, not willing to risk the pain of further loss. She was through with the 'terrible life wasting longing' she told Sybille Bedford, but she felt the richer for having seen David and known that 'there is someone in this world who can make me feel like this'. Was it to keep the feelings at bay that when she went on to Trieste she found a 'beau', a fifty-year-old aristocrat from Trieste's Thirty-Three Families, who was now driving a taxi? His deep-set, dark eyes reminded her of a panda's and she was delighted by his *grand seigneur* manner. He was entirely male, she told Sybille, and she was sick of sissies. They swam in the moonlight and spoke to each other in Italian, which was only good since it prevented him from guessing 'any of the less seductive features of my mind'. She felt herself to be a middle-aged Zuleika Dobson.

Later, when she was back in Rome, she wrote to Berenson: 'I think I know absolutely nothing about men, having spent my whole life with them ... I know something about women, although God knows how. It must be by osmosis. But, qua men, I think I am doltish. If I like them, I magnify them until they are splendid giants (very uncomfortable for them); if I don't like them, I ignore them. But understand, study, observe – never. So it follows that men in my books must be rather ghastly.' The Triestino did not merit a name in her letters about the affair.

Something in Martha was uneasy however; she felt uprooted and not even repeating to herself Malraux's maxim about work could make it right. Her letters from L'Olgiata have an unhappy, fretful tone, at once impatient and resigned. This mood coincided, in a way extremely painful to them both, with a long visit to Rome by her mother. Edna arrived at Ciampino airport at dawn, after a series of plane delays, looking frail and exhausted, but as upright and uncomplaining as ever. Martha, seeing her eyes milky and a little blind, was seized by her usual panic at any sign of her mother's mortality. She rushed to give her a good time. They made expeditions into the city, they visited friends, they played with Sandy, to whom Edna was very attached. Flavia and Sybille were charmed by Edna's unfailing sweetness and 'perfect kindness'. But Martha, escaping as often as possible to her study at the top of the house, was bored. She was afflicted with the same feelings of irritation and claustrophobia that had so over-whelmed her when Wyncie and Teecher came to Cuernavaca.

Sybille Bedford remembers Edna's sense of being unwanted, of feeling that she had become too old and useless and 'like

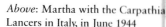

Above: Martha with the Carpathian Lancers in Italy, in June 1944

Left: Major General James Gavin of the 82nd Airborne, at thirty-six the youngest divisional commander in the American army. He told Martha that she would make a fine guerilla fighter. 'I was crazy about him as a soldier,' she wrote later

a piece of furniture' and that Martha was now beyond her reach. Horribly aware of what was happening, conscious, as she had never been before, that it was possible both to love her mother more than anyone in life, yet be irritated by her presence, Martha pretended that nothing was wrong. Edna concentrated on Sandy. Both mother and daughter longed for the stay to end. When Edna eventually flew back to St Louis, Martha was seized with anxiety about her mother, and fear about her own 'deadness'. She had behaved, yet again, she said, like a hyena.

Nor was this mood of detached boredom only present with her mother. Flavia, too, felt ill-used by Martha. They stopped meeting. Martha told Sybille that she had always feared and hated the weighing out of emotions as if they could be counted, some giving more, some giving less; and that while she always longed for intimacy, when it came her desire to run for cover was almost uncontrollable.

Alone with Sandy at L'Olgiata Martha felt her own sense of herself faltering. Nothing was going right. The Topolino was broken into and two dresses, a suit and two pairs of shoes that had been made for her were stolen. She was spending more money than she had – more than $600 a month – and she was beginning to wonder if she hadn't made a dreadful error in leaving Cuernavaca in such haste. Might they be better off in Trieste? Or in Paris? Could she face another hideously cold winter at L'Olgiata? She had decided that the 'Middle Aged Madcap Set' of Judy Montagu and Jenny Crosse repelled her; they were too aimless, insatiable and introspective.

Towards the end of the summer, leaving Sandy with his nanny, she had been to meet Sybille on the shores of Lake Maggiore, where she behaved boorishly to their hostess, Esther Murphy Strachey, pointedly going to bed rather than endure the boredom of an evening in her company. Together Sybille and Martha had made a trip around Switzerland. 'My meteoric and impatient friend' was how Sybille described Martha in her account of the journey for *Encounter*. Martha had been delighted by the Swiss, and charmed and entertained by their orderliness and reliability. 'What a genius they have for the small change of freedom,' she said to Sybille. But she was no more prepared to linger in Switzerland than she lingered anywhere else, and Sybille, who had been journeying in a pleasantly unhurried way before she met Martha, found herself hurtling along the roads in the Topolino. 'Let's shove,' said Martha, as they sat peacefully on the shores of the lake at Lucerne feeding the swans. And so they shoved, up mountains and through valleys, orchards, fields and woods, down lanes and highways, past castles and lakes, pausing only to eat and sleep.

After they parted, Martha once again took stock of her life. She knew now that she dreaded the idea of going back to live in Rome. The people were all wrong. What she really liked were upper middle-class intellectuals and artists and she was fed up with expatriate Americans. They were joyless and they could not communicate, having been brought up never to admit to doubt, pain or grief, and they thought failure was dirty, like a nasty disease. These expatriates, she wrote, who in the end were forced to pay psychiatrists so as to admit in secret what they could not divulge in public, were suffering from extreme loneliness. Her own next step, on the path to *savoir-vivre* '(which will have to do, for me, instead of wisdom)', was not to allow herself to get so depressed and angry when the sky was grey. As for Sandy, and his presence in her life, nothing was said.

* * *

Martha called Sybille Bedford 'Syb' or 'Sybi'; it was her own abbreviation and used only by her. It was Syb who became her closest writing confidante, someone with whom she could pick over not only the act and art of writing but the minutiae of every character and the nuance of every scene. In writing, as in all else, Martha, once engaged, was wholehearted to the point of obsessiveness. For a while, during 1952 and 1953, there were times when she seemed to be writing for Syb alone.

At no time in her life was Martha ever more than fleetingly

Martha during the Second World War. *Above*: in Finland, in December 1939; and *below*: on board the *Pilot*, in July 1942

358

David Gurewitsch, with Martha's mentor, Eleanor Roosevelt. Martha hoped to marry him in Mexico in 1950

Left and *above:* Martha in Mexico with Sandy, the little boy she adopted in Italy

Martha with Tom Matthews, whom she married in February 1954

Martha with the Pamps, Rosario and Lola, in Africa

Martha on the beach at Nyali, in Kenya

Martha and Sandy in London, in the early 1960s

Sybille Bedford,
Martha's writing confidante

Betsy Drake,
a good friend from the 1970s

'The true north of my life':
Martha's mother, Edna, in the 1960s

Diana Cooper,
with whom Martha went to the movies

Sandy Gellhorn and Sandy Matthews

Catscradle, Martha's cottage in Wales

Martha with her favourite brother Alfred

Martha at Catscradle

Martha's 85th birthday party. Guests included James Fox, Nicholas Shakespeare, Victoria Glendinning and John Simpson

Martha in her eighties

satisfied with anything she had written. As she told Berenson, she felt impelled to write, but it was more like a sentence than a celebration. 'Life frays and falls apart,' she wrote to him, 'and the only way I can make it seem real to me is to write. I never have any time of certainty or self-belief, of feeling that it matters whether I write or polish shoes.' She deeply envied those writers, 'happy like goats', who took satisfaction in what they accomplished. Sitting in her study at L'Olgiata, looking out over the cold landscape of winter, hating and resenting the grey skies, yawning and squirming over bilgers that would not flow and unable to decide whether the Mexican novel should be about her love affair with David or expatriate schemers against McCarthy, Martha felt low. She had made herself believe that it was a failure, a sin, not to love life; '*joie de vivre*', she would say, was one of the '*specialités de la maison*', but that was now leaking away. She felt harassed and rather scared. It was Sybille who kept her going, Sybille who comforted her when the 'marshmallow paragraph, dripping sentimentality and sweetness' made her feel ashamed, and who insisted one day on rescuing a manuscript she had decided to take to the rubbish dump.

Sybille did not find her own writing particularly easy. Her first book, *The Sudden View*, about Mexico, written in her early forties and with considerable apprehension, would find its English publisher at least in part through Martha's help. Sybille had sprung upon the world, Martha would tell friends, a quite remarkable writer, disciplined and talented. Long letters – sometimes running to seven or eight closely typed pages – went backwards and forwards between them, as chapters were finished, or new ideas surfaced, with suggestions for places to expand or cut, ideas for titles and changes of emphasis. Often, it was a case of shoring up the other's nerve. 'Most people, all people, write as feebly as they speak which disgusts me,' wrote Martha one day. 'You write like an angel; angel of another century.' 'You must have more confidence,' Sybille wrote to Martha. 'Yes, I do know about that flutter in the stomach, one goes quite cold. But think: you have brought it off before . . . This one will jell too. Everything you dread most has come off so far (in grinding agony, I admit); a few weeks ago you thought you could not do the sex. Well, you did it . . .' Sometimes, Martha complained that Sybille was as protective about her work as she was about Sandy, 'tiger-fierce and basically frightened'. 'You do not need to be any of this; I understand despair . . . darling, don't fight it so. I am well disposed . . . allow this alien wind to play around your edifice, it is not going to hurt it.'

In their exchanges, Martha could be more brutal than Sybille. Martha was, for instance, obsessed about Sybille's poor spelling, and insisted that she used far too many meals in her fiction. 'Bridge party chapter far too long,' came back one message. 'Food, food, food. Who will proofread?' Martha was also far more explosive, and several letters in the thick sheaf of their correspondence are contrite notes from Martha, apologising for having erupted uninvited into one of Sybille's evenings with someone else, and harangued the gathering about the hell of writing before hurrying away back to L'Olgiata in the Topolino. 'I am very sorry to have behaved, last evening, like a river of pus and gloom,' reads one. 'This unfortunate condition is the usual result of having spent a day writing with one's feet.' The redeeming factor of Martha's more intemperate and insensitive outbursts lay, for all her friends, in her humour and great generosity. One day, realising how short of money Sybille was while waiting for a cheque from a publisher, she sent round $200, enough to keep her for three months. Knowing that Sybille would not accept it from her, she told her that it came from Edna. On the publication day of one of Sybille's books, Martha got a Roman baker to ice a cake with the word 'book' wrongly spelt.

But Sybille was not Martha's only writing confidante. Robert Presnell was becoming another member of Martha's charmed circle of favoured men friends. Presnell could be, and was, tough in ways Sybille found hard. 'Who is the judge that sits perpetually on your head?' he wrote, in response to a wail of despair. 'Write those lines, you silly fool, they are all yours, both the good and the bad, and no one exists in purity and essence. Write the bad lines if only to keep writing . . . Your ego sits like a fat, repulsive Queen of the Bees, being fed, pampered, caressed . . . Writing is lonely, wretched, unheralded, often meaningless, insignificant, and too often devoid of even a masturbatory pleasure, mean though that is. Write, Martha, and stop crying at the cold. You've wept long enough.'

Martha was not always weeping. Often, she was fuming. Anger against McCarthyism simmered even as she sat writing her bilgers out along the Via Cassia. Just as the Jews in Israel had crystallised into figures of gaiety and courage, so those in power in America were corrupt and corrupting. How morally right was it for writers, she asked friends guiltily, to lock themselves away?

Early in 1953 she proposed to Mrs Roosevelt that she should set up a Citizen's Committee against Calumny, all of whose members would be sworn non-communists – their one concession to the 'folly of the times being the need to confirm this fact' – and whose job it would be to protect decent, ordinary American liberals from the 'deadly rat bites of unsubstantiated individual accusations'. Apologising for burdening her with another chore, Martha added: 'I cannot, with comfort, resign myself to the advance of the Dark Ages; so I write to you. Because you are a tower of light, because people will believe you, because you have never been afraid; and because you care about the condition of man, whose only claim to dignity, whose only hope, is the honor of the mind.' Martha's faith in Mrs Roosevelt had not lessened with time, nor had the slightly fulsome tone she now used for her alone.

She had long since realised that for her to use her vehemence effectively, it was no use spreading it too thin. Rage had to be selective. Nothing gave her more pleasure than meeting Adlai Stevenson, Governor of Illinois, while in Trieste and talking to him about the House Committee on Un-American Activities. Before they parted Stevenson asked Martha to prepare some notes for him to use in his speeches about Americans driven into exile in Italy by McCarthyism at home. When she returned to Rome, she drafted a thirteen-page letter on all the 'floating words that make an intellectual and emotional climate'. It was the sort of writing she excelled at. Haunted by a sense of *déjà vu*, recalling the German refugees from Hitler in the 1930s, she wrote about the anxiety felt by the Americans she knew in Rome, the way they avoided speaking out because of the fear of having their passports confiscated or being branded 'controversial personalities', and the speed with which America's 'moral stock' was falling every day. 'I think that Orwell and Kafka, in collaboration, are the only writers who could have done justice to this miserable story,' she told Stevenson, adding that it would give her great satisfaction to do anything of this kind for him again. It was the start of another good friendship.

Martha had now left Scribners and, in the summer of 1953, Doubleday in New York brought out the collection of short stories that she had long been working on. Called *The Honeyed Peace*, and dedicated to Sybille and to Winifred Hill, an elderly woman who had befriended her in Cuernavaca, the volume contained stories written as far back as 1937. Many had already appeared in *Harper's* and the *Saturday Evening Post*. If they had a common theme, it lay in the fugitive nature of pleasure or happiness, and many touched on the anguish of readjustment after the certainties of war. One way or another, the characters in all the stories are misfits, misplaced some-where within themselves. *The Honeyed Peace* includes some of the best short stories Martha ever wrote. 'Venus Ascendant' was about a young woman brought to the edge of destruc-tion by a vain and manipulative man, a horror story which she said made her laugh out loud. In 'Miami-New York' a somewhat older woman fantasises about the affair she will have with the young officer seated next to her on her flight home. Many of the characters are lonely women, but the victories they score over their complacent men are not good victo-ries; and the acidity in the telling is sometimes almost too uncomfortable to bear. Reviewers were not certain what they felt. Both the *Nation* and the *New York Times* remarked on a new note of desperation in Martha's writing. And when the collection came out in London, the *Daily Telegraph* dismissed the stories as monotonous, saying that Martha was 'skating over the thin ice of hysteria, nostalgia and sheer sentimentality'.

The publication of *The Honeyed Peace*, Martha's sixth book, marked a new tone in her relations with her publishers. Her views on publishing, always strong, had become stronger. Ken McCormick, editor-in-chief of Doubleday, was on the receiving end of a number of haughty letters of a kind that would become all too familiar to her editors in the years to come. The copy, she told him, was 'creeping with clichés'. It sounded like a toothpaste advertisement. The binding, a 'revolting' shade of mustard, depressed and unnerved her. She railed in successive letters against the galleys, the page proofs, the use of italics and the misspelling of names. She told him what size of lettering to use for her name on the cover, and in what shade of yellow. She scolded him for trying to turn her into a celebrity, and said that it did not matter to her or to anyone else if her hair was pink or black. McCormick, who had only agreed to publish the short stories in order to get an option on her novel, fought back, but he was in a losing war. Martha, he said, was one of the most nervous ladies he had ever had to deal with – 'and I've had to deal with some pretty nervous ladies'. And he was not pleased when he received a casual note from her saying that the novel was not only going to be late, but might well never come at all. In 1988, when McCormick came to organise his papers, he added a note to Martha's file. 'This book caused me more trouble than doing all of Somerset Maugham . . . Miss Gellhorn simply broadcast on a different wave length.'

Sitting at L'Olgiata after her six weeks in Yugoslavia, the Italian lakes and Switzerland, contemplating a second freezing winter in the Roman campagna, Martha wondered whether to move her household into a flat in Rome. Only Sybille's presence now kept her in Italy. Abruptly, leaving Sandy again with his nanny, she took off to see Leonard Bernstein rehearsing Prokofiev in Tel Aviv ('Men at work is what I like.'), pausing in London on the way to see whether the 'curious whims of the heart' drew her to the English and to London. She found herself much feted by Stephen Spender in *Encounter* and by the *Observer*, much in demand by publishers – George Weidenfeld told her he would publish anything she cared to write – and much sought after for dinner parties. She met Freddy Ayer, Peter Quennell and Randolph Churchill. To Sybille she reported that she had fallen in love with hideous grimy London, that she loved the way people ate lunch immediately followed by tea, and that the nonsense of the city made her laugh. A movie man was after her for the rights of 'Venus Ascendant'. She was too excited to sleep. 'Being in the middle again. I love it. Very greedy for life, suddenly.'

On returning to Rome, she consulted Waldner, her fortune-teller, about moving to London. As she reported to Berenson, he told her that Saturn had apparently been 'flopped over me like some sort of cosmic fried egg, but had now rolled or dripped off . . . I feel like a new woman without a lot of glum stars in the voisinage.'

The only problem was Sandy, who had turned into a 'prissy and finicky' five-year-old, would not pick up a snail or anything in a shell, and was becoming spoilt. It does not seem to have occurred to Martha that he might have been craving affection. No longer were her letters to friends filled with his amusing sayings; in a vast correspondence filled with reflections about herself and the people around her, Sandy at this point featured rarely. 'He still loves me so much that he dreads displeasing me,' Martha wrote ominously to Edna. 'I shall have to use this . . .'

Sandy had been looking pale, 'like a very tiny grey rag'. To bring colour into his cheeks, she took him, together with a nanny and another child, to the Isle of Wight, where the rain fell ceaselessly and the wind blew. Sandy and the other little boy quarrelled like rattlesnakes. Martha loathed the nanny, a '22 year old pea-brain monster called Marisa'.

Drinking whisky from a toothmug in her bedroom, she became distraught with boredom. She filled some of the time by writing long letters to her mother, reproaching herself about how appallingly she had acted towards her in the summer, and repeating that the moment she felt anyone too dependent on her she was driven to behave wickedly and horribly in ways she could not control. She had done the same, she realised, with David, Flavia and Bill Walton. 'I think it is because some little empty space, which I have to keep free for myself or die, gets crushed in; and then I become as evil as anyone who is hanging on to a raft and kicking off the next fellow.'

Sandy did not greatly care for the Isle of Wight either and begged to leave. Martha, having decreed that he should have red cheeks, was adamant that he should get them. Only after ten excruciating days, her life going to waste 'on this doll-size Augean stable', with 'ulcers forming, softly, softly, like little rosebuds, in my tum', were they permitted to leave. Nineteen fifty-three, Martha wrote to Edna, had been an altogether hateful year. 'One seems to be a complete plaything of fate, and fate has arrived in my life clothed in the body of Sandy.' It was the nearest she got to admitting that she had perhaps hastened into the adoption with little heed of what it might do to her life.

* * *

The decision to stay in London was not quite what it seemed. Martha was indeed bored in Rome; but she had also found a new beau – a word she continued to use all her life – in England. He was a tall, conventionally good-looking, patrician American, whose father was a bishop. She had first met him twenty-five years earlier at the *New Republic* when she was a cub reporter looking for work, and he the rising star of the editorial department. Tom Matthews was a widower, ex-St Paul's, Princeton and Oxford, with four sons, and he had come to England to explore the possibility of setting up a permanent London office for *Time* magazine, of which he had been the editor-in-chief. He was now fifty-two, a keen tennis player and sociable, and he liked to give and to go to parties. However, he was rather deaf, which meant that he was forced to wear a hearing aid. He wrote poetry, which Martha did not think much of, and, since leaving *Time* – just as well, she said, for she would not have dreamt of going out with anyone who stayed there – he was planning to write a number of books. T.S. Eliot was his mentor. Tom was also rich, dependable and, soon, much in love with Martha. He sent her a great many bunches of flowers and took her dancing, which she loved; and, within a few months, he asked her to marry him. Martha had never really intended even to go to bed with him, she told Sybille, but then she had felt sorry for him, 'and thought: it really doesn't matter about me, I'm alright, it's such a small thing and one would never refuse a loan, why refuse a loan of only this', which suggests that she had reverted to her old ways of thinking about sex. She was also worried about Sandy, conscious that he was now five, that he needed a proper home, and that he was 'through no act of his own, but because of a careless, inconceivably frivolous and selfish act of mine, making life untenable'. She could not organise her child's life, she said; nor could she live her own; it was a total stalemate. She had always known that there had to be a trap for her someday, a trap big and tough enough to catch her, and 'this is it. But I am not a willing trap victim, even of love.' Mocking herself, she told Sybille that, while she was a 'crippled hare', Sybille was a 'forging steady powerful tortoise'.

Martha was not in love, nor did she pretend to be. She noted in her diary, the first evening she went out with Tom, that he feared life and was drawn to the dark, and that he was therefore dangerous and to be avoided. But she liked his kindliness and suspected that he might be more complicated than he appeared to be; she did not feel ashamed of him, as she had at various times felt ashamed of Hemingway, Gavin and David, and he did not 'bugger up' her work. On the contrary, he seemed to value it. One day, reviewing her position, she wrote a long letter to her mother. Martha was too wary of self-indulgence to write poignant letters; but this one has a painful note. 'Ah me,' she wrote. 'I think probably it is best to marry him . . . Around now, that is what I want; things easier, just less damn trouble . . . I guess this life is not my job and I do not do it well and as a result I am never really happy. Terrible thing to say. Probably I was not meant to be a mother . . . I have entered a too difficult profession, I am simply not up to it. Which does not mean that I shall abandon it . . . but it does mean that I shall always do it with something close to agony, never ease, and that I will never feel that I, as a person, am really functioning.' Better, then, to share domesticity with someone else, for domesticity was hellish, basically, plain hellish. Martha's last words must have haunted Edna: 'Goodnight my dearest Fotsie,' she wrote, using the nickname by which she had called her mother as a child. 'It's no wonder you hardly know me any more, because who am I? And what have I become? But what would I have become anyhow, at forty-five? Hard to know. I feel ten years older than God.'

Martha and Tom Matthews were married in Caxton Hall on 4 February 1954, Martha telling Berenson that the place looked like a 'cut rate funeral parlour'. The witnesses were Moura Budberg, whom Martha had known from the earliest days of her friendship with H.G. Wells, and Sybille Bedford, who came straight from Golders Green Crematorium where she had been attending the funeral of a close friend. After the ceremony, they went back to Tom's set in Albany, Piccadilly, where he had arranged an elaborate lunch for a party of people, several of them former beaux of Martha's. They began their honeymoon in a house in Oxfordshire, lent to them by the Birkenheads. Sandy went with them, expressing considerable joy at acquiring a father. He had been found crying bitterly one night before the wedding for fear it was not going to happen. Flavia had sent an affectionate but admonishing letter, urging Martha to try to shed some of her 'silly illusions' about sex, false glamour, and to be prepared to make some sacrifices.

They stayed on for some weeks in Oxfordshire, putting Sandy into a local school. Writing to Sybille, with whom he had become friends, Tom said of Martha: 'She seems happy, and I hope she is. I am, very . . . She laughs at me, and I hope always will.' Martha herself reported that she was 'dottily happy', and spent a lot of time in bed, writing to her friends 'explaining and extolling' her new life. 'I feel,' she said to Sybille, 'like a fudge-eating, negligee clad, lump of female suet pudding . . . *Must* work.' Describing Tom's features to Berenson as looking as if they had been carved on Mount Rushmore, she told him that married life was vastly enjoyable, pea-brained, like going to boarding school for the first time and sitting up all night talking to one's room-mate, and at the same time living in a 'kind of half merry, half haunted ways and means committee'. The only thorn was Tom's request that they might be blessed by an Anglican American priest whom he had long regarded as a kind of confessor, and who was now a don at Cambridge. The blessing took place at 8.15 one morning, after which Tom took communion and Martha sat furiously in the pew, noting Father Casey's mean mouth and odious pomposity, sickened by Tom's apparent need for what she called this 'horrible cannibalistic voodoo, of the ugliest sort' which made her hate both Tom and the Church, and realise that here was a subject they would never be able to discuss. Both Sybille and Flavia felt such vehemence to be unreasonable.

When they returned to London, Martha and Sandy moved into Albany, where Martha was given a room of her own on the second floor, which she immediately painted white, filling it with white furniture and curtains in bold plain blues and greens. Soon, they began looking for a house to buy. In April, still with Sandy in tow, they went to St Moritz to ski and Sybille was surprised, a week or so later, to receive a summons to join them on the slopes, together with a cheque for $50 from Tom to buy herself some ski clothes. Sybille greatly liked Tom; it was hard not to.

Martha was exuberant. 'It turns out that wedlock is the easiest thing I have so far undertaken,' she wrote to Berenson. 'There it is: we are plain silly happy.' A few weeks later, she wrote again: 'I am, as the London servants say, very well suited. Oh very well suited indeed. Miraculously so, and as I never imagined I could be. I am neither bored nor lonely.' She took off for a few days to meet Leonard Bernstein while Sybille stayed with Tom and Sandy. From afar, old friends observed Martha's new happiness with a certain amount of wariness. Edna told Hortense Flexner that she felt as if Martha were flopping about in whipped cream; Hortense replied that she couldn't see her being suffocated in it, for she loved the dangerous edge too well.

Tom's four sons were Tommy, an Oxford scholar like his father and a philosopher, who was now twenty-eight; Johnny, twenty-five, working in Munich for Radio Free Europe; Paul, twenty, who wanted to paint and was working in a circus; and another Sandy, just twelve and living with his uncle and aunt in America. The first that Sandy Matthews remembers hearing of his father's wedding was when his aunt called him into the kitchen and told him that she had just heard on the radio that Tom had married again. Paul, the only one of the brothers in London, went to meet his new stepmother in Albany. He was delighted by Martha, describing her as an 'asset' and 'scintillating'.

Julie Cuyler, Tom's first wife, had come from an old Princeton family. Summers were spent at Newport, Rhode Island, where the family had an estate on the ocean. Everyone played a lot of tennis; there were lobster picnics with the neighbours and much desultory talk. The house was fine, but a little battered: it was called Boothden and had been built by the brother of the man who shot Lincoln, and bought by Tom's father in 1931. Julie herself, good-tempered and family-minded, had died in 1949 of cancer. She was remembered with great affection.

Martha felt a certain amount of understandable apprehension as the end of June approached and they prepared to set out for a long summer of introductions. She admitted to Berenson that the idea of Newport 'revolted' her. It was the wrong kind of ocean – too cold, too rough – and her feelings of hostility towards America had been growing sharper. It was not only the paralysing boredom of St Louis, but the horror of McCarthyism besides.

However, the crossing, first class on the *Mauritania*, was a delight. Martha took luxuriously to her bed, revelling in the break from domestic life, while Tom ate large meals in the dining room, and Sandy was looked after by others. But Newport turned out, very quickly, to be even worse than she had feared. She loathed lobster picnics; she was bored by small talk; she was too cold to swim. To friends, in letters that became less humorous day by day, she spoke of the 'absence of life', of feeling dead and tame and gelded, trapped by piousness. She began to say that it had been a hostile act on Tom's part to take her to Newport, but also that she felt guilt at being such a disobliging wife, particularly after Tom told her she was terrifying the neighbours. The scene is all too easy to imagine: Martha, elegant, capricious and edgy with boredom; old friends coming to visit and inspect, which always brought out the worst in her; Tom pretending all was well until goaded into reacting.

And the meeting with Sandy Matthews was not a success. The twelve-year-old boy was not, as she put it, her 'cup of tea'. She found him priggish, boastful, a 'success King' and coldly egocentric, hardly surprising, given her sudden appearance in his life, and the fact that he was about to be uprooted from everything that was familiar to him. While she had been genuinely fond of Hemingway's three sons and their bookish and competitive ways, she was disconcerted to find that she actually disliked Tom's east coast boys. Tom, awkward with his sons, more obviously fond of his ebullient small stepson, did very little to help. He scarcely knew his own Sandy, having sent him to live with Julie's brother and children after his wife's death. Sandy Gellhorn disappeared into the attics, where he dressed up in a fancy dress Guards' uniform and played with a train set.

Martha appears to have been almost relieved when her ankles swelled up alarmingly and she went into hospital for tests; though from some letters it seems that she may have had a 'nervous breakdown' of the kind she suffered at Bryn Mawr, but there is no clue as to what form this took. Even a visit to Newport by Edna, who, like Sybille, thoroughly liked Tom, and a few days' escape to stay with the Bernsteins, on holiday nearby, did not soften Martha's distaste for Tom's family. Nor did sending the two Sandys off to day camp, which made Sandy Matthews extremely miserable, as he felt the banishment from his family home keenly. It was with a sense of release, after this summer without end, that she accepted an offer from the *Sunday Times* to cover the army's McCarthy hearings.

Her article, which was published in September, was a muted sigh of relief. It was as professional as all her reports, the vehemence of her reactions substantially toned down. McCarthy, who had been a noisy, scandalous and megalomaniac figure, was portrayed as a man finally brought face to face with the madness and meaninglessness of his four years of 'Communist scrounging'. But there was no gloating; no one, she wrote, should allow themselves too great a sense of triumph, for even were McCarthy himself brought low, the corrosive sense of suspicion and unease that he had set in motion still flourished, and no one, as yet, had publicly censored that.

Buoyed up by her bracing piece of journalism, Martha returned with all her customary vigour to the question of where the family would live. Houses were a particular nightmare for her, bringing into play two of the most conflicting forces in her nature: absolute dependence on living in surroundings that were both very comfortable and totally to her own taste; and an absolute distaste for the kitchen of life that went into making them so. Since she alone knew what she would tolerate, she alone could find and furnish a house. In May, she and Tom had bought a handsome, six-storey house in Chester Square in Belgravia, and builders and decorators had been at work while they had been away. It was Martha's thirteenth house. It should have been ready for them to move into in September; but it wasn't, and she returned to oversee the finish and to decorate it as the builders left, putting the two Sandys into the Goring Hotel with a nanny. Soon, she was writing, half-furiously, half-humorously, that her mind was now concerned only with chintz, chair covers and lamps and that most days she felt that she were singlehandedly putting up a pyramid, personally carrying the granite blocks one by one. When two floors had been carpeted, and the curtains hung, the ceiling fell down.

Sandy Matthews had come to live with them in England and both Sandys were at local schools, but the domestic chores that Martha had so fondly imagined would be made tolerable by the partnership with Tom were proving a nightmare, not least because Tom had little interest in curtains, very little practice in dealing with schoolboys, and because Martha was accustomed to doing everything herself. 'The interesting question,' she wrote to Berenson: 'Can one work and be happy?' From the sidelines, Sybille watched on anxiously. 'I so wish you to be at peace,' she wrote to Martha from Rome. 'Enjoying Tom, enjoying Sandy, working when you can – out of that grip of fret and rush and anxiety and being late and then bored, and outraged and bored again. *Tu es tombée dans des bien mauvaises façons spirituelles.* You will say it is in the mind. But the mind can be trained and directed . . . You have such good tools: mind, sensitiveness, discipline, your magnificent courage – perhaps the most useful quality of all.' What Martha did not have, of course, was patience; and, when bored, she could be ruthless.

It was not long before she decided that it was simply too difficult to write at Chester Square, where the bustle and the inefficiency of maids and cooks gave her, she said, dengue fever of the soul. She rented a small flat at 215 Ashley Gardens, not far away, and here, rejoicing in its whiteness and the sense of her own perfect private order, she came to write and read. For longer breaks, she went off on her own to a hotel in the country, usually the Compleat Angler at Marlow, or broke away from family holidays in France or Spain, leaving the others to come straight back to London, while she roamed and fed her need for freedom and solitude.

Taking Sandy Gellhorn out of school in February 1956 for a trip to Majorca of several months, Martha wrote to her mother of her need to flee from Tom's darkness, his tendency to 'depress' life. 'I think it is his disease,' she wrote, 'inherited, or infected into him when he was tiny and helpless . . . And since he is stronger than I am, his deathlessness prevailed over my desire to love life and laugh. I am not strong enough to cure him or to fight off a sort of miasma that comes from that secret hidden sickness . . . So I flee in little bits and all the happiness comes back, and if I can keep him away from his appalling tendency to spoil fun, then that's fine.' They had been married exactly two years.

It is impossible not to feel sorry for Matthews. When he decided to stay on in England in order to go down to Dartington, where his own Sandy was singing in an operetta, Martha was cross and said so. Sandy Matthews continued to find adjustment to England, a new stepmother and a new brother, as well as British schools with their long shorts and Latin, lonely and difficult. He was bullied and felt himself excluded from both Martha and Tom's loving attentions to Sandy Gellhorn. Personally Martha found Tom's youngest son a 'prig' though she did at some point, in spite of her most profound misgivings, agree to consult a child psychotherapist about their relationship. Sandy Matthews remembers these years as extremely unhappy: longing to be loved, he found Martha's evident indifference very painful.

During these early years of her second marriage, Martha did not write a great deal: some short stories, a few articles, but no longer works of fiction. But she was reading. John Cheever, she observed, though witty and clever and eccentric, clearly knew nothing at all about sex, because he wrote about it as if he were describing food. He reminded her of early American furniture. When Diana Cooper sent her Virginia Woolf's diary, Martha was delighted to find that Woolf had been as confused by life as she felt herself to be. 'I feel we are all minnows in life together.' In her letters to friends she sounded more at peace than she had for many years. 'I am happy,' she told Berenson. 'This is a bore to everyone else (happy people have no history) and a satisfaction to me.'

A pattern to their lives was slowly being established. They made London their base, and they travelled, in great comfort, together or apart, with or without the two Sandys and Edna. Usually they went to the sun, to swim, to look at things and in order for Martha to do what she liked best: writing in the hot sun, preferably all day long, on a terrace, naked but for a straw hat. Boothden, to the grief of the older boys, and particularly Sandy, for whom it was yet another blow, was sold. A succession of servants – twenty-three in half a dozen years – came and went, driving Martha to frenzies of exasperation, until she finally went to Spain and found two women from Pamplona, Rosario the cook and Lola the housemaid, and brought them back with her to London. She called them the Pamps and they improved life for everyone. On perfect days, Martha wrote for about three hours, read for about three, and then went out walking, to stir up her sluggish thoughts and plan what she was going to write next. The rest of the day was reserved for 'frittering'. And while in Chester Square, as a concession to Tom, they had people to dinner and to parties. These were years of good new friendships – George Kennan, the American diplomat she had met briefly in Prague before the war, James Thurber – and the only time in her life that Martha really turned her eye, and her pen, on to social life. The vignettes she dispatched to Diana Cooper, Sybille and Edna, could be sharp. After a lunch given at the Ritz for Harold Acton by George Weidenfeld, she wrote a long letter describing the occasion to Berenson. 'George,' she wrote, 'is a man who is so eaten and ravaged by something, the virus of getting ahead (where to?) that he has lost the ability to look at the person he is talking to.' Acton, she noted was courteous and kindly, and gave her a little faith in social life. Rosamond Lehmann, who came for a drink, was so boring that she was shocked into wanting to write again. 'I do not really like her. I think she would not be happy, or contented, or even busy in Paradise, with perhaps three dozen cherubs fetching and carrying.' Somerset Maugham's mouth frightened her. 'We all make our faces in the end . . . Sad and sardonic, I thought it, and also mean.' People often struck her as having mean mouths.

Berenson, confined to I Tatti by old age, a consummate social figure himself, was often the recipient of her more acerbic descriptions. On returning one afternoon from tea with Rosamond Lehmann, at which Ivy Compton-Burnett had been present she wrote: 'I was of course terrorised by this group, and therefore babbled away like Annie-get-your gun for about five minutes until I lost my voice for good. After which, aside from being shaken with wondering private mirth, I spent my time ogling a plate of macaroons as if I hoped to marry them.

'Miss Ivy CB, the recognised lion of the gathering, spoke from time to time like a prissy machine-gun; little bursts of clipped and refined words about nothing much . . . Miss CB looks like a 19th century governess who has not yet been arraigned for murder; but will be . . . She has a vague suggestion of a mouth, and small ball-bearing eyes . . . She is very scary and perhaps 70 . . . Presently there arrived, as a sort of filler, a young fairy named James Pope-Hennessy, who had the wit to keep his mouth shut, and then Christopher Sykes, who is quite fat and has a terrific mouth wiggling stammer and is nice, really nice, and given to laughter; a quality none of the ladies seemed to go in for, much . . . I must have seemed a sort of transatlantic waif, beached in Belgravia. It was superbly uneasy, for everyone as far as I could make out.' Little laughter and much unease: it was all a long way away from the shared memories and rueful confessions of Lenny Bernstein, Presnell or Walton.

When, in May 1954, Martha heard that Robert Capa had been killed by a Vietminh mine in Indo-China, she mourned him with a slow tidal wave of sorrow. She planned to record the particular importance of his friendship in the quasi-factual fiction she had made the basis of so many of her short stories.

In 1959, Martha's fiftieth year, she registered that she was happy. She felt tied to Tom, as to a Siamese twin, she told Berenson, and this both scared and elated her. When they were apart she missed him, and she had never missed a man this way before. Sandy Gellhorn, now eleven, had turned into a greedy boy, 'my little fatty', gorging on his food like a boa constrictor, and this upset her, as did his tendency to tell lies, but she felt huge relief that he appeared content. To her mother, Martha complained of the difficulty of drilling a sense of morality into him, saying, after she caught him stealing money and then lying about it, that the 'next time he lies, I will treat him with contempt'. Martha, when cross and baffled, could be very chilling.

Sandy himself remembers this period as one of growing unease. Martha had sent him away to Le Rosey, a boarding school in Switzerland, sharing a room first with Alexander Onassis and later with two older boys, who bullied him. He knew he was larger and stockier than other boys, and that Martha did not like him to be fat. During the Easter holidays of his twelfth year, she sent him to a clinic in Rome, where the doctor put him on a diet of steamed meat and green vegetables, and where a sympathetic male nurse gave him occasional ice creams. The ten pounds he lost were quickly put back on again and at Le Rosey he was made to sit for his meals at '*la table de régime*', from where he observed the other boys eating the food he craved. One night a master, finding him with salami and chocolates under his bedclothes – the dormitory had planned a midnight feast – called him a '*cochon*', a pig. When at home, he was weighed every day by Martha, and punished if he failed to lose weight. Kept permanently on a diet in the holidays, he was forced to watch Sandy Matthews devour fried potatoes and bread. It was, he says, the beginning of self-consciousness, guilt, deception and a drifting apart from Martha. When with her now, he was watchful.

Sandy Matthews, with whom she had had such terrible battles over the way he sat hunched, with rounded shoulders, idling his time truculently away, was at last happy at Dartington, and he and Martha had forged a friendship built on mutual fear for the world in an age of atomic science. Sandy remembers the day they became friends: he had written to her about a geneticist who was worried about the possibility that a day might come when people could be artificially created, and she answered him seriously, as to another adult.

When the boys were at home, it was Martha who kept the household buoyant, particularly at breakfast, when Tom sat silent; and it was Martha who, when Sandy Matthews needed a small tent, ordered and sent him one, even if it was vast, impractical and came from Harrods. As a stepmother, she bothered, but her honesty verged on the ruthless. Writing to Paul,

Tom's older son, at about this time, she explained that she had no intention of ever being anything but truthful in her dealings with her stepsons, and would make no allowances. 'I dislike pity so much that I do not dispense with even a normal amount of it; I think it is like feeding people poison.'

And she was looking good, though whenever she slipped above 138 pounds – her doctor assured her 140 would be fine – she despaired, telling Diana Cooper, her preferred confidante when it came to ailments and looks, that her face was covered in lines. 'I am 5 pounds overweight, all on my bottom; my hair is the colour of dried mustard and is cut in a manner that looks like a Lesbian school teacher; I have no clothes, and am very cheerful.'

Freed from money worries, Martha had returned to the kind of peacetime journalism she found most pleasurable, leisurely pieces for the *Atlantic Monthly* and the *New Republic*, either about England – the elections, the weather, the trial of *Lady Chatterley's Lover* or about her travels. She went twice to Poland, to see how the young fared behind the Iron Curtain, and came back praising their 'sharp minds and strong spirits' and their defiance, which reminded her of the young Israelis. While there, she visited Auschwitz in the company of a former inmate whose father had been shot by the guards, and listened to his stories of some of the men who had defied the Nazis and been killed. She was much taken by her companion, whom she calls K in the brief diary she kept of the visit. 'The attraction of K is absurd – forceful,' she wrote. 'I cannot stop thinking of him . . . Felt myself sexually attractive to men 25 – or more – years younger . . . The heightened sense of life due to K . . . One feels oneself soft, cowardly and inexperienced. I no longer know what real life is. I only know what is hard and soft.'

The articles allowed her to go on asking questions, which was exactly what she most liked to do. In 1959 a collection of her war pieces was published as *The Face of War*, to reviews that were disappointingly few in number, but those that did appear were very good. In the *New York Times*, Herbert Mitgang called it a 'brilliant anti-war book that is as fresh as if written this morning'. The *Atlantic Monthly* said that Martha was an 'intense and merciful writer'. Martha's message, pulled together in a preface written for the collection, was that war had to be tolerated, because men were stupid enough to need conflict, and because human dignity and freedom were worth fighting and even dying for; but that annihilation was not to be contemplated. The words suited the mood of a generation prepared to march from Aldermaston to London to protest against atomic weapons. Memory and imagination, she wrote, echoing Santayana, were the greatest deterrent to war.

And, after some fallow years, Martha had again been writing fiction, good short stories, not bilgers, of the kind she felt most proud of, one of which was called 'In Sickness and In Health' and won her the O'Henry Prize. It appeared in a collection of long short stories, *Two by Two*, on the theme of marriage and its bonds, which was widely reviewed, but not always well. Penelope Mortimer, in the *Sunday Times*, accused Martha's characters of advertising humanity but said that they 'didn't touch the stuff themselves'. Claud Cockburn, her old colleague from the Spanish civil war, wrote that Martha was particularly good at conveying the eerie sadness of horror and the claustrophobia of apparent blind alleys, while still managing to make clear how much she despised despair. One of the stories which she included was the one about Capa and their friendship. More obituary than fiction, though she had made up the details about Capa's wife, about whom he never spoke, it had taken her three years to get right, throwing away draft after draft.

Martha herself felt low about the book, after its lukewarm reviews. She was not in tune with current fashion, she told friends; nowadays, when she wrote, she felt alone, 'and always as if I were talking to myself'. She was feeling particularly grey when she got a letter from Janet Flanner, praising the book, and particularly the story about Capa: 'Dear Janet. My God, the relief . . . I cannot tell you how you have lifted my heart. I have a public now. You. Not writing into a void.'

In the early summer of 1959, leaving Sandy Gellhorn still at school, Tom, Martha and Edna set off on an 11,000-mile drive around America. Tom was to write a book; Martha wanted to look at schools, juvenile delinquents, beatniks and the general happiness of the country; Edna carried the 'booze bag'. They took turns at the wheel, stayed in motels, laughed a great deal. Only Martha fretted, chafing at not being free to roam, complaining about the revolting food and the repellent buildings, despairing of a land that had moved so far from the hopes of Jefferson and Lincoln. Ruefully, she wrote to a new friend called Nikki Dobrski that Tom and Edna were very alike, 'the life lovers, the life enhancers, the givers', somewhat contradicting her earlier attacks on Tom's dark soul. As for herself, she was far from sure what she was.

CHAPTER THIRTEEN

The Capital of My Soul

In the winter of 1961, when the weather in London was cold and grey, the social life full of 'gentle, kindly horror' and the writing appeared to have fizzled away into silence, Martha discovered Africa. It didn't happen immediately: there were hesitations, disasters, doubts. But when the moment came, when she was able to pause, and look, and listen, and register what she was seeing and feeling, then a sort of delight filled her, so strong that it blocked out both past and future. Whenever she was asked why she loved Africa, she would talk about the great wide sky; the sense of time to live and not live through; the weather and the emptiness. She felt drunk there, she would say, on space and silence. And then there were the animals, when she sat at night listening to the coughing of the hyenas and the sounds of hooves in the dark.

It was in Africa that Martha first put on a mask and snorkel and saw new worlds in the coral that looked to her like the terraced mountains of China. For the next thirteen years, the enchantment of Africa worked for her, particularly East Africa, not all the time but often enough to bring her back again and again and eventually to build her own house; though that too, like all the houses in Martha's life, brought its own quota of torments. Africa became the place where she reflected most, about the world, about people and about herself; and where she felt most happy for more time, but also more wretched: alone, getting older, not able to write. It marked a new chapter in her life, one she was drawn and driven to, and like all new chapters, it changed her. She had always known, and for the most part welcomed, solitude; and despised loneliness as a battle that only cowards refused to fight and only the weak lost. In Africa, every nuance and shade of being alone became familiar to her.

Martha spent Christmas 1961 in bed with flu. When she recovered, Tom took to his own bed, lying grimly like a carved crusader on his marble tomb, irritating her with his fears of pleurisy and pneumonia. Martha, so stoical about her own health, could be ruthless about that of others: if you were a little ill, you put up with it and did not complain; if very ill, you went to hospital. Edna, the ultimate non-complainer, had trained her well. Rosario and Lola fell ill next, Rosario moaning that the change of life was adding to her sufferings.

Recovering, Martha took stock. She had just sold her short story, 'Venus Ascendant', to a television company for $3,000 to turn into a play for Deborah Kerr. She felt bereft of new ideas and longing for excitement. And, above all, she longed to be alone. Towards the middle of January, she put Sandy on a plane back to Switzerland, had herself vaccinated by her alarmist doctor against typhoid, typhus, cholera, tetanus, polio, yellow fever and smallpox, and studied a thirty-year-old school atlas she found among her books. Her idea was to explore Africa, where she had never been, starting with Cameroon in French West Africa, visiting Chad, then Khartoum, from where she would follow the Nile to Entebbe before travelling slowly east towards Nairobi. She planned to be away at least two months, possibly three. She wrote to Teecher that she felt 'bone dry in brain and spirit (if not downright mean and ugly) and in need of a new world'. She had turned fifty-two in November and felt she had become middle-aged; and she hated it. Age, suddenly, was an issue, a fact, something that could not be ignored, something which, like weight, had to be watched, reckoned with, fought. After talking to old Africa travellers, she packed a hot-water bottle, woollen trousers and a heavy sweater, a large Spanish fisherman's hat, paints, cards for solitaire, binoculars, a cosmetics case full of medicines, a lot of lavatory paper, William L. Shirer's *The Rise and Fall of the Third Reich*, a copy of Karen Blixen's *Out of*

Africa, and a great many thrillers. She took her typewriter.

It is hard, now that mass tourism has reduced many of the old game reserves to little more than zoos, and civil wars have rendered large parts of the continent of Africa too dangerous for visitors, to remember how wild Africa once was, how different, how full of still unfamiliar animals. The beginning of the 1960s had seen much of the continent emerge from colonial rule, and new governments were beginning to shape their own futures. The end of something, the start of the new: transitions intrigued Martha.

24 January found her in Douala in the Cameroon, glaring morosely at the surrounding greyish jungle swamp. Her first impression of Africa was of a shabby, expensive, hideous country, not the exotic paradise she had expected. In the diary she began that day she noted: 'This is not strange and exciting.' She learnt the Hausa word for 'who cares?': 'Oho.' On the 26th, she flew to Yaoundé, then on to Gama, taking notes as she went, on schools, water supplies, the locals, the food, lepers, the crops and the smells, most of which revolted her. It was extremely humid and hot, too hot. Her skin turned grey in a sun that reminded her of a fried egg and spots broke out over her face; one of her heels developed a blister, which became infected and oozed. Wherever she went, the good hotels were always full. The ones she was reduced to had small, dark, hot, profoundly depressing rooms, where the smell of DDT made her feel sick and dead mosquitoes littered the floor. She roamed, ate foul meals, and marvelled at all the people who seemed to come to Africa for pleasure.

One day she went to a game park with a young guide. She had been told by the warden that he was extremely reliable. After a while they broke away from the French group they had been travelling with and he led her deep into the bush. They lost their way and she found herself on the edge of a herd of elephants, standing absolutely still, silently guarding two of their young. Martha knew little about wild animals, but she remembered being told that elephants when protecting their young were particularly dangerous. '*Je fuis*,' she whispered to the guide. They ran.

The days passed, and she bumped on along atrocious roads, fighting off grime and spots and depression, forcing down the stodgy food. In Mokolo, she came into contact with other travellers, who shunned her. She felt herself to be a 'bore, so insignificant, so unknown . . . Also,' she wrote in her notebook, 'loss of confidence due to being hideous. How I depended on my looks. Feel heavy, bloated, old, unappealing. Also beginning to feel cross; this filthy hotel, this sloppiness.' She could not be said to be having fun, she wrote to Adlai Stevenson, who had provided her with introductions to American foreign officials, few of whom bothered to acknowledge her, but at least she was not bored. Her spirits rose only when she left French West Africa, which reminded her all too strongly of Conrad, and found herself on a plane for Khartoum, with a spick and span English crew: 'self-respect and civilisation against all odds', she wrote. She could not understand why the whites had ever bothered to settle in Africa at all, so fundamentally unsuited did they seem to its climate or to its native people. Later, she included these first weeks in Africa among the horror journeys of her life.

Kenya, however, entranced her. Here was the Africa she had been waiting for, where flights of flamingos rose into the sky above grazing zebra and antelopes, where forests of bamboo grew behind banks of brilliantly coloured flowering creepers; where she could see wart hogs which made her laugh, and giraffe, the animals she liked best of all, pale and creamy and lightly marked, invisible against the thorn trees. Her mood lightened. It reminded her of being twenty again, arriving in Europe and walking over the snowy Pyrenees into Spain wearing only a cotton dress, full of anticipation for anything that might come her way. Kenya was exactly what she liked. Not desolate and thorny and damply sweltering, but warm and bright, the air soft, the earth green. It was even more beautiful, she wrote to Teecher, than Mexico. She rented a beaten-up old Land Rover, and hired a driver, a 'Presbyterian Kikuyu pansy', and set off on safari. Joshua turned out barely able to drive, wore pointed shoes, shiny drainpipe black trousers and red sunglasses, and she hated and loved him by turn, but they bumped along over the dirt roads, pausing for nights in lodges and remote hotels, and she felt happy, even when they got terrifyingly lost. She adored this 'light-house keeper's' existence, and though she feared that the blacks would ultimately make a 'sewer' out of Africa, she was on their side. It was a pity, she said, that she had discovered Africa so late in her career, and 'so late in its'.

On 18 March, Martha reached Mombasa. She had covered two thousand miles by road in four weeks and spent $2,450 – more than if she had been moving around the Riviera in a Rolls-Royce – but she knew she would now always return. In Nairobi, she had visited Karen Blixen's house and she suggested to Adlai Stevenson that the American government should buy it from its current owners, who wanted to sell, and turn it into the residence for the US's first ambassador to Kenya after independence. It was a magical place, and would much enhance the prestige of any American mission. (Stevenson did follow up her proposal, and the house was visited by a team of American inspectors, who declared it to be too small and too dilapidated and said that it would have to be completely destroyed and rebuilt. Martha, enraged, called the inspectors 'real estate characters' and 'imbeciles without taste' and said that it would obviously take someone far less pompous than a US ambassador to enjoy it.)

Martha returned to London in time for Sandy's Easter holidays. Sandy had left for Switzerland in January already fat: he was now very fat indeed, at fourteen weighing twenty-five pounds more than Martha. They struggled, Sandy apparently desperate to eat, Martha as desperate to prevent him. Pound by pound, he was reduced to a more seemly size. For most of the time, however, when not battling with him, or with her own feelings of disgust at his eating habits, she continued to be charmed and warmed by his affection. Before he left for school again, she felt the moment had come to impart some of the facts of life. She decided to make them brief and simple: never catch a venereal disease, never make girls pregnant, never lie about emotions or make false promises. The black and white certainties so carefully instilled by her parents remained strong.

In the late spring, Edna, now in her early eighties, arrived from St Louis. Edna and Tom had grown very fond of each other, and she and Martha had survived Martha's prickly and unhappy patch, and the three left for the Aegean where Tom had rented a large yacht. Martha, who longed to describe her African adventures, complained that no one would listen to her, and that the millionaires' life was a mug's game compared to the serenity and simplicity of Africa. But they laughed like Martha's proverbial goats, and swam in deserted bays, and hurried from port to port in order to avoid invitations from similar yachts. Martha had been struck by a line in a Doris Lessing novel – 'I don't enjoy pleasure' – and decided that what she enjoyed in life were surprises and work. 'But it's alarming,' she wrote to Teecher, 'to grow less and less gregarious. I can hardly bear social occasions; I feel as if I'd written the script long ago.'

While Tom accompanied Edna back to the States, Martha paused in a rented villa in Corfu to write. She was planning a new volume of short stories, wondering about a book on Africa – she told Adlai Stevenson that the blacks and the whites would surely loathe it equally – and had accepted, with many misgivings, to write a long piece for the *Atlantic Monthly* on the new generation of young Germans, the 'future rulers'. To friends, she sounded flippant, talking about 'a short jaunt to hell' to check whether the Germans were the 'same old honeybuns as before'. But it was clear that the whole idea made her uneasy. She had not set foot in Germany since the Nuremberg trials.

She returned after three weeks spent almost entirely with university students in different parts of the country saying that she would never go there again. The Germans, she said, were incurable. They hadn't changed; and they never would. 'At present,' she wrote to Adlai Stevenson, 'they are in the phase of being quiescent sheep and tigers; but only because they are overweight with butter and cream. Remove those and they will become insane blood-loving sheep and man-eating tigers.'

She had found the young, at their best, pathetic and feeling very isolated, 'condemned to their country'. Stevenson was now one of Martha's closest correspondents, and it was to him that she would write some of her most passionate letters about her increasing despair at the way the world was going, and her growing hatred for American foreign policy.

Stevenson had also been a close friend of Eleanor Roosevelt and when, on 8 November 1962, Martha's fifty-fourth birthday, Mrs Roosevelt died after a short illness, it was to him that Martha addressed her first anguished letter. Martha had not seen much of Mrs Roosevelt in recent years, but they had continued to write fondly to one another, even if, on Mrs Roosevelt's part, there seems to have been a slightly unhappy feeling that Martha, busy in her new life, no longer needed her. Her sudden death shocked Martha. 'This is a day when it would have mattered to be together. To weep,' Martha now wrote to Stevenson. 'I always thought she was the loneliest human being I ever knew in my life; and so used to bad treatment . . . I've wept for her often; and been shaken with anger for her too; and I never liked the President, nor trusted him as a man, because of how he treated her. And always knew she was something so rare that there's no name for it, more than a saint, a saint who took on all the experiences of everyday life, an absolutely unfrightened self-less woman whose heart never went wrong. I feel lonelier and more afraid; someone gone from one's own world who was like the certainty of a refuge; and someone gone from the world who was like a certainty of honor.' One of Martha's heroic models, constant in her life since childhood, gone.

After Christmas, with Sandy back at school, she flew to Nairobi and shut herself away in the Rift Valley in a small house in order to finish her article on 'stinking Germany'. Africa again delighted her. She was 'wildly happy', she said. 'This is my place. Home to the hunter, home from Chester Square.'

The article done and posted, there was better to come. She had made friends in Nairobi with Jack and Dora Block, who now lent her their beach house in Nyali, outside Mombasa.

It stood just a short path away from a white coral sand beach so long that she never reached its ends; and the Indian Ocean, in which she swam from early morning until long after dark, was blue and warm. So intensely pleasurable was her new underwater world, floating with a mask and snorkel above the brilliantly coloured fish and the filigreed coral, that one day she burnt her back and the backs of her legs so badly that the skin peeled away to red flesh. After that, she swam covered up. In Nyali, Martha rediscovered something that she had forgotten: how to loaf. Loafing meant lying in the sun, reading Simone de Beauvoir's *The Second Sex*. It meant not working. It meant, above all, not feeling guilty. 'It may be,' she wrote to Teecher on her ninth wedding anniversary in February, 'that I am using the natural world as an escape from the world of men, but oh what a lovely escape it is.' Tom Matthews, who did not like the sun, and needed the company of his friends, stayed in London, apparently accepting Martha's long absences without complaint.

After a while, to gather material for an article for the *Atlantic Monthly* on Tanganyika's new President, Julius Nyerere, she trekked for six days to remote villages, and then to the high-lands and back to the Rift Valley with its walls of high blue mountains and extinct volcanoes, where she slept in a mud hut, and cooked fried eggs for herself at night over a kerosene stove, listening to the hippopotamuses 'grunting about like house pets'. At the back of her mind seems to have been a running debate about the future of Africa, and just where and how the countries which had just gained independence would fit in the modern world, and how blacks and whites would work together. Her article for the *Atlantic Monthly* has a dated and insensitive ring to it, and says things that would be hard to voice today, but it has all the hallmarks of Martha's honesty. Political correctness was never of any interest to her. 'My diagnosis of the quality of Africans is that they lack the time sense,' she wrote, 'and so are spared the horror and the nuisance of looking ahead . . . Their minds certainly do not work as ours do, and facts do not limit and discipline their thinking.' She felt extremely guilty, she continued, at the revulsion she felt over the way the Africans smelt, but she had been somewhat comforted to find that their own disgust at the white smell, '*l'odeur fade des morts*', was just as strong. What she did not elaborate in her article was her contempt for almost all the whites she had encountered. Echoing Paul Scott's words about the whites in India, when he said that it was the work they did that gave them dignity, Martha would talk of her admiration for the professionals, the doctors, farmers, biologists and teachers, whose skills and dedication gave them substance. In the others, the hangers-on, the wives, those taking and exploiting and giving nothing, she could see no good; and would not bother to look for it.

And there Martha's love affair with Africa might have crystallised, kept alive but not developed further by infrequent visits in search of her lion-coloured plains, blue mountains and vast skies, her heart and spirits lifted by the giraffes and wart hogs and dashed by people both white and black, storing up fortitude during spells of solitude, had it not been for a new, and unhappy, turn in her life.

* * *

Nine years of marriage: considerably longer, already, than any other of Martha's relationships and, for the most part, companionable, even if she and Tom had always been, and remained, emotionally and temperamentally very different people. Sandy Matthews was now twenty-one, and though Martha continued to berate him for his posture, the stoop that made him look like a 'wizened, bent, somewhat ailing gent', she wrote him long and affectionate letters in serious terms on the subjects that interested him. Robust, plain speaking was the tone she continued to adopt with all four of Tom's sons, sometimes apologising afterwards for her hectoring. Gellhorns, she admitted, were noisy and quickly lost their tempers, but they forgot their rows just as quickly; Matthewses, however, were complicated and exhausting and their facetious tones maddened her. Whether solicited or not, from time to time she fired off letters of admonition and advice that seemed to reflect an increasingly stark view of life. 'From observation and experience,' she wrote one day to Paul, 'I am convinced life is really like going up a mountain slowly and then coming down slowly; but once you start going down, it is just all going down: therefore waste no minutes on the trip up, for they vanish, those minutes, and the hope of them too.' After Paul's marriage broke up in 1961, she wrote that she deplored the welter of self-pity in which he seemed to have sunk. 'I wish to shriek a warning: look out before it is too late . . . The problem is you. The threat to you is pity, coddling . . . bite on the nail . . . swallow it and digest it, and get on with your life, for Christ's sake.'

As for her own fat Sandy, there were times when she railed against his greed and laziness, others when she was seduced by his laughter. They quarrelled, he lied and was evasive, she grew impatient. During his holidays, some of their best days together were spent bicycling around the English countryside, having set off early from London by train, though Martha continued to fall off whenever she met an obstacle. Sandy, always, was her unprotected flank: second only to Edna, he touched her where she felt most raw.

The routine of her early days with Tom continued. They had acquired a neurotic poodle, Soot, and sent him to an animal psychiatrist, from whom he returned to Chester Square fixated on Rosario, terrified of Tom and believing that Sandy was another poodle.

Martha and Tom travelled a great deal – to France and Switzerland, Scandinavia and America, Tangiers, where Martha predictably took against the Arabs, and Paris, which now repelled her for its attachment to a dead, waxworks past. When the holiday was to be a family outing, Martha would often set out ahead, taking their Mini Minor across the Channel and roaming through France alone. She had taken up painting, though even she agreed with Tom that her paintings of people bore an unfortunate resemblance to failed plastic surgery. 'So happy, so happy,' she wrote to Alvah Bessie as she set out on one of these expeditions, 'the open road being my first, oldest and strongest love.'

The dream of the perfect house remained strong and one summer, charmed by the white hill villages of southern Spain, she persuaded Tom to let her buy five acres of land between Valencia and Alicante, contributing $18,000 from her own savings. The land lay in a valley planted with fig trees, up above a rocky river bed, Martha told Teecher, and the orange groves smelt 'like all the weddings in the world'. It reminded her of Mexico. But Martha's Spanish house defeated her faster than most of her domestic endeavours. A water diviner was found, and a well dug to a depth of forty metres, but no water flowed. Money trickled away with little signs of activity from the builders. Martha fumed, sitting alone in the half-finished house. After a few frenzied months, she turned her back on her half-built house and fled.

Some time towards the end of the 1950s, trying to resist her constant urge to 'rush off to fires', Martha began sifting through her memories and her notes in search of a new idea for a novel. She remembered her Roman life, and the odd assortment of characters who had flocked to postwar Italy, and she thought again about what had happened to her old friend Judy Montagu and her relationship with an American writer called Milton Gendel, correspondent in Rome for *Art Review*. Gendel worked for Olivetti, and the wife of one of the Olivettis was his mistress, Vittoria, by whom he had twins. He had been married before, and divorce was not recognised in Italy until almost twenty years later. Judy Montagu, a tall, gawky woman, neither well dressed nor elegant, but very determined, visiting Rome on one of her social sweeps, had fallen much in love with Gendel, an amusing, clever man, whose rather gruff ways were very attractive to women, and pursued him with total, frantic dedication. Eventually, after many scenes, Gendel succumbed. Soon, Vittoria Olivetti was abandoned and Judy Montagu and Gendel got married, had a daughter and moved into a magnificent flat on Rome's pretty central island where they led increasingly separate lives. In this tale of passion, betrayal and disillusion, Martha found her material. Making very little attempt to disguise her old friends and acquaintances, beyond casting the story in Paris, and calling Judy, Liz, and Milton, Ben, Martha wrote a short novel about their lives, for once relatively fast and without too much pain. *His Own Man*, she wrote to Alvah Bessie, was a 'tiny book, very beautifully made, like first class cabinet work' and lighter than a powder puff. Simon & Schuster thought it should be successful. It is in some ways her most entertaining novel, witty, acute and extremely lively; but it is neither flattering nor kind.

Martha's obtuseness seems to have been casual rather than malicious. In that way that writers find all too easy, she had forgotten about Judy Montagu and the book's origins, and come to see her novel as a book about the seriousness of marriage, in which, as she put it to Teecher, 'happiness is not necessarily its aim or product, any more than happiness is the aim or product of life'. At least, that is what she later claimed. Judy Montagu did not see it that way. After *His Own Man* appeared in America to mixed reviews, Judy Montagu protested to the British publisher, Rupert Hart-Davis, a great friend of Diana Cooper, and the book was stopped in the UK. Martha made light of the whole affair, and in a statement to her solicitors offered to change at least some of the passages she guessed Judy Montagu had taken offence to. One can see why. Liz in the book was domineering, spoilt, a steamroller over the feelings of others, with 'a large bust, a hoarse voice, and no one would have said she was beautiful'. Liz was also profoundly amoral. But Judy Montagu was not mollified, and even Diana Cooper, friend to them both, could not broker a peaceful solution. (What Vittoria Olivetti made of it all is not recorded, for she wisely kept silent; but her portrait in the book, as Jessica de Camberges, is hardly appealing either: limp and self-effacing to an absurd degree, she manipulates the vain and gullible Ben into fathering her child.) *His Own Man* was not published in Britain; and Judy Montagu did not speak to Martha again. Several mutual friends considered she had gone too far.

Something of Martha's occasional deaf ear to the sensitivities of other people was connected, at least partly, to her antipathy towards social life. Nine years of marriage to the gregarious Tom had done nothing to win her round to the company of strangers. On the contrary, she felt clearer than ever that the world was divided between real friends – to whom she was, for the most part, loyal and devoted – and everyone else, who mattered not at all. Into the category of true friends, who made her laugh and whose language of confidences she spoke and understood, came Irwin Shaw, Sybille Bedford, Diana Cooper, Lucy Moorehead, Moshe Pearlman, Leonard Bernstein and a few others. It was, unfortunately, possible to start among the true friends and be cast into darkness, but this was rare; when it happened Martha could be brutal. Social life, in the sense of dinner parties, the 'quark-quark of nattering', Martha loathed in an almost exaggerated way: it took only a few crass or ill-judged remarks to paralyse a dinner table, particularly as Martha had two ways of dealing with acute social boredom. One was to talk, loudly and relentlessly, and the other was to bolt. Sir Nicholas Henderson, a guest at Chester Square in those years – the food delicious, Rosario being an excellent cook, but the portions small, owing to Martha's self-punishing diets and her complete indifference to meals – remembers an evening at which, early on during dinner, Martha put down her knife and fork and retired to bed. Others remember long evenings of stultifying unease, Tom starchy and prone to ponderousness, Martha tetchy.

Letters from Martha to Berenson and his companion, Nicky Mariano, convey how much she must have hated Tom's easy friendliness, and how implacable was her distaste for domesticity. On the 8 October 1955, to Berenson: 'Everyone is happy. Except me. I am not happy because I feel like a very old, used, dank, grey rag.' (In the Swiss mountains, from which she had just come, she had felt like a 'cross between a Valkyrie and a gorilla.') On the 14 January 1956, to Berenson: 'Tom is far happier than I, but then he is not the hausfrau.' Eleven days later, again to Berenson: 'Ah me. I miss the places, I miss the adored, lost, loony people. I am awfully tired of servant problems and civilisation.' Transforming it all into a comic scene for Diana Cooper, she said that the servant problem was like having fingernails torn out and that she now spent a lot of her time loitering in the park, at the Turkish baths or in the London Library, in order to avoid the 'absolute, pure, nameless, indescribable, loathsome hell' of 27 Chester Square, where life was joyless. She would not solve her boredom by taking a lover, for that would be pathetic; drink ruined the 'shape and texture' of the body, and this she minded; and psychoanalysis was not only costly but a 'murderous bore'. Even Virginia Cowles, with whom she had once found life fun, she now considered tedious and obsessed with the cleverness of her own sons.

Like many fundamentally rather depressive people, Martha thrived on the energy that only contact with others provided. Social encounters gave her a lift, however brief. They also exhausted her, for fearing to bore others herself she put a great deal of effort into them, both in order to control the situation and to make them a success. A letter written to Berenson sometime in the 1950s put some of this very well: 'I don't agree with you about talk. It seems to me it is one of the greatest pleasures and vices in the world; perhaps the greatest. I have always talked more than anyone I know, alas and regrettably . . . But the real business of life is writing, and that is all done alone and needs a vast amount of aloneness to get going and one must bite on the nail of loneliness, and not escape into talk . . .'

In the spring of 1963, Martha flew to the States to visit Edna, now eighty-five and rather frail. On her way to St Louis, she stayed with the Whitneys in Long Island, enjoying the luxury and reporting to friends with a certain pleasure that, having no clothes of the kind worn by the Whitneys' smart friends, she had taken her old safari clothes. Martha, whose ferocious battle with her weight continued, knew well that she looked as good in crumpled khaki as she did in most things.

After a few days in St Louis, she took Edna away on one of their driving holidays, stopping at night in motels they liked the look of, wandering as they always did without much plan. In Alabama she was unpleasantly struck by the way so few blacks seemed to stay out in the streets, preferring to shut themselves away as the Jews did in Germany in the 1930s. She told Adlai Stevenson, now the recipient of her acerbic attacks on the United States, that she was revolted by the assumption the whites seemed to have that the blacks lusted after their women. This American apartheid was a disgrace, she said. Something had to be done.

Then, in Georgia, Edna fell ill. Her bones began to ache and whenever she tried to stand, she fainted. Martha quickly fixed for them to fly home from Atlanta, got a wheelchair for the airport and arranged with Alfred, now a distinguished doctor, to meet them and take Edna into hospital. She then sat by her mother's bed, holding her hand and playing solitaire, trying to convey the depth of her love and need as if 'it were all the warmth of all the summers'. But she was very shaken. 'My days are each a year long,' she told Stevenson. 'I've seen altogether too much death but it was all violent; and I realise that I was never before involved with my whole being.' She wrote to Diana Cooper: 'My mother is dying . . . I'm dying with her in small pieces, longing to keep her company, horrified by the loneliness and how love (real love, this) cannot reach.' Eventually Martha left to return to Europe, urged away by Alfred who wanted Edna to rest. She did not expect to see her mother again and when she said goodbye, smiling, she felt a gash of pain, because she could not – would not – imagine a world in which Edna did not exist, though she was perfectly clear that death was always preferable to slow decline.

As tenacious as her daughter, Edna recovered, but slowly.

Though Martha continued to treat her own health with impatience, there were signs that she was not as fit as she insisted. There had been the 'nervous breakdown' in Newport, diagnosed as a stomach problem in the Johns Hopkins Hospital; and, more recently, an alarming but ultimately solvable problem with a suspected hernia of the diaphragm, which had taken her to a hospital in Switzerland, a specialist in Paris and finally to a doctor she liked and trusted in Rome who cured her and assured her all was well. Martha insisted on dealing with her medical problems alone, and for the most part treated them humorously. But occasionally an apprehensive note sounded in her letters. If Adlai Stevenson was her preferred ear for the ills of government, and Sybille Bedford for all things literary, it was to Diana Cooper and Leonard Bernstein that she addressed matters of health and appearance, her own as well as Sandy's. 'I feel that a sloppy body is hand in glove with a sloppy mind,' she wrote, trying to convey the despair she felt about Sandy's weight, and confessing that she regarded obesity much as other people regarded drunkenness. Now, around the time of Edna's illness, she wrote to Diana Cooper: 'This is something I had never thought of: ill health. The shame-fulness and boredom of it, and the dreary limitations of life.' It was not old age that worried her, as she proposed to spend it with a lot of tough and mean old chums, musing on the human condition, a bottle of whisky at her elbow, but middle age, which already seemed to her uneasy and muddled. To Bernstein, one despairing day, she wrote: 'Lenny, I damn near can't bear it. I think honestly (I try to be honest as a regular thing but one simply does not know fully about this) but I have never been afraid of dying . . . But I have a feeling I am scared now; and what I am scared of is the limitations, the smallness, the nagging endurable pains that make your mind ugly in the end, the *endlessness* of it.' A little later, she apol-ogised for her 'de profundis' letter.

Some time in the spring of 1963, Martha discovered that Tom was having an affair. There had been a tacit understanding, Paul Matthews believes, that since Martha spent so much time away, Tom would be permitted discreet 'walk-outs'; and she now admitted to friends that she had endured his 'lapses' in the past. But occasional walk-outs was not what Tom wanted, and some years earlier, perhaps even as many as five, he had in fact met and become involved with the widow of General Popski, who had commanded a raiding unit, Popski's Private Army, in the Second World War. Pamela had a flat in London and, when Martha was abroad, and probably even when she was not, she and Tom had met regularly.

There are several versions of how Martha discovered – a receipt for a wine order delivered to a strange address in the pocket of a suit she was sending to the cleaners; an innocent remark of Sandy Gellhorn's; an ill-timed question of Sandy Matthews's; a not so innocent remark of Lola's or Rosario's – but the result was, predictably, fury. It was not made better, of course, by the fact that Martha had never really been in love with Tom, in the way she had once loved David Gurewitsch, that she had never crossed that odd line between affection and addiction. There were rows. Martha accused Tom of being interested only in sex and tennis. Tom offered to give Pamela up. Martha, forgetting perhaps how extremely jealous she had felt about James Gavin's night with Marlene Dietrich, spoke disgustedly to friends about this repulsive new sensation of jealousy, and said that she had no intention of enduring it. Compromise was 'witless', and she refused to see that there were ever two sides of any question to do with love or loyalty.

Martha never did anything slowly. She met Pamela; they talked politely about the news of the day and world events, and went their separate ways, Martha to a work flat she had rented in Caxton Street in Victoria, Pamela, some time later, into Chester Square. As for her feelings, Martha soon packaged them in a way she found she could bear; as so often, the fact that she minded what had happened, and that she could see that her long periods of absence had played a part in the affair, made her sound harsh. Pamela, she told friends, was an insignificant, uninteresting woman, 'a 25 watt edition of Gellhorn' and Tom was welcome to her: he had never been up to much himself, had clearly been out of his depth in her company, and was now finding his own level. He was not and had never been a 'life-enhancer'; indeed, he was a 'life-destroyer', and she was determined to live, not die; and she was through with marriage for ever. Tom, she said, suffered from too much fear, fear of life itself; he was full of regrets, and shame, and doubt and guilt; she should have heeded her first instincts. He now had his freedom. But he would have to pay for it. The battles over alimony – eventually set at

$20,000 a year, not a bad sum for those days – were unpleasant.

If to friends Martha raged, to the boys, to her mother and to Teecher she forced herself to sound calm and in control. She assured Tom's sons that they would always be welcome to come to stay with her wherever she and Sandy settled. In August, having been introduced by Diana Cooper to an anti-depressant pill called Stelladex (she said it was 'anti-melancholy, anti-suicide') she took Sandy and one of his American cousins to a house outside Oxford for the summer.

Martha's departure from Tom was so rapid that Sandy never saw Chester Square again, coming home for his holidays to find his things packed up or given away. Tom, his room, his home and London all gone; he thought of the break later as a 'knock-out punch'. And he was still fat. After nearly thirteen years of negotiations, Sandy was at last an American citizen, though it had finally taken a Bill in the Senate to make him one. He was now sixteen, and on better terms with Martha, who said that she felt she had got her 'little fat boy' back. From treating her like a 'public utility', he had taken to noting her existence again. He had, she wrote to Teecher, 'a loving heart after all'. Tom and Sandy had been fond of one another, Tom sometimes seeming to find his stepson easier than his own sons, and the break from Tom, for Sandy, was hard, particularly as it coincided with a change of school. There had long been a plan for Sandy to switch to Milton, in the States, to prepare him for an American college, but he felt his abrupt exile painfully.

It turned out to be a hot summer. The English countryside, dry and green and soft, delighted Martha. Though the Oxfordshire house, lent by friends, had a baronial hall for a sitting room, furnished in black Jacobean oak and cold as a deep freeze, the garden was full of roses, and the Pamps, like Sandy and his cousin Walter, took to English country life. Martha returned to journalism, doing a first article on English village life, fortified by the return of Sandy from the desert wastes of adolescence and by Diana Cooper's Stelladex. In much the same way that only the poor understood about poverty, she wrote to Teecher, so only the unhappy really cherished happiness.

Some years earlier, during one of their long exchanges about writing, Sybille Bedford had written to Martha: 'Only work gives shape and sanity to life. It is both a key and the anchor.' Yes, said Martha now, but courage was what she really believed in.

Towards the end of July, in answer to a note from Sandy Matthews, Martha wrote back an emphatic letter about morality and religion. It says much about her state of mind, as she left Tom and contemplated a future on her own, a 'woman alone'; and it showed how strongly she now held to the moral dicta of her childhood. She would hate to believe in immortality, she said, and found it very comforting to know that nothingness would follow the long struggle on earth of being and becoming. However, she did believe, without reservation, in personal responsibility, 'here and now, for ourselves and our acts', and that there was no escaping the attendant punishments for those who failed to learn, or learnt too little, or led complacent lives and somehow failed to pay their fares. More than ever before, Martha was coming to view the world as a place in which no one, ever, got away with anything.

* * *

Africa, Martha told Leonard Bernstein, was now the capital of her soul; she would find a house to rent, somewhere where the swimming was good, she would take the Pamps – Martha described the two Spanish women as occupying a role in her life halfway between that of maiden aunts and middle-aged daughters – to keep house for her, and Sandy would fly out for his holidays from Milton. Through friends, she heard of a place above the beach at Nyali, not far from the Blocks' house. She rented it sight unseen, remembering with delight the sand the colour and texture of fine white flour and the rings of palms. The agent wrote back to tell her that the property consisted of a white bungalow surrounded by trees on a slight rise above the sea, that it had a swimming pool, a separate guesthouse, and that it was covered in bougainvillea. The Pamps, offered Africa, were wary; Martha was excited, in the way she always was with something new, far away and different.

The three women met on the quay at Mombasa, the Pamps having come from Tilbury by ship, Martha having flown in from a visit to Edna in St Louis. The agent had sent word that the house lacked linen, crockery and kitchen things, and so they shopped in the market on their way through Mombasa. Martha felt cheerful with anticipation. Rosario asked whether they would find other people with black skins in their new home. She was astonished to be told that Africans were black. They hired a small truck to follow the car with the luggage and the many parcels and boxes. The air, wrote Martha later, was soft as feathers; the sky went up forever, water-blue and bright. She felt soaked with sun and hope.

After leaving the main road, the little convoy turned into a drive and on to what seemed to be the dry bed of a creek, rutted and strewn with boulders, up which they slowly made their way towards the house. What had clearly once been a lawn now appeared before them as a desert of sand and weeds, on which lay scattered rusty tins and parts of an abandoned bicycle. Before they reached the house they caught sight of a concrete pit, over the edges of which oozed a trickle of green water, with drowned crabs and lizards at the bottom. The house agent, waiting inside with the inventory, was brisk and not at all apologetic. The outgoing tenant could hardly control his laughter. What furniture was still in one piece had apparently come from the closing-down sale of a government office. There were indeed 'six rugs' but close inspection revealed nasty old spotted mats; the 'feather pillows' were made of horse hair and smelt of mildew; the 'curtains' were nylon and full of holes. Over everything lay a shiny, greasy fur of dirt. The Pamps said nothing.

Martha, who prided herself on her frontier spirit, got back into the car and drove to the nearest village, leaving the Pamps prodding about morosely with their new dusters. She returned with seven painters, four men with pickaxes and several Indian carpenters. Rosario told her that the stove did not work. She went back to town and bought a new one. 'Where are we?' Lola cried miserably. 'We are alone in the middle of Africa.' 'We are not alone', replied Martha briskly. 'People have lived here for years.' 'They are mad,' said Lola. When the electrician failed to turn up, Martha got back into the car and went to fetch him. The Pamps remained speechless, except when they saw an insect, when they screamed. In the evening, the three women crouched silently in their derelict new home, munching sandwiches, Martha washing down hers with a great deal of whisky. Days passed. Martha began referring to the house as Le Petit Trianon.

The day that the mosquito nets were delivered from Mombasa, where they had been ordered especially to fit the beds, was a bad one, for the nets were found to be far too short and narrow and left gaps at either end. Then there was the night that an infestation of bushbabies descended on the house, sweet to look at, three inches long and with enormous eyes, but possessed of screeching voices which they used to great effect around dawn. They were followed by monkeys, who leapt and gambolled across the corrugated iron roof with the thunder of elephants. The rains came and with them the insects spawned. Soon, the house was filled with creeping, flying, scurrying, biting creatures. Martha's body took on the aspect of 'Ypres and Verdun . . . scarred and chewed'. Bats arrived. The Pamps looked grim and reproachful. When she could, Martha escaped into the sea and her new underwater landscape. When she came home, Rosario, who had said nothing for a long time, spoke: 'The signora is mucho raro,' she said. 'Imagine being made so cheerful by fish.' Swallowing some of Diana Cooper's Stelladex, Martha retired to the guest-house.

But then the day came when the rains stopped, a cool breeze began to blow and the insects vanished. The house was now painted white throughout, scrubbed clean and furnished in Martha's bright lime greens, yellows and cherry reds. The new lawn, sown with six sacks of grass seed imported at vast expense, was sprouting fast. The weeds had been checked and where once a jungle of tendrils had choked the shrubs there now flowered marvellous tropical plants. The vervet monkeys, having mysteriously quietened down, perched on the garage roof eating the nuts from the wild almond trees or came to peer through her window to watch Martha typing. The air again felt to Martha like velvet against her skin; the sea was satin and cool.

Though never very musical, she went into Mombasa and bought three gramophone records – of Brahms, Beethoven and Chopin – and played them in the evenings on her wind-up gramophone, sitting with her whisky on the terrace, remembering the Chopin mazurka she and Hemingway had played in Madrid during the shelling. Rimsky-Korsakov, Debussy, Ravel and even Mozart, she decided, were not quite right for the African night. She wore shorts for dinner, or if she needed to go into town, but no underwear. A black mamba, found one day in the sitting room, was dispatched without too much commotion. In the evenings, even Rosario consented to drink a small Cinzano Bianco, and Lola bought herself a bathing suit. When it was very hot, and no one was around, Martha lay naked by the now clean, blue swimming pool, cooking her 'bottom and her bosom' as she wrote contentedly to Diana Cooper, describing her new life, but saying that it was probably not to anyone's taste but her own.

Martha was beginning to envisage a pattern for her life. She would spend seven months of every year in Africa, four in her flat in London, and keep the twelfth for roaming. Her mood was robust. She told friends that she did not regret her marriage to Hemingway, who had shot off his Mausers and cursed but who had taught her a lot and with whom she had written more than at any other time before or since; but that she passionately regretted her nine wasted years with Tom, and the way that she had allowed herself to be duped by his apparently loving manner and civilised exterior. She blamed it all on her own cowardice. 'I have never found what I was seeking and probably never will,' she wrote to Agi Paoloczi-Horvath, a new London friend; 'this is no reason to go into a corner and cry for the rest of one's life.'

Before coming to Africa, Martha had arranged to write a number of reports on the African game parks for the American foreign programme and, once the Nyali house had been made habitable and the Pamps could safely, if complainingly, be left, she made a first trip to Uganda to visit an elephant expert, Dr Bum, and then a second expedition to the Serengeti National Park. She decided not to risk another incompetent and maddening chauffeur like Joshua, so drove herself, covering 450 miles of rutted track alone, in a second-hand Volkswagen she had bought. In 1957 the Government of Tanganyika had appointed a Committee of Inquiry to advise on the future of the park and called on a number of eminent ecologists to give their opinion on how the Masai, who had poached tusks and killed the animals all their lives, could now be induced to co-exist with the wildlife. The *Atlantic Monthly* had agreed to take a piece on the new game conservationists, and she wrote about the park lovingly, as being country 'broken by hills, and muddy streams fringed with fever trees, and islands of thicket, palm, wild fig, wild almond, sausage trees matted together by vines and orchids'. The wildebeest along her route had been hunted, and she watched them run from the noise of the car 'in streaming friezes against the sky'. Not being a poet or a scientist, she said, she had no suitable language to describe the animals, but her plain words were better than many. 'I can only say that to see them racing over their own land is to see freedom in tangible form; and the sight is intoxicating.'

Martha was doing what she liked best: alternating solitude and the sea with trips with scientists and game wardens, who showed her a new and other Africa, and if she fell out badly with some – the 'elephant' man was described as a bore, a scientific fraud, a fool, mean, conceited and a prime shit – she was charmed by the professionalism and imagination of others. She was introduced to five young scientists writing a report on the habitat of some of the park's animals, whom the Africans called by the names of the species of their particular expertise. Martha visited Mr Zebra in the Ngorongoro Crater, and went out collecting droppings with Mr Hyena, who walked briskly ahead clapping his hands to scare away lions or snakes. 'I should report to you that at this hour, 8:10 pm on January 31', she wrote to Teecher, 'I have been consciously and ecstatically happy for two hours and ten minutes.' To Diana Cooper, she added: 'I'm not only really at home in my skin, at last, but the skin is spiffing. It's so wonderful to feel free – and this is freedom.'

In the summer of 1964, Martha was obliged to return to London to give evidence in her divorce hearing, to answer personal questions for an unhappy half hour in the witness box, for which she wore a dark grey suit and neat white blouse, and felt like a governess wrongly accused of murder. When she left the court, she threw up on the bus. Her only consolation was to insist that Pamela was a woman who would not cause trouble among sex-starved men on a desert island.

She took Sandy and his cousin back with her to Nyali, but again she clashed with Sandy over food, insisting that he lose sixteen pounds, and she was angry about his apparent indifference to the sights of Africa. The boys were tedious and selfish and Sandy had the willpower of spaghetti. She longed for the summer to end and for them to leave, and whiled away the hours of their stay playing solitaire more than 'Napoleon ever did on Elba', as she told Teecher. 'Like him, caged and beaten, I wait for the time to pass.'

Isolated from her friends, Martha was becoming increasingly alert to the news she picked up on her radio and she longed for letters. She was extremely upset when she heard from her favourite brother Alfred that his second youngest daughter, Maria, whose eighteenth birthday she had attended not long before, had been diagnosed with inoperable cancer, and was slowly dying. Martha had also reacted to news of President Kennedy's murder with a profound, almost personal grief, writing to Diana Cooper that for the first month afterwards she had seen no reason to go on living; it was another black mark against America, shameful, revolting, and it made her think of cannibalism, a nation eating its best because it could not endure excellence. She felt scarred, as she had once felt contaminated by Dachau. Indeed, she said to Leonard Bernstein that no event in her lifetime had seemed to her as abominable except for the Nazi concentration camps. Though Martha's early opinion of Kennedy had been wary – she disliked his 'pug dog face' and 'his grating voice' – her letter of condolence to Jacqueline Kennedy was fulsome. 'For a month and a day, I have been thinking of you and that uniquely fine man, your husband, and can find no words for a steady passion of grief . . . we are all poorer, and always will be.' (Alive, Kennedy had seemed to her a rather more human figure. Somewhat to her surprise, Martha had been invited to his inauguration party at the White House. Standing alone, she had been approached by one of his aides, who told her that the President had a question for her. They were left alone in a private corner. Kennedy, who had evidently been told of her frequent visits to the Roosevelts, asked her whether she knew of any secret passages or doors leading in and out of the White House, which would allow him to come and go unseen.)

Martha, at work on three long stories, was also now worrying that she was writing badly, haunted by a suspicion that younger writers, Americans like John Updike, Saul Bellow and William Styron, were writing better than she was, and that they could remember things, like smells and noises, in a way she could not. She said that she suspected they understood about evil, while she did not, and she resented how prolific they were, the writing apparently flowing like lava. Her writing, she said, was pedestrian, unadventurous, while they, who led soft little lives, brought forth tigers out of their cocoons. And she had fallen out with the editor of *National Geographic*, after she refused to travel with a photographer to research an article. She was thinking a great deal about writing, fearing a future without ideas.

The three long stories, published in 1965 as *Pretty Tales for Tired People*, show none of this. They are Martha at her most astringent, the deft social miniaturist at work. They include one of her best and cruellest stories, 'The Fall and Rise of Mrs Hapgood', about a woman who, having been betrayed by her husband, recasts her life anew, and in the process gets her revenge, crushing another man for good measure. Though, as with many of Martha's stories, the suffering is superficial, and the worldly pleasures provide a lasting balm.

Once again, there is much of Martha in Mrs Hapgood, from her early view of making love as a matter of obligation – 'she liked knowing that this too was part of her usefulness to Luke, she liked (it had to be admitted, it had to be seen at last) feeling noble' – to her ultimate sense of apartness. 'What if she had never loved Robert, but loved the man she created, a fine graven image, whom she called Robert?' The losers in these stories, as in *His Own Man*, are the men, good-looking, sensuous men with mistresses, who love their work – interestingly, few of Martha's female characters ever have real jobs – and until the final unravelling catastrophe are more than a little self-satisfied. The women, by contrast, are knowing, rueful and full of guile.

Martha was approaching sixty. Her relations with Sandy were now permanently troubled and she was tormented by a feeling that she had failed him, that he knew nothing about love because she had not loved him enough. She was also haunted by Edna's faltering health, and the fact that the people she was most fond of were growing old: Teecher, her devoted friend for over forty years, was in her eighties, and Diana Cooper, who had not long completed three volumes of autobiography, was in her seventies. Martha's group of close men friends was unravelling, with Bill Walton and Allen Grover gone to new lives in which Martha seemed to have little part, while her writing partnership with Sybille Bedford had not survived her move to London. She was also, she told Agi Paoloczi-Horvath, 'sex starved'. Kennedy's assassination had oddly unnerved her, and she was filled with a new horror of being alone in a world gone mad. And though her nerve came back, and she forced herself to write, five pages every day, and not to flee, there were now constant undercurrents of sadness and unease in her letters. She had never found the writing harder, nor the words more leaden, and it frightened her; she had not flowered into a writer, as she had hoped, but shrunk into a withered seed pod. 'As for me,' she wrote one day to Teecher, having struggled for four days over an article about the game parks, 'I am not sure what species I belong to any more. I see that my life is very queer; I see no one; I take my excitement out of the elements.' Since Hemingway's death she was again in touch with his sons, and Patrick, Mousie as she had known him in Cuba, and now a game hunter like his father, suggested that she accompany him on a buffalo hunt. She went, saying she needed a change, and was pleased to find in Patrick a 'gentle realist', a man without self-pity or illusions. Walking through the bush, she got lost and then pulled a muscle in her knee, and had to be rescued, feeling, as she told Teecher, a 'disgrace', with a body that now conked out.

In the autumn of 1964, having put Sandy and his cousin on a plane back to school, and given the Pamps a year's paid holiday in Spain, she found herself totally alone, with a new snake-bite kit in the fridge, a pistol in her drawer and an African house boy called Joseph 'whose emotions I will never know and therefore not have to consider'. There was no real need to search so frantically for journalistic commissions, for Tom's alimony had been agreed. Since she wanted to lose weight, she cooked a piece of meat only every few days and lived on that, staring out over the sea at the sky beyond, blue on blue, as she described it. She played a great deal of solitaire. In the evenings, the moon shone so brightly that her shadow lay black along the grass and her two cats grew into tigers. She determined to live only in the present, and indulge neither in memories about a happier past nor fantasies for a future she no longer believed would come her way. She accepted that she had no patience, but intended to acquire endurance year by year. She had taken to using the word 'young', meaning not rigid or backward looking, when she wanted a word of praise. 'I suppose,' she wrote to Teecher, as Christmas approached, having decided to sit out the winter and spring in Nyali, 'all goes well here; but in fact, all simply goes. I will not allow it to do otherwise.'

CHAPTER FOURTEEN

Stones on the Heart

Even before Martha's divorce was through, she had found someone else, a tall, thin American slightly younger than herself, with very different views and interests. He made her laugh. In her letters to friends, she referred to him as L.

L. was married, and already had a mistress and, from time to time, brief affairs. Martha became his 'seldom-seen, part-time cream on all this coffee', and he regarded her, she said, as a great spiritual luxury, or perhaps rather like maintaining a rare game park. He was very busy, and very rich, and he was soon managing her money for her with great success. He was extremely generous. He sent her vast bunches of flowers, mainly long-stemmed yellow or red roses, the first arriving from Harrods in a large glass slipper, and he seemed to her to be filled with the kind of selflessness that she associated with royalty. L. was not a great reader of books, nor a writer of letters, but he used long-distance telephones with abandon, and though they met no more than a few times each year, she felt looked after in ways she had not felt before, not 'accompanied', which she would have perhaps liked, but looked after. In New York, discreetly, they went dancing in the ballrooms of large hotels, sometimes at tea time.

Martha would say that the infrequency of their meetings suited her perfectly and that for the first time in her life she did not feel burdened by the sex; but to some friends she confided that, though a part of her knew by now that she was not made for 'shared daily life, only shared joy', she wanted L. more than he wanted her, and that she felt like a child with its nose pressed against the window of a bakery, longing for what lay within. 'There are only 3 happy things in life,' she said to Robert Presnell, 'one's own work, private and silent, the natural world where others haven't mucked it up, and Luv. I feel undernourished on all three.'

Martha talked with gratitude of the sense of fun L. gave her, for she felt there was very little fun in any other bit of her life. Sandy, now sixteen, was treating her coldly; she found him selfish and 'dull beyond imagining' and, though she trusted and assumed this stage would pass, she resolved to distance herself from him emotionally until it did. For his part, Sandy had become watchful and very wary of Martha, conscious of how critical she was of him, and anxious not to provoke her disapproval. And it was painful to her to watch her mother's heroic battles against age and fragility, and though she paid regular visits to St Louis, she was torn apart by guilt and fury whenever forced to spend too long in America. New York, she complained, was dirty, full of hideous people and anti-food; St Louis made her feel as if she had ptomaine poisoning, while American politics stank, as did politics as a whole, being essential, in the way that garbage collecting and sewer cleaning were essential, but no less revolting for that. To friends, her opinions, though forceful and intemperate, were leavened by the particular tone of her humour. More than ever, she used letters as ways of railing and mocking.

Worse, and growing worse all the time, was the war in Vietnam, embarked on by one President, Kennedy, for whom she had once felt some admiration, and now pursued by another, Johnson, for whom she felt only contempt. As one of the privileged of the world, she knew herself to be fortunate; but to be American in the mid-sixties was to feel nothing but shame. In long, despairing letters, saying that the barbarians were sweeping the world, she voiced these feelings of exile and alienation to Robert Presnell, Irwin Shaw, Adlai Stevenson – until his sudden death in 1965 – and George Kennan, now ambassador in Belgrade. Kennan shared her despair. 'I feel almost paralysed with the currents and counter-currents you evoke . . . because they are so contradictory and I am sure of so little,' he replied to one of Martha's cries. 'Every known ideal of the entire period of our lives has worn out and lost its reality or its power. Our own country neither wants us nor understands us.' Senator Fulbright, Chairman of the Committee for Foreign Relations in the Senate, who early in 1966 organised the first serious public debate on American intervention in the form of televised hearings before the Senate – at which James Gavin spoke for the dissenters – wrote to assure her that 'there are a number of us in the Senate who are just as sick of this insanity as you are, and it seems to be getting worse every day'. The question for Martha now was whether she should go out into the world and start fighting; or accept what she described to Leonard Bernstein as 'my diamond-studded destiny, sit on my ass . . . and write acid little tales'. Bernstein advised her to stay put. 'Just drink up,' he wrote, 'let your hair grow Nile-green, your belly Nile-wide, and your African soul free.'

It was not in Martha's nature to do nothing. With varying degrees of intensity, which, like rising decibels, grew stronger and more outraged with the passing years, she railed against America's war in Vietnam. At first, after Lyndon Johnson insisted that American troops were merely backing up the South Vietnamese army, and that a stand against communism was essential, she tried hard to make herself believe those newspaper correspondents who, against the evidence, went on shoring up the government line. But then the day came when she knew she could bear the role of 'good German' no longer. 'The Vietnam war would be better if those turds who govern us (all four of them) said simply: America Uber Alles, and were honest turds,' she wrote to Presnell. 'I cannot endure the words spoken and it amazes me that everyone is not deafened by echoes – this is the very language of the Nazis, the Soviets . . . We used to live in a fearsome world, where the choices were absolutely clear; we now live in a smeared and odious world and I can understand why the ostrich buries its head: the view is too sickening everywhere.' Vietnam had become a stone on her heart, and she was simply not prepared to go on being an 'unwilling, revolted, powerless accomplice in crime'. She began to look for ways to go to the war.

* * *

It was surprisingly difficult. Martha was now fifty-eight, and it was more than twenty years since she had last covered a conflict. While she had spent those years mainly writing fiction, a new generation of younger war correspondents had come up and many of the best of them, including David Halberstam and Neil Sheehan, were already in Vietnam, which at the peak of the war would have more than seven hundred reporters in the field. Martha approached various American newspaper editors, who, either aware of her intense hostility towards the American military presence, or with a team of people already in Saigon, politely turned her down. Eventually, in the summer of 1966, the *Manchester Guardian* agreed to take six articles, providing she paid her own expenses. She intended, she explained to them, to do what she had always done in a war: wander around and describe what the fighting was doing to ordinary people, about whom very little ever seemed to appear in the papers. 'I want to write about the Vietnamese, the civilians, whom everyone has forgotten are *people*,' she told Sandy Matthews, the one of Tom's sons to whom she had remained closest, a few days before she left for Saigon. 'I want to try, humbly, to give them faces so we know who we are destroying.'

Before leaving London, she made a new will, with bequests to Diana Cooper and L., and wrote two letters, to be opened only if she failed to return. To her eighty-seven-year-old mother, whom she had not told her plans, she said that she was going to Vietnam because she could no longer bear to live 'feeling, thinking and fearing for the future as I do, and *not* take the only action open to me'. She ended her letter: 'I love you best of anybody; I always have.' Sandy Gellhorn was now nearly eighteen, and soon, as an American citizen, liable to be called up; the irony of the situation struck her as so horrible as to be scarcely bearable. Her second letter was to him. She wanted to tell him, she said, how thankful she was that life had brought them together, and that she was going to Vietnam because she believed anything anyone could do to stop the war was a service to the young. 'I want them to live, everywhere. I want them to have time. I hope they will be more generous and more kind and more sane than the generations before them.'

By the summer of 1966 there were almost a quarter of a million American men stationed in Vietnam, serving openly alongside the South Vietnamese army. People no longer talked about a 'counter-insurgency', but a war. Under General William Westmoreland search and destroy missions involving tanks, artillery and defoliants sprayed from the air were scorching villages and crops and driving refugees to seek shelter in squalid encampments along the coast. Dykes and irrigation ditches were regularly bombed. Three hundred acres of rice, so it was said, could be destroyed in a single defoliation mission. It was becoming a very nasty war. Also, at two billion dollars a month, a very expensive one. Body counts were rising, as were the numbers of civilians burned by napalm. There was talk now, on both sides, of torture; to many Americans, the South Vietnamese were 'gooks' and 'slants'. For their part, the Vietcong were shelling villages, laying booby traps and killing civilians, demonstrating to the government in Saigon that it was unable to protect its own citizens.

To help the government of South Vietnam win the war, the young American soldiers were famously told at their induction talk, they had first to win the hearts and minds of the people. But hearts and minds were to be found in bodies, Martha remarked dryly, and bodies were what concerned her. 'The way to win hearts and minds,' she wrote, 'you must first have a heart and a mind of your own. It takes time, patience and moral courage,' none of which, she seemed to be suggesting, was much in evidence among the Americans.

Martha reached Saigon on 17 August, under a white sky and in temperatures in the middle nineties. 'How the money is wasted on destruction,' she wrote in the notebook she had already started on the plane, complaining that her arm ached appallingly from her many vaccinations. 'We might as well spend it on wells, irrigation schemes, desalinating water. But we never will. More likely the sea of flames.' On the 18th, she presented her letter from the *Guardian* to MACV – Military Assistance Command Vietnam – and to the Saigon government, and in return was made an accredited correspondent, which entitled her to free travel, C-rations and military briefings, the Americans having adopted a public relations policy of welcoming all reporters and appealing to their patriotism. To her relief, there were no barriers to women at the front, not least because this was a war with no front.

That evening she sat in a bar watching Vietnamese bar girls playing gin rummy with their customers. It was hot, like damp glue, and towards the end of the day it began to rain. Before this phase of the war, Saigon had been a pleasant city, a mixture of the East and France, left over from that long occupation, with handsome houses, a cathedral, a river and a small zoo. It was now intensely busy, its streets permanently jammed with very old Peugeots and Citroëns, fumes rising from their exhaust pipes, with pedicabs and army trucks, Japanese motorbikes and official limousines and its pavements were crowded with off-duty American soldiers towering over the Vietnamese. Martha, as always in the East, felt a sense of revulsion at the gross, fleshy Western bodies whose graceless shape she shared. 'We are *all* big and sweaty,' she noted in her diary. There were beggars and cripples sitting in doorways, and once you left the city centre, with its signs in English and the new traffic lights installed by the Americans, you found yourself in a warren of slums, linked to each other by polluted, stagnant canals. War tourists, the kind of visitor Martha most despised, were everywhere: diplomats and politicians from the States, movie stars, foreign observers, businessmen on the make. In the evenings, there were cocktail parties, at which the women wore miniskirts; while not far away, in the suburbs, the fighting went on. By day, Saigon was so noisy that it was hard to hear the bombers passing overhead; but at night they sounded, wrote Martha, 'like a steady passage of freight trains across the sky'.

Every afternoon, at five o'clock, the military held a briefing for the journalists. Because of the particularly elusive nature of the war, successes were measured not in battles won but in body counts, Killed in Action and Missing in Action, KIAs and MIAs, buried in meaningless statistics, designed to minimise or conceal the steady escalation of the war. Long before Martha got to Vietnam, the correspondents knew that civilians were being killed by both sides in great number and with great brutality, but most accepted these casualties as a natural part of the war, and preferred to stick to covering missions and tactical operations, leaving speculation on the morality of the war itself to others. It was, they would say, a new and slippery kind of war, which did not bear too much examining. What was at issue was not whether the US had been right to intervene – most accepted the argument about the bulwark against communism – but the effectiveness of American tactics. The more reflective among them, entangled in what the journalist and future novelist Ward Just called the 'ethical gymnastics' of the war, fell back on irony, and tried to report what they saw as faithfully as possible. Most of them sympathised with American goals even while doubting the wisdom of the way the war was being conducted. In any case, there was very little appetite back home for more emotive coverage. Television, already present in some ten million American homes, showed footage of combat missions, helicopters and the wounded coming home, but not of orphanages, napalm burns or accidental hits on villages full of civilians. When Harrison Salisbury reported in the *New York Times* that US planes were dropping explosives on civilian targets he was much reviled in Washington.

For Martha, it was all much clearer. It was the Spanish civil war all over again, only this time she felt herself to be, for the first time in her life, on the wrong side. America was revealing a streak of 'natural fascism', and she had become the 'good' German. It was her duty to bear witness, and good witnesses, in her book, wrote about the effects of war on civilians, as she had in Spain. In her notebook, scrawled along the bottom of one page, are the words from John 8:32: 'And ye shall know the truth, and the truth shall make you free.' Not that those who told the truth seemed to achieve very much. 'Walter Lippman is an aged unfrightened angel with a sword but no one listens to him,' she told a new friend, George Paoloczi-Horvath. 'I wish I understood Rusk; he's the indecipherable devil. Johnson, clearly, is just a megalomaniac Texan, with no understanding of the world outside Texas.' Paoloczi-Horvath, a Hungarian who had spent many years as a political prisoner and had recently written a book, *The Undefeated*, about his experiences which Martha much admired, had become one of the friends to whom she complained about the evils of the world.

To get her bearings, and because he wanted to talk to her about the Spanish civil war, Martha lunched with Ward Just, who was in Vietnam for *Newsweek*. Martha was 'gorgeous, clear-eyed with the facts straight as rulers', Just wrote later in his book about Vietnam, *To What End*. She talked with 'high good humour' and 'shirty nonchalance' – the way she often talked about the past – about the bombs that had rained so many years before on her and Hemingway in Madrid. Just was struck by how little of the prima donna there was about her – in contrast to other visiting writers such as John Steinbeck and Mary McCarthy – and how obviously she loved being back among soldiers and other war correspondents. When he argued that it was his job to write about tactics and weapons, Martha observed that while no one would ever remember a given engagement in the highlands, the casualties would stick long in the public mind. At the time, he wondered whether she wasn't a bit unbalanced on the subject of Vietnam. The reporters were then, he says, 'very big on balance'.

Martha was not interested in military tactics, logistics, hardware or bombing missions; she attended no briefings, ate no C-rations, and flew on no helicopter sorties. In fact, she travelled very little. Since there was no front, she did not go looking for one. For the next three weeks she visited hospitals, and talked to people who had lost legs, arms and their sight to US bombs, mortars and shells and to Vietcong mines. She wandered around refugee camps; she talked to nuns running orphanages, to doctors, to soldiers, to children with tuberculosis or burnt by napalm. In her notebook, she wrote: 'Total refugees: in camps 71,896, outside 127,682 . . . Woman has 2 wounded children, artillery mistake . . . Little boy, both arms in plaster, and chest wound (little brother killed) mortar (ours).' She made notes about diet, water pollution, American directives, government statistics, and the way that the faces of the people in the streets looked sad, tired and strained. 'How spooky,' she wrote, 'in rain swept suburbs; no street lights – no electricity.' She thought that the stars looked dim and red in colour once darkness fell. She described one small boy, his skin so burned that it 'looked like swollen raw meat' and another who 'moaned like a mourning dove'. Napalm worked, she noted, because it was jellied gasoline and the jelly stuck to the flesh while the gasoline burned. 'We always get the napalm cases in batches,' she reported a doctor telling her. And then she wrote: 'And there's white phosphorus too and it's worse because it goes on gnawing at flesh like rat's teeth, gnawing at the bone.'

One day, she was taken up in a US military plane and looked down on the jungle which seemed to her 'like a solid mass of Persian green sponges, very beautiful winding red mud rivers', but the craters made by the bombs were full of red water like blood and the carpet bombing was indeed like a carpet, one round hole after another. By the end of three weeks, she had filled five small notebooks.

For most of the time, she wandered alone, keeping well away from other reporters, few of whom knew she was there. Even if they had, her name would not have meant much to many of the younger ones, beyond the fact perhaps that she had once been married to Hemingway, and had written bravely about Spain. Clare Hollingworth, a British journalist, remembers being conscious of Martha's presence, and being struck that she tended to attract strong feelings among the older correspondents, both for and against. For her own part, she felt, she says, 'neutral, though I admired the way she looked. Other women in Vietnam looked terrible. Martha looked terrific.' It was not that Martha took more trouble with her appearance than other women reporters, but casual working clothes suited her natural style. If anything, her looks had grown better with the years, her features clearer and more pronounced. She was now very handsome.

Before leaving Vietnam, Martha told Ward Just that all his talk about covering the war from a balanced viewpoint had impressed her, and that she would like to see the other side. Would he go with her to meet some of the military? She named a certain division, the 1st Cavalry Division, saying she had known its commander in Germany, but told Just not to bother to mention her name. 'Let's make it a surprise . . . Maybe he'll give us some grub.' When, in due course, they reached the divisional headquarters, a young captain showed them to their tents. He told them that the general was expecting them to dinner, and asked their names. Martha muttered something inaudible.

Ward Just arrived to collect Martha from her tent and found her looking immensely chic, having changed out of old khaki clothes and into well-cut trousers and wearing a wonderful bright pink scarf. The mess tent was immaculate, with linen on the tables and dry martinis waiting. On seeing Martha, the general, Jack Norton, was much surprised. Norton had been James Gavin's aide-de-camp in Germany.

During dinner, Martha was coquettish. A certain amount was drunk. The young captains and majors were captivated. Suddenly a mortar was heard not far away. To a man, the soldiers leapt for their helmets. Martha laughed out loud, and then teased them about being frightened, saying that in France and Belgium no soldier would ever have behaved that way. The Americans took it well. Later, Martha said to friends that among the many disasters about the war in Vietnam was the fact that the Americans showed the wrong spirit: they were frightened, and they had every reason to be. First-rate officers, in her book, had a sort of gaiety about them, a kind of good cheer. There wasn't much of that, she said, in Saigon.

Martha flew back to London, sat down at her typewriter, and in what, for her, was a remarkably short space of time, wrote six articles for the *Guardian* which appeared in September in the newspaper, and were then printed as a special booklet.

They talked of refugees, burned children, the French nuns and their orphanages, Vietnamese peasants and teachers, US aid officials, and fear. They compared conditions in hospitals to those found in the Crimean war. The tone of the articles was quiet, calm, but with that absolutely chilly precision that was Martha's hallmark when most angry. 'We are not maniacs and monsters,' she wrote, 'but our planes range the sky all day and all night and our artillery is lavish and we have much more deadly stuff to kill with . . . This is indeed a new kind of war . . . and we had better find a new way to fight it.' She warned against what she called 'fear-syndrome propaganda', and said that it was an insult to the men in uniform and that sober accuracy would be better for everyone, both inside Vietnam and out. 'Is this an honourable way,' she asked, 'for a great nation to fight a war 10,000 miles from its safe homeland?'

In America, her old paper, the *St Louis Post-Dispatch*, picked up the less contentious of her articles – though they cut the above sentence. Ironically, it was left to the *Ladies Home Journal*, in January 1967, to print the most emotional of Martha's writing about Vietnam, under the heading 'Suffer the Little Children'. 'We love our children,' the article began, 'we are famous for loving our children.' And then she went on to describe what exactly American weapons had done to the children of Vietnam. She listed, very precisely, the different kinds of wounds caused by mortar, machine gun, bomb and napalm. She explained that the war was turning two thousand children each month into orphans. She quoted doctors explaining the way that gangrene attacked flesh that had been melted by napalm. 'We cannot give back life to the dead Vietnamese children. We cannot now fail to help wounded children as we would help our own. But more and more dead and wounded children will cry out to the conscience of the world, unless the bombing of Vietnamese hamlets is stopped.' Her conclusion was stark. 'I have witnessed modern war in nine countries,' she wrote, 'but I have never seen a war like the one in South Vietnam.' Later she was angry with herself that she had been too gentle in her reports; there had been worse, far worse, that she could have written, and she had chosen not to, out of fear that if she did not censor herself, nothing would be published.

There was a stir in England when Martha's articles appeared, for little had yet been published that was so frankly critical and disbelieving about the American presence in Vietnam. She used a press tour of seven cities and some television interviews arranged to launch the paperback of her collection of war pieces, *The Face of War*, to discuss the war and to call on journalists to cover 'every fact and facet' of the fighting and not allow themselves to be manipulated cravenly by American military interests. 'To be deeply opposed to the war in Vietnam,' she declared, in a press release that she drafted and redrafted in an attempt to tone down its anger, 'is *not* to be anti-American', a statement some in her audience, listening to her muted fury, must have found hard to believe. Meanwhile, friends wrote to praise the articles: 'They're good,' wrote Leonard Bernstein, 'and what's more, *unique*, as far as I can tell . . . You're a good girl, and a brave and imaginative one, and a loving though despairing one, and you must suffer and do more, though it afflicts you.' And in Vietnam, Ward Just did precisely what Martha had hoped he would do, and took to writing about civilian casualties. Meanwhile, the photographer Horst Faas read her articles and thought: 'For Christ sake, here we go again, we've seen this before, we know all this. Why do women always have to look for orphanages?' It was only many years later, not long before Martha's death, that Faas again read Martha's pieces and saw how right she had been to insist on the casualties.

In Britain, a young Australian reporter called John Pilger, working for the *Daily Mirror*, was called in to see his editor, Hugh Cudlipp. Cudlipp had been reading Martha's articles and now handed them to Pilger. 'Here's your story.' Pilger went twice to Vietnam and came back with articles about civilian casualties, for which he won several prizes. In Washington, Senator Ernest Gruening asked that Martha's article on the children be reprinted in the congressional record, and Senator Fulbright praised her article, adding in a letter to her: 'our frustration has become almost complete . . . I wish I had some words of comfort or encouragement for you, but, truly, I am hard put to it to think of anything'. And in New York, a young lawyer called Thomas Miller read what she had written and decided to abandon his practice and go to Vietnam, where he helped to set up a plastic surgery unit to treat injured children.

Throughout the rest of 1966 and 1967, the American military, its artillery now firing an average of one million shells every month, went on insisting that victory lay just around the next corner. But then, in January 1968, the North Vietnamese launched their Tet offensive, causing many casualties and huge military damage. Finally, Americans appeared to understand that the war was not about to be won by them. Almost overnight, it became a question of not whether the war would end, but how serious American losses would be. Suddenly, the public mood seemed to change. Opposition to the war grew louder and better organised, and with it came a growing feeling that what was happening in Vietnam was cruel and inhuman. Though it would be a long time before the full scale of corruption, pilfering, black marketeering, smuggling, prostitution and drug dealing – there came a day when one in ten American soldiers was said to be addicted to heroin – emerged, it became easier for correspondents to file critical stories. New, more openly hostile reporters, such as Gloria Emerson and Frances Fitzgerald, wrote outspoken articles, widely acclaimed by the growing anti-war movement in America. Lyndon Johnson began to talk about 'peace through negotiations'.

Martha now decided to write a book about the war. It was to be an instant paperback, researched in two months and then written in another two. Her idea, she told her new agent in New York, Cyrilly Abels, was to do it as she had done *The Trouble I've Seen* in the 1930s, as semi-fiction, 'telling about it all by telling at length about a few', picking out individuals from the many who had been hurt 'by age, by locality, by type of suffering, by class or person; interspersed with short, very flat and cool vignettes of the bastards: the profiteers, bullies, liars who abound'. But the book never happened. Martha tried, again and again, using all her contacts to get back into Vietnam, but she was never granted another visa.

Very few people, perhaps half a dozen, were refused visas for Vietnam in those years, and to this day just who blocked her is not entirely clear. Other writers, just as critical in their views, had no trouble going in and out. Barry Zorthian, chief military spokesman for the Americans in Vietnam in the late 1960s, is certain that the veto came from the Vietnamese, since the Americans 'never turned down requests: we wouldn't have wanted it thought that we were keeping people out'. Others, who say that the Vietnamese acted only under pressure from the Americans, are not so sure. President Kennedy's former Special Assistant, Arthur Schlesinger, Martha learnt later from journalist friends, had been heard to say that Martha was 'emotional' and not to be taken seriously.

In London, Pamela Egremont, whom Martha had met with Diana Cooper and who spent many years working as a volunteer in hospitals in South Vietnam largely as a result of reading Martha's articles, remembers once asking an official in the South Vietnamese Embassy why they were refusing Martha a visa. At the mention of Martha's name, says Lady Egremont, the man turned white. Martha had been to see him many times, he said. Then one day, when he was forced to tell her that her application had yet again been turned down, she picked up a pile of books and threw them at him. 'The language, madame, the language,' the official said.

The failure to get back to Saigon caused Martha much pain. She told friends that she now felt she had lived too long. 'I am in terrible shape,' she wrote to Alvah Bessie, 'sick from a sense of isolation and desuetude.' But she did not give up. In June 1972 she went to Paris to see Madame Nguyen Thi Binh, the National Liberation Front's delegate to the Vietnamese Peace Conference to ask her whether she could get her a visa for the north. She wanted to see for herself the devastation caused by the American bombing around Hanoi, and the *St Louis Post-Dispatch* had agreed to take a piece. Madame Binh, about whom Martha had earlier written an admiring profile for the *Guardian*'s women's page, was friendly and, to Martha's surprise, kissed her when they parted. But when the visa came through, it was for a male correspondent, not a woman; and the *Post-Dispatch* sent a reporter called Dudman, who, said Martha wearily, knew nothing about South-east Asia, nothing at all about war, and wrote only with his feet. 'I have lost hope,' she told Betsy Drake, the former actress, and an important new friend in her life, introduced by Robert Presnell. 'This is how Women's Lib. was born.' Betsy had recently published a novel and was working as a psychotherapist.

And so she returned to what she could do, which was to work against the war from the sidelines. She wrote to American senators, to friends in government, to the newspapers. During her lifetime Martha wrote many letters to newspapers, most of them furious and disbelieving. The dozens she wrote about the war in Vietnam, written and rewritten in many drafts, sometimes by hand, sometimes typed, and all of them scored over and with many crossings out, are among the most outraged. She sent ideas and any new bits of information to writers who were, to her mind, sound on the war, such as Anthony Lewis of the *New York Times*. She attended anti-war rallies and demonstrations and joined doctors and priests in trying to raise money to take burned Vietnamese children to the US for treatment. She scoured the photographs of the bombing and the injured refugees and the occasional harrowing picture of executions and torture with rage and nausea, and wrote to the newspapers about 'genocide from the air'. She even flew to Washington to take part in Vietnam Moratorium Day. And she continued to write bitter and furious letters to her friends, saying how wretchedly impotent and ashamed she felt to be American, to be a human being, to be alive. 'This is so evil and awful, a kind of mad pestulance,' she wrote to Sandy Matthews, after the Americans sent B-52s to bomb Qung Tri, where there was a large refugee camp. 'If we can't win, we destroy . . . I am sickened and the helplessness is so awful . . .

I want to be rioting with the students. What else is left except to riot?'

Only contact with people who felt as passionately as she did seemed to assuage her anger, and she exchanged frequent, despairing letters with Senator Fulbright and George Kennan. 'We have now parted from every sort of real control over our own policy and over world affairs,' replied Kennan to one of Martha's cries of outrage, 'and we simply slither and stumble down the precipitate slope of events. Perhaps God will be good to us and we will survive. But it will have to be God, because we have lost control.' A world dominated by an America that refused blindly to learn from history, and that was governed by stupidity and immorality: it was all Martha feared most.

Senator Eugene McCarthy – who Martha canvassed for and gave money to – failed to beat Nixon in the presidential elections, and Nixon and Kissinger went on to bomb Cambodia and Laos. Martha referred to Nixon as a 'disgusting sick crook' who would go down in history as a 'miserable lying murdering little swine'. ('Why don't those fucking professors stay at their universities?' she said to a friend about Kissinger.) But the war did finally end. And Daniel Ellsberg, who helped bring about its end after making available to journalists and senators fourteen volumes of mostly classified government documents on the war, became another one of Martha's heroes. 'You have earned the respect and gratitude of men of good will everywhere,' she wrote to him in an immensely long letter, telling him that his report was 'bitter' but necessary homework for everyone.

On 27 January 1973, a peace treaty was at last signed in Paris, not so very different from the uncertain settlement made in Geneva nineteen years before, except that over half a million people were dead, and a once green and fertile country was pitted, scorched and littered with debris. The war in Vietnam had lasted longer than any foreign conflict in American history. For Martha, it had indeed been another Spain, but one in which she felt personally complicit; and it left, she said again, a stone on her heart.

* * *

If Vietnam was the stone she couldn't shift, Israel remained Martha's 'commitment'. In the 1960s, certainly the most political decade of her life, when friends, fiction, travel, Sandy and even her mother were to some extent pushed out by a grating sense of personal responsibility for the wrong she saw about her, Martha returned again to her own private battle on behalf of the Jews in Israel, a people she saw as traduced by an indifferent and expedient world. There was a danger, she would say, that the Israelis were increasingly seen as military bullies. And just as she wanted to turn the 'non-people' of South Vietnam into individuals with hopes and fears, so she wished to show the Israelis as 'human', brave, intelligent people, who produced 'funny wine and good books, scientists, musicians and farmers of genius'.

The trouble, as was so often the case with Martha's most passionately held convictions, was that where there were heroes, there also had to be villains. Injustice demanded perpetrators. Having taken viscerally against the Arabs, she seldom let a chance pass to compare them to the Germans. Nasser, who came to power in Egypt in 1957, was the arch villain. He was, she told Bill Walton, 'a plain pustullant sore'.

Early in the 1960s, long before she thought about going to Vietnam, Martha had decided that she wanted to see for herself what the Palestinians were really like, and asked to visit the UN Relief Works Agency (UNRWA) camps in Lebanon, Gaza and Jordan. The *Atlantic Monthly* had agreed to take two articles from her. Her mood, from the start, was hostile. 'Nothing that I had read or heard prepared me for what I found,' she wrote, only this time she intended the words to be ironic. Martha had expected misery, malnutrition, despair; she found, or chose to see, happiness, good health, a people who would have been perfectly willing to adapt to the hand that history had dealt them were it not for the lies and spirit of hatred fed to them by their leaders. 'You all like Nasser?' she reported a conversation in a camp in her notebook. 'Smiles. Joy. Certainly do. He will unite us and make us strong. He is our leader. (What a bunch of poor dumb clots. And due to UNRWA – health and schooling, these will be the cream of Arab world)

. . . Arab world very stupid. I see no hope for peace. Stupidity rules supreme.' In her very long article for the *Atlantic Monthly*, published in the autumn of 1961, Martha heaped praise on the fine parental 'care and concern' of UNRWA, and warned against Nasser's Holy War against Israel and against a thousand-year Muslim Reich. 'The echo of Hitler's voice is heard again in the land,' she wrote, 'now speaking Arabic.' As for the refugees' apparent misery, it was all in their heads. They had been made 'sick in their minds' by a diet of official Arab propaganda and homemade fantasy. Then she went on to Jerusalem.

'When I stand before you here, O judges of Israel, I do not stand alone. With me are six million accusers.' Martha was not in Jerusalem for the start of the trial against Adolf Eichmann early in 1961, but she was there for its end, in a state of furious indignation that the world was less interested in the many months of evidence presented before it, than the fact that America had just put the first man into space. 'Does it by any chance bore us to hear of the agony of a people?' she demanded. 'Deadness of imagination, deadness of heart are fatal diseases.'

Whether or not Martha had read Primo Levi's account of Auschwitz by 1961, she too had spent much of her life searching for the meaning of what it was to be a man. She sat in the courtroom in Jerusalem, as she had sat in Nuremberg, listening to survivors talk about what they had seen and experienced in the death camps of Treblinka and Chelmno, hearing, behind her, 'like soft surf', the sounds of indrawn sobs of horror and grief. Watching Eichmann in the dock, she wondered how such an ordinary-looking man had been capable of such unrepentant, unlimited evil. She thought about his victims and how their corpses had been pulled from the gas chambers still crouched over the bodies of their children, trying to protect them; and she reflected that the United States had lost its own humanity when it had barred its doors to millions of doomed Jews in the 1930s.

Martha was in court the day that Eichmann testified, in a

voice with a 'cold snarl, a bark' that she thought must have sounded so frightening to those whose deaths he had ordered. She listened with contempt to his last 'Little Lie': that he had only been a minor bureaucrat in someone else's greater scheme of things. But there was no absolution for Eichmann's 'black hell', Nuremberg having established the principle of private responsibility; and Martha, in words not unlike those of Primo Levi, wrote: 'The private conscience is not only the last protection of the conquered world. It is the one guarantee of the dignity of man.'

Later, when she heard that Eichmann had been executed, and his ashes scattered over the sea, she was glad. Though she was against capital punishment, she felt this to be different, for Eichmann was a man who had forfeited his right to be a member of the human race; though she continued to brood about how someone could be both perfectly sane, and perfectly inhuman – that is to say, insane – at the same time. Somewhere in this philosophical paradox, she suspected, lay the root germ of anti-Semitism.

In 1967, still unable to get back into Vietnam, Martha returned to Israel. As in Rome in the early 1950s, she seemed adrift, without the anchor of love or close relationships, sustained chiefly by anger, sometimes exaggerated and unreasoned. She arrived as the Six Day War against Egypt, Jordan and Syria was ending. The Arab forces were broken and the Israelis were now in possession of the Golan Heights, the western bank of the Jordan river, the town of Kuneitra and a strip of Syria, having crossed the Sinai and reached the Suez canal. Martha stayed for just over a month and wrote articles for the *Guardian*, the *Nation*, *Commonweal* and American *Vogue*.

The State Department had issued an order forbidding US citizens from going into Israel, 'as if Americans were too soft', Martha wrote with happy scorn in her notebook. 'Yet they need danger more than any others.' At fifty-nine, defying authority had lost none of its pleasure. Her first morning on the streets of Tel Aviv she was charmed to see a female lieu-tenant wearing battle fatigues and ballet slippers, and she was soon noting down the odd assortment of clothes and shoes worn by an army evidently short of uniforms and admirably indifferent to regimentation. There were, she recorded in her first notebook, men in camouflage and black Oxford shoes, others with their shirt tails hanging over their trousers, while many sported moustaches, sideburns or ducktails. 'As a fighting force,' she wrote, 'it is unique; as human beings, it is a fair treat.' She particularly liked the informality between offi cers and men, the use of first names, and the total absence of salutes.

Martha had good friends in the Israeli army, including Moshe Dayan, newly appointed Minister of Defence, who was a great admirer of James Gavin. Soon, she was given a car, driver and conducting officer to take her into the Sinai to see the remains of war. They passed burned out tanks, guns, spent shells, lorries with blindfolded prisoners. 'Fiercest smell on earth: human dead,' Martha wrote in her notebook, with her usual blend of work and personal observations. 'Sorrow and disgust . . . There is no swank, no crowing. No Israelis are drunk, no looting, no raping of women . . . I know Israelis will not torture.' Scribbled at the bottom of a page are the words: 'How do I look? An ugly 48?' She went on: 'Atrocities: 7 Israeli pilots hung, 1 thrown to crowd, killed with spades, 2 pilots decapitated in Smyrna, heads shown on TV, girl tele-typist, breasts cut off etc. Made me sick.' The next day, she returned to the atrocities: '6 Arabs caught last night with hand grenades at the Wailing Wall. Got shot at once. Jews *are* too lenient – will do them no good . . . Least violent people anywhere.'

In the Sinai, she was introduced to General Sharon, who told her that farm boys made the best officers. Then she was taken to the border with Syria, to view the reinforced gun positions and watch young soldiers playing poker. The first notebook was soon full: numbers of dead and wounded, information about planes, bombs, the conditions of the roads, snatches of conversation with kibbutzim, hospital patients, girl soldiers.

For the *Guardian*, Martha had agreed to revisit the Palestinian camps of her earlier journey, and to write about the effect of the 1967 war on those refugees. Her notes make uncomfortable reading. Martha, whose sympathy for exile and alienation in all other people was real, who minded profoundly about the human condition, who felt herself to be an outsider and a stranger in her own land, remained obdurate about the Palestinians. If anything, the recent war, her own private conflict against America, the current rootlessness of her life, all combined to harden still further her unshakable distaste for the Arab world. In 1967, as in 1949 and 1961, she saw only what she wished to see. Facts, normally so clear and esteemed, shimmered and changed form. It was a frightening display of stubbornness, in someone otherwise so alive to the nuances of every situation, and again raised all the old questions about truth and how Martha perceived and reported it.

Her opinions had not changed, but the language was more extreme. Nasser, President of Egypt for the past twelve years, was still the villain. He should be shot, Martha noted in her diary, to 'avenge the black corpses of the poor slave Italians in the Sinai'. Palestine was a myth, taught at home and school to a people who, if given the chance, would prefer compensation 'for their imagined lost possessions'. The Gaza strip, 'a garden spot, 150 square miles of rolling land covered with citrus groves and green fields', shaded by the 'waving plumes of eucalyptus trees', its roads lined by flowering oleanders, was nothing other than a huge lunatic asylum. It was the nastiest place on earth and needed psychiatrists, not aid workers. The war had neither touched nor troubled the refugees, yet according to Martha those she talked to were sullen, resentful, suspicious, afraid and full of hatred. Liars as well as cowards, the Arabs were 'terrible people'. And so it went on, in notes and entries in her diary, in her articles, in letters to friends. To Presnell, who had dared to question the reasons for the war, Martha replied sharply that he had got the whole thing, like everyone else had, 'ass backwards'. Even the *Guardian*, she told him, had now turned pro-Arab, and insisted that there had been two hundred civilian refugee casualties, when she had counted less than 150. Arab officers, she told him, had a nasty way of fleeing in civilian cars, leaving their troops. 'And the peace is as decent and straight as the war; and Israel gets no credit because the world cannot endure real virtue. So Israel has to be cut down to size, and lied about. Makes me sick.' This was Martha at her worst: blinkered, not listening, self-righteous and without humour.

Continuing to say that a world not safe for Israel would be a world beneath contempt, Martha returned to Israel in the early 1970s. Moshe Dayan remained a friend, as did Moshe Pearlman, and they exchanged letters about Israel's difficulty in finding friends in a world they saw as increasingly sympathetic to the Arab people, though Martha's opinions were often more vehement than those expressed by the two Israelis. For a while, she even thought of writing a book about young Israelis, and she covered 3,500 miles in a rented Volkswagen, talking to soldiers, students and the 'wadi freaks' as she called them, hippies living rough. But though she came back with many full notebooks, the moment had somehow passed, and she could not find a tone or a shape for the book. And something about the country itself was changing for her. Its leaders had become old and 'old myself, I am beginning to get a phobia against the old'. More important, perhaps, she grew bored. 'Sick bored', she wrote, saying that Israelis were not, after all, 'funny people', with 'never a joke, never, never'. They were tough, self-reliant, but they had 'a somewhat Swiss overtone', and their manners, a combination of the worst of the French and the Germans, were arrogant and boorish. Hebrew, furthermore, was not a language spoken by civilised people, since it lent itself naturally to shouting and bullying. Furthermore, she would cover no more wars. She was through with man's inhumanity to man and intended to stick with wild animals, who did not torture and killed only for food. She was in any case profoundly at odds with the newspaper world, and with editors and publishers, everywhere. 'Who,' she asked, 'is this tall, fierce, irritable, impatient, sunburned, driven woman?'

When Martha's own humour returned, so did her need for irony and self-mockery. She believed just as passionately in the absolute right of the Israelis to occupy the land, and in the absolute villainy of the Palestinians, but she would go there no more herself. For the rest of her life, repeating that if ever the state of Israel were menaced, she would insist on dying with it, she fought the Israeli cause from afar.

* * *

'In my opinion, cities are best for frantic greedy visits – do it all, depart and convalesce,' Martha had written in one of her small black notebooks. In the mid-1960s, sickened by Vietnam and the Arab world, she decided that she wanted a home in Africa, as a base for a life that would include stays in the Caxton Street flat in London, visits to St Louis to see Edna, trips to Rome to have shoes made for her narrow feet at Ferragamo, and to consult Dr Simeons, her 'wonder doctor', and occasional holidays on a hot sandy beach, to snorkel and lie naked in the sun. Jack and Dora Block, her Nairobi friends, owned, along with the Norfolk Hotel and a successful safari business, a farm at Lake Naivasha, 64,000 acres of land, part of it on the slopes of Mt Longonot, a volcanic crater high above the Rift Valley. When Martha began to talk about finding a house in Kenya to buy, they offered her a small cottage they had along the shores of the lake, where poinsettias, hibiscus and bougainvillea grew. But Martha was looking for somewhere more remote. She wanted giraffes for neighbours, not people.

During one of the Blocks' holidays abroad, their farm manager, John Nazer, drove Martha around their land, finally taking her up Mt Longonot. It was isolated, windy, open, with vast skies and views across the Rift Valley to the blue mountains beyond, 'golden and hazy and impossibly beautiful'. Around grew tall, thick tawny-coloured grass, and 'huge velvety seamed extinct volcanoes'. By the time the Blocks returned to Nairobi, Martha was in love: it was here, on a bare patch of land, at an altitude of 7,500 feet, up a five-mile track that was nearly impassable in summer sand and winter mud, that she wanted to build a house and, more improbably, create a garden. The Blocks and the Nazers tried very hard to dissuade her; but, as others before them had discovered, when resolved, Martha was not to be deflected. On Longonot, she said, she would not feel suffocated, the way she had come to feel everywhere else. It reminded her of Mexico, out of all the places in her life the one where she had been most happy, only grander, wilder and older.

No house of Martha's ever came easily. If anything, the years had increased her need for perfection, and she embarked on this new house with all the passionate attention to detail that she had brought to Mexico, Spain and Chester Square. The fact that Nairobi, the nearest proper town, lay several hours' drive away, that everything had to be brought up by lorry, grinding up the red dirt track, and that the men she employed as workmen were maddeningly easy-going, only increased her doggedness. She specified the type of glue for the tiles, and the primer for the walls, she made lists, she gave orders, and she drove up and down the mountain, giving herself up to this new kitchen of life with grim determination. She called the house Villa Matata, the villa of troubles.

Bit by bit, with exasperating delays and difficulties, when lorries got stuck in the mud, and the bore-hole water was found to be too alkaline to drink, when the giraffes ate the new garden and the windbreaks sagged in the gales, a small, plain house went up on the mountainside. It crouched low into the ground and was soon furnished in Martha's primary colours. Grass turf was brought from the lake ten miles away to make a lawn, and a garden of tomatoes and flowering creepers planted behind a stockade of dried sisal stalks. And though the whole enterprise of building maddened her, and cost £3,048 she thought she could ill afford, she was charmed when in the evening, having lit her fire, she stood in the dark garden listening to the zebras' laughing bark and the jackals' yap, or watched the sunlight pouring through the sudden bursts of rain across the great plain below, or rose in the faint light of early dawn to see a giraffe pulling at the leaves of the nearby thorn trees.

'The silence and the solitude are as remarkable as they are magical,' she told Sandy Gellhorn, in a long letter continued over several weeks, reflecting over her own life and his, and why she had been drawn to Africa. 'It really is the most beautiful place on earth . . . and it is all mine.' Though she had to drive twenty-three miles into Naivasha twice a week to collect water and supplies; though the lawn got eaten by a flock of birds that looked like English wrens; though her garden refused to flower and turned into desert, and Josphat, her Kikuyu servant, concocted inedible stews made of tinned corned beef, she felt happy. 'I know Africa is my place,' she wrote to her Hungarian friend in London, George Paoloczi-Horvath. 'Because there is everything to learn, everything: as long as my head and my legs hold out, I'll never come to the end of it.' At last she felt 'like herself'; alone, but not lonely. And at night the enormous sky and the silence made her feel as if she were drowning, 'the last one alive in a great shining dark'. The house had no electricity, radio or telephone. 'The cook's cat had a knockdown fight with a small leopard just outside my fence,' Martha reported to Diana Cooper. 'That's the kind of news here.' Sometimes she gardened eight hours a day.

Though she was at last trying to write her remembered affection for Mexico into a novel, it was not going well. And since she had no taste for the few local white families, or, on her rare visits to Nairobi, for the gatherings in the smart Muthaiga Club, she was restless for a new assignment. She had been reading Robert Ardrey's *The Territorial Imperative* with growing interest and for a while grew excited by a project suggested by Dr Raymond Dusmann of the Conservation Foundation in Washington and funded by the Rockefeller Trust, for her to talk to the many ecologists and animal scientists working in East Africa and report on 'who is doing what and where'. Having apparently forgotten her intense loathing for the 'elephant' man, Martha was full of enthusiasm and spent $2,000 on safari equipment and provisions before setting out on what she called 'my ecologists' hunt' through the Serengeti National Park. She was passionate about the national parks, she told Dr Dusmann, 'for I believe they are the last such magical land on earth that can be saved . . . If we spoil them, through stupidity and arrogance now, our heirs and descendants will have the right to spit on our graves.'

It was, perhaps inevitably, one of Martha's more unhappy commissions, though it did not quite make an entry into her book of horror journeys. She left Mt Longonot 'eager to learn and ready to admire', with fifty-five projects to inspect. Within three weeks she was back, in a state of extreme moral indignation, saying that the scientists – young shits out for a Ph.D – did not 'give a fart for the beauty and rarity of this last place where wild animals live', and were nothing but a bunch of lazy and ambitious killers, more interested in conducting experiments on the animals '(like the experiments in Dachau and Auschwitz clinics)' than in devising ways of conserving them. These killer scientists, she wrote to Dr Dusmann in her letter of resignation and returning her grant, were stupid, arrogant, uncoordinated, ill-disciplined and addicted to rifles. The only good thing was that, having left the Serengeti 'with the status of Typhoid Mary', she had also introduced some hornets into their smug little world and others were now starting to ask questions about the usefulness of their research.

And so she returned to Longonot, to protect her tomatoes from slugs and giraffes, to try to coax a Virginia creeper to grow up her wind-blasted walls and to teach a new maid called Priscilla how to keep house. She had grown to like the Africans, and know them in the sense that she felt she could recognise what they were like, even if they remained foreign to her. She would say that they reminded her of characters in Evelyn Waugh's *Black Mischief*, with a 'sort of venal-golden-heartedness', but that sometimes they were unbearably 'stupid'. However, when Priscilla became pregnant, despite the fact that Martha had got hold of a supply of birth control pills for her, Martha arranged tests and an abortion and went with her to hospital. And afterwards, though complaining about all this squandered time, she obtained a new supply of birth control pills and carefully coached Priscilla again in their use. She said that she had at last forged a 'vague dotty amiable bond' with the people around her. At nights, after days struggling between her typewriter and the garden, pausing from time to time to paint – she was in her Impressionist phase – she made one more attempt to read Proust, then gave him up for ever, saying he bored her so profoundly that she developed cramps in her legs, and could hardly prevent herself from 'crying SHIT aloud'.

She was never in Longonot for very long, however, particularly in the late 1960s, when Edna, now nearly ninety, seemed to be failing. Martha, who had kept sane on her trips to St Louis by writing articles about poverty and the American legal system, filling many folders with outraged notes and clippings, now began spending longer visits with her mother. She dreaded and resisted these times, but felt too anxious and guilty to avoid them for long. She had sold all her American investments and moved her money to Switzerland, saying that she would do nothing to aid, abet or profit from the war economy. But she was finding that real love, as she grew older, had become more painful, and when with her mother she was now overwhelmed by feelings of pity and helplessness. Edna, though no less gallant and resolute in extreme old age, was weary. She was also very reasonably full of doubts about Martha spending too long in St Louis. She dreaded what she referred to as Martha's 'sacrificial lamb' stance, writing sadly to Hortense Flexner: 'She won't even try to find some interesting people here . . . With Martha there is such hate that it is terrible. She starts with God and hates him violently. She does not know where to place her hate so just *hates* everything and everybody.' When ill at ease and on foreign ground, unable to get away, Martha quickly merged boredom and displeasure, seldom bothering to conceal her emotions. Cornered, she seemed to possess no mechanism for behaving well. By the same token, when not trapped or obliged to confront people or situations that upset her, she had a particular ability to think about them with apparently genuine pleasure.

Martha spent the autumn of 1968 in St Louis, and she was there when her brother George, having for many months survived only on oxygen, finally died of emphysema and pneumonia. Martha suffered waves of guilt, saying that she had never done anything for him, and that one would scarcely be 'so careless of a stranger'. She had always thought that George had been the cleverest child in the family, and now mourned his wasted and unhappy life, just as she regretted that she had barely known her two older brothers since their childhood. For a moment, she feared that she might have emphysema herself, from many years of heavy smoking, and she noted that she had no intention of choking to death as George had; she intended, she said, to 'be in charge of my dying'. Her aunt, too, was very ill with cancer of the pancreas, and St Louis had taken on the grim aspect of 'an open grave'.

Sandy Gellhorn was now at Columbia University in New York, studying French literature. He saw little of Martha, taking care to conceal from her the fact that he was becoming increasingly dependent on drugs. When they did meet, usually on one of her visits through New York when Martha was on her way to St Louis, he felt himself pretending to be a different person in her presence, trying, as he put it later, to 'be what I believed she wanted me to be and feeling that I was a constant disappointment to her'.

That autumn Martha was sixty. When she told L., he flew her up to New York from St Louis to spend a few days with the Irwin Shaws and the Bernsteins, and then took her away to Tucson, where they dined and danced 'finding each other absolutely delectable', she told Sandy Gellhorn, 'returning to a ridiculous motel, all white plastic inside, and love life. The old also enjoy themselves like mad, only have to be extremely careful about it. I laughed myself silly over the whole thing.' Though still concerned about his weight, and the way that Sandy seemed so unwilling to spend any time with her, Martha did what she always did when not confronted by reality: she remembered their happy times and her affection for him. He became the recipient of many of Martha's more intimate letters.

Martha's affair with L., having survived an anxious time when she sensed that he was moving away from her, was happy; but there was not enough of it. Particularly when in St Louis, she complained of feeling 'visibly and constantly shrivelling into something more like a piece of board than a woman', as she told Presnell. L. whetted the appetite but did not satisfy it, and though she neither blamed him nor complained to him, for he had promised her nothing more, she would have liked not so much the cream on the coffee, but the coffee itself. '(Oh, these new and daring images).' What she really wanted, she told Betsy Drake, was a 'delightful funny pleasure loving male playmate, someone to laugh with and make love with'. If by now, at sixty, she believed that she was unlikely to find one, she was also reflective about relationships in a way she had never been before. She had come to believe that people who married again and again, and moved from person to person, were perhaps incapable of real love, which was why they kept on looking. Inside themselves they had no model for feeling or behaviour. 'I am sure, for instance, that this was true of me, until L. L. happened too late, in practice, for my life: too late to make over the shape of my life, I guess I mean. But not too late to save me from dying in ignorance. I know now more than I ever did before: and it is very simple – an unquestioning and total delight from the sound of a voice, the look of a face, the peace of a body: and the longing to make the other happy. Who learns that young is lucky: I begin to feel that love, like art, is a talent which has to be trained – yet one cannot organise to train oneself.'

Around this time, Bertrand, with whom she had continued to exchange occasional letters, came to spend a few nights with her in London during one of her pauses between Africa and St Louis. He told her that he still found her very beautiful. She was touched, despite her intense irritation at the way he appeared incapable of doing anything for himself. Recently she had been dreaming about men, not erotically, but about the company of men, and she reflected that she was mourning in her dreams the lost world of her male friendships. Then, briefly, she had an admirer, a former ambassador who was brought for a drink by a mutual friend, and about whom she became 'foolishly excited'. The ambassador, having delighted her by making her laugh, told her that he would ring her. He didn't. She sent him a postcard. Still, she heard nothing. 'I have invented a new maxim,' she wrote to Betsy. 'Do not count on adultery until it is hatched . . . I am not lonely. I am alone.'

Martha was back in St Louis in the autumn of 1969, renting a flat on the floor below Edna's, spending part of every day with her mother, reading to her, taking her for drives and cooking when the cook went out. The rest of the time she lay disconsolately on her bed, trying to think up short stories and reading thrillers, fighting the fear of her mother's death and her own encircling depression by making occasional forays with her old school friend Mary Taussig to a local dance hall, where an eighteen-year-old taught them discotheque numbers called funky broadway, tighten up, pearl, boogaloo, shingaling and stomp. Martha told Diana Cooper that in St Louis, as in all provincial America, the animals came two by two: 'the sexless life is bad enough; but the totally manless life is straight hell'.

That autumn Martha was by turn ferociously bored and anguished, finding, as she had so many years earlier in Rome, that her mother's fretfulness and confusion irritated her profoundly. 'Oh God,' she wrote, 'this is surely a much better version of hell than Sartre's *Huit clos*. I am afraid to think about myself: what these six years of coming to St Louis have done to me.' Edna's many friends and acquaintances dropped in and Martha sat watching their 'round shapeless pudgy non faces' with loathing, observing that these 'nice' people were made of 'Wilton carpeting, cold cream, ice cream, cotton wool, everything bland and soft'. Trying to rein in her agitated thoughts about the presidential elections that autumn, Nixon versus Johnson, one the 'plague', the other 'typhus', Martha felt weighed down with dread. Before she left, believing again that it was for the last time, Edna told her: 'You're a wonderful daughter. You've always made me happy.' Martha told Teecher that in the months that followed she clung to the words. What she minded now, more than her mother's death, was her slow and painful journey towards it.

But Edna struggled on. And it was not until Martha returned the following autumn that she knew her mother was finally about to die. Edna was now silent, apparently all but unable to speak, and she lay still. Her sight had gone, and she had stopped eating, 'her last possible act of self-will being to close her teeth', Martha wrote to Sandy Gellhorn. She sat by her mother's bed, watching the waxy skeleton that was now her dying form. Occasionally, Edna made a sound like a faint moan; and then tears would run down her face from her closed eyes. 'I can hardly imagine that I'll ever laugh again and am haunted by her face.' She loved Edna better than she loved anyone, 'even you, old boy; and always have since my earliest childhood, never loved anyone that much, that long, that well'. Martha's tactlessness could be brutal.

On 22 September, Martha knew that she could bear it no longer. Silently, she said goodbye to her mother, knowing that once she left, Edna would quickly let go and die. Telling the assembled family that she would be back, she fled to New York. She was at the Bernstein's flat when she heard, two days later, that her mother was dead.

Martha went to bed and spent a week sleeping, trying to protect herself from a grief that she had spent her whole adult life dreading. She did not return to St Louis for the funeral. As at other moments of real pain in her life, she said very little to anyone, as if she had no words adequate for what she was now feeling, and very little desire to search for them. Her letters to her close friends were brief. 'The fact that she does not exist affects me as if I were a compass which had lost true north,' she wrote to Jack Block's sister Ruth Rabb. 'No sense of direction left; no point; I don't seem to know why I am here or what for.' Edna, she told Betsy, was the only person who had ever possessed her; the love she had known with her mother had indeed been her only constant. Later, she told Alfred that she could not escape in her thoughts the horror of Edna's slow death. 'I have never stopped blaming myself,' she told him, 'for lacking the courage to give her the bye bye pills so she could go away.'

Martha's health, normally so robust, had recently become uncertain, with bouts of what she feared was mountain sickness up Longonot in Kenya, but which turned out to be an allergy to iron in vitamins. This was followed by malaria, then prolonged bleeding which she almost hoped might turn out to be fatal but proved not to be serious. Then came a fall, while cycling alone around the tulip fields in Holland, followed by acute anaemia, and a sore patch on her left nostril which would not heal and which a biopsy revealed to be cancerous, a solar keratosis, though treatable with a course of radio-therapy. It made her look, she told Diana Cooper, like an aging gorgonzola, and she wore something like beige glue to cover it. And then, in the autumn of 1973, after some years of nagging gynaecological problems, Martha accepted that she would have to have a hysterectomy. The operation went well, but in the following days an abscess developed in the wound, she ran a high temperature and for a while it seemed that she might not recover. But she did, despite considerable pain, spending twenty-four days in hospital, and the convalescence left her weak and unaccustomedly uncertain, though Shirlee Matthews, Sandy's wife, nursed her lovingly and the Pamps sent in bowls of creamed carrot soup. 'Now I'm a frail, bowed, little old lady, aged 102,' she wrote to Alfred.

Though making light of it to friends Martha remained extremely conscious of her appearance. Adopting her familiar tactic of self-caricature, she said that her hair stuck up in spikes like the fur of a sick cat, and that her face was 'incurably raddled'. To counter the spreading 'lard', she put herself through ferocious sessions of Canadian Air Force exercises, determined to get her weight down to the new desired 125 pounds – her weight at twenty – and keep it there. She remarked crossly that Lauren Bacall had huge hips, but that they didn't show. 'Maybe I care so much about looks because my own are gone and I lived on them, well and truly and with easy confidence,' she wrote to Sandy Matthews. 'I will never adjust to this face I see when brushing my teeth. It cannot be mine. I don't feel like that face at all.' Martha was now revolted by visible signs of physical decay: they made her feel dirty, unclean. She hated the no-man's-land of the middle years, little better than a 'cheesy sort of Dark Ages', and even a face-lift, done by a comforting woman surgeon in Harley Street, made her feel only momentarily better. In Africa, she at least sometimes lost the sense of getting old. 'I have no age,' she wrote to Sandy, 'neither old nor young; and I wonder if I have any sex . . . I feel like a man alone; with the shameless addition: a strong man alone.' Her one comfort was that in Africa at least she felt healthy, skin pleasantly sunburned, weight right, muscles in good shape. It felt good, a release from what she now saw as the prison of age, the life sentence of growing old.

Writing fiction, however, remained almost impossibly hard, and though she sat for long hours at her typewriter on Mt Longonot, she tore up nearly everything she started. *The Lowest Trees Have Tops*, a novel based in Mexico, and once again closely modelled on her own life, was something she had begun some years earlier, and she finished it now in a state of almost manic distraction from the war in Vietnam. She began another about a man going mad from solitude and pointlessness, and wrote to ask George Paoloczi-Horvath whether he thought it possible for a man to live as she now lived, middle-aged, isolated and without sex? It also occurred to her that 'I have a hopeless nature (Scorpio) and that nothing works or ever has; and there is no solution for this because I carry the germs of furious frustration inside me . . . What a BORE it is to be, inside, a permanent fierce hungry demanding angry hurt greedy hopeful twenty five; and outside to look (as I do) like a distinguished withered apple.' She had the time, the peace, the freedom, the money she had longed for all her life, and perhaps at last some understanding of people – but now she could not write. She had become superannuated, out of step with the world, and her juice had run out. What was more, she had no publisher, having left Simon & Schuster after her editor, Henry Simon, retired, and the firm became 'the General Motors' of the book world.

And Martha was, in a way she had never been before, lonely, so deeply lonely that it felt like a deformity, a hump on her back for which there was no cure. 'It isn't death I fear,' she wrote to Presnell, 'it's joylessness, not living while alive. That's *much* worse.' Having forgotten her experiment with Leonard

Bernstein in Cuernavaca, she spent her sixty-first birthday alone smoking some pot, feeling sick and very dizzy.

Bernstein wrote her comforting and bracing letters, trying to list possible causes for her unhappiness and suggesting that it might all come down to the depression of a manic-depressive in a depressed state. The thought that she might be depressed was not new to Martha, though she tended to attribute it to the realisation that she had become old. She called it 'clinical melancholia'. 'Despair is just a place to me, by now, like Des Moines, where one often is,' she wrote to Betsy, for some time now the friend to whom she addressed her most troubled letters, 'a ghastly place, to hate but not fear, maybe.' And, a little later: 'Betsy, what am I going to do with some 25 to 30 more years? I am terrified of the bleak stretch of time, a cold tundra of time.' Betsy herself was very low, and Martha's words to her were firm: 'Ground rules: no one has a right to commit suicide before aged 65 unless suffering a terminal illness, to avoid torture, or because hopelessly maimed in an accident or war. After 65, one has surely done one's bit, paid one's entry fees, and is free to depart.' But, she added, Betsy should not worry about her: 'I haven't the pills in mind.' Even to Betsy, Martha packaged her bleaker thoughts in humour and throwaway disclaimers.

It is in her notebooks that a different voice is found, one of lonely doubt. 'How I wish I knew if everyone (or most people) suffered this same lurching sensation,' she wrote, sometime in 1971. 'I do not feel like that unhesitatingly confidant, tirelessly energetic, curious, fierce, careless creature who was me, young . . . Oh, I am lost, lost, in the maze of my untrained mind . . . Though I never imagined for a minute that I was an intellectual, it is embarrassing to see how little my brain counts: it seems to do nothing much except collect, file, select, check and if the emotions become confused, the writing tails off. That would explain so much unfinished work; I stopped feeling for the people – for or against – and the dried emotion left me maimed . . . My emotions are painfully simple, I now realise, just degrees of love and hate . . . Charged, appointed or elected by no one, I feel generally and totally responsible

but am helpless . . . and this helplessness is suffocating me
. . . All I believe is that life would be worse if no one described
it – the words may not enlighten and save, but silence would
be abominable.'

Where Betsy and Martha disagreed most profoundly was
over analysis and therapy, Martha voicing a predictable aversion to what she considered, along with writing autobiography,
a self-indulgent and agonisingly boring pastime. 'I don't believe
we are out of touch with ourselves,' she wrote to Betsy. 'I
think we are far too concerned with our own navels . . . You
are what you do; you learn by listening, *hearing*, feeling for
others, putting yourself in the place and lives of others. I'll get
the hang of me, for working purposes, as I move along; besides
I change, with the times, with external events, such as passing
time and greater experience. I think we are out of touch with
others, with all others . . . I can't help being in touch with
myself, for God's sake, no matter how much I would like to
meet someone in me who is not me.' Irwin Shaw, her confidant on medical matters, advised her to stay well away from
psychiatrists: 'They are usually small, uncertain men who
weigh matters beyond their comprehension in small, crooked
scales.'

Pills, however, were different. Some years earlier, already
unable to write and having difficulty sleeping, she had
consulted a doctor who had given her a prescription for a drug
called Spansule Drinamyl – better than Diana Cooper's
Stelladex – which had made her able to work again, 'the
plumber returned to his tools'. It seemed the perfect pill, she
told Presnell, with no side effects. Happiness, she had now
decided, was simply the absence of pain.

And then there was Sandy. Martha had always been volatile
in her affections, needing constantly to reappraise and reassess.
There was little unconditional love in her repertoire of
emotions – even Edna, after all, had on occasion fallen from
grace – and no unconditional friendship. Martha's love had
to be earned. Sandy, even as a young child, had not been
exempt.

In 1967 Sandy had been drafted into the US army, having dropped out of Columbia in spite of Martha's entreaties. Her fear was that he would be sent to Vietnam, but after he had tried and failed to have his call-up deferred, she persuaded him not to dodge the draft, telling him that she was already on an American blacklist herself, and that the American military would not only make an example of him, but that his failure to join up might in some way injure Edna and the rest of the family in America. Sandy did his basic training at Fort Bliss in Texas, and Martha rented him an apartment in New York for his periods of leave. Having then agreed to a specialist technical three-year engagement, he was allowed to study to become a cameraman and, with Martha calling in favours from well-connected friends, he joined a film unit and was sent to Berlin. He began to enjoy his new life.

However, Sandy was not a letter writer, and Martha was infuriated, baffled and hurt by his long silences, just as she had been irritated by what she called his 'periods of being some sort of sea-slug sunk in sludge'. Particularly when alone for weeks on end in Kenya, Martha felt his failings keenly, and wrote to tell him so. The tone is often scolding, and she could, with him as with others, be brutal. His manners were ghastly, she told him, he was selfish, idle, and he lacked all motivation, guts, imagination and will. He sulked and was sullen, and Martha loathed sulkers. 'I have no respect for you,' she wrote, after one long silence, 'and at present little affection . . . You have absolutely no style, your mind is as interesting as blotting paper, you *do* nothing, you are unable to make anything of the days, the life, the places . . . You are a perfectly average nonentity . . . Love is like tennis you know, on a major scale: it is played by two people, not by one saint and one pig. And I've never been able to go on loving people I don't respect . . . Honey, you are neither a job nor obligation: you're a selfish, lazy, pointless young man . . .' What haunted her now was a feeling that most of Sandy's ills stemmed from her failures as a mother.

She was not always quite so fierce. 'Oh Sandy,' she wrote not long afterwards, 'I wish you'd make a sign. You know, wave a hand down here to the grave. You can't think how I live or non-live, the way I most fear and despise, waiting for time to pass . . . Oh WRITE to me, what the hell is this? Can't you conceive that I need help?'

But Sandy, too, needed help. It was in Berlin that he first came into contact with hard drugs. At weekends, it was usual for the entire film unit to take LSD. By June 1970, six months before his contract came to an end, Sandy went absent without leave, and took off first for Paris, then returned to London. Martha, frightened and appalled, took him to a psychiatrist. Again calling in favours, she managed to persuade the American military to send him for a month to a psychiatric hospital in Mannheim – which Sandy later remembered as terrifying – and then to allow him to leave the army without a dishonourable discharge.

A brief attempt to live together in London ended in rows and recriminations, and Sandy went off to Spain, where Martha had given him the house she and Tom had partially built in the early 1960s. Their relationship had never been more distant. Getting increasingly involved in drugs, Sandy kept going by selling his few possessions, and occasionally finding a few days work as a waiter. He became too ashamed and too afraid to make any further contact with Martha.

Martha herself was wretched. 'He has been the major work of my life,' she wrote one day to Betsy. 'I made every known mistake. I might add that I have paid for them heavily . . . The worst is to see that it was all useless . . . I feel that he will never get what he probably needs most from me: admiration. I cannot fake it, and he hasn't earned it.'

They met, from time to time, and Martha agonised about his long silences. 'Sandy is just grief to me,' she wrote one day. 'I remember the lovely looking and funny and happy little boy. And see this fat nervy vulgarly dressed citizen.' Torn between guilt and disgust, she made a new will, making his share dependent on his weight, saying that he was currently a 'total loss, a poor small unwanted life'. It was, she would say, a long, remorseless tale of errors, into which she had fallen, one by one. She remembered Mexico with longing and infinite regret. 'It seems to me that my whole life I have spent squirming around, wriggling, shifting, scratching, trying to find a way to be comfortable in my skin and on earth, and failing,' she wrote to her old friend Winifred Hill in Cuernavaca. 'But there, for those years, was as near as I've ever come to it. Clearly my nature is wasteful and self-destructive. I do not cling to blessings or good fortune: I move on, with equal speed, from what is right as well as from what is wrong.'

Then the day came that Sandy was sent to prison, for possession and dealing. He went to great lengths to keep it from Martha, getting his lawyer to post his occasional letters to her from town, so that she would not see the address of a jail. Later, when she discovered where he was, she did her best to help him, and went to visit him. After he was released, Sandy married, but Martha did not approve of the marriage and they now seldom met or even spoke. Seeing in her life with Sandy a terrible chapter of failure, Martha did what she could to move on.

* * *

And, in the late autumn of 1973, Martha finally began to feel better. She had mourned her mother for three years, and something of the sharpness of that grief had finally eased. And she was at last writing again, at work on a short story set in Africa that she sensed had possibilities. Now, in the mornings, she returned to her typewriter without dread. She had also started a little part-time teaching in one of the village schools. In January she rented a house on the beach at Kilifi and thought of trying to take a long lease on something more permanent by the sea. The air was like satin, she told Betsy, the sea silky, and the garden had bouquets of frangipani trees. Alan and Lucy Moorehead were staying in the Blocks' house at Malindi, not far away, with the actress Celia Fleming. Feeling robust, Martha did not allow herself to be thrown when, on two separate nights, she found intruders in her garden, one of them trying to force a door, and discovered that the servants were not, as she had assumed, sleeping in a little house at the back.

On Saturday 19 January, Martha set out at about ten o'clock to drive over to Malindi to spend the day with Celia and the Mooreheads. The road was empty, there were very few people about and she was travelling at about fifty miles an hour. Along a straight stretch a small boy suddenly appeared out of the ditch to her left and darted across, a few yards in front of the car. Martha braked hard, wrenching the wheel to the right. She heard a soft thud before the car veered off the tarmac, across the grass and dust verge and down into a deep ditch. She knocked the right side of her head, behind her ear, bounced around like a rag doll, and passed out. When she came to a few moments later she found that the car had turned over and was now facing back the way she had come. She sat quite still; everything was quiet around her, and as it had been, except that in the middle of the road lay the curled up body of the small boy. Later, she thought she remembered a mewing sound; then he was dead.

From the other side of the road the boy's two older sisters now appeared, screaming. Adults arrived, and the boy's mother, all shouting and gesticulating. Stunned, Martha went on sitting, while they crowded round. A woman suddenly leant in and wrenched her hair. When the police arrived, they took away her passport and put the child's body on to a stretcher, while the other children went on screaming loudly. The Mooreheads came to collect her from the police station, and took her to a doctor who told her that the x-rays showed no cracks to her skull and gave her Valium and sleeping pills. Ruth Rabb found a lawyer. Later, it seemed that the two girls, standing on one side of the road, had called to their younger brother to cross quickly before the car came. All Martha could think about was whether the boy had died instantly, without pain. She felt profound relief that she had not actually run over him.

The accident left her haunted, sleepless and scared. 'I am so afraid of remembering what I can never forget,' she told Betsy. She was too frightened to let herself fall asleep and read most of the night until the Seconal and the Valium dragged her into sleep. Though assured by everyone that it had not been her fault and that there was nothing she could have done, she longed to have died herself instead of the child. 'I should have been dead,' she said. 'I have always said that when you think you have gone through the worst in life, just wait, there will be worse; but I never imagined anything like this . . . What I cannot get out of my mind is this: I did everything in my power without the slightest thought of self-preservation: but there is the fact . . . the child is dead. How does one live with that.' It was a statement, not a question. Her accounts in letters to friends were factual, dry; but utterly despairing. They wrote back immediately. 'You absolutely *must*, repeat must, not give in,' wrote Leonard Bernstein. 'Write a story about it,' said Diana Cooper. 'The method is said to heal.' Instead, Martha consulted her Roman astrologer Waldner, who told her that looking back over her stars for the previous six months he could see ill health, sadness and 'misfortune with a young person'. She found the idea that it had all been predestined a little comforting. L. cabled his love.

When Martha went back to her typewriter, she found she again could not write. The story she had started was dead; it had turned to dust. She sat at her desk forcing herself simply to keep typing, anything, 'long slow hard work, the one solution in life, and the one consolation'. Much later, she wrote three long short stories about Africa. 'By the Sea' is about a middle-aged woman, Diana, mourning her son who has died from leukemia, testing the limits of her endurance by coming alone to Africa. Like Martha, Diana hits and kills but does not run over a small boy, who has been called by his sisters from the other side of the road. Diana's shocked grief at the accident is heartfelt, but the story is really about loneliness, the absence in her life of 'someone who looks at you as no one else ever can'. The story was written at one of the times she felt most alienated from Sandy.

The police kept Martha's passport for a while but decided not to prosecute. She tried to give the boy's family money. The headaches that tormented her for some time after the accident died down and the purple bruises that ran from both shoulders down to her knees faded. But something in her African life had broken, and the loneliness was now intolerable to her. Longonot had become too remote, its mountain weather too cloudy and uncertain, and the altitude was causing her to see little black spots. Africa had served its purpose and provided her with an escape when she felt she was going mad with her obsessive need to do something about Vietnam. By proving to her that she could do nothing, it had in some way made her conscious of herself again. For a while it had allowed her to do what, as she pointed out, ostriches do not do, and bury her head in the sand. Though she would continue to return to Africa for many years to swim and snorkel in the winter months she sold her house on the volcano back to the Blocks and returned to London. It was another failure, to add to all the others: the failed houses, the broken relationships, and Sandy, her 'greatest failure of all'. The end was made more unpleasant by a bitter wrangle over money, Martha feeling that she was grossly underpaid by the Blocks, who were correct but not generous in offering her about half of all she had eventually spent on the house; they never spoke again. When the Blocks, trying to make peace, invited her for lunch, she replied that she only lunched with friends.

Martha felt she had become a leper. 'I am terrified,' she wrote to Betsy, 'because now I think I am under some sort of spell of darkness and anyone who comes anywhere near me is going to have trouble or worse.' She had entered the long voyage in the valley of the shadows. How is it possible, she asked, to be so unhappy, and yet to live?

CHAPTER FIFTEEN

I Act, Therefore I Am

Martha's life would get better; but not yet. She had been right to fear her middle years, her late fifties and sixties, saying that they were neither fish nor fowl, for they brought her considerable unhappiness. Her inability to write – she called it lockjaw of the brain – that had begun at Longonot persisted well into the 1970s and she felt permanently at odds with herself, restless, berating herself for lack of discipline and talent. If she could not write, all that was left was to travel, and travel, in which she invested so much hope, was often disappointing. After Africa, Martha decided to explore new places in the sun. She became a connoisseur of the better package holidays, the best white beaches, the most exotic reefs, the 'desert island, with mod cons'. She went to the Caribbean, to the Virgin Islands, to Thailand, to the Red Sea, to France, Greece, the Canary Islands and Australia, like a Mexican jumping bean, she said to friends, as she paused to see them in New York or London between journeys. Since she could not enjoy food, because of her weight, and had no sex life, she told Diana Cooper that she sublimated everything into a love affair with places. 'I mean to keep moving,' she said, 'guaranteed cure for accidie.' She talked of putting up a sign in her bathroom, 'when things get bad, run', and spoke of snorkelling her way around the world from Hawaii to the Seychelles, first class, with all her luggage in a single zipper bag. One restless summer, she went to Turkey, Corsica, Switzerland and the Sinai desert, keeping well away from ruins or monuments, saying that nothing depressed her more than history, 'always more of the ghastly same, only different clothes and weapons'.

Some of these journeys were a success, at least for a while; in Gozo, for several summers running, she sat on a terrace looking out over the very blue sea drinking a cheap local red wine she decided she preferred to whisky, from time to time walking across the street to smooth yellow rocks and diving into the sea. 'Do you remember Miss Dietrich's most famous song?' she asked Diana Cooper. '"Men (something) / round me / like mutts around a phlegm / I cawn't helppit." I was always fond of that mutts bit. What I want now is a handsome funny mutt with whom to swim, eat, drink and etcetera; as I ardently do not wish to work.' Others started well, with all the excitement of somewhere new, only to fall apart under a grey sky, a party of noisy Germans, a bedroom window that would not open. There was too much wind, which 'scraped' her nerves; the expatriates were predatory; the sea was too cold.

Like many people for whom weather and light shape mood, Martha was easily thrown by her surroundings. She rarely sat out the storms; just as she fled boredom and loneliness, so she hurried away from disappointment. Weather was her most capricious enemy. As she grew older and more conscious of the signs of age, so she craved the sense of looking good that came with skin browned by the sun; but her skin was able to tolerate less and less direct sunlight. Longing for the sun, she spent more and more time in the shade, looking out at the bright light she had once lain in so freely. 'I know my chances of rising above gloom, let alone depression, are tightly linked to weather,' she told Betsy. 'I only feel well when I can live without clothes and in sun and warmth.'

And, increasingly, journeys were blighted by ill health. One winter, having heard good reports about the Australian coral reefs, Martha decided to go to Perth to explore its snorkelling. The trip was to give her a 'last long surfeit of pleasure'. It began in Hawaii, and she nearly drowned after snorkelling too far out and getting caught in the surf. She moved on to Fiji, where the underwater life was indeed superb, but where she was savagely bitten by a plague of sea lice. It also rained. She had barely landed in Perth when her ear began to throb. It was the same ear, and the same pain, that had caused her such misery in the 1930s. She found a doctor who gave her antibiotics and strong painkillers. The pain remained excruciating. She stayed in her hotel bedroom for two and a half weeks, dazed and stupefied by the drugs but in agony, then flew south to Esperance, planning to camp, alone on a woody island, and hire a boat in which to explore the surrounding reefs. 'Snorkel or die is the present motto, and I do not care if I do die,' she wrote to a friend. It was weeks before her ear recovered, and she never returned to Australia. Just occasionally, when illness was putting constraints on her life she found intolerable, or when she watched friends like Felicia Bernstein slowly dying of cancer in pain and fear, yet wanting always one more day of life, she wondered about suicide. Haunted by her mother's slow death, she did not blame Hemingway for not wanting to 'stay around for a long rotting finale'; he had, as she told Betsy, every reason for wanting to leave, and his suicide was very sane. 'Why stay until the evil present becomes a worse future and eats away all the value of the past?' It was, she would say, a matter of doing it all neatly and efficiently, in a manner and at a time of one's own choosing, and of facing up to that final moment of understanding that life had become unlivable. That was what she dreaded: the few moments of 'desperate suffocation, a hell of fear, before unconsciousness'.

Curiously, the one country where she categorically loathed the weather, where she felt perpetually chilled and lowered by the grey skies, was the place she now decided to make her home. Of all the cities in the world, London had come to feel the most easy. She liked its parks. Diana Cooper lived in London, as did Sybille Bedford and Lucy Moorehead. Irwin Shaw, who had a house in Klosters, and Leonard Bernstein, whose home was still New York, passed through. There were endless new movies, Martha having discovered the pleasures of the cinema, to which she went in the afternoons with Diana Cooper, who talked throughout the film. When the Russian epic *War and Peace* was showing very late one night, the two women took a thermos of bullshots and some sandwiches and met at the cinema at midnight.

And so, early in the 1970s, Martha bought a flat at 72 Cadogan Square. It had two floors, the top one being a sloping attic that might one day, she still hoped, provide an occasional home for Sandy, and which she filled with her books and papers and turned into a study. The central heating was excellent. Returning to the flat from Malta one November, she said that she would go to bed for the winter, like Oblomov, and perhaps rent a small bear from the zoo for company. Appalled by the 'sense of loneliness everywhere', she volunteered to work one evening a week in a new legal advice centre in Fulham, where she listened to accounts of homelessness and domestic quarrels and turned them into questions for lawyers to address. At four o'clock on sleepless nights, she now kept the 'dark night of the soul' at bay with Insidon, referring to it casually as 'some type of brain pill', and declaring that it transformed life from fiery blackness to a bearable charcoal grey. 'I am tossing around in life trying to find some way to be,' she told Betsy. 'As opposed to giving up.' She did not plan to give up. 'I violently want *you* to be happy because I am so unhappy,' she told Sandy Matthews. 'I mean to overcome this sadness, to cure myself of it, with the same determination one could use to get rid of T.B. I'm damned if I'll end up being sad – spreading anxiety, alarm and boredom.' Her models were Edna and Diana Cooper, now in her eighties.

It was in Cadogan Square that Martha had her one taste of committee life. It left her, and those she sat with, bruised. After she had been in her flat some months, the dozen or so tenants of the building decided they needed a common front to deal with the landlord and the problems of an aging building. Martha became an active member. But soon, she grew infuriated by the delays and inefficiency, and deeply impatient with the chatter of her fellow committee members. Martha fumed and squabbled. She quibbled about tiny amounts of money. She became, says David Albert, the lawyer who was company secretary, the scourge of every meeting, and she had no sense at all of what democracy was all about, though she did make him – and one or two others – laugh. The rest of the members, goaded and embattled, dug their toes in. Martha resigned.

And, after a winter of bright frosty days and deep snow in a rented house in Wareham, in Dorset, brought to an end by furious arguments with her landlady, a 'pious devious spinster', Martha drove 1,200 miles crossing backwards and forwards as she went from Dorset to Herefordshire and bought a two-hundred-year-old 'dolls house' six miles from Chepstow. She had decided that she needed country, to escape from the 'nervy gloom' of cities; people in London had become 'snarly like overcrowded rats'. The cottage was very small, twenty-five feet long and ten feet wide, with no guest room, which was precisely what she wanted, for she disliked having guests even more than being one herself. It cost £25,000, as if, she complained to Presnell, it were made of 'carved teak inlaid with pearls'. It was, she told friends, ideal for a dwarf with the soul of a lighthouse keeper, and though her soul was perfectly suitable, she was physically too big to dress and undress in a bedroom the size of a broom cupboard. After months of squabbling with the builders, she thought of calling it Matata Two, the second house of trouble, but settled on Catscradle, the name of the children's game played with string, which usually ends in inextricable knots and confusion.

In winter, there were days when the fog rolled up across the fields from the Bristol Channel and she could not leave the house for fear that she would never find her way home. She reported that the cottage was acquiring a patina of green mould, and she was probably turning mouldy as well. But she was surprisingly content in her new house, despite a brief altercation with the neighbours whose sheep ate her garden. She acquired two kittens, one brownish black, the other pale marmalade, called Brother and Sister. In the spring, she began planting vegetables in rows, with sweet peas in between, and an Albertine rose to climb up the side of the house. She had a window opened low by her bed, so as to be able to wake to a view of fields and the estuary below, with the cats purring like electric kettles at her feet. In the long hot summer of 1983, day after day of heat after three months of steady rain, the Albertine bloomed all over the cottage, waterfalls of honeysuckle fell from the fence, the sweet peas flowered in bushes of oxtail red, and there were bumper crops of strawberries, cucumbers, tomatoes, courgettes, spinach and sweetcorn. Martha stayed out all day, gardening in a bathing suit, and discovered a beach two hours' drive away, where she walked along the sand but complained that it was fit only for polar bears to swim from. When she saw Roald Dahl one day on television, she noted smugly that he now walked with a limp. 'He looks very old,' she said to Betsy, with some satisfaction. 'He may mellow into a nice man; success may soften him.'

In Wales, Martha was not bored. The chronic state of boredom that had afflicted her like an illness all her life when with people – too many people, the wrong people, the right people for too long – evaporated. At Catscradle she chose who to be with, and when – by letter. 'It is 8:10pm,' she wrote to the novelist and biographer Victoria Glendinning one day. 'Time to chat. The best reason for letters . . . writing a letter is too lovely, like a Mars bar.'

Though Martha strongly discouraged visitors, and if they insisted on coming put them up firmly in a bed and breakfast up the road, her fondness for Diana Cooper obliged her to extend a weekend invitation. It was October. Diana Cooper chose to come by coach from Victoria Station, bringing her Chihuahua, Doggie. The journey, which should have taken three hours, took six after gales blew a tanker and a lorry across the carriageway on the Severn Bridge. Doggie, previously a funny, dancing dog, was suffering from extreme and inexplicable depression; she had gone lame, like her mistress, and stared grimly from large, black-rimmed, sad eyes, taking no notice of Martha's two cats. The cats, on the other hand, were terrified. With Doggie in the house, they ate the furniture, peed on the carpets, knocked over the plants and scratched. After Doggie left, Martha went to the vet in Monmouth to get some Valium for the cats in order to take them up to London; with the appalling weather, she thought that she might become depressed like Doggie.

Diana Cooper, now eighty-eight, was in many ways Martha's closest companion, and Martha admired her battles with old age, and her refusal to complain, other than in self-mocking terms. 'I'm much deafer,' Lady Diana reported, 'more delapidatedly sunken faced, bigger paunched, thinner-haired, leprous-armed daily', telling an interviewer who asked about her fabled beauty that personally she had always seen herself as a 'bit of a blanc mange'. What was more, she was enduring a 'bugger of a death', as she told Martha, 'helpless and waiting'. Martha, who was completely indifferent about what others thought of her friends, was unmoved when Rebecca West wrote to tell her that she couldn't bear Diana Cooper, who seemed to her 'greedy and arrogant, with filthy manners', the English version of the 'just as frightful' Lauren Bacall. ('But please let me see more of *you*,' Rebecca West went on, 'who are my idea of a perfect woman.')

With the years, Martha's approval of courage grew stronger. To be brave, in the face of illness, loss, restrictions of age and fading looks, seemed to her as important as military bravery on the battlefield. Cowards bored and repelled her even more as time went by. 'I revere courage,' Martha said to Hortense Flexner. 'Perhaps I make it God, and endow it with every other quality, as stemming from it.' Heroes had kept their lustre. In the early 1970s, she thought briefly that she had found a new one.

Not long after Nadezhda Mandelstam's account of her husband Osip's persecution by Stalin, *Hope Against Hope*, appeared in the West, Martha read it straight through at a single sitting. Mrs Mandelstam, she thought, might just restore her faith in the perfectibility of man; she had been so brave, under conditions of hell, that she had 'kept the record straight'. She was particularly struck by Mrs Mandelstam's conclusion – if you can do nothing else, scream – and repeated it often to friends to illustrate why it was so important to bear witness to the injustices of the age. Martha had never had much to do with the Soviet Union, beyond her encounter with the

Russian soldiers by the Elbe in 1945, but since she believed it was right to praise people whenever possible for their work, she wrote to Moscow.

A letter quickly came back from Mrs Mandelstam, urging Martha to visit her. 'Do come, do come, do come. I will be horribly glad to see you. Do do do come. What about orange marmalade . . . we always had it in the morning when I was a child. As I am gaga (I am it) I wish to feel as a child I once was and have marmalade for my lunch . . . I kiss you.' More letters came; the two women were soon, as Martha put it, pen pals. She was wary of going to the Soviet Union, telling Betsy that in so much as she ever thought of Moscow at all it was as a sort of Chicago on the Volga, flat, hideous and freezing in winter. Mrs Mandelstam grew more insistent, and, one summer in the early 1970s, Martha caught a plane to Moscow. As instructed, she packed ulcer medicine for her hostess, as well as painkillers for her arthritic knee, a cashmere shawl, some Arpège scent, fourteen pairs of nylon stockings, a spring coat, the orange marmalade, and some recordings by Menuhin. Mrs Mandelstam had written to say that she found the sound of Menuhin's violin 'clever, kind, and Christian'. Martha also put in a generous supply of whisky, thrillers by Ed McBain and Mickey Spillane, and a large envelope of reviews of *Hope Against Hope* which Mrs Mandelstam had never seen. She left out pornography, in which Mrs Mandelstam had expressed an interest. Swallowing a handful of pills to calm herself down, she left for the airport in dread, laden, as she put it like a Santa Claus mule. Long before it began, she knew it would be a horror journey.

Being July, Moscow was not freezing cold; on the contrary, it was exceptionally, claustrophobically, hot. By the time Martha rose from her hotel bed each day, and set out for Mrs Mandelstam's 'sleazy cement block' an hour's journey away, the temperature was well over a hundred, and the sky overcast, still and heavy. Mrs Mandelstam was now seventy-four, about ten years older than Martha. She was a short, solid, square woman with big hips and wide shoulders and her legs were bowed into an almost perfect V. Her eyes, of the palest blue, looked sad and innocent. She smoked, and coughed, incessantly. The flat, overcrowded and airless, was always full of visitors. 'The squalor of the flat is excessive, unnecessary,' Martha wrote irritably in her notebook. 'Dead flowers everywhere – clothes, papers, books – it is appalling to me.'

One day, leaving behind the invariable group of attendants – 'all so gay except for me' – she took Mrs Mandelstam out to lunch. 'She was dressed up,' Martha wrote later, 'an embroidered white nylon blouse, mustard coloured straight skirt, rather dirty same colour corduroy shoes and figured black bandana. She pants like an animal, very frightening: her heart? At lunch we talked about O.M. and love. "I did not adore him, I answered for his love." During separation 1 yr during civil war, she had lovers and enjoyed herself. He could never be without her – every minute – she longed to be alone – she had no friends, he either took them, or kicked them out (like E.H.) . . . Her "happy times" all had to do with laughing (like mine).' Martha's relief at not finding herself at a deathbed, as her hostess had seemed to suggest in her letters, was soon dispelled by Mrs Mandelstam talking of coming to live in London. Martha began to feel like an agent for American Express.

Martha was hot, tired and miserable. Her normal solution, flight, was impossible. She was confused by the meals that kept appearing at odd times – a plate of fried mushrooms at five o'clock, another of fried potatoes at eight – and she had always hated drinking whisky out of a tooth mug with warm tap water and no ice. She doubted Mrs Mandelstam's truthfulness when she talked about her faith, and was annoyed when, having been touched by her delight in the first bottle of scent she professed she had ever seen, she caught sight of a bottle of Chanel No. 5 sitting on her bookshelf. As the days crawled by, she went on admiring her as a writer, and respected her huge nerve, but she did not like her. She found her pathetic, ungenerous and egocentric. 'Suffering has not ennobled,' she wrote in her notebook. When Mrs Mandelstam told her that she had been to bed with Osip the first night they met in Kiev in 1919, and that she had not been in love with him then,

Martha noted: 'I'm beginning to have the sense that all her life since 1938 is atoning for *not* having loved him enough when alive. Mad idea?'

She began to count the days, then the hours, to departure. She lay on her bed in her hateful hotel, naked in the stupefying heat, feeling oppressed by Mrs Mandelstam's hermetic world and infected by her palpable sense of fear. 'No papers, no books, radio jammed,' she wrote. 'No perspective.' When Mrs Mandelstam asked her if she was ever afraid, she replied: 'No, only angry.' But in her notebook, she wrote: 'But not true. I long to escape. The main sensation is pure Big Brother fear.'

Martha, who was not afraid of death, and had no hesitation about going to a war zone, was very afraid of prison; it was, she said, her one and only real fear, and in Moscow she felt as if she was breathing an air that smelt of secret police. And as the day for her departure approached, she grew increasingly apprehensive that something would happen to keep her a prisoner in the Soviet Union. At the airport, waiting to board her plane, she smoked twelve cigarettes. When they took off she seized on the British Airways magazine and 'read avidly', as she wrote later in *Travels with Myself and Another*, 'the little booklet that lists all the junky things you can buy on our splendid capitalist airlines'. Moscow had been all she most loathed. Even the people she had expected to like talked a strange dislocated dialogue of non-sequiturs and repeated themselves endlessly, while the drabness and glumness of the city had made it impossible for her to enjoy her usual pastime of observing how the people lived.

After her return to London, Martha and Mrs Mandelstam kept up their 'pen-pallery'. 'I am keeping the bed and the docs don't know why I have temperature . . . It is not cancer,' Mrs Mandelstam reported. 'But I feel very weak, perhaps it is tedium vitae. Tedium vitae is a very insolent thing . . . I have nothing to do except reading and I begin hating the books . . . Dostoevsky made me feel even worse.' She wrote again: 'You write that you can't write. You need a war to speak against it. But is it worth having one? I don't think so . . .

But you are not used to thinking and it is time to begin. So I wish you get rid of your depression and stop to be a recluse.' Then came another: 'If I had to live my life from the beginning once more I would become a nun. But when young I didn't think that clean life was possible. I would have preferred to become a whore. The only thing I am glad for that I have no children . . . The young are not satisfactory. When I meet one of them I thank God that they are not mine. The babies are nice. But when they become grown-ups they are not what they ought to be – weaklings, nasty lot and so on.'

Martha suspected that she had been a disappointment to Mrs Mandelstam, not the acolyte that had been wanted, and that she was too obviously out of sympathy with a closed circle that acted as if it had a monopoly on suffering. Though she redoubled her efforts with publishers and agents on Mrs Mandelstam's behalf, and sent books and occasional presents of money, she did so largely out of a sense of guilt, and slowly the exchange of letters petered out.

* * *

All her life, Martha filled small, differently coloured leather- or cardboard-bound notebooks with her research and observations, written in pen or pencil, in her round, legible hand. Today these notebooks, held together by rubber bands, are kept in large boxes among her papers in the Muggar Library at Boston University, where she began depositing her archive in the 1960s. There are dozens of them, for the most part covering her later journeys, to Vietnam, Israel, the Far East, South America and Spain, the earlier notebooks lost or discarded during her many moves. But there are also a few, which have no date and seem to belong nowhere in particular, that are about writing: about her hopes and uncertainties, about new and abandoned ideas, about characters and plots for novels, and about herself as a writer. 'What *is* real life? Technique for being brave: never think about oneself.' And again: 'Story about Solly, success thinning a man' – presumably a reference to Solly Zuckerman, the scientist and an old friend of hers. Under 'inexplicable insecurities', she had written: 'loneliness, intellectuals have to be protesters, as a writer always alone, the loneliest trade'.

One notebook sketches the story of an American reporter called Charles Danver, who travels to Spain, Finland and England and goes into Dachau. He meets Marian Hawtrey: 'father rich – never worked – collected majolica: tyrant, pious – mother sweet, subdued, pious. Marian only child – classical profile – tall, long narrow feet, aristocratic looking, reserved. 2 years at Vassar . . . never success at parties, with men, born frightened, so remained.' In the end, Marian refuses either to marry Charles or to sleep with him. 'I won't take the risk, she says. I'm not really good at it, as sport. Liking is rare enough. Besides, I'm used to loneliness.' Diaries as notebooks, lists of things to look up, snatches of conversation: what stands out is how little Martha imagined, how much on the contrary she reported, then used as fiction. Did she not realise this when she so vehemently protested at the least suggestion that her fiction was modelled closely on her life? There are entries on depression, on death, on the Nazi camps, on a child killed by a car.

The many lists of questions also show the extent to which she worried about accuracy: 'Look up 1) Industrial rev. 2) world events from autumn 1965 through 1970 – to 1973 3) medical pre-war training in France. Post 1945 – how to become analyst. 4) spinal meningitis. breakdown (sedition & ECT) etc. When was the pill introduced? Home property tax on rue de l'Université? . . . Details about legal aid, solicitors, county courts, transports to Auschwitz (write to friend in Paris for details). Neuroses – as defined in Freud's last book? Transference. Harrod's work day in Dec. 1968.'

Most interesting perhaps are the notes that concern her own vision of herself as a writer. Even when helpless to change the world, people had no right to the 'comfort of ignorance'. More than most writers, perhaps, she believed not in the determining power of thought but in action: men, as she had told Sandy Matthews, were what they did, not what they thought. Neither Descartes nor Freud appealed to her. If the vision sounds narrow, the black and white uncomfortably stark, the characters in the best of her short stories do not lack subtlety or nuance. But it is how they behave, not what they think, that intrigues Martha. 'I cannot analyse,' Martha once wrote to Betsy. 'It is not my bag.' 'I consider thinking nearly impossible,' she wrote on another occasion, echoing something Hemingway had once said to her. In the sense that she lacked the transforming magic of the true novelist, Martha was not a good writer of fiction; but she was a superb reporter, and at her best occupied that fine line where fact ends and fiction begins. She had, as the writer James Cameron once remarked, a 'cold eye and a warm heart'.

Those notebooks are intriguing. Others are more painful to read. These are the ones that deal with the bleakness that nearly every writer feels at some point in a writing life. For Martha, these arid and demoralising times came often; and they were extremely unpleasant. There are two notebooks, in particular, largely given to reflection about herself. The first reads: 'This book is all false starts. Week after week of dead pages . . . Questions, doubts and fears chew at my mind . . . I have no discipline in work hours, no order in my mind, no theories of literature, no universal view of anything . . .' The other, written later, says: 'Oh I am lost, lost, in the maze of my untrained mind. I cannot imagine who I was, when young . . . now, I feel that half the time I am lying, an impostor . . . Normally I swim, float, trudge, whatever it is, wherever I am, and some sort of ectoplasm – a grey substance made of sympathy, curiosity, concern, admiration, amusement, indignation – links one to the surrounding scene.' On a stray page, not attached to anything, are these fragments: 'a sudden feeling of having committed a sin – the sin of unhappiness, deadness, blindness, unfeelingness – the sin of wallowing in one's own misery . . . A sin against life: to lose one's taste for it, one's love of it.'

Having hitched her vision of herself so firmly to writing, and having inherited from both parents extremely high standards, Martha effectively created for herself a perilous and demanding world. If to write was her duty, her reason for being alive, then not to write was to fail. To fail as a writer was to fail at life, to be adrift in a formless and uncertain universe with nothing to hold on to. When Martha could not write, when what she called lockjaw of the brain paralysed her for week after week, or when she read back what she had written and decided it was worthless, she despaired: not only of herself as a writer, but as a person, a friend, a human being. She felt herself to be literally pointless, and would sit brooding, disconnected, haunted by the futility of the human condition. And, just as when the writing was going well, she felt physically strong and healthy, so when it went badly, she felt ill. She got ulcer pains. And with her mother dead, Sandy missing for months at a time, L. affectionate but absent, she had no anchor. All but a very few writers find writing hard; Martha found it excruciating. 'I have lost my eye, ear, nerve, and probably am no longer a writer': this sentence, written to a friend in the early 1980s, was repeated, in a dozen different forms, again and again in letters all her life.

To understand just how hard she found it, just how many false starts she made, how many stories and novels she sketched out and abandoned, one has to do no more than look into the cardboard boxes in Boston. There, among the notebooks in their rubber bands and the files of neatly gathered letters, are the folders containing her discarded writings. There is a file marked *A certain age*, containing stories about people in old age; another with the complete typescript of *Peace on Earth*, her fictionalised experiences of France in the 1930s, 'judged useless after a year's work', as she has written on the cover; 'Acting on Information Received', a short story about a man who needed fame to breathe and who, his talent having deserted him, commits suicide. (This last story was sent to Irwin Shaw to read, who returned it saying toughly that it was really all about Hemingway and was only notes and not a proper story.) There are stories with titles like 'The Long Journey', 'In Love with a Voice', 'The Long Temptation', probably rejected bilgers; chapters for her projected book on Israel, with notes: 'What beats me is the tone. Personal? Am I there too?' She was there too, always, though to the end of her life she resisted ever acknowledging it; perhaps because to admit that her strength lay more in what she perceived and translated than in what she was able to imagine was not acceptable to her. It would, in her own eyes, have diminished her as a novelist. 'And I see people,' she has written, in a diary started in Switzerland in the 1970s. 'Considering they are figments of my imagination, I find it rather weird actually to see them.'

Among the many files is a note: 'I now realise that's why I have 4 or 5 unfinished novels – if not the actual first person singular, then the heroine is too close to me, hence useless and unreal.' In Belize, Martha abandoned a novel after 12,000 words; in Nyali, she jettisoned two hundred pages on nuclear weapons. In Kenya, in 1974, she started a novel based around the character of an analyst – in itself surprising, given her hostility to self-examination. That was in February; in May, she gave it up and started a second version. This reached seven chapters before she abandoned it in December. She decided to hold on to sixty of the 350 finished pages, however, and turn it into a novella. By the middle of March she had completed 150 pages, and was not displeased with what she had written. In June, she read it through and decided that it was worthless. She scrapped it all and settled down to work, frenetically this time, writing for most of the day and parts of the night, 'like a mad scientist'. She got to the end in late July: eighteen months of almost solid work for one short story. 'Writing,' Martha observed to Betsy only too understandably, 'is beyond question the hardest thing on earth; give me laying railroad ties any time.' Rebecca West once said to Martha that she felt as if she had spent her life trying to write with her left hand. Martha replied that in her case she had written with the little finger of her left hand. On bad days, she said that writing was nothing but a 'long absorbing act of vomiting'.

If Martha was consumed by doubts about her own ability to write, she was by contrast absolutely clear about how it had to be done. For a start, you could not both write and live. Writing, she told Sandy Matthews, was 'hermit's work', with at the very most another hermit nearby for occasional visits. Four hours a day of actual writing was all that should be attempted, with the rest of the time given to training for the next day. 'One has to walk, laze, dream,' she wrote, 'leave the mind open as a door for the wayward idea and word.' Writing was unremitting labour, and no young writer could miss out on a long 'self-conducted apprenticeship'.

More important, indeed the single most important factor, was compulsion. You wrote because you had to write, because you had no choice. You wrote because you were angry. 'Because,' she told Presnell, 'one sees, feels and must speak; because one wants to know what one thinks; because it is the hardest work there is and thus, like Everest, it lures . . . something to say which is killing one inside . . . I do not think it a bad profession; I think it marvellous . . . It gets harder and harder because one knows more, the complexity in the brain is harder to put into words than the violence and clarity of youth; and because one has much better taste and fiercer self criticism . . . But since there are no happy endings, that is no worse than any other.'

And, beyond the discipline, the solitude and the compulsion, the writing muscles that had to be kept in training and the attention to accurate research, there were a few practical rules, which she told those of her friends who wrote to her about their books. Nothing, she said, was any good without disciplining the inner compulsion; for strangers to English, like George Paoloczi-Horvath, there should be immersion in language, 'bathing and drowning' in good written English. Style was paramount, 'because the first function of writing is to snare and lure, never to bore, and to give out information in the form of pleasure and excitement'. 'We are all entertainers,' she told Paoloczi-Horvath. 'Some more serious than others, that's all.' Thesaurus and the dictionary were permitted, but sparingly; the 'nasty weaselling face of the clichés' was to be ruthlessly banned.

And, of course, there was the question of truth. Predictably, given her own avowed abhorrence of lies, and her huge admiration for her mother's moral clarity, Martha declared when asked that there was something repellent about not telling the truth. Lying, as she had often said, was a cardinal sin. If, however, this occasionally left her in a somewhat delicate intellectual position – 'all this objectivity shit' – it was not one she was particularly anxious to explore. Did she and Hemingway lie when they failed to write about the atrocities committed on the republican side during the Spanish civil war? When they omitted to report what the Chinese people really felt about Madame Chiang Kai-shek? This slippery line, which existed in Martha on several levels – why, for instance, did she tell Sybille Bedford that she was four years younger than she was? – is curious. Certainly, it annoyed people, and critics have seized, often very vehemently, on perceived discrepancies, presumably precisely because Martha spoke out so loudly about the need to be truthful.

Soft on herself in this regard, Martha could indeed be ferociously hard on others. To fabricate, knowingly, was despicable. To accuse others of doing so, without real evidence, was slanderous. When, in 1975, Phillip Knightley published *The First Casualty*, about the reporter as hero and maker of myths, he speculated, as many others have done before and since, about whether Robert Capa's celebrated photograph of the falling republican soldier in Spain was in fact staged. Had the man really been killed, or, as various negatives found later suggest, had the photograph been taken as a series of posed pictures during manoeuvres, and mislabelled? Capa was not present when the photograph was first captioned by *Vue* magazine as a picture of a dying man. By the time he returned from the Spanish front *Life* magazine had turned it into the enduring symbol of the courageous republican side. Capa himself died without ever clarifying the matter.*

---

*The mystery may in fact have at last been solved. Richard Whelan, Capa's biographer, has been convinced by a homicide detective, an expert in violent death, that Capa's soldier was in fact shot. He believes the most likely explanation is that the republican soldiers had been unaware of a rebel battery nearby, that it had unexpectedly opened fire, and that the soldier, standing up to let Capa get a good picture, had been shot dead before he had a chance to aim his rifle.

After the publication of *The First Casualty*, Martha was invited to appear on a television programme with Knightley. When the subject of Capa's photograph came up it was immediately clear that Martha was not prepared to discuss it. Capa, her friend, was an honourable man and honourable men do not lie about their work. So outraged was she by the tenor of the debate that she threatened to walk out in the middle of the interview. Knightley, who had been something of a friend before, was dismissed and barely spoken to again. When they met, she turned away. (Martha, when she saw herself on the screen, was appalled. 'I looked 108 years old,' she told her brother Alfred. 'This a.m. I decided I looked like Dorothy Parker. The bags under her eyes were such that we always thought her related to the camel.')

There was, however, another incident concerning Martha and journalistic truth, more humorous and considerably more rancorous. In February 1980, Lillian Hellman, the American playwright and author of several volumes of memoirs, filed a lawsuit against the novelist Mary McCarthy for defamation. A few weeks earlier, appearing on the Dick Cavett show on television, McCarthy had been asked who, in her opinion, were the 'over praised' writers. Lillian Hellman, McCarthy replied: she was both bad and dishonest. Asked to elaborate, she said that every word Hellman wrote was 'a lie, including the "and" and the "the".' Hellman immediately sued for 'mental pain and anguish', asking for $1.75 million. Much enjoying the squabble between these two feisty women – Hellman was known to have once referred to McCarthy's fiction as novels by a 'lady magazine writer', and McCarthy to have called Hellman's plays works of 'oily virtuosity' – the literary world remembered that while McCarthy had sided with the Orwell faction over the Spanish civil war, opposing too close a tie with the Soviets, Hellman had promoted a united front as the only way to defeat Franco. 'It's not just two old ladies engaged in a cat fight,' observed Irving Howe, co-editor of *Dissent*. 'I think for many of us those disputes were the formative passions of our lives.' For the American left, Hellman, veteran of McCarthyism, and McCarthy, whose novel *The Group* had enchanted a generation of young women, were heroines of their time.

Martha had met Lillian Hellman in Spain and had not greatly cared for her. When *Pentimento*, Hellman's memoir, first appeared she had complained that her recollections of Hemingway and life at the Hotel Florida were wildly inaccurate. A mutual friend, the *Washington Post* journalist Jon Randal, reminded McCarthy of this and she now wrote to ask Martha whether she would be prepared to testify on her behalf. 'Would you be willing to give my lawyers an affidavit describing the untruths and prevarications?' Martha, in the event, was happy to do this and more. She did not much like Mary McCarthy either, telling Betsy that she was a 'coony opportunist', with the 'spookiest handwriting', and that she certainly would not want to spend any time on a desert island with her. But, she added, 'H. is the greater liar', and she had 'used the Spanish war as a garment to drape herself in'. And Martha did feel very strongly about Spain. Having stayed silent for almost thirty years on the subject of Hemingway and the civil war, she felt that the moment had come to nail the 'braggarts, the mythomanes and corpse vultures'.

Martha's attack on Hellman came in the form of a thirty-page broadside delivered to the *Paris Review*, after its editor, George Plimpton, invited her to comment on a piece Stephen Spender had written for the magazine. In this, Spender had described a lunch at the Brasserie Lipp in Paris, apparently attended by both Hemingway and Martha, at which his wife Inez, having refused to eat sweetbreads, had been called 'yellow' by Hemingway. Hemingway, said Spender, had then boasted that Martha had been 'yellow' before he knew her, and that he had prepared her for the ordeals of the Spanish civil war by taking her to the morgue in Madrid every morning before breakfast. Something about this apparently trivial story enraged Martha. Hemingway's 'old corpse' had been battered enough. She replied to Plimpton's invitation with a blast of invective, first against 'stupid old' Spender, and then, for good measure, against Hellman.

Coining a new word, 'apocryphiar', to describe a person

who invents a story about himself as a hero, she spent six weeks combing through her papers and notes, as well as published accounts of Spain and the timing of various battles and bombings, and then '12 bloody days' writing and rewriting. She delivered a scathing, funny, highly damning attack on both Spender and Hellman. Spender, she explained in a letter to Plimpton, was an 'ass. He always was an ass but a nice timid ass. In his advanced years he has become a pompous ass, which is deplorable.' What was more, neither she nor Hemingway had ever had lunch with Spender or 'his unknown first wife'. The idea of anyone visiting a morgue before breakfast was grotesque: 'Mr Spender has a weird and wondrous imagination.' Spender, she wrote in her piece, could be written off as a 'silly juggins', trading on imaginary intimacies, were it not for the way he set about trying to belittle Hemingway who was, as everyone knew, a writer far superior and more important than himself.

As for Hellman, Martha made it plain that her account of Madrid was beneath contempt. Hellman's suggestion that she ignored Hemingway's warning and dashed over to a radio studio during the shelling of Madrid to make a broadcast was pure fantasy. Her apocryphisms were 'whoppers'; and for sixteen pages, line by line, lie by lie, Martha spelt them out. The woman of whom Hemingway was famously quoted as saying that she had '*cojones*' had nothing but 'the "*cojones*" of a brass monkey'. Literary America enjoyed every word.

Plimpton had originally expected a short letter from Martha, to appear in some discreet corner of the magazine. He was clearly appalled, while appreciating the possible publicity from printing such an article. He sent Martha's typescript off to Spender (but not to Hellman), and played for time. Muriel Gardner, who had dined with Spender and Inez on the same night as the disputed lunch, was able to vouch for the lunch having taken place, and she also recalled the story about the morgue.

Martha, unlike Hellman, did have '*cojones*'. Barely was her article on Plimpton's desk than she began her assault. Was he delaying using it because of his own lack of *cojones*? How much was he planning to pay her? Why wasn't he answering her letters? How could he be so unbusiness-like? 'Please be less charming,' she wrote, 'and more honourable.' She complained about the expense of the transatlantic calls his dithering obliged her to make. She fumed about the size of the type when she eventually received a proof. She had the footnotes moved. And when, at last, the piece appeared, she complained bitterly that by changing her title from 'Close Encounters of the Apocryphal Kind' to 'On Apocryphism' he had effectively spoilt her entire line of reasoning. It was, she said, 'vandalism'.

Lillian Hellman said grandly that she had never seen anything so silly, and that life was too tough to stoop to this kind of nonsense. Privately, she cursed Plimpton for not giving her, as he had given Spender, a first chance to see the piece and reply. Mary McCarthy was duly grateful and felt buoyed up for the forthcoming trial, but remarked to Spender that really all Martha had done was add to the 'general sense of probability that the woman is lying'. And, in the event, the trial never took place, as Lillian Hellman died before it went to court. As for Martha's friends, though greatly entertained by the onslaught, they were faintly surprised by the passion she had brought to the whole affair. As Gloria Emerson put it in a letter: 'Why use all that energy on attacking an elderly woman?' But Martha's own position was clear, at least to her. Apocryphiars, like liars in all their forms, had to be stamped out.

Martha was in fact very interested in the process of memory. Her brother Alfred believes that her memory was excellent, and that her recall of incidents and the most fleeting of conversations and meetings that had taken place far in the past was exceptional. Martha herself, from a very early age, worried incessantly that one of her failings as a writer was that her mind stored nothing. Without memory, she said, 'there is nothing but shapeless rubble in the mind'. Where had all the people gone, she asked, 'who were strangers once and are now forgotten strangers?'. The two views are not really contradictory. Martha longed for a disciplined memory, one that obeyed her commands, just as she longed for order and reliability in everything. Memory, elusive, capricious, defied her sense of neatness; she saw what others learn to recognise and live with as a personal failing. One of the last articles Martha ever wrote was actually called 'Memory', about the Spanish civil war, and it appeared in the *London Review of Books* in December 1996. It is not only beautifully written but extremely vivid. 'I have no grasp of time and no control over my memory,' she wrote in her last paragraph. 'I cannot order it to deliver. Unexpectedly, it flings up pictures, disconnected with no before or after. It makes me feel a fool. What is the use in having lived so long, travelled so widely, listened and looked so hard, if in the end you don't know what you know?' This was written when Martha was eighty-six. She had been writing and working for almost seventy years and found the process as hard, as daunting, as uncertain as it had been all her life. 'The job gets harder every year,' she told Milton Wolff, who wrote to complain of his difficulties in finding a publisher. 'And now it's close to torture.'

* * *

It would never have seemed conceivable to Martha, even though she found the process so painful, to give up writing altogether. For one thing, there was a great deal that she still wished to say; for another, like most writers, she went on hoping that she might just possibly one day write a book that she actually considered good. And it was through writing, improbably, that her life took a real and lasting turn for the better.

Dachau had unquestionably been a determining moment in her life. She had known that she would never really trust in people's fundamental honesty and compassion again, and indeed she never did. If there were such men for whom the untranslatable word '*Mensch*' applied, they were rare and well concealed. After Dachau, her natural instinct to write about underdogs – those reduced by circumstance, not the complainers, for Martha never lost her distaste for the victim mentality – hardened. It was not politics that really touched her, though she railed against politicians, but the way they shaped the human condition 'horribly, inexorably'. Refugees, casualties of war, the displaced, the tortured, became the focus of almost all her articles. What she saw, as the years passed, depressed her: a world, in Santayana's words, unable to learn from history, condemned to keep repeating the same mistakes, full of lemmings, led by super-lemmings, scurrying towards the abyss. 'Anywhere you look,' she said to Sandy Matthews, 'the species, like scorpions, is stinging itself to death.' For a while, she became convinced that a third world war was imminent, nuclear and therefore liable to bring about extinction. 'I feel madness in the air,' she wrote. 'Nothing strikes me as rational anywhere.'

Occasionally, from among the super-lemmings there would emerge a hero, on whom Martha would alight with pleasure. Gorbachev was greeted as 'the only great statesman'. Clinton, for a while, looked set to become 'one of the great educators of the age', and she wrote an article about him for the *New Republic*, 'Cry Shame', defending him against character assassination by reporters and referring to the Clintons as the 'spiritual heirs to the Roosevelts'. (After her death, Sandy Matthews found a personal letter from Clinton among her papers, thanking her for supporting 'me in difficult circumstances' at the time of the Monica Lewinsky scandal). Heroic acts charmed her. When the Israeli special forces stormed the hijacked plane at Entebbe airport in the summer of 1976, Martha wrote exuberantly to Moshe Pearlman about the 'immense shiningness of the rescue'. The following year, when Charles Bronson starred in a film about the Israeli raid, Martha and Diana Cooper went to a matinee performance and wept. She admired those who fought back, and particularly the old who did so. When Dora Russell reached ninety, Martha remarked admiringly that, though a bit dotty, when it came to courage this ugly old lady took the cake.

And, just as there were still heroes, there were of course still villains. After Nasser, Kissinger and Nixon, whose impeachment she travelled to the States to attend, came Reagan and Mrs Thatcher ('a counter-jumper with a cooing voice'). Villains were excellent material for articles. Always preferring the role of actor to spectator, she liked to harry them on the ground. In February 1976 Martha spent several weeks in Spain, writing about life after Franco for the *New York Times* magazine, and lost six pounds working twelve hours a day for thirteen days whittling the article down from 150 pages to thirty. Later came articles for the *Guardian* about the strike of the British miners, 'the bravest of the working class' (mocked by Ferdinand Mount in the *Daily Telegraph* as sentimentally patronising); for the *New Statesman* about Reagan's policy towards Nicaragua; for *Granta* on the American troops in Panama, where, she complained, 'our noble asshole President' was allocating $1,000 million to rebuild in the wake of the invasion; and on the torture of human rights defenders in El Salvador. 'We hold shameful passports,' she told a friend; she would rather be a Dane.

Being seventy, or even eighty, never seemed to her a reason for giving up war reporting, and she minded intensely when, in 1982, she could find no takers for a proposed piece on the Israeli invasion of Lebanon, of which she greatly approved. 'What can one do, Moshe,' she asked her old friend Pearlman, 'if one is regarded as too old to be useful?' Brooding over this, she said to Milton Wolff: 'It seems to me that I have spent my life, futilely, squealing in print against the bastards and for the decent people; and I might as well have stayed in bed reading thrillers.' And, after her death, she told a friend, she wanted a park bench in Kew Gardens in her name, with the words 'under-rated writer'. These were her low days. To the end of her life, questioned about how she saw her role as a reporter, and why she went on writing, she always said the same thing: she wrote because, like Mrs Mandelstam, she believed that it was her duty to record the injustice she witnessed, and that, though she believed she had personally done nothing of any use, she had always felt it a matter of necessity to keep going. 'It seemed to me personally that it was my job to get things on the record,' she said at a round table discussion for journalists at Freedom Forum in 1996, 'in the hopes that at some point or other, somebody couldn't absolutely lie about it.'

Her sense of indignation never diminished. She was greatly entertained when, in the late 1970s, she learnt from the new Freedom of Information Act that a file had been opened on her at the time of the Spanish civil war by the FBI, and that the CIA had fourteen entries under her name. According to their agent in Spain, Martha had been running a communist network and had been involved in 'questionable projects' within communist circles. Her first reaction, one of extreme contempt, was soon followed by curiosity. She wrote to America and eventually received xeroxed copies detailing her supposed activities. Many of the pages, for 'reasons of security,' had been blacked out, but there were lists of her activities in Spain and Mexico and she was referred to as a writer who had supported 'Communist controlled movements, manifestos and political candidates'. Martha made much of what she was able to read, putting together a twenty-seven-page attack on the idiocy, audacity and perversity of the snoopers. '*How dare they?*,' she demanded. 'Who do they think they are?'

And, sometime around the middle of the 1970s, her book writing block broke. She was fiddling with one of the novellas for her African volume when she suddenly saw how to make it work. Scarcely rising from her desk, she wrote steadily, pausing only to send off lists of questions to Ruth Rabb: 'What wooden floors would have been laid in 1920 in a farm house built at 6,000ft?' 'What kind of creepers would have thrived at that altitude?' 'What was the Swahili for "worthless bum"?' Published as *The Weather in Africa* in the summer of 1978, the book did not sell as she had hoped it would, and the first reviews were 'mediocre to mean'. But she was already deep into another book about the horror journeys of her life, and this one she found fun. She went to a hotel in France and settled down: in two weeks, she had written almost half. 'My memory is like an amputated arm,' she told Betsy; 'but flashes return.'

Travels with Myself and Another was Martha's only volume

of autobiography. Born out of a sudden desire to record some of the more hideously comic journeys of her life and told in the first person, *Travels* includes almost her only published reference to Hemingway, as UC, the unwilling companion of the terrible trip to China in 1942. (He also made an appearance in 'Memory', as E.) It was finished at great speed, Martha laughing out loud as she wrote, or when she woke in the night and remembered episodes and sentences. Publishers were slow to react: eight in the United States and six in Britain turned it down before Allen Lane offered a three-book deal of £5,000, for *Travels*, *The Weather in Africa* and a reprint of *The Honeyed Peace*. The first reviews for *Travels* were somewhat disappointing. Laurén Bacall urged her to follow her example and talk about herself in public, but Martha shied away from the humiliation, saying that it was too like taking a truth drug or going in for psychoanalysis. But then good reviews appeared in *The Times* and the *Telegraph*, copies began to sell, and, for the first time in many years, Martha experienced a faint stirring of pride in being a writer. *Travels*, published in 1978, hit a nerve and its timing, when the reading world was just rediscovering a taste for the personal journey, was excellent; it has been in print almost ever since, and is perhaps the best known and loved of her books. It sells steadily.

In its wake came new editions by Virago of *Liana* and *A Stricken Field*, and yet another of *The Face of War*, for which she wrote a new conclusion. Though she complained bitterly that it took her four months and 40 to 50,000 'failed words' to complete, that she hated every sentence and wrote them with 'blood pouring from the fingers', fighting off nasty weaselling clichés from all sides, her spirits remained high, even if her conclusion was dark. 'After a lifetime of war-watching,' she wrote, 'I see war as an endemic human disease, and governments are carriers.' She started work on a collection of other pieces, those written in peace time, *The View from the Ground*, which became its companion. She stopped referring to her books as 'collectors' items', and started instead talking about new books she might write, like one about growing old. And, just as they had in the 1930s, after *The*

Trouble I've Seen was published, editors and reviewers began to notice and admire her work, praising her persistence and her intelligent eye, her intemperate moral indignation, and enjoying the fact that, unlike many of the newer writers, she took no pleasure in promoting herself. Her attacks on the Arab world were unbalanced, they agreed, but it was refreshing to read such first-class reporting, such discerning and compassionate commentaries on the nature of the modern world. Martha cared, very much, about what happened to people; but she was never sentimental. Her eye was sharp, her prose style powerful and dignified and spare, and she did not care who she offended. It made readers nostalgic for a time when reporters went out with notebooks and wrote about what they saw, and you believed them.

CHAPTER SIXTEEN

The Sin of Unhappiness

With this new literary success, and at about the time that she was complaining she had become a 'solitary, aimless, joyless, aging woman', a transformation took place in Martha's life. It was something she had never envisaged; and it involved people.

It had been a long time since Martha had relied on people to provide her with anything more than the most transient pleasure. 'I like very few people on earth for more than a limited number of hours at a time,' she had once said to Diana Cooper. If anything, her faith in friendship had been diminishing. Several of her closest friends had died suddenly – George Paoloczi-Horvath, her fellow 'world watcher', of a stroke; Lucy Moorehead in a car crash; Felicia Bernstein of cancer – and Martha was often at odds with the survivors. She didn't like feeling 'a lone antique monument' she told Sandy Matthews, and felt sad that she could do nothing to comfort their children, since there was no comfort. 'Nothing makes up for the loss,' she told Bernard Perlin, her American painter friend. 'It's there, a permanent wound.' Having been unjudgemental when Leonard Bernstein went off for a while with a twenty-eight-year-old boy, she told him that, puffed up with his own fame, he had become insufferable and an embarrassing bore, 'like the intellectual's Liberace'. Later, however, she regretted her harsh words. About a week before he died Bernstein asked her what she felt about suicide. Her reply was stern. Suicide was fine when you could no longer have the life you wanted. She intended to do it herself if anything ever came along that stopped her from living. And she added: 'You cannot lie there, as a sorrowing vegetable. You have to make an effort on your own behalf . . . I know a lot about pain, Lennypot, and I know it is bad for people, eats away the spirit, but how about courage, what is it for if not to use when needed? . . . You don't need sympathy, you need someone to say buck-up . . .' Bernstein, who was in considerable pain from emphysema and its complications, was very low, and feeling guilty about Felicia. A few days later he died. Martha handled this death as she handled all deaths: a few sad, understanding remarks; then silence.

The 'Senile Set' she was left with consisted for the most part of women, and Martha observed that she knew in advance what each would say, and what she herself would say in reply. 'The company of my friends, my own age and older, now depresses me horribly,' she wrote in a diary kept during a long solitary tramp along the Doubs river in Switzerland. 'My own age seem to me simply beasts of burden . . . afflicted with age as if it were a disease.' She had decided that she would stick to solitude, though she was beginning to be plagued by what she described as having nothing to think about. 'What next?' thoughts began to seem pointless, and she had never cared for metaphysical speculation. She reread Henry James and decided that he was overrated, rejected Rose Macaulay as a 'stylish woman's magazine writer', and dismissed Lesley Blanche as a 'sex obsessed lady with a rather fishy fancy style'. She also decided she hated Gogol, detested Eugene O'Neill and Tennessee Williams, considered Steinbeck rotten, could not read Hardy and was sick of 'waiting for the gleam or glitter' in modern novels, which never came through. Instead, she read thrillers, one after another, as many as ten or twelve a week, 'as people take dope'.

It was now, however, that a group of new friends came into her life. They were not so very different from the people she had known and always been fond of, nor from those of her friends' children, such as Jamie Bernstein and John Moorehead, my brother, and myself, whom she had been summoning round for drinks in Cadogan Square for many years. They were young, forty and even fifty years younger than she was, and they were drawn to her through her new and republished books. They were not only openly admiring of her achievements, but charmed by her humour, and the fact that she understood and knew it all, and yet remained so apparently untouched by age. It meant nothing to them that she was nearing eighty. On the contrary, they were stunned by her elegance, her wonderful looks. And, more important, they made her laugh. She rather enjoyed being a teacher. She was bored with her own familiar problems. She came away from a publication party for James Fenton in Oxford 'swollen with booze and conceit', having enjoyed herself 'like billy-o' and been 'rediscovered by kids'. She felt, she told the Rabbs, 'like a geriatric debutante'.

One of the first of these new friends was John Pilger, the Australian reporter. Pilger, having been sent off by his editor on the *Mirror*, Hugh Cudlipp, to South-east Asia with Martha's articles, invited her to a preview of his film about Vietnam in 1978; they discovered they shared a sense of outrage about political power and injustice. They also fought, long into the night, furiously and giving no quarter, over Israel and the Palestinians: Pilger was Martha's sparring partner, the only new friend with whom she happily had rows.

Then came Rosie Boycott, who was exploring articles for *Spare Rib*; they talked about the ambiguities of feminism and agreed on how much they hated whining and how important it was to fight back. Rosie was Martha's kind of young woman, a 'non-moaner', someone who like herself saw no conflict between being a woman and achieving what you wanted. It was her sort of feminism. John Hatt, founder of Eland Books, came into Martha's life when he wrote to ask her about the rights to *Travels*; James Fox, when she wrote to tell him he had written *White Mischief* 'felicitously'; Victoria Glendinning, after a nice review of *The Weather in Africa*; Nicholas Shakespeare at dinner with John Hatt; Jeremy Harding when he made a programme about her for *Omnibus* and she was 'stonily resistant' to any mention of Hemingway's name. Martha felt enormous affection for them all. They became 'my chaps', and, in the evenings, over the Famous Grouse, they brought her the story of their lives. With each, the emphasis was a little different.

With the men, particularly James Fox and Nicholas Shakespeare, she was instinctively flirtatious, almost coquettish, conscious of her own attraction, enjoying the fact of being with men again, the camaraderie of the battle of life, mocking the world, and mocking themselves. They railed against Reagan, against broken love affairs. For Shakespeare, Martha was the best listener he had ever encountered, and she was the person he wanted to talk to when something happened to him. She was curious, and wanted to know everything; but not jealous. Martha called Fox 'my favourite James in all the world' and told him that his mumbling low voice unfailingly gave her pleasure. Almost forty years apart in age, they were each other's confidants, both practitioners she would say of the art of self-destructive relationships. Scorpios, she told him, belonged in turbulent times. 'I feel like a crushed caterpillar, right now.'

With John Hatt, she talked about writing and editing – he was practically the only editor whose corrections she tolerated – and about his journeys. 'Aside from you,' she told him, 'I think all publishers are shits.' She forgave him for voting for Mrs Thatcher because they laughed so much together. 'I always mean to ask you if you believe in God as well as Mrs Thatcher,' she wrote early in their friendship. 'Do tell, next time.' If Pilger was the reporter of the casualties of war – 'my spiritual heir', she once called him – Hatt became her traveller, visiting the places she could no longer get to. With Victoria Glendinning, she talked about writing, about domesticity – Martha remained totally sceptical about its pleasures, saying they were simply not her bag – and the past; Victoria introduced Martha to the microwave. 'It's bliss,' Martha told her, 'to get the whole feeding thing done in max. 4 mins.' Victoria was the woman friend of the kind she had lost with the early deaths of Lucy Moorehead and Felicia Bernstein. 'You're my chum,' she told her, 'since I've not yet caught on to the fact that I'm made stately, out of the chum class, by years.'

When John Simpson and Jon Snow entered her life in the early 1990s, they brought the news from the front lines she could no longer visit. Snow, presenting the seven o'clock news on Channel 4, grew to expect Martha's phone call as he came off the air, waiting to cross-examine him about some item of political perfidy on which he had touched. Simpson, dropping in for a drink on his return from a distant conflict, relived his battles for her, while she listened and debriefed him. 'Tell me the news from the Rialto,' she would say to all of them, and the news was that of battles and skirmishes, intrigues and political chicanery. For Simpson, for Pilger, for Shakespeare, there had never been a confidante quite like her, someone so shrewd and wise, and yet so funny. They saw Martha because they wanted to talk to her, and to listen to her, and because they felt a little flattered about her attentiveness. Though most of her new friends were men, because Martha believed that men were funnier, if less reliable, there were young women too, many of them writers and journalists, like Mary Blume, who worked for the *International Herald Tribune* in Paris; and Cynthia Kee, with whom Martha went walking around London. 'You didn't pry,' says Rosie Boycott. 'Whatever you got was fine.'

They did not start out as a group, and Martha herself greatly preferred seeing them individually. But she did occasionally introduce them to each other, when she felt there might be pleasure or advantage in it, and from time to time one or the other would give a dinner to which Martha would be asked, and then they would all sit up late into the night, drinking and talking, while Martha stayed and stayed. And next morning would come the invariable letter of apology. 'I practically week-ended with you,' Martha told Fox after one late night. She took to putting an alarm clock in her bag, set for eleven o'clock, but either ignored its squeals or forgot to prime it to ring. Her fear, as she told all of them, was that she would bore them. 'You are absolutely not boring,' wrote Victoria in one early reply, writing the words in capitals and underlining them. She was right. Martha was not boring, even if the emphatic blasts of her current campaigns could be wearying.

'It must have been like having a hot meal with a tank,' Martha told Fox after a long evening on the subject of war. If she talked too much, she would say, it was because she spent so much time alone. 'Mind wobbling on edge of crash or melt-down.'

It was perhaps surprising, given Martha's own low threshold for boredom, her impatience with those who did not appeal to her, that her instinct for how friendship worked was, with this group at least, so sure. She never gossiped with any of them about the others. She seldom sought them out, prefer-ring to let the impetus come from them. 'Can you tactfully find out if Rosie is off me?' she asked John Hatt one day. Her visitors came away feeling that they had been understood, that they had touched on topics of importance, and that they were, for a moment at least, better than they had thought them-selves to be. They were all touched by her unfailing generosity, at times of financial crisis, to pay school fees, bail out ailing businesses, provide a desperately wanted break. Once Martha had money, she gave regularly to charities. She also went on supporting the Pamps after Lola had a small stroke and Rosario began to suffer from '*nervios*', one year doubling their money, having received a letter from Lola saying that they were very thin. She wrote hurriedly to ask them what they ate and how much they weighed, and laughed when she learnt that they ate a great deal more than she did. She also sent a cheque for $100 every Christmas to Gregorio, Hemingway's boatman in Havana.

To those new friends afflicted by calamities, Martha wrote affectionately. When she judged the moment right, she became bracing. When Bernard Perlin's partner Bud died in 1986, Martha's letters were frequent and loving. Then, as Perlin grieved, she offered work, trips, visits. As the mourning went on, however, she warned against tunnel vision, nervous collapse, the waste of life, and the need, always, for courage. 'You must not feel trapped,' she said to Sandy Matthews. 'There isn't enough time for that sort of waste and unhappi-ness.' No words of comfort, she told me when my mother, Lucy Moorehead, died in a car crash, 'because I don't believe in them; maybe solidarity'. She could also, of course, be peremptory and didactic: judging that I was making mistakes in the way I was bringing up my daughter, she fired off two blasts on my failings as a mother. I was so angry and mortified I tore them up.

Not all the encounters were a success. Shakespeare remembers a terrible evening after Martha and Germaine Greer expressed a desire to meet. Foolishly, he organised a dinner at his own house and invited John Hatt to join them. Germaine Greer was surprisingly nervous. Her solution was to gabble, and to go on gabbling, about the men she had slept with. Martha sat at the table with her cigarette, her eyes narrowed against the smoke, and listened. She never spoke. Peter Straus, who published a compendium of Martha's novellas, *Two By Two*, recalls an evening with Martha and Edna O'Brien. O'Brien asked Martha where she had bought her beautiful clothes. 'Oxfam,' replied Martha. 'I don't give a fuck about clothes.' When Harold Pinter came to call, Martha reported later to James Fox that she could hardly believe 'how boring we both were'. She strongly disliked Bruce Chatwin's 'marble' writing, saying it was carved and perfect but that he had the coldness of an etymologist studying freakish insects. (Not all evenings with strangers were a disaster: Rosie introduced Martha to Bob Geldof and she 'wowed the table.')

Perhaps the most unfortunate meeting of all was with Shusha Guppy, who went to interview Martha for a collection of articles about writers for the *Paris Review*. As they had agreed, Guppy sent Martha a typescript of the proposed article. She received in return a furious and intemperate letter. Shusha, according to Martha, was 'stupid, tasteless, ignorant and dishonest'. She had lifted passages from other people. Of all the interviews Martha had ever read, she could remember none as 'rambling, pointless and erroneous as this'. Being with Shusha, she told James Fox, was like being bathed 'in a malodorous marshmallow sauce'. Shusha did not greatly care for Martha either.

And, just occasionally, a friendship which had started with immense promise withered. Bill Buford, then editor of *Granta*, offered one day to find Martha more satisfactory publishing deals than she had been getting for a number of her books. Within weeks he had negotiated excellent terms with publishers in America and England. There was talk of other foreign deals. Martha was delighted. Bill, she said, was a 'volcano of energy and ideas'. 'Dearest William,' she wrote to him, 'you're wonderful, you're wonderful, you're wonderful.' After decades of neglect, of being 'in the position of the great dead', she was at last going to be read, and she had at last found an agent for whom writing a book was not like 'giving needlepoint to a horse'. For a while Buford, riding high, became both Martha's agent and her editor. But there was something in his style that irked her. He was too casual, too forgetful of royalty statements, too cavalier with his corrections. He changed things without consulting her. Martha's attention to detail, to the size of print, the photograph on the jacket, the date when payments were made, had, if anything, increased with the years. She bawled him out, then apologised for being 'an old fart . . . hideous and nasty'. He gave a party for the launch of one of her books. She was greatly touched, saying that she had never had a book party in her life. But then he forgot to send her a cheque, let Virago publish a new edition of *Liana* 'disgustingly', allowed an idiotic lawyer to sign a deal on a 'terrible' script. ('No cross-eyed actress called Martha Gellhorn is getting naked out of bed.')

Martha felt abandoned: 'Bill, I need some word. This is very lonely and uncertain work.' She was tired with cultivating her barren garden 'like a poor mad mole'. Waiting for Bill to come to dinner was 'strangely like waiting for Godot'. 'You are behaving exactly like all the publishers in my life,' she told him. 'They promise a girl the sun and the moon, feed her caviar and champagne, send American Beauty roses, until she signs on the dotted line. After which they are out to lunch.' She became stern. 'This is too serious for your easy promise/not deliver system. *I mean it*.' Then she grew angry. 'I have been angry with you before, but never this angry. I find you plainly intolerable . . .' When he once again failed to send her a cheque, she went to the Small Claims Court in Wales and filed a suit. (More combative than litigious, she nonetheless ran up over £1,200 in lawyers' fees when *Stern Magazine* used the banned name 'Hemingway' in a footnote about a reprinted article. The bill was paid by her agent, Gillon Aitken, after Martha categorically refused to pay even half.) She grew still angrier when *Granta* used quotes from earlier works as captions to a new piece. 'The idea that you can do the chopping act to sell books is infuriating. You really are beyond bearing now. You don't know the difference between the truth and whatever suits you . . . With deep unfriendliness.' She told him that he had become a very shady character, 'glitzy shady'.

Buford fought back. He agreed that he was unreliable, that he could not promise total efficiency, but said that he could and he would see that her books were properly published. He told her that he cared about her writing. He pointed out that her peremptoriness was causing upset in his office. He sent her flowers. When she turned eighty, and told him that she could not face a celebratory party, he sent her eighty red roses. She was touched. 'Now I see you as a Russian Prince . . . I am covered in beautiful red roses and you are reduced to semi-starvation.' But then he did something that she could not forgive. He simply failed to answer one of her invitations. The weeks passed. She left messages. It was, in fact, no worse than many other incidents of carelessness; but for Martha the end had come. She told him that she did not want to see him again. And though, publicly, the rift was repaired, the friendship was over. The volcano of energy had defeated her.

Away from the charmed circle, Martha's older friendships suffered. Irwin Shaw, that 'wonderfully laughing man', had died in 1984, and Diana Cooper in 1986, the same week as Robert Presnell, leaving a vast gap in Martha's life. (Asked by the family what memento she would like of Diana Cooper, Martha replied her hats; the collection was so vast, and so exotic, that she gave it to the V & A.) Nigel Ryan, founder of ITN, did something to fill the emptiness by taking Martha to the movies in the afternoons. They sometimes fell out over 'all that objectivity shit', Ryan being more of a believer in reliable witnesses than the righting of wrongs.

Sybille Bedford and Betsy Drake still lived not far from Martha in London. Martha had not been impressed by Sybille Bedford's biography of Aldous Huxley, telling her that she had got the sex all wrong. Soon after Edna's death, she had asked Sybille to be her literary executor, adding that she was leaving her the flat in Cadogan Square in her will. In the early 1980s, however, Martha changed her mind, saying that she needed someone younger. For a while, they continued to meet, and to talk over the phone, but the long conversations about writing were over. Sybille found herself always doing the calling. One day, when she phoned to propose a meeting, Martha announced: 'Sybille, you are too boring.' The friendship was finished. 'When somebody bores me,' Martha said to Betsy coldly, 'it's the same as if they had contagious leprosy. I move silently off into the night.'

With Betsy it was slightly different. The two women had become close when Betsy answered her cry for help and came from California to look after Martha at the time of the infection that followed her hysterectomy. Martha's letters to her, then and later, were among the longest and most intimate she ever wrote. They agreed on their hatred for most American politics and politicians, they commiserated with each other about the shaded gradations of loneliness, they talked about depression, Sandy, work, love, men, appearance, weight and their mothers. They wrote to each other about sex. 'What a fascinating topic,' wrote Martha in the autumn of 1972. 'I don't know whether I'm prim; I sure haven't lived it. I started living outside the sexual conventions long before anyone did such dangerous stuff . . . I didn't like the sex at all . . . partly (largely?) due to a Victorian upbringing; sex and love were different. If I practised sex, out of moral conviction, that was one thing; but to enjoy it probably (in my subconscious) seemed a defeat.' And then she went on: 'What has always really absorbed me in life is what is happening *outside*. I accompanied men and was accompanied in action, in the extrovert part of life; I plunged into that . . . But not sex; that seemed to be their delight and all I got was a pleasure of being wanted, I suppose and the tenderness (not nearly enough) that a man gives when he is satisfied. I daresay I was the worst bed partner in five continents . . . So I just went on having abortions, because shits got me into them, and being wanted; but I never in my life looked at a man and said, that one is for me.' When she looked back on her life, Martha told Betsy, she saw that it contained 'more lovers than I can count or remember', but she did not regard herself as promiscuous. She had not enjoyed sex, she said, until she was over forty. She had been to bed with men for many reasons – friendship, comfort, companionship, fun, pity – but not for desire. Just as her dim view of marriage went some way to explaining why she paid so little attention to the existence of wives of the men she took up with, so it explained how such a fundamentally unpromiscuous woman seemed to have so many affairs.

In her friendship with Betsy, Martha took the leading role. She advised, admonished, directed, reminisced, answered questions; and, sometimes, bossed. For the most part, the relationship worked very well, and Betsy was immensely fond of Martha. Martha particularly enjoyed the fact that she felt able to talk to Betsy at any time, about anything, though she also spoke of becoming a 'total egomaniac . . . watered by your too generous affection'. But she was also capable, particularly with Betsy, of surges of rudeness and imperiousness, especially when irritated; and Betsy could be prickly.

Both women liked walking. One day, early in the 1980s, Martha suggested an expedition to Monmouth Castle in Wales, followed by a walk through the English countryside with knapsacks, stopping to sleep in inns along the way. She instructed Betsy on what to pack in her knapsack. In the train, they opened a bottle of wine and played poker but Martha was cross to find fish in the sandwiches that Betsy had brought. They caught a bus from Monmouth to the castle, but something about Betsy's attitude to the outing, her complaints about her heavy knapsack, grated. Getting off the bus, Martha strode ahead. In the ruins, she chose to be alone, glaring at Betsy from between the battlements. That evening they made their way, still in muted hostility, to Shrewsbury, where the hotel they settled on was built steeply on a hillside. Betsy suffered from vertigo. Next day, Martha said that she would walk alone; that evening she dined in her room.

On the following morning, Betsy woke to find herself covered in mosquito bites. 'You are nothing but a hypochondriac,' Martha said furiously. 'Get yourself back to London.' Betsy did. A few days later Martha telephoned. There was something almost like an apology. 'I just moon, tumble, gallop, creep through life saying almost exactly what I think almost all the time.'

Betsy, like Buford, fought back. 'You have said demeaning, cruel, belittling things to me about me and about other people. But I prefer the word savage, maybe because, periodically, I see you in my mind's eye as a lion surprised while feasting on a zebra.' The friendship carried on, jarred from time to time by outbursts of irritation on Martha's part, when she berated Betsy for emotional tyranny. 'The rule, your rule, is: tread softly, by God, or you will disturb my feelings. It's an enormous tedious bore . . . Friendship is fun and a loose mutual aid society. It isn't soul picking (your soul, note). I won't have this nonsense and this tyranny.' They did not travel together again. With time, Martha's toughness over the frailties of others – and her own – had grown more pronounced; what she didn't like, she pushed away.

The 1980s had brought Martha another unexpected pleasure. Sandy served a third prison sentence in Cardiff jail in 1986. He fully assumed that Martha would now turn her back on him. She didn't. She went to visit him from Catscradle, and when he came out she paid for him to go to the Charter Clinic in London, though she refused to take part in any of the family therapy or group sessions. Martha's mistrust of analysis remained implacable, though perhaps this public examination of herself as a mother, something she examined with guilt and remorse when alone and in letters to friends, was simply too painful to bear. The past was indeed another country; the question, always, was what you did about the present.

Sandy now became a mini-cab driver and after some years she invested money in a car rental business for him. After the death of his wife, he wrote to ask her whether she wanted to have a son back. He had now been off drugs for more than ten years. For the rest of Martha's life, they remained friends and met regularly, though it was some years before Martha was willing to introduce him to the chaps. For the first time in his life since he was a small boy, Sandy ceased to be afraid of her; and she ceased to expect of him things that it was not in his nature to deliver. They became close. The years of anger and resentment, if not redeemed, had at least been survived.

The 8 November 1993 was Martha's eighty-fifth birthday. The chaps, men and women, gave a party for her at the Groucho club in Soho. Mary Blume came over from Paris for the evening, and Gloria Emerson from New York. Rosie Boycott had James Fox's portable Olivetti copied in the shape of a cake, a piece of marzipan paper emerging from the top with the words 'Happy Birthday, Martha' in sugar type. In the weeks leading up to the event, Martha had decided to give each of her guests a label. Rosie was the 'Can-do girl'; Nicholas Shakespeare, 'Fortune's favourite kid'; Gillon Aitken, 'Power broker'. There was a touch of steel in the words she chose, but much thought and much affection had gone into them. Martha used to tell her younger friends that she had outgrown loneliness, insomuch as she had ever known it at all, having been well schooled by Hemingway and Matthews, both of them 'positively professors in how to be frozen cold lonely and survive it'. But once the chaps entered her life, she was no longer alone.

* * *

Martha found getting old extremely hard. Old age was not, as she had hoped, 'spiffing'; on the contrary, it was a terrible disease, the worst. She minded, as a woman who had always been looked at, becoming invisible, and she minded even more being seen as old. Two young Frenchmen overtook her one day in the street, and looked back, having perhaps been struck by her tall, elegant silhouette. '*Bah. C'est une vieille*,' one said to the other, turning indifferently away. (Martha shouted at them: '*Quels cons.*') When she saw a portrait of herself taken by the photographer Jane Bown, around the time of her eighty-first birthday, she was upset. Who was the specially nice char-lady, she asked, this sad, tired, very old woman? She was now closer to Job, she told friends, than anyone she knew.

Martha fought the lines on her face with a face lift, which she was cross to find so painful and so expensive, and she dealt with the jagged scar left across her stomach by her hysterectomy with more surgery, again painful, to smooth out the tuck. She had an operation to raise her 'drooped' eyelids. She was irritated by her 'swollen belly and drooping chin'. 'Find something else to rely on?', she wrote to Betsy. 'Like my soul?' She kept up an unremitting assault on her thickening middle by walking determinedly around the Welsh hills with a pedometer strapped to her waist, and she dieted on grape-fruit and Marmite, and at least once on a new dieting pill called Permathene-12. When in London, she went twice a week to a gym to do stretching exercises. It was not just a question of basic discipline, but a public service. And, of course, it worked. Martha, in her seventies and eighties, looked terrific, naturally elegant in very plain clothes often bought from Marks & Spencer or Oxfam, her fair hair well cut, wearing an expres-sion that could be considered haughty except for the humour around her mouth and the irony in her eyes. Her voice, like her vocabulary, was distinctive; droll, wry, self-mocking. It was a bummer stage of life, she said to Betsy. 'Everyone grows old. Not everyone grows up. The object is to aim for that, since one cannot avoid growing old.'

When she judged her appearance tolerable, and her muscles in good shape, she made dates to meet L., whose distant courtship continued to delight her. She remained very attached to him, appreciative of his niceness to her and of some funda-mental quality of honour and innocence that had been lacking in Hemingway and Matthews, though she said of their rela-tionship that it had 'such lightness in weight that it would hardly burden an ant'.

One summer, fed up with the interminable trudges around the wet Welsh hills, she built a swimming pool at the end of her cottage, a thin glass conservatory twenty-eight feet long and ten feet wide, in which she swam up and down twice a day, setting her alarm clock to go off after forty-five minutes. As an extravagance, she told friends, it could be compared to a yacht. As she swam, with the rain battering on the glass above her head, she listened to Radio 3, saying that she had never cared for opera but that it was not nearly so bad when you could not see the singers, until James Fox taught her how to work a cassette player, and then she listened to Schubert and Chopin and thought about the times she had listened to Chopin during the Spanish civil war. Solitary swimming was dangerous for haunting thoughts, the 'coal black mountains' of regret that sometimes tormented her, the 'wrong, sad, hurting things'. She fretted about the harm she might have done to Sandy Gellhorn. She minded never having had a daughter. She wished that she had not wasted ten years on Tom Matthews. 'I live with my failures until they choke me,' she told Betsy. When the electricity system in the pool failed because of damp, and the temperature of the water sank below that of a steam bath, she mended it with her hair dryer. Scorpios were great survivors, she reminded herself and her friends, and indestructible; but they made trouble for themselves, and they were never happy or content except in short bursts.

Martha had always been physically robust, but she was also prone to ill health. As she grew older, she suffered annoying small accidents, perhaps inevitable in someone so restless. She cracked her coccyx slipping on a smooth rock in Gozo, then tore a ligament and wrenched her back in Rome falling down a step on to a stone floor in her hotel bathroom. Her blood pressure sank to that of 'a two-toed sloth'. She began to suffer from tinnitus, which destroyed the silence she had sought and loved in Wales. In the late 1970s, she had started getting pains in her back, which were first diagnosed as osteoporosis, 'backbone crumbling . . . bones like a spider's web', and later as a nerve pressing on a disc. Her back grew increasingly troublesome, causing her occasionally to limp and slightly drag her feet, until in 1991 a doctor prescribed anti-inflammatory pills. For a while she felt better and was able to work on her muscles by more walking and more swimming. But then it grew worse again, and a new doctor gave her slow-release morphine pills, to which she grew briefly and unpleasantly addicted. She thought that she had started to go 'briskly downhill' at the age of eighty-two, and become 'superannuated' at eighty-five. Yet that summer, 1994, she went swimming in three separate seas: the Mediterranean, the Aegean and the Red Sea.

The solar keratosis on her nose never properly healed, but it was kept under control by repeated courses of radiotherapy and dry-ice treatment. Her old ear infection, dormant for many years, flared up again whenever she swam too long in the sea. Small skin cancers had to be burnt off her face. Worse, considerably worse than any of this, however, was the slow reduction of sight. All through the 1980s, Martha had been conscious of a problem with her eyes. In the spring of 1991, she was told that she would need a cataract operation on one eye. For the first two weeks after leaving hospital, she was elated: her earlier excellent vision seemed to have been restored, in that eye at least. But then her sight began to fail. For a while, Martha raged against the eye surgeon, insisting that he had botched the operation. But then it became clear that she was in fact suffering from macular degeneration, an irreversible condition involving central vision. It meant that reading became first hard, then difficult without the strongest magnifying glass, and finally all but impossible. She was told that she would never go blind, but her right eye could soon detect very little.

To her younger friends Martha treated her ailments lightly. She made jokes with John Hatt about having to ask strangers whether she was looking at a cloud or a mountain range, and buying double-lensed magnifying spectacles that made her look like an alien from outer space. 'I want to be a tough old woman, with strong legs,' she said to James Fox. 'Chin up.' To laugh was to make it all bearable. It was to Betsy, to Milton Wolff, the Rabbs and Nikki Dobrski, older friends with whom she saw no need to pretend, that she wrote about the inconvenience, the pain, the effort, the thoughts of death. The only thing she could now do without pain, she told Howard Gotlieb, curator of her papers at Boston University, was swim. By her eighty-fifth birthday, Martha was picking out large letters in bright light only with considerable difficulty.

After Martha's death, Betsy felt regret that she had not taken what she later believed to be evidence of clinical depression more seriously. Was the chronic sense of boredom that ran like a constant refrain through her letters and diaries in fact evidence of persistent depression? Whether Martha's very real feelings of despair about herself and her writing in fact crossed that unmistakable barrier into depressive illness is hard to say. It seems unlikely, at least on a serious level. 'I had a long interior discussion with myself as to whether pain of mind or pain of the body is worse and decided firmly on pain of the body,' Martha wrote one day to the Rabbs. Depressive people seldom feel that way.

Among the many things that Martha loathed about old age was her new sense of helplessness. What she would not do was give up travelling, and particularly travelling on her own, though to her growing blindness were now added mild deafness and sometimes incontinence. Travel was synonymous with freedom, and freedom, like possession and loneliness, was a theme that had never ceased to attract and intrigue her. In letters and conversations she often talked about the conquering of loneliness and the limits set on life by dependency. Even so some of the journeys brought her real pleasure. 'I feel almost giddy with hope,' she said to John Hatt, as she made a plan to snorkel in Maccaroy in Venezuela, where she had been told the water was crystal-clear. In February 1990, Martha spent a month in a house on the banks of a river in Belize, watching the deep, dark, fast-running brown water flow below her balcony, listening to an invisible 'orchestra of howling monkeys' in the jungle around her. In the evenings she was taken by boat to see giant orange iguanas sitting on fallen tree trunks. She would go on travelling, alone, she told friends who worried about her, so as to 'keep myself awake'. 'The certainty of the shape of the days,' she said, 'drives me mad.'

In the early 1990s, having consulted a new young friend,

Anna Benn, a Russian expert who had come to help her with her papers and letters, where she should go for adventure, she travelled to St Petersburg 'on a four day toot', and then, delighted with *glasnost*, she returned twice more. There was a summer expedition to northern Spain, 'enemy territory', staying with a Spaniard whose father had been shot by his own side in the civil war; a train journey through South Africa; a dismal holiday in Nîmes, when for thirteen out of sixteen days the skies stayed black, and Martha's bag was snatched in the street with her passport and travellers' cheques. Defiantly, she filled her hotel bedroom with carnations, and bought cherries, figs and peaches in the market, but still felt as if a biblical curse had settled on her.

*　　*　　*

One of these holidays brought a horrifying event. It was how she dealt with it that makes it important; her courage, not the event itself.

In January 1988, Martha borrowed the Rabbs' house at Nyali, outside Mombasa. She knew it well from earlier visits and was out walking at dawn every morning on the hard, white, packed sand, forced to go early because she could no longer tolerate full sun. The house, among trees and flowered bushes, stood twenty-five metres back from the beach, and when the tide was out the sand seemed to stretch for ever. At that hour the beach was completely deserted and Martha was soon doing five miles every morning. 'Stronger legs and happier every day,' she told Betsy, saying that she had halved her consumption of whisky and cigarettes and that she had written two chapters of a novel in a week, 'as easily as eating ice cream sundaes'. Alex, the Rabbs' cook, made Martha a sandwich for lunch and prepared her dinner before leaving for home at around seven in the evening. 'I am so happy it is hardly decent,' she wrote to Bill Buford. 'Last night, lying on the terrace in moonlight, drinking, I thought maybe I was going to die soon, this being a state of grace surely not meant for normal people or normal life.' She had been swimming naked at midnight, and thought she had located the Southern Cross.

On 6 March, Martha rose, as usual, very early and walked down the path from the house to the beach. She was not wearing her watch or her rings, having taken to leaving them inside the house since a man had once, at dusk, torn her watch off and tried to pull her mother's wedding ring from her finger. She had refused to listen to the Rabbs' warnings about not going out alone too early or too late.

As she descended the last steps on to the sand, a man appeared from behind the trees and attacked her. She was knocked down and raped. It all happened extremely quickly. As he ran off, she went back to the house, evidently remaining entirely calm, put iodine on the cuts and grazes caused by the sharp coral stones of the steps, got into her car and drove into Mombasa to find a doctor. She saw one who worked in the hotels, a man she knew and liked, who gave her antibiotics and a tetanus injection and did some tests for venereal infections. He was kind, but 'cruelly ham-handed' and caused her some pain.

Before driving back to Nyali, she bought herself a dark blue bikini, so as to be able to expose her cuts and bruises fully to the sun, and two new garden spigots for the gardener. She then wrote to tell the Rabbs what had happened. 'Women have been raped all over the world since time began,' she said. 'Simply because I was involved does not make this case special. In fact I got off lightly. I was afraid twice, but I have been frightened by high explosives far more often than that. Fear is only damaging if you let it change your attitudes and actions, which certainly I shall not.' She was insistent that what she referred to as the 'Ugly Event on the steps' should in no manner be allowed to spoil the real and lasting pleasures of Nyali.

Martha permitted herself neither reproach nor self-pity. She mentioned the rape only twice, in two separate letters. There is no other reference to it of any kind in any other existing letter, note or diary. It was simply as if it had never happened. She spoke of it only to Betsy, writing to her a few days later a long letter about plans to go to the Masai Mara to see the animals, about President Reagan's new peace plan for the Middle East, and about Primo Levi's sudden death. It made her feel guilty, she said, that she had never written to tell Levi how much what he had written mattered to her, but she also felt immensely grateful to him. What she found hard to bear was the thought of his sense of failure and his loneliness. The rape was barely touched on. By not giving it words, she was able to minimise it, as she had done all her life. To have talked about it, dwelt on it, would have made it worse, for then it would have been harder to file it away.

Then Martha went back to reading her thrillers, and writing her novel, telling Buford that she was dreading returning to the grey skies and the kitchen of life in London. Whatever her tendency to dwell on failures and regrets, something that grew more pronounced in the last decade of her life, allowing herself to indulge in self-pity was not part of it. Chance disasters were, like injuries of war, events that had to be dealt with, unpleasant, unfortunate, but not of lasting interest or importance. Tough on others, Martha was ruthless on herself. Complaining was not, as she might have put it, her bag.

And so she went on travelling, almost always alone, and, whenever she could get a commission for an article, writing. Despite her infirmities, she still regarded herself, rightly, as a 'first class observer'. And she had never lost, as she told Betsy, her 'tormented understanding of pain'.

Early in 1994, soon after her eighty-fifth birthday, she decided that she wanted to go to Brazil. She was now almost blind in one eye, slightly deaf, prone to ear infections and often in considerable pain from her back. She had been reading about the murder of street children in Brazil, and had become obsessed by the way that these deaths seemed to go unnoticed in the West and unpunished in Brazil itself. She questioned friends about the Brazilian death squads, and approached *Granta* to see if they would take an article on her return. Ian Jack, who had taken over from Buford as editor, was summoned for a drink in Cadogan Square and was struck by the fact that she might have been a character played by Lauren

Bacall, smoking and drinking, elegant, full of energy. He told her that he would read anything she brought back.

Fortunately for Martha, Nicholas Shakespeare had a sister, Amanda, who had been running a programme for street children in the Pelourinho district of Salvador, in north-eastern Brazil, where four children had been murdered the previous year. A guard on the railways was awaiting trial for their killings. Shakespeare offered to put Martha in touch with Amanda, but the telephone numbers he had given her did not seem to work. The days passed, Martha's departure date grew closer, and Shakespeare appeared to have vanished. She rang, wrote, left messages. Martha, who was very attached to him, was prepared to put up with much from Shakespeare that she would not tolerate from Bill Buford. Even so, her last fax to the elusive Shakespeare says much about her underlying new frailty. It was all in capital letters, since otherwise she would not have been able to see it. 'WHERE ARE YOU? I AM DESPERATE. UNTIL NOW NOTHING FROM YOUR TELEPHONE, NOT EVEN A FAX WHINE. EVERY NUMBER YOU HAVE GIVEN ME FOR AMANDA IS WRONG . . . I HAVE NO OTHER CONTACT IN ALL BRAZIL EXCEPT AMANDA. HAVE A HEART. GET THIS RIGHT FOR ME. JUST BECAUSE YOU ARE FORTUNE'S FAVOURED KID DOESN'T MEAN ALL GOES LIKE CLOCKWORK FOR EVERYONE, YOU OAF. HELL, WHAT SHALL I DO? DESPERATELY AND ALSO VERY IRRITABLY, MARTHA.'

Shakespeare responded and Martha set off for Brazil early in February. She was planning to swim and snorkel first, along the coast, before flying on to Salvador. When Amanda collected her from the airport ten days later, Martha had a heavily bandaged arm. The sea had been rough, the undertow tricky, and Martha had been saved from slipping under the water by a young Brazilian who had grabbed her arm as she fought to keep her footing. In so doing, he had torn away a long piece of her very thin skin, leaving a large, raw patch, rather like a burn. A doctor had dressed the wound and told her to stay out of the water until it healed.

At the airport Martha was brisk. No, she would not like

to stay with one of Amanda's friends, a woman judge who was going to help her with her article. She preferred hotels. Amanda, though well briefed by her brother, was nervous. The first interpreter, an anxious girl who spoke bad English, was dismissed. A second, a fat and fastidious boy who fussed about taking buses and going to the slums, was put sharply in his place. Nonetheless, Martha and Amanda soon became friends. Amanda was impressed by Martha's ferocious hard work, her thoroughness, her apparently instinctive understanding and sympathy for the street children, her dogged need to master every fact. She was charmed by her elegance. On the days she was not talking to lawyers or street children, Martha sat by the hotel pool in white shorts and open sandals with slight heels, browning her legs in the sun, unable to swim because of her bandaged arm and just occasionally dropping off into a light sleep. She asked Amanda questions about her life; they talked about Brazil, and politics, and the world. After they had been together a few days, Martha began to talk a little about her own life, about Sandy, about herself when she was Amanda's age. The only prickly note was struck when a police colonel, answering questions about the murdered children, said politely that he was a great admirer of Hemingway. Martha snapped at him.

The days passed and Martha kept wanting to know more, more about the boys, more about the guard accused of killing them, more about the courts and the prisons, more about Brazil. She was intrigued by the tropical plants growing round the hotel and asked Amanda to find her someone she could ask about Brazil's vegetation. She kept questioning the guilt of the accused man, uncertain to the end as to whether he was in fact the kind of man who could kill children. She said that killing children was not something that she could imagine, and she had trouble seeing this short, ordinary man, whom she was allowed to interview inside his remand prison, as a child murderer. The diary of her visit to Brazil began rather subdued, almost sad in tone. 'Have no lipstick – proof vanity has died.' Her hearing aid had broken: 'What next?' But then, as her interviews began, as the familiar process of being sucked into a story took over, her old tone, robust, energetic, full of questions, returned. 'Street kid aged 16 – MP collect them – 3 or 4 – take them off to a hut – steal their clothes – beat them on hands. Broke his hand . . . houses of families of boys open sewer – boards over stagnant water . . . one child accused of stealing watch – ultimately died of beatings . . .' After Martha left, several weeks later, lists of questions for Amanda started arriving: dates, facts, spellings, missing bits of information.

By the spring of 1994, Martha could see very little. She returned to Cadogan Square with her usual collection of notes, unable to read them, and barely able to see the typewriter keys. Her method of working had always been slow and painstaking. It was now excruciatingly slow. Every sentence had to be read back to her, to be reworked, retyped and read back again. Day after day, week after week, Martha sat at her desk, labouring. After six different drafts, she decided that she would send the forty-five-page manuscript, typed in capital letters and much crossed out in heavy black lines, to Ian Jack.

Jack found himself in an unhappy position. He admired Martha, but he did not think that the article was good enough to stand on its own in *Granta*, and he did not feel it right or fair to publish it and have it seen as 'Gellhorn's last article'. She had gone to Brazil needing to be outraged, and the facts did not quite justify the rage. Nervous of her reaction, he wrote to tell her that he could not print it. In truth, it was not Martha's best piece. The constraints on the very process of writing it made it uneven and a little jerky. But it did contain flashes of the old excellent reporting, and ended with her usual envoi: 'What do the violent deaths of a few thousand street children matter? The poor are not quite people in Brazil.' It was published in the *London Review of Books*.

'And that's it,' Martha now wrote to Mary Blume. Brazil had been a 'journey too far' and she intended to write no more. She pinned a sheet of paper to the copy of the article: 'This is an historic document . . . It is my last and worst article . . . The result is unsatisfactory to me in every way.' She told Gloria Emerson that it had 'no decent sentence' in forty-five pages.

Martha did, of course, go on working. She wrote a few more travel pieces, a couple of articles, published in various newspapers and magazines, and she went back to the Welsh hills to revisit the pit villages she had written about during the strike for a BBC radio programme. 'We go on learning, thoughts growing (like fingernails in the grave) as long as we breathe,' she said, worrying sometimes that the passionate anger she had felt so steadily all her life was now turning to weary disgust. But Brazil was the last long investigative reporting she attempted.

* * *

In the autumn of 1994, around the time of her eighty-sixth birthday, Martha put Catscradle on the market. She loved the Welsh hills and the cottage itself, but now found the business of coping with it too tough, the incessant rainy weather fit only for growing mushrooms. She was profoundly bored with swimming up and down her expensively heated pool. The climate alone was bound to lead anyone to 'neurosis, melancholia, probably schizophrenia'. She found a home for her cats with the Rothschilds, and parted from them sadly but without sentimentality. Before leaving Wales, she burnt a number of her letters – to her mother, to Tom Matthews, to L. – saying that she could no longer see to read them and that she didn't want anyone else to do so. As they were burning letters written to her so many years before by her father, Martha asked Sandy Gellhorn, who was helping her, to read them aloud. It was perfectly clear from their words that for some time before his death Dr Gellhorn had felt perfectly reconciled with his daughter. Listening, Martha suddenly began to cry. She must have felt guilty all her life about having failed her father, Sandy now realised, and for reasons now long buried had chosen never to register the fact that her father had forgiven and accepted her. The rest of the letters, the ones Martha decided to spare, were put into large brown envelopes and sent to the Boston archives.

In the face of renewed interest in her books, she remained

the most private of people, closing her door to interviewers, Ph.D students and biographers, refusing permission to quote from her work, saying that she could not help 'these dullish sounding seekers after historical truth'. She remained adamant, to the point of legal threats, that no mention ever be made of Hemingway's name in connection with her own. She spoke of herself as a '*fierce*' old lady. She tried to fight off a biographer, Carl Rollyson, who went ahead and wrote the book anyway, and when she saw it she called it a 'paean of hate' and sent a ten-page letter to Gillon Aitken listing the errors of fact. Occasionally, she talked of writing an autobiography of her own, on 'sex, memory and war', to put the record right. She never overcame her distaste for writing about herself, for using the word 'I', and told Mary Blume that she could not write backwards. 'Everything I write is hot off the griddle, the past is truly another country and I have forgotten it.' Her idea of good reporting remained the same as in the 1930s: what mattered was not the reporter, but the facts: 'eliminating as much as possible the sound of me screaming'. Her dislike of personal publicity gave her a reputation for fearing some kind of unpleasant exposure, but she did not mind, just as she had never much minded what anyone said about her, and she continued to write, and talk, to friends with exceptional candour and self-knowledge.

In London, Martha's life continued unchanged, with frequent visits from the chaps, bringing with them reports from the war fronts of conflict and love, walks in Kew and along the Embankment, trips with her brother Alfred, who returned to the centre of her life in the early 1990s, and with whom she was now closer than she had ever been. They spent Christmas 1995 going up the Nile. She saw a lot of Shirlee and Sandy Matthews, who, like Sandy Gellhorn, helped her with the physical chores of life. 'Dearest James,' she wrote to Fox one day. 'Thank you for comforting me with Bloody Marys, for wine tasting, for food choosing, for lunch, for your company, for being a sweet friend in need.' John Simpson, knowing of her great admiration for Nelson Mandela, arranged for her to masquerade as a producer for the BBC and stand alongside a barrier which he walked past during one of his visits to London. One winter, she flew, alone, to Oman. Only travel lifted her sense of being trapped, she told Victoria Glendinning, because travel brought change, and change the chance of newness. She remained busy, and angry, writing to Clinton about Cuba, keeping an eye on Blair's government, attending a meeting of the International Brigade survivors at the Imperial War Museum, complaining afterwards that the eulogy to Laurie Lee had been ridiculous, and that he had done nothing but lie about his time in Spain. Jesse Jackson, she remarked, was nothing but 'an opera singer and a turd'. Humphrey Burton, who went to interview her about Leonard Bernstein, was a 'self-satisfied twit'.

She seemed quieter, sometimes, troubled by her ill health, irritated by her dependency on others, 'blind, helpless and unwriting' as she put it to Betsy, adding that she felt like a piece of very old rope. In August 1997, she wrote to her old friend Milton Wolff: 'There are two things the matter with me. One, my body is too old, I can no longer do what I want to do. I am as close to sedentary as I can get without actually being tied to a chair. Two, I am bored.' Being unable to read made her feel isolated. She struggled to listen to books on tape but never felt the same 'absolute escape from here and now and from myself' that her own reading provided, saying that she was used to travelling through books at her own speed, not one dictated to by others. For a while, she reviewed books on tape for the *Observer*. Forced to dictate her letters, she complained that they sounded like prison reports.

When she occasionally talked about death, it was to say that death, for her, meant nothing: the only thing to fear was the manner of dying. She briskly rejected sympathy, saying that at last her feeble memory was coming into its own, protecting her from remorse, things she wanted to forget. Occasionally she told friends that she had two main regrets in her life, two things she minded more than anything else: that she had never written a great book or had the kind of close and lasting relationship with a man that she had seen in her parents' and Hortense Flexner's marriages. To have had that sort of love would have been better than looking back on emptiness. But she was not despondent, other than passingly, in front of others. 'If there's one emotion I cannot endure it is sadness,' she said to Victoria Glendinning. 'That is to say personal sadness. Anger is healthy and useful. Sadness is out.' When spring came round, she looked forward to visiting Kew Gardens, and liked to hear about the first crocuses and daffodils. One evening, Betsy, looking out of her window in Chelsea, saw the full moon bright in the sky. She telephoned Martha, who took her binoculars and stood staring out of her own window in Cadogan Square, looking out at the night.

Afterword

On Saturday 14 February 1998 Martha decided that the moment had come to die. Though she knew that she would never go totally blind, by this point the world around her was little more than a series of blurred images. She also knew that she had cancer of the ovary and the liver, and that there was nothing that could be done for it. No amount of walking, eating grapefruit, having tucks of skin made neater, or, above all, willpower would help her now. She could no longer read, work or travel; the driving motor of so much of her life, the need to witness and record, was gone. Time had, quite simply, run out: she had been watching this day come. What future remained promised to be a struggle that even Martha was no longer willing to engage in.

The flat was, as ever, very clean and very neat. Those of her papers that were not in Boston were arranged into bundles and marked, as her mother's had been in St Louis on her death twenty-nine years before. She had already given away pieces of jewellery. Her will, leaving bequests of great imagination and fondness to her friends, was in order – to Nikki, who loved to travel, money for a ticket to the States; to John Hatt, always pressed for money for Eland Books, £10,000; to James Fox, three charming pieces of silver; to Rosie Boycott, who had had a burglary, a set of silver knives and forks. Martha went round the rooms, sticking labels on various bits of furniture. She put the rubbish into a plastic bag and placed it outside her front door, on the landing. She had a long, laughing, talk on the telephone with Alfred, who was in New York. When

Nicholas Shakespeare rang, at around 4.30, they talked about Clinton and Iraq. Martha was angry about the course of the war in Bosnia. Nicholas was staying in the country, and she wanted to know about the spring flowers. She told him that she would not be coming to stay with him that week, as they had planned.

There was a jug of new white tulips in her bedroom, on the dressing table below her wall of photographs, of Sandy as a baby, then as a child, then as a man, of Capa, of Diana Cooper, John Hatt, Eleanor Roosevelt, the Bernsteins and Bernard Perlin, who had painted the picture of the swimming fish, which she had left to Sandy Matthews. There was a picture of three giraffes. Alfred was there, and Edna, and L. Martha put on a cream silk nightdress and lay in her bed, leaving the window slightly open. She turned on one of her audio books, a recording of Sebastian Faulk's *Three Fatal Englishmen*, a biography of three men whose lives had been cut short by a particular combination of chance and character.

Then Martha took the pill she had got hold of. 'I think it takes some kind of desperate courage to commit suicide, for after all, it is the totally unknown risk,' she had once written to Betsy, 'that blank uncertainty, only one's own wilful belief in nothingness is protection. I think, Betsy, that dying is a very hard business, however achieved.' Was Martha, who had found living so hard, afraid? Were there those last few minutes of 'desperate suffocation' before unconsciousness? There was no sign of fear on her face when she was found by Victoria Glendinning on Sunday morning.

In her will, Martha had asked that there be a gathering for her friends at which to remember her. It took place at Cadogan Square a week later, and the forty or so people who came laughed and drank, as she had wished, and talked about the many times they had sat in these rooms, laughing and drinking with her. Some were meeting for the first time, Martha's determination to keep her friends separate having persisted to the end. A few days later, Alfred, Sandy Gellhorn and Sandy Matthews took a boat down the Thames and threw Martha's ashes, as she had stipulated, into the fast-flowing water on an outgoing tide 'for my last travels'. With them, among the ashes, went some long-stemmed red roses.

Acknowledgements

In the summer of 1969 I was pregnant with my first child. My husband Jeremy and I came to London from Rome, where we were living, to wait for her birth. There was a heatwave, day after day of the sort of weather I now know Martha Gellhorn most liked. One evening, she asked us to dinner. I wish I could remember what we talked about, but I do remember how, as we left the restaurant, I realised that the baby was coming. Early next afternoon my daughter was born. We called her Martha. My mother's name was also Martha, though she was always known as Lucy, and the two women were very good friends. The omens seemed right. Two reflective, funny, clever women: Martha was bolder; my mother more loving. They had a lot of fun. The name seemed a good start for a child.

I was never one of Martha Gellhorn's 'chaps', the close circle of younger friends, women as well as men, who gathered around her in the last twenty years of her life. I was always a little frightened of her. But there was never a time when she was not somewhere in my life, as my mother's friend, someone to hear about, and laugh with, and admire. Like the many people who talked to me for this book, I miss her slightly drawling, self-mocking voice, her ironic glance, her certainty that misfortune can and must be handled with fortitude and dignity and that it is we who owe the world a duty, and never the world that owes us anything. To fight, to keep going, to be compassionate; whenever possible, to laugh: that, for me, was Martha's message. Often, of course, she failed, as we all do. She could be dismissive, imperious, insensitive; and even cruel. But she tried, and she did not complain; and that is what I remember.

I would most particularly like to thank Alfred Gellhorn, Martha's youngest brother, for his constant help, encouragement, and friendship, as well as Sandy Gellhorn, her adopted son, and Sandy Matthews, her stepson and literary executor, and his wife Shirlee, for all their advice, reminiscences and hospitality. I am extremely grateful for the access Sandy Matthews kindly gave me to Martha's papers, and for permission to quote from her letters, diaries and unpublished works.

Howard Gotlieb, Director of the Department of Special Collections at Boston University, where Martha's archive is lodged, was immensely helpful during my visits to the library, as were his archivists, Sean Noel and Nathaniel Parks. I would like to thank them. Margaret Rich and AnnaLee Pauls of the Special Collections Library at Princeton University very kindly took time and trouble to track down a series of letters for me, as did Steven Plotkin and James Roth at the John F. Kennedy Library in Boston: I am most grateful to them all. I also consulted archives and papers in the British Library; the London Library; the Eton College Library; the Seeley G. Mudd Manuscript Library in Princeton; the Beinecke Rare Book and Manuscript Library at Yale University; the Manuscripts and Archives Division, and the Berg Collection, of the New York Public Library; the Franklyn D. Roosevelt Library in Hyde Park, New York; the State Historical Library of Wisconsin; the University of Oregon; the Rare Book and Manuscript Library of Columbia University, New York; the University of South Carolina; the Ohio State University; the Harry Ransom Humanities Research Centre at the University of Texas at Austin; the Library of Congress; the Bancroft Library at the University of California; the College of Physicians of Philadelphia Library; the George Arents Research Library, Bird Library, Syracuse University; Radcliffe College; the University of Louisville; the Rare Book and Special Collections Library at the University of Illinois at Urbana-Champaign; the Special Collections at the Washington University Libraries; the Harvard University Center for Italian Renaissance Studies at I Tatti in Florence. I would like to thank their staffs and archivists for their help in locating relevant material.

ACKNOWLEDGEMENTS

For their memories of Martha, and for lending me their letters and giving me permission to quote from them, I would particularly like to thank: Gillon Aitken, David Albert, Sybille Bedford, Anna Benn, Jane Bernstein, Dora Block, Mary Blume, Rosie Boycott, Bill Buford, Cornell Capa, Harriet Crawley, Betsy Drake, Nikki Dobrski, Gloria Emerson, Pamela Egremont, Horst Faas, George Feifer, James Fox, Peter Gellhorn, Flavia Della Gherardesca, Victoria Glendinning, Rob and Lorraine Grover, Shusha Guppy, Jerry Hannifin, Jeremy Harding, John Hatt, Clare Hollingworth, Jenny Hughes, Sue Hoyle, Clarice Incisa, Ian Jack, Hugues de Jouvenel, Ward Just, Cynthia Kee, Phillip Knightley, John P. Matthews, Pamela Matthews, Paul Matthews, Jeffrey Meyers, Patricia Milbourne, Pauline Neville, John Owen, Agi Paoloczi-Horvath, David Pearlman, Bernard Perlin, Sir Edward Pickering, John Pilger, Marsha Presnell, Ruth and Sol Rabb, Jon Randal, Marilyn Sale, Ann Sebba, Amanda Shakespeare, Nicholas Shakespeare, Adam Shaw, John Simpson, Elsie Smith, Jon Snow, Natasha Spender, Peter Straus, Hugh Thomas, Raleigh Trevelyan, Peter Viertel, Vicky Weston, Richard Whelan, Milton Wolff, Barry Zorthian.

In St Louis, four friends of Martha's helped me to reconstruct her early days: Virginia Deutch, William Polk, the late Archie O'Reilly and Mary Taussig Hall. I am very grateful to them. Also in St Louis, the staff of John Burroughs School found copies of Martha's early writings for me in the school review, and told me about the school's creation, the archivists at the *St Louis Post-Dispatch* produced her first articles, while the Saint Louis Public Library and the Western Historical Manuscript Library at the University of Missouri in St Louis unearthed material relating to her life and family. Mrs Coralee Paul did some research for me in and around the city. In Florence, the archivists at the Harvard University Center let me consult the correspondence between Martha and Bernard Berenson. I am grateful to them all.

I would also particularly like to thank the following people for their hospitality and help during the months of my research: Jill Kneerim, William Bell and Lexie Eliot in Boston; Jane Kramer and Vincent Crapanzano in New York; Helen Wilmerding in Princeton; Lyndall Passerini in Cortona. My son, Daniel Swift, did some research for me in New York. My warm thanks go to my editor at Chatto & Windus, Penny Hoare, my editors at Henry Holt, Ileene Smith and Jennifer Barth, and to my agent, Clare Alexander. As always, I am particularly grateful to Anne Davie, Teddy Hodgkin and Julian Schuckburgh, for reading the manuscript and making many helpful suggestions.

Sources and Select Bibliography

Martha was a devoted and regular letter writer, sending many hundreds of letters every year to friends, and keeping the replies. In the 1960s, when she decided to give her papers to the Special Collections at Boston University, she asked her friends to return what they had kept. There are some twenty cartons of papers in her archive; perhaps a third of the contents are letters – to and from Martha – covering her entire life. Many other friends kept copies of their correspondence. During her lifetime, Martha also frequently kept small diaries, for the most part during her work trips or while reporting wars. These combine work and personal life. And, at various times in her life, she began fragments of memoirs. These are all among her papers in Boston.

Preface

3 *I have only to go* . . .   Martha to James Fox 3 July 1986

3 *'Flâner,' she would say* . . .   Martha to Victoria Glendinning 30 Sept. 1987

3 *That's my trouble* . . .   Martha to Shirlee Matthews n.d.

4 *I believe passionately* . . .   Martha to Sandy Matthews n.d.

4 *Scorpios, she wrote* . . .   Martha to Alfred Gellhorn 14 Nov. 1975

4 *I've never known complete* . . .   Martha to Hortense Flexner 17 Feb. 1965

5 *chewing cement* . . .   Martha to James Fox 15 Jan. 1988

5 *I long to scream* . . .   Martha to Mary Blume 2 Feb. 1980

5 *hell's own damage* . . .   Martha to Betsy Drake 8 Feb. 1973

6 I *feel angry* . . .   Martha to Nadezhda Mandelstam n.d.

6 *What happened to laughter* . . .   Martha to Leonard Bernstein 27 Dec. 1979

7 *like a great affair* . . .   Nicholas Shakespeare conversation with author, 10 July 2001

7 *My chosen and projected* . . .   Martha to James Fox 3 July 1986

8 *She wasn't always* . . . Agi Paoloczi-Horvath conversation with author, 15 Mar. 2001
9 *I do most definitely feel* . . . Martha to Nikki Dobrski n.d.
10 *dark grey sludge* . . . Martha to Hortense Flexner n.d.
10 *Yes, life is tough* . . . Martha to Hortense Flexner n.d.
10 *Being a survivor* . . . Martha to Victoria Glendinning 13 Aug. 1994
10 *Tell him* . . . Martha to Leonard Bernstein 19 Feb. 1979

Chapter One

John Burroughs School in St Louis has a full collection of the school's early papers, including copies of the school review with Martha's first writings. For the early history of St Louis and the Fischel and Gellhorn families, see the archives of the *St Louis Post-Dispatch*; see also the Joseph Stanley Pennell papers, University of Oregon.

13 *They told each other* . . . Betsy Drake conversation with author, 10 Jan. 2001
18 *rather clever and a bit* . . . Mary Taussig Hall conversation with author, 3 Nov. 2000
20 *always childhood's* . . . 'Sunday at Crève Cœur'. Unpublished fragment
24 *'My father,' she wrote* . . . Unpublished memoir
26 *You show yourself* . . . Edna Gellhorn to Martha n.d.
27 *Personal rebellion* . . . Martha to Sandy Gellhorn 26 Oct. 1969
30 *triumph of youth* . . . Exam book: Bryn Mawr
30 *I'll get something* . . . Martha to Edna Gellhorn n.d.
30 *In this, she drew* . . . *New Republic* 30 April 1930
34 *I just waited* . . . Unpublished memoir

Chapter Two

For a good account of Bertrand de Jouvenel's relationship with his stepmother Colette, see Judith Thurman, *Secrets of the Flesh. A Life of Colette*, Knopf, New York, 1999. See also correspondence between Bertrand de Jouvenel and Martha in the Special Collections, Boston University.

37 *unforgettable ebony* . . . Janet Flanner, *Paris Was Yesterday*, Angus & Robertson, London, 1972
39 *Years later* . . . Unpublished memoir
42 *Colette had first struck* . . . Bertrand de Jouvenel, *Un Voyageur dans le siècle*, Editions Robert Lafont, Paris, 1979
44 *reaching for me* . . . Martha to Campbell Beckett n.d.
44 *For we live* . . . Bertrand to Martha n.d.

44 *tight-lipped* ... Unpublished memoir
48 *Tant que je suis* ... Unpublished memoir
49 *My beloved, I am* ... Bertrand to Martha n.d.
50 *I have learned* ... Bertrand to Martha n.d.
50 *I knew myself* ... Unpublished memoir

Chapter Three

52 *I think I am probably* ... Martha to Stanley Pennell n.d.
54 *land of the lotus eaters* ... Martha to Stanley Pennell n.d.
54 *Palm trees* ... Martha to Stanley Pennell 16 April 1931
55 *I find myself* ... Martha to Stanley Pennell 27 April 1931
57 *gargantuan proportions* ... Diary 21–28 June 1931
59 *doubting and criticising* ... Unpublished memoir
61 *Even in matters* ... Martha to Bertrand n.d.
62 *You are built* ... Bertrand to Martha n.d.
62 *no wild passion* ... Bertrand to Edna Gellhorn 17 June 1932
63 *Ah my beloved* ... Martha to Bertrand n.d.
65 *I know there are two* ... Martha to Bertrand n.d.
66 *three 'great devotions'* ... Edna Gellhorn to Martha 13 Nov. 1932
66 *Alfred remembers* ... Alfred Gellhorn conversation with author, 10 Nov. 2000
68 *a mean, bitter* ... Martha to Bertrand 30 Mar. 1933
70 *she felt so well* ... Martha to Bertrand n.d.
72 *I see perfection* ... Martha to Bertrand 27 Feb. 1933
74 *The group on the train* ... Letter to unnamed friend in US government, probably 1942
80 *My needs are simple* ... Bertrand to Martha n.d.
82 *I don't know what* ... Martha to Campbell Beckett 29 April 1934
83 *He is so weak* ... Martha to David Gurewitsch 1950
84 *My beloved* ... Bertrand to Martha 16 April 1934

Chapter Four

For a good picture of Harold Hopkins and the writers he sent to report on the Depression, see John F. Bauman and Thomas H. Coode, *In the Eye of the Great Depression*, Northern Illinois University Press, Deka 16, Illinois 1988. See also Martha Gellhorn's reports to Harry Hopkins in the Franklin D. Roosevelt in Hyde Park Library, New York.

92 *The present generation* ... Martha to Harry Hopkins 19 Nov. 1934
95 *numb and doubting* ... *with the rabbit* Martha to Bertrand n.d.
96 *Franklin, talk* ... Unpublished memoir

96 *She gave off light* . . . See Emily Williams interview with Martha Gellhorn 20 Feb. 1980 in the Franklin D. Roosevelt Library

96 *What Mad Pursuit had* . . . Martha Gellhorn interview with Jacqueline Orsagh Jan. 1976. A good overview of the press coverage is to be found in Jacqueline Orsagh's Ph.D thesis, *A Critical Biography of Martha Gellhorn*, Michigan State University, Ann Arbor, Michigan

98 *As she felt stronger* . . . Martha to Lorena Hickok 1 Aug. 1935

101 *She must learn patience* . . . Eleanor Roosevelt to Hortense Flexner, quoted in Joseph Lash, *Love, Eleanor: Eleanor Roosevelt and Her Friends,* Doubleday, New York, 1982

102 *'gray,' noted Martha* . . . Unpublished memoir

105 *Your affair with that* . . . Dr Gellhorn to Martha 10 April 1936

108 *I cannot tell you* . . . Eleanor Roosevelt: 'My Day'

108 *H.G. Wells was an* . . . Martha's account is to be found in an unpublished note, written in Aug. 1965, and put among her papers

109 *He had decided that* . . . H.G. Wells, *Experiment in Autobiography: Discoveries and Conclusions of a Very Ordinary Brain*, Macmillan, New York, 1934

109 *My story of my relations* . . . H.G. Wells, *H.G. Wells in Love. Postscript to an Experiment in Autobiography*, ed. G.P. Wells, Faber & Faber, London, 1984 (typescript, with references to Martha, deposited in the Gordon Ray papers at the Morgan Library in New York)

109 *I'm sorry to leave* . . . H.G. Wells to Martha 28 Mar. 1935

111 *She wrote later* . . . Martha to G.P. Wells, see unpublished note

111 *I'm restless and bothered* . . . H.G. Wells to Martha 27 Nov. 1935

112 *Moura and I have* . . . H.G. Wells to Martha 16 May 1936

112 *In one, recounted* . . . John Hatt conversation with author, 15 Oct. 2001

114 *You have accomplished* . . . Edna Gellhorn to H.G. Wells 12 July (no year)

115 *Writing to tell* . . . Martha to G.P. Wells 26 April 1983

115 *As for his affairs* . . . Martha to G.P. Wells 2 Jan. 1985

116 *You are a very great* . . . Bertrand to Martha Jan. 1936

118 *writing in the* Daily Mirror . . . 10 Mar. 1936

118 *The only terms* . . . Martha to Allen Grover 6 Aug. 1936

118 *As for Martha* . . . Rob and Lorraine Grover conversation with author, 13 Sep. 2002

119 *No one reached* . . . Martha to David Gurewitsch 5 April 1950

119 *get sorry for herself* . . . Eleanor Roosevelt to Edna Gellhorn n.d.

Chapter Five

For accounts of the Spanish civil war, see Virginia Cowles, *Looking for*

SOURCES AND SELECT BIBLIOGRAPHY

Trouble, Harper & Brothers, New York, 1941; Carlos Baker, *Ernest Hemingway*, Collins, London, 1969; Gustav Regler, *The Owl of Minerva*, Rupert Hart-Davis, London, 1959; Bernice Kent, *The Hemingway Women*, W. W. Norton & Co., New York, 1983; Phillip Knightley, *The First Casualty: From Crimea to Vietnam, The War Correspondent as Hero, Propagandist and Myth Maker*, Harcourt, Brace, Jovanovich, New York, 1975; Hugh Thomas, *The Spanish Civil War*, Harper & Row, New York, 1977; Richard Whelan, *Robert Capa*, Faber & Faber, London, 1985; Henry Hart (ed.), *The Writer in a Changing World*, Equinox Cooperative Press, United States of America, 1937; Josephine Herbst, *The Starched Blue Sky of Spain and Other Memoirs*, HarperCollins, London, 1991; Frederick R. Benson, *Writers in Arms: The Literary Impact of the Spanish Civil War*, University of London Press, London, 1967; A. Scott Berg, *Maxwell Perkins: Editor of Genius*, Hamish Hamilton, London, 1979. Martha's own unpublished diary of the war runs to some thirty typed pages. For an excellent overview of the 1930s, see Piers Brendon, *The Dark Valley: A Panorama of the 1930s*, Knopf, New York, 2000.

123 *style had been 'affected'* . . . Martha to Bertrand 1933
124 *He's a big powerful* . . . quoted in Jeffrey Meyers, *Ernest Hemingway*, MacMillan, London, 1985
125 *I hate to go away* . . . Hemingway to Mr & Mrs Pfeiffer n.d.
126 *weak with envy* . . . Martha to Charles Scribner 23 Jan. 1937
126 *odd bird* . . . Martha to Eleanor Roosevelt n.d.
126 *Martha's thank-you* . . . Martha to Pauline 14 Jan. 1937
127 *If there is a war* . . . Martha to Eleanor Roosevelt 4 Jan. 1937
127 *seemed terribly little* . . . Martha to Eleanor Roosevelt 13 Jan. 1937
127 *I do not write* . . . Martha to Charles Scribner 13 Feb. 1937
128 *Spain was, she told* . . . Martha to Eleanor Roosevelt 13 Jan. 1937
128 *You do get yourself* . . . Eleanor Roosevelt to Martha 16 Jan. 1937
128 *And I entered* . . . Martha to David Gurewitsch n.d.
129 *Me, I am going* . . . Martha to Mrs Barnes 30 Jan. 1937
133 *I know, as surely* . . . Herbert Matthews, *The Education of a Correspondent*, Harcourt Brace & Co., New York, 1946
133 *I've been happy* . . . Bertrand to Martha n.d.
135 *looking like hell* . . . Unpublished memoir
142 *Ernest is quite* . . . Milton Wolff. See *Madrid 1937: Letters of the Abraham Lincoln Brigade from the Spanish Civil War*, ed. Jefferson Hendricks, Routledge, London, 1996
149 *10,000 had been* . . . *Manchester Guardian*, 19 Mar. 1937
152 *Stalin's man* . . . 'Memory', *London Review of Books* 12 Dec. 1996

Chapter Six

For more material on this period see Martha's extensive correspondence with Eleanor Roosevelt and Hortense Flexner.

155 *The Loyalists will . . .* *World Telegraph* 20 May 1937
155 *Ever sensible . . .* Eleanor Roosevelt to Martha 24 June 1937
155 *Later, she admitted . . .* Mary Blume conversation with author, 27 Sept. 1999
156 *About 10.30 . . .* Dawn Powell, *Selected Letters*, ed. Tim Page, Holt, New York, 1999
159 *lousier and lousier . . .* Martha to Hemingway 2 July 1937
160 *looks and her spirit . . .* Marion Meade, *Dorothy Parker: What Fresh Hell is This?*, Villard Books, New York, 1988
160 *He is a nice kid . . .* Hemingway to Jack Wheeler 2 June 1938
161 *You could pass . . .* Diary 25 Oct. 1937
161 *Mississippi and Ohio . . .* 'Men Without Medals', *Collier's* 15 Jan. 1938
163 *As Martha told a friend . . .* Martha to David Gurewitsch 7 April 1950
167 *Rawlings' room . . .* Ernest Hemingway, *The Fifth Column and Four Stories of the Spanish Civil War*, Scribners, New York, 1966
170 *The young men will . . .* Martha to Eleanor Roosevelt n.d.
171 *when it is as if . . .* Martha to Rosamund Lehmann n.d.
176 *The country is a fortress . . .* Martha to Eleanor Roosevelt 17 June 1938
176 *In her article . . .* *Collier's* 6 Aug. 1936
179 *an attractive . . .* George Kennan, *Memoirs 1925–1950*, Little Brown & Co., Boston, 1967
184 *been young and there . . .* Martha to Edwin Rolfe 29 Mar. (no year)

Chapter Seven

The account of Martha's marriage to Hemingway and their early years together is based largely on letters between Martha, Hortense Flexner, Eleanor Roosevelt, Edna Gellhorn and Allen Grover: few are dated.

186 *write something . . .* Eleanor Roosevelt to Martha 15 Nov. 1938
190 *like a mediaeval . . .* Gustav Regler, *The Owl of Minerva*, Rupert Hart-Davis, London, 1959
191 *A humorist in this world . . .* *Los Angeles Times* 7 Jan. 1939
191 *Nothing in my life . . .* Martha to Hortense Flexner and Wyncie King 8 June 1939
194 *a walking tape-recorder . . .* *The Face of War*, Simon & Schuster, New York, 1959
194 *Her first sight . . .* Martha to Hemingway 30 Nov. 1939

195 *Cox, recalling* . . . Geoffrey Cox conversation with author, 22 April 2001

195 *If people wept* . . . 'Death in the Present Tense', *Collier's* 10 Feb. 1940

195 *This book is what* . . . Martha to Hemingway 4 Dec. 1939

196 *It is my sort* . . . Martha to Hortense Flexner 4 Dec. 1939

197 *tolls as long distance* . . . Hemingway to Max Perkins 21 April 1940

197 *I'm a damned* . . . Hemingway to Max Perkins 22 April 1940

197 *splendidly constructed* . . . Martha to Allen Grover 9 Mar. 1940

199 *Later reviews* . . . *New York Herald Tribune* 8 Mar. 1940

199 *Whatever pleasure* . . . *Time* 17 Mar. 1940

199 *I intend to outlast* . . . Martha to Eleanor Roosevelt 17 Mar. 1940

200 *branded as a 'disaster* . . . Martha to Charles Colebaugh 3 April 1940

202 *she complained that he was* . . . Martha to Hortense Flexner 17 May 1940

204 *a place to envy* . . . Martha to Max Perkins 30 Oct. 1940

206 *Ernest and I* . . . Martha to Eleanor Roosevelt 27 Dec. 1940

210 *Life is awful* . . . Martha to Alexander Woollcott 8 Mar. (no year)

Chapter Eight

216 *By now she had* . . . Martha to Max Perkins 21 April 1941

217 *Hemingway told* . . . Hemingway to Max Perkins 29 April 1941

218 *prickly and defiant* . . . See Hemingway to Allen Grover 5 Mar. 1942; Allen Grover to Martha 30 April 1942

218 *I don't want* . . . See correspondence between Martha and Hortense Flexner autumn 1942

219 *Several critics* . . . See Marianne Hauser, *New York Times Book Review* 2 Nov. 1941

220 *It seemed a dreadful* . . . *The Face of War*, Simon & Schuster, New York, 1959

222 *I love the life* . . . Martha to Bill Davis 26 June 1942

222 *an acid attack* . . . *New Republic* 10 Aug. 1942

223 *Are we going to rat* . . . Martha to Eleanor Roosevelt

224 *Gosh, gosh* . . . Martha to Charles Colebaugh 25 June 1942

224 *like a constant* . . . Martha to Hemingway 2 Aug. 1942

224 *I am driven* . . . Martha to Hemingway 1 Aug. 1942

225 *Hurricanes threatened* . . . For best account of her journey see *Travels with Myself and Another*, Dodd, Mead, New York, 1978

227 *I think thinking* . . . Hemingway to Martha 25 Aug. 1942

228 *one cat just* . . . Hemingway to Hadley 25 Nov. 1943

229 *One night she had dinner* . . . Martha to Hemingway 16 Oct. 1942

230 *full of juice* . . . *really needing people* Martha to Allen Grover 14 July 1943

231 *Take care of yourself* . . . Martha to Hemingway 31 Dec. 1942
232 *It is the first time* . . . Martha to Max Perkins Jan. 1943
232 *no social awareness* . . . Martha to Edwin Rolfe 8 Dec. 1942
233 *I wish we could* . . . Martha to Hemingway 7 July 1943
234 *saving 'terrifically'* . . . Hemingway to Hadley 23 July 1942
235 *She told a friend* . . . Betsy Drake conversation with author, 10 Jan. 2001
235 *With some annoyance* . . . Hemingway to Martha 16 Mar. 1943
236 *Love consists* . . . Hemingway to Martha n.d. 1943
236 *who hunted for mice* . . . Hemingway to Charles Scribner 24 Nov. 1943
237 *As often when* . . . Martha to Hemingway 3 Sep. 1943
239 *Hearing of the death* . . . Martha to Hemingway 5 Oct. 1943

Chapter Nine

For an account of women correspondents, see Nancy Caldwell Sorel, *The Women Who Wrote the War*, Arcade Publishing, New York, 1999; for Paris at the end of the war, see Anthony Beevor and Artemis Cooper, *Paris After the Liberation, 1944–49*, Hamish Hamilton, London, 1994.

242 *In Spain, she wrote* . . . Martha to Hortense Flexner 30 Oct. 1940
245 *Diana is* . . . Martha to Hemingway 9 Dec. 1943
246 *One night she dined* . . . Martha to Hemingway 1 Dec. 1943
246 *I am in love* . . . Martha to Hemingway 20 Nov. 1943
247 *Hemingway, still alone* . . . Hemingway to Edna Gellhorn Dec. n.d. 1943
251 *among gal correspondents* . . . *Collier's* 4 Mar. 1944
253 *The way it looks* . . . Martha to Eleanor Roosevelt 27 April 1944
254 *I feel myself* . . . Martha to Allen Grover 27 May 1944
257 *Then she decided* . . . See memoirs, letters, articles in *Collier's*
262 *Before leaving London* . . . Martha to Col. Lawrence 24 June 1944
262 *female journalists* . . . Martha to Allen Grover 26 June 1944
266 *I hate to lose anyone* . . . Hemingway to Patrick 15 Sept. 1944
270 *a letter full of recriminations* . . . Hemingway to Edna Gellhorn 21 Sept. 1944
270 *When she broached* . . . see Richard Whelan, *Robert Capa*, Faber & Faber, London, 1985
271 *Who shall I* . . . Martha to Allen Grover 30 Oct. 1944
273 *Funny how* . . . Hemingway to Max Perkins 15 Oct. 1944

Chapter Ten

277 *when I'm alone* . . . Martha to Allen Grover 24 Jan. 1945

280 *wild and crazy* ... Martha to David Gurewitsch 7 April 1950

280 *You are the purpose* ... James Gavin to Martha 28 June 1945

286 *Darling, I love* ... James Gavin to Martha 9 July 1945

289 *la fille du regiment* ... Martha to David Gurewitsch 7 April 1950

291 *pale empty color* ... Martha to Robert Sherrod 14 Feb. 1946

291 *It is hopeless* ... Martha to Robert Sherrod 21 Feb. 1946

292 *Capa has a thing* ... William Walton to Martha 2 Feb. 1946

293 *Martha was now* ... Martha to Robert Sherrod April 1946

295 *big and unrewarding* ... Martha to Max Perkins 16 Jan. 1947

297 *Bored, she became* ... Martha to David Gurewitsch n.d.

299 *She really needed a jailer* ... Martha to Charles Scribner 31 Dec. 1946

302 *Since it is not safe* ... *New Republic* 4 Aug. 1947

303 *He had taken on* ... Hemingway to Charles Scribner 28 June 1947

303 *In 1999, Jeffrey* ... Jeffrey Meyers, 'The Quest for Hemingway', *The Virginia Quarterly Review*, Autumn 1985; 'The Hemingways: An American Tragedy', *The Virginia Quarterly Review*, 1999, vol.75. See also correspondence between Ernest Hemingway and Buck Lanham, Special Collections, Princeton University.

303 *It was not the worst* ... Hemingway to Buck Lanham 25 Aug. 1948

303 *definitely belonged* ... Hemingway to Buck Lanham Nov. 8 1948

303 *He did, however* ... Hemingway to Matthew, Winter 1945

303 *I hope Ernest* ... Martha to Charles Scribner 23 Sept. 1947 (no year)

304 *He wasn't present* ... Martha to Betsy Drake 8 May 1974

305 *sneering tone* ... Martha to Bernard Berenson 26 April 1954

305 *Some of the final* ... Ernest Hemingway, *Across the River and Into the Trees*, Scribners, New York, 1950

310 *She feared* ... Martha to Wallace Meyer 5 Sept. 1948

311 *Dearly beloved* ... Martha to William Walton 13 Mar. 1948

Chapter Eleven

313 *The* flamboyante ... *The Lowest Trees Have Tops*, Dodd, Mead, New York, 1967

314 *I had forgotten* ... Martha to William Walton n.d.

315 *I have discovered how* ... Martha to Diana Cooper 11 Aug. 1949

316 *I dug this grave* ... See letters to 'L.E.R.', Boston University

319 *There had been too much dying* ... *Saturday Evening Post* 27 Aug. 1949

320 *Sybille wrote later* ... Sybille Bedford conversation with author, 18 Feb. 2000

322 *What amuses me* ... Martha to Flavia della Gherardesca n.d.

323 *Lucy Moorehead* ... Private collection

368 *I am, as the* . . . Martha to Bernard Berenson 30 May 1954

369 *The first that Sandy* . . . Sandy Matthews conversation with author, 18 Sept. 2000

370 *a fancy dress Guards'* . . . Sandy Gellhorn conversation with author, 14 Sept. 2002

372 *The interesting question* . . . Martha to Bernard Berenson 6 Jan. 1955

373 *I feel we are all* . . . Martha to Diana Cooper 18 Nov. 1955

374 *Somerset Maugham's mouth* . . . Martha to Nicky Mariano 12 July 1959

374 *Ivy Compton-Burnett* . . . Martha to Bernard Berenson 17 Aug. (no year)

375 *Sandy Gellhorn, now* . . . Sandy Gellhorn conversation with author, 14 Sept. 2002

378 *She was feeling* . . . Janet Flanner to Martha 18 May 1966

Chapter Thirteen

For a good life of Diana Cooper, see Philip Ziegler, *Diana Cooper*, Hamish Hamilton, London, 1981.

380 *gentle, kindly* . . . Martha to Hortense Flexner 21 Jan. 1962

381 *she planned to be away* . . . Martha to Hortense Flexner 8 Jan. 1962

383 *Self-respect and civilisation* . . . Martha to Adlai Stevenson 5 Feb. 1962

383 *She rented a* . . . Martha to Hortense Flexner 17 May 1962

385 *To friends, she* . . . Martha to Adlai Stevenson 11 Oct. 1962

385 *'At present,' she* . . . Martha to Adlai Stevenson 26 Dec. 1962

386 *stinking Germany* . . . 'Is there a new Germany?' *Atlantic Monthly* Feb. 1964

386 *She was 'wildly'* . . . Martha to Adlai Stevenson 19 Jan. 1963

389 *From observation* . . . Martha to Paul Matthews 15 Nov. 1965

389 *I wish to shriek* . . . Martha to Paul Matthews 18 Jan. 1961

389 *a dead, waxworks* . . . Martha to Diana Cooper 31 Jan. (no year)

389 *So happy* . . . Martha to Alvah Bessie 13 June 1958

391 *a 'tiny book* , , .' Martha to Alvah Bessie 13 April 1961

394 *all the warmth* . . . Martha to Paul Matthews 14 June 1963

394 *My mother is dying* . . . Martha to Diana Cooper 8 July 1963

395 *This is something* . . . Martha to Diana Cooper 2 Feb. 1964

395 *I damn near* . . . Martha to Leonard Bernstein 21 Jan. 1964

397 *the break from Tom* . . . Sandy Gellhorn conversation with author

399 *The agent had sent word* . . . 'I have Monkeys on My Roof', *Ladies Home Journal*, July 1964

400 *Ypres and Verdun* . . . Martha to Diana Cooper 1 Feb. 1964

402 *broken by hills* . . . *Atlantic Monthly* Feb. 1966

Chapter Fourteen

434 *visibly and constantly* . . .   Martha to Robert Presnell 7 Oct. 1965

435 *What she really wanted* . . .   Martha to Betsy Drake 12 Mar. 1965

436 *forays with her old* . . .   Mary Taussig Hall conversation with author, 12 Nov. 2000

436 *the sexless life* . . .   Martha to Diana Cooper 12 Oct. 1965

436 *'Oh God,' she wrote* . . .   Martha to Sandy Matthews 30 Oct. 1970

439 *It isn't death* . . .   Martha to Robert Presnell 1 Jan. 1966

440 *Despair is just* . . .   Martha to Betsy Drake 10 Dec. 1972

440 *Betsy, what am* . . .   Martha to Betsy Drake 12 Mar. 1973

441 *the plumber* . . .   Martha to Robert Presnell 6 Aug. 1965

442 *In 1967 Sandy* . . .   Sandy Gellhorn conversation with author, 14 Sept. 2002

442 *I have no respect* . . .   Martha to Sandy Gellhorn n.d.

442 *Oh Sandy* . . .   Martha to Sandy Gellhorn 30 Oct. 1969

443 *She remembered Mexico* . . .   Martha to Winifred Hill 5 Jan. 1970

445 *On Saturday 19* . . .   Private collections

446 *I should have been* . . .   Martha to Betsy Drake 22 Jan. 1974

446 *long slow hard* . . .   Martha to Alfred Gellhorn 19 Feb. (no year)

Chapter Fifteen

449 *I know my chances* . . .   Martha to Betsy Drake 9 Jan. 1973

451 *It was in Cadogan Square* . . .   David Albert conversation with author, 11 Jan. 2001, Sue Hoyle conversation with author, 10 Mar. 2000

454 *I revere courage* . . .   Martha to Hortense Flexner 11 Aug. 1963

455 *A letter quickly came back* . . .   See correspondence with Nadezhda Mandelstam, Boston University

457 *as she wrote later* . . .   *Travels with Myself and Another*, Dodd, Mead, New York, 1978

460 *I cannot analyse* . . .   Martha to Betsy Drake 19 May 1971

460 *I consider thinking* . . .   Martha to Betsy Drake 2 Jan. 1976

464 *Soft on herself* . . .   Phillip Knightley conversation with author, 17 April 2001

464 Footnote: Richard Whelan conversation with author, 19 Nov. 2000

466 *Would you be willing* . . .   Mary McCarthy to Martha 10 Aug. 1980

466 *Coining a new* . . .   On Apocryphism *Paris Review*, Autumn Winter 1980–81. See also correspondence with George Plimpton. Natasha Spender conversation with author 27 May 2002

468 *Please be less* . . .   Martha to George Plimpton 15 Sept. 1980

470 *Anywhere you look* . . .   Martha to Sandy Matthews 12 Nov. 1980

471 *mocked by Ferdinand Mount* . . .   *Daily Telegraph* 8 Dec. 1984

471 *What can one do* . . .   Martha to Moshe Pearlman 16 Aug. 1982

471 *Brooding over* . . .   Martha to Milton Wolff 6 Dec. 1984

Chapter Sixteen

475 *I like very few* ...   Martha to Diana Cooper 2 Feb. 1970

477 *like a geriatric* ...   Martha to Ruth Rabb 4 Feb. 1987

477 *they discovered they shared* ...   John Pilger conversation with author, 18 Mar. 2001

477 *articles for* Spare Rib ...   Rosie Boycott conversation with author, 11 May 2001

477 *felicitously* ...   Martha to James Fox 24 July 1984

478 *For Shakespeare* ...   Nicholas Shakespeare conversation with author, 17 Feb. 2002

478 *I feel like a crushed* ...   Martha to James Fox 27 Oct. 1989

478 *Aside from you* ...   Martha to John Hatt n.d.

478 *It's bliss* ...   Martha to Victoria Glendinning n.d.

479 *Snow, presenting* ...   Jon Snow conversation with author, 3 April 2001

480 *When Bernard* ...   Bernard Perlin conversation with author, 26 Mar. 2001

481 *'Oxfam,' replied* ...   Peter Straus conversation with author, 5 July 2000

481 *Perhaps the most unfortunate* ...   Shusha Guppy telephone conversation with author, 12 May 2001

481 *And, just occasionally* ...   Bill Buford conversation with author, 19 Nov. 2000, and see correspondence Martha and Buford in archives of *Granta*

483 *They sometimes fell out* ...   Nigel Ryan conversation with author, 15 Mar. 2001

484 *Martha announced* ...   Sybille Bedford conversation with author, 2 Nov. 2000

484 *The two women had become* ...   Betsy Drake conversation with author, 10 Jan. 2001

488 *Find something else* ...   Martha to Betsy Drake 6 Mar. 1974

488 *such lightness* ...   Martha to Betsy Drake 8 Feb. 1975

491 *In the early 1990s* ...   Anna Benn conversation with author, 3 June 2000

492 *One of these holidays* ...   Private communication

492 *I am so happy* ...   Martha to Bill Buford 31 Jan. 1988

495 *At the airport* ...   Amanda Shakespeare conversation with author

500 *an opera singer* ...   Martha to Bill Buford 18 July 1988

Index